SOURCES
of the
WESTERN
TRADITION

SOURCES of the WESTERN TRADITION

EIGHTH EDITION

VOLUME II: FROM THE RENAISSANCE TO THE PRESENT

Marvin Perry

Baruch College, City University of New York

George W. Bock, Editorial Associate

WADSWORTH
CENGAGE Learning™

Australia • Brazil • Japan • Korea • Mexico • Singapore • Spain • United Kingdom • United States

WADSWORTH
CENGAGE Learning·

**Sources of the Western Tradition:
Volume II: From the Renaissance
to the Present, Eighth Edition**
Marvin Perry

Senior Publisher: Suzanne Jeans

Senior Sponsoring Editor: Nancy Blaine

Assistant Editor: Lauren Floyd

Editorial Assistant: Emma Goehring

Executive Marketing Manager:
Diane Wenckebach

Marketing Coordinator: Lorreen Pelletier

Senior Marketing Communications Manager:
Heather Baxley

Associate Content Project Manager:
Anne Finley

Senior Art Director: Cate Rickard Barr

Senior Print Buyer: Judy Inouye

Senior Rights Acquisition Specialist, Text:
Katie Huha

Senior Image Rights Acquisition Specialist:
Jennifer Meyer Dare

Production Service: PreMediaGlobal

Cover Designer: Roy R. Neuhaus

Cover Image: Kerr-Lawson, James
(1864–1939). *Caterina Reading a Book*,
c. 1888. Scottish. © The Fine Art Society,
London, UK/Bridgeman Art Library

Compositor: PreMediaGlobal

For product information and technology assistance, contact us at
Cengage Learning Customer & Sales Support, 1-800-354-9706

For permission to use material from this text or product,
submit all requests online at **www.cengage.com/permissions.**
Further permissions questions can be emailed to
permissionrequest@cengage.com.

Library of Congress Control Number: 2010928288

ISBN-13: 978-0-495-91321-4

ISBN-10: 0-495-91321-9

Wadsworth
20 Channel Center Street
Boston, MA 02210
USA

Cengage Learning is a leading provider of customized learning solutions with
office locations around the globe, including Singapore, the United Kingdom,
Australia, Mexico, Brazil, and Japan. Locate your local office at:
international.cengage.com/region

Cengage Learning products are represented in Canada by
Nelson Education, Ltd.

For your course and learning solutions, visit **www.cengage.com.**

Purchase any of our products at your local college store or at our preferred
online store **www.cengagebrain.com.**

Printed in the United States of America
1 2 3 4 5 6 7 14 13 12 11 10

Contents

PART TWO: MODERN EUROPE   91

CHAPTER 4   *Era of the French Revolution*   91

CHAPTER 5   *The Industrial Revolution*   122

CHAPTER 14 *Europe: A New Era*   *438*

PART FOUR:
THE CONTEMPORARY WORLD   471

CHAPTER 15 *The West in an Age of Globalism*   471

Preface

Teachers of the Western Civilization survey have long recognized the pedagogical value of primary sources, which are the raw materials of history. The eighth edition of *Sources of the Western Tradition* contains a wide assortment of documents—some 217 in Volume I and 213 in Volume II and principally primary sources—that have been carefully selected and edited to fit the needs of the survey and to supplement standard texts.

I have based my choice of documents for the two volumes on several criteria. To introduce students to those ideas and values that characterize the Western tradition, *Sources of the Western Tradition* emphasizes primarily the works of the great thinkers. While focusing on the great ideas that have shaped the Western heritage, however, the reader also provides a balanced treatment of political, economic, and social history. I have tried to select documents that capture the characteristic outlook of an age and provide a sense of the movement and development of Western history. The readings are of sufficient length to convey their essential meaning, and I have carefully extracted those passages that focus on the documents' main ideas.

An important feature of the reader is the grouping of several documents that illuminate a single theme; such a constellation of related readings reinforces understanding of important themes and invites comparison, analysis, and interpretation. For example, in Volume I, Chapter 9, *The Renaissance*, Section 1, "The Humanists' Fascination with Antiquity" contains three interrelated readings: the first by Petrarch, shows his commitment to classical culture; in the second, Leonardo Bruni discusses the value of studying Greek literature and proposes a humanist educational program; and in the third, Petrus Paulus Vergerius also discusses the importance of liberal studies. In Volume II, Chapter 13, *World War II*, Section 11, "Resistance" contains four readings:

in the first, Albert Camus explains why he joined the French Resistance; the second reproduces the leaflets distributed during the war by Hans and Sophie Scholl denouncing the Nazis; the third selection is by Marek Edelman, one of the surviving commanders of the memorable Warsaw Ghetto uprising; and the final selection by Tadeusz Bor-Komorowski, Commander of the Polish Home Army, recounts the Poles' valiant effort to drive the Germans from Warsaw.

An overriding concern of mine in preparing this compilation was to make the documents accessible—to enable students to comprehend and to interpret historical documents on their own. I have provided several pedagogical features to facilitate this aim. Introductions of three types explain the historical setting, the authors' intent, and the meaning and significance of the readings. First, introductions to each chapter—thirteen in Volume I and fifteen in Volume II—provide comprehensive overviews of periods. Second, introductions to each numbered section or grouping treat the historical background for the reading(s) that follow(s). Third, each reading has a brief headnote that provides specific details about that reading.

Within some readings, interlinear notes, clearly set off from the text of the document, serve as transitions and suggest the main themes of the passages that follow. Used primarily in longer extracts of the great thinkers, these interlinear notes help to guide students through the readings.

To aid students' comprehension, brief, bracketed editorial definitions or notes that explain unfamiliar or foreign terms are inserted into the running text. When terms or concepts in the documents require fuller explanations, these appear at the bottom of pages as editors' footnotes. Where helpful, I have retained the notes of authors, translators, or editors from whose works the documents were acquired. (The latter have asterisks, daggers, et cetera, to distinguish them from my numbered explanatory notes.) The review questions that appear at the ends of sections enable students to check their understanding of the documents; sometimes the questions ask for comparisons with other readings, linking or contrasting key concepts.

For ancient sources, I have generally selected recent translations that are both faithful to the text and readable. For some seventeenth- and eighteenth-century English documents, the archaic spelling has been retained, when this does not preclude comprehension, in order to show students how the English language has evolved over time.

For the eighth edition I have reworked most chapters, dropping some documents and adding new ones. All new documents have been carefully edited: extraneous passages deleted, notes inserted to explain historical events, names identified, and technical terms defined. Throughout the book, I have extended the constellation format that groups related documents into one section.

The eighth edition of Volume I contains 23 new documents. In Chapter 2, I have added passages from *Exodus* to the constellation "Humaneness of Hebrew Law" and have significantly enriched the introduction. In Chapter 3, I have inserted a new section, "Early Greek Philosophy: The Emancipation of Thought from Myth," which includes excerpts from Aristotle on Thales of Miletus, as well as excerpts from Anaximander and Pythagoras. The section "Greek Drama" now features *Antigone* by Sophocles. In the section "The Status of Women in Classical Greek Society," *Medea* has joined *Lysistrata*. Added to the section "The Decline of the Republic" in Chapter 4 is Velleius Paterculus' account of Octavian's triumph over Mark Antony. Chapter 6 includes three new selections: the first covers The Dead Sea Scrolls; the second is on Rabbinic Judaism: Ethical Concerns; and the third features Pope Gelasius I's elucidation of the proper relationship between church and state. A section on jihad has been added to Chapter 7. It includes sayings attributed to the Prophet and Ibn Taymiyyah's understanding of

the religious and moral duty to participate in jihad. In that same chapter, added to the constellation "Converting the Germanic Peoples to Christianity," is an account by Bishop Martin of Braga of the persistence of paganism in the countryside.

In Chapter 8, I have added an account of German towns forming an alliance to protect merchants to the section "The Revival of Trade and the Growth of Towns." Also in Chapter 8, Thomas Aquinas' argument for the death sentence for unrepentant heretics has been inserted in the section "Religious Dissent," and a selection from Adelard of Bath, an early exponent of investigating the natural world, has been incorporated into the section, "Medieval Learning: Synthesis of Reason and Christian Faith." The section "The Jews in the Middle Ages" also has a new selection—an account of Philip II's expulsion of the Jews from France; the section "The Fourteenth Century: An Age of Adversity" has a new selection on the extermination of the Albigensians (or Cathars). In Chapter 9, I have enriched the constellation "The Humanists' Fascination with Antiquity" with a passage from Petrus Paulus Vergerius' educational treatise in which he stresses the importance of liberal studies. In Chapter 10, in the section "The German Peasants Revolt," I have inserted passages from a pamphlet by an unknown author that clearly states the peasants' grievances. The section "Spanish Oppression of Amerindians" in Chapter 11 has been enhanced with a statement by Spain's chief crown jurist justifying on theological grounds Spanish domination of the Amerindians. Chapter 12 now begins with Nicholas Copernicus' discussion of his breakthrough in astronomy that precipitated the Scientific Revolution.

Volume II contains 33 new selections. The new selection for Chapter 2, *The Scientific Revolution*, which is reproduced from Volume I, is described above. Added to Chapter 4 is Gracchus Babeuf's call for the elimination of private property during the French Revolution. Chapter 5 now includes Friedrich Engels' famous description of slums in Britain's rapidly growing urban centers. In Chapter 6, an excerpt from Goethe's *Faust* has been incorporated into the "Romanticism" constellation. Also inserted into that chapter is a new section, "Repression," which contains the Karlsbad Decrees that were designed to stifle liberalism and nationalism in the German states. Introducing the section "Realism in Literature" in Chapter 7 is now an early definition of realism by Vissarion Belinsky, a Russian intellectual. Broadening the section "Anti-Semitism: Regression to the Irrational" in Chapter 8 is a description of the murderous Kishinev Pogrom in Russia. In Chapter 9, an excerpt from *The Black Man's Burden* by Edmund Morel, who was distressed by the mistreatment of Africans in the Congo, has been added to the section "European Rule in Africa." Also inserted into Chapter 9 is a new section, "Chinese Resentment of Western Imperialism," that contains selections focusing on the anti-Western and anti-Christian outlook of the Boxers. An account of the militarist spirit of French students prior to World War I has been added to the section "Militarism" in Chapter 11. Also inserted into the chapter is a new constellation, "Women at War," that depicts the employment of women in British factories and the opposition to female employment in Germany.

Chapter 12 contains a new section, "The Great Depression," that depicts the suffering of working people in Britain and Germany. Another new section, "Resistance," has been incorporated into Chapter 13 (for a description of the four selections in that section, see page above). A survivor's account of the firebombing of Dresden has been added to the section "The End of the Third Reich," also in Chapter 13. In Chapter 14, *Europe: A New Era*, the first section, "The Aftermath: Devastation and Demoralization" has been completely revised. It now includes a description of a ruined Germany by distinguished journalist Theodore H. White, accounts of the ordeal of Jewish survivors dwelling in camps for displaced persons, and the expulsion of Germans from Czechoslovakia. In the same chapter, added to the section "Communist Repression" is Roy Medvedev's discussion of Stalin's last years. Another selection by Theodore H. White, this time on Germany's economic resurgence, has been incorporated into "The New Germany: Economic Miracle and Confronting the Past." The chapter ends with a new section, "The Soviet Union: Restructuring and Openness," that features excerpts from Mikhail S. Gorbachev's *Perestroika*.

Chapter 15 has been completely revised to reflect issues of current importance. The new section "Russia: Creeping Autocracy and Burgeoning Nationalism" contains the article Vladimir Putin: A New Tsar in the Kremlin? In another new section, "Child Soldiers," Ishmael Beah describes his terrifying ordeal as a boy soldier in Sierra Leone. Augmenting the section "Radical Islamic Terrorists" is a report by the European Union on this growing problem and an appeal by Abdurrahman Wahid, the former president of Indonesia, for Muslims to unite and defeat the radicals who are distorting Islam's true meaning. In the section "Islam in Europe: Failure of Assimilation," Walter Laqueur, a prominent American historian with strong ties to Europe, discusses the threat to Europe's future posed by a burgeoning Muslim population. In 2008, the United States State Department prepared a comprehensive study of global anti-Semitism, excerpts of which are reproduced in the new section, "Resurgence of Anti-Semitism." The closing section, "In Defense of European Values," contains excerpts from *The Betrayal of the West*, French sociologist Jacques Ellul's defense of Western civilization from its detractors.

I wish to thank the following instructors for their critical reading of the manuscript: Richard Brabander, Bridgewater State College; Elena Osokina, University of South Carolina; and Janusz Duzinkiewicz, Purdue University. I would be remiss if I did not also thank Sylvia Gray, Portland Community College, who took the initiative to suggest to the publisher a significant improvement in the Hebrew Law selection.

I am grateful to the staff of Wadsworth/ Cengage Learning who lent their talents to the project. As in previous editions, Nancy Blaine, senior sponsoring editor, provided useful guidelines. A special thanks to Lauren Floyd, assistant editor, who efficiently prepared the revision for production. I also thank Anne Finley, associate content project manager, who, with the very capable assistance of freelancer Karunakaran Gunasekaran, skillfully guided the book through production. Also deserving of my gratitude are Greg Teague, copy editor, who read the manuscript with a trained eye; Katie Huha, senior rights specialist, who managed the difficult task of obtaining text permissions smoothly; Jennifer Meyer Dare, senior photo editor, who oversaw the selection and research of the chapter-opening photos; and Cate Rickard Barr, senior art director, who managed the design of the cover.

I am pleased that my friend George Bock continues to evaluate with a trained eye proposed new selections and introductions and to proofread so diligently. I thank my wife Phyllis Perry for her encouragement and computer expertise, which saved me time and aggravation. Unfortunately, Angela Von Laue, who had assisted me since the death of her husband Theo in 2000, has taken a too early retirement from the book. I miss her research and proofreading skills.

M.P.

Prologue
Examining Primary Sources

When historians try to reconstruct and apprehend past events, they rely on primary or original sources—official documents prepared by institutions and eyewitness reports. Similarly, when they attempt to describe the essential outlook or world-view of a given era, people, or movement, historians examine other types of primary sources—the literature, art, philosophy, and religious expressions of the time. These original sources differ from secondary or derivative sources—accounts of events and times written at a later date by people who may or may not have had access to primary sources. *Sources of the Western Tradition* consists principally of primary sources, which are the raw materials of history; they provide historians with the basic facts, details, and thinking needed for an accurate reconstruction of the past.

Historians have to examine a document with a critical spirit. The first question asked is: Is the document authentic and reliable? An early illustration of critical historical awareness was demonstrated by the Renaissance thinker Lorenzo Valla (c. 1407–1457) in *Declamation Concerning the False Decretals of Constantine*. The so-called Donation of Constantine, which was used by popes to support their claim to temporal authority, stated that the fourth-century Roman emperor Constantine had given the papacy dominion over the western Empire. By showing that some of the words in the document were unknown in Constantine's time and therefore could not have been used by the emperor, Valla proved that the document was forged by church officials several hundred years after Constantine's death. A more recent example of the need for caution is shown by the discovery of the "Hitler Diaries" in the mid–1980s. Several prominent historians "authenticated" the manuscript before it was exposed as a forgery—the paper dated from the 1950s and

Hitler died in 1945. Nor can all eyewitness accounts be trusted, something Thucydides, the great Greek historian, noted 2,400 years ago.

[E]ither I was present myself at the events which I have described or else I heard of them from eye-witnesses whose reports I have checked with as much thoroughness as possible. Not that even so the truth was easy to discover: different eye-witnesses give different accounts of the same events, speaking out of partiality for one side or the other or else from imperfect memories.

An eyewitness's personal bias can render a document worthless. For example, in *The Auschwitz Lie* (1973), Thies Christophersen, a former SS guard at Auschwitz-Birkenau, denied the existence of gas chambers and mass killings in the notorious Nazi death camp, which he described as a sort of resort where prisoners, after work, could swim, listen to music in their rooms, or visit a brothel. Years later he was captured on videotape—he mistakenly thought the interviewers were fellow neo-Nazis—confessing that he had lied about the gas chambers because of loyalty to the SS and his desire to protect Germany's honor.

After examining the relevant primary sources and deciding on their usefulness, historians have to construct a consistent narrative and provide a plausible interpretation. Ideally, this requires that they examine documentary evidence in a wholly neutral, detached, and objective way. But is it possible to write history without being influenced by one's own particular viewpoint and personal biases?

No doubt several historians examining the same material might draw differing conclusions, and each could argue his or her position persuasively. This is not surprising, for history is not an exact science and historians, like all individuals, are influenced by their upbringing and education, by their thoughts and feelings. Conflicting interpretations of historical events and periods are expected and acceptable features of historiography. But what is not acceptable is the deliberate distortion and suppression of evidence in order to substantiate one's own prejudices.

A flagrant example of writers of history misusing sources and distorting evidence in order to fortify their own prejudices is the recent case of British historian David Irving, author of numerous books on World War II, several of them well reviewed. Increasingly Irving revealed an undisguised admiration for Hitler and an antipathy toward Jews, which led him to minimize and disguise atrocities committed by the Third Reich. Addressing neo-Nazi audiences in several lands, he asserted that the Holocaust is "a major fraud. . . . There were no gas chambers. They were fakes and frauds." In *Lying About Hitler: History, Holocaust and the David Irving Trial* (2001), Richard J. Evans, a specialist in modern German history with a broad background in archival research, exposed instance after instance of how Irving, in his attempt to whitewash Hitler, misquoted sources, "misrepresented data, . . . skewed documents [and] ignored or deliberately suppressed material when it ran counter to his arguments. . . . [W]hen I followed Irving's claims and statements back to the original documents on which they purported to rest . . . Irving's work in this respect was revealed as a house of cards, a vast apparatus of deception and deceit."

The sources in this anthology can be read on several levels. First, they enhance understanding of the historical period in which they were written, shedding light on how people lived and thought and the chief concerns of the time. Several of the sources, written by some of humanity's greatest minds, have broader implications. They are founts of wisdom, providing insights of enduring value into human nature and the human condition. The documents also reveal the evolution of those core ideas and values—reason, freedom, and respect for human dignity—that constitute the Western heritage. Equally important, several documents reveal the precariousness of these values and the threats to them. It is the hope of the editors that an understanding of the evolution of the Western tradition will foster a renewed commitment to its essential ideals.

The documents in these volumes often represent human beings struggling with the vital questions of their day. As such they invite the reader to react actively and imaginatively to the times in which they were produced and to the individuals who produced them. The documents should also be approached with a critical eye. The reader has always to raise several pointed questions regarding the author's motivation, objectivity, logic, and accuracy. In addition, depending on the content of a particular document, the reader should consider the following questions: What does the document reveal about the times in which it was written? About the author? About the nature, evolution, and meaning of the Western tradition? About human nature and human relations? About good and evil? About progress? About war and peace? About gender relations? About life and death? Doubtless other questions will come to mind. In many instances, no doubt, the documents will impel readers to reflect on current issues and their own lives.

Introduction
The Middle Ages and the Modern World
—◦◦◦—

Historians have traditionally divided Western history into three broad periods: ancient, medieval, and modern. What is meant by modernity? What has the modern world inherited from the Middle Ages? How does the modern West differ fundamentally from the Middle Ages?[1]

Medieval civilization began to decline in the fourteenth century, but no dark age comparable to the three centuries following Rome's fall descended on Europe; its economic and political institutions and technological skills had grown too strong. Instead, the waning of the Middle Ages opened up possibilities for another stage in Western civilization: the modern age.

The modern world is linked to the Middle Ages in innumerable ways. European cities, the middle class, the state system, English common law, universities—all had their origins in the Middle Ages. During medieval times, important advances were made in business practices, including partnerships, systematic bookkeeping, and the bill of exchange. By translating and commenting on the writings of Greek and Arabic thinkers, medieval scholars preserved a priceless intellectual heritage, without which the modern mind could never have evolved. In addition, numerous strands connect the thought of the scholastics and that of early modern philosophers.

Feudal traditions lasted long after the Middle Ages. Up to the French Revolution, for instance, French aristocrats enjoyed special privileges and exercised power over local government. In England, the aristocracy controlled local government until the Industrial Revolution transformed English society in the nineteenth century. Retaining the medieval ideal of the noble warrior, aristocrats continued to dominate the officer corps of European armies through the nineteenth century and even into the twentieth. Aristocratic notions of duty, honor, loyalty, and courtly love had endured into the twentieth century.

During the Middle Ages, Europeans began to take the lead over the Muslims, the Byzantines, the Chinese, and all the other peoples in the use of technology. Medieval technology and inventiveness stemmed in part from Christianity, which taught that God had created the world specifically for human beings to subdue and exploit. Consequently, medieval people employed animal power and labor-saving machinery to relieve human drudgery. Moreover, Christianity taught that God was above nature, not within it, so the Christian had no spiritual obstacle to exploiting nature—unlike, for instance, the Hindu. In contrast to classical humanism, the Christian outlook did not consider manual work degrading; even monks combined it with study.

The Christian stress on the sacred worth of the individual and on the higher law of God has never ceased to influence Western civilization. Even though in modern times the various Christian churches have not often taken the lead in political and social reform, the ideals identified with the Judeo-Christian tradition have become part of the Western heritage. As such, they have inspired social reformers who may no longer identify with their ancestral religion.

Believing that God's law was superior to state or national decrees, medieval philosophers provided a theoretical basis for opposing tyrannical kings who violated Christian principles. The idea that both the ruler and the ruled are bound by a higher law would, in a secularized form, become a principal element of modern liberal thought.

---

[1] Material for this introduction is taken from Marvin Perry et al., *Western Civilization*, 7th ed. (Boston: Houghton Mifflin, 2004), pp. 290–295.

Feudalism also contributed to the history of liberty. According to feudal theory, the king, as a member of the feudal community, was duty-bound to honor agreements made with his vassals. Lords possessed personal rights, which the king was obliged to respect. Resentful of a king who ran roughshod over customary feudal rights, lords also negotiated contracts with the crown, such as the famous Magna Carta (1215), to define and guard their customary liberties. To protect themselves from the arbitrary behavior of a king, feudal lords initiated what came to be called *government by consent* and the *rule of law*.

During the Middle Ages, then, there gradually emerged the idea that law was not imposed on inferiors by an absolute monarch but required the collaboration of the king and his subjects; that the king, too, was bound by the law; and that lords had the right to resist a monarch who violated agreements. A related phenomenon was the rise of representative institutions, with which the king was expected to consult on the realm's affairs. The most notable such institution was the British Parliament; although subordinate to the king, it became a permanent part of the state. Later, in the seventeenth century, Parliament would successfully challenge royal authority. Thus, continuity exists between the feudal tradition of a king bound by law and the modern practice of limiting the authority of the head of state.

Although the elements of continuity are clear, the characteristic outlook of the Middle Ages is as different from that of the modern age as it was from the outlook of the ancient world. Religion was the integrating feature of the Middle Ages, whereas science and secularism—a preoccupation with worldly life—determine the modern outlook. The period from the Italian Renaissance of the fifteenth century through the eighteenth-century Age of Enlightenment constituted a gradual breaking away from the medieval world-view—a rejection of the medieval conception of nature, the individual, and the purpose of life. The transition from medieval to modern was neither sudden nor complete, for there are no sharp demarcation lines separating historical periods. While many distinctively medieval ways endured in the sixteenth, seventeenth, and even eighteenth centuries, these centuries saw as well the rise of new intellectual, political, and economic forms, which marked the emergence of modernity.

Medieval thought began with the existence of God and the truth of his revelation as interpreted by the church, which set the standards and defined the purposes for human endeavor. The medieval mind rejected the fundamental principle of Greek philosophy: the autonomy of reason. Without the guidance of revealed truth, reason was seen as feeble.

Scholastics engaged in genuine philosophical speculation, but they did not allow philosophy to challenge the basic premises of their faith. Unlike either ancient or modern thinkers, medieval schoolmen ultimately believed that reason alone could not provide a unified view of nature or society. A rational soul had to be guided by a divine light. For all medieval philosophers, the natural order depended on a supernatural order for its origin and purpose. To understand the natural world properly, it was necessary to know its relationship to the higher world. The discoveries of reason had to accord with Scripture as interpreted by the church. In medieval thought, says historian-philosopher Ernst Cassirer,

[N]either science nor morality, neither law nor state, can be erected on its own foundations. Supernatural assistance is always needed to bring them to true perfection. . . . Reason is and remains the servant of revelation; within the sphere of natural intellectual and psychological forces, reason leads toward, and prepares the ground for, revelation.[2]

In the modern view, both nature and the human intellect are self-sufficient. Nature is a mathematical system that operates without

---

[2]Ernst Cassirer, *The Philosophy of the Enlightenment* (Boston: Beacon, 1955), p. 40.

miracles or any other form of divine intervention. To comprehend nature and society, the mind needs no divine assistance; it accepts no authority above reason. The modern mentality finds it unacceptable to reject the conclusions of science on the basis of clerical authority and revelation or to ground politics, law, or economics on religious dogma. It refuses to settle public issues by appeals to religious belief.

The medieval philosopher understood both nature and society to be a hierarchical order. God was the source of moral values, and the church was responsible for teaching and upholding these ethical norms. Kings acquired their right to rule from God. The entire social structure constituted a hierarchy: The clergy guided society according to Christian standards; lords defended Christian society from its enemies; and serfs, lowest in the social order, toiled for the good of all. In the hierarchy of knowledge, a lower form of knowledge derived from the senses, and the highest type of knowledge, theology, dealt with God's revelation. To the medieval mind, this hierarchical ordering of nature, society, and knowledge had a divine sanction.

Rejecting the medieval division of the universe into higher and lower realms and superior and inferior substances, the modern view postulated the uniformity of nature and nature's laws: the cosmos knows no privilege of rank; heavenly bodies follow the same laws of nature as earthly objects. Space is geometric and homogeneous, not hierarchical, heterogeneous, and qualitative. The universe was no longer conceived as finite and closed but as infinite, and the operations of nature were explained mathematically. The modern thinker studies mathematical law and chemical composition, not grades of perfection. Spiritual meaning is not sought in an examination of the material world. Roger Bacon, for example, described seven coverings of the eye and then concluded that God had fashioned the eye in this manner in order to express the seven gifts of the Spirit. This way of thinking is alien to the modern scientific outlook. So, too, is the medieval belief that natural disasters,

such as plagues and famines, are God's punishments for people's sins.

The outlook of the modern West also broke with the rigid division of medieval society into three orders: clergy, nobles, and commoners. The intellectual justification for this arrangement, as expressed by the English prelate John of Salisbury (c. 1115–1180), has been rejected by modern Westerners: "For inferiors owe it to their superiors to provide them with service, just as the superiors in their turn owe it to their inferiors to provide them with all things needful for their protection and succor."[3] Opposing the feudal principle that an individual's obligations and rights are a function of his or her rank in society, the modern view stressed equality of opportunity and equal treatment under the law. It rejected the idea that society should be guided by clergy, who were deemed to possess a special wisdom; by nobles, who were entitled to special privileges; and by monarchs, who were thought to receive their power from God.

The modern West also rejected the personal and customary character of feudal law. As the modern state developed, law assumed an impersonal and objective character. For example, if the lord demanded more than the customary forty days of military service, the vassal might refuse to comply, because he would see the lord's request as an unpardonable violation of custom and agreement, as well as an infringement on his liberties. In the modern state, with a constitution and a representative assembly, if a new law increasing the length of military service is passed, it merely replaces the old law. People do not refuse to obey it because the government has broken faith or violated custom.

In the modern world, the individual's relationship to the universe has been radically transformed. Medieval people lived in a geocentric universe that was finite in space and time. The universe was small, enclosed by a sphere of

---

[3]John of Salisbury, *Policraticus*, trans. John Dickinson (New York: Russell & Russell, 1963), pp. 243–244.

stars, beyond which were the heavens. The universe, it was believed, was some four thousand years old, and, in the not-too-distant future, Christ would return and human history would end. People in the Middle Ages knew why they were on earth and what was expected of them; they never doubted that heaven would be their reward for living a Christian life. Preparation for heaven was the ultimate aim of life. J. H. Randall, Jr., a historian of ideas, eloquently sums up the medieval view of a purposeful universe, in which the human being's position was clearly defined:

> The world was governed throughout by the omnipotent will and omniscient mind of God, whose sole interests were centered in man, his trial, his fall, his suffering and his glory. Worm of the dust as he was, man was yet the central object in the whole universe. . . . And when his destiny was completed, the heavens would be rolled up as a scroll and he would dwell with the Lord forever. Only those who rejected God's freely offered grace and with hardened hearts refused repentance would be cut off from this eternal life.[4]

This comforting medieval vision is alien to the modern outlook. Today, in a universe some

[4]J. H. Randall, Jr., *The Making of the Modern Mind* (Boston: Houghton Mifflin, 1940), p. 34.

12 billion years old, in which the earth is a tiny speck floating in an endless cosmic ocean, where life evolved over tens of millions of years, many Westerners no longer believe that human beings are special children of God; that heaven is their ultimate goal; that under their feet is hell, where grotesque demons torment sinners; and that God is an active agent in human history. To many intellectuals, the universe seems unresponsive to the religious supplications of people, and life's purpose is sought within the limits of earthly existence. Science and secularism have driven Christianity and faith from their central position to the periphery of human concerns.

The modern outlook developed gradually from the Renaissance to the eighteenth-century Age of Enlightenment. Mathematics rendered the universe comprehensible. Economic and political thought broke free of the religious frame of reference. Science became the great hope of the future. The thinkers of the Enlightenment wanted to liberate humanity from superstition, ignorance, and traditions that could not pass the test of reason. They saw themselves as emancipating culture from theological dogma and clerical authority. Rejecting the Christian idea of a person's inherent sinfulness, they held that the individual was basically good and that evil resulted from faulty institutions, poor education, and bad leadership. Thus, the concept of a rational and free society in which individuals could realize their potential slowly emerged.

CHAPTER 1

The Rise of Modernity

THE TRIUMPH OF GALETEA, Raphael, 1513. This fresco from the Palazzo della Farnesina in Rome exemplifies the Renaissance artist's elevation of the human form. The mythological subject is also humanistic in its evocation of the ancient Greek tradition. *(The Triumph of Galatea, 1512–14 (fresco) (see also 108063-4), Raphael (Raffaello Sanzio of Urbino) (1483–1520) / Villa Farnesina, Rome, Italy / Giraudon / The Bridgeman Art Library International)*

From the fifteenth through the seventeenth centuries, medieval attitudes and institutions broke down, and distinctly modern cultural, economic, and political forms emerged. For many historians, the Renaissance, which originated in the city-states of Italy, marks the starting point of the modern era. The Renaissance was characterized by a rebirth of interest in the humanist culture and outlook of ancient Greece and Rome. Although Renaissance individuals did not repudiate Christianity, they valued worldly activities and interests to a much greater degree than did the people of the Middle Ages, whose outlook was dominated by Christian otherworldliness. Renaissance individuals were fascinated by *this* world and by life's possibilities; they aspired to live a rich and creative life on earth and to fulfill themselves through artistic and literary activity.

Individualism was a hallmark of the Renaissance. The urban elite sought to demonstrate their unique talents, to assert their own individuality, and to gain recognition for their accomplishments. The most admired person during the Renaissance was the multitalented individual, the "universal man," who distinguished himself as a writer, artist, linguist, athlete. Disdaining Christian humility, Renaissance individuals took pride in their talents and worldly accomplishments—"I can work miracles," said the great Leonardo da Vinci.

During the High Middle Ages there had been a revival of Greek and Roman learning. Yet there were two important differences between the period called the Twelfth-Century Awakening and the Renaissance. First, many more ancient works were restored to circulation during the Renaissance than during the cultural revival of the Middle Ages. Second, medieval scholastics had tried to fit the ideas of the ancients into a Christian framework; they used Greek philosophy to explain Christian teachings. Renaissance scholars, on the other hand, valued ancient works for their own sake, believing that Greek and Roman authors could teach much about the art of living.

A distinguishing feature of the Renaissance period was the humanist movement, an educational and cultural program based on the study of ancient Greek and Latin literature. By studying the humanities—history, literature, rhetoric, moral, and political philosophy—humanists aimed to revive the worldly spirit of the ancient Greeks and Romans, which they believed had been lost in the Middle Ages.

Humanists were thus fascinated by the writings of the ancients. From the works of Thucydides, Plato, Cicero, Seneca, and other ancient authors, humanists sought guidelines for living life well in this world and looked for stylistic models for their own literary efforts. To the humanists, the ancients had written brilliantly, in an incomparable literary style, on friendship, citizenship, love, bravery, statesmanship, beauty, excellence, and every other topic devoted to the enrichment of human life.

Like the humanist movement, Renaissance art also marked a break with medieval culture. The art of the Middle Ages had served a religious function; its purpose was to lift the mind to God. It depicted a spiritual universe in which the supernatural was the supreme reality. The Gothic cathedral, with its flying buttresses, soared toward heaven, rising in ascending tiers; it reflected the medieval conception of a hierarchical universe with God at its apex. Painting also expressed gradations of spiritual values. Traditionally, the left side of a painting portrayed the damned, the right side the saved; dark colors expressed evil, light colors good. Spatial proportion was relative to spirituality—the less spiritually valuable a thing was, the less form it had (or the more deformed it was). Medieval art perfectly expressed the Christian view of the universe and the individual. The Renaissance shattered the dominance of religion over art, shifting attention from heaven to the natural world and to the human being; Renaissance artists often dealt with religious themes, but they placed their subjects in a naturalistic setting. Renaissance art also developed a new concept of visual space—perspective—that was defined from the standpoint of the individual observer. It was a quantitative space in which the artist, employing reason and mathematics, portrayed the essential form of the object as it appeared in three dimensions to the human eye: that is, it depicted the object in perspective.

The Renaissance began in the late fourteenth century in the northern Italian city-states, which had grown prosperous from the revival of trade in the Middle Ages. Italian merchants and bankers had the wealth to acquire libraries and fine works of art and to support art, literature, and scholarship. Surrounded by reminders of ancient Rome—amphitheaters, monuments, and sculpture—the well-to-do took an interest in classical culture and thought. In the late fifteenth and the sixteenth centuries, Renaissance ideas spread to Germany, France, Spain, and England through books available in great numbers due to the invention of the printing press.

1 The Humanists' Fascination with Antiquity

Humanists believed that a refined person must know the literature of Greece and Rome. They strove to imitate the style of the ancients, to speak and write as eloquently as the Greeks and Romans. Toward these ends, they sought to read, print, and restore to circulation every scrap of ancient literature that could still be found.

Petrarch
THE FATHER OF HUMANISM

During his lifetime, Francesco Petrarca, or Petrarch (1304–1374), had an astounding reputation as a poet and scholar. Often called the "father of humanism," he inspired other humanists through his love for classical learning; his criticism of medieval Latin as barbaric in contrast to the style of Cicero, Seneca, and other Romans; and his literary works based on classical models. Petrarch saw his own age as a restoration of classical brilliance after an interval of medieval darkness.

A distinctly modern element in Petrarch's thought is the subjective and individualistic character of his writing. In talking about himself and probing his own feelings, Petrarch demonstrates a self-consciousness characteristic of the modern outlook.

Like many other humanists, Petrarch remained devoted to Christianity: "When it comes to thinking or speaking of religion, that is, of the highest truth, of true happiness and eternal salvation," he declared, "I certainly am not a Ciceronian or a Platonist but a Christian." Petrarch was a forerunner of the Christian humanism best represented by Erasmus. Christian humanists combined an intense devotion to Christianity with a great love for classical literature, which they much preferred to the dull and turgid treatises written by scholastic philosophers and theologians. In the following passage, Petrarch criticizes his contemporaries for their ignorance of ancient writers and shows his commitment to classical learning.

. . . O inglorious age! that scorns antiquity, its mother, to whom it owes every noble art—that dares to declare itself not only equal but superior to the glorious past. I say nothing of the vulgar, the dregs of mankind, whose sayings and opinions may raise a laugh but hardly merit serious censure. . . .

. . . But what can be said in defense of men of education who ought not to be ignorant of antiquity and yet are plunged in this same darkness and delusion?

You see that I cannot speak of these matters without the greatest irritation and indignation. There has arisen of late a set of dialecticians [experts in logical argument], who are not only ignorant but demented. Like a black army of ants from some old rotten oak, they swarm forth from their hiding places and devastate the fields of sound learning. They condemn Plato and Aristotle, and laugh at Socrates and Pythagoras.[1] And, good God! under what silly and incompetent leaders these opinions are put forth. . . . What shall we say of men who scorn Marcus Tullius Cicero,[2] the bright sun of eloquence? Of those who scoff at Varro and Seneca,[3] and are scandalized at what

[1]The work of Aristotle (384–322 B.C.), a leading Greek philosopher, had an enormous influence among medieval and Renaissance scholars. A student of the philosopher Socrates, Plato (c. 427–347 B.C.) was one of the greatest philosophers of ancient Greece. His work grew to be extremely influential in the West during the Renaissance period, as new texts of his writings were discovered and translated into Latin and more Westerners could read the originals in Greek. Pythagoras (c. 582–507 B.C.) was a Greek philosopher whose work influenced both Socrates and Plato.

[2]Cicero (106–43 B.C.) was a Roman statesman and rhetorician. His Latin style was especially admired and emulated during the Renaissance.

[3]Varro (116–27 B.C.) was a Roman scholar and historian. Seneca (4 B.C.–A.D. 65) was a Roman statesman, dramatist, and Stoic philosopher whose literary style was greatly admired during the Renaissance.

they choose to call the crude, unfinished style of Livy and Sallust [Roman historians]? . . .

Such are the times, my friend, upon which we have fallen; such is the period in which we live and are growing old. Such are the critics of today, as I so often have occasion to lament and complain—men who are innocent of knowledge and virtue, and yet harbour the most exalted opinion of themselves. Not content with losing the words of the ancients, they must attack their genius and their ashes. They rejoice in their ignorance, as if what they did not know were not worth knowing. They give full rein to their license and conceit, and freely introduce among us new authors and outlandish teachings.

Leonardo Bruni
STUDY OF GREEK LITERATURE AND A HUMANIST EDUCATIONAL PROGRAM

Leonardo Bruni (1374–1444) was a Florentine humanist who extolled both intellectual study and active involvement in public affairs, an outlook called civic humanism. In the first reading from his *History of His Own Times in Italy*, Bruni expresses the humanist's love for ancient Greek literature and language.

In a treatise, *De Studiis et Literis* (On Learning and Literature), written around 1405 and addressed to the noble lady Baptista di Montefeltro (1383–1450), daughter of the Count of Urbino, Bruni outlines the basic course of studies that the humanists recommended as the best preparation for a life of wisdom and virtue. In addition to the study of Christian literature, Bruni encourages a wide familiarity with the best minds and stylists of ancient Greek and Latin cultures.

LOVE FOR GREEK LITERATURE

Then first came a knowledge of Greek, which had not been in use among us for seven hundred years. Chrysoloras the Byzantine,[1] a man of noble birth and well versed in Greek letters, brought Greek learning to us. When his country was invaded by the Turks, he came by sea, first to Venice. The report of him soon spread, and he was cordially invited and besought and promised a public stipend, to come to Florence and open his store of riches to the youth. I was then studying Civil Law,[2] but . . . I burned with love of academic studies, and had spent no little pains on dialectic and rhetoric. At the coming of Chrysoloras I was torn in mind, deeming it shameful to desert the law, and yet a crime to lose such a chance of studying Greek literature; and often with youthful impulse I would say to myself: "Thou, when it is permitted thee to gaze on Homer, Plato and Demosthenes,[3] and the other [Greek] poets, philosophers, orators, of whom such glorious things are spread abroad, and speak with them and be instructed in their admirable teaching, wilt thou desert and rob thyself? Wilt thou neglect this opportunity so divinely offered? For seven hundred years, no one in Italy has possessed Greek letters; and yet

[1]Chrysoloras (c. 1355–1415), a Byzantine writer and teacher, introduced the study of Greek literature to the Italians, helping to open a new age of Western humanistic learning.
[2]Civil Law refers to the Roman law as codified by Emperor Justinian in the early sixth century A.D. and studied in medieval law schools.

[3]Demosthenes (384–322 B.C.) was an Athenian statesman and orator whose oratorical style was much admired by Renaissance humanists.

we confess that all knowledge is derived from them. How great advantage to your knowledge, enhancement of your fame, increase of your pleasure, will come from an understanding of this tongue? There are doctors of civil law everywhere; and the chance of learning will not fail thee. But if this one and only doctor of Greek letters disappears, no one can be found to teach thee." Overcome at length by these reasons, I gave myself to Chrysoloras, with such zeal to learn, that what through the wakeful day I gathered, I followed after in the night, even when asleep.

ON LEARNING AND LITERATURE

. . . The foundations of all true learning must be laid in the sound and thorough knowledge of Latin: which implies study marked by a broad spirit, accurate scholarship, and careful attention to details. Unless this solid basis be secured it is useless to attempt to rear an enduring edifice. Without it the great monuments of literature are unintelligible, and the art of composition impossible. To attain this essential knowledge we must never relax our careful attention to the grammar of the language, but perpetually confirm and extend our acquaintance with it until it is thoroughly our own. . . . To this end we must be supremely careful in our choice of authors, lest an inartistic and debased style infect our own writing and degrade our taste; which danger is best avoided by bringing a keen, critical sense to bear upon select works, observing the sense of each passage, the structure of the sentence, the force of every word down to the least important particle. In this way our reading reacts directly upon our style. . . .

But we must not forget that true distinction is to be gained by a wide and varied range of such studies as conduce to the profitable enjoyment of life, in which, however, we must observe due proportion in the attention and time we devote to them.

First amongst such studies I place History: a subject which must not on any account be neglected by one who aspires to true cultivation.

For it is our duty to understand the origins of our own history and its development; and the achievements of Peoples and of Kings.

For the careful study of the past enlarges our foresight in contemporary affairs and affords to citizens and to monarchs lessons of incitement or warning in the ordering of public policy. From History, also, we draw our store of examples of moral precepts.

In the monuments of ancient literature which have come down to us History holds a position of great distinction. We specially prize such [Roman] authors as Livy, Sallust, and Curtius;[4] and, perhaps even above these, Julius Caesar; the style of whose Commentaries, so elegant and so limpid, entitles them to our warm admiration. . . .

The great Orators of antiquity must by all means be included. Nowhere do we find the virtues more warmly extolled, the vices so fiercely decried. From them we may learn, also, how to express consolation, encouragement, dissuasion, or advice. If the principles which orators set forth are portrayed for us by philosophers, it is from the former that we learn how to employ the emotions—such as indignation, or pity—in driving home their application in individual cases. Further, from oratory we derive our store of those elegant or striking turns of expression which are used with so much effect in literary compositions. Lastly, in oratory we find that wealth of vocabulary, that clear easy-flowing style, that verve and force, which are invaluable to us both in writing and in conversation.

I come now to Poetry and the Poets. . . . For we cannot point to any great mind of the past for whom the Poets had not a powerful attraction. Aristotle, in constantly quoting Homer, Hesiod, Pindar, Euripides, and other [Greek] poets, proves that he knew their works hardly less intimately than those of the philosophers. Plato, also, frequently appeals to them, and in this way covers them with his approval. If we

---

[4]Q. Curtius Rufus, a Roman historian and rhetorician of the mid-first century A.D., composed a biography of Alexander the Great.

turn to Cicero, we find him not content with quoting Ennius, Accius,[5] and others of the Latins, but rendering poems from the Greek and employing them habitually. . . . Hence my view that familiarity with the great poets of antiquity is essential to any claim to true education. For in their writings we find deep speculations upon Nature, and upon the Causes and Origins of things, which must carry weight with us both from their antiquity and from their authorship. Besides these, many important truths upon matters of daily life are suggested or illustrated. All this is expressed with such grace and dignity as demands our admiration. . . . To sum up what I have endeavoured to set forth. That high standard of education to which I referred at the outset is only to be reached by one who has seen many things and read much. Poet, Orator, Historian, and the rest, all

must be studied, each must contribute a share. Our learning thus becomes full, ready, varied and elegant, available for action or for discourse in all subjects. But to enable us to make effectual use of what we know we must add to our knowledge the power of expression. These two sides of learning, indeed, should not be separated: they afford mutual aid and distinction. Proficiency in literary form, not accompanied by broad acquaintance with facts and truths, is a barren attainment; whilst information, however vast, which lacks all grace of expression, would seem to be put under a bushel or partly thrown away. Indeed, one may fairly ask what advantage it is to possess profound and varied learning if one cannot convey it in language worthy of the subject. Where, however, this double capacity exists—breadth of learning and grace of style—we allow the highest title to distinction and to abiding fame. If we review the great names of ancient [Greek and Roman] literature, Plato, Democritus, Aristotle, Theophrastus, Varro, Cicero, Seneca, Augustine, Jerome, Lactantius, we shall find it hard to say whether we admire more their attainments or their literary power.

---

[5]Ennius (239–169 B.C.) wrote the first great Latin epic poem, which was based on the legends of Rome's founding and its early history. Accius (c. 170–90 B.C.), also a Roman, authored a history of Greek and Latin literature.

REVIEW QUESTIONS

1. What do historians mean by the term "Renaissance humanism"?
2. What made Petrarch aware that a renaissance, or rebirth, of classical learning was necessary in his time?
3. Why did Leonardo Bruni abandon his earlier course of studies to pursue the study of Greek literature?
4. What subjects made up the basic course of studies advocated by Bruni?

---

2 Human Dignity

In his short lifetime, Giovanni Pico della Mirandola (1463–1494) mastered Greek, Latin, Hebrew, and Arabic and aspired to synthesize the Hebrew, Greek, and Christian traditions. His most renowned work, *Oration on the Dignity of Man*, composed in 1486, has been called the humanist manifesto.

Pico della Mirandola
ORATION ON THE DIGNITY OF MAN

In the opening section of the *Oration*, Pico declares that unlike other creatures, human beings have not been assigned a fixed place in the universe. Our destiny is not determined by anything outside us. Rather, God has bestowed upon us a unique distinction: the liberty to determine the form and value our lives shall acquire. The notion that people have the power to shape their own lives is a key element in the emergence of the modern outlook.

I have read in the records of the Arabians, reverend Fathers, that Abdala the Saracen,[1] when questioned as to what on this stage of the world, as it were, could be seen most worthy of wonder, replied: "There is nothing to be seen more wonderful than man." In agreement with this opinion is the saying of Hermes Trismegistus: "A great miracle, Asclepius, is man."[2] But when I weighed the reason for these maxims, the many grounds for the excellence of human nature reported by many men failed to satisfy me—that man is the intermediary between creatures, the intimate of the gods, the king of the lower beings, by the acuteness of his senses, by the discernment of his reason, and by the light of his intelligence the interpreter of nature, the interval between fixed eternity and fleeting time, and (as the Persians say) the bond, nay, rather, the marriage song of the world, on David's [biblical king] testimony but little lower than the angels. Admittedly great though these reasons be, they are not the principal grounds, that is, those which may rightfully claim for themselves the privilege of the highest admiration. For why should we not admire more the angels themselves and the blessed choirs of heaven? At last it seems to me I have come to understand why man is the most fortunate of creatures and consequently worthy of all admiration and what precisely is that rank which is his lot in the universal chain of Being—a rank to be envied not only by brutes but even by the stars and by minds beyond this world. It is a matter past faith and a wondrous one. Why should it not be? For it is on this very account that man is rightly called and judged a great miracle and a wonderful creature indeed. . . .

. . . God the Father, the supreme Architect, had already built this cosmic home we behold, the most sacred temple of His godhead, by the laws of His mysterious wisdom. The region above the heavens He had adorned with Intelligences, the heavenly spheres He had quickened with eternal souls, and the excrementary and filthy parts of the lower world He had filled with a multitude of animals of every kind. But, when the work was finished, the Craftsman kept wishing that there were someone to ponder the plan of so great a work, to love its beauty, and to wonder at its vastness. Therefore, when everything was done (as Moses and Timaeus[3] bear witness), He finally took thought concerning the creation of man. But there was not among His archetypes that from which He could fashion a new offspring, nor was there in His treasure-houses anything which He might bestow on His new son as an inheritance, nor was there in the seats of all the world a place where the latter might sit to contemplate the universe. All was

---

[1]Abdala the Saracen possibly refers to the eighth-century A.D. writer Abd-Allah Ibn al-Muqaffa.

[2]Ancient writings dealing with magic, alchemy, astrology, and occult philosophy were erroneously attributed to an assumed Egyptian priest, Hermes Trismegistus. Asclepius was a Greek god of healing.

---

[3]Timaeus, a Greek Pythagorean philosopher, was a central character in Plato's famous dialogue *Timaeus*.

now complete; all things had been assigned to the highest, the middle, and the lowest orders. But in its final creation it was not the part of the Father's power to fail as though exhausted. It was not the part of His wisdom to waver in a needful matter through poverty of counsel. It was not the part of His kindly love that he who was to praise God's divine generosity in regard to others should be compelled to condemn it in regard to himself.

At last the best of artisans [God] ordained that that creature to whom He had been able to give nothing proper to himself should have joint possession of whatever had been peculiar to each of the different kinds of being. He therefore took man as a creature of indeterminate nature and, assigning him a place in the middle of the world, addressed him thus: "Neither a fixed abode nor a form that is thine alone nor any function peculiar to thyself have we given thee, Adam, to the end that according to thy longing and according to thy judgment thou mayest have and possess what abode, what form, and what functions thou thyself shalt desire. The nature of all other beings is limited and constrained within the bounds of laws prescribed by Us. Thou, constrained by no limits, in accordance with thine own free will, in whose hand We have placed thee, shalt ordain for thyself the limits of thy nature. We have set thee at the world's center that thou mayest from thence more easily observe whatever is in the world. We have made thee neither of heaven nor of earth, neither mortal nor immortal, so that with freedom of choice and with honor, as though the maker and molder of thyself, thou mayest fashion thyself in whatever shape thou shalt prefer. Thou shalt have the power to degenerate into the lower forms of life, which are brutish. Thou shalt have the power, out of thy soul's judgment, to be reborn into the higher forms, which are divine."

O supreme generosity of God the Father, O highest and most marvelous felicity of man! To him it is granted to have whatever he chooses, to be whatever he wills. Beasts as soon as they are born (so says Lucilius)[4] bring with them from their mother's womb all they will ever possess. Spiritual beings [angels], either from the beginning or soon thereafter, become what they are to be for ever and ever. On man when he came into life the Father conferred the seeds of all kinds and the germs of every way of life. Whatever seeds each man cultivates will grow to maturity and bear in him their own fruit. If they be vegetative, he will be like a plant. If sensitive, he will become brutish. If rational, he will grow into a heavenly being. If intellectual, he will be an angel and the son of God. And if, happy in the lot of no created thing, he withdraws into the center of his own unity, his spirit, made one with God, in the solitary darkness of God, who is set above all things, shall surpass them all.

---

[4]Lucilius, a first-century A.D. Roman poet and Stoic philosopher, was a close friend of Seneca, the philosopher-dramatist.

REVIEW QUESTIONS

1. According to Pico della Mirandola, what quality did humans alone possess? What did its possession allow them to do?
2. How does Pico's view point to the emergence of the modern outlook?

3 Break with Medieval Political Theory

Turning away from the religious orientation of the Middle Ages, Renaissance thinkers discussed the human condition in secular terms and opened up possibilities for thinking about moral and political problems in new ways. Thus, Niccolò Machiavelli (1469–1527), a Florentine statesman and political theorist, broke with medieval political theory. Medieval political thinkers held that the ruler derived power from God and had a religious obligation to rule in accordance with God's precepts. Machiavelli, though, ascribed no divine origin to kingship, nor did he attribute events to the mysterious will of God; and he explicitly rejected the principle that kings should adhere to Christian moral teachings. For Machiavelli, the state was a purely human creation. Successful kings or princes, he asserted, should be concerned only with preserving and strengthening the state's power and must ignore questions of good and evil, morality and immorality. Machiavelli did not assert that religion was supernatural in origin and rejected the prevailing belief that Christian morality should guide political life. For him, religion's value derived from other factors: a ruler could utilize religion to unite his subjects and to foster obedience to law.

Niccolò Machiavelli
THE PRINCE

In contrast to medieval thinkers, Machiavelli did not seek to construct an ideal Christian community but to discover how politics was *really* conducted. In *The Prince*, written in 1513 and published posthumously in 1532, he studied politics in the cold light of reason, as the following passage illustrates.

It now remains to be seen what are the methods and rules for a prince as regards his subjects and friends. And as I know that many have written of this, I fear that my writing about it may be deemed presumptuous, differing as I do, especially in this matter, from the opinions of others. But my intention being to write something of use to those who understand, it appears to me more proper to go to the real truth of the matter than to its imagination; and many have imagined republics and principalities which have never been seen or known to exist in reality; for how we live is so far removed from how we ought to live, that he who abandons what is done for what ought to be done, will

rather learn to bring about his own ruin than his preservation.

Machiavelli removed ethics from political thinking. A successful ruler, he contended, is indifferent to moral and religious considerations. But will not the prince be punished on the Day of Judgment for violating Christian teachings? In startling contrast to medieval theorists, Machiavelli simply ignored the question. The action of a prince, he said, should be governed solely by necessity.

A man who wishes to make a profession of goodness in everything must necessarily come to grief among so many who are not good. Therefore it is necessary for a prince, who wishes to maintain himself, to learn how not to be good, and to use this knowledge and not use it, according to the necessity of the case.

Leaving on one side, then, those things which concern only an imaginary prince, and speaking of those that are real, I state that all men, and especially princes, who are placed at a greater height, are reputed for certain qualities which bring them either praise or blame. Thus one is considered liberal, another . . . miserly; . . . one a free giver, another rapacious; one cruel, another merciful; one a breaker of his word, another trustworthy; one effeminate and pusillanimous, another fierce and high-spirited; one humane, another haughty; one lascivious, another chaste; one frank, another astute; one hard, another easy; one serious, another frivolous; one religious, another an unbeliever, and so on. I know that every one will admit that it would be highly praiseworthy in a prince to possess all the above-named qualities that are reputed good, but as they cannot all be possessed or observed, human conditions not permitting of it, it is necessary that he should be prudent enough to avoid the scandal of those vices which would lose him the state, and guard himself if possible against those which will not lose it [for] him, but if not able to, he can indulge them with less scruple. And yet he must not mind incurring the scandal of those vices, without which it would be difficult to save the state, for if one considers well, it will be found that some things which seem virtues would, if followed, lead to one's ruin, and some others which appear vices result in one's greater security and wellbeing. . . .

. . . I say that every prince must desire to be considered merciful and not cruel. He must, however, take care not to misuse this mercifulness. Cesare Borgia was considered cruel, but his cruelty had brought order to the Romagna,[1]

united it, and reduced it to peace and fealty. If this is considered well, it will be seen that he was really much more merciful than the Florentine people, who, to avoid the name of cruelty, allowed Pistoia[2] to be destroyed. A prince, therefore, must not mind incurring the charge of cruelty for the purpose of keeping his subjects united and faithful; for, with a very few examples, he will be more merciful than those who, from excess of tenderness, allow disorders to arise, from whence spring bloodshed and rapine; for these as a rule injure the whole community, while the executions carried out by the prince injure only individuals. . . .

Machiavelli's rigorous investigation of politics led him to view human nature from the standpoint of its limitations and imperfections. The astute prince, he said, recognizes that human beings are by nature selfish, cowardly, and dishonest, and regulates his political strategy accordingly.

From this arises the question whether it is better to be loved more than feared, or feared more than loved. The reply is, that one ought to be both feared and loved, but as it is difficult for the two to go together, it is much safer to be feared than loved, if one of the two has to be wanting. For it may be said of men in general that they are ungrateful, voluble, dissemblers, anxious to avoid danger, and covetous of gain; as long as you benefit them, they are entirely yours; they offer you their blood, their goods, their life, and their children, as I have before said, when the necessity is remote; but when it approaches, they revolt. And the prince who has relied solely on their words, without making other preparations, is ruined;

---

[1]Cesare Borgia (c. 1476–1507) was the bastard son of Rodrigo Borgia, then a Spanish cardinal, and later Pope

Alexander VI (1492–1503). With his father's aid he attempted to carve out for himself an independent duchy in north-central Italy, with Romagna as its heart. Through cruelty, violence, and treachery, he succeeded at first in his ambition, but ultimately his principality collapsed. Romagna was eventually incorporated into the Papal State under Pope Julius II (1503–1513).

[2]Pistoia, a small Italian city in Tuscany, came under the control of Florence in the fourteenth century.

for the friendship which is gained by purchase and not through grandeur and nobility of spirit is bought but not secured, and at a pinch is not to be expended in your service. And men have less scruple in offending one who makes himself loved than one who makes himself feared; for love is held by a chain of obligation which, men being selfish, is broken whenever it serves their purpose; but fear is maintained by a dread of punishment which never fails.

Still, a prince should make himself feared in such a way that if he does not gain love, he at any rate avoids hatred; for fear and the absence of hatred may well go together, and will be always attained by one who abstains from interfering with the property of his citizens and subjects or with their women. And when he is obliged to take the life of any one, let him do so when there is a proper justification and manifest reason for it; but above all he must abstain from taking the property of others, for men forget more easily the death of their father than the loss of their patrimony. Then also pretexts for seizing property are never wanting, and one who begins to live by rapine will always find some reason for taking the goods of others, whereas causes for taking life are rarer and more fleeting.

But when the prince is with his army and has a large number of soldiers under his control, then it is extremely necessary that he should not mind being thought cruel; for without this reputation he could not keep an army united or disposed to any duty. Among the noteworthy actions of Hannibal[3] is numbered this, that although he had an enormous army, composed of men of all nations and fighting in foreign countries, there never arose any dissension either among them or against the prince, either in good fortune or in bad. This could not be due to anything but his inhuman cruelty, which together with his infinite other virtues, made him always venerated and terrible in the sight of his soldiers, and

---

[3]Hannibal (247–182 B.C.) was a brilliant Carthaginian general whose military victories almost destroyed Roman power. He was finally defeated at the battle of Zama in 202 B.C. by the Roman general Scipio Africanus.

without it his other virtues would not have sufficed to produce that effect. Thoughtless writers admire on the one hand his actions, and on the other blame the principal cause of them. . . .

Again in marked contrast to the teachings of Christian (and ancient) moralists, Machiavelli said that the successful prince will use any means to achieve and sustain political power. If the end is desirable, all means are justified.

How laudable it is for a prince to keep good faith and live with integrity, and not with astuteness, every one knows. Still the experience of our times shows those princes to have done great things who have had little regard for good faith, and have been able by astuteness to confuse men's brains, and who have ultimately overcome those who have made loyalty their foundation.

You must know, then, that there are two methods of fighting, the one by law, the other by force: the first method is that of men, the second of beasts; but as the first method is often insufficient, one must have recourse to the second. It is therefore necessary for a prince to know well how to use both the beast and the man. . . .

A prince being thus obliged to know well how to act as a beast must imitate the fox and the lion, for the lion cannot protect himself from traps, and the fox cannot defend himself from wolves. One must therefore be a fox to recognise traps, and a lion to frighten wolves. Those that wish to be only lions do not understand this. Therefore, a prudent ruler ought not to keep faith when by so doing it would be against his interest, and when the reasons which made him bind himself no longer exist. If men were all good, this precept would not be a good one; but as they are bad, and would not observe their faith with you, so you are not bound to keep faith with them. Nor have legitimate grounds ever failed a prince who wished to show [plausible] excuse for the non-fulfilment of his promise. Of this one could furnish an infinite number of modern examples, and show how many times peace has been broken, and how many promises rendered worthless, by the faithlessness of princes, and those that have been best able to imitate the fox have succeeded best. But it is necessary to be able to disguise this character well, and to be a great feigner and dissembler; and men are so simple and so ready to obey present necessities, that one who deceives will always find those who allow themselves to be deceived. . . .

. . . Thus it is well to seem merciful, faithful, humane, sincere, religious, and also to be so; but you must have the mind so disposed that when it is needful to be otherwise you may be able to change to the opposite qualities. And it must be understood that a prince, and especially a new prince, cannot observe all those things which are considered good in men, being often obliged, in order to maintain the state, to act against faith, against charity, against humanity, and against religion. And, therefore, he must have a mind disposed to adapt itself according to the wind, and as the variations of fortune dictate, and, as I said before, not deviate from what is good, if possible, but be able to do evil if constrained.

A prince must take great care that nothing goes out of his mouth which is not full of the above-named five qualities, and, to see and hear him, he should seem to be all mercy, faith, integrity, humanity, and religion. And nothing is more necessary than to seem to have this last quality, for men in general judge more by the eyes than by the hands, for every one can see, but very few have to feel. Everybody sees what you appear to be, few feel what you are, and those few will not dare to oppose themselves to the many, who have the majesty of the state to defend them; and in the actions of men, and especially of princes, from which there is no appeal, the end justifies the means. Let a prince therefore aim at conquering and maintaining the state, and the means will always be judged honourable and praised by every one, for the vulgar is always taken by appearances and the issue of the event; and the world consists only of the vulgar, and the few who are not vulgar are isolated when the many have a rallying point in the prince. A certain prince of the present time, whom it is well not to name, never does anything but preach peace and good faith, but he is really a great enemy to both, and either of them, had he observed them, would have lost him state or reputation on many occasions.

REVIEW QUESTIONS

1. In what ways was Niccolò Machiavelli's advice to princes a break from the teachings of medieval political and moral philosophers?
2. How does Machiavelli's image of human nature compare with that of Pico della Mirandola?
3. Would Machiavelli's political advice help or hurt a politician in a modern democratic society?

4 The Lutheran Reformation

The reformation of the Western Christian church in the sixteenth century was precipitated by Martin Luther (1483–1546). A pious German Augustinian monk and theologian, Luther had no intention of founding a new church or overthrowing the political and ecclesiastical order of late medieval Europe. He was educated in the tradition of the New Devotion, a movement heightening spirituality, and as a theology professor at the university in Wittenberg, Germany, he opposed rationalistic, scholastic theology. Sympathetic at first to the ideas of Christian humanists like Erasmus, Luther too sought a reform of morals and an end to abusive practices within the church. But a visit to the papal court in Rome in 1510 left him profoundly shocked at its worldliness and disillusioned with the papacy's role in the church's governance.

Martin Luther
ON PAPAL POWER, JUSTIFICATION BY FAITH, THE INTERPRETATION OF THE BIBLE, AND THE NATURE OF THE CLERGY

To finance the rebuilding of the church of St. Peter in Rome, the papacy in 1515 offered indulgences to those who gave alms for this pious work. An indulgence was a mitigation or remission of the penance imposed by a priest in absolving a penitent who confessed a sin and indicated remorse. Indulgences were granted by papal decrees for those who agreed to perform some act of charity, alms-giving, prayer, pilgrimage, or other pious work. Some preachers of this partic-ular papal indulgence deceived people into believing that a "purchase" of this indulgence would win them, or even the dead, a secure place in heaven.

In 1517, Luther denounced the abuses connected with the preaching of papal indulgences. The quarrel led quickly to other and more profound theological issues. His opponents defended the use of indulgences on the basis of papal authority, shifting the debate to questions about the nature of papal power within the church. Luther responded with a vigorous attack on the whole system of papal governance. The principal points of his criticism were set out in his *Address to the Christian Nobility of the German Nation Concerning the Reform of the Christian Estate*, published in August 1520. In the first excerpt that follows, Luther argued that the papacy was blocking any reform of the church and appealed to the nobil-ity of Germany to intervene by summoning a "free council" to reform the church.

A central point of contention between Luther and Catholic critics was his theo-logical teaching on justification (salvation) by faith and on the role of good works in the scheme of salvation. Luther had suffered anguish about his unworthiness before God. Then, during a mystical experience, Luther suddenly perceived that his salvation came not because of his good works but as a free gift from God due to Luther's faith in Jesus Christ.

Thus, while never denying that a Christian was obliged to perform good works, Luther argued that such pious acts were not helpful in achieving salva-tion. His claim that salvation or justification was attained through faith in Jesus Christ as Lord and Savior, and through that act of faith alone, became the rally-ing point of the Protestant reformers.

The Catholic position, not authoritatively clarified until the Council of Trent (1545–1563), argued that justification came not only through faith, but through hope and love as well, obeying God's commandments and doing good works. In *The Freedom of a Christian*, published in 1520, Luther outlined his teaching on justification by faith and on the inefficacy of good works; the second excerpt is from this work.

Another dispute between Luther and papal theologians was the question of interpretation of the Bible. In the medieval church, the final authority in any dispute over the meaning of Scriptural texts or church doctrine was ordinarily the pope alone, speaking as supreme head of the church or in concert with the bishops in an ecumenical council. The doctrine of papal infallibility (that the pope could not err in teaching matters of faith and morals) was already well known, but belief in this doctrine had not been formally required. Luther argued that the literal text of Scripture was alone the foundation of Christian truth, not the teaching of popes or councils. Moreover, Luther said that all believers were priests, and the clergy did not hold any power beyond that of the laity; therefore the special privileges of the clergy were unjustified. The third excerpt contains Luther's views on the interpretation of Scripture and the nature of priestly offices.

ON PAPAL POWER

The Romanists [traditional Catholics loyal to the papacy] have very cleverly built three walls around themselves. Hitherto they have protected themselves by these walls in such a way that no one has been able to reform them. As a result, the whole of Christendom has fallen abominably.

In the first place, when pressed by the temporal power they have made decrees and declared that the temporal power had no jurisdiction over them, but that, on the contrary, the spiritual power is above the temporal. In the second place, when the attempt is made to reprove them with the Scriptures, they raise the objection that only the pope may interpret the Scriptures. In the third place, if threatened with a council, their story is that no one may summon a council but the pope.

In this way they have cunningly stolen our three rods from us, that they may go unpunished. They have [settled] themselves within the safe stronghold of these three walls so that they can practice all the knavery and wickedness which we see today. Even when they have been compelled to hold a council they have weakened its power in advance by putting the princes under oath to let them remain as they were. In addition, they have given the pope full authority over all decisions of a council, so that it is all the same whether there are many councils or no councils. They only deceive us with puppet shows and sham fights. They fear terribly for their skin in a really free council! They have so intimidated kings and princes with this technique that they believe it would be an offense against God not to be obedient to the Romanists in all their knavish and ghoulish deceits. . . .

The Romanists have no basis in Scripture for their claim that the pope alone has the right to call or confirm a council. This is just their own ruling, and it is only valid as long as it is not harmful to Christendom or contrary to the laws of God. Now when the pope deserves punishment, this ruling no longer obtains, for not to punish him by authority of a council is harmful to Christendom. . . .

Therefore, when necessity demands it, and the pope is an offense to Christendom, the first man who is able should, as a true member of the whole body, do what he can to bring about a truly free council. No one can do this so well as the temporal authorities, especially since they are also fellow-Christians, fellow-priests, fellow-members of the spiritual estate, fellow-lords over all things. Whenever it is necessary or profitable they ought to exercise the office and work which they have received from God over everyone.

JUSTIFICATION BY FAITH

You may ask, "What then is the Word of God, and how shall it be used, since there are so many words of God?" I answer: The Apostle explains this in Romans 1. The Word is the gospel of God concerning his Son, who was made flesh, suffered, rose from the dead, and was glorified through the Spirit who sanctifies. To preach Christ means to feed the soul, make it righteous, set it free, and save it, provided it believes the preaching. Faith alone is the saving and efficacious use of the Word of God, according to Rom. 10(:9): "If you confess with your lips that Jesus is Lord and believe in your heart that God raised him from the dead, you will be saved." Furthermore, "Christ is the end of the law, that every one who has faith may be justified" (Rom. 10:4). Again, in Rom. 1(:17), "He who through faith is righteous shall live." The Word of God cannot be received and cherished by any works whatever but only by faith. Therefore it is clear that, as the soul needs only the Word of God for its life and righteousness, so it is justified by faith alone and not any works; for if it could be justified by anything else, it would not need the Word, and consequently it would not need faith.

This faith cannot exist in connection with works—that is to say, if you at the same time claim to be justified by works, whatever their character—for that would be the same as "limping with two different opinions" (I Kings 18:21), as worshiping Baal and kissing one's own hand (Job 31:27–28), which, as Job says, is a very great iniquity. Therefore the moment you begin to have faith you learn that all things in you are altogether blameworthy, sinful, and damnable, as the Apostle says in Rom. 3(:23), "Since all have sinned and fall short of the glory of God," and, "None is righteous, no, not one: . . . all have turned aside, together they have gone wrong" (Rom. 3:10–12). When you have learned this

you will know that you need Christ, who suffered and rose again for you so that, if you believe in him, you may through this faith become a new man in so far as your sins are forgiven and you are justified by the merits of another, namely, of Christ alone.

Since, therefore, this faith can rule only in the inner man, as Rom. 10(:10) says, "For man believes with his heart and so is justified," and since faith alone justifies, it is clear that the inner man cannot be justified, freed, or saved by any outer work or action at all, and that these works, whatever their character, have nothing to do with this inner man. On the other hand, only ungodliness and unbelief of heart, and no outer work, make him guilty and a damnable servant of sin. Wherefore it ought to be the first concern of every Christian to lay aside all confidence in works and increasingly to strengthen faith alone and through faith to grow in the knowledge, not of works, but of Christ Jesus, who suffered and rose for him, as Peter teaches in the last chapter of his first Epistle (1 Pet. 5:10). No other work makes a Christian. . . .

Our faith in Christ does not free us from works but from false opinions concerning works, that is, from the foolish presumption that justification is acquired by works. Faith redeems, corrects, and preserves our consciences so that we know that righteousness does not consist in works, although works neither can nor ought to be wanting; just as we cannot be without food and drink and all the works of this mortal body, yet our righteousness is not in them, but in faith; and yet those works of the body are not to be despised or neglected on that account. In this world we are bound by the needs of our bodily life, but we are not righteous because of them. "My kingship is not of this world" (John 18:36), says Christ. He does not, however, say, "My kingship is not here, that is, in this world." And Paul says, "Though we live in the world we are not carrying on a worldly war" (II Cor. 10:3), and in Gal. 2(:20), "The life I now live in the flesh I live by faith in the Son of God." Thus what we do, live, and are in works and ceremonies, we do because of the necessities of this life and of the effort to rule our body. Nevertheless we are righteous, not in these, but in the faith of the Son of God.

THE INTERPRETATION OF THE BIBLE AND THE NATURE OF THE CLERGY

They (the Roman Catholic Popes) want to be the only masters of Scriptures. . . . They assume sole authority for themselves and would persuade us with insolent juggling of words that the Pope, whether he be bad or good, cannot err in matters of faith. . . .

. . . They cannot produce a letter to prove that the interpretation of Scripture . . . belongs to the Pope alone. They themselves have usurped this power . . . and though they allege that this power was conferred on Peter when the keys were given to him, it is plain enough that the keys were not given to Peter alone but to the entire body of Christians (Matt. 16:19; 18:18). . . .

. . . Every baptized Christian is a priest already, not by appointment or ordination from the Pope or any other man, but because Christ Himself has begotten him as a priest . . . in baptism. . . .

The Pope has usurped the term "priest" for his anointed and tonsured hordes [clergy and monks]. By this means they have separated themselves from the ordinary Christians and have called themselves uniquely the "clergy of God," God's heritage and chosen people who must help other Christians by their sacrifice and worship. . . . Therefore the Pope argues that he alone has the right and power to ordain and do what he will. . . .

[But] the preaching office is no more than a public service which happens to be conferred on someone by the entire congregation all the members of which are priests. . . .

. . . The fact that a pope or bishop anoints, makes tonsures, ordains, consecrates [makes holy], and prescribes garb different from those of the laity . . . nevermore makes a Christian and a spiritual man. Accordingly, through baptism all of us are consecrated to the priesthood, as St. Peter says . . . (I Peter 2:9).

To make it still clearer, if a small group of pious Christian laymen were taken captive and settled in a wilderness and had among them no priest consecrated by a bishop, if they were to agree to choose one from their midst, married or unmarried, and were to charge him with the office of baptizing, saying Mass, absolving [forgiving of sins], and preaching, such a man would be as truly a priest as he would if all bishops and popes had consecrated him.

REVIEW QUESTIONS

1. Why did Martin Luther see the papacy as the crucial block to any meaningful reform of the church?
2. How did Luther's teaching undermine the power of the clergy and traditional forms of piety?

5 Justification of Absolute Monarchy by Divine Right

Effectively blocking royal absolutism in the Middle Ages were the dispersion of power between kings and feudal lords, the vigorous sense of personal freedom and urban autonomy of the townspeople, and the limitations on royal power imposed by the church. However, by the late sixteenth century, monarchs were asserting their authority over competing groups with ever greater effectiveness. In the seventeenth century European kings implemented their claim to absolute power as monarchs chosen by and responsible to God alone. This theory, called the divine right of kings, became the dominant political ideology of seventeenth-century Europe.

Bishop Jacques-Benigne Bossuet
POLITICS DRAWN FROM THE VERY WORDS OF HOLY SCRIPTURE

Louis XIV was the symbol of absolutism, a term applied to those early modern states where monarchs exercised power free of constitutional restraints. Theorists of absolutism like Bishop Jacques-Benigne Bossuet (1627–1704) argued that monarchs received their authority directly from God. Following are excerpts from Bossuet's *Politics Drawn from the Very Words of Holy Scripture* (1707).

THIRD BOOK, IN WHICH ONE BEGINS TO EXPLAIN THE NATURE AND THE PROPERTIES OF ROYAL AUTHORITY

Article II, Royal Authority is Sacred

1st Proposition, God establishes kings as his ministers, and reigns through them over the peoples   We have already seen that all power comes from God.

"The prince, St. Paul adds, is God's minister to thee for good. But if thou do that which is evil, fear: for he beareth not the sword in vain. For he is God's minister: an avenger to execute wrath upon him that doth evil."

Thus princes act as ministers of God, and his lieutenants on earth. It is through them that he exercises his Empire. . . .

It is in this way that we have seen that the royal throne is not the throne of a man, but the throne of God himself. "God hath chosen Solomon my son, to sit upon the throne of the kingdom of the Lord over Israel." And again: "Solomon sat on the throne of the Lord."

And in order that no one believe that it was peculiar to the Israelites to have kings established by God, here is what Ecclesiasticus says: "Over every nation he set a ruler." . . .

Thus he governs all peoples, and gives them, all of them, their kings; though he governs Israel in a more particular and announced fashion.

2nd Proposition, The person of kings is sacred   It appears from all this that the person of kings is sacred, and that to attempt anything against them is a sacrilege. . . . [T]hey are sacred through their charge, as being the representatives of divine majesty, deputized by his providence for the execution of his plans. It is thus that God calls Cyrus his anointed. . . .

One must protect kings as sacred things; and whoever neglects to guard them is worthy of death. . . .

3rd Proposition, One must obey the prince by reason of religion and conscience . . . Even if rulers do not acquit themselves of this duty [punishment of evildoers and praise of the good], one must respect in them their charge and their ministry. "Servants, be subject to your masters with all fear, not only to the good and gentle, but also to the angry and unjust."

There is thus something religious in the respect one gives to the prince. The service of God and respect for kings are inseparable things, and St. Peter places these two duties together: "Fear God, Honor the King."

God, moreover, has put something divine into kings. "I have said: You are Gods, and all of you the sons of the most High." It is God himself whom David makes speak in this way. . . .

4th Proposition, Kings should respect their own power, and use it only for the public good Their power coming from on high, as has been said, they must not believe that they are the owners of it, to use it as they please; rather must they use it with fear and restraint, as something which comes to them from God, and for which God will ask an accounting of them.

FOURTH BOOK, ON THE CHARACTERISTICS OF ROYALTY (CONTINUATION)

First Article, Royal Authority is Absolute

1st Proposition, The prince need account to no one for what he ordains . . . Without this absolute authority, he can neither do good nor suppress evil: his power must be such that no one can hope to escape him; and, in fine, the sole defense of individuals against the public power, must be their innocence. . . .

2nd Proposition, When the prince has decided, there can be no other decision The judgments of sovereigns are attributed to God himself. . . .

[N]o one has the right to judge or to review after him.

One must, then, obey princes as if they were justice itself, without which there is neither order nor justice in affairs.

They are gods, and share in some way in divine independence. "I have said: You are gods, and all of you the sons of the most High."

Only God can judge their judgments and their persons. . . .

It follows from this that he who does not want to obey the prince, is . . . condemned irremissibly to death as an enemy of public peace and of human society. . . .

The prince can correct himself when he knows that he has done badly; but against his authority there can be no remedy except his authority.

3rd Proposition, There is no co-active force against the prince One calls co-active [coercive] force a power to constrain and to execute what is legitimately ordained. To the prince alone belongs legitimate command; to him alone belongs co-active force as well.

It is for that reason also that St. Paul gives the sword to him alone. "If thou do that which is evil, fear; for he beareth not the sword in vain."

In the state only the prince should be armed: otherwise everything is in confusion, and the state falls back into anarchy.

He who creates a sovereign prince puts everything together into his hands, both the sovereign authority to judge and all the power of the state.

REVIEW QUESTION

1. According to Bossuet, why do kings merit absolute obedience, and what duty do they owe to God?

6   A Secular Defense of Absolutism

Thomas Hobbes (1588–1679), a British philosopher and political theorist, witnessed the agonies of the English civil war, including the execution of Charles I in 1649. These developments fortified Hobbes's conviction that absolutism was the most desirable and logical form of government. Only the unlimited power of a sovereign, said Hobbes, could contain human passions that disrupt the social order and threaten civilized life; only absolute rule could provide an environment secure enough for people to pursue their individual interests.

Leviathan (1651), Hobbes's principal work of political thought, broke with medieval political theory. Medieval thinkers assigned each group of people—clergy, lords, serfs, guildsmen—a place in a fixed social order; an individual's social duties were set by ancient traditions believed to have been ordained by God. During early modern times, the great expansion of commerce and capitalism spurred the new individualism already pronounced in Renaissance culture; group ties were shattered by competition and accelerating social mobility. Hobbes gave expression to a society where people confronted each other as competing individuals.

Thomas Hobbes
LEVIATHAN

Hobbes was influenced by the new scientific thought that saw mathematical knowledge as the avenue to truth. Using geometry as a model, Hobbes began with what he believed were self-evident axioms regarding human nature, from which he deduced other truths. He aimed at constructing political philosophy on a scientific foundation and rejected the authority of tradition and religion as inconsistent with a science of politics. Thus, although Hobbes supported absolutism, he dismissed the idea advanced by other theorists of absolutism that the monarch's power derived from God. He also rejected the idea that the state should not be obeyed when it violated God's law. *Leviathan* is a rational and secular political statement. In this modern approach, rather than in Hobbes's justification of absolutism, lies the work's significance.

Hobbes had a pessimistic view of human nature. Believing that people are innately selfish and grasping, he maintained that competition and dissension, rather than cooperation, characterize human relations. Even when reason teaches that cooperation is more advantageous than competition, Hobbes observed that people are reluctant to alter their ways, because passion, not reason, governs their behavior. In the following passages from *Leviathan*, Hobbes describes the causes of human conflicts.

Nature hath made men so equall, in the faculties of body, and mind; as that though there bee found one man sometimes manifestly stronger in body, or of quicker mind than another; yet when all is reckoned together, the difference between man, and man, is not so considerable, as that one man can thereupon claim to himselfe any benefit, to which another may not pretend, as well as he. For as to the strength of body, the weakest has strength enough to kill the strongest, either by secret machination, or by confederacy with others, that are in the same danger with himselfe. . . .

And as to the faculties of the mind . . . men are . . . [more] equall than unequall. . . .

From this equality of ability, ariseth equality of hope in the attaining of our Ends. And therefore if any two men desire the same thing, which neverthelesse they cannot both enjoy, they become enemies; and in the way to their End, . . . endeavour to destroy, or subdue one another. . . . If one plant, sow, build, or possesse a convenient Seat, others may probably be expected to come prepared with forces united, to dispossesse, and deprive him, not only of the fruit of his labour, but also of his life, or liberty. . . .

So that in the nature of man, we find three principall causes of quarrell. First, Competition; Secondly, Diffidence; Thirdly, Glory.

The first, maketh men invade for Gain; the second, for Safety; and the third, for Reputation. The first use Violence, to make themselves Masters of other men's persons, wives, children, and cattell; the second, to defend them; the third, for trifles, as a word, a smile, a different opinion, and any other signe of undervalue, either direct in their Persons, or by reflexion in their Kindred, their Friends, their Nation, their Profession, or their Name.

Hereby it is manifest, that during the time men live without a common Power to keep them all in awe, they are in that condition which is called Warre; and such a warre, as is of every man, against every man. . . .

Hobbes then describes a state of nature—the hypothetical condition of humanity prior to the formation of the state—as a war of all against all. For Hobbes, the state of nature is a logical abstraction, a device employed to make his point. Only a strong ruling entity—the state—will end the perpetual strife and provide security. For Hobbes, the state is merely a useful arrangement that permits individuals to exchange goods and services in a secure environment. The ruling authority in the state, the sovereign, must have supreme power, or society will collapse and the anarchy of the state of nature will return.

Whatsoever therefore is consequent to a time of Warre, where every man is Enemy to every man; the same is consequent to the time, wherein men live without other security, than what their own strength, and their own invention shall furnish them withall. In such condition, there is no place for Industry; because the fruit thereof is uncertain: and consequently no Culture of the Earth; no Navigation, nor use of the commodities that may be imported by Sea; no commodious Building; no Instruments of moving, and removing such things as require much force; no Knowledge of the face of the Earth; no account of Time; no Arts; no Letters; no Society; and which is worst of all, continuall feare, and danger of violent death; And the life of man, solitary, poore, nasty, brutish, and short. . . .

The Passions that encline men to Peace, are Feare of Death; Desire of such things as are necessary to commodious living; and a Hope by their Industry to obtain them. And Reason suggesteth convenient Articles of Peace, upon which men may be drawn to agreement. . . .

And because the condition of Man, (as hath been declared in the precedent Chapter) is a condition of Warre of every one against every one; in which case every one is governed by his own Reason; and there is nothing he can make use of, that may not be a help unto him, in preserving his life against his enemyes; It followeth, that in such a condition, every man has a Right to every thing; even to one another's body. And therefore, as long as this naturall Right of every man to every thing endureth, there can be no security to any man, (how strong or wise soever he be,) of living out the time, which Nature ordinarily alloweth men to live. . . .

. . . If there be no Power erected, or not great enough for our security; every man will and may lawfully rely on his own strength and art, for caution against all other men. . . .

The only way to erect . . . a Common Power, as may be able to defend them from the invasion of [foreigners] and the injuries of one another, and thereby to secure them in such sort, as that by their owne industrie, and by the fruites of the Earth, they may nourish themselves and live contentedly; is, to conferre all their power and strength upon one Man, or upon one Assembly of men, that may reduce all their Wills, by plurality of voices, unto one Will . . . and therein to submit their Wills, every one to his Will, and their Judgements, to his Judgment. This is more than Consent, or Concord; it is a reall Unitie of them all, in one and the same Person, made by Covenant of every man with every man, in such manner, as if every man should say to every man, *I Authorise and give up my Right of Governing my selfe, to this Man, or to this Assembly of men, on this condition, that thou give up thy Right to him, and Authorise all his Actions in like manner.* This done, the Multitude so united in one Person, is called a COMMON-WEALTH. . . . For by this Authorite, given him by every particular man in the Common-wealth, he hath the use of so much Power and Strength . . . conferred on him, that by terror thereof, he is inabled to forme the wills of them all, to Peace at home, and mutuall [aid] against their enemies abroad. And in him consisteth the Essence of the Common-wealth; which (to define it,) is *One Person, of whose Acts a great Multitude, by mutuall Covenants one with another, have made themselves every one the Author, to the end he may use*

the strength and means of them all, as he shall think expedient, for their Peace and Common Defence.

And he that carryeth this Person, is called SOVERAIGNE, and said to have *Soveraigne Power*; and every one besides, his SUBJECT. . . .

. . . They that have already Instituted a Common-wealth, being thereby bound by Covenant . . . cannot lawfully make a new Covenant, amongst themselves, to be obedient to any other, in any thing whatsoever, without his permission. And therefore, they that are subjects to a Monarch, cannot without his leave cast off Monarchy, and return to the confusion of a disunited Multitude; nor transferre their Person from him that beareth it, to another Man, or other Assembly of men: for they . . . are bound, every man to every man, to [acknowledge] . . . that he that already is their Soveraigne, shall do, and judge fit to be done; so that [those who do not obey] break their Covenant made to that man, which is injustice: and they have also every man given the Soveraignty to him that beareth their Person; and therefore if they depose him, they take from him that which is his own, and so again it is injustice. . . . And whereas some men have pretended for their disobedience to their Soveraign, a new Covenant, made, not with men, but with God; this also is unjust: for there is no Covenant with God, but by mediation of some body that representeth God's Person; which none doth but God's Lieutenant, who hath the Soveraignty under God. But this pretence of Covenant with God, is so evident a [lie], even in the pretenders own consciences, that it is not onely an act of an unjust, but also of a vile, and unmanly disposition. . . .

. . . Consequently none of [the sovereign's] Subjects, by any pretence of forfeiture, can be freed from his Subjection.

REVIEW QUESTIONS

1. What was Thomas Hobbes's view of human nature and what conclusions did he draw from it about the best form of government?
2. What has been the political legacy of Hobbes's notion of the state?

7 The Triumph of Constitutional Monarchy in England: The Glorious Revolution

The struggle against absolute monarchy in England during the early seventeenth century reached a climax during the reign of Charles I (1625–1649). Parliament raised its own army as civil war broke out between its supporters and those of the king. Captured by the Scottish Presbyterian rebels in 1646 and turned over to the English parliamentary army in 1647, Charles was held prisoner for two years until the Puritan parliamentary general Oliver Cromwell (1599–1658) decided to put him on trial for treason. The king was found guilty and executed in 1649.

The revolutionary parliamentary regime evolved into a military dictatorship headed by Cromwell. After Cromwell's death, Parliament in 1660 restored the monarchy and invited the late king's heir to end his exile and take the throne. Charles II (1660–1685), by discretion and skillful statesmanship, managed to evade many difficulties caused by the hostility of those who opposed his policies. He attempted to ease religious discrimination by ending the laws that penalized dissenters who rejected the official Church of England. But the religious prejudices of Parliament forced the king to desist, and the laws penalizing both Protestant dissenters and Roman Catholics remained in force. The king's motives for establishing religious toleration were suspect, since he himself was married to a French Catholic and his brother and heir James, Duke of York, was also a staunch Catholic.

When James II (1685–1688) succeeded to the throne, he tried unsuccessfully to get Parliament to repeal the Test Act, a law that forbade anyone to hold a civil or military office or to enter a university unless he was a member in good standing of the Church of England. This law effectively barred both Catholics and Protestant dissenters from serving in the king's government. When Parliament refused to act, James got the legal Court of the King's Bench to approve his decree suspending the Test Act. The court affirmed that the king, due to his sovereign authority, had absolute power to suspend any law at his sole discretion. The prerogatives claimed by the king were seen by many as an attempt to impose absolute monarchy on the English people.

King James further roused enemies by appointing many Catholics to high government posts and by issuing his Declaration of Indulgence for Liberty of Conscience on April 4, 1687. This declaration established complete freedom of worship for all Englishmen, ending all civil penalties and discriminations based on religious dissent. Instead of hailing the declaration as a step forward in solving the religious quarrels within the kingdom, many persons viewed this suspension of the laws as a further act of absolutism because James acted unilaterally without consulting Parliament. This act united the king's enemies and alienated his former supporters.

When the king's wife gave birth to a son, making the heir to the throne another Catholic, almost all factions (except the Catholics) abandoned James II and invited the Dutch Protestant Prince William of Orange and his wife Mary, James II's Protestant daughter, to come to England. James and his Catholic family and friends fled to France. Parliament declared the throne vacant and offered it to William and Mary as joint sovereigns. As a result of the "Glorious Revolution," the English monarchy became clearly limited by the will of Parliament.

THE ENGLISH DECLARATION OF RIGHTS

In depriving James II of the throne, Parliament had destroyed forever in Britain the theory of divine right as an operating principle of government and had firmly established a limited constitutional monarchy. The appointment of William and Mary was accompanied by a declaration of rights (later enacted as the Bill of Rights), which enumerated and declared illegal James II's arbitrary acts. The Declaration of Rights, excerpted below, compelled William and Mary and future monarchs to recognize the right of the people's representatives to dispose of the royal office and to set limits on its powers. These rights were subsequently formulated into laws passed by Parliament. Prior to the American Revolution, colonists protested that British actions in the American colonies violated certain rights guaranteed in the English Bill of Rights. Several of these rights were later included in the Constitution of the United States.

And whereas the said late king James the Second having abdicated the government and the throne being thereby vacant, His Highness the prince of Orange (whom it hath pleased Almighty God to make the glorious instrument of delivering this kingdom from popery and arbitrary power) did (by the advice of the lords spiritual and temporal and divers principal persons of the commons)[1] cause letters to be written to the lords spiritual and temporal, being Protestants; and other letters to the several counties, cities, universities, boroughs and Cinque ports[2] for the choosing of such persons to represent them, as were of right to be sent to parliament, to meet and sit at Westminster upon the two and twentieth day of January in this year one thousand six hundred eighty and eight,[3] in

order to [guarantee] . . . that their religion, laws and liberties might not again be in danger of being subverted; upon which letters elections having been accordingly made.

And thereupon the said lords spiritual and temporal and commons pursuant to their respective letters and elections being now assembled in a full and free representative of this nation, taking into their most serious consideration the best means for attaining the ends aforesaid, do in the first place (as their ancestors in like case have usually done) for the vindicating and asserting their ancient rights and liberties, declare:

That the pretended power of suspending of laws or the execution of laws by regal authority without consent of parliament is illegal.

That the pretended power of dispensing with laws or the execution of laws by regal authority as it hath been assumed and exercised of late is illegal.

That the commission for erecting the late court of commissioners for ecclesiastical causes and all other commissions and courts of like nature are illegal and pernicious.

That the levying money for or to the use of the crown by pretence of prerogative without

---

[1]"The lords spiritual" refers to the bishops of the Church of England who sat in the House of Lords, and "the lords temporal" refers to the nobility entitled to sit in the House of Lords. The commons refers to the elected representatives in the House of Commons.

[2]The Cinque ports along England's southeastern coast (originally five in number) enjoyed special privileges because of their military duties in providing for coastal defense.

[3]The year was in fact 1689 because until 1752, the English used March 25 as the beginning of the new year.

grant of parliament for a longer time or in other manner than the same is or shall be granted is illegal.

That it is the right of the subjects to petition the king and all commitments and prosecutions for such petitioning are illegal.

That the raising or keeping a standing army within the kingdom in time of peace unless it be with consent of parliament is against the law.

That the subjects which are Protestants may have arms for their defence suitable to their conditions and as allowed by law.

That election of members of parliament ought to be free.

That the freedom of speech and debates or proceedings in parliament ought not to be impeached or questioned in any court or place out of parliament.

That excessive bail ought not to be required nor excessive fines imposed nor cruel and unusual punishments inflicted.

That jurors ought to be duly impanelled and returned and jurors which pass upon men in trials for high treason ought to be freeholders.

That all grants and promises of fines and forfeitures of particular persons before conviction are illegal and void.

And that for redress of all grievances and for the amending, strengthening and preserving of the laws parliaments ought to be held frequently.

And they do claim, demand, and insist upon all and singular the premises as their undoubted rights and liberties and that no declarations, judgments, doings, or proceedings to the prejudice of the people in any of the said premises ought in any wise to be drawn hereafter into consequence or example.

REVIEW QUESTIONS

1. How did the Declaration of Rights limit royal authority? With what result?
2. In what ways did the Glorious Revolution impact upon the American rebellion in the 1770s?

CHAPTER 2
The Scientific Revolution

GALILEO GALILEI'S (1564–1642) support of Copernicanism and rejection of the medieval division of the universe into higher and lower realms make him a principal shaper of modern science. *(The Granger Collection, New York)*

The Scientific Revolution of the sixteenth and seventeenth centuries replaced the medieval view of the universe with a new cosmology and produced a new way of investigating nature. It overthrew the medieval conception of nature as a hierarchical order ascending toward a realm of perfection. Rejecting reliance on authority, the thinkers of the Scientific Revolution affirmed the individual's ability to know the natural world through the method of mathematical reasoning, the direct observation of nature, and carefully controlled experiments.

The medieval view of the universe had blended the theories of Aristotle and Ptolemy, two ancient Greek thinkers, with Christian teachings. In that view, a stationary earth stood in the center of the universe just above hell. Revolving around the earth were seven planets: the moon, Mercury, Venus, the sun, Mars, Jupiter, and Saturn. Because people believed that earth did not move, it was not considered a planet. Each planet was attached to a transparent sphere that turned around the earth. Encompassing the universe was a sphere of fixed stars; beyond the stars lay three heavenly spheres, the outermost of which was the abode of God. An earth-centered universe accorded with the Christian idea that God had created the universe for men and women and that salvation was the aim of life.

Also agreeable to the medieval Christian view was Aristotle's division of the universe into a lower, earthly realm and a higher realm beyond the moon. Two sets of laws operated in the universe, one on earth and the other in the celestial realm. Earthly objects were composed of four elements: earth, water, fire, and air; celestial objects were composed of the divine ether—a substance too pure, too clear, too fine, too spiritual to be found on earth. Celestial objects naturally moved in perfectly circular orbits around the earth; earthly objects, composed mainly of the heavy elements of earth and water, naturally fell downward, whereas objects made of the lighter elements of air and fire naturally flew upward toward the sky.

The destruction of the medieval world picture began with the publication in 1543 of *On the Revolutions of the Heavenly Spheres*, by Nicolaus Copernicus, a Polish mathematician, astronomer, and clergyman. In Copernicus's system, the sun was in the center of the universe, and the earth was another planet that moved around the sun. Most thinkers of the time, committed to the Aristotelian–Ptolemaic system and to the biblical statements that seemed to support it, rejected Copernicus's conclusions.

The work of Galileo Galilei, an Italian mathematician, astronomer, and physicist, was decisive in the shattering of the medieval cosmos and the shaping of the modern scientific outlook. Galileo advanced the modern view that knowledge of nature derives from direct observation and from mathematics. For Galileo, the universe was a "grand book which . . . is written in the language of mathematics, and its characters are triangles, circles, and other geometric figures without which it is humanly impossible to understand a single word of it." Galileo also pioneered experimental physics, advanced the modern idea that nature is uniform throughout the universe, and attacked reliance on scholastic authority rather than on experimentation in resolving scientific controversies.

Johannes Kepler (1571–1630), a contemporary of Galileo, discovered three laws of planetary motion that greatly advanced astronomical knowledge. Kepler showed that the path of a planet was an ellipse, not a circle as Ptolemy (and Copernicus) had believed, and that planets do not move at uniform speed but accelerate as they near the sun. He devised formulas to calculate accurately both a planet's speed at each point in its orbit around the sun and a planet's location at a particular time. Kepler's laws provided further evidence that Copernicus had been right, for they made sense only in a sun-centered universe, but Kepler could not explain why planets stayed in their orbits rather than flying off into space or crashing into the sun. The resolution of that question was left to Sir Isaac Newton.

Newton's great achievement was integrating the findings of Copernicus, Galileo, and Kepler into a single theoretical system. In *Principia Mathematica* (1687), he formulated the mechanical laws of motion and attraction that govern celestial and terrestrial objects.

The creation of a new model of the universe was one great achievement of the Scientific Revolution; another accomplishment was the formulation of the scientific method. The scientific method encompasses two approaches to knowledge, which usually complement each other: the empirical (inductive) and the rational (deductive). Although all sciences use both approaches, the inductive method is generally more applicable in such descriptive sciences as biology, anatomy, and geology, which rely on the accumulation of data. In the inductive approach, general principles are derived from analyzing external experiences—observations and the results of experiments. In the deductive approach, used in mathematics and theoretical physics, truths are derived in successive steps from indubitable axioms. Whereas the inductive method builds its concepts from an analysis of sense experience, the deductive approach constructs its ideas from self-evident principles that are conceived by the mind itself without external experience. The deductive and inductive approaches to knowledge, and their interplay, have been a constantly recurring feature in Western intellectual history since the rationalism of Plato and the empiricism of Aristotle. The success of the scientific method in modern times arose from the skillful synchronization of induction and deduction by such giants as Leonardo da Vinci, Copernicus, Kepler, Galileo, and Newton.

The Scientific Revolution was instrumental in shaping the modern outlook. It destroyed the medieval conception of the universe and established the scientific method as the means for investigating nature and acquiring knowledge, even in areas having little to do with the study of the physical world. By demonstrating the powers of the human mind, the Scientific Revolution gave thinkers great confidence in reason and led eventually to a rejection of traditional beliefs in magic, astrology, and witches. In the eighteenth century, this growing skepticism led thinkers to question miracles and other Christian beliefs that seemed contrary to reason.

1 The Copernican Revolution

In proclaiming that the earth was not stationary but revolved around the sun, Nicolaus Copernicus (1473–1543) revolutionized the science of astronomy. Fearing controversy and scorn, Copernicus long refused to publish his great work, *On the Revolutions of the Heavenly Spheres* (1543). However, persuaded by friends, he finally relented and permitted publication; a copy of his book reached him on his deathbed. As Copernicus anticipated, his ideas aroused the ire of many thinkers.

Both Catholic and Protestant philosophers and theologians, including Martin Luther, attacked Copernicus for contradicting the Bible and Aristotle and Ptolemy, and they raised several specific objections. First, certain passages in the Bible imply a stationary earth and a sun that moves (for example, Psalm 93 says, "Yea, the world is established; it shall never be moved"; and in attacking Copernicus, Luther pointed out that "sacred Scripture tells us that Joshua commanded the sun to stand still, and not the earth"). Second, a body as heavy as the earth cannot move through space at such speed as Copernicus suggested. Third, if the earth spins on its axis, why does a stone dropped from a height land directly below instead of at a point behind where it was dropped? Fourth, if the earth moved, objects would fly off it. And finally, the moon cannot orbit both the earth and the sun at the same time.

Nicolaus Copernicus
ON THE REVOLUTIONS OF THE HEAVENLY SPHERES

On the Revolutions of the Heavenly Spheres was dedicated to Pope Paul III, whom Copernicus asked to protect him from vilification. In the dedication, Copernicus explains his reason for delaying publication of *Revolutions*.

To His Holiness, Pope Paul III, Nicholas Copernicus'
Preface to His Books on the Revolutions

I can readily imagine, Holy Father, that as soon as some people hear that in this volume, which I have written about the revolutions of the spheres of the universe, I ascribe certain motions to the terrestrial globe, they will shout that I must be immediately repudiated together with this belief. For I am not so enamored of my own opinions that I disregard what others may think of them. I am aware that a philosopher's ideas are not subject to the judgement of ordinary persons, because it is his endeavor to seek the truth in all things, to the extent permitted to human reason by God. Yet I hold that completely erroneous views should be shunned. Those who know that the consensus of many centuries has sanctioned the conception that the earth remains at rest in the middle of the heaven as its center would, I reflected, regard it as an insane pronouncement if I made the opposite assertion that the earth moves. Therefore I debated with myself for a long time whether to publish the volume which I wrote to prove the earth's motion or rather to follow the example of the Pythagoreans[1] and certain others, who used to transmit philosophy's secrets only to kinsmen and friends, not in writing but by word of mouth. . . . And they did so, it seems to me, not, as some suppose, because they were in some way jealous about their teachings, which would be spread around; on the contrary, they wanted the very beautiful thoughts attained by great men of deep devotion not to be ridiculed by those who are reluctant to exert themselves vigorously in any literary pursuit unless it is lucrative; or if they are stimulated to the non-acquisitive study of philosophy by the exhortation and example of others, yet because of their dullness of mind they play the same part among philosophers as drones among bees. When I weighed these considerations, the scorn which

I had reason to fear on account of the novelty and unconventionality of my opinion almost induced me to abandon completely the work which I had undertaken.

But while I hesitated for a long time and even resisted, my friends [encouraged me]. . . . Foremost among them was the cardinal of Capua [a city in southern Italy], Nicholas Schönberg, renowned in every field of learning. Next to him was a man who loves me dearly, Tiedemann Giese, bishop of Chelmno [a city in northern Poland], a close student of sacred letters as well as of all good literature. For he repeatedly encouraged me and, sometimes adding reproaches, urgently requested me to publish this volume and finally permit it to appear after being buried among my papers and lying concealed not merely until the ninth year[2] but by now the fourth period of nine years. The same conduct was recommended to me by not a few other very eminent scholars. They exhorted me no longer to refuse, on account of the fear which I felt, to make my work available for the general use of students of astronomy. The crazier my doctrine of the earth's motion now appeared to most people, the argument ran, so much the more admiration and thanks would it gain after they saw the publication of my writings dispel the fog of absurdity by most luminous proofs. Influenced therefore by these persuasive men and by this hope, in the end I allowed my friends to bring out an edition of the volume, as they had long besought me to do. . . .

But you [your Holiness] are rather waiting to hear from me how it occurred to me to venture to conceive any motion of the earth, against the traditional opinion of astronomers and almost against common sense. . . . [Copernicus then describes some of the problems connected with the Ptolemaic system.]

---

[1]Pythagoreans were followers of Pythagoras, a Greek mathematician and philosopher of the sixth century B.C.; they were particularly interested in cosmology.

[2]The Roman poet Horace, who lived in the first century B.C., suggested in *Ars Poetica* that writers should keep a new manuscript in a cupboard "until the ninth year" before publishing it. Only then, he argued, would they have enough objectivity to judge its value. Copernicus is referring to this famous piece of advice.

For a long time, then, I reflected on this confusion in the astronomical traditions concerning the derivation of the motions of the universe's spheres. I began to be annoyed that the movements of the world machine, created for our sake by the best and most systematic Artisan of all [God], were not understood with greater certainty by the philosophers, who otherwise examined so precisely the most insignificant trifles of this world. For this reason I undertook the task of rereading the works of all the philosophers which I could obtain to learn whether anyone had ever proposed other motions of the universe's spheres than those expounded by the teachers of astronomy in the schools. And in fact first I found in Cicero that Hicetas supposed the earth to move. Later I also discovered in Plutarch[3] that certain others were of this opinion. . . .

Therefore, having obtained the opportunity from these sources, I too began to consider the mobility of the earth. . . . I thought that I too would be readily permitted to ascertain whether explanations sounder than those of my predecessors could be found for the revolution of the celestial spheres on the assumption of some motion of the earth.

Having thus assumed the motions which I ascribe to the earth later on in the volume, by long and intense study I finally found that if the motions of the other planets are correlated with the orbiting of the earth, and are computed for the revolution of each planet, not only do their phenomena follow therefrom but also the order and size of all the planets and spheres, and heaven itself is so linked together that in no portion of it can anything be shifted without disrupting the remaining parts and the universe as a whole. Accordingly in the arrangement of the volume too I have adopted the following order. In the first book I set forth the entire distribution of the spheres together with the motions which I attribute to the earth, so that this book contains, as it were, the general structure of the universe. Then in the remaining books I correlate the motions of the other planets and of all the spheres with the movement of the earth so that I may thereby determine to what extent the motions and appearances of the other planets and spheres can be saved if they are correlated with the earth's motions. I have no doubt that acute and learned astronomers will agree with me if, as this discipline especially requires, they are willing to examine and consider, not superficially but thoroughly, what I adduce in this volume in proof of these matters. However, in order that the educated and uneducated alike may see that I do not run away from the judgement of anybody at all, I have preferred dedicating my studies to Your Holiness rather than to anyone else. For even in this very remote corner of the earth where I live you are considered the highest authority by virtue of the loftiness of your office and your love for all literature and astronomy too. Hence by your prestige and judgement you can easily suppress calumnious attacks although, as the proverb has it, there is no remedy for a backbite.

Perhaps there will be babblers who claim to be judges of astronomy although completely ignorant of the subject and, badly distorting some passage of Scripture to their purpose, will dare to find fault with my undertaking and censure it. I disregard them even to the extent of despising their criticism as unfounded. For it is not unknown that Lactantius,[4] otherwise an illustrious writer but hardly an astronomer, speaks quite childishly about the earth's shape, when he mocks those who declared that the earth has the form of a globe. Hence scholars need not be surprised if any such persons will likewise ridicule me. Astronomy is written for astronomers. To them my work too will seem, unless I am mistaken, to make some contribution.

---

[3]Hicetas, a Pythagorean philosopher of the fourth century B.C., taught that the earth rotated on its axis while the other heavenly bodies were at rest. Cicero was a Roman statesman of the first century B.C. Plutarch (A.D. c. 50– c. 120) was a Greek moral philosopher and biographer whose works were especially popular among Renaissance humanists.

---

[4]Renaissance humanists admired Lactantius (c. 240– c. 320), a Latin rhetorician and Christian apologist, for his classical, Ciceronian literary style.

Cardinal Bellarmine
ATTACK ON THE COPERNICAN THEORY

In 1615, Cardinal Bellarmine, who in the name of the Inquisition warned Galileo not to defend the Copernican theory, expressed his displeasure with heliocentrism in a letter to Paolo Antonio Foscarini. Foscarini, head of the Carmelites, an order of mendicant friars in Calabria, and professor of theology, had tried to show that the earth's motion was not incompatible with biblical statements.

Cardinal Bellarmine to Foscarini (12 April 1615)

My Very Reverend Father,

I have read with interest the letter in Italian and the essay in Latin which Your [Reverence] sent me; I thank you for the one and for the other and confess that they are full of intelligence and erudition. You ask for my opinion, and so I shall give it to you, but very briefly, since now you have little time for reading and I for writing.

First, . . . to want to affirm that in reality the sun is at the center of the world and only turns on itself without moving from east to west, and the earth . . . revolves with great speed around the sun . . . is a very dangerous thing, likely not only to irritate all scholastic philosophers and theologians, but also to harm the Holy Faith by rendering Holy Scripture false. For your [Reverence] has well shown many ways of interpreting Holy Scripture, but has not applied them to particular cases; without a doubt you would have encountered very great difficulties if you had wanted to interpret all those passages you yourself cited.

Second, I say that, as you know, the Council [of Trent] prohibits interpreting Scripture against the common consensus of the Holy Fathers; and if Your [Reverence] wants to read not only the Holy Fathers, but also the modern commentaries on Genesis, the Psalms, Ecclesiastes, and Joshua, you will find all agreeing in the literal interpretation that the sun is in heaven and turns around the earth with great speed, and that the earth is very far from heaven and sits motionless at the center of the world. Consider now, with your sense of prudence, whether the Church can tolerate giving Scripture a meaning contrary to the Holy Fathers and to all the Greek and Latin commentators. Nor can one answer that this is not a matter of faith, since if it is not a matter of faith "as regards the topic," it is a matter of faith "as regards the speaker"; and so it would be heretical to say that Abraham did not have two children and Jacob twelve, as well as to say that Christ was not born of a virgin, because both are said by the Holy Spirit through the mouth of the prophets and the apostles.

Third, I say that if there were a true demonstration that the sun is at the center of the world and the earth in the third heaven, and that the sun does not circle the earth but the earth circles the sun, then one would have to proceed with great care in explaining the Scriptures that appear contrary, and say rather that we do not understand them than that what is demonstrated is false. But I will not believe that there is such a demonstration, until it is shown to me. . . . and in case of doubt one must not abandon the Holy Scripture as interpreted by the Holy Fathers. I add that the one who wrote, "The sun also ariseth, and the sun goeth down, and hasteth to his place where he arose," was Solomon [King of ancient Israel], who not only spoke inspired by God, but was a man above all others wise and learned in the human sciences and in the knowledge of created things; he received all this wisdom from God; therefore it is not likely that he was affirming something that was contrary to truth already demonstrated or capable of being demonstrated.

REVIEW QUESTIONS

1. What led Nicolaus Copernicus to investigate the motions of the universe's spheres?
2. Why did he fear to publish this theory about the earth's motion?
3. On what grounds did Cardinal Bellarmine reject the Copernican theory?

2 Galileo: Confirming the Copernican System

The brilliant Italian scientist Galileo Galilei (1564–1642) rejected the medieval division of the universe into higher and lower realms and proclaimed the modern idea of nature's uniformity. Learning that a telescope had been invented in Holland, Galileo built one for himself and used it to investigate the heavens. Through his telescope, Galileo saw craters and mountains on the moon; he concluded that celestial bodies were not pure, perfect, and immutable, as had been believed. There was no difference in quality between heavenly and earthly bodies; nature was the same throughout.

With his telescope, Galileo discovered four moons orbiting Jupiter, an observation that overcame a principal objection to the Copernican system. Galileo showed that a celestial body could indeed move around a center other than the earth; that earth was not the common center for all celestial bodies; that a celestial body (earth's moon or Jupiter's moons) could orbit a planet at the same time that the planet revolved around another body (namely, the sun).

Galileo appealed to the Roman Catholic authorities asking them to halt their actions against the theories of Copernicus, but was unsuccessful. His support of Copernicus aroused the ire of both clergy and scholastic philosophers. In 1616, the church placed Copernicus's book on the index of forbidden books, and Galileo was ordered to cease his defense of the Copernican theory. In 1632, Galileo published *Dialogue Concerning the Two Chief World Systems* in which he upheld the Copernican view. Widely distributed and acclaimed, the book antagonized Galileo's enemies, who succeeded in halting further printing. Summoned to Rome, the aging and infirm scientist was put on trial by the Inquisition and ordered to renounce the Copernican theory. Galileo bowed to the Inquisition, which condemned the *Dialogue* and sentenced him to life imprisonment—largely house arrest at his own villa near Florence, where he was treated humanely.

Galileo Galilei
LETTER TO THE GRAND DUCHESS CHRISTINA AND *DIALOGUE CONCERNING THE TWO CHIEF WORLD SYSTEMS— PTOLEMAIC AND COPERNICAN*

The first reading illustrates Galileo's active involvement in a struggle for freedom of inquiry many years before the *Dialogue* was published. In 1615, in a letter addressed to Grand Duchess Christina of Tuscany, Galileo argued that passages from the Bible had no authority in scientific disputes.

The second reading (from the *Dialogue*) reveals Galileo's views on Aristotle. Medieval scholastics regarded Aristotle as the supreme authority on questions concerning nature, an attitude that was perpetuated by early modern scholastics. Galileo insisted that such reliance on authority was a hindrance to scientific investigation, that it is through observation, experiment, and reason that one arrives at physical truth.

BIBLICAL AUTHORITY

Some years ago, as Your Serene Highness well knows, I discovered in the heavens many things that had not been seen before our own age. The novelty of these things, as well as some consequences which followed from them in contradiction to the physical notions commonly held among academic philosophers, stirred up against me no small number of professors—as if I had placed these things in the sky with my own hands in order to upset nature and overturn the sciences. They seemed to forget that the increase of known truths stimulates the investigation, establishment, and growth of the arts; not their diminution or destruction.

Showing a greater fondness for their own opinions than for truth, they sought to deny and disprove the new things which, if they had cared to look for themselves, their own senses would have demonstrated to them. To this end they hurled various charges and published numerous writings filled with vain arguments, and they made the grave mistake of sprinkling these with passages taken from places in the Bible which they had failed to understand properly, and which were ill suited to their purposes. . . .

. . . Men who were well grounded in astronomical and physical science were persuaded as soon as they received my first message. There were others who denied them or remained in doubt only because of their novel and unexpected character, and because they had not yet had the opportunity to see for themselves. These men have by degrees come to be satisfied. But some, besides allegiance to their original error, possess I know not what fanciful interest in remaining hostile not so much toward the things in question as toward their discoverer. No longer being able to deny them, these men now take refuge in obstinate silence, but being more than ever exasperated by that which has pacified and quieted other men, they divert their thoughts to other fancies and seek new ways to damage me. . . .

. . . Possibly because they are disturbed by the known truth of other propositions of mine which differ from those commonly held, and therefore mistrusting their defense so long as they confine themselves to the field of philosophy, these men have resolved to fabricate a shield for their fallacies out of the mantle of pretended religion and the authority of the Bible. These they apply, with little judgment, to the refutation of arguments that they do not understand and have not even listened to.

First they have endeavored to spread the opinion that such propositions in general are contrary to the Bible and are consequently damnable and heretical. . . . Hence they have had no trouble in finding men who would preach the damnability and heresy of the new doctrine from their very pulpits with unwonted confidence, thus doing impious and inconsiderate injury not only to that doctrine and its followers but to all mathematics and mathematicians in general. . . .

. . . They go about invoking the Bible, which they would have minister to their deceitful purposes. Contrary to the sense of the Bible and the intention of the holy [Church] Fathers, if I am not mistaken, they would extend such authorities until even in purely physical matters—where faith is not involved—they would have us altogether abandon reason and the evidence of our senses in favor of some biblical passage, though under the surface meaning of its words this passage may contain a different sense.

I hope to show that I proceed with much greater piety than they do, when I argue not against condemning [Copernicus'] book, but against condemning it in the way they suggest—that is, without understanding it, weighing it, or so much as reading it. For Copernicus never discusses matters of religion or faith, nor does he use arguments that depend in any way upon the authority of sacred writings which he might have interpreted erroneously. He stands always upon physical conclusions pertaining to the celestial motions, and deals with them by astronomical and geometrical demonstrations, founded primarily upon sense experiences and very exact observations. He did not ignore the Bible, but he knew very well that if his doctrine were proved, then it could not contradict the Scriptures when they were rightly understood. . . .

The reason produced for condemning the opinion that the earth moves and the sun stands still is that in many places in the Bible one may read that the sun moves and the earth stands still. Since the Bible cannot err, it follows as a necessary consequence that anyone takes an erroneous and heretical position who maintains that the sun is inherently motionless and the earth movable.

With regard to this argument, I think in the first place that it is very pious to say and prudent to affirm that the holy Bible can never speak untruth—whenever its true meaning is understood. But I believe nobody will deny that it is often very abstruse, and may say things which are quite different from what its bare words signify. Hence in expounding the Bible if one were always to confine oneself to the unadorned grammatical meaning, one might fall into error. . . .

. . . Now the Bible, merely to condescend to popular capacity, has not hesitated to obscure some very important pronouncements, attributing to God himself some qualities extremely remote from (and even contrary to) His essence. Who, then, would positively declare that this principle has been set aside, and the Bible has confined itself rigorously to the bare and restricted sense of its words, when speaking but casually of the earth, of water, of the sun, or of any other created thing? Especially in view of the fact that these things in no way concern the primary purpose of the sacred writings, which is the service of God and the salvation of souls—matters infinitely beyond the comprehension of the common people.

This being granted, I think that in discussions of physical problems we ought to begin not from the authority of scriptural passages, but from sense-experiences and necessary demonstrations. . . . Nothing physical which sense-experience sets before our eyes, or which necessary demonstrations prove to us, ought to be called in question (much less condemned) upon the testimony of biblical passages which may have some different meaning beneath their words. . . .

. . . I do not feel obliged to believe that that same God who has endowed us with senses, reason, and intellect has intended to forgo their use and by some other means to give us knowledge which we can attain by them. He would not require us to deny sense and reason in physical matters which are set before our eyes and minds by direct experience or necessary demonstrations. . . .

It is obvious that such [anti-Copernican] authors, not having penetrated the true senses of Scripture, would impose upon others an obligation to subscribe to conclusions that are repugnant to manifest reason and sense, if they had any authority to do so. God forbid that this sort of abuse should gain countenance and authority, for then in a short time it would be necessary to proscribe all the contemplative sciences. People who are unable to understand perfectly both the Bible and the sciences far outnumber those who do understand. The former, glancing superficially through the Bible, would arrogate to themselves the authority to decree upon every question of physics on the strength of some word which they have misunderstood, and which was employed by the sacred authors for some different purpose. And the smaller number of understanding men could not dam up the furious torrent of such people, who would gain the majority of followers simply because it is much more pleasant to gain a reputation for wisdom without effort or study than to consume oneself tirelessly in the most laborious disciplines.

Galileo attacked the unquestioning acceptance of Aristotle's teachings in his *Dialogue Concerning the Two Chief World Systems— Ptolemaic and Copernican*. In the *Dialogue*, Simplicio is an Aristotelian and Salviati is a spokesman for Galileo; Sagredo, a third participant, introduces the problem of relying on the authority of Aristotle.

ARISTOTELIAN AUTHORITY

SAGREDO One day I was at the home of a very famous doctor in Venice, where many persons came on account of their studies, and others occasionally came out of curiosity to see some anatomical dissection performed by a man who was truly no less learned than he was a careful and expert anatomist. It happened on this day that he was investigating the source and origin of the nerves, about which there exists a notorious controversy between the Galenist and Peripatetic doctors.[1] The anatomist showed that the great trunk of nerves, leaving the brain and passing through the nape, extended on down the spine and then branched out through the whole body, and that only a single strand as fine as a thread arrived at the heart. Turning to a gentleman whom we knew to be a Peripatetic philosopher, and on whose account he had been exhibiting and demonstrating everything with unusual care, he asked this man whether he was at last satisfied and convinced that the nerves originated in the brain and not in the heart. The philosopher, after considering for awhile, answered: "You have made me see this matter so plainly and palpably that if Aristotle's text were not contrary to it, stating clearly that the nerves originate in the heart, I should be forced to admit it to be true." . . .

SIMPLICIO But if Aristotle is to be abandoned, whom shall we have for a guide in philosophy? Suppose you name some author.

SALVIATI We need guides in forests and in unknown lands, but on plains and in open places only the blind need guides. It is better for such people to stay at home, but anyone with eyes in his head and his wits about him could serve as a guide for them. In saying this, I do not mean that a person should not listen to Aristotle; indeed, I applaud the reading and careful study of

---

[1]Galenist doctors followed the medical theories of Galen (A.D. c. 130–c. 200), a Greek anatomist and physician whose writings had great authority among medieval and early modern physicians. Peripatetic doctors followed Aristotle's teachings.

his works, and I reproach only those who give themselves up as slaves to him in such a way as to subscribe blindly to everything he says and take it as an inviolable decree without looking for any other reasons. This abuse carries with it another profound disorder, that other people do not try harder to comprehend the strength of his demonstrations. And what is more revolting in a public dispute, when someone is dealing with demonstrable conclusions, than to hear him interrupted by a text (often written to some quite different purpose) thrown into his teeth by an opponent? If, indeed, you wish to continue in this method of studying, then put aside the name of philosophers and call yourselves historians, or memory experts; for it is not proper that those who never philosophize should usurp the honorable title of philosopher.

GALILEO CONDEMNED BY THE INQUISITION

The following selection is drawn from the records of the Inquisition, which found Galileo guilty of teaching Copernicanism.

Whereas you, Galileo, son of the late Vincenzo Galilei, Florentine, aged seventy years, were in the year 1615 denounced to this Holy Office for holding as true the false doctrine taught by some that the Sun is the center of the world and immovable and that the Earth moves, and also with a diurnal [daily] motion; for having disciples to whom you taught the same doctrine; for holding correspondence with certain mathematicians of Germany concerning the same; for having printed certain letters, entitled "On the Sunspots," wherein you developed the same doctrine as true; and for replying to the objections from the Holy Scriptures, which from time to time were urged against it, by glossing the said Scriptures according to your own meaning: and whereas there was thereupon produced the copy of a document in the form of a letter, purporting to be written by you to one formerly your disciple, and in this divers propositions are set forth, following the position of Copernicus, which are contrary to the true sense and authority of Holy Scripture:

This Holy Tribunal being therefore of intention to proceed against the disorder and mischief thence resulting, which went on increasing to the prejudice of the Holy Faith, by command of His Holiness and of the Most Eminent Lords Cardinals of this supreme and universal Inquisition, the two propositions of the stability of the Sun and the motion of the Earth were by the theological Qualifiers qualified as follows:

The proposition that the Sun is the center of the world and does not move from its place is absurd and false philosophically and formally heretical, because it is expressly contrary to the Holy Scripture.

The proposition that the Earth is not the center of the world and immovable but that it moves, and also with a diurnal motion, is equally absurd and false philosophically and theologically considered at least erroneous in faith.

But whereas it was desired at that time to deal leniently with you, it was decreed at the Holy Congregation held before His Holiness on the twenty-fifth of February, 1616, that his Eminence the Lord Cardinal Bellarmine should order you to abandon altogether the said false doctrine and, in the event of your refusal, that an injunction should be imposed upon you by the Commissary of the Holy Office to give up the said doctrine and not to teach it to others, not to defend it, nor even discuss it; and failing your acquiescence in this injunction, that you should be imprisoned.

And, in order that a doctrine so pernicious might be wholly rooted out and not insinuate itself further to the grave prejudice of Catholic truth, a decree was issued by the Holy Congregation of the Index prohibiting the books which treat of this doctrine and declaring the doctrine itself to be false and wholly contrary to the sacred and divine Scripture.

And whereas a book appeared here recently, printed last year at Florence, the title of which shows that you were the author, this title being: "Dialogue of Galileo Galilei on the Great World Systems"; and whereas the Holy Congregation was afterward informed that through the publication of the said book the false opinion of the motion of the Earth and the stability of the Sun was daily gaining ground, the said book was taken into careful consideration, and in it there was discovered a patent violation of the aforesaid injunction that had been imposed upon you, for in this book you have defended the said opinion previously condemned and to your face declared to be so, although in the said book you strive by various devices to produce the impression that you leave it undecided, and in express terms as probable: which, however, is a most grievous error, as an opinion can in no wise be probable which has been declared and defined to be contrary to divine Scripture.

Therefore by our order you were cited before this Holy Office, where, being examined upon your oath, you acknowledged the book to be written and published by you. You confessed that you began to write the said book about ten or twelve years ago, after the command had been imposed upon you as above; that you

requested license to print it without, however, intimating to those who granted you this license that you had been commanded not to hold, defend, or teach the doctrine in question in any way whatever.

We say, pronounce, sentence, and declare that you, the said Galileo, by reason of the matters adduced in trial, and by you confessed as above, have rendered yourself in the judgment of this Holy Office vehemently suspected of heresy, namely, of having believed and held the doctrine—which is false and contrary to the sacred and divine Scriptures—that the Sun is the center of the world and does not move from east to west and that the Earth moves and is not the center of the world; and that an opinion may be held and defended as probable after it has been declared and defined to be contrary to the Holy Scripture; and that consequently you have incurred all the censures and penalties imposed and promulgated in the sacred canons and other constitutions, general and particular, against such delinquents. From which we are content that you be absolved, provided that, first, with a sincere heart and unfeigned faith, you abjure, curse, and detest before us the aforesaid errors and heresies and every other error and heresy contrary to the Catholic and Apostolic Roman Church in the form to be prescribed by us for you.

And, in order that this your grave and pernicious error and transgression may not remain altogether unpunished and that you may be more cautious in the future and an example to others that they may abstain from similar delinquencies, we ordain that the book of the "Dialogue of Galileo Galilei" be prohibited by public edict. . . .

REVIEW QUESTIONS

1. What was Galileo Galilei's objection to using the Bible as a source of knowledge of physical things? According to him, how did one acquire knowledge of nature?
2. What point was Galileo making in telling the story of the anatomical dissection?
3. What was Galileo's view on the use of Aristotle's works as a basis for scientific endeavors?
4. Why did the Inquisition regard the teaching of Copernicanism as dangerous?

3 Prophet of Modern Science

Sir Francis Bacon (1561–1626), an English statesman and philosopher, vigorously supported the advancement of science and the scientific method. He believed that increased comprehension and mastery of nature would improve living conditions for people and therefore wanted science to encompass systematic research; toward this end, he urged the state to fund scientific institutions. Bacon denounced universities for merely repeating Aristotelian concepts and discussing abstruse problems—Is matter formless? Are all natural substances composed of matter?—that did not increase understanding of nature or contribute to human betterment. The webs spun by these scholastics, he said, were ingenious but valueless. Bacon wanted an educational program that stressed direct contact with nature and fostered new discoveries.

Bacon was among the first to appreciate the new science's value and to explain its method clearly. Like Leonardo da Vinci, Bacon gave supreme value to the direct observation of nature; for this reason he is one of the founders of the empirical tradition in modern philosophy. Bacon upheld the inductive approach—careful investigation of nature, accumulation of data, and experimentation—as the way to truth and useful knowledge. Because he wanted science to serve a practical function, Bacon praised artisans and technicians who improved technology.

Francis Bacon
ATTACK ON AUTHORITY AND ADVOCACY OF EXPERIMENTAL SCIENCE

Bacon was not himself a scientist; he made no discoveries and had no laboratory. Nevertheless, for his advocacy of the scientific method, Bacon is deservedly regarded as a prophet of modern science. In the first passage from *Redargutio Philosophiarum* (The Refutation of Philosophies), written in 1609, a treatise on the "idols of the theater"—fallacious ways of thinking based on given systems of philosophy—Bacon attacks the slavish reliance on Aristotle.

But even though Aristotle were the man he is thought to be I should still warn you against receiving as oracles the thoughts and opinions of one man. What justification can there be for this self-imposed servitude [that] . . . you are content to repeat Aristotle after two thousand [years]? . . . But if you will be guided by me you will deny, not only to this man but to any mortal now living or who shall live hereafter, the right to dictate your opinions. . . . You will never be sorry for trusting your own strength, if you but once make trial of it. You may be inferior to Aristotle on the whole, but not in everything. Finally, and this is the head and front of the whole matter, there is at least one thing in which you are far ahead of him—in precedents, in experience, in the lessons of time. Aristotle, it is said, wrote a book in which he gathered together the laws and institutions of two hundred and fifty-five cities; yet I have no doubt that the customs of Rome are worth more than all of them combined so far as military and political science are concerned. The position is the same in natural philosophy. Are you of a mind to cast aside not only your own endowments but the gifts of time? Assert yourselves before it is too late. Apply yourselves to the study of things themselves. Be not for ever the property of one man.

In these excerpts from *The New Organon* (New System of Logic), in 1620 Bacon criticizes contemporary methods used to inquire into nature. He expresses his ideas in the form of aphorisms—concise statements of principles or general truths.

I. Man, being the servant and interpreter of Nature, can do and understand so much and so much only as he has observed in fact or in thought of the course of nature: beyond this he neither knows anything nor can do anything.

VIII. . . . The sciences we now possess are merely systems for the nice ordering and setting forth of things already invented; not methods of invention or directions for new works.

XII. The logic now in use serves rather to fix and give stability to the errors which have their foundation in commonly received notions than to help the search after truth. So it does more harm than good.

XIX. There are and can be only two ways of searching into and discovering truth. The one [begins with] the . . . most general axioms, and from these principles, the truth of which it takes for settled and immoveable, proceeds to judgment and to the discovery of middle axioms. And this way is now in fashion. The other derives axioms from the senses and particulars, rising by a gradual and unbroken ascent, so that it arrives at the most general axioms last of all. This is the true way, but as yet untried.

XXIII. There is a great difference between . . . certain empty dogmas, and the true signatures and marks set upon the works of creation as they are found in nature.

XXIV. It cannot be that axioms established by argumentation should avail for the discovery of new works; since the subtlety of nature is greater many times over than the subtlety of argument. But axioms duly and orderly formed from particulars easily discover the way to new particulars, and thus render sciences active.

XXXI. It is idle to expect any great advancement in science from the superinducing [adding] and engrafting of new things upon old. We must begin anew from the very foundations, unless we would revolve for ever in a circle with mean and contemptible progress.

CIX. There is therefore much ground for hoping that there are still laid up in the womb of nature many secrets of excellent use, having no affinity or parallelism with any thing that is now known, but lying entirely out of the beat of the imagination, which have not yet been found out. They too no doubt will some time or other, in the course and revolution of many ages, come to light of themselves, just as the others did; only by the method of which we are now treating they can be speedily and suddenly and simultaneously presented and anticipated.

REVIEW QUESTIONS

1. What intellectual attitude did Francis Bacon believe obstructed new scientific discoveries in his time?
2. What method of scientific inquiry did Bacon advocate?

4   The Circulation of the Blood:
Validating the Empirical Method

William Harvey (1578–1657), a British physician, showed that blood circulates in the body because of the pumping action of the heart muscle. Previous belief derived from Galen's theories. Galen (c. 130–c. 200), a Greco-Roman physician, claimed that there were two centers of blood, with the liver being the source of blood in the veins, and the heart being the source of arterial blood. In contrast, Harvey demonstrated that all blood passes through a single central organ, the heart, flowing away from the heart through the arteries and back to it through the veins, and that this constant, rotating circulation is caused by the rhythmic contractions of the heart muscle acting as a pump.

   This discovery of the circulation of the blood marked a break with medieval medical ideas (inherited from the ancient world) and signified the emergence of modern physiology. Harvey employed the inductive method championed by Sir Francis Bacon: he drew conclusions after carefully observing and experimenting with living animals.

William Harvey
THE MOTION OF THE HEART
AND BLOOD IN ANIMALS

In *The Motion of the Heart and Blood in Animals* (1628), Harvey described the heart as a mechanical pump, a description that corresponded to Newton's view that the universe was a mechanical system. In this reading, Harvey discusses his reasons for writing the book and provides insights into his method.

When I first gave my mind to vivisections [cutting live animals open for experimentation], as a means of discovering the motions and uses of the heart and sought to discover these from actual inspection, and not from the writings of others, I found the task so truly arduous, so full of difficulties, that I was almost tempted to think . . . that the motion of the heart was only to be comprehended by God. For I could neither rightly perceive at first when the systole and when the diastole took place, nor when and where dilatation and contraction occurred,[1] by reason of the rapidity of the motion, which in many animals is accomplished in the twinkling of an eye, coming and going like a flash of lightning; so that the systole presented itself to me now from this point, now from that; the diastole the same; and then everything was reversed, the motions occurring, as it seemed, variously and confusedly together. My mind was therefore greatly unsettled, nor did I know what I should myself conclude, nor what believe from others. . . .

   At length, and by using greater and daily diligence, having frequent recourse to vivisections, employing a variety of animals for the purpose, and collating numerous observations, I thought that I had attained to the truth, that I should extricate myself and escape from this labyrinth [a

---

[1]In dilatation, the heart muscle is relaxed, creating the diastole, or expansion of the heart's chambers, during which they fill with blood. The heart's contraction, or systole, forces the blood out of the chambers in a pumping action.

maze, a confused state], and that I had discovered what I so much desired, both the motion and the use of the heart and arteries; since which time I have not hesitated to expose my views upon these subjects, not only in private to my friends, but also in public, in my anatomical lectures, after the manner of the Academy[2] of old.

These views, as usual, pleased some more, others less; some chid and calumniated me, and laid it to me as a crime that I had dared to depart from the precepts and opinion of all anatomists; others desired further explanations of the novelties, which they said were both worthy of consideration, and might perchance be found of signal use. At length, yielding to the requests of my friends, that all might be made participators in my labours, and partly moved by the envy of others, who, receiving my views with uncandid minds and understanding them indifferently, have essayed to traduce me publicly, I have been moved to commit these things to the press, in order that all may be enabled to form an opinion both of me and my labours. . . .

But lest any one should say that we give them words only, and make mere specious assertions without any foundation, and desire to innovate without sufficient cause, three points present themselves for confirmation, which being stated, I conceive that the truth I contend for will follow necessarily, and appear as a thing obvious to all. First,—the blood is incessantly transmitted by the action of the heart from the vena cava to the arteries in such quantity, that it cannot be supplied from the ingesta,[3] and in such wise that the whole mass must very quickly pass through the organ; Second,—the blood under the influence of the arterial pulse enters and is impelled in a continuous, equable, and incessant stream through every part and member of the body, in much larger quantity than were sufficient for nutrition, or than the whole mass of fluids could supply; Third,—the veins in like manner return this blood incessantly

to the heart from all parts and members of the body. These points proved, I conceive it will be manifest that the blood circulates, revolves, propelled and then returning, from the heart to the extremities, from the extremities to the heart, and thus that it performs a kind of circular motion.

Let us assume either arbitrarily or from experiment, the quantity of blood which the left ventricle[4] of the heart will contain when distended to be, say two ounces, three ounces, one ounce and a half—in the dead body I have found it to hold upwards of two ounces. Let us assume further, how much less the heart will hold in the contracted than in the dilated state; and how much blood it will project into the aorta[5] upon each contraction;—and all the world allows that with the systole something is always projected, a necessary consequence demonstrated in the third chapter, and obvious from the structure of the valves; and let us suppose as approaching the truth that the fourth, or fifth, or sixth, or even but the eighth part of its charge is thrown into the artery at each contraction; this would give either half an ounce, or three drachms, or one drachm [dram: ⅛ ounce] of blood as propelled by the heart at each pulse into the aorta; which quantity, by reason of the valves at the root of the vessel, can by no means return into the ventricle. Now in the course of half an hour, the heart will have made more than one thousand beats, in some as many as two, three, and even four thousand. Multiplying the number of drachms propelled by the number of pulses, we shall have either one thousand half ounces, or one thousand times three drachms, or a like proportional quantity of blood, according to the amount which we assume as propelled with each stroke of the heart, sent from this organ into the artery; a larger quantity in every case than is contained in the whole body! In the same way, in the sheep or dog, say that but a single scruple [$\frac{1}{3}$ dram, $\frac{1}{24}$ ounce] of blood passes with each

---

[2]*The Academy* refers to the Athens school founded by Plato at which public lectures were given.

[3]The vena cava is the major vein that carries blood returning from the body into the heart. Ingesta refers to solid or liquid nutrients taken into the body.

[4]The heart consists of four chambers: a left and right ventricle (the lower chambers) and a left and right atrium (the upper chambers).

[5]The aorta is the major artery that carries blood out of the heart to the body.

stroke of the heart, in one half hour we should have one thousand scruples, or about three pounds and a half of blood injected into the aorta; but the body of neither animal contains above four pounds of blood, a fact which I have myself ascertained in the case of the sheep.

Upon this supposition, therefore, assumed merely as a ground for reasoning, we see the whole mass of blood passing through the heart, from the veins to the arteries, and in like manner through the lungs.

But let it be said that this does not take place in half an hour, but in an hour, or even in a day; any way it is still manifest that more blood passes through the heart in consequence of its action, than can either be supplied by the whole of the ingesta, or that can be contained in the veins at the same moment.

REVIEW QUESTIONS

1. What evidence led William Harvey to conclude that blood constantly circulates through the heart?
2. What method did he use to reach his conclusions?
3. Why did some of Harvey's colleagues refuse to believe his conclusions?
4. Why did Harvey publish his book?

5   The Autonomy of the Mind

René Descartes (1596–1650), a French mathematician and philosopher, united the new currents of thought initiated during the Renaissance and the Scientific Revolution. Descartes said that the universe was a mechanical system whose inner laws could be discovered through mathematical thinking and formulated in mathematical terms. With Descartes' assertions on the power of thought, human beings became fully aware of their capacity to comprehend the world through their mental powers. For this reason he is regarded as the founder of modern philosophy.

The deductive approach stressed by Descartes presumes that inherent in the mind are mathematical principles, logical relationships, the principle of cause and effect, concepts of size and motion, and so on—ideas that exist independently of human experience with the external world. Descartes, for example, would say that the properties of a right-angle triangle ($a^2 + b^2 = c^2$) are implicit in human consciousness prior to any experience one might have with a triangle. These innate ideas, said Descartes, permit the mind to give order and coherence to the physical world. Descartes held that the mind arrives at truth when it "intuits" or comprehends the logical necessity of its own ideas and expresses these ideas with clarity, certainty, and precision.

René Descartes
DISCOURSE ON METHOD

In the *Discourse on Method* (1637), Descartes proclaimed the mind's autonomy and importance, and its ability and right to comprehend truth. In this work he offered a method whereby one could achieve certainty and thereby produce a comprehensive understanding of nature and human culture. In the following passage from the *Discourse on Method*, he explained the purpose of his inquiry. How he did so is almost as revolutionary as the ideas he wished to express. He spoke in the first person, autobiographically, as an individual employing his own reason, and he addressed himself to other individuals, inviting them to use their reason. He brought to his narrative an unprecedented confidence in the power of his own judgment and a deep disenchantment with the learning of his times.

PART ONE

From my childhood I lived in a world of books, and since I was taught that by their help I could gain a clear and assured knowledge of everything useful in life, I was eager to learn from them. But as soon as I had finished the course of studies which usually admits one to the ranks of the learned, I changed my opinion completely. For I found myself saddled with so many doubts and errors that I seemed to have gained nothing in trying to educate myself unless it was to discover more and more fully how ignorant I was.

Nevertheless I had been in one of the most celebrated schools in Europe, where I thought there should be wise men if wise men existed anywhere on earth. I had learned there everything that others learned, and, not satisfied with merely the knowledge that was taught, I had perused as many books as I could find which contained more unusual and recondite knowledge. . . . And finally, it did not seem to me that our times were less flourishing and fertile than were any of the earlier periods. All this led me to conclude that I could judge others by myself, and to decide that there was no such wisdom in the world as I had previously hoped to find. . . .

I revered our theology, and hoped as much as anyone else to get to heaven, but having learned on great authority that the road was just as open to the most ignorant as to the most learned, and that the truths of revelation which lead thereto are beyond our understanding, I would not have dared to submit them to the weakness of my reasonings. I thought that to succeed in their examination it would be necessary to have some extraordinary assistance from heaven, and to be more than a man.

I will say nothing of philosophy except that it has been studied for many centuries by the most outstanding minds without having produced anything which is not in dispute and consequently doubtful. I did not have enough presumption to hope to succeed better than the others; and when I noticed how many different opinions learned men may hold on the same subject, despite the fact that no more than one of them can ever be right, I resolved to consider almost as false any opinion which was merely plausible. . . .

This is why I gave up my studies entirely as soon as I reached the age when I was no longer under the control of my teachers. I resolved to seek no other knowledge than that which I might find within myself, or perhaps in the great book of nature. I spent a few years of my adolescence traveling, seeing courts and armies, living with people of diverse types and stations of life, acquiring varied experience, testing myself in the episodes which fortune sent me, and, above all, thinking about the things around me so that I could derive some profit from them. For it seemed to me that I might find much more of the truth in the cogitations [reflections] which each man made on things which were important to him, and where he would be the loser if he judged badly, than in the cogitations of a man of letters in his study, concerned with speculations which produce no effect, and which have no consequences to him. . . .

. . . After spending several years in thus studying the book of nature and acquiring experience, I eventually reached the decision to study my own self, and to employ all my abilities to try to choose the right path. This produced much better results in my case, I think, than would have been produced if I had never left my books and my country. . . .

PART TWO

. . . As far as the opinions which I had been receiving since my birth were concerned, I could not do better than to reject them completely for once in my lifetime, and to resume them afterwards, or perhaps accept better ones in their place, when I had determined how they fitted into a rational scheme. And I firmly believed that by this means I would succeed in conducting my life much better than if I built only upon the old foundations and gave credence to the principles which I had acquired in my childhood without ever having examined them to see whether they were true or not. . . .

. . . Never has my intention been more than to try to reform my own ideas, and rebuild them on foundations that would be wholly mine. . . . The decision to abandon all one's preconceived notions is not an example for all to follow. . . .

As for myself, I should no doubt have . . . [never attempted it] if I had had but a single teacher or if I had not known the differences which have always existed among the most learned. I had discovered in college that one cannot imagine anything so strange and unbelievable but that it has been upheld by some philosopher; and in my travels I had found that those who held opinions contrary to ours were neither barbarians nor savages, but that many of them were at least as reasonable as ourselves. I had considered how the same man, with the same capacity for reason, becomes different as a result of being brought up among Frenchmen or Germans than he would be if he had been brought up among Chinese or cannibals; and how, in our fashions, the thing which pleased us ten years ago and perhaps will please us again ten years in the future, now seems extravagant and ridiculous; and I felt that in all these ways we are much more greatly influenced by custom and example than by any certain knowledge. Faced with this divergence of opinion, I could not accept the testimony of the majority, for I thought it worthless as a proof of anything somewhat difficult to discover, since it is much more likely that a single man will have

discovered it than a whole people. Nor, on the other hand, could I select anyone whose opinions seemed to me to be preferable to those of others, and I was thus constrained to embark on the investigation for myself.

Nevertheless, like a man who walks alone in the darkness, I resolved to go so slowly and circumspectly that if I did not get ahead very rapidly I was at least safe from falling. Also, I did not want to reject all the opinions which had slipped irrationally into my consciousness since birth, until I had first spent enough time planning how to accomplish the task which I was then undertaking, and seeking the true method of obtaining knowledge of everything which my mind was capable of understanding. . . .

Descartes' method consists of four principles that place the capacity to arrive at truth entirely within the province of the human mind. One finds a self-evident principle, such as a geometric axiom. From this general principle, other truths are deduced through logical reasoning. This is accomplished by breaking a problem down into its elementary components and then, step by step, moving toward more complex knowledge.

. . . I thought that some other method [besides that of logic, algebra, and geometry] must be found to combine the advantages of these three and to escape their faults. Finally, just as the multitude of laws frequently furnishes an excuse for vice, and a state is much better governed with a few laws which are strictly adhered to, so I thought that instead of the great number of precepts of which logic is composed, I would have enough with the four following ones, provided that I made a firm and unalterable resolution not to violate them even in a single instance.

The first rule was never to accept anything as true unless I recognized it to be evidently such: that is, carefully to avoid precipitation and prejudgment, and to include nothing in my conclusions unless it presented itself so clearly and distinctly to my mind that there was no occasion to doubt it.

The second was to divide each of the difficulties which I encountered into as many parts as possible, and as might be required for an easier solution.

The third was to think in an orderly fashion, beginning with the things which were simplest and easiest to understand, and gradually and by degrees reaching toward more complex knowledge, even treating as though ordered materials which were not necessarily so.

The last was always to make enumerations so complete, and reviews so general, that I would be certain that nothing was omitted. . . .

What pleased me most about this method was that it enabled me to reason in all things, if not perfectly, at least as well as was in my power. In addition, I felt that in practicing it my mind was gradually becoming accustomed to conceive its objects more clearly and distinctly. . . .

Descartes was searching for an incontrovertible truth that could serve as the first principle of philosophy. His arrival at the famous dictum "I think, therefore I am" marks the beginning of modern philosophy.

PART FOUR

. . . As I desired to devote myself wholly to the search for truth, I thought that I should . . .

reject as absolutely false anything of which I could have the least doubt, in order to see whether anything would be left after this procedure which could be called wholly certain. Thus, as our senses deceive us at times, I was ready to suppose that nothing was at all the way our senses represented them to be. As there are men who make mistakes in reasoning even on the simplest topics in geometry, I judged that I was as liable to error as any other, and rejected as false all the reasoning which I had previously accepted as valid demonstration. Finally, as the same precepts which we have when awake may come to us when asleep without their being true, I decided to suppose that nothing that had ever entered my mind was more real than the illusions of my dreams. But I soon noticed that while I thus wished to think everything false, it was necessarily true that I who thought so was something. Since this truth, *I think, therefore I am*, was so firm and assured that all the most extravagant suppositions of the sceptics[1] were unable to shake it, I judged that I could safely accept it as the first principle of the philosophy I was seeking.

---

[1]The skeptics belonged to the ancient Greek philosophic school that held true knowledge to be beyond human grasp and treated all knowledge as uncertain.

REVIEW QUESTIONS

1. Why was René Descartes critical of the learning of his day?
2. What are the implications of Descartes' famous words: "I think, therefore I am"?
3. Compare Descartes' method with the approach advocated by Francis Bacon.

---

6 The Mechanical Universe

By demonstrating that all bodies in the universe—earthly objects as well as moons, planets, and stars—obey the same laws of motion and gravitation, Sir Isaac Newton (1646–1723) completed the destruction of the medieval view of the universe. The idea that the same laws governed the movement of earthly and heavenly bodies was completely foreign to medieval thinkers, who drew a sharp division between a higher celestial world and a lower terrestrial one. In the *Principia Mathematica* (1687), Newton showed that the same forces that hold celestial bodies in their orbits around the sun make apples fall to the ground. For Newton, the universe was like a giant clock, all of whose parts obeyed strict mechanical principles and worked together in perfect precision. To Newton's contemporaries, it seemed as if mystery had been banished from the universe.

Isaac Newton
PRINCIPIA MATHEMATICA

In the first of the following passages from *Principia Mathematica*, Newton stated the principle of universal law and lauded the experimental method as the means of acquiring knowledge.

RULES OF REASONING IN PHILOSOPHY

Rule I.   We are to admit no more causes of natural things than such as are both true and sufficient to explain their appearances.

To this purpose the philosophers say that Nature does nothing in vain, and more is in vain when less will serve; for Nature is pleased with simplicity, and affects not the pomp of superfluous causes.

Rule II.   Therefore to the same natural effects we must, as far as possible, assign the same causes.

As to respiration in a man and in a beast; the descent of stones [meteorites] in *Europe* and in *America*; the light of our culinary fire and of the sun; the reflection of light in the earth, and in the planets.

Rule III.   The qualities of bodies, which . . . are found to belong to all bodies within the reach of our experiments, are to be esteemed the universal qualities of all bodies whatsoever.

For since the qualities of bodies are only known to us by experiments, we are to hold for universal all such as universally agree with experiments. . . . We are certainly not to relinquish the evidence of experiments for the sake of dreams and vain fictions of our own

devising; nor are we to recede from the analogy of Nature, which [is] . . . simple, and always consonant to itself. We no other way know the extension of bodies than by our senses, nor do these reach it in all bodies; but because we perceive extension in all that are sensible, therefore, we ascribe it universally to all others also. That abundance of bodies are hard, we learn by experience; and because the hardness of the whole arises from the hardness of the parts, we, therefore, justly infer the hardness of the undivided particles not only of the bodies we feel but of all others. That all bodies are impenetrable, we gather not from reason, but from sensation. The bodies which we handle we find impenetrable, and thence, conclude impenetrability to be an universal property of all bodies whatsoever. That all bodies are moveable, and endowed with certain powers (which we call . . . {*inertia*}) of persevering in their motion, or in their rest, we only infer from the like properties observed in the bodies which we have seen. The extension, hardness, impenetrability, mobility, . . . of the whole, result from the extension, hardness, impenetrability, mobility, . . . of the parts; and thence we conclude the least particles of all bodies to be also all extended, and hard and impenetrable, and moveable, . . . And this is the foundation of all philosophy. . . .

Lastly, if it universally appears, by experiments and astronomical observations, that all bodies about the earth gravitate towards the earth, and that in proportion to the quantity of matter which they severally contain; that the moon likewise, according to the quantity of its matter, gravitates towards the earth; that, on the other hand, our sea gravitates towards the moon; and all the planets mutually one towards another; and the comets in like manner towards the sun; we must, in consequence of this rule, universally allow that all bodies whatsoever are endowed with a principle of mutual gravitation. . . .

Rule IV.   In experimental philosophy we are to look upon propositions collected by general induction from phenomena as accurately or very nearly true, notwithstanding any contrary hypotheses that may be imagined, till such time as other phenomena occur, by which they may either be made more accurate, or liable to exceptions.

This rule we must follow, that the argument of induction may not be evaded by hypotheses.

Newton describes further his concepts of gravity and scientific methodology.

GRAVITY

Hitherto, we have explained the phenomena of the heavens and of our sea by the power of gravity, but have not yet assigned the cause of this power. This is certain, that it must proceed from a cause that penetrates to the very centres of the sun and planets, without suffering the least diminution of its force; that operates not according to the quantity of the surfaces of the particles upon which it acts (as mechanical causes used to do) but according to the quantity of the solid matter which they contain, and propagates its virtue on all sides to immense distances, decreasing always in the duplicate portion of the distances. . . .

Hitherto I have not been able to discover the cause of those properties of gravity from

the phenomena, and I frame no hypothesis; for whatever is not deduced from the phenomena is to be called an hypothesis; and hypotheses, whether metaphysical or physical, whether of occult qualities or mechanical, have no place in experimental philosophy. In this philosophy particular propositions are inferred from the phenomena, and afterward rendered general by induction. Thus it was the impenetrability, the mobility, and the impulsive forces of bodies, and the laws of motion and of gravitation were discovered. And to us it is enough that gravity does really exist, and acts according to the laws which we have explained, and abundantly serves to account for all the motions of the celestial bodies, and of our sea.

A devout Anglican, Newton believed that God had created this superbly organized universe. The following selection is also from the *Principia*.

GOD AND THE UNIVERSE

This most beautiful system of the sun, planets, and comets could only proceed from the counsel and dominion of an intelligent and powerful Being. And if the fixed stars are the centers of other like systems, these, being formed by the like wise counsel, must be all subject to the dominion of One, especially since the light of the fixed stars is of the same nature with the light of the sun and from every system light passes into all the other systems; and lest the systems of the fixed stars should, by their gravity, fall on each other mutually, he hath placed those systems at immense distances from one another.

This Being governs all things not as the soul of the world, but as Lord over all; and on account of his dominion he is wont to be called "Lord God" . . . or "Universal Ruler." . . . It is the dominion of a spiritual being which constitutes a God. . . . And from his true dominion it follows that the true God is a living, intelligent and powerful Being. . . . he governs all things, and knows all things that are or can be done. . . . He endures for ever, and is every where present; and by existing always and every where, he constitutes duration and space. . . . In him are all things contained and moved; yet neither affects the other: God suffers nothing from the motion of bodies; bodies find no resistance from the omnipresence of God. . . . As a blind man has no idea of colors so we have no idea of the manner by which the all-wise God preserves and understands all things. He is utterly void of all body and bodily figure, and can therefore neither be seen, nor heard, nor touched; nor ought to be worshipped under the representation of any corporeal thing. We have ideas of his attributes, but what the real substance of any thing is we know not. . . . Much less, then, have we any idea of the substance of God. We know him only by his most wise and excellent contrivances of things. . . . [W]e reverence and adore him as his servants; and a god without dominion, providence, and final causes, is nothing else but Fate and Nature. Blind metaphysical necessity, which is certainly the same always and everywhere, could produce no variety of things. All that diversity of natural things which we find suited to different times and places could arise from nothing but the ideas and will of a Being necessarily existing. . . . And thus much concerning God; to discourse of whom from the appearances of things does certainly belong to Natural Philosophy.

REVIEW QUESTIONS

1. What did Isaac Newton mean by universal law? What examples of universal law did he provide?
2. What method for investigating nature did Newton advocate?
3. Summarize Newton's arguments for God's existence.
4. For Newton, what is God's relationship to the universe?

CHAPTER 3

The Enlightenment

RENÉ DESCARTES earned an international reputation for his work in philosophy and mathematics. Here he is conducting a scientific demonstration at the court of Queen Christina of Sweden, c. 1700. *(The Art Archive/Picture Desk)*

The Enlightenment of the eighteenth century culminated the movement toward modernity that started in the Renaissance era. The thinkers of the Enlightenment, called *philosophes*, attacked medieval otherworldliness, dethroned theology from its once-proud position as queen of the sciences, and based their understanding of nature and society on reason alone, unaided by revelation or priestly authority.

From the broad spectrum of Western history, several traditions flowed into the Enlightenment: the rational spirit born in classical Greece, the Stoic emphasis on natural law that applies to all human beings, and the Christian belief that all individuals are equal in God's eyes. A more immediate influence on the Enlightenment was Renaissance humanism, which focused on the individual and worldly human accomplishments and which criticized medieval theology-philosophy for its preoccupation with questions that seemed unrelated to the human condition. In many ways, the Enlightenment grew directly out of the Scientific Revolution. The philosophes praised both Newton's discovery of the mechanical laws that govern the universe and the scientific method that made this discovery possible. They wanted to transfer the scientific method—the reliance on experience and the critical use of the intellect—to the realm of society. They maintained that independent of clerical authority, human beings through reason could grasp the natural laws that govern the social world, just as Newton had uncovered the laws of nature that operate in the physical world. The philosophes said that those institutions and traditions that could not meet the test of reason, because they were based on authority, ignorance, or superstition, had to be reformed or dispensed with.

For medieval philosophers, reason had been subordinate to revelation; the Christian outlook determined the medieval concept of nature, morality, government, law, and life's purpose. During the Renaissance and Scientific Revolution, reason increasingly asserted its autonomy. For example, Machiavelli rejected the principle that politics should be based on Christian teachings; he recognized no higher world as the source of a higher truth. Galileo held that on questions regarding nature, one should trust to observation, experimentation, and mathematical reasoning and should not rely on Scripture. Descartes rejected reliance on past authority and maintained that through thought alone one could attain knowledge that has absolute certainty. Agreeing with Descartes that the mind is self-sufficient, the philosophes rejected the guidance of revelation and its priestly interpreters. They believed that through the use of reason, individuals could comprehend and reform society.

The Enlightenment philosophes articulated basic principles of the modern outlook: confidence in the self-sufficiency of the human mind, belief that individuals possess natural rights that governments should not violate, and the desire to reform society in accordance with rational principles. Their views influenced the reformers of the French Revolution, the Founding Fathers of the United States, and modern liberalism.

1   The Enlightenment Outlook

The critical use of the intellect was the central principle of the Enlightenment. The philosophes rejected beliefs and traditions that seemed to conflict with reason and attacked clerical and political authorities for interfering with the free use of the intellect.

Immanuel Kant
"WHAT IS ENLIGHTENMENT?"

The German philosopher Immanuel Kant (1724–1804) is a giant in the history of modern philosophy. Several twentieth-century philosophic movements have their origins in Kantian thought, and many issues raised by Kant still retain their importance. For example, in *Metaphysical Foundations of Morals* (1785), Kant set forth the categorical imperative that remains a crucial principle in moral philosophy. Kant asserted that when confronted with a moral choice, people should ask themselves: "Canst thou also will that thy maxim should be a universal law?" By this, Kant meant that people should ponder whether they would want the moral principle underlying their action to be elevated to a universal law that would govern others in similar circumstances. If they concluded that it should not, then the maxim should be rejected and the action avoided.

Kant valued the essential ideals of the Enlightenment and viewed the French Revolution, which put these ideals into law, as the triumph of liberty over despotism. In an essay entitled "What Is Enlightenment?" (1784), he contended that the Enlightenment marked a new way of thinking and eloquently affirmed the Enlightenment's confidence in and commitment to reason.

Enlightenment is man's leaving his self-caused immaturity. Immaturity is the incapacity to use one's intelligence without the guidance of another. Such immaturity is self-caused if it is not caused by lack of intelligence, but by lack of determination and courage to use one's intelligence without being guided by another. *Sapere Aude!* [Dare to know!] Have the courage to use your own intelligence! is therefore the motto of the enlightenment.

Through laziness and cowardice a large part of mankind, even after nature has freed them from alien guidance, gladly remain immature. It is because of laziness and cowardice that it is so easy for others to usurp the role of guardians.

It is so comfortable to be a minor! If I have a book which provides meaning for me, a pastor who has conscience for me, a doctor who will judge my diet for me and so on, then I do not need to exert myself. I do not have any need to think; if I can pay, others will take over the tedious job for me. The guardians who have kindly undertaken the supervision will see to it that by far the largest part of mankind, including the entire "beautiful sex," should consider the step into maturity, not only as difficult but as very dangerous.

After having made their domestic animals dumb and having carefully prevented these quiet creatures from daring to take any step beyond the lead-strings to which they have fastened them, these guardians then show them the danger which threatens them, should they attempt to walk alone. Now this danger is not really so very great; for they would presumably learn to walk after some stumbling. However, an example of this kind intimidates and frightens people out of all further attempts.

It is difficult for the isolated individual to work himself out of the immaturity which has become almost natural for him. He has even become fond of it and for the time being is incapable of employing his own intelligence, because he has never been allowed to make the attempt. Statutes and formulas, these mechanical tools of a serviceable use, or rather misuse, of his natural faculties, are the ankle-chains of a continuous immaturity. Whoever threw it off would make an uncertain jump over the smallest trench because he is not accustomed to such free movement. Therefore there are only a few who have pursued a firm path and have succeeded in escaping from immaturity by their own cultivation of the mind.

But it is more nearly possible for a public to enlighten itself: this is even inescapable if only the public is given its freedom. For there will always be some people who think for themselves, even among the self-appointed guardians of the great mass who, after having thrown off the yoke of immaturity themselves, will spread about them the spirit of a reasonable estimate of their own value and of the need for every man to think for himself. . . . [A] public can only arrive at enlightenment slowly. Through revolution, the abandonment of personal despotism may be engendered and the end of profit-seeking and domineering oppression may occur, but never a true reform of the state of mind. Instead, new prejudices, just like the old ones, will serve as the guiding reins of the great, unthinking mass. . . .

All that is required for this enlightenment is *freedom*; and particularly the least harmful of all that may be called freedom, namely, the freedom for man to make *public use* of his reason in all matters. But I hear people clamor on all sides: Don't argue! The officer says: Don't argue, drill! The tax collector: Don't argue, pay! The pastor: Don't argue, believe! . . . Here we have restrictions on freedom everywhere. Which restriction is hampering enlightenment, and which does not, or even promotes it? I answer: The *public use* of a man's reason must be free at all times, and this alone can bring enlightenment among men. . . .

I mean by the public use of one's reason, the use which a scholar makes of it before the entire reading public. . . .

The question may now be put: Do we live at present in an enlightened age? The answer is: No, but in an age of enlightenment. Much still prevents men from being placed in a position. . . to use their own minds securely and well in matters of religion. But we do have very definite indications that this field of endeavor is being opened up for men to work freely and reduce gradually the hindrances preventing a general enlightenment and an escape from self-caused immaturity.

REVIEW QUESTIONS

1. What did Immanuel Kant mean by the terms *enlightenment* and *freedom*?
2. In Kant's view, what factors delayed the progress of human enlightenment?
3. What are the political implications of Kant's views?

2 Political Liberty

John Locke (1632–1704), a British statesman, philosopher, and political theorist, was a principal source of the Enlightenment. Eighteenth-century thinkers were particularly influenced by Locke's advocacy of religious toleration, his reliance on experience as the source of knowledge, and his concern for liberty. In his first *Letter Concerning Toleration* (1689), Locke declared that Christians who persecute others in the name of religion vitiate Christ's teachings. Locke's political philosophy as formulated in the *Two Treatises on Government* (1690) complements his theory of knowledge; both were rational and secular attempts to understand and improve the human condition. The Lockean spirit pervades the American Declaration of Independence, the Constitution, and the Bill of Rights and is the basis of the liberal tradition that aims to protect individual liberty from despotic state authority.

Viewing human beings as brutish and selfish, Thomas Hobbes (see page 400) had prescribed a state with unlimited power; only in this way, he said, could people be protected from each other and civilized life preserved. Locke, regarding people as essentially good and humane, developed a conception of the state differing fundamentally from Hobbes'. Locke held that human beings are born with natural rights of life, liberty, and property; they establish the state to protect these rights. Consequently, neither executive nor legislature, neither king nor assembly has the authority to deprive individuals of their natural rights. Whereas Hobbes justified absolute monarchy, Locke explicitly endorsed constitutional government in which the power to govern derives from the consent of the governed and the state's authority is limited by agreement.

John Locke
SECOND TREATISE ON GOVERNMENT

Locke said that originally, in establishing a government, human beings had never agreed to surrender their natural rights to any state authority. The state's founders intended the new polity to preserve these natural rights and to implement the people's will. Therefore, as the following passage from Locke's *Second Treatise on Government* illustrates, the power exercised by magistrates cannot be absolute or arbitrary.

. . . *Political power* is that power, which every man having in the state of nature, has given up into the hands of the society, and therein to the governors, whom the society hath set over itself, with this express or tacit trust, that it shall be employed for their good, and the preservation of their property: now this *power*, which every man has *in the state of nature*, and which he parts with to the society in all such cases where the society can secure him, is to use such means, for the preserving of his own property, as he thinks good, and nature allows him; and to punish the breach of the law of nature in others, so as (according to the best of his reason) may most conduce to the preservation of himself, and the rest of mankind.

So that the *end and measure of this power*, when in every man's hands in the state of nature, being the preservation of all of his society, that is, all mankind in general, it can have no other *end or measure*, when in the hands of the magistrate, but to preserve the members of that society in their lives, liberties, and possessions; and so cannot be an absolute, arbitrary power over their lives and fortunes, which are as much as possible to be preserved; but a *power to make laws*, and annex such *penalties* to them, as may tend to the preservation of the whole, by cutting off those parts, and those only, which are so corrupt, that they threaten the sound and healthy, without which no severity is lawful. And this *power has its original only from compact*, and agreement, and the mutual consent of those who make up the community. . . .

These are the *bounds*, which the trust, that is put in them by the society, and the law of God and nature, have *set to the legislative* power of every common-wealth, in all forms of government.

First, They are to govern by *promulgated established laws*, not to be varied in particular cases, but to have one rule for rich and poor, for the favourite at court, and the country man at plough.

Secondly, These *laws* also ought to be designed *for* no other end ultimately, but *the good of the people*.

Thirdly, They must *not raise taxes* on the *property of the people, without the consent of the people,* given by themselves, or their deputies. And this properly concerns only such governments, where the *legislative* is always in being, or at least where the people have not reserved any part of the legislative to deputies, to be from time to time chosen by themselves.

Fourthly, The *legislative* neither must *nor can transfer the power of making laws* to any body else, or place it any where, but where the people have. . . .

If government fails to fulfill the end for which it was established—the preservation of the individual's right to life, liberty, and property—the people have a right to dissolve that government.

. . . The *legislative acts against the trust* reposed in them, when they endeavour to invade the property of the subject, and to make themselves, or any part of the community, masters, or arbitrary disposers of the lives, liberties, or fortunes of the people.

The reason why men enter into society, is the preservation of their property; and the end why they chuse and authorize a legislative, is, that there may be laws made, and rules set, as guards and fences to the properties of all the members of the society, to limit the power, and moderate the dominion of every part and member of the society: for since it can never be supposed to be the will of the society, that the legislative should have a power to destroy that which every one designs to secure, by entering into society, and for which the people submitted themselves to legislators of their own making; whenever the *legislators endeavour to take away, and destroy the property of the people*, or to reduce them to slavery under arbitrary power, they put themselves into a state of war with the people, who are thereupon absolved from any farther obedience, and are left to the common refuge, which God hath provided for all men, against force and violence. Whensoever therefore the *legislative* shall transgress this fundamental rule of society; and either by ambition, fear, folly or corruption, *endeavour to grasp* themselves, *or put into the hands of any other, an absolute power* over the lives, liberties, and estates of the people; by this breach of trust they *forfeit the power* the people had put into their hands for quite contrary ends, and it devolves to the people, who have a right to resume their original liberty, and, by the establishment of a new legislative, (such as they shall think fit) provide for their own safety and security, which is the end for which they are in society. What I have said here, concerning the legislative in general, holds true also concerning the supreme executor, who having a double trust put in him, both to have a part in the legislative, and the supreme execution of the law, acts against both, when he goes about to set up his own arbitrary will as the law of the society. He *acts* also *contrary to his trust*, when he either employs the force, treasure, and offices of the society, to corrupt the *representatives*, and gain them to his purposes; or openly pre-engages the *electors,* and prescribes to their choice, such, whom he has, by sollicitations, threats, promises, or otherwise, won to his designs; and employs them to bring in such, who have promised beforehand what to vote, and what to enact. . . .

Locke responds to the charge that his theory will produce "frequent rebellion." Indeed, says Locke, the true rebels are the magistrates who, acting contrary to the trust granted them, violate the people's rights.

. . . Such *revolutions happen* not upon every little mismanagement in public affairs. *Great mistakes* in the ruling part, many wrong and inconvenient laws, and all the *slips* of human frailty, will be *borne by the people* without mutiny or murmur. But if a long train of abuses, prevarications and artifices, all tending the same way, make the design visible to the people, and they cannot but feel what they lie under, and see whither they are going; it is not to be wondered at, that they should then rouze themselves, and endeavour to put the rule into such hands which may secure to them the ends for which government was at first erected. . . .

. . . I answer, that *this doctrine* of a power in the people of providing for their safety a-new, by a new legislative, when their legislators have acted contrary to their trust, by invading their property, is *the best defence against rebellion*, and the probablest means to hinder it: for *rebellion* being an opposition, not to persons, but authority, which is founded only in the constitutions and laws of the government; those, whoever they be, who by force break through, and by force justify their violation of them, are truly and properly *rebels*: for when men, by entering into society and civil government, have excluded force, and introduced laws for the preservation of property, peace, and unity amongst themselves, those who set up force again in opposition to the laws, do {rebel}, that is, bring back again the state of war, and are properly rebels: which they who are in power, (by the pretence they have to authority, the temptation of force they have in their hands, and the flattery of those about them) being likeliest to do; the properest way to prevent the evil, is to shew them the danger and injustice of it, who are under the greatest temptation to run into it.

The end of government is the good of mankind; and which is *best for mankind*, that the people should always be exposed to the boundless will of tyranny, or that the rulers should be sometimes liable to be opposed, when they grow exorbitant in the use of their power, and employ it for the destruction, and not the preservation of the properties of their people?

Thomas Jefferson
DECLARATION OF INDEPENDENCE

Written in 1776 by Thomas Jefferson (1743–1826) to justify the American colonists' break with Britain, the Declaration of Independence enumerated principles that were quite familiar to English statesmen and intellectuals. The preamble to the Declaration, excerpted below, articulated clearly Locke's philosophy of natural rights. Locke had viewed life, liberty, and property as the individual's essential natural rights; Jefferson substituted the "pursuit of happiness" for property.

A DECLARATION BY THE REPRESENTATIVES OF THE UNITED STATES OF AMERICA, IN GENERAL CONGRESS ASSEMBLED

When in the Course of human Events, it becomes necessary for one People to dissolve the Political Bands which have connected them with another, and to assume among the Powers of the Earth, the separate and equal Station to which the Laws of Nature and of Nature's God entitle them, a decent Respect to the Opinions of Mankind requires that they should declare the causes which impel them to the Separation.

We hold these Truths to be self-evident, that all Men are created equal, that they are endowed by their Creator with certain unalienable Rights, that among these are Life, Liberty, and the Pursuit of Happiness—That to secure these Rights, Governments are instituted among Men, deriving their just Powers from the Consent of the Governed, That whenever any Form of Government becomes destructive of these Ends, it is the Right of the People to alter or to abolish it, and to institute new Government, laying its Foundation on such Principles, and organizing its Powers in such Form, as to them shall seem most likely to effect their Safety and Happiness. Prudence, indeed, will dictate that Governments long established should not be changed for light and transient Causes; and accordingly all Experience hath shewn, that Mankind are more disposed to suffer, while Evils are sufferable, than to right themselves by abolishing the Forms to which they are accustomed. But when a long Train of Abuses and Usurpations, pursuing invariably the same Object, evinces a Design to reduce them under absolute Despotism, it is their right, it is their duty, to throw off such Government, and to provide new Guards for their future Security. Such has been the patient Sufferance of these Colonies; and such is now the Necessity which constrains them to alter their former Systems of Government. The History of the present King of Great-Britain is a History of repeated Injuries and Usurpations, all having in direct Object the Establishment of an absolute Tyranny over these States. . . .

REVIEW QUESTIONS

1. Compare the views of John Locke with those of Thomas Hobbes regarding the character of human nature, political authority, and the right to rebellion.
2. Compare Locke's theory of natural rights with the principles stated in the American Declaration of Independence.

3 Attack on Religion

Christianity came under severe attack during the eighteenth century. The philosophes rejected Christian doctrines that seemed contrary to reason. Deism, the dominant religious outlook of the philosophes, taught that religion should accord with reason and natural law. To deists, it seemed reasonable to believe in God, for this superbly constructed universe required a creator in the same manner that a watch required a watchmaker. But, said the deists, after God had constructed the universe, he did not interfere in its operations; the universe was governed by mechanical laws. Deists denied that the Bible was God's work, rejected clerical authority, and dismissed miracles—like Jesus walking on water—as incompatible with natural law. To them, Jesus was not divine but an inspired teacher of morality. Many deists still considered themselves Christians; the clergy, however, viewed the deists' religious views with horror.

Voltaire
A PLEA FOR TOLERANCE AND REASON

François Marie Arouet (1694–1778), known to the world as Voltaire, was the recognized leader of the French Enlightenment. Few of the philosophes had a better mind, and none had a sharper wit. A relentless critic of the Old Regime (the social structure in prerevolutionary France), Voltaire attacked superstition, religious fanaticism and persecution, censorship, and other abuses of eighteenth-century French society. Spending more than two years in Great Britain, Voltaire acquired a great admiration for English liberty, toleration, commerce, and science. In *Letters Concerning the English Nation* (1733), he drew unfavorable comparisons between a progressive Britain and a reactionary France.

Voltaire's angriest words were directed against established Christianity, to which he attributed many of the ills of modern society. Voltaire regarded Christianity as "the Christ-worshiping superstition" that someday would be destroyed "by the weapons of reason." He rejected revelation and the church hierarchy and was repulsed by Christian intolerance, but he accepted Christian morality and believed in God as the prime mover who set the universe in motion.

The following passages compiled from Voltaire's works—grouped according to topic—provide insight into the outlook of the philosophes. The excerpts come from sources that include his *Treatise on Tolerance* (1763), *The Philosophical Dictionary* (1764), and *Commentary on the Book of Crime and Punishments* (1766).

TOLERANCE

It does not require any great art or studied elocution to prove that Christians ought to tolerate one another. I will go even further and say that we ought to look upon all men as our brothers. What! call a Turk, a Jew, and a Siamese, my brother? Yes, of course; for are we not all children of the same father, and the creatures of the same God?

———

What is tolerance? . . . We are all full of weakness and errors; let us mutually pardon our follies. This is the last law of nature. . . .

It is clear that every private individual who persecutes a man, his brother, because he is not of the same opinion, is a monster. . . .

Of all religions, the Christian ought doubtless to inspire the most tolerance, although hitherto the Christians have been the most intolerant of all men.

———

. . . Tolerance has never brought civil war; intolerance has covered the earth with carnage. . . .

What! Is each citizen to be permitted to believe and to think that which his reason rightly or wrongly dictates? He should indeed, provided that he does not disturb the public order; for it is not contingent on man to believe or not to believe; but it is contingent on him to respect the usages of his country; and if you say that it is a crime not to believe in the dominant religion, you accuse then yourself the first

Christians, your ancestors, and you justify those whom you accuse of having martyred them.

You reply that there is a great difference, that all religions are the work of men, and that the Apostolic Roman Catholic Church is alone the work of God. But in good faith, ought our religion because it is divine reign through hate, violence, exiles, usurpation of property, prisons, tortures, murders, and thanksgivings to God for these murders? The more the Christian religion is divine, the less it pertains to man to require it; if God made it, God will sustain it without you. You know that intolerance produces only hypocrites or rebels, what distressing alternatives! In short, do you want to sustain through executioners the religion of a God whom executioners have put to death and who taught only gentleness and patience?

I shall never cease, my dear sir, to preach tolerance from the housetops, despite the complaints of your priests and the outcries of ours, until persecution is no more. The progress of reason is slow, the roots of prejudice lie deep. Doubtless, I shall never see the fruits of my efforts, but they are seeds which may one day germinate.

DOGMA

. . . Is Jesus the Word? If He be the Word, did He emanate from God in time or before time? If He emanated from God, is He co-eternal and consubstantial with Him, or is He of a similar substance? Is He distinct from Him, or is He not? Is He made or begotten? Can He beget in His turn? Has He paternity? or productive virtue without paternity? Is the Holy Ghost made? or begotten? or produced? or proceeding from the Father? or proceeding from the Son? or proceeding from both? Can He beget? can He produce? is His hypostasis consubstantial with the hypostasis of the Father and the Son? and how is it that, having the same nature—the same essence as the Father and the Son, He cannot do the same things done by these persons who are Himself?

Assuredly, I understand nothing of this; no one has ever understood any of it, and that is why we have slaughtered one another.

The Christians tricked, cavilled, hated, and excommunicated one another, for some of these dogmas inaccessible to human intellect.

FANATICISM

Fanaticism is to superstition what delirium is to fever, what rage is to anger. He who has ecstasies and visions, who takes dreams for realities, and his own imaginations for prophecies is an enthusiast; he who reinforces his madness by murder is a fanatic. . . .

The most detestable example of fanaticism is that exhibited on the night of St. Bartholomew,[1] when the people of Paris rushed from house to house to stab, slaughter, throw out of the window, and tear in pieces their fellow citizens who did not go to mass.

There are some cold-blooded fanatics; such as those judges who sentence men to death for no other crime than that of thinking differently from themselves. . . .

Once fanaticism has infected a brain, the disease is almost incurable. I have seen convulsionaries who, while speaking of the miracles of Saint Paris [a fourth-century Italian bishop], gradually grew heated in spite of themselves. Their eyes became inflamed, their limbs shook, fury disfigured their face, and they would have killed anyone who contradicted them.

There is no other remedy for this epidemic malady than that philosophical spirit which, extending itself from one to another, at length softens the manners of men and prevents the access of the disease. For when the disorder has made any progress, we should, without loss of time, flee from it, and wait till the air has become purified.

------

[1]"St. Bartholomew" refers to the day of August 24, 1572, when the populace of Paris, instigated by King Charles IX at his mother's urging, began a week-long slaughter of Protestants.

PERSECUTION

What is a persecutor? He whose wounded pride and furious fanaticism arouse princes and magistrates against innocent men, whose only crime is that of being of a different opinion. "Impudent man! you have worshipped God; you have preached and practiced virtue; you have served man; you have protected the orphan, have helped the poor; you have changed deserts, in which slaves dragged on a miserable existence, into fertile lands peopled by happy families; but I have discovered that you despise me, and have never read my controversial work. You know that I am a rogue; that I have forged G[od]'s signature, that I have stolen. You might tell these things; I must anticipate you. I will, therefore, go to the confessor [spiritual counselor] of the prime minister, or the magistrate; I will show them, with outstretched neck and twisted mouth, that you hold an erroneous opinion in relation to the cells in which the Septuagint was studied; that you have even spoken disrespectfully ten years ago of Tobit's dog,[2] which you asserted to have been a spaniel, while I proved that it was a greyhound. I will denounce you as the enemy of God and man!" Such is the language of the persecutor; and if precisely these words do not issue from his lips, they are engraven on his heart with the pointed steel of fanaticism steeped in the bitterness of envy. . . .

O God of mercy! If any man can resemble that evil being who is described as ceaselessly employed in the destruction of your works, is it not the persecutor?

SUPERSTITION

In 1749 a woman was burned in the Bishopric of Würzburg [a city in central Germany], convicted of being a witch. This is an extraordinary phenomenon in the age in which we live. Is it possible that people who boast of their reformation and of trampling superstition under foot, who indeed supposed that they had reached the perfection of reason, could nevertheless believe in witchcraft, and this more than a hundred years after the so-called reformation of their reason?

In 1652 a peasant woman named Michelle Chaudron, living in the little territory of Geneva [a major city in Switzerland], met the devil going out of the city. The devil gave her a kiss, received her homage, and imprinted on her upper lip and right breast the mark that he customarily bestows on all whom he recognizes as his favorites. This seal of the devil is a little mark which makes the skin insensitive, as all the demonographical jurists of those times affirm.

The devil ordered Michelle Chaudron to bewitch two girls. She obeyed her master punctually. The girls' parents accused her of witchcraft before the law. The girls were questioned and confronted with the accused. They declared that they felt a continual pricking in certain parts of their bodies and that they were possessed. Doctors were called, or at least, those who passed for doctors at that time. They examined the girls. They looked for the devil's seal on Michelle's body—what the statement of the case called *satanic marks*. Into them they drove a long needle, already a painful torture. Blood flowed out, and Michelle made it known, by her cries, that satanic marks certainly do not make one insensitive. The judges, seeing no definite proof that Michelle Chaudron was a witch, proceeded to torture her, a method that infallibly produces the necessary proofs: this wretched woman, yielding to the violence of torture, at last confessed every thing they desired.

The doctors again looked for the satanic mark. They found a little black spot on one of her thighs. They drove in the needle. The torment of the torture had been so horrible that the poor creature hardly felt the needle; thus the crime was established. But as customs were becoming somewhat mild at that time, she was burned only after being hanged and strangled.

---

[2]The Septuagint, the version of the Hebrew Scriptures used by Saint Paul and other early Christians, was a Greek translation done by Hellenized Jews in Alexandria sometime in the late third or the second century B.C. *Tobit's dog* appears in the Book of Tobit, a Hebrew book contained in the Catholic version of the Bible.

In those days every tribunal of Christian Europe resounded with similar arrests. The [twigs] were lit everywhere for witches, as for heretics. People reproached the Turks most for having neither witches nor demons among them. This absence of demons was considered an infallible proof of the falseness of a religion.

A zealous friend of public welfare, of humanity, of true religion, has stated in one of his writings on behalf of innocence, that Christian tribunals have condemned to death over a hundred thousand accused witches. If to these judicial murders are added the infinitely superior number of massacred heretics, that part of the world will seem to be nothing but a vast scaffold covered with torturers and victims, surrounded by judges, guards and spectators.

Thomas Paine
THE AGE OF REASON

Exemplifying the deist outlook was Thomas Paine (1737–1809), an Englishman who moved to America in 1774. Paine's *Common Sense* (1776) was an eloquent appeal for American independence. Paine is also famous for *The Rights of Man* (1791–1792), in which he defended the French Revolution. In *The Age of Reason* (1794–1796), he denounced Christian mysteries, miracles, and prophecies as superstition and called for a natural religion that accorded with reason and science.

I believe in one God, and no more; and I hope for happiness beyond this life.

I believe in the equality of man; and I believe that religious duties consist in doing justice, loving mercy, and endeavoring to make our fellow-creatures happy.

But, lest it should be supposed that I believe many other things in addition to these, I shall, in the progress of this work, declare the things I do not believe, and my reasons for not believing them.

I do not believe in the creed professed by the Jewish church, by the Roman church, by the Greek church, by the Turkish church, by the Protestant church, nor by any church that I know of. My own mind is my own church. . . .

When Moses told the children of Israel that he received the two tablets of the [Ten] commandments from the hands of God, they were not obliged to believe him, because they had no other authority for it than his telling them so; and I have no other authority for it than some historian telling me so. The commandments carry no internal evidence of divinity with them; they contain some good moral precepts, such as any man qualified to be a lawgiver, or a legislator, could produce himself, without having recourse to supernatural intervention. . . .

When also I am told that a woman called the Virgin Mary, said, or gave out, that she was with child without any cohabitation with a man, and that her betrothed husband, Joseph, said that an angel told him so, I have a right to believe them or not; such a circumstance required a much stronger evidence than their bare word for it; but we have not even this—for neither Joseph nor Mary wrote any such matter themselves; it is only reported by others that *they said so*—it is hearsay upon hearsay, and I do not choose to rest my belief upon such evidence.

It is, however, not difficult to account for the credit that was given to the story of Jesus Christ being the son of God. He was born when the heathen mythology had still some fashion and repute in the world, and that mythology had prepared the people for the belief of such a story. Almost all the extraordinary men that lived under the heathen mythology were reputed to be the sons of some of their gods. It was not a new thing, at that time, to believe a man to have been celestially begotten; the intercourse of gods with women was then a matter of familiar opinion. Their Jupiter [chief Roman god], according to their accounts, had cohabited with hundreds: the story, therefore, had nothing in it either new, wonderful, or obscene; it was conformable to the opinions that then prevailed among the people called Gentiles, or Mythologists, and it was those people only that believed it. The Jews who had kept strictly to the belief of one God, and no more, and who had always rejected the heathen mythology, never credited the story. . . .

Nothing that is here said can apply, even with the most distant disrespect, to the real character of Jesus Christ. He was a virtuous and an amiable man. The morality that he preached and practised was of the most benevolent kind; and though similar systems of morality had been preached by Confucius [Chinese philosopher], and by some of the Greek philosophers, many years before; by the Quakers [members of the Society of Friends] since; and by many good men in all ages, it has not been exceeded by any. . . .

. . . The resurrection and ascension [of Jesus Christ], supposing them to have taken place, admitted of public and ocular demonstration, like that of the ascension of a balloon, or the sun at noon-day, to all Jerusalem at least. A thing which everybody is required to believe, requires that the proof and evidence of it should be equal to all, and universal; and as the public visibility of this last related act was the only evidence that could give sanction to the former part, the whole of it falls to the ground, because that evidence never was given. Instead of this, a small number of persons, not more than eight or nine, are introduced as proxies for the whole world, to say they saw it, and all the rest of the world are called upon to believe it. But it appears that Thomas [one of Jesus' disciples] did not believe the resurrection, and, as they say, would not believe without having ocular and manual demonstration himself. *So neither will I,* and the reason is equally as good for me, and for every other person, as for Thomas.

It is in vain to attempt to palliate or disguise this matter. The story, so far as relates to the supernatural part, has every mark of fraud and imposition stamped upon the face of it. Who were the authors of it is as impossible for us now to know, as it is for us to be assured that the books in which the account is related were written by the persons whose names they bear; the best surviving evidence we now have respecting this affair is the Jews. They are regularly descended from the people who lived in the times this resurrection and ascension is said to have happened, and they say, *it is not true.*

Baron d'Holbach
GOOD SENSE

More extreme than the deists were the atheists, who denied God's existence altogether. The foremost exponent of atheism was Paul-Henri Thiry, Baron d'Holbach (1723–1789), a prominent contributor to the *Encyclopedia*. Holbach hosted many leading intellectuals, including Diderot, Rousseau, and Condorcet (all represented later in this chapter), at his country estate outside of Paris. He regarded the idea of God as a product of ignorance, fear, and superstition and said that terrified by natural phenomena—storms, fire, floods—humanity's primitive ancestors attributed these occurrences to unseen spirits, whom they tried to appease through rituals. In denouncing religion, Holbach was also affirming core Enlightenment ideals—reason and freedom—as the following passage from *Good Sense* (1772) reveals.

In a word, whoever will deign to consult common sense upon religious opinions, and will bestow on this inquiry the attention that is commonly given to any objects we presume interesting, will easily perceive that those opinions have no foundation; that Religion is a mere castle in the air. Theology is but the ignorance of natural causes reduced to a system; a long tissue of fallacies and contradictions. In every country, it presents us with romances void of probability. . . .

Savage and furious nations, perpetually at war, adore, under divers names, some God, conformable to their ideas, that is to say, cruel, carnivorous, selfish, bloodthirsty. We find, in all the religions of the earth, "a God of armies," a "jealous God," an "avenging God," a "destroying God," a "God," who is pleased with carnage, and whom his worshippers consider it as a duty to serve to his taste. Lambs, bulls, children, men, heretics, infidels, kings, whole nations, are sacrificed to him. Do not the zealous servants of this barbarous God think themselves obliged even to offer up themselves as a sacrifice to him? Madmen may every where be seen who, after meditating upon their terrible God, imagine that to please him they must do themselves all possible injury, and inflict on themselves, for this honour, the most exquisite torments. The gloomy ideas more usefully formed of the Deity, far from consoling them under the evils of life, have every where disquieted their minds, and produced follies destructive to their happiness.

How could the human mind make any considerable progress, while tormented with frightful phantoms, and guided by men, interested in perpetuating its ignorance and fears? Man has been forced to vegetate in his primitive stupidity: he has been taught nothing but stories about invisible powers upon whom his happiness was supposed to depend. Occupied solely by his fears, and by unintelligible reveries, he has always been at the mercy of his priests, who have reserved to themselves the right of thinking for him, and directing his actions.

Thus man has remained a child without experience, a slave without courage, fearing to reason, and unable to extricate himself from the labyrinth, in which he has so long been wandering. He believes himself forced to bend under the yoke of his gods, known to him only by the fabulous accounts given by his ministers, who, after binding each unhappy mortal in the chains of his prejudice, remain his masters, or else abandon him defenceless to the absolute power of tyrants, no less terrible than the gods, of whom they are the representatives upon earth.

Oppressed by the double yoke of spiritual and temporal power, it has been impossible for the people to know and pursue their happiness. As Religion, so Politics and Morality became sacred things, which the profane were not permitted to handle. Men have had no other Morality, than what their legislators and priests brought down from the unknown regions of heaven. The human mind, confused by its theological opinions ceased to know its own powers, mistrusted experience, feared truth and disdained reason, in order to follow authority. Man has been a mere machine in the hands of tyrants and priests, who alone have had the right of directing his actions. Always treated as a slave, he has contracted the vices of a slave.

Such are the true causes of the corruption of morals, to which Religion opposes only ideal and ineffectual barriers. Ignorance and servitude are calculated to make men wicked and unhappy. Knowledge, Reason, and Liberty, can alone reform them, and make them happier. But every thing conspires to blind them and to confirm them in their errors. Priests cheat them, tyrants corrupt, the better to enslave them. Tyranny ever was, and ever will be, the true cause of man's depravity, and also of his habitual calamities. Almost always fascinated by religious fiction, poor mortals turn not their eyes to the natural and obvious causes of their misery; but attribute their vices to the imperfection of their natures, and their unhappiness to the anger of the gods. They offer up to heaven vows, sacrifices, and presents, to obtain the end of their sufferings, which in reality, are attributable only to the negligence, ignorance, and perversity of their guides, to the folly of their customs, to the unreasonableness of their laws, and above all, to the general want of knowledge. Let men's minds be filled with true ideas; let their reason be cultivated; let justice govern them; and there will be no need of opposing to the passions, such a feeble barrier, as the fear of the gods. Men will be good, when they are well instructed, well governed, and when they are punished or despised for the evil, and justly rewarded for the good, which they do to their fellow citizens.

To discover the true principles of Morality, men have no need of theology, of revelation, or of gods: They have need only of common sense. They have only to commune with themselves, to reflect upon their own nature, to consult their visible interests, to consider the objects of society, and of the individuals who compose it; and they will easily perceive, that virtue is advantageous, and vice disadvantageous to such beings as themselves. Let us persuade men to be just, beneficent, moderate, sociable; not because such conduct is demanded by the gods, but, because it is pleasure to men. Let us advise them to abstain from vice and crime; not because they will be punished in the other world, but because they will suffer for it in this.—*There are,* says a great man [Montesquieu], *means to prevent crimes, and these means are punishments; there are means to reform manners, and these means are good examples. . . .*

. . . Men are unhappy, only because they are ignorant; they are ignorant, only because every thing conspires to prevent their being enlightened; they are wicked, only because their reason is not sufficiently developed.

REVIEW QUESTIONS

1. What arguments did Voltaire offer in favor of religious toleration?
2. Why did Voltaire ridicule Christian theological disputation?
3. What did Voltaire mean by the term *fanaticism*? What examples did he provide? How was it to be cured?
4. What Christian beliefs did Thomas Paine reject? Why?
5. How did Baron d'Holbach's critique of religion affirm basic Enlightenment ideals?

4 Epistemology

The philosophes sought a naturalistic understanding of the human condition, one that examined human nature and society without reference to God's will. Toward this end, they sought to explain how the mind acquires knowledge; and as reformers, they stressed the importance of education in shaping a better person and a better society.

John Locke
ESSAY CONCERNING HUMAN UNDERSTANDING

In his *Essay Concerning Human Understanding* (1690), a work of immense significance in the history of philosophy, John Locke argued that human beings are not born with innate ideas (the idea of God and principles of good and evil, for example) divinely implanted in their minds. Rather, said Locke, the human mind at birth is a blank slate upon which are imprinted sensations derived from contact with the world. These sensations, combined with the mind's reflections on them, are the source of ideas. In effect, knowledge is derived from experience. In the tradition of Francis Bacon, Locke's epistemology (theory of knowledge) implied that people should not dwell on insoluble questions, particularly sterile theological issues, but should seek practical knowledge that promotes human happiness and enlightens human beings and gives them control over their environment.

Locke's empiricism, which aspired to useful knowledge and stimulated an interest in political and ethical questions that focused on human concerns, helped to mold the utilitarian and reformist spirit of the Enlightenment. If there are no innate ideas, said the philosophes, then human beings are not born with original sin, contrary to what Christians believed. All that individuals are derives from their particular experiences. If people are provided with a proper environment and education, they will become intelligent and productive citizens. "[O]f all the Men we meet with," wrote Locke, "Nine Parts of Ten are what they are, Good or Evil, useful or not, by their Education. 'Tis that which makes the great Difference in Mankind." This was how the reform-minded philosophes interpreted Locke. They preferred to believe that evil stemmed from faulty institutions and poor education, both of which could be remedied, rather than from a defective human nature. Excerpts from *Essay Concerning Human Understanding* follow.

Let us then suppose the mind to be, as we say, white paper, void of all characters, without any ideas:—How comes it to be furnished? Whence comes it by that vast store which the busy and boundless fancy of man has painted on it with an almost endless variety? Whence has it all the *materials* of reason and knowledge? To this I answer, in one word, from EXPERIENCE. In that all our knowledge is founded; and from that it ultimately derives itself. Our observation employed either, about external sensible objects or about the internal operations of our minds perceived and reflected on by ourselves, is that which supplies our understandings with all the *materials* of thinking. These two are the fountains of knowledge, from whence all the ideas we have, or can naturally have, do spring.

First, our Senses, conversant about particular sensible objects, do convey into the mind several distinct perceptions of things, according to those various ways wherein those objects do affect them. And thus we come by those *ideas* we have of *yellow, white, heat, cold, soft, hard, bitter, sweet,* and all those which we call sensible qualities; which when I say the senses convey into the mind, I mean, they from external objects convey into the mind what produces there those perceptions. This great source of most of the ideas we have, depending wholly upon our senses, and derived by them to the understanding, I call SENSATION.

Secondly, the other fountain from which experience furnisheth the understanding with ideas is,—the perception of the operations of our own mind within us, as it is employed about the ideas it has got. . . .

And such are *perception, thinking, doubting, believing, reasoning, knowing, willing*, and all the different actings of our own minds;—which we being conscious of, and observing in ourselves, do from these receive into our understandings as distinct ideas as we do from bodies affecting our senses. This source of ideas every man has wholly in himself; and though it be not sense, as having nothing to do with external objects, yet it is very like it, and might properly enough be called *internal sense*. But as I call the other Sensation, so I call this REFLECTION, the ideas it affords being such only as the mind gets by reflecting on its own operations within itself. By reflection then, in the following part of this discourse, I would be understood to mean, that notice which the mind takes of its own operations, and the manner of them, by reason whereof there come to be ideas of these operations in the understanding. These two, I say, viz. external material things, as the objects of SENSATION, and the operations of our own minds within, as the objects of REFLECTION, are to me the only originals from whence all our ideas take their beginnings. . . .

The understanding seems to me not to have the least glimmering of any ideas which it doth not receive from one of these two. *External objects* furnish the mind with the ideas of sensible qualities, which are all those different perceptions they produce in us; and *the mind* furnishes the understanding with ideas of its own operations.

These, when we have taken a full survey of them, and their several modes, (combinations, and relations,) we shall find to contain all our whole stock of ideas; and that we have nothing in our minds which did not come in one of these two ways. Let any one examine his own thoughts, and thoroughly search into his understanding; and then let him tell me, whether all the original ideas he has there, are any other than of the objects of his senses, or of the operations of his mind, considered as objects of his reflection. And how great a mass of knowledge soever he imagines to be lodged there, he will, upon taking a strict view, see that he has not any idea in his mind but what one of these two have imprinted;—though perhaps, with infinite variety compounded and enlarged by the understanding, as we shall see hereafter.

He that attentively considers the state of a child, at his first coming into the world, will have little reason to think him stored with plenty of ideas, that are to be the matter of his future knowledge. It is *by degrees* he comes to be furnished with them.

Claude Helvétius
ESSAYS ON THE MIND
AND A TREATISE ON MAN

Even more than did Locke, Claude-Adrien Helvétius (1715–1777) emphasized the importance of the environment in shaping the human mind. Disparities in intelligence and talent, said Helvétius, are due entirely to environmental conditions and not to inborn qualities. Since human beings are malleable and perfectible, their moral and intellectual growth depends on proper conditioning.

For this reason he called for political reforms, particularly the implementation of a program of enlightened public education.

In 1758 Helvétius published *Essays on the Mind*, which treated ethics in a purely naturalistic way. Shocked by his separation of morality from God's commands and from fear of divine punishment as well as by his attacks on the clergy, the authorities suppressed the book. His second major work, *A Treatise on Man*, was published posthumously in 1777. Apparently Helvétius wanted to avoid another controversy. The following passages from both works illustrate Helvétius' belief that "education makes us what we are."

ESSAYS ON THE MIND

The general conclusion of this discourse is, that genius is common, and the circumstances, proper to unfold it, very extraordinary. If we may compare what is profane to what is sacred, we may say in this respect, Many are called, but few are chosen.

The inequality observable among men, therefore, depends on the government under which they lie; on the greater or less happiness of the age in which they are born; on the education; on their desire of improvement, and on the importance of the ideas that are the subject of their contemplations.

The man of genius is then only produced by the circumstances in which he is placed.* Thus all the art of education consists in placing young men in such a concurrence of circumstances as are proper to unfold the buds of genius and virtue. [I am led to this conclusion by] the desire of promoting the happiness of mankind. I am convinced that a good education would diffuse light, virtue, and consequently, happiness in society; and that the opinion, that geniuses

and virtue are merely gifts of nature, is a great obstacle to the making any farther progress in the science of education, and in this respect is the great favourer of idleness and negligence. With this view, examining the effects which nature and education may have upon us, I have perceived that education makes us what we are; in consequence of which I have thought that it was the duty of a citizen to make known a truth proper to awaken the attention, with respect to the means of carrying this education to perfection.

A TREATISE ON MAN

Some maintain that, *The understanding is the effect of a certain sort of interior temperament and organization.*

Locke and I say: *The inequality in minds or understandings, is the effect of a known cause, and this cause is the difference of education. . . .*

Among the great number of questions treated of in this work, one of the most important was to determine whether genius, virtue, and talents, to which nations owe their grandeur and felicity, were the effect of the difference of . . . the organs of the five senses [that is, differences due to birth] . . . or if the same genius, the same virtues, and the same talents were the effect of education, over which the laws and the form of government are all powerful.

If I have proved the truth of the latter assertion, it must be allowed that the happiness of nations is in their own hands, and that it entirely depends on the greater or less interest they take in improving the science of education.

---

*The opinion I advance must appear very pleasing to the vanity of the greatest part of mankind, and therefore, ought to meet with a favourable reception. According to my principles, they ought not to attribute the inferiority of their abilities to the humbling cause of a less perfect [endowment], but to the education they have received, as well as to the circumstances in which they have been placed. Every man of moderate abilities, in conformity with my principles, has a right to think, that if he had been more favoured by fortune, if he had been born in a certain age or country, he [would have] himself been like the great men whose genius he is forced to admire.

REVIEW QUESTIONS

1. According to John Locke, knowledge originates in experience and has two sources—the senses and reflection. What does this mean, and what makes this view of knowledge so revolutionary?
2. How does Locke's view of the origin of knowledge compare to that of René Descartes? Which view do you favor, or can you suggest another alternative?
3. What is the relationship between Locke's theory of knowledge and his conceptions of human nature and politics?
4. In what way may Claude Helvétius be regarded as a disciple of John Locke, and how did he expand the significance of Locke's ideas?

---

5 Compendium of Knowledge

A 38-volume *Encyclopedia*, whose 150 or more contributors included leading Enlightenment thinkers, was undertaken in Paris during the 1740s as a monumental effort to bring together all human knowledge and to propagate Enlightenment ideas. The *Encyclopedia*'s numerous articles on science and technology and its limited coverage of theological questions attest to the new interests of eighteenth-century intellectuals. Serving as principal editor, Denis Diderot (1713–1784) steered the project through difficult periods, including the suspension of publication by French authorities. After the first two volumes were published, the authorities denounced the work for containing "maxims that would tend to destroy royal authority, foment a spirit of independence and revolt, . . . and lay the foundations for the corruption of morals and religion." In 1759, Pope Clement XIII condemned the *Encyclopedia* for having "scandalous doctrines {and} inducing scorn for religion." It required careful diplomacy and clever ruses to finish the project and still incorporate ideas considered dangerous by religious and governmental authorities. With the project's completion in 1772, Diderot and Enlightenment opinion triumphed over clerical censors and powerful elements at the French court.

Denis Diderot
ENCYCLOPEDIA

The *Encyclopedia* was a monument to the Enlightenment, as Diderot himself recognized. "This work will surely produce in time a revolution in the minds of man, and I hope that tyrants, oppressors, fanatics, and the intolerant will not gain thereby. We shall have served humanity." Some articles from the *Encyclopedia* follow.

Encyclopedia . . . In truth, the aim of an *encyclopedia* is to collect all the knowledge scattered over the face of the earth, to present its general outlines and structure to the men with whom we live, and to transmit this to those who will come after us, so that the work of past centuries may be useful to the following centuries, that our children, by becoming more educated, may at the same time become more virtuous and happier, and that we may not die without having deserved well of the human race. . . .

. . . We have seen that our *Encyclopedia* could only have been the endeavor of a philosophical century. . . .

I have said that it could only belong to a philosophical age to attempt an *encyclopedia*; and I have said this because such a work constantly demands more intellectual daring than is commonly found in [less courageous periods]. All things must be examined, debated, investigated without exception and without regard for anyone's feelings. . . . We must ride roughshod over all these ancient puerilities, overturn the barriers that reason never erected, give back to the arts and sciences the liberty that is so precious to them. . . . We have for quite some time needed a reasoning age when men would no longer seek the rules in classical authors but in nature. . . .

Fanaticism   . . . is blind and passionate zeal born of superstitious opinions, causing people to commit ridiculous, unjust, and cruel actions, not only without any shame or remorse, but even with a kind of joy and comfort. *Fanaticism,* therefore, is only superstition put into practice. . . .

Fanaticism has done much more harm to the world than impiety. What do impious people claim? To free themselves of a yoke, while *fanatics* want to extend their chains over all the earth. Infernal zealomania! . . .

Government   . . . The good of the people must be the great purpose of the *government*. The governors are appointed to fulfill it; and the civil constitution that invests them with this power is bound therein by the laws of nature and by the law of reason, which has determined that purpose in any form of *government* as the cause of its welfare. The greatest good of the people is its liberty. Liberty is to the body of the state what health is to each individual; without health man cannot enjoy pleasure; without liberty the state of welfare is excluded from nations. A patriotic governor will therefore see that the right

to defend and to maintain liberty is the most sacred of his duties. . . .

If it happens that those who hold the reins of *government* find some resistance when they use their power for the destruction and not the conservation of things that rightfully belong to the people, they must blame themselves, because the public good and the advantage of society are the purposes of establishing a *government*. Hence it necessarily follows that power cannot be arbitrary and that it must be exercised according to the established laws so that the people may know its duty and be secure within the shelter of laws, and so that governors at the same time should be held within just limits and not be tempted to employ the power they have in hand to do harmful things to the body politic. . . .

History   . . . *On the usefullness of history.* The advantage consists of the comparison that a statesman or a citizen can make of foreign laws, morals, and customs with those of his country. This is what stimulates modern nations to surpass one another in the arts, in commerce, and in agriculture. The great mistakes of the past are useful in all areas. We cannot describe too often the crimes and misfortunes caused by absurd quarrels. It is certain that by refreshing our memory of these quarrels, we prevent a repetition of them. . . .

Humanity   . . . is a benevolent feeling for all men, which hardly inflames anyone without a great and sensitive soul. This sublime and noble enthusiasm is troubled by the pains of other people and by the necessity to alleviate them. With these sentiments an individual would wish to cover the entire universe in order to abolish slavery, superstition, vice, and misfortune. . . .

Intolerance   . . . Any method that would tend to stir up men, to arm nations, and to soak the earth with blood is impious.

It is impious to want to impose laws upon man's conscience: this is a universal rule of conduct. People must be enlightened and not constrained. . . .

What did Christ recommend to his disciples when he sent them among the Gentiles? Was it to kill or to die? Was it to persecute or to suffer? . . .

Which is the true voice of humanity, the persecutor who strikes or the persecuted who moans?

Peace   . . . War is the fruit of man's depravity; it is a convulsive and violent sickness of the body politic. . . .

If reason governed men and had the influence over the heads of nations that it deserves, we would never see them inconsiderately surrender themselves to the fury of war; they would not show that ferocity that characterizes wild beasts. . . .

Political Authority   No man has received from nature the right to command others. Liberty is a gift from heaven, and each individual of the same species has the right to enjoy it as soon as he enjoys the use of reason. . . .

The prince owes to his very subjects the *authority* that he has over them; and this *authority* is limited by the laws of nature and the state. The laws of nature and the state are the conditions under which they have submitted or are supposed to have submitted to its government. . . .

Moreover the government, although hereditary in a family and placed in the hands of one person, is not private property, but public property that consequently can never be taken from the people, to whom it belongs exclusively, fundamentally, and as a freehold. Consequently it is always the people who make the lease or the agreement: they always intervene in the contract that adjudges its exercise. It is not the state that belongs to the prince, it is the prince who belongs to the state: but it does rest with the prince to govern in the state, because the state has chosen him for that purpose: he has bound himself to the people and the administration of affairs, and they in their turn are bound to obey him according to the laws. . . .

The Press   [*press* includes newspapers, magazines, books, and so forth] . . . People ask if freedom of the *press* is advantageous or prejudicial to a state. The answer is not difficult. It is of the greatest importance to conserve this practice in all states founded on liberty. I would even say that the disadvantages of this liberty are so inconsiderable compared to its advantages that this ought to be the common right of the universe, and it is certainly advisable to authorize its practice in all governments. . . .

REVIEW QUESTIONS

1. Why was the publication of the *Encyclopedia* a vital step in the philosophes' hopes for reform?
2. To what extent were John Locke's political ideals reflected in the *Encyclopedia*?
3. Why was freedom of the press of such significance to the enlightened philosophes?

6 Rousseau: Political Reform
—⁓—

To the philosophes, advances in the arts were hallmarks of progress. However, Jean Jacques Rousseau argued that the accumulation of knowledge improved human understanding but corrupted the morals of human beings. In *A Discourse on the Arts and Sciences* (1750) and *A Discourse on the Origin of Inequality* (1755), Rousseau diagnosed the illnesses of modern civilization. He said that human nature, which was originally good, had been corrupted by society. As a result, he stated at the beginning of *The Social Contract* (1762), "Man is born free; and everywhere he is in chains." How can humanity be made moral and free again? In *The Social Contract*, Rousseau suggested one cure: reforming the political system. He argued that in the existing civil society the rich and powerful who controlled the state oppressed the majority. Rousseau admired the small, ancient Greek city-state (polis), where citizens participated actively and directly in public affairs. A small state modeled after the ancient Greek polis, said Rousseau, would be best able to resolve the tensions between individual freedom and the requirements of the collective community.

Jean Jacques Rousseau
THE SOCIAL CONTRACT

In the opening chapters of *The Social Contract*, Rousseau rejected the principle that one person has a natural authority over others. All legitimate authority, he said, stemmed from human traditions, not from nature. Rousseau had only contempt for absolute monarchy and in *The Social Contract* sought to provide a theoretical foundation for political liberty.

[To rulers who argued that they provided security for their subjects, Rousseau responded as follows:]

It will be said that the despot assures his subjects civil tranquillity. Granted; but what do they gain, if the wars his ambition brings down upon them, his insatiable avidity, and the vexatious conduct of his ministers press harder on them than their own dissensions would have done? What do they gain, if the very tranquillity they enjoy is one of their miseries? Tranquillity is found also in dungeons; but is that enough to make them desirable places to live in? The Greeks imprisoned in the cave of the Cyclops lived there very tranquilly, while they were awaiting their turn to be devoured. . . .

Even if each man could alienate himself [relinquish his freedom], he could not alienate his children: they are born men and free; their liberty belongs to them, and no one but they has the right to dispose of it. Before they come to years of discretion, the father can, in their name, lay down conditions for their preservation and well-being, but he cannot give them irrevocably

and without conditions: such a gift is contrary to the ends of nature, and exceeds the rights of paternity. It would therefore be necessary, in order to legitimize an arbitrary government, that in every generation the people should be in a position to accept or reject it; but, were this so, the government would be no longer arbitrary.

To renounce liberty is to renounce being a man, to surrender the rights of humanity and even its duties. For him who renounces everything no indemnity is possible. Such a renunciation is incompatible with man's nature; to remove all liberty from his will is to remove all morality from his acts.

Like Hobbes and Locke, Rousseau refers to an original social contract that terminates the state of nature and establishes the civil state. The clash of particular interests in the state of nature necessitates the creation of civil authority.

I suppose men to have reached the point at which the obstacles in the way of their preservation in the state of nature [are] greater than the resources at the disposal of each individual for his maintenance in that state. That primitive condition can then subsist no longer; and the human race would perish unless it changed its manner of existence. . . .

This sum of forces can arise only where several persons come together: but, as the force and liberty of each man are the chief instruments of his self-preservation, how can he pledge them without harming his own interests, and neglecting the care he owes to himself? This difficulty, in its bearing on my present subject, may be stated in the following terms:

"The problem is to find a form of association which will defend and protect with the whole common force the person and goods of each associate, and in which each, while uniting himself with all, may still obey himself alone, and remain as free as before." This is the fundamental problem of which the *Social Contract* provides the solution.

In entering into the social contract, the individual surrenders his rights to the community as a whole, which governs in accordance with the general will—an underlying principle that expresses what is best for the community. The general will is a plainly visible truth that is easily discerned by reason and common sense purged of self-interest and unworthy motives. For Rousseau, the general will by definition is always right and always works to the community's advantage. True freedom consists of obedience to laws that coincide with the general will. Obedience to the general will transforms an individual motivated by self-interest, appetites, and passions into a higher type of person—a citizen committed to the general good. What happens, however, if a person's private will—that is, expressions of particular, selfish interests—clashes with the general will? As private interests could ruin the body politic, says Rousseau, "whoever refuses to obey the general will shall be compelled to do so by the whole body." Thus Rousseau rejects entirely the Lockean principle that citizens possess rights independently of and against the state. Because Rousseau grants the sovereign (the people

constituted as a corporate body) virtually unlimited authority over the citizenry, some critics view him as a precursor of modern dictatorship.

The clauses of this contract . . . properly understood, may be reduced to one—the total alienation of each associate, together with all his rights, to the whole community; for, in the first place, as each gives himself absolutely, the conditions are the same for all; and, this being so, no one has any interest in making them burdensome to others.

Moreover, the alienation being without reserve, the union is as perfect as it can be, and no associate has anything more to demand: for, if the individuals retained certain rights, as there would be no common superior to decide between them and the public, each, being on one point his own judge, would ask to be so on all; the state of nature would thus continue, and the association would necessarily become inoperative or tyrannical.

Finally, each man, in giving himself to all, gives himself to nobody; and as there is no associate over which he does not acquire the same right as he yields others over himself, he gains an equivalent for everything he loses, and an increase of force for the preservation of what he has.

If then we discard from the social compact what is not of its essence, we shall find that it reduces itself to the following terms:

"Each of us puts his person and all his power in common under the supreme direction of the general will, and, in our corporate capacity, we receive each member as an indivisible part of the whole."

At once, in place of the individual personality of each contracting party, this act of association creates a moral and collective body, composed of as many members as the assembly contains voters, and receiving from this act its unity, its common identity, its life, and its will. . . .

In order then that the social compact may not be an empty formula, it tacitly includes the undertaking, which alone can give force to the rest, that whoever refuses to obey the general will shall be compelled to do so by the whole body. This means nothing less than that he will be forced to be free; for this is the condition which, by giving each citizen to his country, secures him against all personal dependence. In this lies the key to the working of the political machine; this alone legitimizes civil undertakings, which, without it, would be absurd, tyrannical, and liable to the most frightful abuses.

The passage from the state of nature to the civil state produces a very remarkable change in man, by substituting justice for instinct in his conduct, and giving his actions the morality they had formerly lacked. Then only, when the voice of duty takes the place of physical impulses and right of appetite, does man, who so far had considered only himself, find that he is forced to act on different principles, and to consult his reason before listening to his inclinations. Although, in this state, he deprives himself of some advantages which he got from nature, he gains in return others so great, his faculties are so stimulated and developed, his ideas so extended, his feelings so ennobled, and his whole soul so uplifted, that, did not the abuses of this new condition often degrade him below that which he left, he would be bound to bless continually the happy moment which took him from it forever, and, instead of a stupid and unimaginative animal, made him an intelligent being and a man.

Let us draw up the whole account in terms easily commensurable. What man loses by the social contract is his natural liberty and an unlimited right to everything he tries to get and succeeds in getting; what he gains is civil liberty and the proprietorship of all he possesses. If we are to avoid mistake in weighing one against the other, we must clearly distinguish natural liberty, which is bounded only by the strength of the individual, from civil liberty, which is limited by the general will; and possession, which is merely the effect of force or the right of the first occupier, from property, which can be founded only on a positive title.

We might, over and above all this, add, to what man acquires in the civil state, moral liberty, which alone makes him truly master of himself; for the mere impulse of appetite is slavery, while obedience to a law which we prescribe to ourselves is liberty. . . .

The first and most important deduction from the principles we have so far laid down is that the general will alone can direct the State according to the object for which it was instituted, i.e. the common good: for if the clashing of particular interests made the establishment of societies necessary, the agreement of these very interests made it possible. The common element in these different interests is what forms the social tie; and, were there no point of agreement between them all, no society could exist. It is solely on the basis of this common interest that every society should be governed. . . .

It follows from what has gone before that the general will is always right and tends to the public advantage; but it does not follow that the deliberations of the people are always equally correct. Our will is always for our own good, but we do not always see what that is; the people is never corrupted, but it is often deceived, and on such occasions only does it seem to will what is bad.

There is often a great deal of difference between the will of all and the general will; the latter considers only the common interest, while the former takes private interest into account, and is no more than a sum of particular wills: but take away from these same wills the pluses and minuses that cancel one another, and the general will remains as the sum of the differences.

If, when the people, being furnished with adequate information, held its deliberations, the citizens had no communication one with another, the grand total of the small differences would always give the general will, and the decision would always be good. But when factions arise, and partial associations are formed at the expense of the great association, the will of each of these associations becomes general in relation to its members, while it remains particular in relation to the State: it may then be said that there are no longer as many votes as there are men, but only as many as there are associations. The differences become less numerous and give a less general result. Lastly, when one of these associations is so great as to prevail over all the rest, the result is no longer a sum of small differences, but a single difference; in this case there is no longer a general will, and the opinion which prevails is purely particular.

It is therefore essential, if the general will is to be able to express itself, that there should be no partial society [factions] within the State, and that each citizen should think only his own thoughts. . . . But if there are partial societies, it is best to have as many as possible and to prevent them from being unequal. . . . These precautions are the only ones that can guarantee that the general will shall be always enlightened, and that the people shall in no way deceive itself.

REVIEW QUESTIONS

1. What did Jean Jacques Rousseau mean by the "general will"? What function did it serve in his political theory?
2. Why do some thinkers view Rousseau as a champion of democracy, whereas others see him as a spiritual precursor of totalitarianism?

7 Humanitarianism

A humanitarian spirit pervaded the philosophes' outlook. Showing a warm concern for humanity, they attacked militarism, slavery, religious persecution, torture, and other violations of human dignity, as can be seen in passages from the *Encyclopedia* and Voltaire's works earlier in this chapter. Through reasoned arguments they sought to make humankind recognize and renounce its own barbarity. In the following selections, other eighteenth-century reformers denounce judicial torture, the abuse of prisoners, and slavery.

Caesare Beccaria
ON CRIMES AND PUNISHMENTS

In *On Crimes and Punishments* (1764), Caesare Beccaria (1738–1794), an Italian economist and criminologist, condemned torture, commonly used to obtain confessions in many European countries, as irrational and inhuman.

The true relations between sovereigns and their subjects, and between nations, have been discovered. Commerce has been reanimated by the common knowledge of philosophical truths diffused by the art of printing, and there has sprung up among nations a tacit rivalry of industriousness that is most humane and truly worthy of rational beings. Such good things we owe to the productive enlightenment of this age. But very few persons have studied and fought against the cruelty of punishments and the irregularities of criminal procedures, a part of legislation that is as fundamental as it is widely neglected in almost all of Europe.

Very few persons have undertaken to demolish the accumulated errors of centuries by rising to general principles, curbing, at least, with the sole force that acknowledged truths possess, the unbounded course of ill-directed power which has continually produced a long and authorized example of the most cold-blooded barbarity. And yet the groans of the weak, sacrificed to cruel ignorance and to opulent indolence; the barbarous torments, multiplied with lavish and useless severity, for crimes either not proved or wholly imaginary; the filth and horrors of a prison, intensified by that cruellest tormentor of the miserable, uncertainty—all these ought to have roused that breed of magistrates who direct the opinions of men. . . .

But what are to be the proper punishments for such crimes?

Is the death-penalty really *useful* and *necessary* for the security and good order of society? Are torture and torments *just*, and do they attain the *end* for which laws are instituted? What is the best way to prevent crimes? Are the same punishments equally effective for all times? What influence have they on customary behavior? These problems deserve to be analyzed with that geometric precision which the mist of sophisms, seductive eloquence, and timorous doubt cannot withstand. If I could boast only of having been the first to present to Italy, with a little more clarity, what other nations have boldly written and are beginning to practice, I would account myself fortunate. But if, by defending the rights of man and of unconquerable truth, I should help to save from the spasm and agonies of death some wretched victim of tyranny or of no less fatal ignorance, the thanks and tears of one innocent mortal in his transports of joy would console me for the contempt of all mankind. . . .

A cruelty consecrated by the practice of most nations is torture of the accused during his trial, either to make him confess the crime or to clear up contradictory statements, or to discover accomplices, or to purge him of infamy in some metaphysical and incomprehensible way, or, finally, to discover other crimes of which he might be guilty but of which he is not accused.

No man can be called *guilty* before a judge has sentenced him, nor can society deprive him of public protection before it has been decided that he has in fact violated the conditions under which such protection was accorded him. What right is it, then, if not simply that of might, which empowers a judge to inflict punishment on a citizen while doubt still remains as to his guilt or innocence? Here is the dilemma, which is nothing new: the fact of the crime is either certain or uncertain; if certain, all that is due is the punishment established by the laws, and tortures are useless because the criminal's confession is useless; if uncertain, then one must not torture the innocent, for such, according to the laws, is a man whose crimes are not yet proved. . . .

. . . The impression of pain may become so great that, filling the entire sensory capacity of the tortured person, it leaves him free only to choose what for the moment is the shortest way of escape from pain. The response of the accused is then as inevitable as the impressions of fire and water. The sensitive innocent man will then confess himself guilty when he believes that, by so doing, he can put an end to his torment. Every difference between guilt and innocence disappears by virtue of the very means one pretends to be using to discover it. (Torture) is an infallible means indeed—for absolving robust scoundrels and for condemning innocent persons who happen to be weak. Such are the fatal defects of this so-called criterion of truth, a criterion fit for a cannibal. . . .

Of two men, equally innocent or equally guilty, the strong and courageous will be acquitted, the weak and timid condemned, by virtue of this rigorous rational argument: "I, the judge, was supposed to find you guilty of such and such a crime; you, the strong, have been able to resist the pain, and I therefore absolve you; you, the weak, have yielded, and I therefore condemn you. I am aware that a confession wrenched forth by torments ought to be of no weight whatsoever, but I'll torment you again if you don't confirm what you have confessed."

A strange consequence that necessarily follows from the use of torture is that the innocent person is placed in a condition worse than that of the guilty, for if both are tortured, the circumstances are all against the former. Either he confesses the crime and is condemned, or he is declared innocent and has suffered a punishment he did not deserve. The guilty man, on the contrary, finds himself in a favorable situation; that is, if, as a consequence of having firmly resisted the torture, he is absolved as innocent, he will have escaped a greater punishment by enduring a lesser one. Thus the innocent cannot but lose, whereas the guilty may gain. . . .

It would be superfluous to [cite] . . . the innumerable examples of innocent persons who have confessed themselves criminals because of the agonies of torture; there is no nation, there is no age that does not have its own to cite.

John Howard
PRISONS IN ENGLAND AND WALES

The efforts of John Howard (1726–1790), a British philanthropist, led Parliament in 1774 to enact prison reform. In 1777 Howard published *State of the Prisons in England and Wales*, excerpts from which follow.

There are prisons, into which whoever looks will, at first sight of the people confined there, be convinced, that there is some great error in the management of them: the sallow meagre countenances declare, without words, that they are very miserable: many who went in healthy, are in a few months changed to emaciated dejected objects. Some are seen pining under diseases, "*sick and in prison;*" expiring on the floors, in loathsome cells, of pestilential fevers, and . . . smallpox: victims, I must not say to the cruelty, but I will say to the inattention, of sheriffs, and gentlemen in the commission of the peace.

The cause of this distress is, that many prisons are scantily supplied, and some almost totally unprovided with the necessaries of life.

There are several Bridewells [prisons for those convicted of lesser crimes such as vagrancy and disorderly conduct] (to begin with them) in which prisoners have no allowance of FOOD at all. In some, the keeper farms what little is allowed them: and where he engages to supply each prisoner with one or two pennyworth of bread a day, I have known this shrunk to half, sometimes less than half the quantity, cut or broken from his own loaf.

It will perhaps be asked, does not their work maintain them? for every one knows that those offenders are committed to *hard labour*. The answer to that question, though true, will hardly be believed. There are very few Bridewells in which any work is done, or can be done. The prisoners have neither tools, nor materials of any kind; but spend their time in sloth, profaneness and debauchery, to a degree which, in some of those houses that I have seen, is extremely shocking. . . .

I have asked some keepers, since the late act for preserving the health of prisoners, why no care is taken of their sick: and have been answered, that the magistrates tell them *the act does not extend to Bridewells.*

In consequence of this, at the quarter sessions you see prisoners, covered (hardly covered) with rags; almost famished; and sick of diseases, which the discharged spread wherever they go, and with which those who are sent to the County-Gaols infect these prisons. . . .

Felons have in some Gaols two pennyworth of bread a day; in some three halfpennyworth; in some a pennyworth; in some a shilling a week. . . . I often weighed the bread in different prisons, and found the penny loaf 7½ to 8½ ounces, the other loaves in proportion. It is probable that when this allowance was fixed by its value, near double the quantity that the money will now purchase, might be bought for it: yet the allowance continues unaltered. . . .

This allowance being so far short of the cravings of nature, and in some prisons lessened by farming to the gaoler, many criminals are half starved: such of them as at their commitment were in health, come out almost famished, scarce able to move, and for weeks incapable of any labour.

Many prisons have NO WATER. This defect is frequent in Bridewells, and Town-Gaols. In the felons courts of some County-Gaols there is no water: in some places where there is water, prisoners are always locked up within doors, and have no more than the keeper or his servants think fit to bring them: in one place they are limited to three pints a day each—a scanty provision for drink and cleanliness! . . .

From hence any one may judge of the probability there is against the health and life of prisoners, crowded in close rooms, cells, and subterraneous dungeons, for fourteen or sixteen hours out of the four and twenty. In some of those caverns the floor is very damp: in others there is sometimes an inch or two of water; and the straw, or bedding is laid on such floors, seldom on barrack bedsteads. . . . Some Gaols have no SEWERS; and in those that have, if they be not properly attended to, they are, even to a visitant, offensive beyond expression: how noxious then to people constantly confined in those prisons!

In many Gaols, and in most Bridewells, there is no allowance of STRAW for prisoners to sleep on; and if by any means they get a little, it is not changed for months together, so that it is almost worn to dust. Some lie upon rags, others upon the bare floors. When I have complained of this to the keepers, their justification has been, "The county allows no straw; the prisoners have none but at my cost."

The evils mentioned hitherto affect the *health* and *life* of prisoners: I have now to complain of what is pernicious to their MORALS; and that is, the confining all sorts of prisoners together: debtors and felons; men and women; the young beginner and the old offender: and with all these, in some counties, such as are guilty of misdemeanors only. . . .

In some Gaols you see (and who can see it without pain?) boys of twelve or fourteen eagerly listening to the stories told by practised and experienced criminals, of their adventures, successes, stratagems, and escapes.

I must here add, that in some few Gaols are confined idiots and lunatics . . . The insane, where they are not kept separate, disturb and terrify other prisoners. No care is taken of them, although it is probable that by medicines, and proper regimen, some of them might be restored to their senses, and to usefulness in life. . . .

A cruel custom obtains in most of our Gaols, which is that of the prisoners demanding of a new comer GARNISH, FOOTING, or (as it is called in some London Gaols) CHUMMAGE. "Pay or strip," are the fatal words. I say *fatal*, for they are so to some; who having no money, are obliged to give up part of their scanty apparel; and if they have no bedding or straw to sleep on, contract diseases, which I have known to prove mortal.

Loading prisoners with HEAVY IRONS, which make their walking, and even lying down to sleep, difficult and painful, is another custom which I cannot but condemn. In some County-Gaols the *women* do not escape this severity.

Denis Diderot
ENCYCLOPEDIA
"MEN AND THEIR LIBERTY ARE NOT OBJECTS OF COMMERCE. . . ."

Montesquieu, Voltaire, David Hume, Benjamin Franklin, Thomas Paine, and several other philosophes condemned slavery and the slave trade. In Book 15 of *The Spirit of the Laws* (1748), Montesquieu scornfully refuted all justifications for slavery. Ultimately, he said, slavery, which violates the fundamental principle of justice underlying the universe, derived from base human desires to dominate and exploit other human beings. In 1780, Paine helped draft the act abolishing slavery in Pennsylvania. Five years earlier, he wrote:

> Our Traders in Men . . . must know the wickedness of that SLAVETRADE, if they attend to reasoning, or the dictates of their own hearts, and [those who] shun and stifle all these willfully sacrifice Conscience, and the character of integrity to that Golden Idol. . . . Most shocking of all is the alleging the sacred Scriptures to favour this wicked practice.

The *Encyclopedia* denounced slavery as a violation of the individual's natural rights.

[This trade] is the buying of unfortunate Negroes by Europeans on the coast of Africa to use as slaves in their colonies. This buying of Negroes, to reduce them to slavery, is one business that violates religion, morality, natural laws, and all the rights of human nature.

Negroes, says a modern Englishman full of enlightenment and humanity, have not become slaves by the right of war; neither do they deliver themselves voluntarily into bondage, and consequently their children are not born slaves. Nobody is unaware that they are bought from their own princes, who claim to have the right to dispose of their liberty, and that traders have them transported in the same way as their other goods, either in their colonies or in America, where they are displayed for sale.

If commerce of this kind can be justified by a moral principle, there is no crime, however atrocious it may be, that cannot be made legitimate. Kings, princes, and magistrates are not the proprietors of their subjects: they do not, therefore, have the right to dispose of their liberty and to sell them as slaves.

On the other hand, no man has the right to buy them or to make himself their master. Men and their liberty are not objects of commerce; they can be neither sold nor bought nor paid for at any price. We must conclude from this that a man whose slave has run away should only blame himself, since he had acquired for money illicit goods whose acquisition is prohibited by all the laws of humanity and equity.

There is not, therefore, a single one of these unfortunate people regarded only as slaves who does not have the right to be declared free, since he has never lost his freedom, which he could not lose and which his prince, his father, and any person whatsoever in the world had not the power to dispose of. Consequently the sale that has been completed is invalid in itself. This Negro does not divest himself and can never divest himself of his natural right; he carries it everywhere with him, and he can demand everywhere that he be allowed to enjoy it. It is, therefore, patent inhumanity on the part of judges in free countries where he is transported, not to emancipate him immediately by declaring him free, since he is their fellow man, having a soul like them.

Marquis de Condorcet
THE EVILS OF SLAVERY

Marie Jean Antoine-Nicolas Caritat, Marquis de Condorcet (1743–1794), was a French mathematician and historian of science. He contributed to the *Encyclopedia* and campaigned actively for religious toleration and the abolition of slavery. In 1788, Condorcet helped found The Society of the Friends of Blacks, which attacked slavery. Seven years earlier he had published a pamphlet denouncing slavery as a violation of human rights. Following are excerpts from this pamphlet.

"Dedicatory Epistle to the Negro Slaves"

My Friends,

Although I am not the same color as you, I have always regarded you as my brothers. Nature formed you with the same spirit, the same reason, the same virtues as whites. . . . Your tyrants will reproach me with uttering only commonplaces and having nothing but chimerical [unrealistic] ideas: indeed, nothing is more common than the maxims of humanity and justice; nothing is more chimerical than to propose to men that they base their conduct on them.

Reducing a man to slavery, buying him, selling him, keeping him in servitude: these are truly crimes, and crimes worse than theft. In effect, they take from the slave, not only all forms of property but also the ability to acquire it, the control over his time, his strength, of everything that nature has given him to maintain his life and his needs. To this wrong they add that of taking from the slave the right to dispose of his own person. . . .

It follows from our principles that the inflexible justice to which kings and nations are subject like their citizens requires the destruction of slavery. We have shown that this destruction will harm neither commerce nor the wealth of a nation because it would not result in any decrease in cultivation. We have shown that the master had no right over his slave; that the act of keeping him in servitude is not the enjoyment of a property right but a crime; that in freeing the slave the law does not attack property but rather ceases to tolerate an action which it should have punished with the death penalty. The sovereign therefore owes no compensation to the master of slaves just as he owes none to a thief whom a court judgment has deprived of the possession of a stolen good. The public tolerance of a crime may make punishment impossible but it cannot grant a real right to the profit from the crime.

REVIEW QUESTIONS

1. What were Caesare Beccaria's arguments against the use of torture in judicial proceedings? In your opinion, can torture ever be justified?
2. What ideals of the Enlightenment philosophes are reflected in Beccaria's arguments?
3. List the abuses in British jails that John Howard disclosed.
4. How did Condorcet demonstrate the humanitarianism of the Enlightenment?
5. How did Condorcet show that slaves' rights are destroyed?

8 Literature as Satire: Critiques of European Society

The French philosophes, particularly Voltaire, Diderot, and Montesquieu, often used the medium of literature to decry the ills of their society and advance Enlightenment values. In the process they wrote satires that are still read and admired for their literary merits and insights into human nature and society. The eighteenth century also saw the publication of Jonathan Swift's *Gulliver's Travels* (1726), one of the greatest satirical works written in English.

Voltaire
CANDIDE

In *Candide* (1759), Voltaire's most important work of fiction, he explored the question: Why do the innocent suffer? And because Voltaire delved into this mystery with wit, irony, satire, and wisdom, the work continues to be hailed as a literary masterpiece.

The illegitimate Candide (son of the sister of the baron in whose castle he lives in Westphalia) is tutored by the philosopher Pangloss, a teacher of "metaphysico-theologo-cosmolonigology": that is, a person who speaks nonsense. The naive Pangloss clings steadfastly to the belief that all that happens, even the worst misfortunes, are for the best.

Candide falls in love with Cunegund, the beautiful daughter of the baron of the castle; but the baron forcibly removes Candide from the castle when he discovers their love. Candide subsequently suffers a series of disastrous misfortunes, but he continues to adhere to the belief firmly instilled in him by Pangloss, that everything happens for the best and that this is the best of all possible worlds. Later, he meets an old beggar, who turns out to be his former teacher, Pangloss, who tells Candide that the Bulgarians have destroyed the castle and killed Cunegund and her family. Candide and Pangloss then travel together to Lisbon, where they survive the terrible earthquake, only to have Pangloss hanged (but he escapes death) by the Inquisition. Soon thereafter, Candide is reunited with Cunegund, who, despite having been raped and sold into prostitution, has not been killed. Following further adventures and misfortunes, the lovers are again separated when Cunegund is captured by pirates.

After experiencing more episodes of human wickedness and natural disasters, Candide abandons the philosophy of optimism, declaring "that we must cultivate our gardens." By this Voltaire meant that we can never achieve utopia, but neither should we descend to the level of brutes. Through purposeful and honest work, and the deliberate pursuit of virtue, we can improve, however modestly, the quality of human existence.

The following excerpt from Candide starts with Candide's first misfortune after being driven out of the castle at Westphalia. In addition to ridiculing philosophical optimism, Voltaire expresses his revulsion for militarism.

CHAPTER II

What Befell Candide Among the Bulgarians

Candide, thus driven out of this terrestrial paradise, wandered a long time, without knowing where he went; sometimes he raised his eyes, all bedewed with tears, toward Heaven, and sometimes he cast a melancholy look toward the magnificent castle where dwelt the fairest of young baronesses. He laid himself down to sleep in a furrow, heartbroken and supperless. The snow fell in great flakes, and, in the morning when he awoke, he was almost frozen to death; however, he made shift to crawl to the next town, which was called Waldberghoff-trarbk-dikdorff, without a penny in his pocket, and half dead with hunger and fatigue. He took up his stand at the door of an inn. He had not been long there before two men dressed in blue fixed their eyes steadfastly upon him.

"Faith, comrade," said one of them to the other, "yonder is a well-made young fellow, and of the right size."

Thereupon they went up to Candide, and with the greatest civility and politeness invited him to dine with them.

"Gentlemen," replied Candide, with a most engaging modesty, "you do me much honor, but, upon my word, I have no money."

"Money, sir!" said one of the men in blue to him. "Young persons of your appearance and merit never pay anything. Why, are you not five feet five inches high?"

"Yes, gentlemen, that is really my size," replied he with a low bow.

"Come then, sir, sit down along with us. We will not only pay your reckoning, but will never suffer such a clever young fellow as you to want money. Mankind were born to assist one another."

"You are perfectly right, gentlemen," said Candide; "that is precisely the doctrine of Master Pangloss; and I am convinced that everything is for the best."

His generous companions next entreated him to accept a few crowns, which he readily complied with, at the same time offering them his note for the payment, which they refused, and sat down to table.

"Have you not a great affection for—"

"Oh, yes!" he replied. "I have a great affection for the lovely Miss Cunegund."

"Maybe so," replied one of the men, "but that is not the question! We are asking you whether you have not a great affection for the King of the Bulgarians?"*

"For the King of the Bulgarians?" said Candide. "Not at all. Why, I never saw him in my life."

"Is it possible! Oh, he is a most charming king! Come, we must drink his health."

"With all my heart, gentlemen," Candide said, and he tossed off his glass.

"Bravo!" cried the blues. "You are now the support, the defender, the hero of the Bulgarians; your fortune is made; you are on the high road to glory."

So saying, they put him in irons and carried him away to the regiment. There he was made to wheel about to the right, to the left, to draw his ramrod, to return his ramrod, to present, to fire, to march, and they gave him thirty blows with a cane. The next day he performed his exercise a little better, and they gave him but twenty. The day following he came with ten and was looked upon as a young fellow of surprising genius by all his comrades.

Candide was struck with amazement and could not for the soul of him conceive how he came to be a hero. One fine spring morning, he took it into his head to take a walk, and he marched straight forward, conceiving it to be a privilege of the human species, as well as of the brute creation, to make use of their legs how and when they pleased. He had not gone above two leagues when he was overtaken by four other heroes, six feet high, who bound him neck and heels, and carried him to a dungeon. A court-martial sat upon him, and he was asked which he liked best, either to run the gauntlet six and thirty times through the

_____

*I.e., Prussians.

whole regiment, or to have his brains blown out with a dozen musket balls. In vain did he remonstrate to them that the human will is free, and that he chose neither. They obliged him to make a choice, and he determined, in virtue of that divine gift called free will, to run the gauntlet six and thirty times. He had gone through his discipline twice, and the regiment being composed of two thousand men, they composed for him exactly four thousand strokes, which laid bare all his muscles and nerves, from the nape of his neck to his rump. As they were preparing to make him set out a third time, our young hero, unable to support it any longer, begged as a favor they would be so obliging as to shoot him through the head. The favor being granted, a bandage was tied over his eyes, and he was made to kneel down. At that very instant, his Bulgarian Majesty, happening to pass by, inquired into the delinquent's crime, and being a prince of great penetration, he found, from what he heard of Candide, that he was a young meta-physician, entirely ignorant of the world. And, therefore, out of his great clemency, he condescended to pardon him, for which his name will be celebrated in every journal, and in every age. A skillful surgeon made a cure of Candide in three weeks by means of emollient unguents prescribed by Dioscorides. His sores were now skinned over, and he was able to march when the King of the Bulgarians gave battle to the King of the Abares.[†]

CHAPTER III

How Candide Escaped from the Bulgarians, and What Befell Him Afterwards

Never was anything so gallant, so well accoutered, so brilliant, and so finely disposed as the two armies. The trumpets, fifes, oboes, drums, and cannon, made such harmony as never was heard in hell itself. The entertainment began by a discharge of cannon, which, in the twinkling of an eye, laid flat about six thousand men on each side. The musket bullets swept away, out of the best of all possible worlds, nine or ten thousand scoundrels that infested its surface. The bayonet was next the sufficient reason for the deaths of several thousands. The whole might amount to thirty thousand souls. Candide trembled like a philosopher and concealed himself as well as he could during this heroic butchery.

At length, while the two kings were causing *Te Deum*[‡] to be sung in each of their camps, Candide took a resolution to go and reason somewhere else upon causes and effects. After passing over heaps of dead or dying men, the first place he came to was a neighboring village, in the Abarian territories, which had been burned to the ground by the Bulgarians in accordance with international law. Here lay a number of old men covered with wounds, who beheld their wives dying with their throats cut, and hugging their children to their breasts all stained with blood. There several young virgins, whose bellies had been ripped open after they had satisfied the natural necessities of the Bulgarian heroes, breathed their last; while others, half burned in the flames, begged to be dispatched out of the world. The ground about them was covered with the brains, arms, and legs of dead men.

Candide made all the haste he could to another village, which belonged to the Bulgarians, and there he found that the heroic Abares had treated it in the same fashion. From thence continuing to walk over palpitating limbs or through ruined buildings, at length he arrived beyond the theater of war, with a little provision in his pouch, and Miss Cunegund's image in his heart.

[†]I.e., French. The Seven Years' War had begun in 1756.

[‡]A Te Deum ("We praise thee, God") is a special liturgical hymn praising and thanking God for granting some special favor, like a military victory or the end of a war.

Denis Diderot
SUPPLEMENT TO THE VOYAGE OF BOUGAINVILLE

Enlightenment thinkers often used examples from the non-European world in order to attack European values that seemed contrary to nature and reason. Denis Diderot reviewed Louis Antoine de Bougainville's *Voyage Around the World* (1771) and in the next year wrote *Supplement to the Voyage of Bougainville* (published posthumously in 1796). In this work, Diderot explored some ideas, particularly the sex habits of Tahitians, treated by the French explorer. Diderot also denounced European imperialism and the exploitation of non-Europeans, and questioned traditional Christian sexual standards. In *Supplement*, Diderot constructed a dialogue between a Tahitian (Orou), who possesses the wisdom of a French philosophe, and a chaplain, whose defense of Christian sexual mores reveals Diderot's critique of the Christian view of human nature. Diderot thus used a representative of an alien culture to attack those European customs and beliefs that the philosophes detested. In the opening passage, before Orou's dialogue, a Tahitian elder rebukes Bougainville and his companions for bringing the evils of European civilization to his island.

"We [Tahitians] are free—but see where you [Europeans] have driven into our earth the symbol of our future servitude. You are neither a god nor a devil—by what right, then, do you enslave people? Orou! You who understand the speech of these men, tell every one of us, as you have told me, what they have written on that strip of metal—'This land belongs to us.' This land belongs to you! And why? Because you set foot in it? If some day a Tahitian should land on your shores, and if he should engrave on one of your stones or on the bark of one of your trees: 'This land belongs to the people of Tahiti,' what would you think? You are stronger than we are! And what does that signify? When one of our lads carried off some of the miserable trinkets with which your ship is loaded, what an uproar you made, and what revenge you took! And at that very moment you were plotting, in the depths of your hearts, to steal a whole country! You are not slaves; you would suffer death rather than be enslaved, yet you want to make slaves of us! Do you believe, then, that the Tahitian does not know how to die in defense of his liberty? This Tahitian, whom you want to treat as a chattel, as a dumb animal—this Tahitian is your brother. You are both children of Nature—what right do you have over him that he does not have over you?

"You came; did we attack you? Did we plunder your vessel? Did we seize you and expose you to the arrows of our enemies? Did we force you to work in the fields alongside our beasts of burden? We respected our own image in you. Leave us our own customs, which are wiser and more decent than yours. We have no wish to barter what you call our ignorance for your useless knowledge. We possess already all that is good or necessary for our existence. Do we merit your scorn because we have not been able to create superfluous wants for ourselves? When we are hungry, we have something to eat; when we are cold, we have clothing to put on. You have been in our huts—what is lacking there, in your opinion? You are welcome to drive yourselves as hard as you please in pursuit of what you call the comforts of life, but allow sensible people to stop when they see they have nothing to gain but imaginary benefits from the continuation of their painful labors. If you persuade us to go beyond the bounds of strict necessity, when shall we come to the end of our labor? When shall we have time for enjoyment? We have reduced our daily and yearly labors to the least possible amount, because to us nothing seemed more desirable than leisure. Go and bestir yourselves in your own country; there you may torment yourselves as much as you like; but leave us in peace, and do not fill our heads with a hankering after your false needs and imaginary virtues. Look at these men—see how healthy, straight and strong they are. See these women—how straight, healthy, fresh and lovely they are. Take this bow in your hands—it is my own—and call one, two, three, four of your comrades to help you try to bend it. I can bend it myself. I work the soil, I climb mountains, I make my way through the dense forest, and I can run four leagues [about 12 miles] on the plain in less than an hour. Your young comrades have been hard put to it to keep up with me, and yet I have passed my ninetieth year. . . .

"Woe to this island! Woe to all the Tahitians now living, and to all those yet to be born, woe from the day of your arrival! We used to know but one disease—the one to which all men, all animals and all plants are subject—old age. But you have brought us a new one [venereal disease]: you have infected our blood. We shall perhaps be compelled to exterminate with our own hands some of our young girls, some of our women, some of our children, those who have lain with your women, those who have lain with your men. Our fields will be spattered with the foul blood that has passed from your veins into ours. Or else our children, condemned to die, will nourish and perpetuate the evil disease that you have given their fathers and mothers, transmitting it forever to their descendants." . . .

Before the arrival of Christian Europeans, love-making was natural and enjoyable. Europeans introduced an alien element, guilt.

But a while ago, the young Tahitian girl blissfully abandoned herself to the embraces of a Tahitian youth and awaited impatiently the day when her mother, authorized to do so by her having reached the age of puberty, would remove her veil and uncover her breasts. She was proud of her ability to excite men's desires, to attract the amorous looks of strangers, of her own relatives, of her own brothers. In our presence, without shame, in the center of a throng of innocent Tahitians who danced and played the flute, she accepted the caresses of the young man whom her young heart and the secret promptings of her senses had marked out for her. The notion of crime and the fear of disease have come among us only with your coming. Now our enjoyments, formerly so sweet, are attended with guilt and terror. That man in black [a priest], who stands near to you and listens to me, has spoken to our young men, and I know not what he has said to our young girls, but our youths are hesitant and our girls blush. Creep away into the dark forest, if you wish, with the perverse companion of your pleasures, but allow the good, simple Tahitians to reproduce themselves without shame under the open sky and in broad daylight.

In the following conversation between Orou and the chaplain, Christian sexual mores and the concept of God are questioned. Orou addresses the chaplain.

[OROU] "You are young and healthy and you have just had a good supper. He who sleeps alone, sleeps badly; at night a man needs a woman at his side. Here is my wife and here are my daughters. Choose whichever one pleases you most, but if you would like to do me a favor, you will give your preference to my youngest girl, who has not yet had any children."

The mother said: "Poor girl! I don't hold it against her. It's no fault of hers."

The chaplain replied that his religion, his holy orders, his moral standards and his sense of decency all prevented him from accepting Orou's invitation.

Orou answered: "I don't know what this thing is that you call 'religion,' but I can only have a low opinion of it because it forbids you to partake of an innocent pleasure to which Nature, the sovereign mistress of us all, invites everybody. It seems to prevent you from bringing one of your fellow creatures into the world, from doing a favor asked of you by a father, a mother and their children, from repaying the kindness of a host, and from enriching a nation by giving it an additional citizen. I don't know what it is that you call 'holy orders,' but your chief duty is to be a man and to show gratitude. . . . I hope that you will not persist in disappointing us. Look at the distress you have caused to appear on the faces of these four women—they are afraid you have noticed some defect in them that arouses your distaste. But even if that were so, would it not be possible for you to do a good deed and have the pleasure of honoring one of my daughters in the sight of her sisters and friends? Come, be generous!"

THE CHAPLAIN "You don't understand—it's not that. They are all four of them equally beautiful. But there is my religion! My holy orders! . . .

. . . [God] spoke to our ancestors and gave them laws; he prescribed to them the way in which he wishes to be honored; he ordained that certain actions are good and others he forbade them to do as being evil."

OROU "I see. And one of these evil actions which he has forbidden is that of a man who goes to bed with a woman or girl. But in that case, why did he make two sexes?"

THE CHAPLAIN "In order that they might come together—but only when certain conditions are satisfied and only after certain initial ceremonies have been performed. By virtue of these ceremonies one man belongs to one woman and only to her; one woman belongs to one man and only to him."

OROU "For their whole lives?"

THE CHAPLAIN "For their whole lives."

OROU "So that if it should happen that a woman should go to bed with some man who was not her husband, or some man should go to bed with a woman that was not his wife . . . but that could never happen because the workman [God] would know what was going on, and since he doesn't like that sort of thing, he wouldn't let it occur."

THE CHAPLAIN "No. He lets them do as they will, and they sin against the law of God (for that is the name by which we call the great workman) and against the law of the country; they commit a crime."

OROU "I should be sorry to give offense by anything I might say, but if you don't mind, I'll tell you what I think."

THE CHAPLAIN "Go ahead."

OROU "I find these strange precepts contrary to nature, and contrary to reason. . . . Furthermore, your laws seem to me to be contrary to the general order of things. For in truth is there anything so senseless as a precept that forbids us to heed the changing impulses that are inherent in our being, or commands that require a degree of constancy which is not possible, that violate the liberty of both male and female by chaining them perpetually to one another? Is there anything more unreasonable than this perfect fidelity that would restrict us, for the enjoyment of pleasures so capricious, to a single partner—than an oath of immutability taken by two individuals made of flesh and blood under a sky that is not the same for a moment, in a cavern that threatens to collapse upon them, at the foot of a cliff that is crumbling into dust, under a tree that is withering, on a bench of stone that is being worn away? Take my word for it, you have reduced human beings to a worse condition than that of the animals. I don't know what your great workman is, but I am very happy that he never spoke to our forefathers, and I hope that he never speaks to our children, for if he does, he may tell them the same foolishness, and they may be foolish enough to believe it." . . .

OROU "Are monks faithful to their vows of sterility?"

THE CHAPLAIN "No."

OROU "I was sure of it. Do you also have female monks?"

THE CHAPLAIN "Yes."

OROU "As well behaved as the male monks?"

THE CHAPLAIN "They are kept more strictly in seclusion, they dry up from unhappiness and die of boredom."

OROU "So nature is avenged for the injury done to her! Ugh! What a country! If everything is managed the way you say, you are more barbarous than we are."

Montesquieu
THE PERSIAN LETTERS

Like other philosophes, Charles Louis de Secondat, baron de la Brède et de Montesquieu (1689–1755), was an ardent reformer who used learning, logic, and wit to denounce the abuses of his day. His principal work, *The Spirit of the Laws* (1748), was a contribution to political liberty. To safeguard liberty from despotism, which he regarded as a pernicious form of government that institutionalizes cruelty and violence, Montesquieu advocated the principle of separation of powers—that is, the legislative, executive, and judiciary should not be in the hands of one person or body. Montesquieu's humanitarianism and tolerant spirit is also seen in an earlier work, *The Persian Letters* (1721), published anonymously in Holland. In the guise of letters written by imaginary Persian travelers in Europe, Montesquieu makes a statement: He denounces French absolutism, praises English parliamentary government, and attacks religious persecution, as in this comment on the Spanish Inquisition excerpted below.

LETTER XXIX

Rica to Ibben, at Smyrna

. . . I have heard that in Spain and Portugal there are dervishes who do not understand a joke, and who have a man burned as if he were straw. Whoever falls into the hands of these men is fortunate only if he has always prayed to God with little bits of wood in hand, has worn two bits of cloth attached to two ribbons, and has sometimes been in a province called Galicia!* Otherwise, the poor

devil is really in trouble. Even though he swears like a pagan that he is orthodox, they may not agree, and burn him for a heretic. It is useless for him to submit distinctions, for he will be in ashes before they even consider giving him a hearing.

Other judges presume the innocence of the accused; these always presume him guilty. In doubt they hold to the rule of inclining to severity, evidently because they consider mankind as evil. On the other hand, however, they hold such a high opinion of men that they judge them incapable of lying, for they accept testimony from deadly enemies, notorious women, and people living by some infamous profession. In passing

---

*The references are to a rosary, a scapular, and the pilgrimage shrine of St. James of Campostello in the Spanish province of Galicia.

sentence, the judges pay those condemned a little compliment, telling them that they are sorry
to see them so poorly dressed in their brimstone
shirts,[†] that the judges themselves are gentle
men who abhor bloodletting, and are in despair
at having to condemn them. Then, to console
themselves, they confiscate to their own profit all
the possessions of these poor wretches.

Happy the land inhabited by the children of
the prophets! There these sad spectacles are unknown.[‡] The holy religion brought by the angels
trusts truth alone for its defense, and does not
need these violent means for its preservation.

PARIS, THE 4TH OF THE MOON OF CHALVAL, 1712

[†]Those condemned by the Inquisition appeared for sentenc-
ing dressed in shirts colored to suggest the flames of their
presumed postmortem destination.

[‡]The Persians are the most tolerant of all the [Muslims].

REVIEW QUESTIONS

1. What does *Candide* reveal about Voltaire's general outlook?
2. How did Diderot attempt to use the Tahitians to criticize the sexual morals of
   Europeans?
3. How did Diderot use the concept of the law of nature to undermine Christian sexual
   morality?
4. How does Montesquieu characterize Spanish and Portuguese inquisitors?

---

9 On the Progress of Humanity

During the French Revolution, the Marquis de Condorcet attracted the enmity of
the dominant Jacobin party and in 1793 was forced to go into hiding. Secluded
in Paris, he wrote *Sketch for a Historical Picture of the Progress of the Human
Mind*. Arrested in 1794, Condorcet died during his first night in prison from
either exhaustion or self-inflicted poison.

Marquis de Condorcet
PROGRESS OF THE HUMAN MIND

Sharing the philosophes' confidence in human goodness and in reason, Condorcet
was optimistic about humanity's future progress. Superstition, prejudice, intolerance, and tyranny—all barriers to progress in the past—would gradually be
eliminated, and humanity would enter a golden age. The following excerpts are
from Condorcet's *Sketch*.

. . . The aim of the work that I have undertaken, and its result will be to show by appeal
to reason and fact that nature has set no term
to the perfection of human faculties; that the
perfectibility of man is truly indefinite; and
that the progress of this perfectibility, from

now onwards independent of any power that might wish to halt it, has no other limit than the duration of the globe upon which nature has cast us. This progress will doubtless vary in speed, but it will never be reversed as long as the earth occupies its present place in the system of the universe, and as long as the general laws of this system produce neither a general cataclysm nor such changes as will deprive the human race of its present faculties and its present resources. . . .

. . . It will be necessary to indicate by what stages what must appear to us today a fantastic hope ought in time to become possible, and even likely; to show why, in spite of the transitory successes of prejudice and the support that it receives from the corruption of governments or peoples, truth alone will obtain a lasting victory; we shall demonstrate how nature has joined together indissolubly the progress of knowledge and that of liberty, virtue and respect for the natural rights of man. . . .

After long periods of error, after being led astray by vague or incomplete theories, publicists have at last discovered the true rights of man and how they can all be deduced from the single truth, that *man is a sentient being, capable of reasoning and of acquiring moral ideas.* . . .

At last man could proclaim aloud his right, which for so long had been ignored, to submit all opinions to his own reason and to use in the search for truth the only instrument for its recognition that he has been given. Every man learnt with a sort of pride that nature had not forever condemned him to base his beliefs on the opinions of others; the superstitions of antiquity and the abasement of reason before the [deception] of supernatural religion [had] disappeared from society as from philosophy.

Thus an understanding of the natural rights of man, the belief that these rights are inalienable and [cannot be forfeited], a strongly expressed desire for liberty of thought and letters, of trade and industry, and for the alleviation of the people's suffering, for the [elimination] of all penal laws against religious dissenters and the abolition of torture and barbarous punishments,

the desire for a milder system of criminal legislation and jurisprudence which should give complete security to the innocent, and for a simpler civil code, more in conformance with reason and nature, indifference in all matters of religion which now were relegated to the status of superstitions and political [deception], a hatred of hypocrisy and fanaticism, a contempt for prejudice, zeal for the propagation of enlightenment: all these principles, gradually filtering down from philosophical works to every class of society whose education went beyond the catechism and the alphabet, became the common faith . . . [of enlightened people]. In some countries these principles formed a public opinion sufficiently widespread for even the mass of the people to show a willingness to be guided by it and to obey it. . . .

Force or persuasion on the part of governments, priestly intolerance, and even national prejudices, had all lost their deadly power to smother the voice of truth, and nothing could now protect the enemies of reason or the oppressors of freedom from a sentence to which the whole of Europe would soon subscribe. . . .

Our hopes for the future condition of the human race can be subsumed under three important heads: the abolition of inequality between nations, the progress of equality within each nation, and the true perfection of mankind. Will all nations one day attain that state of civilization which the most enlightened, the freest and the least burdened by prejudices, such as the French and the Anglo-Americans [by virtue of their revolutions], have attained already? Will the vast gulf that separates these peoples from the slavery of nations under the rule of monarchs, from the barbarism of African tribes, from the ignorance of savages, little by little disappear? . . .

Is the human race to better itself, either by discoveries in the sciences and the arts, and so in the means to individual welfare and general prosperity; or by progress in the principles of conduct or practical morality; or by a true perfection of the intellectual, moral, or physical faculties of man, an improvement which may result from a perfection either of the instruments used to heighten the intensity of these faculties and to direct their use or of the natural constitution of man?

In answering these three questions we shall find in the experience of the past, in the observation of the progress that the sciences and civilization have already made, in the analysis of the progress of the human mind and of the development of its faculties, the strongest reasons for believing that nature has set no limit to the realization of our hopes. . . .

The time will therefore come when the sun will shine only on free men who know no other master but their reason; when tyrants and slaves, priests and their stupid or hypocritical instruments will exist only in works of history and on the stage; and when we shall think of them only to pity their victims and their dupes; to maintain ourselves in a state of vigilance by thinking on their excesses; and to learn how to recognize and so to destroy, by force of reason, the first seeds of tyranny and superstition, should they ever dare to reappear amongst us.

REVIEW QUESTIONS

1. According to Condorcet, what economic, political, and cultural policies were taught by the philosophes?
2. What image of human nature underlies Condorcet's theory of human progress?

CHAPTER 4

Era of the French Revolution

THE STORMING OF THE BASTILLE, JULY 14, 1789. The fall of the Bastille, a symbol of the Old Regime's darkness and despotism, furthered the cause of reform. *(akg-images)*

In 1789, many participants and observers viewed the revolutionary developments in France as the fulfillment of the Enlightenment's promise—the triumph of reason over tradition and ignorance, of liberty over despotism. It seemed that the French reformers were eliminating the abuses of an unjust system and creating a new society founded on the ideals of the philosophes.

Eighteenth-century French society, the Old Regime, was divided into three orders, or estates. The First Estate (the clergy) and the Second Estate (the nobility) enjoyed special privileges sanctioned by law and custom. The church collected tithes (taxes on the land), censored books regarded as a threat to religion and morality, and paid no taxes to the state (although the church did make a "free gift" to the royal treasury). Nobles were exempt from most taxes, collected manorial dues from peasants (even from free peasants), and held the highest positions in the church, the army, and the government.

Opinion among the aristocrats was divided. Some nobles, influenced by the liberal ideals of the philosophes, sought to reform France; they wanted to end royal despotism and establish a constitutional government. To this extent, the liberal nobility had a great deal in common with the bourgeoisie. These liberal nobles saw the king's financial difficulties in 1788 as an opportunity to regenerate the nation under enlightened leadership. When they resisted the king's policies, they claimed that they were opposing royal despotism. But at the same time, many nobles remained hostile to liberal ideals and opposed reforms that threatened their privileges and honorific status.

Peasants, urban workers, and members of the bourgeoisie belonged to the Third Estate, which comprised about 96 percent of the population. The bourgeoisie—which included merchants, bankers, professionals, and government officials below the top ranks—provided the leadership and ideology for the French Revolution. For most of the eighteenth century, the bourgeoisie did not challenge the existing social structure, including the special privileges of the nobility. But by 1789 the bourgeoisie wanted to abolish those privileges and to open prestigious positions to men of talent regardless of their birth; it wanted to give France a constitution that limited the monarch's power, established a parliament, and protected the rights of the individual.

The immediate cause of the French Revolution was a financial crisis. The wars of Louis XIV and subsequent foreign adventures, including French aid to the American colonists during their revolution, had emptied the royal treasury. The refusal of the clergy and the nobles to surrender their tax exemptions compelled Louis XVI to call a meeting of the Estates General—a medieval assembly that had last met in 1614—to deal with impending bankruptcy. Many nobles intended to use the Estates General to weaken the French throne and regain powers lost a century earlier under the absolute rule of Louis XIV. But the nobility's plans were unrealized; their revolt against the crown paved the way for the Third Estate's eventual destruction of the Old Regime.

Between June and November 1789 the bourgeoisie, aided by uprisings of the common people of Paris and the peasants in the countryside, gained control over the state and instituted reforms. During this opening and moderate phase of the Revolution (1789–1791), the bourgeoisie abolished the special privileges of the aristocracy and clergy, formulated a declaration of human rights, subordinated the church to the state, reformed the country's administrative and judicial systems, and drew up a constitution creating a parliament and limiting the king's power.

Between 1792 and 1794 came a radical stage. Three principal factors propelled the Revolution in a radical direction: pressure from the urban poor, the *sans-culottes*, who wanted the government to do something about their poverty; a counterrevolution led by clergy and aristocrats who wanted to undo the reforms of the Revolution; and war with the European powers that sought to check French expansion and to stifle the revolutionary ideals of liberty and equality.

The dethronement of Louis XVI, the establishment of a republic in September 1792, and the king's execution in January 1793 were all signs of growing radicalism. As the new Republic tottered under the twin blows of internal insurrection and foreign invasion, the revolutionary leadership grew more extreme. In June 1793 the Jacobins took power. Tightly organized, disciplined, and fiercely devoted to the Republic, the Jacobins mobilized the nation's material and human resources to defend it against the invading foreign armies. To deal with counterrevolutionaries, the Jacobins unleashed the Reign of Terror. Of the 500,000 people imprisoned for crimes against the Republic, some 16,000 were sentenced to death by guillotine and another 20,000 perished in prison before they could be tried. More than 200,000 died in the civil war in the provinces, and 40,000 were summarily executed by firing squad, guillotine, and mass drownings ordered by military courts authorized by the Convention. Although the Jacobins succeeded in saving the Revolution, their extreme measures aroused opposition. In the last part of 1794, power again passed into the hands of the moderate bourgeoisie, who wanted no part of Jacobin radicalism.

In 1799, Napoleon Bonaparte, a popular general with an inexhaustible yearning for power, overthrew the government and pushed the Revolution in still another direction, toward military dictatorship. Although Napoleon subverted the revolutionary ideal of liberty, he preserved the social gains of the Revolution—the abolition of the special privileges of the nobility and the clergy.

The era of French Revolution was a decisive period in the shaping of the modern West. By destroying aristocratic privileges and opening careers to talent, it advanced the cause of equality under the law. By weakening the power of the clergy, it promoted the secularization

of society. By abolishing the divine right of monarchy, drafting a constitution, and establishing a parliament, it accelerated the growth of the
liberal-democratic state. By eliminating serfdom and the sale of government offices and by reforming the tax system, it fostered a rational
approach to administration. In the nineteenth century, the ideals and
reforms of the French Revolution spread in shock waves across Europe;
in country after country, the old order was challenged by the ideals of
liberty and equality.

1   Abuses of the Old Regime

The roots of the French Revolution lay in the aristocratic structure of French
society. The Third Estate came to resent the special privileges of the aristocracy,
a legacy of the Middle Ages, and the inefficient and corrupt methods of government. To many French people influenced by the ideas of the philosophes, French
society seemed an affront to reason. By 1789, reformers sought a new social
order based on rationality and equality.

GRIEVANCES OF THE THIRD ESTATE

At the same time that elections were held for the Estates General, the three
estates drafted *cahiers de doléances*, the lists of grievances that deputies would
take with them when the Estates General convened. The cahiers from all three
estates expressed loyalty to the monarchy and the church and called for a written
constitution and an elected assembly. The cahiers of the clergy and the nobility insisted on the preservation of traditional rights and privileges. The Cahier
of the Third Estate of Dourdan, in the *généralité* of Orléans (one of the thirty-
four administrative units into which prerevolutionary France was divided),
expressed the reformist hopes of the Third Estate. Some of the grievances in
the cahier follow.

29 March, 1789

The order of the third estate of the City, *Bailliage*
[judicial district], and County of Dourdan, imbued with gratitude prompted by the paternal
kindness of the King, who deigns to restore its
former rights and its former constitution, forgets
at this moment its misfortunes and impotence,
to harken only to its foremost sentiment and its
foremost duty, that of sacrificing everything to
the glory of the *Patrie* [nation] and the service
of His Majesty. It supplicates him to accept
the grievances, complaints, and remonstrances
which it is permitted to bring to the foot of the
throne, and to see therein only the expression of
its zeal and the homage of its obedience.

It wishes:

1. That his subjects of the third estate, equal by such status to all other citizens, present themselves before the common father without other distinction which might degrade them.

2. That all the orders [the three estates], already united by duty and a common desire to contribute equally to the needs of the State, also deliberate in common concerning its needs.

3. That no citizen lose his liberty except according to law; that, consequently, no one be arrested by virtue of special orders, or, if imperative circumstances necessitate such orders, that the prisoner be handed over to the regular courts of justice within forty-eight hours at the latest.

4. That no letters or writings intercepted in the post [mails] be the cause of the detention of any citizen, or be produced in court against him, except in case of conspiracy or undertaking against the State.

5. That the property of all citizens be inviolable, and that no one be required to make sacrifice thereof for the public welfare, except upon assurance of indemnification based upon the statement of freely selected appraisers. . . .

15. That every personal tax be abolished; that thus the *capitation* and the *taille* and its accessories be merged with the *vingtièmes*[1] in a tax on land and real or nominal property.

16. That such tax be borne equally, without distinction, by all classes of citizens and by all kinds of property, even feudal and contingent rights.

17. That the tax substituted for the *corvée* [taxes paid in labor, often road building] be borne by all classes of citizens equally and without distinction. That said tax, at present beyond the capacity of those who pay it and the needs

to which it is destined, be reduced by at least one-half. . . .

JUSTICE

1. That the administration of justice be reformed, either by restoring strict execution of ordinances, or by reforming the sections thereof that are contrary to the dispatch and welfare of justice. . . .

7. That venality [sale] of offices be suppressed. . . .

8. That the excessive number of offices in the necessary courts be reduced in just measure, and that no one be given an office of magistracy if he is not at least twenty-five years of age, and until after a substantial public examination has verified his morality, integrity, and ability. . . .

10. That the study of law be reformed; that it be directed in a manner analogous to our legislation, and that candidates for degrees be subjected to rigorous tests which may not be evaded; that no dispensation of age or time be granted.

11. That a body of general customary law be drafted of all articles common to all the customs of the several provinces and *bailliages*. . . .

12. That deliberations of courts . . . which tend to prevent entry of the third estate thereto be rescinded and annulled as injurious to the citizens of that order, in contempt of the authority of the King, whose choice they limit, and contrary to the welfare of justice, the administration of which would become the patrimony of those of noble birth instead of being entrusted to merit, enlightenment, and virtue.

13. That military ordinances which restrict entrance to the service to those possessing nobility be reformed.

That naval ordinances establishing a degrading distinction between officers born into the order of nobility and those born into that of the third estate be revoked, as thoroughly injurious to an order of citizens and destructive of the competition so necessary to the glory and prosperity of the State.

---

[1]A *taille* was a tax levied on the value of a peasant's land or wealth. A *capitation* was a head or poll tax paid for each person. A *vingtième* was a tax on income and was paid chiefly by peasants.

FINANCES

1. That if the Estates General considers it necessary to preserve the fees of *aides* [tax on commodities], such fees be made uniform throughout the entire kingdom and reduced to a single denomination. . . .

2. That the tax of the *gabelle* [tax on salt] be eliminated if possible, or that it be regulated among the several provinces of the kingdom. . . .

3. That the taxes on hides, which have totally destroyed that branch of commerce and caused it to go abroad, be suppressed forever.

4. That . . . all useless offices, either in police or in the administration of justice, be abolished and suppressed.

AGRICULTURE

4. That the right to hunt may never affect the property of the citizen; that, accordingly, he may at all times travel over his lands, have injurious herbs uprooted, and cut *luzernes* [alfalfa], *sainfoins* [fodder], and other produce whenever it suits him; and that stubble may be freely raked immediately after the harvest. . . .

11. . . . That individuals as well as communities be permitted to free themselves from the rights of *banalité* [peasants were required to use the lord's mill, winepress, and oven], and *corvée*, by payments in money or in kind, at a rate likewise established by His Majesty on the basis of the deliberations of the Estates General. . . .

15. That the militia, which devastates the country, takes workers away from husbandry, produces premature and ill-matched marriages, and imposes secret and arbitrary taxes upon those who are subject thereto, be suppressed and replaced by voluntary enlistment at the expense of the provinces.

Emmanuel Sieyès
WHAT IS THE THIRD ESTATE?

In a series of pamphlets, including *The Essay on Privileges* (1788) and *What Is the Third Estate?* (1789), Abbé Emmanuel Sieyès (1748–1836) expressed the bourgeoisie's disdain for the nobility. Although educated at Jesuit schools to become a priest, Sieyès had come under the influence of Enlightenment ideas. In *What Is the Third Estate?* he denounced the special privileges of the nobility, asserted that the people are the source of political authority, and maintained that national unity stands above estate or local interests. The ideals of the Revolution— liberty, equality, and fraternity—are found in Sieyès's pamphlet, excerpts of which follow.

The plan of this book is fairly simple. We must ask ourselves three questions.

1. What is the Third Estate? *Everything.*
2. What has it been until now in the political order? *Nothing.*
3. What does it want to be? *Something.* . . .

. . . Only the well-paid and honorific posts are filled by members of the privileged order [nobles]. Are we to give them credit for this? We could do so only if the Third Estate was unable or unwilling to fill these posts. We know the answer. Nevertheless, the privileged have dared to preclude the Third

Estate. "No matter how useful you are," they said, "no matter how able you are, you can go so far and no further. Honors are not for the like of you." . . .

. . . Has nobody observed that as soon as the government becomes the property of a separate class, it starts to grow out of all proportion and that posts are created not to meet the needs of the governed but of those who govern them? . . .

It suffices to have made the point that the so-called usefulness of a privileged order to the public service is a fallacy; that, without help from this order, all the arduous tasks in the service are performed by the Third Estate; that without this order the higher posts could be infinitely better filled; that they ought to be the natural prize and reward of recognised ability and service; and that if the privileged have succeeded in usurping all well-paid and honorific posts, this is both a hateful iniquity towards the generality of citizens and an act of treason to the commonwealth.

Who is bold enough to maintain that the Third Estate does not contain within itself everything needful to constitute a complete nation? It is like a strong and robust man with one arm still in chains. If the privileged order were removed, the nation would not be something less but something more. What then is the Third Estate? All; but an "all" that is fettered and oppressed. What would it be without the privileged order? It would be all; but free and flourishing. Nothing will go well without the Third Estate; everything would go considerably better without the two others. . . .

. . . The privileged, far from being useful to the nation, can only weaken and injure it; . . . the nobility may be a *burden* for the nation. . . .

The nobility, however, is . . . a foreigner in our midst because of its *civil and political* prerogatives.

What is a nation? A body of associates living under *common* laws and represented by the same *legislative assembly*, etc.

Is it not obvious that the nobility possesses privileges and exemptions which it brazenly calls its rights and which stand distinct from the rights of the great body of citizens? Because of these special rights, the nobility does not belong to the common order, nor is it subjected to the common laws. Thus its private rights make it a people apart in the great nation.

REVIEW QUESTIONS

1. The principle of equality pervaded the cahiers of the Third Estate. Discuss this statement.
2. How important did Emmanuel Sieyès say the nobility (the privileged order) was to the life of the nation?
3. What importance did Sieyès attach to the contribution of the Third Estate (the bourgeoisie) to the life of the nation?

2 The Role of the Philosophes

The Enlightenment thinkers were not themselves revolutionaries. However, by subjecting the institutions and values of the Old Regime to critical scrutiny and by offering the hope that society could be reformed, the philosophes created the intellectual precondition for revolution.

Alexis de Tocqueville
CRITIQUE OF THE OLD REGIME

The following passage from *The Old Regime and the French Revolution*, by Alexis de Tocqueville (1805–1859), treats the role of the philosophes in undermining the Old Regime. Born of a noble family, de Tocqueville was active in French politics. After traveling in the United States, he wrote *Democracy in America* (1835), a great work of historical literature. In 1856, he published *The Old Regime and the French Revolution*, which explored the causes of the French Revolution.

France had long been the most literary of all the nations of Europe; although her literary men had never exhibited such intellectual powers as they displayed about the middle of the 18th century, or occupied such a position as that which they then assumed. Nothing of the kind had ever been seen in France, or perhaps in any other country. They were not constantly mixed up with public affairs as in England: at no period, on the contrary, had they lived more apart from them. They were invested with no authority whatever, and filled no public offices in a society crowded with public officers; yet they did not, like the greater part of their brethren in Germany, keep entirely aloof from the arena of politics and retire into the regions of pure philosophy and polite literature. They busied themselves incessantly with matters appertaining to government, and this was, in truth, their special occupation. Thus they were continually holding forth on the origin and primitive forms of society, the primary rights of the citizen and of government, the natural and artificial relations of men, the wrong or right of customary laws, and the principles of legislation. While they thus penetrated to the fundamental basis of the constitution of their time, they examined its structure with minute care and criticised its general plan.

. . . [The thinkers of the Enlightenment] all agreed that it was expedient to substitute simple and elementary rules, deduced from reason and natural law, for the complicated traditional customs which governed the society of their time. Upon a strict scrutiny it may be seen that what might be called the political philosophy of the eighteenth century consisted, properly speaking, in this one notion.

These opinions were by no means novel; for three thousand years they had unceasingly traversed the imaginations of mankind, though without being able to stamp themselves there. How came they at last to take possession of the minds of all the writers of this period? Why, instead of progressing no farther than the heads of a few philosophers, as had frequently been the case, had they at last reached the masses, and assumed the strength and the fervour of a political passion to such a degree, that general and abstract theories upon the nature of society became daily topics of conversation, and even inflamed the imaginations of women and of the peasantry? How was it that literary men, possessing neither rank, nor honours, nor fortune, nor responsibility, nor power, became, in fact, the principal political men of the day? . . .

It was not by chance that the philosophers of the 18th century . . . coincided in entertaining notions so opposed to those which still served as bases to the society of their time: these ideas had been naturally suggested to them by the aspects of the society which they had all before their eyes. The sight of so many unjust or absurd privileges, the {burden} of which was more and more felt whilst their cause was less and less understood, urged, or rather precipitated the minds of one and all to the idea of the natural equality of man's condition. Whilst they looked upon so many strange and irregular institutions, born of other times, which no one had attempted either to bring into harmony with each other or to adapt to modern wants, and which appeared likely to perpetuate their existence though they had lost their worth, they learned to abhor what was ancient and traditional, and naturally became desirous of re-constructing the social edifice of their day upon an entirely new plan—a plan which each one traced solely by the light of his reason. . . .

Had {the French} been able, like the English, gradually to modify the spirit of their ancient institutions by practical experience without destroying them, they would perhaps have been less inclined to invent new ones. But there was not a man who did not daily feel himself injured in his fortune, in his person, in his comfort, or his pride by some old law, some ancient political custom, or some other remnant of former authority, without perceiving at hand any remedy that he could himself apply to his own particular hardship. It appeared that the whole constitution of the country must either be endured or destroyed.

The French, however, had still preserved one liberty amidst the ruin of every other: they were still free to philosophize almost without restraint upon the origin of society, the essential nature of governments, and the primordial rights of mankind.

All those who felt themselves aggrieved by the daily application of existing laws were soon enamoured of these literary politics. The same taste soon reached even those who by nature or by their condition of life seemed the farthest removed from abstract speculations. Every taxpayer wronged by the unequal distribution of the *taille*[1] was fired by the idea that all men ought to be equal; every little landowner devoured by the rabbits of his noble

---

[1]For an explanation of taxes, see footnote 1 on page 95.

neighbour was delighted to be told that all privileges were without distinction contrary to reason. Every public passion thus assumed the disguise of philosophy; all political action was violently driven back into the domain of literature; and the writers of the day, undertaking the guidance of public opinion, found themselves at one time in that position which the heads of parties commonly hold in free countries. No one in fact was any longer in a condition to contend with them for the part they had assumed. . . .

If now it be taken into consideration that this same French nation, so ignorant of its own public affairs, so utterly devoid of experience, so hampered by its institutions, and so powerless to amend them, was also in those days the most lettered and witty nation of the earth, it may readily be understood how the writers of the time became a great political power, and ended by being the first power in the country.

Above the actual state of society—the constitution of which was still traditional, confused, and irregular, and in which the laws remained conflicting and contradictory, ranks sharply sundered, the conditions of the different classes fixed whilst their burdens were unequal—an imaginary state of society was thus springing up, in which everything appeared simple and co-ordinate, uniform, equitable, and agreeable to reason. The imagination of the people gradually deserted the former state of things in order to seek refuge in the latter. Interest was lost in what was, to foster dreams of what might be; and men thus dwelt in fancy in this ideal city, which was the work of literary invention. . . .

This circumstance, so novel in history, of the whole political education of a great people being formed by its literary men, contributed more than anything perhaps to bestow upon the French Revolution its peculiar stamp, and to cause those results which are still perceptible.

REVIEW QUESTIONS

1. According to de Tocqueville, how did the philosophes undermine the Old Regime?
2. Why did de Tocqueville believe the French people were receptive to the philosophes' ideas?

---

3 Liberty, Equality, Fraternity

In August 1789 the newly created National Assembly adopted the Declaration of the Rights of Man and of the Citizen, which expressed the liberal and universal ideals of the Enlightenment. The Declaration proclaimed that sovereignty derives from the people: that is, that the people are the source of political power; that men are born free and equal in rights; and that it is the purpose of government to protect the natural rights of the individual. Because these ideals contrasted markedly with the outlook of an absolute monarchy, a privileged aristocracy, and an intolerant clergy, some historians view the Declaration of Rights as the death knell of the Old Regime. Its affirmation of liberty, reason, and natural rights inspired liberal reformers in other lands.

DECLARATION OF THE RIGHTS OF MAN AND OF THE CITIZEN

Together with John Locke's *Second Treatise on Government*, the American Declaration of Independence, and the Constitution of the United States, the Declaration of the Rights of Man and of the Citizen, which follows, is a pivotal document in the development of modern liberalism.

The Representatives of the people of FRANCE, formed into a NATIONAL ASSEMBLY, considering that ignorance, neglect, or contempt of human rights, are the sole causes of public misfortunes and corruptions of Government, have resolved to set forth in a solemn declaration, these natural, imprescriptible, and unalienable rights: that this declaration, being constantly present to the minds of the members of the body social, they may be ever kept attentive to their rights and their duties: that the acts of the legislative and executive powers of Government, being capable of being every moment compared with the end of political institutions, may be more respected: and also, that the future claims of the citizens, being directed by simple and incontestible principles, may always tend to the maintenance of the Constitution, and the general happiness.

For these reasons the NATIONAL ASSEMBLY doth recognize and declare, in the presence of the Supreme Being, and with the hope of his blessing and favor, the following *sacred* rights of men and of citizens:

I. *Men are born, and always continue, free, and equal in respect of their rights. Civil distinctions, therefore, can be founded only on public utility.*

II. *The end of all political associations, is, the preservation of the natural and imprescriptible rights of man; and these rights are liberty, property, security, and resistance of oppression.*

III. *The nation is essentially the source of all sovereignty; nor can any* INDIVIDUAL *or* ANY BODY OF MEN, *be entitled to any authority which is not expressly derived from it.*

IV. Political Liberty consists in the power of doing whatever does not injure another. The exercise of the natural rights of every man, has no other limits than those which are necessary to secure to every *other* man the free exercise of the same rights; and these limits are determinable only by the law.

V. The law ought to prohibit only actions hurtful to society. What is not prohibited by the law, should not be hindered; nor should any one be compelled to that which the law does not require.

VI. The law is an expression of the will of the community. All citizens have a right to concur, either personally, or by their representatives, in its formation. It should be the same to all, whether it protects or punishes; and *all being equal in its sight, are equally eligible to all honors, places, and employments, according to their different abilities, without any other distinction than that created by their virtues and talents.*

VII. No man should be accused, arrested, or held in confinement, except in cases determined by the law, and according to the forms which it has prescribed. All who promote, solicit, execute, or cause to be executed, arbitrary orders, ought to be punished; and every citizen called upon or apprehended by virtue of the law, ought immediately to obey, and renders himself culpable by resistance.

VIII. The law ought to impose no other penalties but such as are absolutely and evidently necessary; and no one ought to be punished, but in virtue of a law promulgated before the offence, and legally applied.

IX. Every man being presumed innocent till he has been convicted, whenever his detention becomes indispensible, all rigor {harshness} to him, more than is necessary to secure his person, ought to be provided against by the law.

X. No man ought to be molested on account of his opinions, not even on account of his *religious* opinions, provided his avowal of them does not disturb the public order established by the law.

XI. The unrestrained communication of thoughts and opinions being one of the most precious rights of man, every citizen may speak, write, and publish freely, provided he is responsible for the abuse of this liberty in cases determined by the law.

XII. A public force being necessary to give security to the rights of men and of citizens, that force is instituted for the benefit of the community, and not for the particular benefit of the persons with whom it is entrusted.

XIII. A common contribution being necessary for the support of the public force, and for defraying the other expenses of government, it ought to be divided equally among the members of the community, according to their abilities.

XIV. Every citizen has a right, either by himself or his representative, to a free voice in determining the necessity of public contributions, the appropriation of them, and their amount, mode of assessment, and duration.

XV. Every community has a right to demand of all its agents, an account of their conduct.

XVI. Every community in which a separation of powers and a security of rights is not provided for, wants a constitution.

XVII. The rights to property being inviolable and sacred, no one ought to be deprived of it, except in cases of evident public necessity, legally ascertained, and on condition of a previous just indemnity.

REVIEW QUESTIONS

1. What does the Declaration say about the nature of political liberty? What are its limits, and how are they determined?
2. How does the Declaration show the influence of John Locke (see page 54).
3. The ideals of the Declaration have become deeply embedded in the Western outlook. Discuss this statement.

---

4 Expansion of Human Rights

The abolition of the special privileges of the aristocracy and the ideals proclaimed by the Declaration of the Rights of Man and of the Citizen aroused the hopes of reformers in several areas: in what was considered radicalism, even by the framers of the Declaration of the Rights of Man, some women began to press for equal rights; humanitarians called for the abolition of the slave trade; and Jews, who for centuries had suffered disabilities and degradation, petitioned for full citizenship.

Mary Wollstonecraft
A VINDICATION OF THE RIGHTS OF WOMAN

When in 1789 the French revolutionaries issued their "Declaration of the Rights of Man," it was only a matter of time before a woman published a "Declaration of the Rights of Woman." That feat was accomplished in 1791 in France by Olympe de Gouges. In England, Mary Wollstonecraft (1759–1797), strongly influenced by her, published her own statement, *A Vindication of the Rights of Woman*, in 1792. Her protest against the prevailing submissiveness of women was reinforced by the philosophy of the Enlightenment and the ideals of the French Revolution, which she observed firsthand from 1792 to 1794. A career woman, she made her living as a prolific writer closely associated with the radicals of her time, one of whom, William Godwin, she married shortly before her death. Wollstonecraft became famous for her vigorous protests against the subjection of women. Children, husbands, and society generally, she pleaded in *A Vindication of the Rights of Woman*, were best served by well-educated, self-reliant, and strong women capable of holding their own in the world.

. . . I have turned over various books written on the subject of education, and patiently observed the conduct of parents and the management of schools; but what has been the result?—a profound conviction that the neglected education of my fellow creatures is the grand source of the misery I deplore, and that women, in particular, are rendered weak and wretched. . . .

The conduct and manners of women, in fact, evidently prove that their minds are not in a healthy state. . . . One cause of this . . . I attribute to a false system of education, gathered from the books written on this subject by men who, considering females rather as women than human creatures, have been more anxious to make them alluring mistresses than affectionate wives and rational mothers. . . .

. . . A degree of physical superiority of men cannot . . . be denied, and it is a noble prerogative! But not content with this natural preeminence, men endeavour to sink us still lower, merely to render us alluring objects for a moment. . . .

My own sex, I hope, will excuse me, if I treat them like rational creatures, instead of flattering their *fascinating* graces, and viewing them as if they were in a state of perpetual childhood, unable to stand alone. I earnestly wish to point out in what true dignity and human happiness consists. I wish to persuade women to endeavour to acquire strength, both of mind and body. . . .

Dismissing, then, those pretty feminine phrases, which the men condescendingly use to soften our slavish dependence, and despising that weak elegancy of mind, exquisite sensibility, and sweet docility of manners, supposed to be the sexual characteristics of the weaker vessel, I wish to show that elegance is inferior to virtue, that the first object of laudable ambition is to obtain a character as a human being, regardless of the distinction of sex. . . .

The education of women has of late been more attended to than formerly; yet they are still reckoned a frivolous sex, and ridiculed or pitied by the writers who endeavour by satire or instruction to improve them. It is acknowledged that they spend many of the first years of their lives in acquiring a smattering of accomplishments; meanwhile strength of body and mind are sacrificed to libertine notions of beauty, to the desire of establishing themselves—the only way women can rise in the world—by marriage. And this desire making mere animals of them, when they marry they act as such children may

be expected to act,—they dress, they paint, and nickname God's creatures. Surely these weak beings are only fit for a seraglio [harem]! Can they be expected to govern a family with judgment, or take care of the poor babes whom they bring into the world? . . .

Contending for the rights of woman, my main argument is built on this simple principle, that if she be not prepared by education to become the companion of man, she will stop the progress of knowledge and virtue; for truth must be common to all, or it will be inefficacious with respect to its influence on general practice. And how can woman be expected to co-operate unless she knows why she ought to be virtuous? unless freedom strengthens her reason till she comprehends her duty, and sees in what manner it is connected with her real good. If children are to be educated to understand the true principle of patriotism, their mother must be a patriot; and the love of mankind, from which an orderly train of virtues spring, can only be produced by considering the moral and civil interest of mankind; but the education and situation of woman at present shuts her out from such investigations. . . .

Consider—I address you as a legislator—whether, when men contend for their freedom and [are] to be allowed to judge for themselves respecting their own happiness, it be not inconsistent and unjust to subjugate women, even though you firmly believe that you are acting in the manner best calculated to promote their happiness? Who made man the exclusive judge, if woman partake with him of the gift of reason?

In this style argue tyrants of every denomination, from the weak king to the weak father of a family; they are all eager to crush reason, yet always assert that they usurp its throne only to be useful. Do you not act a similar part when you *force* all women, by denying them civil and political rights, to remain immured [imprisoned] in their families groping in the dark? for surely, sir, you will not assert that a duty can be binding which is not founded on reason? If, indeed, this be their destination, arguments may be drawn from reason; and thus augustly supported, the more understanding women acquire, the more they will be attached to their duty—comprehending it—for unless they comprehend it, unless their morals be fixed on the same immutable principle as those of man, no authority can make them discharge it in a virtuous manner. They may be convenient slaves, but slavery will have its constant effect, degrading the master and the abject dependent.

But if women are to be excluded, without having a voice, from a participation of the natural rights of mankind, prove first, to ward off the charge of injustice and inconsistency, that they [lack] reason, else this flaw in your NEW CONSTITUTION will ever show that man must, in some shape, act like a tyrant, and tyranny, in whatever part of society it rears its brazen front, will ever undermine morality. . . .

In what does man's pre-eminence over the brute creation consist? The answer is as clear as that a half is less than the whole, in Reason. . . . Yet . . . deeply rooted processes have clouded reason. . . . Men, in general, seem to employ their reason to justify prejudices, which they have imbibed, they can scarcely trace how, rather than to root them out.

The power of generalising ideas, of drawing comprehensive conclusions from individual observations . . . has not only been denied to women; but writers have insisted that it is inconsistent, with a few exceptions, with their sexual character. Let men prove this, and I shall grant that woman only exists for man. I must, however, previously remark, that the power of generalising ideas, to any great extent, is not very common amongst men or women. But this exercise is the true cultivation of the understanding; and everything conspires to render the cultivation of the understanding more difficult in the female than the male world. . . .

I shall not go back to the remote annals of antiquity to trace the history of woman; it is sufficient to allow that she has always been either a slave or a despot, and to remark that each of these situations equally retards the progress of reason. The grand source of female folly and vice has ever appeared to me to arise from narrowness of mind; and the very constitution of civil governments has put almost insuperable obstacles in the way to prevent the cultivation of the female understanding; yet virtue can be built on no other foundation. . . .

When do we hear of women who, starting out of obscurity, boldly claim respect on account of their great abilities or daring virtues? Where are they to be found? . . .

With respect to women, when they receive a careful education, they are either made fine ladies, brimful of sensibility, and teeming with capricious fancies, or mere notable women. The latter are often friendly, honest creatures, and have a shrewd kind of good sense, joined with worldly prudence, that often render them more useful members of society than the fine sentimental lady, though they possess neither greatness of mind nor taste. The intellectual world is shut against them. Take them out of their family or neighbourhood, and they stand still; the mind finding no employment, for literature affords a fund of amusement which they have never sought to relish, but frequently to despise. The sentiments and taste of more cultivated minds appear ridiculous, even in those whom chance and family connections have led them to love; but in mere acquaintance they think it all affectation.

A man of sense can only love such a woman on account of her sex, and respect her because she is a trusty servant. He lets her, to preserve his own peace, scold the servants, and go to church in clothes made of the very best materials. . . . [W]omen, whose minds are not enlarged by cultivation, or . . . by reflection, are very unfit to manage a family, for, by an undue stretch of power, they are always tyrannising to support a superiority that only rests on the arbitrary distinction of fortune.

Women have seldom sufficient serious employment to silence their feelings; a round of little cares, or vain pursuits frittering away all strength of mind and organs, they become naturally only objects of sense. In short, the whole tenor of female education (the education of society) tends to render the best disposed romantic and inconstant; and the remainder vain and [contemptible]. In the present state of society this evil can scarcely be remedied, I am afraid, in the slightest degree; should a more laudable ambition ever gain ground they may be brought nearer to nature and reason, and become more virtuous and useful as they grow more respectable. . . .

Women . . . all want to be ladies. Which is simply to have nothing to do, but listlessly to go they scarcely care where, for they cannot tell what.

But what have women to do in society? I may be asked, but to loiter with easy grace. . . . Women might certainly study the art of healing, and be physicians as well as nurses. . . . They might also study politics . . . for the reading of history will scarcely be more useful than the study of romances. . . . Business of various kinds, they might likewise pursue, if they were educated in a more orderly manner, which might save many from common and legal prostitution. . . . The few employments open to a woman, so far from being liberal, are menial. . . .

Some of these women might be restrained from marrying by a proper spirit of delicacy, and others may not have had it in their power to escape in this pitiful way from servitude; is not that Government then very defective, and very unmindful of the happiness of one-half of its members, that does not provide for honest, independent women, by encouraging them to fill respectable stations? . . .

It is a melancholy truth; yet such is the blessed effect of civilisation! the most respectable women are the most oppressed; and, unless they have understandings far superior to the common run of understandings, taking in both sexes, they must, from being treated like contemptible beings, become contemptible. How many women thus waste life away the prey of discontent, who might have practised as physicians, regulated a farm, managed a shop, and stood erect, supported by their own industry, instead of hanging their heads. . . .

Would men but generously snap our chains, and be content with rational fellowship instead of slavish obedience, they would find us more observant daughters, more affectionate sisters, more faithful wives, more reasonable mothers—in a word, better citizens. We should then love them with true affection, because we should learn to respect ourselves; and the peace of mind of a worthy man would not be interrupted by the idle vanity of his wife, nor the babes sent to nestle in a strange bosom, having never found a home in their mother's. . . .

. . . The sexual distinction which men have so warmly insisted upon, is arbitrary. . . . Asserting the rights which women in common with men ought to contend for, I have not attempted to [make light of] their faults; but to prove them to be the natural consequence of their education and station in society. If so, it is reasonable to suppose that they will change their character, and correct their vices and follies, when they are allowed to be free in a physical, moral, and civil sense.

Let woman share the rights, and she will emulate the virtues of man; for she must grow more perfect when emancipated. . . .

Society of the Friends of Blacks
ADDRESS TO THE NATIONAL ASSEMBLY IN FAVOR OF THE ABOLITION OF THE SLAVE TRADE

Planters in the French West Indies and shipbuilding and sugar refining interests opposed any attempts to eliminate slavery or the slave trade since they profited handsomely from these institutions. On February 5, 1790, the Society of the Friends of Blacks, using the language of the Declaration of the Rights of Man, called for the abolition of the slave trade. Recognizing the power of proslavery forces, the society made it clear that it was not proposing the abolition of slavery itself. In 1791, the slaves of Saint Domingue revolted, and in 1794, the Jacobins in the National Convention abolished slavery in the French colonies. The island's white planters resisted the decree, and in 1801 Napoleon sent twenty thousand troops to Saint Domingue in an unsuccessful attempt to restore slavery. In 1804, the black revolutionaries established the independent state of Haiti.

Following are excerpts from the Society of the Friends of Blacks' address to the National Assembly.

The humanity, justice, and magnanimity that have guided you in the reform of the most profoundly rooted abuses gives hope to the Society of the Friends of Blacks that you will receive with benevolence its demand in favor of that numerous portion of humankind, so cruelly oppressed for two centuries.

This Society, slandered in such cowardly and unjust fashion, only derives its mission from the humanity that induced it to defend the blacks even under the past despotism. Oh! Can there be a more respectable title in the eyes of this august Assembly which has so often avenged the rights of man in its decrees?

You have declared them, these rights; you have engraved on an immortal monument that all men are born and remain free and equal in rights; you have restored to the French people these rights that despotism had for so long despoiled; . . . you have broken the chains of feudalism that still degraded a good number of our fellow citizens; you have announced the destruction of all the stigmatizing distinctions that religious or political prejudices introduced into the great family of humankind. . . .

We are not asking you to restore to French blacks those political rights which alone, nevertheless, attest to and maintain the dignity of man; we are not even asking for their liberty. No; slander, bought no doubt with the greed of the shipowners, ascribes that scheme to us and spreads it everywhere; they want to stir up everyone against us, provoke the planters and their numerous creditors, who take alarm even at gradual emancipation. They want to alarm all the French, to whom they depict the prosperity of the colonies as inseparable from the slave trade and the perpetuity of slavery.

No, never has such an idea entered into our minds; we have said it, printed it since the beginning of our Society, and we repeat it in order to reduce to nothing this grounds of argument, blindly adopted by all the coastal cities, the grounds on which rest almost all their addresses [to the National Assembly]. The immediate emancipation of the blacks would not only be a fatal operation for the colonies; it would even be a deadly gift for the blacks, in the state of abjection and incompetence to which cupidity has reduced them. It would be to abandon to themselves and without assistance children in the cradle or mutilated and impotent beings.

It is therefore not yet time to demand that liberty; we ask only that one cease butchering thousands of blacks regularly every year in order to take hundreds of captives; we ask that one henceforth cease the prostitution, the profaning of the French name, used to authorize these thefts, these atrocious murders; we demand in a word the abolition of the slave trade. . . .

In regard to the colonists, we will demonstrate to you that if they need to recruit blacks in Africa to sustain the population of the colonies at the same level, it is because they wear out the blacks with work, whippings, and starvation; that, if they treated them with kindness and as good fathers of families, these blacks would multiply and that this population, always growing, would increase cultivation and prosperity. . . .

Have no doubt, the time when this commerce will be abolished, even in England, is not far off. It is condemned there in public opinion, even in the opinion of the ministers. . . .

If some motive might on the contrary push them [the blacks] to insurrection, might it not be the indifference of the National Assembly about their lot? Might it not be the insistence on weighing them down with chains, when one consecrates everywhere this eternal axiom: *that all men are born free and equal in rights.* So then therefore there would only be fetters and gallows for the blacks while good fortune glimmers only for the whites? Have no doubt, our happy revolution must re-electrify the blacks whom vengeance and resentment have electrified for so long, and it is not with punishments that the effect of this upheaval will be repressed. From one insurrection badly pacified will twenty others be born, of which one alone can ruin the colonists forever.

It is worthy of the first free Assembly of France to consecrate the principle of philanthropy which makes of humankind only one single family, to declare that it is horrified by this annual carnage which takes place on the coasts of Africa, that it has the intention of abolishing it one day, of mitigating the slavery that is the result, of looking for and preparing, from this moment, the means.

PETITION OF THE JEWS OF PARIS, ALSACE, AND LORRAINE TO THE NATIONAL ASSEMBLY, JANUARY 28, 1790

After several heated debates, the National Assembly granted full citizenship to the Jews on September 27, 1791. Influenced by the French example, almost all European states in the nineteenth century would also emancipate the Jews dwelling within their borders. In the following *Petition of the Jews of Paris, Alsace, and Lorraine to the National Assembly, January 28, 1790*, the Jews pointed to historic wrongs and invoked the ideals of the Revolution as they called for equal rights.

A great question is pending before the supreme tribunal of France. *Will the Jews be citizens or not?*

Already, this question has been debated in the National Assembly; and the orators, whose intentions were equally patriotic, did not agree at all on the result of their discussion. Some wanted Jews admitted to civil status. Others found this admission dangerous. A third opinion consisted of preparing the complete improvement of the lot of the Jews by gradual reforms.

In the midst of all these debates, the national assembly believed that it ought to adjourn the question. . . .

It was also said that the adjournment was based on the necessity of knowing with assurance what were the true desires of the Jews; given, it was added, the disadvantages of according to this class of men rights more extensive than those they want.

But it is impossible that such a motive could have determined the decree of the national assembly.

First, the wish of the Jews is perfectly well-known, and cannot be equivocal. They have presented it clearly in their addresses of 26 and 31 August, 1789. The Jews of Paris repeated it in a *new address* of 24 December. They ask that all the degrading distinctions that they have suffered to this day be abolished and that they be declared CITIZENS. . . .

Their desires, moreover, as we have just said, are well known; and we will repeat them here. They ask to be CITIZENS. . . .

In truth, [the Jews] are of a religion that is condemned by the one that predominates in France. But the time has passed when one could say that it was only the dominant religion that could grant access to advantages, to prerogatives, to the lucrative and honorable posts in society. For a long time they confronted the Protestants with this maxim, worthy of the Inquisition, and the Protestants had no civil standing in France. Today, they have just been reestablished in the possession of this status; they are assimilated to the Catholics in everything; the intolerant maxim that we have just recalled can no longer be used against them. Why would they continue to use it as an argument against the Jews?

In general, civil rights are entirely independent from religious principles. And all men of whatever religion, whatever sect they belong to, whatever creed they practice, provided that their creed, their sect, their religion does not offend the principles of a pure and severe morality, all these men, we say, equally able to serve the fatherland, defend its interests, contribute to its splendor, should all equally have the title and the rights of citizen. . . .

[The Jews] are reproached at the same time for the vices that make them unworthy of civil status and the principles which render them at once unworthy and incompetent. A rapid glance at the bizarre as well as cruel destiny of these unfortunate individuals will perhaps remove the disfavor with which some seek to cover them. . . .

Always persecuted since the destruction of Jerusalem, pursued at times by fanaticism and at others by superstition, by turn chased from the kingdoms that gave them an asylum and then called back to these same kingdoms, excluded from all the professions and arts and crafts, deprived even of the right to be heard as witnesses against a Christian, relegated to separate districts like another species of man with whom one fears having communication, pushed out of certain cities which have the privilege of not receiving them, obligated in others to pay for the air that they breathe as in Augsburg where they pay a *florin* an hour or in Bremen a *ducat* a day, subject in several places to shameful tolls. Here is the list of a part of the harassment still practiced today against the Jews.

And [critics of the Jews] would dare to complain of the state of degradation into which some of them can be plunged! They would dare to complain of their ignorance and their vices! Oh! Do not accuse the Jews, for that would only precipitate onto the Christians themselves all the weight of these accusations. . . .

Let us now enter into more details. The Jews have been accused of the crime of usury. But first of all, all of them are not usurers; and it would be as unjust to punish them all for the offense of some as to punish all the Christians for the usury committed by some of them and the speculation of many. . . .

Reflect, then, on the condition of the Jews. Excluded from all the professions, ineligible for all the positions, deprived even of the capacity to acquire property, not daring and not being able to sell openly the merchandise of their commerce, to what extremity are you reducing them? You do not want them to die, and yet you refuse them the means to live: you refuse them the means, and you crush them with taxes. You leave them therefore really no other resource than usury. . . .

Everything that one would not have dared to undertake, moreover, or what one would only have dared to undertake with an infinity of precautions a long time ago, can now be done and one must dare to undertake it in this moment of universal regeneration, when all ideas and all sentiments take a new direction; and we must hasten to do so. Could one still fear the influence of a prejudice against which reason has appealed for such a long time, when all the former abuses are destroyed and all the former

prejudices overturned? Will not the numerous changes effected in the political machine uproot from the people's minds most of the ideas that dominated them? Everything is changing; the lot of the Jews must change at the same time; and the people will not be more surprised by this particular change than by all those which they see around them everyday. This is therefore the moment, the true moment to make justice triumph: attach the improvement of the lot of the Jews to the revolution; amalgamate, so to speak, this partial revolution to the general revolution. Your efforts will be crowned with success, and the people will not protest, and time will consolidate your work and render it unshakable.

REVIEW QUESTIONS

1. According to Mary Wollstonecraft, what benefits would society derive from giving equal rights to women?
2. Why did Wollstonecraft object to the traditional attitudes of men toward women?
3. How, in Wollstonecraft's opinion, should women change?
4. In proposing the abolition of the slave trade, what did the Society of the Friends of Blacks petition the National Assembly to do? Was it feasible? Do you feel it was adequate? Explain.
5. On what grounds did the Jews of Paris, Alsace, and Lorraine petition the National Assembly to grant the Jews citizenship? What historic wrongs did they decry? What views of religion and politics did they uphold?
6. What did the demands of Mary Wollstonecraft, the Society of the Friends of Blacks, and the Jews of Paris, Alsace, and Lorraine have to do with the French Revolution and the ideas of the Enlightenment, and how did they exemplify the expansion of human rights?

5   The Jacobin Regime

In the summer of 1793 the French Republic was threatened with internal insurrection and foreign invasion. During this period of acute crisis, the Jacobins provided strong leadership. They organized a large national army of citizen soldiers who, imbued with love for the nation, routed the invaders on the northern frontier. To deal with internal enemies, the Jacobins instituted the Reign of Terror, in which Maximilien Robespierre (1758–1794) played a pivotal role.

It was not because they were bloodthirsty or power mad that many Jacobins, including Robespierre, supported the use of terror. Rather, they were idealists who believed that terror was necessary to rescue the Republic and the Revolution from destruction. Deeply committed to republican democracy, Robespierre saw himself as the bearer of a higher faith, molding a new society founded on reason, good citizenship, patriotism, and virtue. Robespierre viewed those who prevented the implementation of this new society as traitors and sinners who had to be killed for the good of humanity.

Maximilien Robespierre
REPUBLIC OF VIRTUE

In his speech of February 5, 1794, Robespierre provided a comprehensive statement of his political theory, in which he equated democracy with virtue and justified the use of terror in defending democracy.

What is the objective toward which we are reaching? The peaceful enjoyment of liberty and equality; the reign of that eternal justice whose laws are engraved not on marble or stone but in the hearts of all men, even in the heart of the slave who has forgotten them or of the tyrant who disowns them.

We wish an order of things where all the low and cruel passions will be curbed, all the beneficent and generous passions awakened by the laws, where ambition will be a desire to deserve glory and serve the *patrie* [nation]; where distinctions grow only out of the very system of equality; where the citizen will be subject to the authority of the magistrate, the magistrate to that of the people, and the people to that of justice; where the *patrie* assures the well-being of each individual, and where each individual shares with pride the prosperity and glory of the *patrie*; where every soul expands by the continual communication of republican sentiments, and by the need to merit the esteem of a great people; where the arts will embellish the liberty that ennobles them, and commerce will be the source of public wealth and not merely of the monstrous riches of a few families.

We wish to substitute in our country . . . all the virtues and miracles of the republic for all the vices and absurdities of the monarchy.

We wish, in a word, to fulfill the intentions of nature and the destiny of humanity, realize the promises of philosophy, and acquit providence of the long reign of crime and tyranny. We wish that France, once illustrious among enslaved nations, may, while eclipsing the glory of all the free peoples that ever existed, become a model to nations, a terror to oppressors, a consolation to the oppressed, an ornament of the universe; and that, by sealing our work with our blood, we may witness at least the dawn of universal happiness—this is our ambition, this is our aim.

What kind of government can realize these prodigies [great deeds]? A democratic or republican government only. . . .

A democracy is a state where the sovereign people, guided by laws of their own making, do for themselves everything that they can do well, and by means of delegates everything that they cannot do for themselves.

It is therefore in the principles of democratic government that you must seek the rules of your political conduct.

But in order to found democracy and consolidate it among us, in order to attain the peaceful reign of constitutional laws, we must complete the war of liberty against tyranny; . . . [S]uch is the aim of the revolutionary government that you have organized. . . .

But the French are the first people in the world who have established true democracy by calling all men to equality and to full enjoyment of the rights of citizenship; and that is, in my opinion, the true reason why all the tyrants leagued against the republic will be vanquished.

There are from this moment great conclusions to be drawn from the principles that we have just laid down.

Since virtue [good citizenship] and equality are the soul of the republic, and your aim is to found and to consolidate the republic, it follows that the first rule of your political conduct must be to relate all of your measures to the maintenance of equality and to the development of virtue; for the first care of the legislator must be to strengthen the principles on which the government rests. Hence all that tends to excite a love of country, to purify moral standards, to exalt souls, to direct the passions of the human heart toward the public good must be adopted or established by you. All that tends to concentrate and debase them into selfish egotism, to awaken an infatuation for trivial things, and scorn for great ones, must be rejected or repressed by you. In the system of the French revolution, that which is immoral and [unwise], and that which tends to corrupt is counterrevolutionary. Weakness, vices, and prejudices are the road to monarchy. . . .

. . . Externally all the despots surround you; internally all the friends of tyranny conspire. . . . It is necessary to annihilate both the internal and external enemies of the republic or perish with its fall. Now, in this situation your first political maxim should be that one guides the people by reason, and the enemies of the people by terror.

If the driving force of popular government in peacetime is virtue, that of popular government during a revolution is both *virtue and terror*: virtue, without which terror is destructive; terror, without which virtue is impotent. Terror is only justice that is prompt, severe, and inflexible; it is thus an emanation of virtue; it is less a distinct principle than a consequence of the general principle of democracy applied to the most pressing needs of the *patrie*.

In a series of notes written in the summer of 1793, Robespierre expressed his policy toward counterrevolutionaries.

DESPOTISM IN DEFENSE OF LIBERTY

What is our goal? The enforcement of the constitution for the benefit of the people.

Who will our enemies be? The vicious and the rich.

What means will they employ? Slander and hypocrisy.

What things may be favorable for the employment of these? The ignorance of the *sans-culottes*.[1]

The people must therefore be enlightened. But what are the obstacles to the enlightenment of the people? Mercenary writers who daily mislead them with impudent falsehoods.

What conclusions may be drawn from this? 1. These writers must be proscribed as the most dangerous enemies of the people. 2. Rightminded literature must be scattered about in profusion.

What are the other obstacles to the establishment of liberty? Foreign war and civil war.

How can foreign war be ended? By putting republican generals in command of our armies and punishing those who have betrayed us.

How can civil war be ended? By punishing traitors and conspirators, particularly if they are deputies or administrators; by sending loyal troops under patriotic leaders to subdue the aristocrats of Lyon, Marseille, Toulon, the Vendée, the Jura, and all other regions in which the standards of rebellion and royalism have been raised; and by making frightful examples of all scoundrels who have outraged liberty and spilled the blood of patriots.

---

[1]*Sans-culottes* literally means without the fancy breeches worn by the aristocracy. The term refers generally to a poor city dweller (who wore simple trousers). Champions of equality, the sans-culottes hated the aristocracy and the rich bourgeoisie.

1. Proscription [condemnation] of perfidious and counterrevolutionary writers and propagation of proper literature.
2. Punishment of traitors and conspirators, particularly deputies and administrators.
3. Appointment of patriotic generals; dismissal and punishment of others.
4. Sustenance and laws for the people.

General Louis de Ligniéres Turreau
UPRISING IN THE VENDÉE

In the Vendée in Western France, peasants loyal to the monarchy, to their priests, and to Catholic tradition (all of which the Revolution had attacked) and led by nobles waged war against the Republic. It was a merciless conflict. Republican authorities executed, generally without a trial, thousands of suspects by firing squad and mass drowning. Frenzied republican soldiers, under orders from their superiors, burned villages, slaughtered livestock, and indiscriminantly killed tens of thousands of peasants. Following is a letter from General Turreau to the minister of war on January 19, 1794, in which he describes the brutal campaign his troops waged against the peasants in the Vendée.

My purpose is to burn everything, to leave nothing but what is essential to establish the necessary quarters for exterminating the rebels. This great measure is one which you should prescribe; you should also make an advance statement as to the fate of the women and children we will come across in this rebellious countryside. If they are all to be put to the sword, I cannot undertake such action without authorization.

All brigands caught bearing arms, or convicted of having taken up arms to revolt against their country, will be bayoneted. The same will apply to girls, women, and children in the same circumstances. Those who are merely under suspicion will not be spared either, but no execution may be carried out except by previous order of the general.

All villages, farms, woods, heathlands, generally anything which will burn, will be set on fire, although not until any perishable supplies found there have been removed. But, it must be repeated, these executions must not take place until so ordered by the general.

I hasten to describe to you the measures which I have just put in hand for the extermination of all remaining rebels scattered about the interior of the Vendée. I was convinced that the only way to do this was by deploying a sufficient number of columns to spread right across the countryside and effect a general sweep, which would completely purge the cantons as they passed. Tomorrow, therefore, these twelve columns will set out simultaneously, moving from east to west. Each column commander has orders to search and burn forests, villages, market towns and farms, omitting, however those places which I consider important posts and those which are essential for establishing communications.

In a letter dated December 26, 1793, a high government official describes mass drowning.

I am writing to you about the more than twelve hundred brigands shot at Savenay; but, according to the intelligence that I have since been given and that I do not doubt, it seems that more than two thousand were shot. They call that "sending to the hospital." Here, an entirely different method is used to get rid of this bad element. These criminals are put into boats which are then sunk. This is called "sending to the water tower." In truth, if the brigands have sometimes complained about dying of hunger, they cannot at least complain about dying of thirst. About twelve hundred were made to drink today. I do not know who thought up this kind of punishment, but it is much more speedy than the guillotine which henceforth seems destined to cut off the heads of nobles, priests and all those who, according to the rank which they formerly occupied, had a great influence over the common people.

REVIEW QUESTIONS

1. Compare and contrast Maximilien Robespierre's vision of the Republic of Virtue with the ideals of the Declaration of the Rights of Man and of the Citizen in Section 3. What did Robespierre mean by virtue?
2. On what grounds did Robespierre justify terror?
3. Like medieval inquisitors, Robespierre regarded people with different views not as opponents but as sinners. Discuss this statement.
4. How did the Jacobins justify their ruthless policies in the Vendée?

---

6 Demands for Economic Justice

The reformers who came to power in 1789 sought to fashion a constitutional government that limited the monarch's power, protected individual rights, created a more rational system of administration and justice, and ended the special privileges of the aristocracy and the clergy. Alleviating the hardships of the poor was not among their concerns.

As the Revolution proceeded, the *sans-culottes*—small shopkeepers, artisans, and wage earners—demanded that the government address their calamitous poverty by increasing wages, setting price controls on foodstuffs, and punishing food speculators and profiteers. To prevent extremes of wealth and poverty, they insisted that the government should raise taxes for the wealthy and redistribute land. The various revolutionary governments rejected most of these demands, which they regarded as a radical interference with private property.

Gracchus Babeuf
CONSPIRACY OF THE EQUALS

The moderate bourgeoisie consolidated their control of the French government in 1795 under a new constitution, which established a five-member Directory with executive power, but the discontent of the poor was not answered. In 1796, the Directory crushed a conspiracy to overthrow the government headed by François-Noel (better known as Gracchus[1]) Babeuf (1760–1797). As editor of the

---

[1]In 1795 he took the name Gracchus after the ancient Roman social reformer.

journal *Tribun du peuple,* which commenced publication in 1794, Babeuf had argued for a new social order in which private property would be abolished. Only such a radical measure, he declared, would end the tyranny of the rich over the poor. In 1796, Babeuf and his colleagues were arrested for conspiring to reestablish the Constitution of 1793, which mandated universal male suffrage, and freedom of thought, and to overthrow the Directory; they regarded these measures as the first step in the creation of a social order based on economic equality. Babeuf conducted his own defense, using the trial as a forum to convey his political philosophy. Babeuf and one other defendant were sentenced to death; the others were either acquitted or deported.

Babeuf's Conspiracy of the Equals is important for two reasons. First, Babeuf's passionate attack on mistreatment of the poor and his call for the abolition of private property presage nineteenth-century socialist movements. Second, the organization of a secret society conspiring to overthrow the government heralds revolutionary movements in the nineteenth and twentieth centuries.

Following are excerpts from Babeuf's defense at his trial.

The aim of the Revolution, furthermore, is to realize the happiness of the majority. If, therefore, this aim is not fulfilled, if the people do not succeed in attaining the better life which was the object of their struggle, then the Revolution is not over. There may be those whose only concern is to substitute their own rule for that of monarchy, but it makes no difference what such people say or want. If the Revolution is brought to an end in mid-passage, it will be judged by history as little more than a catalogue of bloody crimes.

With this in mind I strove to make known the nature of the common welfare, which is the purpose of social existence, or the happiness of the greatest number, which is the purpose of the Revolution. I pondered how it could be that at a given time the majority were worse off than they ought to be; and the conclusions that I reached I ventured to set forth in one of the first issues of the *Tribune.* . . .

There are, I wrote, *historical periods during which the final result of oppressive law is the appropriation of the bulk of social wealth by a minority. Social peace, natural when men are happy, then gives way to class war. The masses can no longer find a way to go on living; they see that they possess nothing and that they suffer under the harsh and flinty oppression of a greedy ruling class. The hour strikes for great and*

memorable revolutionary events, already foreseen in the writings of the times, when a general overthrow of the system of private property is inevitable, when the revolt of the poor against the rich becomes a necessity that can no longer be postponed.

I had also observed that the main actors on the revolutionary scene had realized before I did that the goal of the Revolution ought to be to redress the evil wrought by archaic and rotten social institutions, and to promote the happiness of the people. . . .

The prosecution has reproduced a document entitled "Outline of Babeuf's Doctrine." This piece has been the subject of much debate in some of the correspondence connected with this trial; and it has been viewed as the most radical of all subversive doctrines. Let us examine it further.

Nature, we read there, *has endowed every man with an equal right to the use of nature's gifts. The function of society is to defend this equality of right from the unending attacks of those who, in the state of nature, are wicked and strong; and to enhance, by collective action, collective happiness.*

Nature has placed everyone under an obligation to work. None may exempt himself from work without committing an antisocial action. Work and its fruits should be common to all. Oppression exists when one man is ground down by toil and lacks the barest necessaries of life, while another revels in luxury and idleness. It is impossible for anyone, without committing a crime, to appropriate for his own exclusive use the fruits of the earth or of manufacture.

In a truly just social order there are neither rich nor poor. The rich, who refuse to give up their superfluous wealth for the benefit of the poor, are enemies of the people.

None may be permitted to monopolize the cultural resources of society and hence to deprive others of the education essential for their wellbeing. Education is a universal human right.

The purpose of the Revolution is to abolish inequality and to restore the common welfare. The Revolution is not yet at an end, since the wealthy have diverted its fruits, including political power, to their own exclusive use, while the poor in their toil and misery lead a life of actual slavery and count for nothing in the State.

I have pointed out, under cross-examination, that this document did not come from my pen, but that, since it was indeed a statement of the doctrines I had espoused, I gave it my approval and agreed to its being printed and published. This document was, in effect, a faithful summary of the ideas that I had set forth in the various issues of the *Tribune.* . . .

. . . As I shall try to show you, the desire to be of service to mankind has animated all my thinking. This you may see from the frank confession of my political faith, which I consider it my duty to lay before you precisely as I have propagated it. In the *Tribune of the People* I wrote:

. . . If the earth belongs to none and its fruits to all; if private ownership of public wealth is only the result of certain institutions that violate fundamental human rights; then it follows that this private ownership is a usurpation; and it further follows that all that a man takes of the land and its fruits beyond what is necessary for sustenance is theft from society. . . .

All that a citizen lacks for the satisfaction of his various daily needs, he lacks because he has been deprived of a natural property right by the engrossers of the public domain. All that a citizen enjoys beyond what is necessary for the satisfaction of his daily needs he enjoys as a result of a theft from the other members of society. In this way a more or less numerous group of people is deprived of its rightful share in the public domain. . . .

The plea of superior ability and industry is an empty rationalization to mask the machinations of those who conspire against human equality and happiness. It is ridiculous and unfair to lay claim to a higher wage for the man whose work requires more concentrated thought and more mental effort. Such effort in no way expands the capacity of the stomach. No wage can be defended over and above what is necessary for the satisfaction of a person's needs.

The worth of intelligence is only a matter of opinion, and it still remains to be determined if natural, physical strength is not of equal worth. Clever people have set a high value upon the creations of their minds; if the toilers had also had a hand in the ordering if things, they would doubtless have insisted that brawn is entitled to equal consideration with brain and that physical fatigue is no less real than mental fatigue.

If wages are not equalized, the clever and persevering are given a licence to rob and despoil with impunity those less fortunately endowed with natural gifts. In this way the economic equilibrium of society is upset, for nothing has been more conclusively proven than the maxim: a man only succeeds in becoming rich through the spoliation of others.

All our civic institutions, our social relationships, are nothing else but the expression of legalized barbarism and piracy, in which every man cheats and robs his neighbor. In its festering swamp our swindling society generates vice, crime, and misery of every kind. A handful of well-intentioned people band together and wage war on these evils, but their efforts are futile. They can make no headway because they do not tackle the problem at its roots, but apply palliatives based upon the distorted thinking of a sick society.

It is clear from the foregoing that whatever a man possesses over and above his rightful share of the social product has been stolen. It is therefore right and proper to take this wealth back again from those who have wrongfully appropriated it. . . .

. . . Society must be made to operate in such a way that it eradicates once and for all the desire of a man to become richer, or wiser, or more powerful than others.

Putting this more exactly, we must try to bring our fate under control, *try to make the lot of every member of society independent of accidental circumstances, happy or unhappy. We must try to guarantee to each man and his posterity, however numerous, a sufficiency of the means of existence, and nothing more. We must try and close all possible avenues by which a man may acquire more than his fair share of the fruits of toil and the gifts of nature.*

The only way to do this is to organize a communal regime which will suppress private property, set each to work at the skill or job he understands, require each to deposit the fruits of his labor in kind at the common store, and establish an agency for the distribution of basic necessities. This agency will maintain a complete list of people and of supplies, will distribute the latter with scrupulous fairness, and will deliver them to the home of each worker.

A system such as this has been proven practicable by actual experience, for it is used by our twelve armies with their 1,200,000 men. And what is possible on a small scale can also be done on a large one. A regime of this type alone can ensure the general welfare, or, in other words, the permanent happiness of the people—the true and proper object of organized society.

Such a regime, I continued, *will sweep away iron bars, dungeon walls, and bolted doors, trials and disputations, murders, thefts and crimes of every kind; it will sweep away the judges and the judged, the jails and the gibbets—all the torments of body and agony of soul that the injustice of life engenders; it will sweep away enviousness and gnawing greed, pride and deceit, the very catalogue of sins that Man is heir to; it will remove—and how important is this!—the brooding, omnipresent fear that gnaws always and in each of us concerning our fate tomorrow, next month, next year, and in our old age; concerning the fate of our children and of our children's children.*

Such, gentleman of the jury, was the body of truth that I concerned myself with and that I thought to have divined from my study of the ageless book of nature. These were truths that I did no more than discover and make known. I loved humanity; and I was convinced that a social system such as I had conceived alone would ensure the happiness of man. I was eager, therefore, to gain the attention of my fellows, to win them to my way of thinking.

REVIEW QUESTIONS

1. What was Babeuf's conception of a just social order?
2. How did Babeuf extend the ideals of the Enlightenment and the French Revolution?

7 Napoleon: Destroyer and Preserver of the Revolution

In 1799, a group of conspirators that included Napoleon Bonaparte (1769–1821), an ambitious and popular general, staged a successful coup d'état. Within a short time, Napoleon became a one-man ruler, and in 1804 he crowned himself emperor of the French. Under Napoleon's military dictatorship, political freedom (a principal goal of the French Revolution) was suppressed. Nevertheless, Napoleon preserved, strengthened, and spread to other lands many of the Revolution's reforms. He supported religious tolerance, secular education, and access to positions according to ability; he would not restore the privileges of the aristocracy and church.

Napoleon Bonaparte
LEADER, GENERAL, TYRANT, REFORMER

Napoleon was a brilliant military commander who carefully planned each campaign, using speed, deception, and surprise to confuse and demoralize his opponents. By rapid marches, Napoleon would concentrate a superior force against a segment of the enemy's strung-out forces. Recognizing the importance of good morale, he sought to inspire his troops by appealing to their honor, their vanity, and their love of France.

In 1796, Napoleon, then a young officer, was given command of the French army in Italy. In the Italian campaign, he demonstrated a genius for propaganda and psychological warfare, as the following proclamations to his troops indicate.

LEADER AND GENERAL

March 27, 1796

Soldiers, you are naked, ill fed! The Government owes you much; it can give you nothing. Your patience, the courage you display in the midst of these rocks, are admirable; but they procure you no glory, no fame is reflected upon you. I seek to lead you into the most fertile plains in the world. Rich provinces, great cities will be in your power. There you will find honor, glory, and riches. Soldiers of Italy, would you be lacking in courage or constancy?

April 26, 1796

Soldiers:

In a fortnight you have won six victories, taken twenty-one standards, fifty-five pieces of artillery, several strong positions, and conquered the richest part of Piedmont [a region in northern Italy]; you have captured 15,000 prisoners and killed or wounded more than 10,000 men. . . .

. . . You have won battles without cannon, crossed rivers without bridges, made forced marches without shoes, camped without brandy and often without bread. Soldiers of liberty, only republican phalanxes [infantry troops] could

have endured what you have endured. Soldiers, you have our thanks! The grateful *Patrie* [nation] will owe its prosperity to you. . . .

The two armies which but recently attacked you with audacity are fleeing before you in terror; the wicked men who laughed at your misery and rejoiced at the thought of the triumphs of your enemies are confounded and trembling.

But, soldiers, as yet you have done nothing compared with what remains to be done. . . .

. . . Undoubtedly the greatest obstacles have been overcome; but you still have battles to fight, cities to capture, rivers to cross. Is there one among you whose courage is abating? . . . No. . . . All of you are consumed with a desire to extend the glory of the French people; all of you long to humiliate those arrogant kings who dare to contemplate placing us in fetters; all of you desire to dictate a glorious peace, one which will indemnify the *Patrie* for the immense sacrifices it has made; all of you wish to be able to say with pride as you return to your villages, "I was with the victorious army of Italy!"

Friends, I promise you this conquest; but there is one condition you must swear to fulfill—to respect the people whom you liberate, to repress the horrible pillaging committed by scoundrels incited by our enemies. Otherwise you would not be the liberators of the people; you would be their scourge. . . . Plunderers will be shot without mercy; already, several have been. . . .

Peoples of Italy, the French army comes to break your chains; the French people is the friend of all peoples; approach it with confidence; your property, your religion, and your customs will be respected.

We are waging war as generous enemies, and we wish only to crush the tyrants who enslave you.

The following passages from Napoleon's diary shed light on his generalship, ambition, and leadership qualities.

1800

What a thing is imagination! Here are men who don't know me, who have never seen me, but who only knew of me, and they are moved by my presence, they would do anything for me! And this same incident arises in all centuries and in all countries! Such is fanaticism! Yes, imagination rules the world. The defect of our modern institutions is that they do not speak to the imagination. By that alone can man be governed; without it he is but a brute.

1800

The impact of an army, like the total of mechanical coefficients, is equal to the mass multiplied by the velocity.

A battle is a dramatic action which has its beginning, its middle, and its conclusion. The result of a battle depends on the instantaneous flash of an idea. When you are about to give battle concentrate all your strength, neglect nothing; a battalion often decides the day.

In warfare every opportunity must be seized; for fortune is a woman: if you miss her to-day, you need not expect to find her to-morrow.

There is nothing in the military profession I cannot do for myself. If there is no one to make gunpowder, I know how to make it; gun carriages, I know how to construct them; if it is founding a cannon, I know that; or if the details of tactics must be taught, I can teach them.

The presence of a general is necessary: he is the head, he is the all in all of an army. It was not the Roman army conquered Gaul, but Cæsar; it was not the Carthaginians made the armies of the Republic tremble at the very gates of Rome, but Hannibal; it was not the Macedonian army marched to the Indus [River], but Alexander; . . . it was not the Prussian army that defended Prussia during seven years against the three strongest Powers of Europe, but Frederick the Great.

Concentration of forces, activity, activity with the firm resolve to die gloriously: these are the three great principles of the military art that have always made fortune favourable in all my operations. Death is nothing; but to live defeated and ingloriously, is to die every day.

I am a soldier, because that is the special faculty I was born with; that is my life, my habit. I have commanded wherever I have been. I commanded, when twenty-three years old, at the siege of Toulon; . . . I carried the soldiers of the army of Italy with me as soon as I appeared among them; I was born that way. . . .

It was by becoming a Catholic that I pacified the Vendée [region in western France], and a [Muslim] that I established myself in Egypt; it was by becoming ultramontane[1] that I won over public opinion in Italy. If I ruled a people of Jews, I would rebuild the temple of Solomon! Paradise is a central spot whither the souls of men proceed along different roads; every sect has a road of its own. . . .

1802

My power proceeds from my reputation, and my reputation from the victories I have won. My power would fall if I were not to support it with more glory and more victories. Conquest has made me what I am; only conquest can maintain me. . . .

---

[1]Favoring the pope over competing authorities.

1804

My mistress is power; I have done too much to conquer her to let her be snatched away from me. Although it may be said that power came to me of its own accord, yet I know what labour, what sleepless nights, what scheming, it has involved. . . .

1809

Again I repeat that in war morale and opinion are half the battle. The art of the great captain has always been to make his troops appear very numerous to the enemy, and the enemy's very few to his own. So that to-day, in spite of the long time we have spent in Germany, the enemy do not know my real strength. We are constantly striving to magnify our numbers. Far from confessing that I had only 100,000 men at Wagram [French victory over Austria in 1809] I am constantly suggesting that I had 220,000. In my Italian campaigns, in which I had only a handful of troops, I always exaggerated my numbers. It served my purpose, and has not lessened my glory. My generals and practised soldiers could always perceive, after the event, all the skilfulness of my operations, even that of having exaggerated the numbers of my troops.

In several ways, Napoleon anticipated the strategies of twentieth-century dictators. He concentrated power in his own hands, suppressed opposition, and sought to mold public opinion by controlling the press and education. The following Imperial Catechism of 1806, which schoolchildren were required to memorize and recite, is a pointed example of Napoleonic indoctrination.

TYRANT

Lesson VII. Continuation of the Fourth Commandment.

Q. What are the duties of Christians with respect to the princes who govern them, and what in particular are our duties towards Napoleon I, our Emperor?

A. Christians owe to the princes who govern them, and we owe in particular to Napoleon I, our Emperor, *love, respect, obedience, fidelity, military service* and the tributes laid for the preservation and defence of the Empire and of his throne; we also owe to him fervent prayers for his safety and the spiritual and temporal prosperity of the state.

Q. Why are we bound to all these duties towards our Emperor?

A. First of all, because God, who creates empires and distributes them according to His will, in loading our Emperor with gifts, both in peace and in war, has established him as our sovereign and has made him the minister of His power and His image upon the earth. *To honor and to serve our Emperor is then to honor and to serve God himself.* Secondly, because our Lord Jesus Christ by His doctrine as well as by His example, has Himself taught us what we owe to our sovereign: He was born the subject of Caesar Augustus;[2] He paid the prescribed impost; and just as He ordered to render to God that which belongs to God, so He ordered to render to Caesar that which belongs to Caesar.

Q. Are there not particular reasons which ought to attach us more strongly to Napoleon I, our Emperor?

A. Yes; for it is he whom God has raised up under difficult circumstances to re-establish the public worship of the holy religion of our fathers and to be the protector of it. He has restored and preserved public order by his profound and active wisdom; he defends the state by his powerful arm; he has become the anointed of the Lord through the consecration which he received from the sovereign pontiff, head of the universal church.

Q. What ought to be thought of those who may be lacking in their duty towards our Emperor?

---

[2]Caesar Augustus (27 B.C.–A.D. 14) was the Roman emperor at the time that Jesus was born.

A. According to the apostle Saint Paul, they would be resisting the order established by God himself and would render themselves *worthy of eternal damnation.*

Q. Will the duties which are required of us towards our Emperor be equally binding with respect to his lawful successors in the order established by the constitutions of the Empire?

A. Yes, without doubt; for we read in the holy scriptures, that God, Lord of heaven and earth, by an order of His supreme will and through His providence, gives empires not only to one person in particular, but also to his family.

In the following letter (April 22, 1805) to Joseph Fouché, minister of police, Napoleon reveals his intention to regulate public opinion.

Repress the journals a little; make them produce wholesome articles. I want you to write to the editors of the . . . newspapers that are most widely read in order to let them know that the time is not far away when, seeing that they are no longer of service to me, I shall suppress them along with all the others. . . . Tell them that the . . . Revolution is over, and that there is now only one party in France; that I shall never allow the newspapers to say anything contrary to my interests; that they may publish a few little articles with just a bit of poison in them, but that one fine day somebody will shut their mouths.

With varying degrees of success, Napoleon's administrators in conquered lands provided positions based on talent, equalized taxes, and abolished serfdom and the courts of the nobility. They promoted freedom of religion, fought clerical interference with secular authority, and promoted secular education. By undermining the power of European clergy and aristocrats, Napoleon weakened the Old Regime irreparably in much of Europe. A letter from Napoleon to his brother Jérôme, King of Westphalia, illustrates Napoleon's desire for enlightened rule.

REFORMER

Fontainebleau, November 15, 1807
To Jérôme Napoléon, King of Westphalia

I enclose the Constitution for your Kingdom. It embodies the conditions on which I renounce all my rights of conquest, and all the claims I have acquired over your state. You must faithfully observe it. I am concerned for the happiness of your subjects, not only as it affects your reputation, and my own, but also for its influence on the whole European situation. Don't listen to those who say that your subjects are so accustomed to slavery that they will feel no gratitude for the benefits you give them. There is more intelligence in the Kingdom of Westphalia than they would have you believe; and your throne will never be firmly established except upon the trust and affection of the common people. What German opinion impatiently demands is that men of no rank, but of marked ability, shall have an equal claim upon your favour and your employment, and that every trace of serfdom, or of a feudal hierarchy between the sovereign and the lowest class of his subjects, shall be done away. The benefits of the Code Napoléon [legal code introduced by Napoleon], public trial, and the introduction of juries, will be the leading features of your government. And to tell you the truth, I count more upon their effects, for the extension and consolidation of your rule, than upon the most resounding victories. I want your subjects to enjoy a degree of liberty, equality, and prosperity hitherto unknown to the German people. I want this liberal regime to produce, one way or another, changes which will be of the utmost benefit to the system of the Confederation, and to the strength of your monarchy. Such a method of government will be a stronger barrier between you and Prussia than the Elbe [River], the fortresses, and the protection of France. What people will want to return under the arbitrary Prussian rule, once it has tasted the benefits of a wise and liberal administration? In Germany, as in France, Italy, and Spain, people long for equality and liberalism. I have been managing the affairs of Europe long enough now to know that the burden of the privileged classes was resented everywhere. Rule constitutionally. Even if reason, and the enlightenment of the age, were not sufficient cause, it would be good policy for one in your position; and you will find that the backing of public opinion gives you a great natural advantage over the absolute Kings who are your neighbours.

REVIEW QUESTIONS

1. In his proclamations how did Napoleon Bonaparte try to raise the morale of his troops?
2. How did Napoleon use propaganda to achieve his goals?
3. For what purpose was religious authority cited in the catechism of 1806? What would Machiavelli (see page 10) have thought of this device?
4. How seriously did Napoleon adhere to the ideals of the Enlightenment and French Revolution? Show how Napoleon spread the reforms of the French Revolution.

CHAPTER 5
The Industrial Revolution

LAMBETH GASWORKS. Gustave Doré, 1872. This engraving shows the harsh conditions within industry during the latter half of the nineteenth century. At the time of this scene, most of the lighting in major cities like London was provided by gas. (*Lambeth Gasworks, from 'London, a Pilgrimage', written by William Blanchard Jerrold (1826–84), pub. 1872 (engraving), Dore, Gustave (1832–83) (after) /© Central Saint Martins College of Art and Design, London /The Bridgeman Art Library*)

In the last part of the eighteenth century, as a revolution for liberty and equality swept across France and sent shock waves across Europe, a different kind of revolution, a revolution in industry, was transforming life in Great Britain. In the nineteenth century, the Industrial Revolution spread to the United States and to the European continent. Today, it encompasses virtually the entire world; everywhere the drive to substitute technology for human labor continues at a rapid pace.

After 1760, dramatic changes occurred in Britain in the way goods were produced and labor organized. New forms of power, particularly steam, replaced animal strength and human muscle. Better ways of obtaining and using raw materials were discovered, and a new form of organizing production and workers—the factory—came into common use. In the nineteenth century, technology moved from triumph to triumph with a momentum unprecedented in human history. The resulting explosion in economic production and productivity transformed society with breathtaking speed.

Rapid industrialization caused hardships for the new class of industrial workers, many of them recent arrivals from the countryside. Arduous and monotonous, factory labor was geared to the strict discipline of the clock, the machine, and the production schedule. Employment was never secure. Sick workers received no pay and were often fired; aged workers suffered pay cuts or lost their jobs. During business slumps, employers lowered wages with impunity, and laid-off workers had nowhere to turn for assistance. Because factory owners did not consider safety an important concern, accidents were frequent. Yet the Industrial Revolution was also a great force for human betterment. Ultimately it raised the standard of living, even for the lowest classes, lengthened life expectancy, and provided more leisure time and more possibilities for people to fulfill their potential.

The Industrial Revolution dramatically altered political and social life at all levels, but especially for the middle class, whose engagement in capitalist ventures brought greater political power and social recognition. During the course of the nineteenth century, the bourgeoisie came to hold many of the highest offices in Western European states, continuing a trend that had been fostered by the French Revolution.

Cities grew in size, number, and importance. Municipal authorities were unable to cope with the rapid pace of urbanization, and without adequate housing, sanitation, or recreational facilities, the exploding urban centers were another source of working-class misery. In pre-industrial Britain, most people had lived in small villages. They knew where their roots were; relatives, friends, and the village church gave them a sense of belonging. The industrial centers separated people from nature and from their places of origin, shattering traditional ways of life that had given men and women a sense of security.

The plight of the working class created a demand for reform, but the British government, committed to laissez-faire economic principles that militated against state involvement, was slow to act. In the last part of the nineteenth century, however, the development of labor unions, the rising political voice of the working class, and the growing recognition that the problems created by industrialization required government intervention speeded up the pace of reform. Rejecting the road of reform, Karl Marx called for a working-class revolution that would destroy the capitalist system.

1 Early Industrialization

Several factors help to explain why the Industrial Revolution began in Great Britain. That country had an abundant labor supply, large deposits of coal and iron ore, and capital available for investing in new industries. A large domestic middle class and overseas colonies provided markets for manufactured goods. Colonies were also a source for raw materials, particularly cotton for the textile industry. The Scientific Revolution and an enthusiasm for engineering fostered a spirit of curiosity and inventiveness. Britain had enterprising and daring entrepreneurs who organized new businesses and discovered new methods of production.

Edward Baines
BRITAIN'S INDUSTRIAL ADVANTAGES AND THE FACTORY SYSTEM

In 1835, Edward Baines (1800–1890), an early student of industrialization, wrote *The History of the Cotton Manufacture in Great Britain*—about one of the leading industries in the early days of the Industrial Revolution. In the passages that follow, Baines discusses the reasons for Britain's industrial transformation and the advantages of the factory system.

Three things may be regarded as of primary importance for the successful prosecution of manufactures, namely, water-power, fuel, and iron. Wherever these exist in combination, and where they are abundant and cheap, machinery may be manufactured and put in motion at small cost; and most of the processes of making and finishing cloth, whether chemical or mechanical, depending, as they do, mainly on the two great agents of water and heat, may likewise be performed with advantage.

. . . A great number of streams . . . furnish water-power adequate to turn many hundred mills: they afford the element of water, indispensable for scouring, bleaching, printing, dyeing, and other processes of manufacture: and when collected in their larger channels, or employed to feed canals, they supply a superior inland navigation, so important for the transit of raw materials and merchandise.

Not less important for manufactures than the copious supply of good water, is the great abundance of coal. . . . This mineral fuel animates the thousand arms of the steam-engine, and furnishes the most powerful agent in all chemical and mechanical operations.

In mentioning the advantages which Lancashire [the major cotton manufacturing area] possesses as a seat of manufactures, we must not omit its ready communication with the sea by means of its well-situated port, Liverpool, through the medium of which it receives, from Ireland, a large proportion of the food that supports its population, and whose commerce brings from distant shores the raw materials of its manufactures, and again distributes them, converted into useful and elegant clothing, amongst all the nations of the earth. Through the same means a plentiful supply of timber is obtained, so needful for building purposes.

To the above natural advantages, we must add, the acquired advantage of a canal communication, which ramifies itself through all the populous parts of this country, and connects it with the inland counties, the seats of other flourishing manufactures, and the sources whence iron, lime, salt, stone, and other articles in which Lancashire is deficient, are obtained. By this means Lancashire, being already possessed of the primary requisites for manufactures, is enabled, at a very small expense, to command things of secondary importance, and to appropriate to its use the natural advantages of the whole kingdom. The canals, having been accomplished by individual enterprise, not by national funds, were constructed to supply a want already existing: they were not, therefore, original sources of the manufactures, but have extended together with them, and are to be considered as having essentially aided and accelerated that prosperity from whose beginnings they themselves arose. The recent introduction of railways will have a great effect in making the operations of trade more intensely active, and perfecting the division of labour,

already carried to so high a point. By the railway and the locomotive engine, the extremities of the land will, for every beneficial purpose, be united.

In comparing the advantages of England for manufactures with those of other countries, we can by no means overlook the excellent commercial position of the country—intermediate between the north and south of Europe; and its insular situation, which, combined with the command of the seas, secures our territory from invasion or annoyance. The German ocean, the Baltic, and the Mediterranean are the regular highways for our ships; and our western ports command an unobstructed passage to the Atlantic, and to every quarter of the world.

A temperate climate, and a hardy race of men, have also greatly contributed to promote the manufacturing industry of England.

The political and moral advantages of this country, as a seat of manufactures, are not less remarkable than its physical advantages. The arts are the daughters of peace and liberty. In no country have these blessings been enjoyed in so high a degree, or for so long a continuance, as in England. Under the reign of just laws, personal liberty and property have been secure; mercantile enterprise has been allowed to reap its reward; capital has accumulated in safety; the workman has "gone forth to his work and to his labour until the evening;" and, thus protected and favoured, the manufacturing prosperity of the country has struck its roots deep, and spread forth its branches to the ends of the earth.

England has also gained by the calamities of other countries, and the intolerance of other governments. At different periods, the Flemish and French protestants, expelled from their native lands, have taken refuge in England, and have repaid the protection given them by practising and teaching branches of industry, in which the English were then less expert than their neighbours. The wars which have at different times desolated the rest of Europe, and especially those which followed the French revolution, (when mechanical invention was producing the most wonderful effects in England) checked the progress of manufacturing improvement on the continent, and left England for many years without a competitor. At the same time, the English navy held the sovereignty of the ocean, and under its protection the commerce of this country extended beyond all former bounds, and established a firm connexion between the manufacturers of Lancashire and their customers in the most distant lands.

When the natural, political, and adventitious causes, thus enumerated, are viewed together, it cannnot be [a] matter of surprise that England has obtained a preeminence over the rest of the world in manufactures.

A crucial feature of the Industrial Revolution was a new production system—the making of goods in factories. By bringing all the operations of manufacturing under one roof, industrialists made the process of production more efficient. Baines describes the factory system's advantages over former methods.

. . . Hitherto the cotton manufacture had been carried on almost entirely in the houses of the workmen: the hand or stock cards,[1] the spinning wheel, and the loom required no larger apartment than that of a cottage. A spinning jenny[2] of small size might also be used in a cottage, and in many instances was so used: when the number of spindles was considerably increased, adjacent work-shops were used. But the water-frame, the carding engine, and the other machines which [Richard] Arkwright brought out in a finished state, required both more space than could be found in a cottage,

and more power than could be applied by the human arm. Their weight also rendered it necessary to place them in strongly-built mills, and they could not be advantageously turned by any power then known but that of water.

The use of machinery was accompanied by a greater division of labour than existed in the primitive state of the manufacture; the material went through many more processes; and of course the loss of time and the risk of waste would have been much increased, if its removal from house to house at every stage of the manufacture had been necessary. It became obvious that there were several important advantages in carrying on the numerous operations of an extensive manufacture in the same building. Where water power was required, it was economical to build one mill, and put up one water-wheel, rather than several. This arrangement also enabled the master spinner himself to superintend every stage of the manufacture: it gave him a greater security against the wasteful or fraudulent consumption of the material: it saved time in the transference of the work from hand to hand: and it prevented the extreme inconvenience which would have resulted from the failure of one class of workmen to perform their part, when several other classes of workmen were dependent upon them. Another circumstance which made it advantageous to have a large number of machines in one manufactory was, that mechanics must be employed on the spot, to construct and repair the machinery, and that their time could not be fully occupied with only a few machines.

All these considerations drove the cotton spinners to that important change in the economy of English manufactures, the introduction of the factory system; and when that system had once been adopted, such were its pecuniary advantages, that mercantile competition would have rendered it impossible, even had it been desirable, to abandon it.

---

[1]Prior to spinning, raw fibers had to be carded with a brushlike tool that cleaned and separated them.
[2]The spinning jenny, which was hand-powered, was the first machine that spun fiber onto multiple spindles at the same time; that is, it produced more thread or yarn in less time than the single-thread spinning wheel.

Adam Smith
THE DIVISION OF LABOR

Baines's emphasis on the division of labor in the expanding use of machinery can be traced to Adam Smith, who in the eighteenth century pioneered the study of economics. Adam Smith (1723–1790) was a bright and thoughtful academic who had attended Glasgow University in his native Scotland and then Oxford University in England before being appointed professor of logic at Glasgow at age twenty-eight and professor of moral philosophy a year later. After some years of travel on the Continent, Smith wrote over a span of years his masterpiece; *An Inquiry into the Nature and Causes of the Wealth of Nations* (see also next section), published in 1776, made him instantly famous. He began *The Wealth of Nations* by analyzing the benefits of the division of labor—the system in which each worker performs a single set task or a single step in the manufacturing process.

The greatest improvement in the productive powers of Labour, and the greater skill, dexterity, and judgment with which it is anywhere directed, or applied, seem to have been the effects of the division of labour. . . .

This great increase of the quantity of work, which, in consequence of the division of labour, the same number of people are capable of performing, is owing to three different circumstances; first, to the increase of dexterity in every particular workman; secondly, to the saving of the time which is commonly lost in passing from one species of work to another; and lastly, to the invention of a great number of machines which facilitate and abridge labour, and enable one man to do the work of many. . . .

To take an example, therefore, from a very trifling manufacture; but one in which the division of labour has been very often taken notice of, the trade of the pin-maker; a workman not educated to this business (which the division of labour has rendered a distinct trade), nor acquainted with the use of the machinery employed in it (to the invention of which the same division of labour has probably given occasion), could scarce, perhaps, with his utmost

industry, make one pin in a day, and certainly could not make twenty. But in the way in which this business is now carried on, not only the whole work is a peculiar trade, but it is divided into a number of branches, of which the greater part are likewise peculiar trades. One man draws out the wire, another straightens it, a third cuts it, a fourth points it, a fifth grinds it at the top for receiving the head: to make the head requires two or three distinct operations; to put it on is a peculiar business; to whiten the pins is another; it is even a trade by itself to put them into the paper; and the important business of making a pin is, in this manner, divided into about eighteen distinct operations, which, in some manufactories, are all performed by distinct hands, though in others the same man will sometimes perform two or three of them. I have seen a small manufactory of this kind where ten men only were employed, and where some of them consequently performed two or three distinct operations. But though they were very poor [craftsmen], and therefore but indifferently accommodated with the necessary machinery, they could, when they exerted themselves, make among them about twelve pounds of pins in a day. There are in a pound upwards of four thousand pins of a middling size. Those ten persons, therefore, could make among them upwards of forty-eight thousand pins in a day. Each person, therefore, making a tenth part of forty-eight thousand pins, might be considered as making four thousand eight hundred pins in a day. But if they had all wrought separately and independently, and without any of them having been educated to this peculiar business, they certainly could not each of them have made twenty, perhaps not one pin in a day; that is, certainly, not the two hundred and fortieth, perhaps not the four thousand eight hundredth part of what they are at present capable of performing, in consequence of a proper division and combination of their different operations. . . .

REVIEW QUESTIONS

1. Apart from its natural resources, what other assets for industrial development did England possess?
2. What were the factory system's advantages over the domestic system of production?
3. How, according to Adam Smith, did the division of labor lead to increased productivity?

---

2   The New Science of Political Economy

The new spirit of scientific inquiry manifest in the seventeenth and eighteenth centuries extended also into the economic field, creating the new science of political economy. Its pioneer was Adam Smith, author of the classic book *The Wealth of Nations* (see also previous section). Smith was an optimist, in favor of leaving individuals' economic activities to their own devices. For that reason he condemned government interference in the economy—so common in his day under the protectionist government's mercantilism policy, which sought to increase the nation's wealth by expanding exports while minimizing imports. The "invisible hand," which according to Smith turned individual gain into social advantage, also favored free trade among nations, based on an international division of labor.

Adam Smith's optimistic assumptions were soon called into question by Thomas Robert Malthus (1766–1834). A Church of England clergyman and professor of history and political economy at a small college run by the East India Company, Malthus gave the study of political economy not only a moral but also a pessimistic twist, for he stressed the immutable poverty of nations. He contributed two books to the science of political economy. The first, *An Essay on the Principle of Population, as It Affects the Future Improvement of Society*, was published in 1798. It was followed in 1803 by a second and enlarged edition entitled *An Essay on the Principle of Population, or, a View of Its Past and Present Effects on Human Happiness.* In these works Malthus argued that population growth was the true reason for the misery of the poor.

ADAM SMITH
THE WEALTH OF NATIONS

The Wealth of Nations carries the important message of *laissez faire*, which means that the government should intervene as little as possible in economic affairs and leave the market to its own devices. It advocates the liberation of economic production from all limiting regulation in order to benefit "the people and the sovereign," not only in Great Britain but in the community of countries. Admittedly, in his advocacy of free trade Smith made allowance for the national interest, justifying "certain public works and certain public institutions," including the government and the state. He defended, for instance, the Navigation Acts, which stipulated that goods brought from its overseas colonies into England be carried in British ships. Neither did he want to ruin established industries by introducing free trade too suddenly. Adam Smith was an eighteenth-century cosmopolitan who viewed political economy as an international system. His preference was clearly for economic cooperation among nations as a source of peace. In the passage that follows, Smith argues that economic activity unrestricted by government best serves the individual and society.

Every individual is continually exerting himself to find out the most advantageous employment for whatever capital he can command. It is his own advantage, indeed, and not that of the society, which he has in view. But the study of his own advantage, naturally, or rather necessarily, leads him to prefer that employment which is most advantageous to the society. . . .

. . . As every individual, therefore, endeavours as much as he can both to employ his capital in the support of domestic industry, and so to direct that industry that its produce may be of the greatest value, every individual necessarily labours to render the annual revenue of the society as great as he can. He generally, indeed, neither intends to promote the public interest, nor knows how much he is promoting it. By preferring the support of domestic to that of foreign industry, he intends only his own security; and by directing that industry in such a manner as its produce may be of the greatest value, he intends only his own gain, and he is in this, as in many other cases, led by an invisible hand to promote an end which was no part of his intention. Nor is it always the worse for the society that it was no part of it. By pursuing his own interest he frequently promotes that of the society more effectually than when he really intends to promote it. I have never known much good done by those who affected to trade for the public good. . . .

. . . The statesman who should attempt to direct private people in what manner they ought to employ their capitals, would not only load himself with a most unnecessary attention, but assume an authority which could safely be trusted, not only to no single person, but to no council or senate whatever, and which would nowhere be so dangerous as in the hands of a man who had folly and presumption enough to fancy himself fit to exercise it. . . .

It is thus that every system which endeavours, either by extraordinary encouragements to draw towards a particular species of industry a greater share of the capital of the society than would naturally go to it, or, by extraordinary restraints, force from a particular species of industry some share of the capital which would otherwise be employed in it, is in reality subversive to the great purpose which it means to promote. It retards, instead of accelerating, the progress of the society towards real wealth and greatness; and diminishes, instead of increasing, the real value of the annual produce of its land and labour.

All systems either of preference or of restraint, therefore, being thus completely taken away, the obvious and simple system of natural liberty establishes itself of its own accord. Every man, as long as he does not violate the laws of justice, is left perfectly free to pursue his own interest his own way, and to bring both his industry and capital into competition with those of any other man, or order of men. The sovereign is completely discharged from a duty, in the attempting to perform which he must always be exposed to innumerable delusions, and for the proper performance of which no human wisdom or knowledge could ever be sufficient; the duty of superintending the industry of private people, and of directing it towards the employments most suitable to the interest of the society. According to the system of natural liberty, the sovereign has only three duties to attend to; three duties of great importance, indeed, but plain and intelligible to common understandings: first, the duty of protecting the society from the violence and invasion of other independent societies: secondly, the duty of protecting, as far as possible, every member of the society from the injustice or oppression of every other member of it, or the duty of establishing an exact administration of justice; and, thirdly, the duty of erecting and maintaining certain public works and certain public institutions which it can never be for the interest of any individual, or small number of individuals, to erect and maintain; because the profit could never repay the expense to any individual or small number of individuals, though it may frequently do much more than repay it to a great society.

Thomas R. Malthus
ON THE PRINCIPLE OF POPULATION

Malthus assumed that population tended forever to outgrow the resources needed to sustain it. The balance between population and its life-sustaining resources was elementally maintained, he gloomily argued, by famine, war, and other fatal calamities. As a clergyman, he believed in sexual abstinence as the means of limiting population growth. He also saw little need to better the condition of the poor, whom he considered the most licentious part of the population, because he believed that they would then breed faster and, by upsetting the population/resource balance, bring misery to all. This view—that poverty was an iron law of nature—buttressed supporters of strict laissez faire who opposed government action to aid the poor.

POPULATION'S EFFECTS ON SOCIETY

I have read some of the speculations on the perfectibility of man and of society with great pleasure. I have been warmed and delighted with the enchanting picture which they hold forth. I ardently wish for such happy improvements. But I see great and, to my understanding, unconquerable difficulties in the way to them. These difficulties it is my present purpose to state, declaring, at the same time, that so far from exulting in them, as a cause of triumphing over the friends of innovation, nothing would give me greater pleasure than to see them completely removed. . . .

[These difficulties are]

First, That food is necessary to the existence of man.

Secondly, That the passion between the sexes is necessary and will remain nearly in its present state.

These two laws, ever since we have had any knowledge of mankind, appear to have been fixed laws of our nature; and as we have not hitherto seen any alteration in them, we have no right to conclude that they will ever cease to be what they are now, without an immediate act of power in that Being who first arranged the system of the universe, and for the advantage of His creatures, still executes, according to fixed laws, all its various operations. . . .

Assuming, then, my postulata as granted, I say that the power of population is indefinitely greater than the power in the earth to produce subsistence for man.

Population, when unchecked, increases in a geometrical ratio. Subsistence only increases in an arithmetical ratio. A slight acquaintance with numbers will show the immensity of the first power in comparison of the second.

By that law of our nature which makes food necessary to the life of man, the effects of these two unequal powers must be kept equal.

This implies a strong and constantly operating check on population from the difficulty of subsistence. This difficulty must fall somewhere and must necessarily be severely felt by a large portion of mankind. . . .

This natural inequality of the two powers of population and of production in the earth, and that great law of our nature which must constantly keep their efforts equal, form the great difficulty that to me appears insurmountable in the way to perfectibility of society. . . .

Consequently, if the premises are just, the argument is conclusive against the perfectibility of the mass of mankind.

POPULATION'S EFFECTS ON HUMAN HAPPINESS

The ultimate check to population appears then to be a want of food, arising necessarily from the different ratios according to which population and food increase. But this ultimate check is never the immediate check, except in cases of actual famine.

The immediate check may be stated to consist in all those customs, and all those diseases, which seem to be generated by a scarcity of the means of subsistence; and all those causes, independent of this scarcity, which tend prematurely to weaken and destroy the human frame.

These checks to population, which are constantly operating with more or less force in every society, and keep down the number to the level of the means of subsistence, may be classed under two general heads—the preventive and the positive checks.

The preventive check, as far as it is voluntary, is peculiar to man, and arises from that distinctive superiority in his reasoning faculties which enables him to calculate distant consequences. Man cannot look around him and see the distress which frequently presses upon those who have large families; he cannot contemplate his present possessions or earnings which he now nearly consumes himself, and calculate the amount of each share, when with a little addition they must be divided, perhaps, among seven or eight, without feeling a doubt whether, if he follow the bent of his inclinations, he may be able to support the offspring which he will probably bring into the world. . . .

The conditions are calculated to prevent, and certainly do prevent, a great number of persons in all civilized nations from pursuing the dictate of nature in an early attachment to one woman. . . .

The positive checks to population are extremely various, and include every cause, whether arising from vice or misery, which in any degree contributes to shorten the natural duration of human life. Under this head, therefore, may be enumerated all unwholesome occupations, severe labor and exposure to the seasons, extreme poverty, bad nursing of children, great towns, excesses of all kinds, the whole train of common diseases and epidemics, wars, plague, and famine. . . .

POPULATION AND POVERTY

Almost everything that has been hitherto done for the poor, has tended, as if with solicitous care, to throw a veil of obscurity over this subject and to hide from them the true cause of their poverty. When the wages of labour are hardly sufficient to maintain two children, a man marries and has five or six. He of course finds himself miserably distressed. . . . He accuses his parish. . . . He accuses the avarice of the rich. . . . He accuses the partial and unjust institutions of society. . . . In searching for

objects of accusation, he never [alludes] to the quarter from which all his misfortunes originate. The last person that he would think of accusing is himself. . . .

We cannot justly accuse them (the common people) of improvidence [thriftlessness] and want of industry, till . . . after it has been brought home to their comprehensions, that they are themselves the cause of their own poverty; that the means of redress are in their own hands, and in the hands of no other persons whatever; that the society in which they live and the government which presides over it, are totally without power in this respect; and however ardently they [government] may desire to relieve them, and whatever attempts they may make to do so, they are really and truly unable to execute what they benevolently wish, but unjustly promise.

REVIEW QUESTIONS

1. What did Adam Smith say were the results of a laissez-faire policy?
2. What, according to Smith, were the duties of the sovereign under the system of natural liberty? Do you think there are other duties that should be added?
3. What are the "fixed laws" of human nature according to Thomas Malthus? For Malthus, how did the power of population growth compare with that of the means to increase food?
4. What distinction did Malthus draw between preventive and positive checks to population growth?
5. Why is Malthus considered to have been a pessimist?
6. Do any of Malthus's arguments apply to our world today?

3 The Dark Side of Industrialization

Among the numerous problems caused by rapid industrialization, none aroused greater concern among humanitarians than child labor in factories and mines. In preindustrial times, children had always been part of the labor force, indoors and out, a practice that was continued during the early days of the Industrial Revolution. In the cotton industry, for instance, the proportion of children and adolescents under eighteen was around 40–45 percent of the labor force; in some large firms the proportion was even greater. Employers discovered early that youngsters adapted more easily to machines and factory discipline than did adults, who were used to traditional handicraft routines. Child labor took children away from their parents, undermined family life, and deprived children of schooling. Factory routines dulled their minds, and the long hours spent in often unsanitary environments endangered their health.

Sadler Commission
REPORT ON CHILD LABOR

Due to concern about child labor, in 1832 a parliamentary committee chaired by Michael Thomas Sadler investigated the situation of children employed in British factories. The following testimony is drawn from the records of the Sadler Commission.

May 18, 1832

Michael Thomas Sadler, Esquire, in the chair.
Mr. Matthew Crabtree, called in; and Examined.

What age are you?—Twenty-two.[1]

What is your occupation?—A blanket manufacturer.

Have you ever been employed in a factory?—Yes.

At what age did you first go to work in one?—Eight.

How long did you continue in that occupation?—Four years.

Will you state the hours of labour at the period when you first went to the factory, in ordinary times?—From 6 in the morning to 8 at night.

Fourteen hours?—Yes.

With what intervals for refreshment and rest?—An hour at noon.

Then you had no resting time allowed in which to take your breakfast, or what is in Yorkshire called your "drinking"?—No.

When trade was brisk what were your hours?—From 5 in the morning to 9 in the evening.

Sixteen hours?—Yes.

With what intervals at dinner?—An hour.

How far did you live from the mill?—About two miles.

Was there any time allowed for you to get your breakfast in the mill?—No.

Did you take it before you left home?—Generally.

During those long hours of labour could you be punctual, how did you awake?—I seldom did awake spontaneously. I was most generally awoke or lifted out of bed, sometimes asleep, by my parents.

Were you always in time?—No.

What was the consequence if you had been too late?—I was most commonly beaten.

Severely?—Very severely, I thought.

In whose factory was this?—Messrs. Hague & Cook's, of Dewsbury.

Will you state the effect that those long hours had upon the state of your health and feelings?—I was, when working those long hours, commonly very much fatigued at night, when I left my work, so much so that I sometimes should have slept as I walked if I had not stumbled and started awake again, and so sick often that I could not eat, and what I did eat I vomited.

Did this labour destroy your appetite?—It did.

In what situation were you in that mill?—I was a piecener [see below].

Will you state to the Committee whether pieceing is a very laborious employment

---

[1] In the original source, each paragraph was numbered; this reading includes paragraphs 2481–2519 and 2597–2604.

for children, or not?—It is a very laborious employment. Pieceners are continually running to and fro, and on their feet the whole day.

The duty of the piecener is to take the cardings[2] from one part of the machinery, and to place them on another?—Yes.

So that the labour is not only continual, but it is unabated to the last?—It is unabated to the last.

Do you not think, from your own experience, that the speed of the machinery is so calculated as to demand the utmost exertions of a child, supposing the hours were moderate?—It is as much as they could do at the best; they are always upon the stretch, and it is commonly very difficult to keep up with their work.

State the condition of the children towards the latter part of the day, who have thus to keep up with the machinery?—It is as much as they can do when they are not very much fatigued to keep up with their work, and towards the close of the day, when they come to be more fatigued, they cannot keep up with it very well, and the consequence is that they are beaten to spur them on.

Were you beaten under those circumstances?—Yes.

Frequently?—Very frequently.

And principally at the latter end of the day?—Yes.

And is it your belief that if you had not been so beaten, you should not have got through the work?—I should not if I had not been kept up to it by some means.

Does beating then principally occur at the latter end of the day, when the children are exceedingly fatigued?—It does at the latter end of the day, and in the morning sometimes, when they are very drowsy, and have not got rid of the fatigue of the day before.

What were you beaten with principally?—A strap.

Any thing else?—Yes, a stick sometimes; and there is a kind of roller which runs on the top of the machine called a billy, perhaps two

or three yards in length, and perhaps an inch and a half, or more, in diameter; the circumference would be four or five inches, I cannot speak exactly.

Were you beaten with that instrument?—Yes.

Have you yourself been beaten, and have you seen other children struck severely with that roller?—I have been struck very severely with it myself, so much so as to knock me down, and I have seen other children have their heads broken with it.

You think that it is a general practice to beat the children with the roller?—It is.

You do not think then that you were worse treated than other children in the mill?—No, I was not, perhaps not so bad as some were. . . .

Can you speak as to the effect of this labour in the mills and factories on the morals of the children, as far as you have observed?—As far as I have observed with regard to morals in the mills, there is every thing about them that is disgusting to every one conscious of correct morality.

Do you find that the children, the females especially, are very early demoralized in them?—They are.

Is their language indecent?—Very indecent; and both sexes take great familiarities with each other in the mills, without at all being ashamed of their conduct.

Do you connect their immorality of language and conduct with their excessive labour?—It may be somewhat connected with it, for it is to be observed that most of that goes on towards night, when they begin to be drowsy; it is a kind of stimulus which they use to keep them awake; they say some pert thing or other to keep themselves from drowsiness, and it generally happens to be some obscene language.

Have not a considerable number of the females employed in mills illegitimate children very early in life?—I believe there are; I have known some of them have illegitimate children when they were between 16 and 17 years of age.

How many grown up females had you in the mill?—I cannot speak to the exact number

---

[2]*Cardings* were woolen fibers that had been combed in preparation for spinning and weaving.

that were grown up; perhaps there might be thirty-four or so that worked in the mill at that time.

How many of those had illegitimate children?—A great many of them, eighteen or nineteen of them, I think.

Did they generally marry the men by whom they had the children?—No, it sometimes happens that young women have children by married men, and I have known an instance, a few weeks since, where one of the young women had a child by a married man.

James Phillips Kay
MORAL AND PHYSICAL DISSIPATION

Rapid industrialization produced a drastic change of environment for workers, who moved from the casual, slow-paced English villages and small towns to large, congested, and impersonal industrial cities. The familiar social patterns and cherished values by which preindustrial people had oriented themselves grew weak or disappeared, for these patterns and values clashed with the requirements of the new industrial age. Many people in England, from the highest to the lowest classes, still felt wedded to the old ways and hated the congested industrial centers. In 1832 James Phillips Kay, a physician, published a pamphlet describing the moral and physical condition of the working class in Manchester. His study, excerpted below, provided additional evidence of the painful effects industrialization had on factory workers and their families.

The township of Manchester chiefly consists of dense masses of houses, inhabited by the population engaged in the great manufactories of the cotton trade. . . . Prolonged and exhausting labour, continued from day to day, and from year to year, is not calculated to develop the intellectual or moral faculties of man. The dull routine of a ceaseless drudgery, in which the same mechanical process is incessantly repeated, resembles the torment of Sisyphus[1]—the toil, like the rock, recoils perpetually on the wearied operative. The mind gathers neither stores nor strength from the constant extension and retraction of the same muscles. The intellect slumbers, in supine inertness; but the grosser parts of our nature attain a rank development.

To condemn man to such severity of toil is, in some measure, to cultivate in him the habits of an animal. He becomes reckless. He disregards the distinguishing appetites and habits of his species. He neglects the comforts and delicacies of life. He lives in squalid wretchedness, on meagre food, and expends his superfluous gains in debauchery. . . .

[T]he population. . . . is crowded into one dense mass, in cottages separated by narrow, unpaved, and almost pestilential streets; in an atmosphere loaded with the smoke and exhalations of a large manufacturing city. The operatives are congregated in rooms and workshops during twelve hours in the day, in an enervating, heated atmosphere, which is frequently loaded with dust or filaments of cotton, or impure from constant respiration, or from other causes. They are engaged in an employment which absorbs their attention, and

---

[1]This refers to the myth of Sisyphus, a cruel king of Corinth, who was condemned in Hades to push a big rock up to the top of a hill, only to have it roll back down again.

unremittingly employs their physical energies. They are drudges who watch the movements, and assist the operations, of a mighty material force, which toils with an energy ever unconscious of fatigue. The persevering labour of the operative must rival the mathematical precision, the incessant motion, and the exhaustless power of the machine.

Hence, besides the negative results—the total abstraction of every moral and intellectual stimulus—the absence of variety—banishment from the grateful air and the cheering influences of light, the physical energies are exhausted by incessant toil, and imperfect nutrition. Having been subjected to the prolonged labour of an animal—his physical energy wasted—his mind in supine inaction—the artizan has neither moral dignity nor intellectual nor organic strength to resist the seductions of appetite. His wife and children, too frequently subjected to the same process, are unable to cheer his remaining moments of leisure. Domestic economy is neglected, domestic comforts are unknown. A meal of the coarsest food is prepared with heedless haste, and devoured with equal precipitation. Home has no other relation to him than that of shelter—few pleasures are there—it chiefly presents to him a scene of physical exhaustion, from which he is glad to escape. Himself impotent of all the distinguishing aims of his species, he sinks into sensual sloth, or revels in more degrading licentiousness. His house is ill furnished, uncleanly, often ill ventilated, perhaps damp; his food, from want of forethought and domestic economy, is meagre and innutritious; he is debilitated and hypochondriacal, and falls the victim of dissipation. . . .

The absence of religious feeling, the neglect of all religious ordinances, we conceive to afford substantive evidence of so great a moral degradation of the community, as generally to ensure a concomitant civic debasement. . . .

Friedrich Engels
THE CONDITION OF THE WORKING CLASS IN ENGLAND

The miseries of the industrial towns distressed Friedrich Engels (1820–1895), a well-to-do German intellectual and son of a prosperous German manufacturer. In the early 1840s, Engels moved to Manchester, a great English industrial center, where he eventually established himself in business. In that decade, he also entered into a lifelong collaboration with Karl Marx, the founder of modern socialism (see page 183). Engels yearned for the fellowship and the pleasures of nature that he had experienced in preindustrial Germany. In the new urban centers, he found only alienation and human degradation—even in cosmopolitan London in 1844. The following passage is from his *Condition of the Working Class in England*.

. . . It is only when [a person] has visited the slums of this great city that it dawns upon him that the inhabitants of modern London have had to sacrifice so much that is best in human nature in order to create those wonders of civilisation with which their city teems. The vast majority of Londoners have had to let so many of their potential creative faculties lie dormant, stunted and unused in order that a small, closely-knit group of their fellow citizens could develop to the full the qualities with which nature has endowed them. The restless and noisy activity of the crowded streets is highly distasteful, and it is surely abhorrent to human nature itself. Hundreds of thousands of men and women drawn from all classes and ranks of society pack the streets of London. Are they not all human beings with the same innate characteristics and potentialities? Are they not all equally interested in the pursuit of happiness? And do they not all aim at happiness by following similar methods? Yet they rush past each other as if they had nothing in common. They are tacitly agreed on one thing only—that everyone should keep to the right of the pavement so as not to collide with the stream of people moving in the opposite direction. No one even thinks of sparing a glance for his neighbour in the streets. The more that Londoners are packed into a tiny space, the more repulsive and disgraceful becomes the brutal indifference with which they ignore their neighbours and selfishly concentrate upon their private affairs. We know well enough that this isolation of the individual—this narrow-minded egotism—is everywhere the fundamental principle of modern society. But nowhere is this selfish egotism so blatantly evident as in the frantic bustle of the great city. The disintegration of society into individuals, each guided by his private principles and each pursuing his own aims has been pushed to its furthest limits in London. Here indeed human society has been split into its component atoms.

From this it follows that the social conflict—the war of all against all—is fought in the open. . . . Here men regard their fellows not as human beings, but as pawns in the struggle for existence. Everyone exploits his neighbour with

the result that the stronger tramples the weaker under foot. The strongest of all, a tiny group of capitalists, monopolise everything, while the weakest, who are in the vast majority, succumb to the most abject poverty.

What is true of London, is true also of all the great towns, such as Manchester, Birmingham and Leeds. Everywhere one finds on the one hand the most barbarous indifference and selfish egotism and on the other the most distressing scenes of misery and poverty. . . .

Every great town has one or more slum areas into which the working classes are packed. Sometimes, of course, poverty is to be found hidden away in alleys close to the stately homes of the wealthy. Generally, however, the workers are segregated in separate districts where they struggle through life as best they can out of sight of the more fortunate classes of society. The slums of the English towns have much in common—the worst houses in a town being found in the worst districts. They are generally unplanned wildernesses of one- or two-storied terrace houses built of brick. Wherever possible these have cellars which are also used as dwellings. These little houses of three or four rooms and a kitchen are called cottages, and throughout England, except for some parts of London, are where the working classes normally live. The streets themselves are usually unpaved and full of holes. They are filthy and strewn with animal and vegetable refuse. Since they have neither gutters nor drains the refuse accumulates in stagnant, stinking puddles. Ventilation in the slums is inadequate owing to the hopelessly unplanned nature of these areas. A great many people live huddled together in a very small area, and so it is easy to imagine the nature of the air in these workers' quarters.

REVIEW QUESTIONS

1. According to the testimony given the Sadler Commission, how young were the children employed in the factories? How many hours and at what times of day did they work?
2. What do you think were the reasons for the employment of children from the employers' point of view? From the parents' point of view?
3. What measures were employed in the factories to keep children alert at their tasks?

4. According to James Phillips Kay, what harmful effects did industrialization have on factory workers and their families?
5. According to Friedrich Engels, how had the industrial city caused deterioration in the quality of human relationships? What did he mean by the statement that "human society has been split into its component atoms"?

4 Factory Discipline

For the new industries to succeed, workers needed to adopt the rigorous discipline exercised by the new industrial capitalists themselves. But adapting to labor with machines in factories proved traumatic for the poor, uneducated, and often unruly folk, who previously had toiled on farms and in village workshops and were used to a less demanding pace.

FACTORY RULES

The problem of adapting a preindustrial labor force to the discipline needed for coordinating large numbers of workers in the factory was common to all industrializing countries. The Foundry and Engineering Works of the Royal Overseas Trading Company, in the Moabit section of Berlin, issued the following rules in 1844. The rules aimed at instilling obedience and honesty as well as "good order and harmony" among the factory's workers. The rules not only stressed timekeeping (with appropriate fines for latecomers), but also proper conduct in all aspects of life and work in the factory.

In every large works, and in the co-ordination of any large number of workmen, good order and harmony must be looked upon as the fundamentals of success, and therefore the following rules shall be strictly observed.

Every man employed in the concern . . . shall receive a copy of these rules, so that no one can plead ignorance. Its acceptance shall be deemed to mean consent to submit to its regulations.

(1) The normal working day begins at all seasons at 6 A.M. precisely and ends, after the usual break of half an hour for breakfast, an hour for dinner and half an hour for tea, at 7 P.M., and it shall be strictly observed.

Five minutes before the beginning of the stated hours of work until their actual commencement, a bell shall ring and indicate that every worker employed in the concern has to proceed to his place of work, in order to start as soon as the bell stops.

The doorkeeper shall lock the door punctually at 6 A.M., 8:30 A.M., 1 P.M. and 4:30 P.M.

Workers arriving 2 minutes late shall lose half an hour's wages; whoever is more than 2 minutes late may not start work until after the next break, or at least shall lose his wages until then. Any disputes about the correct time shall be settled by the clock mounted above the gatekeeper's lodge.

These rules are valid both for time- and for piece-workers, and in cases of breaches of these rules, workmen shall be fined in proportion to their earnings. The deductions from the wage shall be entered in the wage-book of the gatekeeper whose duty they are; they shall be unconditionally accepted as it will not be possible to enter into any discussions about them.

(2) When the bell is rung to denote the end of the working day, every workman, both on piece- and on day-wage, shall leave his workshop and the yard, but is not allowed to make preparations for his departure before the bell rings. Every breach of this rule shall lead to a fine of five silver groschen [pennies] to the sick fund. Only those who have obtained special permission by the overseer may stay on in the workshop in order to work.—If a workman has worked beyond the closing bell, he must give his name to the gatekeeper on leaving, on pain of losing his payment for the overtime.

(3) No workman, whether employed by time or piece, may leave before the end of the working day, without having first received permission from the overseer and having given his name to the gatekeeper. Omission of these two actions shall lead to a fine of ten silver groschen payable to the sick fund.

(4) Repeated irregular arrival at work shall lead to dismissal. This shall also apply to those who are found idling by an official or overseer, and refuse to obey their order to resume work.

(5) Entry to the firm's property by any but the designated gateway, and exit by any prohibited route, e.g. by climbing fences or walls, or by crossing the Spree [River], shall be punished by a fine of fifteen silver groschen to the sick fund for the first offences, and dismissal for the second.

(6) No worker may leave his place of work otherwise than for reasons connected with his work.

(7) All conversation with fellow-workers is prohibited; if any worker requires information about his work, he must turn to the overseer, or to the particular fellow-worker designated for the purpose.

(8) Smoking in the workshops or in the yard is prohibited during working hours; anyone caught smoking shall be fined five silver groschen for the sick fund for every such offence.

(9) Every worker is responsible for cleaning up his space in the workshop, and if in doubt, he is to turn to his overseer.—All tools must always be kept in good condition, and must be cleaned after use. This applies particularly to the turner, regarding his lathe.

(10) Natural functions must be performed at the appropriate places, and whoever is found soiling walls, fences, squares, etc., and similarly, whoever is found washing his face and hands in the workshop and not in the places assigned for the purpose, shall be fined five silver groschen for the sick fund.

(11) On completion of his piece of work, every workman must hand it over at once to his foreman or superior, in order to receive a fresh piece of work. Pattern makers must on no account hand over their patterns to the foundry without express order of their supervisors. No workman may take over work from his fellow-workman without instruction to that effect by the foreman.

(12) It goes without saying that all overseers and officials of the firm shall be obeyed without question, and shall be treated with due deference. Disobedience will be punished by dismissal.

(13) Immediate dismissal shall also be the fate of anyone found drunk in any of the workshops.

(14) Untrue allegations against superiors or officials of the concern shall lead to stern reprimand, and may lead to dismissal. The same punishment shall be meted out to those who knowingly allow errors to slip through when supervising or stocktaking.

(15) Every workman is obliged to report to his superiors any acts of dishonesty or embezzlement on the part of his fellow workmen. If he omits to do so, and it is shown after subsequent discovery of a misdemeanour that he knew about it at the time, he shall be liable to be taken to court as an accessory after the fact and the wage due to him shall be retained as punishment. Conversely, anyone denouncing a theft in such a way as to allow conviction of the thief shall receive a reward of two Thaler [dollar equivalent], and, if necessary, his name shall be kept confidential.—Further, the

gatekeeper and the watchman, as well as every official, are entitled to search the baskets, parcels, aprons etc. of the women and children who are taking the dinners into the works, on their departure, as well as search any worker suspected of stealing any article whatever. . . .

(18) Advances shall be granted only to the older workers, and even to them only in exceptional circumstances. As long as he is working by the piece, the workman is entitled merely to his fixed weekly wage as subsistence pay; the extra earnings shall be paid out only on completion of the whole piece contract. If a workman leaves before his piece contract is completed, either of his own free will, or on being dismissed as punishment, or because of illness, the partly completed work shall be valued by the general manager with the help of two overseers, and he will be paid accordingly. There is no appeal against the decision of these experts.

(19) A free copy of these rules is handed to every workman, but whoever loses it and requires a new one, or cannot produce it on leaving, shall be fined 2 ½ silver groschen, payable to the sick fund.

REVIEW QUESTIONS

1. Judging by the Berlin factory rules, what were the differences between preindustrial and industrial work routines?
2. How might these rules have affected the lives of families?

---

5 The Capitalist Ethic

The remarkable advance in industry and material prosperity in the nineteenth century has been hailed as the triumph of the middle class, or bourgeoisie, which included bankers, merchants, factory owners, professionals, and government officials. Unlike the upper classes, which lived on inherited wealth, middle-class people supported themselves by diligent, assiduous activity—what has been called "the capitalist (or bourgeois) ethic." A vigorous spirit of enterprise and the opportunity for men of ability to rise from common origins to riches and fame help explain the growth of industrialism in England. These industrial capitalists adopted the attitude of medieval monks that "idleness is the enemy of the soul," to which they added "time is money."

The ideal of dedicated and responsible hard work directed by an internal rather than an external discipline was seen as the ultimate source of human merit and was widely publicized in the nineteenth century. It encouraged upward mobility among the lower classes and sustained the morale of ambitious middle-class people immersed in the keen competition of private enterprise. By shaping highly motivated private citizens, the capitalist ethic also provided a vital source of national strength.

Samuel Smiles
SELF-HELP AND *THRIFT*

Samuel Smiles (1812–1904) was the most famous messenger of the capitalist ethic at its best. His father, a Scottish papermaker and general merchant, died early, leaving his eleven children to fend for themselves. Samuel was apprenticed to a medical office, in due time becoming a physician in general practice. Turned journalist, he edited the local newspaper in the English city of Leeds, hoping to cure the ills of society by promoting the social and intellectual development of the working classes. Leaving his editorial office, he stepped into railroad management as a friend of George Stephenson, the inventor of the locomotive and promoter of railroads, whose biography Smiles wrote in 1857. Two years later he published *Self-Help*, which had grown out of a lecture to a small mutual-improvement society in which people sought each other's help in bettering their condition. The book was an instant success and was translated into many languages, including Japanese. Having retired after twenty-one years as a railway administrator and prolific author, Smiles suffered a stroke. Recovered, he traveled widely, writing more books about deserving but often unknown achievers. All along, he practiced in his personal life the virtues that he preached. The following selections reveal not only Samuel Smiles's philosophy of life but also the values inspiring the achievements of capitalism.

SELF-HELP

"Heaven helps those who help themselves" is a well-tried maxim, embodying in a small compass the results of vast human experience. The spirit of self-help is the root of all genuine growth in the individual; and, exhibited in the lives of many, it constitutes the true source of national vigour and strength. Help from without is often enfeebling in its effects, but help from within invariably invigorates. Whatever is done *for* men or classes, to a certain extent takes away the stimulus and necessity of doing for themselves; and where men are subjected to over-guidance and over-government, the inevitable tendency is to render them comparatively helpless.

Even the best institutions can give a man no active help. Perhaps the most they can do is, to leave him free to develop himself and improve his individual condition. But in all times men have been prone to believe that their happiness and well-being were to be secured by means of institutions rather than by their own conduct. Hence the value of legislation as an agent in human advancement has usually been much over-estimated. . . . [N]o laws, however stringent, can make the idle industrious, the thriftless provident, or the drunken sober. Such reforms can only be effected by means of individual action, economy, and self-denial; by better habits, rather than by greater rights. . . .

National progress is the sum of individual industry, energy, and uprightness, as national decay is of individual idleness, selfishness, and vice. What we are accustomed to decry as great social evils, will, for the most part, be found to be but the outgrowth of man's own perverted life; and though we may endeavour to cut them down and extirpate them by means of Law, they will only spring up again with fresh luxuriance in some other form, unless the conditions of personal life and character are radically improved. If this view be correct, then it follows that the highest patriotism and philanthropy consist, not so much in altering laws and modifying institutions, as in helping and stimulating men to elevate and improve themselves by their own free and independent individual action.

It may be of comparatively little consequence how a man is governed from without, whilst everything depends upon how he governs himself from within. The greatest slave is not he who is ruled by a despot, great though that evil be, but he who is the thrall of his own moral ignorance, selfishness, and vice. . . .

Smiles' book *Thrift*, published in 1875, restates and expands on the themes stressed in *Self-Help*.

THRIFT

Every man is bound to do what he can to elevate his social state, and to secure his independence. For this purpose he must spare from his means in order to be independent in his condition. Industry enables men to earn their living; it should also enable them to learn to live. Independence can only be established by the exercise of forethought, prudence, frugality, and self-denial. To be just as well as generous, men must deny themselves. The essence of generosity is self-sacrifice.

The object of this book is to induce men to employ their means for worthy purposes, and not to waste them upon selfish indulgences. Many enemies have to be encountered in accomplishing this object. There are idleness, thoughtlessness, vanity, vice, intemperance. The last is the worst enemy of all. Numerous cases are cited in the course of the following book, which show that one of the best methods of abating the curse of Drink is to induce old and young to practice the virtue of Thrift. . . .

It is the savings of individuals which compose the wealth—in other words, the well-being—of every nation. On the other hand, it is the wastefulness of individuals which occasions the impoverishment of states. So that every thrifty person may be regarded as a public benefactor, and every thriftless person as a public enemy. . . .

. . . All that is great in man comes of labor—greatness in art, in literature, in science. Knowledge—"the wing wherewith we fly to heaven"—is only acquired through labor. Genius is but a capability of laboring intensely: it is the power of making great and sustained efforts. Labor may be a chastisement, but it is indeed a glorious one. It is worship, duty, praise, and immortality—for those who labor with the highest aims and for the purest purposes. . . .

. . . Of all wretched men, surely the idle are the most so—those whose life is barren of utility, who have nothing to do except to gratify their senses. Are not such men the most querulous, miserable, and dissatisfied of all, constantly in a state of *ennui* [boredom], alike useless to themselves and to others—mere cumberers [troublesome occupiers] of the earth, who, when removed, are missed by none, and whom none regret? Most wretched and ignoble lot, indeed, is the lot of the idlers.

Who have helped the world onward so much as the workers; men who have had to work from necessity or from choice? All that we call progress—civilization, well-being, and prosperity—depends upon industry, diligently applied—from the culture of a barley-stalk to the construction of a steamship; from the stitching of a collar to the sculpturing of "the statue that enchants the world."

All useful and beautiful thoughts, in like manner, are the issue of labor, of study, of observation, of research, of diligent elaboration. . . .

By the working-man we do not mean merely the man who labors with his muscles and sinews. A horse can do this. But *he* is pre-eminently the working-man who works with his brain also, and whose whole physical system is under the influence of his higher faculties. The man who paints a picture, who writes a book, who makes a law, who creates a poem, is a working-man of the highest order; not so necessary to the physical sustainment of the community as the plowman or the shepherd, but not less important as providing for society its highest intellectual nourishment. . . .

But a large proportion of men do not provide for the future. They do not remember the past.

They think only of the present. They preserve nothing. They spend all that they earn. They do not provide for themselves; they do not provide for their families. They may make high wages, but eat and drink the whole of what they earn. Such people are constantly poor, and hanging on the verge of destitution. . . .

REVIEW QUESTIONS

1. What, according to Samuel Smiles, were the key values that should guide the individual?
2. How did Smiles define success in life?
3. What, in his opinion, were the enemies of individual and national achievement?
4. Do Smiles' writings offer good advice to the poor in the United States today? Explain why or why not.

6 Reformers

Rapid industrialization created numerous hardships for factory hands, including long hours, harsh discipline, unsafe working conditions, and child labor. The distress of workers, which was publicized by parliamentary investigating committees and enlightened intellectuals, spurred a demand for reform. Early socialists like Robert Owen proposed establishing model communities for workers and their families. Other reformers like William Lovett urged parliamentary reforms that would give workers a voice in the political process.

Robert Owen
A NEW VIEW OF SOCIETY

In 1799, Robert Owen (1771–1858) became part owner and manager of the New Lanark cotton mills in Scotland. Distressed by the widespread mistreatment of workers, Owen resolved to improve the lives of his employees and show that it was possible to do so without destroying profits. He raised wages, upgraded working conditions, refused to hire children under ten, and provided workers with neat homes, food, and clothing, all at reasonable prices. He set up schools for children and for adults. In every way, he demonstrated his belief that healthier, happier workers produced more than the less fortunate ones. Owen believed that industry and technology could and would enrich humankind if they were organized according to the proper principles. Visitors came from all over Europe to see Owen's factories.

Just like many philosophes, Owen was convinced that the environment was the principal shaper of character—that the ignorance, alcoholism, and crime of the poor derived from bad living conditions. Public education and factory reform, said Owen, would make better citizens of the poor. Owen came to believe that the entire social and economic order must be replaced by a new system based on harmonious group living rather than on competition. He established a model community at New Harmony, Indiana, but it was short-lived.

In the following selection from *A New View of Society*, Owen proposes the establishment of a model community that would ameliorate the plight of the poor and unemployed.

The immediate cause of the present distress is the depreciation of human labour. This has been occasioned by the general introduction of mechanism into the manufactures of Europe and America, but principally into those of Britain, where the change was greatly accelerated by the inventions of Arkwright and Watt.

The introduction of mechanism into the manufacture of objects of desire in society reduced their price; the reduction of price increased the demand for them, and generally to so great an extent as to occasion more human labour to be employed after the introduction of machinery than had been employed before. . . .

A little reflection will show that the working classes have now no adequate means of contending with mechanical power; one of three results must therefore ensue:—

1. The use of mechanism must be greatly diminished; or,

2. Millions of human beings must be starved, to permit its existence to the present extent; or,

3. Advantageous occupation must be found for the poor and unemployed working classes, to whose labour mechanism must be rendered subservient, instead of being applied, as at present, to supersede it. . . .

It would . . . be a . . . sign of barbarism, and an act of gross tyranny, were any government to permit mechanical power to starve millions of human beings. The thought will not admit of one moment's contemplation; it would inevitably create unheard-of misery to all ranks. . . .

Under the existing laws,[1] the unemployed working classes are maintained by, and consume part of, the property and produce of the wealthy and industrious, while their powers of body and mind remain unproductive. They frequently acquire the bad habits which ignorance and idleness never fail to produce; they amalgamate with the regular poor, and become a nuisance to society.

Most of the poor have received bad and vicious habits from their parents; and so long as their present treatment continues, those bad and vicious habits will be transmitted to their children and, through them, to succeeding generations.

Any plan, then, to ameliorate their condition, must prevent bad and vicious habits from being taught to their children, and provide the means by which only good and useful ones may be given to them. . . .

Under this view of the subject, any plan for the amelioration of the poor should combine means to prevent their children from acquiring bad habits, and to give them good ones—to provide useful training and instruction for them—to provide proper labour for the adults—to direct their labour and expenditure

[1]The Poor Law was established in 1601 and taxed all householders in each parish to provide relief to the aged, sick, and infant poor in the parish, as well as employing the able-bodied poor in the workhouse. The law was supplemented in the late eighteenth century to provide allowances to workers who received wages beneath subsistence level. This proved to be so expensive that in the Poor Law reform in 1834, pauperism was stigmatized as a moral failing, and the only relief provided was employment in the workhouse.

so as to produce the greatest benefit to themselves and to society; and to place them under such circumstances as shall remove them from unnecessary temptations, and closely unite their interest and duty.

The plan represented is on a scale considered to be sufficient to accommodate about 1,200 persons.

And these are to be supposed men, women, and children, of all ages, capacities, and dispositions; most of them very ignorant; many with bad and vicious habits, possessing only the ordinary bodily and mental faculties of human beings, and who require to be supported out of the funds appropriated to the maintenance of the poor—individuals who are at present not only useless and a direct burthen on the public, but whose moral influence is highly pernicious, since they are the medium by which ignorance and certain classes of vicious habits and crimes are fostered and perpetuated in society.

It is evident that while the poor are suffered to remain under the circumstances in which they have hitherto existed, they and their children, with very few exceptions, will continue unaltered in succeeding generations.

In order to effect any radically beneficial change in their character, they must be removed from the influence of such circumstances, and placed under those which, being congenial to the natural constitution of man and the well-being of society, cannot fail to produce that amelioration in their condition which all classes have so great an interest in promoting.

Such circumstances, after incessant application to the subject, I have endeavoured to combine in the arrangement of the establishment represented in the drawings, so far as the present state of society will permit. These I will not attempt to explain more particularly.

Each lodging-room within the squares is to accommodate a man, his wife, and two children under three years of age; and to be such as will permit them to have much more comforts than the dwellings of the poor usually afford.

It is intended that the children above three years of age should attend the school, eat in the mess-room, and sleep in the dormitories;

the parents being, of course, permitted to see and converse with them at meals and all other proper times;—that before they leave school they shall be well instructed in all necessary and useful knowledge;—that every possible means shall be adopted to prevent the acquirement of bad habits from their parents or otherwise;—that no pains shall be spared to impress upon them such habits and dispositions as may be most conductive to their happiness through life, as well as render them useful and valuable members of the community to which they belong.

It is proposed that the women should be employed—

First,—In the care of their infants, and in keeping their dwellings in the best order.

Second,—In cultivating the gardens to raise vegetables for the supply of the public kitchen.

Third,—In attending to such of the branches of the various manufactures as women can well undertake; but not to be employed in them more than four or five hours in the day.

Fourth,—In making up clothing for the inmates of the establishment.

Fifth,—In attending occasionally, and in rotation, in the public kitchen, mess-rooms, and dormitories; and, when properly instructed, in superintending some parts of the education of the children in the schools.

It is proposed that the elder children should be trained to assist in gardening and manufacturing for a portion of the day, according to their strength; and that the men should be employed, all of them, in agriculture, and also in manufactures, or in some other occupation for the benefit of the establishment.

The ignorance of the poor, their ill-training, and their want of a rational education make it necessary that those of the present generation should be actively and regularly occupied through the day in some essentially useful work; yet in such a manner as that their employment should be healthy and productive. The plan which has been described will most amply admit of this. . . .

It is impossible to find language sufficiently strong to express the inconsistency, as well as the injustice, of our present proceedings towards the poor and working classes. They are left in gross ignorance; they are permitted to be trained up in habits of vice, and in the commission of crimes; and, as if purposely to keep them in ignorance and vice, and goad them on to commit criminal acts, they are perpetually surrounded with temptations which cannot fail to produce all those effects. . . .

The poor and unemployed working classes, however, cannot, must not, be abandoned to their fate, lest the consequences entail misfortune on us all. Instead of being left, as they now are, to the dominion of ignorance, and to the influence of circumstances which are fatal to their industry and morals—a situation in which it is easy to perceive the inefficacy, or rather the injuriousness, of granting them a provision in a mere pecuniary shape—they should, on the contrary, be afforded the means of procuring a certain and comfortable subsistence by their labour, under a system which will not only direct that labour and its earnings to the best advantage, but, at the same time, place them under circumstances the most favourable to the growth of morals and of happiness. In short, instead of allowing their habits to proceed under the worst influence possible, or rather, as

it were, to be left to chance, thus producing unintentionally crimes that render necessary the severities of our penal code, let a system for the prevention of pauperism and of crimes be adopted, and the operation of our penal code will soon be restricted to very narrow limits.

The outlines of such a plan, it is presumed, have been, however imperfectly, suggested and sketched in this Report. . . .

The principles and plan are now more fully before the public. If the former contain error, or the latter be impracticable, it becomes the duty of many to expose either. If, however, the plan shall prove, on investigation, to be correct in principle, to be easy of practice, and that it can relieve the poor and unemployed of the working classes from the grievous distresses and degradation under which they suffer, it becomes equally the duty of all who profess to desire the amelioration of the lower orders, to exert themselves without further delay to carry it into execution, in order that another year of extensive and unnecessary suffering and demoralization, from the want of a sufficiency of wholesome food and proper training and instruction, may not uselessly pass away.

REVIEW QUESTION

1. What bad habits did Owen attribute to the poor? How did he propose to remedy the situation?

CHAPTER 6

Romanticism, Reaction, Revolution

WANDERER ABOVE A SEA OF FOG, BY CASPAR DAVID FRIEDRICH. Breaking with traditional rules and standards, Romantic artists sought to express their inner voice. The finest works of art, they held, are not photographic imitations of nature but authentic and spontaneous expressions of the artist's feelings, fantasies, and dreams. *(Caspar David Friedrich, (1774–1840) Wanderer Above a Sea of Fog. Ca. 1817. Oil on canvas, 94.8 x 74.8 cm. Inv.: 5161. On permanent loan from the Foundation for the Promotion of the Hamburg Art Collections. Photo: Elke Walford. Bildarchiv Preussischer Kulturbesitz/Art Resource, NY)*

In 1815 the European scene had changed. Napoleon was exiled to the island of St. Helena, and a Bourbon king, in the person of Louis XVIII, again reigned in France. The Great Powers of Europe, meeting at Vienna, had drawn up a peace settlement that awarded territory to the states that had fought Napoleon and restored to power some rulers dethroned by the French emperor. The Congress of Vienna also organized the Concert of Europe to guard against a resurgence of the revolutionary spirit that had kept Europe in turmoil for some twenty-five years. The conservative leaders of Europe wanted no more Robespierres who resorted to terror and no more Napoleons who sought to dominate the continent.

However, reactionary rulers' efforts to turn the clock back to the Old Regime could not contain the forces unleashed by the French Revolution. Between 1820 and 1848 a series of revolts rocked Europe. The principal causes were liberalism, which demanded constitutional government and the protection of the freedom and rights of the individual citizen, and nationalism, which called for the reawakening and unification of the nation and its liberation from foreign domination.

In the 1820s, the Concert of Europe crushed a quasi-liberal revolution in Spain and liberal uprisings in Italy, and Tsar Nicholas I subdued liberal officers who challenged tsarist autocracy. The Greeks, however, successfully fought for independence from the Ottoman Turks.

Between 1830 and 1832, another wave of revolutions swept over Europe. Italian liberals and nationalists failed to free Italy from foreign rule or to wrest reforms from autocratic princes, and the tsar's troops crushed a Polish bid for independence from Russian rule. But in France, rebels overthrew the reactionary Bourbon Charles X in 1830 and replaced him with a more moderate ruler, Louis Philippe; a little later Belgium gained its independence from Holland.

The year 1848 was decisive in the struggle for liberty and nationhood. In France, democrats overthrew Louis Philippe and established a republic that gave all men the right to vote. However, in Italy and Germany, revolutions attempting to unify each land failed, as did a bid in Hungary for independence from the Hapsburg Empire. After enjoying initial successes, the revolutionaries were crushed by superior might, and their liberal and nationalist objectives remained largely unfulfilled. By 1870, however, many nationalist aspirations had been realized. The Hapsburg Empire granted Hungary autonomy in 1867, and by 1870–1871, the period of the Franco-Prussian War, Germany, and Italy became unified states. That authoritarian and militaristic Prussia unified Germany, rather than liberals like those who had fought in the revolutions of 1848, affected the future of Europe.

In the early nineteenth century a new cultural orientation, romanticism, emphasized the liberation of human emotions and the free expression of personality in artistic creations. The romantics' attack on the rationalism of the Enlightenment and their veneration of the past influenced conservative thought, and their concern for a people's history and traditions contributed to the development of nationalism. By encouraging innovation in art, music, and literature, the romantics greatly enriched European cultural life.

1 Romanticism

Romantics attacked the outlook of the Enlightenment, protesting that the philosophes' excessive intellectualizing and their mechanistic view of the physical world and human nature distorted and fettered the human spirit and thwarted cultural creativity. The rationalism of the philosophes, said the romantics, had reduced human beings to soulless thinking machines, and vibrant nature to lifeless wheels, cogs, and pulleys. In contrast to the philosophes' scientific and analytic approach, the romantics asserted the intrinsic value of emotions and imagination and extolled the spontaneity, richness, and uniqueness of the human spirit. To the philosophes, the emotions obstructed clear thinking.

For romantics, feelings and imagination were the human essence, the source of cultural creativity, and the avenue to true understanding. Their beliefs led the romantics to rebel against strict standards of aesthetics that governed artistic creations. They held that artists, musicians, and writers must trust their own sensibilities and inventiveness and must not be bound by textbook rules; the romantics focused on the creative capacities inherent in the emotions and urged individuality and freedom of expression in the arts. In the Age of Romanticism, the artist and poet succeeded the scientist as the arbiters of Western civilization.

William Wordsworth
TABLES TURNED

The works of the great English poet William Wordsworth (1770–1850) exemplify many tendencies of the Romantic Movement. In the interval during which he tried to come to grips with his disenchantment with the French Revolution, Wordsworth's creativity reached its height. In the preface to *Lyrical Ballads* (1798), Wordsworth produced what has become known as the manifesto of romanticism. He wanted poetry to express powerful feelings and also contended that because it is a vehicle for the imagination, poetry is the source of truth. Wordsworth thus represented a shift in perspective comparable to the shift made by Descartes in philosophy, but for Wordsworth imagination and feeling, not mathematics and logic, yielded highest truth.

The philosophes had regarded nature as a giant machine, all of whose parts worked in perfect precision and whose laws could be uncovered through the scientific method. The romantics rejected this mechanical model. To them, nature was a living organism filled with beautiful forms whose inner meaning was grasped through the human imagination; they sought from nature a higher truth than mechanical law. In "Tables Turned" (1798), Wordsworth exalts nature as humanity's teacher.

Up! up! my Friend, and quit your books;
Or surely you'll grow double:
Up! up! my Friend, and clear your looks;
Why all this toil and trouble?

The sun, above the mountain's head,
A freshening lustre mellow
Through all the long green fields has spread,
His first sweet evening yellow.

Books! 'tis a dull and endless strife:
Come, hear the woodland linnet [Old World
    finch],
How sweet his music! on my life,
There's more of wisdom in it.

And hark! how blithe the throstle [thrush] sings!
He, too, is no mean preacher:
Come forth into the light of things,
Let Nature be your Teacher.

She has a world of ready wealth,
Our minds and hearts to bless—
Spontaneous wisdom breathed by health,
Truth breathed by cheerfulness.

One impulse from a vernal wood
May teach you more of man,
Of moral evil and of good,
Than all the sages can.

Sweet is the lore which Nature brings;
Our meddling intellect
Mis-shapes the beauteous forms of things:—
We murder to dissect.

Enough of Science and of Art;
Close up those barren leaves [book pages];
Come forth, and bring with you a heart
That watches and receives.

William Blake
MILTON

William Blake (1757–1827) was a British engraver, poet, and religious mystic. He also affirmed the creative potential of the imagination and expressed distaste for the rationalist-scientific outlook of the Enlightenment, as is clear from these lines in his poem "Milton," written in 1804.

. . . the Reasoning Power in Man:
This is a false Body; an Incrustation [scab] over
    my Immortal
Spirit; a Selfhood, which must be put off &
    annihilated alway[s]
To cleanse the Face of my Spirit by Self-
    examination,
To bathe in the Waters of Life, to wash off the
    Not Human,
I come in Self-annihilation & the grandeur of
Inspiration,

To cast off Rational Demonstration by Faith in
    the Saviour,
To cast off the rotten rags of Memory by
    Inspiration,
To cast off Bacon, Locke & Newton from
    Albion's covering,[1]
To take off his filthy garments & clothe him
    with Imagination,

---

[1]Bacon, Locke, and Newton were British thinkers who valued reason and science, and Albion is an ancient name for England.

To cast aside from Poetry all that is not
Inspiration,
That it no longer shall dare to mock with the
aspersion of Madness

. . .

To cast off the idiot Questioner who is always
questioning
But never capable of answering, who sits with a
sly grin
Silent plotting when to question, like a thief
in a cave,
Who publishes doubt & calls it knowledge,
whose Science is Despair,

Whose pretence to knowledge is Envy, whose
whole Science is
To destroy the wisdom of ages to gratify
ravenous Envy
That rages round him like a Wolf day & night
without rest:
He smiles with condescension, he talks of
Benevolence & Virtue,
And those who act with Benevolence & Virtue
they murder time on time.
These are the destroyers of Jerusalem, these are
the murderers
Of Jesus, who deny the Faith & mock at Eternal
Life. . . .

Johann Wolfgang von Goethe
FAUST

In *Faust*, Johann Wolfgang von Goethe (1749–1832), Germany's greatest poet, gave expression to the romantic's anguish and yearnings. The play begins in the study of the learned Dr. Faustus. He is a master of all knowledge but feels spiritually empty. He yearns for the innocence and life-affirming wisdom of youth, the inspiration of nature, and the joy and excitement of life's experiences. Science, philosophy, and theology no longer stimulate the troubled professor.

THE FIRST PART OF THE TRAGEDY
Night

(FAUST *in a narrow, high-vaulted Gothic chamber, sitting uneasily at the desk in his armchair.*)

FAUST Ah me! I've now studied thoroughly and with ardent effort philosophy, law, medicine, and even, alas! theology. And here I stand, poor fool, and am no wiser than before. I've the title of Master, even Doctor, and for ten years now I've been leading my pupils by the nose, up and down and back and forth—and realize that we can't know anything! And that is eating my heart out. True, I'm smarter than all these fops of Doctors, Masters, clerks, and preachers; nor am I tormented by scruple or doubt, or any fear of hell or devil. In return, I'm deprived of all joy. For I don't pretend to know anything worth knowing, or to be able to teach anything that might improve men or convert them. Then too, I've neither goods nor gold, nor is any worldly honor or glory mine. No dog would lead such a life as this! And so I've devoted myself to magic, hoping that through the power and speech of the spirit many a secret might become known to me; so that no longer, in a bitter sweat, I'll need to say things that I don't know to be true; and so that I may discern what holds the universe together in its deepest center, view all the working and germinal forces, and be done with this traffic in words.

O light of the full moon, would that you were gazing for the last time upon my pain, you whom I have seen, as I sat awake at this desk, rise through so many a midnight hour. Then, as now, it was over books and papers, mournful friend, that you appeared to me. Ah! could I but walk on mountain heights in your beloved radiance, hover with spirits about mountain caverns, rove over meadows in your dimness, and, unburdened of all this fog of learning, find health by bathing in your dew!

Woe! still stuck this dungeon here? Accursed, musty hole-in-the-wall, where even the blessed light of heaven breaks but dimly through the painted panes! Hemmed in by this pile of books, which is gnawed by worms and covered with dust, and into which smoke-blackened papers are thrust all the way up to the vaulted ceiling; cluttered everywhere with flasks and jars, the place stuffed full of old instruments, and the junk of generations on top of that—that's your world! Men call that a world!

And still you ask why your heart is cramped with fear? Why an inexplicable pain inhibits every stir of life within you? Instead of living Nature, into which God put man at his creation, what surrounds you in smoke and mold is nothing but animal bones and human skeletons.

Up! flee! out into the open country! And this mysterious book, from the hand of Nostradamus* himself, is not guide enough for you? Then you will come to know the course of the stars, and with Nature instructing you the spirit power will dawn on you that tells you how spirit speaks with spirit. In vain does arid speculation try to explain the sacred symbols to you:

Spirits, you are hovering near me: answer me, if you hear me! (*He opens the volume, and his glance falls on the sign of the Macrocosm.*[†]) Ha! what rapture, at this sight, floods all my senses at once! I feel a youthful, holy joy of life coursing like a new fire through my nerves and veins. Was it a god that wrote these symbols which still the turmoil within me, fill my poor heart with joy, and with a mysterious force unveil the powers of Nature round about me? Am I a god? Such brightness grows in me! In these pure lines I see before me creative Nature at work. Only now do I grasp the meaning of the Sage's word, "The spirit world is not barred; it is your mind that is closed, your heart that is dead! Up, neophyte, and bathe your earthly breast tirelessly in the glow of morning!" (*He studies the sign.*) How all things interweave to form the whole, each one working and living in the other, as if the heavenly forces were ascending and descending, passing the golden buckets from hand to hand, and pressing forward from heaven through the earth, their wings fragrant with blessings, until the entire universe resounds in one great harmony!

What a spectacle! But alas, no more than a spectacle. Where can I grasp you, infinite Nature? You breasts, where? Fountains of all life, to which both earth and heaven cling, toward which my languishing breast is straining—you swell, you give suck, and must I pine for you in vain?

---

*Nostradamus is the Latinized name of a French astrologer, Michel de Notredame (1503–66), who published a collection of prophecies which are still occasionally quoted; he wrote no such book as is attributed to him here.

[†]Medieval astrologers contrasted the "Macrocosm," their conception of the universe, with the "Microcosm" . . . man as a world-in-little.

REVIEW QUESTIONS

1. In "Tables Turned," what connection did Wordsworth see between nature and the human mind? How did his idea of nature differ from that of the scientist's? According to Wordsworth, what effect did nature have on the imagination?
2. Why did William Blake attack reason?
3. How does the passage from *Faust* illustrate the romantic temperament?
4. The Romantic Movement was a reaction against the dominant ideas of the Enlightenment. Discuss this statement.

2 Conservatism

In the period after 1815, conservatism was the principal ideology of those who repudiated the Enlightenment and the French Revolution. Conservatives valued tradition over reason, aristocratic and clerical authority over equality, and the community over the individual. Edmund Burke (1729–1797), a leading Anglo-Irish statesman and political thinker, was instrumental in shaping the conservative outlook. His *Reflections on the Revolution in France* (1790) attacked the violence and fundamental principles of the Revolution. Another leading conservative was Joseph de Maistre (1753–1821), who fled his native Sardinia in 1792 (and again in 1793) after it was invaded by the armies of the new French Republic. De Maistre denounced the Enlightenment for spawning the French Revolution, defended the church as a civilizing agent that made individuals aware of their social obligations, and affirmed tradition as a model more valuable than instant reforms embodied in "paper constitutions."

The symbol of conservatism in the first half of the nineteenth century was Prince Klemens von Metternich (1773–1859) of Austria. A bitter opponent of Jacobinism and Napoleon, he became the pivotal figure at the Congress of Vienna (1814–1815), where European powers met to redraw the map of Europe after their victory over France. Metternich said that the Jacobins had subverted the pillars of civilization and that Napoleon, by harnessing the forces of the Revolution, had destroyed the traditional European state system. No peace was possible with Napoleon, who championed revolutionary doctrines and dethroned kings, and whose rule rested not on legitimacy but on conquest and charisma. No balance of power could endure an adventurer who obliterated states and sought European domination.

Edmund Burke
REFLECTIONS ON THE REVOLUTION IN FRANCE

Burke regarded the revolutionaries as wild-eyed fanatics who had uprooted all established authority, tradition, and institutions, thereby plunging France into anarchy. Not sharing the faith of the philosophes in human goodness, Burke held that without the restraints of established authority, people revert to savagery. For Burke, monarchy, aristocracy, and Christianity represented civilizing forces that tamed the beast in human nature. By undermining venerable institutions, he said, the French revolutionaries had opened the door to anarchy and terror. Burke's *Reflections*, excerpts of which follow, was instrumental in the shaping of conservative thought.

. . . You [revolutionaries] chose to act as if you had never been moulded into civil society, and had every thing to begin anew. You began ill, because you began by despising every thing that belonged to you. . . . If the last generations of your country appeared without much lustre in your eyes, you might have passed them by, and derived your claims from a more early race of ancestors. Under a pious predilection for those ancestors, your imaginations would have realized in them a standard of virtue and wisdom, beyond the vulgar practice of the hour: and you would have risen with the example to whose imitation you aspired. Respecting your forefathers, you would have been taught to respect yourselves. You would not have chosen to consider the French as a people of yesterday, as a nation of low-born servile wretches, until the emancipating year of 1789. . . . By following wise examples you would have given new examples of wisdom to the world. You would have rendered the cause of liberty venerable in the eyes of every worthy mind in every nation. . . . You would have had a free constitution; a potent monarchy; a disciplined army; a reformed and venerated clergy; a mitigated but spirited nobility, to lead your virtue. . . .

Compute your gains: see what is got by those extravagant and presumptuous speculations which have taught your leaders to despise all their predecessors, and all their contemporaries, and even to despise themselves, until the moment in which they became truly despicable. By following those false lights, France has bought undisguised calamities at a higher price than any nation has purchased the most unequivocal blessings! . . . France, when she let loose the reins of regal authority, doubled the licence, of a ferocious dissoluteness in manners, and of an insolent irreligion in opinions and practices; and has extended through all ranks of life. . . . all the unhappy corruptions that usually were the disease of wealth and power. This is one of the new principles of equality in France. . . .

. . . The science of government being therefore so practical in itself, and intended for such practical purposes, a matter which requires experience, and even more experience than any person can gain in his whole life, however sagacious and observing he may be, it is with infinite caution that any man ought to venture upon pulling down an edifice which has answered in any tolerable degree for ages the common purposes of society, or on building it up again, without having models and patterns of approved utility before his eyes. . . .

. . . The nature of man is intricate; the objects of society are of the greatest possible complexity; and therefore no simple disposition or direction of power can be suitable either to man's nature, or to the quality of his affairs.

When ancient opinions of life are taken away, the loss cannot possibly be estimated. From that moment we have no compass to govern us; nor can we know distinctly to what port we steer. . . .

. . . Nothing is more certain than that our manners, our civilization, and all the good things which are connected with manners and with civilization have, in this European world of ours, depended for ages upon two principles and were, indeed, the result of both combined: I mean the spirit of a gentleman and the spirit of religion. . . .

Burke next compares the English people with the French revolutionaries.

. . . Thanks to our sullen resistance to innovation, thanks to the cold sluggishness of our national character, we still bear the stamp of our forefathers. . . . We are not the converts of Rousseau; we are not the disciples of Voltaire; Helvetius has made no progress amongst us.[1] Atheists are not our preachers; madmen are not our lawgivers. We know that *we* have made no discoveries, and we think that no discoveries are to be made, in morality, nor many in the great principles of government. . . . We fear God; we look

---

[1]Rousseau, Voltaire, and Helvétius were French philosophes of the eighteenth century noted, respectively, for advocating democracy, attacking the abuses of the Old Regime, and applying scientific reasoning to moral principles (see Chapter 3).

up with awe to kings, with affection to parliaments, with duty to magistrates, with reverence to priests, and with respect to nobility. . . .

. . . We are afraid to put men to live and trade each on his own private stock of reason, because we suspect that this stock in each man is small, and that the individuals would do better to avail themselves of the general bank and capital of nations and of ages.

Klemens von Metternich
THE ODIOUS IDEAS OF THE PHILOSOPHES

Two decades of revolutionary warfare had shaped Metternich's political thinking. After the fall of Napoleon, Metternich worked to restore the European balance and to suppress revolutionary movements. In the following memorandum to Tsar Alexander I, dated December 15, 1820, Metternich denounces the French philosophes for their "false systems" and "fatal errors" that weakened the social fabric and gave rise to the French Revolution. In their presumption, the philosophes forsook the experience and wisdom of the past, trusting only their own thoughts and inclinations.

The progress of the human mind has been extremely rapid in the course of the last three centuries. This progress having been accelerated more rapidly than the growth of wisdom (the only counterpoise to passions and to error); a revolution prepared by the false systems . . . has at last broken out. . . .

. . . There were . . . some men [the philosophes], unhappily endowed with great talents, who felt their own strength, and . . . who had the art to prepare and conduct men's minds to the triumph of their detestable enterprise—an enterprise all the more odious as it was pursued without regard to results, simply abandoning themselves to the one feeling of hatred of God and of His immutable moral laws.

France had the misfortune to produce the greatest number of these men. It is in her midst that religion and all that she holds sacred, that morality and authority, and all connected with them, have been attacked with a steady and systematic animosity, and it is there that the weapon of ridicule has been used with the most ease and success.

Drag through the mud the name of God and the powers instituted by His divine decrees, and the revolution will be prepared! Speak of a social contract,[1] and the revolution is accomplished! The revolution was already completed in the palaces of Kings, in the drawing-rooms and boudoirs of certain cities, while among the great mass of the people it was still only in a state of preparation. . . .

. . . The French Revolution broke out, and has gone through a complete revolutionary cycle in a very short period, which could only have appeared long to its victims and to its contemporaries. . . .

. . . The revolutionary seed had penetrated into every country. . . . It was greatly developed under the *régime* of the military despotism

[1]The social contract theory consisted essentially of the following principles: (1) people voluntarily enter into an agreement to establish a political community; (2) government rests on the consent of the governed: (3) people possess natural freedom and equality, which they do not surrender to the state. These principles were used to challenge the divine right of kings and absolute monarchy.

of Bonaparte. His conquests displaced a number of laws, institutions, and customs; broke through bonds sacred among all nations, strong enough to resist time itself; which is more than can be said of certain benefits conferred by these innovators.

Joseph de Maistre
ESSAY ON THE GENERATIVE PRINCIPLE OF POLITICAL CONSTITUTIONS

The following critique of the philosophes, the French Revolution, and manufactured constitutions is taken from Joseph de Maistre's *Essay on the Generative Principle of Political Constitutions* (1808–1809).

One of the greatest errors of a century which professed them all was to believe that a political constitution could be created and written *a priori*, whereas reason and experience unite in proving that a constitution is a divine work and that precisely the most fundamental and essentially constitutional of a nation's laws could not possibly be written. . . .

. . . Was it not a common belief everywhere that a constitution was the work of the intellect, like an ode or a tragedy? Had not Thomas Paine declared, with a profundity that charmed the universities, that a constitution does not exist as long as one cannot put it in his pocket? The unsuspecting, overweening self-confidence of the eighteenth century balked at nothing, and I do not believe that it produced a single stripling of any talent who did not make three things when he left school: an educational system, a constitution, and a world. . . .

. . . I do not believe that the slightest doubt remains as to the unquestionable truth of the following propositions:

The fundamental principles of political constitutions exist prior to all written law.

Constitutional law (*loi*) is and can only be the development or sanction of a pre-existing and unwritten law (*droit*). . . .

. . . [H]e who believes himself able by writing alone to establish a clear and lasting doctrine IS A GREAT FOOL. If he really possessed the seeds of truth, he could never believe that a little black liquid and a pen could germinate them in the world, protect them from harsh weather, and make them sufficiently effective. As for whoever undertakes writing *laws or civil constitutions* in the belief that he can give them adequate conviction and stability because he has written them, he disgraces himself, whether or no other people say so. He shows an equal ignorance of the nature of inspiration and delirium, right and wrong, good and evil. This ignorance is shameful, even when approved by the whole body of the common people.

. . . [N]o real and great institution can be based on written law, since men themselves, instruments, in turn, of the established institution, do not know what it is to become and since imperceptible growth is the true promise of durability in all things. . . .

Everything brings us back to the general rule. *Man cannot create a constitution, and no legitimate constitution can be written.* The collection of fundamental laws which necessarily constitute a civil or religious society never has been or will be written *a priori*.

De Maistre assails the philosophes for attacking religion. Without Christianity, he says, people become brutalized, and civilization degenerates into anarchy.

Religion alone civilizes nations. No other known force can influence the savage. . . . [W]hat shall we think of a generation which has thrown everything to the winds, including the very foundations of the structure of society, by making education exclusively scientific? It was impossible to err more frightfully. For every educational system which does not have religion as its basis will collapse in an instant, or else diffuse only poisons throughout the State . . . if the guidance of education is not returned to the priests, and if science is not uniformly relegated to a subordinate rank, incalculable evils await us. We shall become brutalized by science, and that is the worst sort of brutality. . . .

Not until the first half of the eighteenth century did impiety really become a force. We see it at first spreading in every direction with amazing energy. From palaces to hovels, it insinuates itself everywhere, infesting everything. . . .

REVIEW QUESTIONS

1. Why was Edmund Burke opposed to the French Revolution?
2. What was Klemens von Metternich's opinion of "the progress of the human mind . . . in the . . . last three centuries" and its effect upon the society of his time?
3. What did Metternich mean by, "Drag through the mud the name of God and the powers instituted by His divine decrees, and the revolution will be prepared!"?
4. Why did Joseph de Maistre believe that man cannot create a constitution and no legitimate constitution can be written?
5. What views of late eighteenth- and early nineteenth-century conservatives are valued by American conservatives today?

---

3 Liberalism

Conservatism was the ideology of the old order that was hostile to the Enlightenment and the French Revolution; in contrast, liberalism aspired to carry out the promise of the philosophes and the Revolution. Liberals called for a constitution that protected individual liberty and denounced censorship, arbitrary arrest, and other forms of repression. They believed that through reason and education, social evils could be remedied. Liberals rejected an essential feature of the Old Regime—the special privileges of the aristocracy and the clergy—and held that the individual should be judged on the basis of achievement, not birth. At the core of the liberal outlook lay the conviction that the individual would develop into a good and productive human being and citizen if not coerced by governments and churches.

John Stuart Mill
ON LIBERTY

Freedom of thought and expression were principal concerns of nineteenth-century liberals. The classic defense of intellectual freedom is *On Liberty* (1859), written by John Stuart Mill (1806–1873), a prominent British philosopher. Mill argued that no individual or government has a monopoly on truth, for all human beings are fallible. Therefore, the government and the majority have no legitimate authority to suppress views, however unpopular; they have no right to interfere with a person's liberty so long as that person's actions do no injury to others. Nothing is more absolute, contended Mill, than the inviolable right of all adults to think and live as they please so long as they respect the rights of others. For Mill, toleration of opposing and unpopular viewpoints is a necessary trait in order for a person to become rational, moral, and civilized.

The object of this essay is to assert one very simple principle, as entitled to govern absolutely the dealings of society with the individual.... That principle is that the sole end for which mankind are warranted, individually or collectively, in interfering with the liberty of action of any of their number is self-protection. That the only purpose for which power can be rightfully exercised over any member of a civilized community, against his will, is to prevent harm to others. His own good, either physical or moral, is not a sufficient warrant. He cannot rightfully be compelled to do or forbear because it will be better for him to do so, because it will make him happier, because, in the opinions of others, to do so would be wise or even right. These are good reasons for remonstrating with him, or reasoning with him, or persuading him, or entreating him, but not for compelling him or visiting him with any evil in case he do otherwise. To justify that, the conduct from which it is desired to deter him must be calculated to produce evil to someone else. The only part of the conduct of anyone for which he is amenable to society is that which concerns others. In the part which merely concerns himself, his independence is, of right, absolute. Over himself, over his own body and mind, the individual is sovereign....

. . . This, then, is the appropriate region of human liberty. It comprises, first, the inward domain of consciousness, demanding liberty of conscience in the most comprehensive sense, liberty of thought and feeling, absolute freedom of opinion and sentiment on all subjects, practical or speculative, scientific, moral, or theological. The liberty of expressing and publishing opinions may seem to fall under a different principle, since it belongs to that part of the conduct of an individual which concerns other people, but, being almost of as much importance as the liberty of thought itself and resting in great part on the same reasons, is practically inseparable from it. Secondly, the principle requires liberty of tastes and pursuits, of framing the plan of our life to suit our own character, of doing as we like, subject to such consequences as may follow, without impediment from our fellow creatures, so long as what we do does not harm them, even though they should think our conduct foolish, perverse, or wrong. Thirdly, from this liberty of each individual follows the liberty, within the same limits, of combination among individuals; freedom to unite for any purpose not involving harm to others: the persons combining being supposed to be of full age and not forced or deceived.

No society in which these liberties are not, on the whole, respected is free, whatever may be its form of government; and none is completely free in which they do not exist absolute and unqualified. The only freedom which deserves the name is that of pursuing our own good in our own way, so long as we do not attempt to deprive others of theirs or impede their efforts to obtain it. Each is the proper guardian of his own health, whether bodily *or* mental and spiritual. Mankind are greater gainers by suffering each other to live as seems good to themselves than by compelling each to live as seems good to the rest. . . .

. . . Let us suppose, therefore, that the government is entirely at one with the people, and never thinks of exerting any power of coercion unless in agreement with what it conceives to be their voice. But I deny the right of the people to exercise such coercion, either by themselves or by their government. The power itself is illegitimate. The best government has no more title to it than the worst. It is as noxious, or more noxious, when exerted in accordance with public opinion than when in opposition to it. If all mankind minus one were of one opinion, mankind would be no more justified in silencing that one person than he, if he had the power, would be justified in silencing mankind. Were an opinion a personal possession of no value except to the owner, if to be obstructed in the enjoyment of it were simply a private injury, it would make some difference whether the injury was inflicted only on a few persons or on many. But the peculiar evil of silencing the expression of an opinion is that it is robbing the human race, posterity as well as the existing generation—those who dissent from the opinion, still more than those who hold it. If the opinion is right, they are deprived of the opportunity of exchanging error for truth; if wrong, they lose, what is almost as great a benefit, the clearer perception and livelier impression of truth produced by its collision with error.

REVIEW QUESTIONS

1. What was the purpose of John Stuart Mill's essay?
2. For Mill, what is the "peculiar evil of silencing the expression of an opinion," however unpopular?
3. On what grounds would Mill permit society to restrict individual liberty? Do you think it is ever legitimate for the state to restrain an individual from harming himself?

4 Rise of Modern Nationalism

Nationalism espoused the individual's allegiance to the national community and sought to unify divided nations and to liberate subject peoples. In the early nineteenth century, most nationalists were liberals who viewed the struggle for unification and freedom from foreign oppression as an extension of the struggle for individual rights. Few liberals recognized that nationalism was a potentially dangerous force that could threaten liberal ideals of freedom and equality.

Ernst Moritz Arndt
THE WAR OF LIBERATION

By glorifying a nation's language and ancient traditions and folkways, romanticism contributed to the evolution of modern nationalism, particularly in
Germany. German romantics longed to create a true folk community in which the
individual's soul would be immersed in the nation's soul. Through the national
community, individuals could find the meaning in life for which they yearned.
The romantic veneration of the past produced a mythical way of thinking about
politics and history, one that subordinated reason to powerful emotions. In
particular, some German romantics attacked the liberal–rational tradition of the
Enlightenment and the French Revolution as hostile to the true German spirit.

The Napoleonic wars kindled nationalist sentiments in the German states.
Hatred of the French occupier evoked a feeling of outrage and a desire for
national unity among some Germans, who before the occupation had thought
not of a German fatherland but of their own states and princes. These Germans
called for a war of liberation against Napoleon. Attracting mostly intellectuals,
the idea of political unification had limited impact on the rest of the people, who
remained loyal to local princes and local territories. Nevertheless, the embryo of
nationalism was conceived in the German uprising against Napoleon in 1813.
The writings of Ernst Moritz Arndt (1769–1860), composed in the same year, vividly express the emerging nationalism. The following excerpts describe Arndt's
view of the War of Liberation and present his appeal for German unity.

Fired with enthusiasm, the people rose, "with
God for King and Fatherland." Among the
Prussians there was only one voice, one feeling,
one anger and one love, to save the Fatherland
and to free Germany. The Prussians wanted war;
war and death they wanted; peace they feared
because they could hope for no honorable peace
from Napoleon. War, war, sounded the cry from
the Carpathians [mountains] to the Baltic [Sea],
from the Niemen to the Elbe [rivers]. War! cried
the nobleman and landed proprietor who had become impoverished. War! the peasant who was
driving his last horse to death. . . . War! the citizen who was growing exhausted from quartering
soldiers and paying taxes. War! the widow who
was sending her only son to the front. War! the
young girl who, with tears of pride and pain, was
leaving her betrothed. Youths who were hardly
able to bear arms, men with gray hair, officers
who on account of wounds and mutilations had
long ago been honorably discharged, rich landed

proprietors and officials, fathers of large families and managers of extensive businesses—all
were unwilling to remain behind. Even young
women, under all sorts of disguises, rushed to
arms; all wanted to drill, arm themselves and
fight and die for the Fatherland. . . .

The most beautiful thing about all this holy
zeal and happy confusion was that all differences
of position, class, and age were forgotten . . .
that the one great feeling for the Fatherland,
its freedom and honor, swallowed all other
feelings, caused all other considerations and
relationships to be forgotten.

In another passage, Arndt appealed for
German unity.

German man, feel again God, hear and fear the
eternal, and you hear and fear also your *Volk*
[folk, people, nation]; you feel again in God

the honor and dignity of your fathers, their glorious history rejuvenates itself again in you, their firm and gallant virtue reblossoms in you, the whole German Fatherland stands again before you in the august halo of past centuries! Then, when you feel and fear and honor all this, then you cry, then you lament, then you wrathfully reproach yourself that you have become so miserable and evil: then starts your new life and your new history. . . . From the North Sea to the Carpathians, from the Baltic to the Alps, from the Vistula to the Schelde [rivers], one faith, one love, one courage, and one enthusiasm must gather again the whole German folk in brotherly community; they must learn to feel how great, mighty, and happy their fathers were in obedience to one German emperor and one Reich, at a time when the many discords had not yet turned one against the other, when the many cowards and knaves had not yet betrayed them; . . . above the ruins and ashes of their destroyed Fatherland they must weepingly join hands and pray and swear all to stand like one man and to fight until the sacred land will be free. . . . Feel the infinite and sublime which slumbers hidden in the lap of the days, those light and mighty spirits which now glimmer in isolated meteors but which soon will shine in all suns and stars; feel the new birth of times, the higher, cleaner breath of spiritual life and do not longer be fooled and confused by the insignificant and small. No longer Catholics and Protestants, no longer Prussians and Austrians, Saxons and Bavarians, Silesians and Hanoverians, no longer of different faith, different mentality, and different will—be Germans, be one, will to be one by love and loyalty, and no devil will vanquish you.

this seems to contradict liberalism, even though nationlists were an "extension" of liberals

Giuseppe Mazzini
YOUNG ITALY

In 1815, Italy was a fragmented nation. Hapsburg Austria ruled Lombardy and Venetia in the north and a Bourbon king sat on the throne of the Kingdom of the Two Sicilies in the south. The duchies of Tuscany, Parma, and Modena were ruled by Hapsburg princes subservient to Austria. The papal states in central Italy were ruled by the pope. The House of Savoy, an Italian dynasty, ruled the Kingdom of Piedmont, which became the cornerstone of Italian unification. Inspired by past Italian glories—the Roman Empire and the Renaissance— Italian nationalists demanded an end to foreign occupation and the unification of the Italian peninsula. As in other lands, national revival and unification appealed principally to intellectuals and the middle class.

A leading figure in the *Risorgimento*—the struggle for Italian nationhood— was Giuseppe Mazzini (1805–1872). Often called the "soul of the Risorgimento," Mazzini devoted his life to the creation of a unified and republican Italy; he believed that a free and democratic Italy would serve as a model to the other nations of Europe. In 1831, he founded Young Italy, a society dedicated to the cause of Italian unity. The following reading includes the oath taken by members of Young Italy.

Young Italy is a brotherhood of Italians who believe in a law of Progress and Duty, and are convinced that Italy is destined to become one nation,—convinced also that she possesses sufficient strength within herself to become one, and that the ill success of her former efforts is to be attributed not to the weakness, but to the misdirection of the revolutionary elements within her,—that the secret of force lies in constancy and unity of effort. They join this association in the firm intent of consecrating both thought and action to the great aim of reconstituting Italy as one independent sovereign nation of free men and equals. . . .

Young Italy is Republican. . . . Republican,—Because theoretically every nation is destined, by the law of God and humanity, to form a free and equal community of brothers; and the republican is the only form of government that insures this future. . . .

The means by which Young Italy proposes to reach its aim are—education and insurrection, to be adopted simultaneously, and made to harmonize with each other. Education must ever be directed to teach by example, word, and pen the necessity of insurrection. Insurrection, whenever it can be realized, must be so conducted as to render it a means of national education. . . .

Insurrection—by means of guerrilla bands—is the true method of warfare for all nations desirous of emancipating themselves from a foreign yoke. This method of warfare supplies the want—inevitable at the commencement of the insurrection—of a regular army; it calls the greatest number of elements into the field, and yet may be sustained by the smallest number. It forms the military education of the people, and consecrates every foot of the native soil by the memory of some warlike deed. . . .

Each member will, upon his initiation into the association of Young Italy, pronounce the following form of oath, in the presence of the initiator:

In the name of God and of Italy;

In the name of all the martyrs of the holy Italian cause who have fallen beneath foreign and domestic tyranny;

By the duties which bind me to the land wherein God has placed me, and to the brothers whom God has given me;

By the love—innate in all men—I bear to the country that gave my mother birth, and will be the home of my children;

By the hatred—innate in all men—I bear to evil, injustice, usurpation and arbitrary rule;

By the blush that rises to my brow when I stand before the citizens of other lands, to know that I have no rights of citizenship, no country, and no national flag;

By the aspiration that thrills my soul towards that liberty for which it was created, and is impotent to exert; towards the good it was created to strive after, and is impotent to achieve in the silence and isolation of slavery;

By the memory of our former greatness, and the sense of our present degradation;

By the tears of Italian mothers for their sons dead on the scaffold, in prison, or in exile;

By the sufferings of the millions,—

I, . . . believing in the mission intrusted by God to Italy, and the duty of every Italian to strive to attempt its fulfillment; convinced that where God has ordained that a nation shall be, He has given the requisite power to create it; that the people are the depositaries of that power, and that in its right direction for the people, and by the people, lies the secret of victory; convinced that virtue consists in action and sacrifice, and strength in union and constancy of purpose: I give my name to Young Italy, an association of men holding the same faith, and swear:

To dedicate myself wholly and forever to the endeavor with them to constitute Italy one free, independent, republican nation; to promote by every means in my power—whether by written or spoken word, or by action—the education of my Italian brothers towards the aim of Young Italy; towards association, the sole means of its accomplishment, and to virtue, which alone can render the conquest lasting; to abstain from enrolling myself in any other association from this time forth; to obey all the instructions, in conformity with the spirit of Young Italy, given me by those who represent with me the union of my Italian brothers; and to keep the secret of these instructions, even at the cost of my life; to assist my brothers of the association both by action and counsel—

NOW AND FOREVER

This do I swear, invoking upon my head the wrath of God, the abhorrence of man, and the infamy of the perjurer, if I ever betray the whole or a part of this my oath.

REVIEW QUESTIONS

1. Ernst Moritz Arndt's writings show the interconnection between romanticism and nationalism. Discuss this statement.
2. Why do you suppose many students were attracted to Young Italy?
3. Giuseppe Mazzini was a democrat, a nationalist, and a romantic. Discuss this statement.

5 Repression

Russia, Austria, Prussia, and Great Britain agreed to act together to preserve the territorial settlement of the Congress of Vienna and the balance of power. After paying its indemnity, France was admitted into this Quadruple Alliance, also known as the Concert of Europe. Metternich intended to use the Concert of Europe to maintain harmony among nations and internal stability within nations. Toward this end, conservatives in their respective countries censored books and newspapers, imprisoned liberal activists, and suppressed nationalist uprisings.

KARLSBAD DECREES

In 1819, Metternich and representatives from other German states meeting at Karlsbad drew up several decrees designed to stifle liberalism and nationalism. The Karlsbad Decrees called for the dissolution of the *Burschenschaften*, German student fraternities, the censoring of books and newspapers, and the dismissal of professors who spread liberal doctrines.

Provisional Decree relative to the Measures to be taken concerning the Universities.

Sect. 1. The Sovereign shall make choice for each university of an extraordinary commissioner, furnished with suitable instructions and powers, residing in the place where the university is established. . . .

The duty of this commissioner shall be to . . . observe carefully the spirit with which the professors and tutors are guided in their public and private lectures; . . . and to devote a constant attention to every thing which may tend to the maintenance of morality, good order and decency among the youths.

Sect. 2. The governments of the states, members of the confederation, reciprocally engage to remove from their universities and other establishment of instruction, the professors and other public teachers, against whom it may be proved, that in departing from their duty, in overstepping the bounds of their duty, in abusing their legitimate influence over the minds of youth, by the propagation of pernicious dogmas, hostile to order and public tranquility, or in sapping the foundation of existing establishments, they have shown themselves incapable of executing the important functions entrusted to them. . . .

A professor or tutor thus excluded, cannot be admitted in any other state of the confederation to any other establishment of public instruction.

Sect. 3. The laws long since made against secret or unauthorized associations at the universities, shall be maintained in all their force and rigour, and shall be particularly extended with so much the more severity against the well-known society formed some years ago under the name of the General Burschenschaft, as it has for its basis an idea, absolutely inadmissible, of community and continued correspondence between the different universities.

The governments shall mutually engage to admit to no public employment any individuals who may continue or enter into any of those associations after the publication of the present decree.

Decree relative to the Measures for preventing the Abuses of the Press.

Sect. 1. . . . No writing appearing in the form of a daily paper or periodical pamphlet . . . shall be issued from the press without the previous consent of the public authority. . . .

Sect. 7. The editor of a journal, or other periodical publication, that may be suppressed by command of the Diet, shall not be allowed, during the space of five years, to conduct any similar publication in any states of the confederation. . . .

Decree relative to the formation of a Central Commission, for the purpose of Ulterior Inquiry respecting Revolutionary Plots, discovered in some of the States of the Confederation.

Art. 1. In 15 days from the date of this decree, an extraordinary commission of inquiry, appointed by the Diet and composed of 7 members, including the President, shall assemble in the city of Mentz, a fortress of the confederation.

2. The object of this commission is, to make careful and detailed inquires respecting the facts, the origin and the multiplied ramifications of the secret revolutionary and demagogic associations, directed against the political constitution and internal repose, as well of the confederation in general, as of the individual members thereof.

REVIEW QUESTIONS

1. What was Metternich afraid of?
2. Draw parallels between The Karlsbad Decrees and the actions of certain regimes in the twentieth and twenty-first centuries.

---

6   1848: The Year of Revolutions

In 1848, revolutions for political liberty and nationhood broke out in many parts of Europe. An uprising in Paris set this revolutionary tidal wave in motion. In February 1848, democrats seeking to create a French republic and to institute universal manhood suffrage precipitated a crisis; the pursuant uprising in Paris forced King Louis Philippe to abdicate. The leaders of the new French Republic championed political democracy but, with some notable exceptions like Louis Blanc (1811–1882), had little concern for the plight of the laboring poor.

The publication of the *Organization of Labor* (1839) had established Blanc as a leading French social reformer. Blanc urged the government to finance national workshops—industrial corporations, in which the directors would be elected by the workers—to provide employment for the urban poor. The government responded to Blanc's insistence that all workers have the "right to work" by indeed establishing national workshops, but these provided jobs for only a fraction of the unemployed, and many workers were given wages for doing nothing. Property owners regarded the workshops as a waste of government funds and as nests of working-class radicalism. When the government closed the workshops in June 1848, Parisian workers revolted.

Flora Tristan
"WORKERS, YOUR CONDITION . . . IS MISERABLE AND DISTRESSING"

Flora Tristan (1803–1844) did not live to see the working-class revolution of 1848 (see page 168), but her appeals for social justice contributed to the unrest of French workers, which exploded in the June Days. Addressing audiences in several cities, Tristan urged workers to strengthen their cause by uniting in a national Workers' Union. In October 1848 eight thousand French workers expressed their gratitude to Tristan by witnessing the unveiling of a monument in her honor at her gravesite. As the following selections from her writings indicate, Tristan was also a pioneer French feminist.

Workers, your condition in present-day society is miserable and distressing: in good health, you have no right to work; in illness, weakness, injury, old age, you have no right to go to a hospital; in poverty, lacking everything, you have no right to beg because begging is against the law. This precarious situation reduces you to a state of savagery in which a man, like a forest dweller, is forced each morning to think up the means to provide himself with sustenance for the day ahead. Such an existence is a real torment. The lot of the animal that chews the cud in the cattle-shed is a thousand times better than yours; he is certain to eat tomorrow; his master takes care of him in the barn, with straw and hay for winter. The lot of the bee in his hole in a tree, is a thousand times better than yours, and so is that of the ant who works in summer in order to live through the winter.

Workers, you are unhappy, yes, without a doubt; but what is the cause of your misery? If a bee or an ant, instead of working in harmony with other bees and ants to lay up provisions for winter in their communal dwelling place, thought to separate himself and work alone, he would die of cold and hunger in his lonely corner. Why do you remain isolated? Isolated you are weak and exhausted under the burdens of all sorts of misery. So, come out of your isolation, unite! In unity is strength! There are so many of you.

I come to propose to you a general union between working men and working women, without distinction of trades, living in the same country; a union for and constituted by the working class, and which would construct several establishments (Palaces of the Workers' Union) distributed across France. There, children of both sexes from six to eighteen years old would be educated, and it would be a refuge for all ill, wounded, or old workers.

There are in France around five million working men and two million working women. Let these seven million workers unite themselves in thought and action to create a great commune for the benefit of all men and women. . . .

Tristan was determined that workingmen accept workingwomen as equals. She described the lives of workingwomen, showing how their lives were blighted by the lack of education, and the ill-treatment of husbands, who were themselves scorned by the other classes in France. The footnotes are Tristan's.

In the life of the workers, the woman is everything. She is their sole providence [caregiver and controlling influence]. If she fails them, everything fails. It is said, "The woman makes or breaks the home," and that is the exact truth; that is why it has become a proverb. Yet what education, what instruction, what direction, what moral or physical development does the woman of the people receive? None. As a child she is left to the mercy of a mother or grandmother who, themselves, received no education; one of them, according to her nature, will be brutal and bad-tempered, will beat and ill-treat her without reason; the other will be weak and careless, and let her do just what she pleases. (In this, as in everything that I set down, I speak in general terms; of course I admit that there are numerous exceptions.) The poor child will grow up in the midst of bewildering contradictions. One day angered by blows and unjust treatment, the next day spoiled by indulgences no less pernicious.

Instead of going to school, she, rather than her brothers, will be kept at home, because she is better suited to household jobs, such as rocking babies, running errands, watching over the soup, etc. At age twelve she goes out to domestic service; there she continues to be exploited by her employer, and often as ill-treated as she was at her parent's house.

Nothing embitters character, hardens the heart, nor results in a bad temper like the continual suffering that a child endures as a result of unjust and brutal treatment. . . .

Such will be the normal situation for a poor young girl of twenty. Then she will marry, without love, and only because it is necessary to marry in order to escape the tyranny of her parents. What happens next? I assume she will have children; in her turn she will be totally incapable of raising her sons and her daughters properly: she will be as brutal toward them as her mother and grandmother were to her.[*] . . . .

The majority of the women of the people are brutal, spiteful, at times harsh. It's true; but how is it that this state of affairs so little matches the gentle, sensitive, generous nature of women in general?

Poor working-class wives! They have so many causes of irritation! First the husband. (One must admit that there are few workers' households that are happy.) The husband, having received more education, being the head of the household by law, and also by the money that he brings into the household, thinks himself (and indeed he is) far superior to the wife who brings in only a small daily wage, and is only a very humble servant in the house.

The result of this is that the husband treats his wife with, at least, much disdain. The poor wife who feels humiliated by each word, each look that her husband gives her, revolts openly or within herself, according to her nature; from that come violent painful scenes, which lead to a constant state of irritation between the

---

[*]The women of the people show themselves to be very tender mothers for little children up to the age of two to three years. Their womanly instinct understands that a child during its first two years needs continual care. But beyond this age they ill-treat them (save for exceptions).

master and the servant (one can even say slave, because the wife is, so to speak, the property of the husband). This state becomes so upsetting that the husband, instead of staying home to chat with his wife, is in a hurry to flee, and as he has no other place to go, he goes to the tavern and drinks absinthe with other husbands as unhappy as he, in the hope of drowning his sorrows.[†]

These means of distraction make things worse. The wife, who has to wait for the money until Sunday in order to provide for her family during the week, is in despair at seeing her husband spend the greater part of it at the tavern. Then his irritation is filled to overflowing, and his cruelty and spitefulness are redoubled. . . .

Then, after the bitter distress caused by the husband, come pregnancies, illnesses, loss of work and poverty, poverty that is always

planted at the door like the head of Medusa. Added to all this is the incessant strain caused by four or five crying, turbulent, annoying children who whirl around their mother, and all that in the cramped worker's dwelling where there is no place to move. Oh! One would have to be an angel on earth not to be irritated, brutal, and bad-tempered in such a situation. In the midst of such a family, however, what happens to the children? They see their father only in the evenings and on Sunday. This father, always in a state of irritation or inebriation, does not speak to them except in anger, and they receive from him only abuse and blows, hearing their mother plead with him continually, they acquire hatred and scorn for him. As for their mother, they fear her, they obey her, but they do not love her. One is made in such a way that one cannot love those who treat one badly. . . . Not having any reason to stay with his mother, the child will seek for any pretext to move away from home. Bad company is easy to get into, for girls as for boys. Idleness leads to vagrancy, and following vagrancy comes crime. . . .

Do you begin to understand, you, the men who exclaim in horror before trying to examine the question, why I claim rights for the women? It is because I wish that she were placed on an absolutely equal footing with the man, and that she enjoy it by virtue of the legal right that every person has at birth. . . .

All the evils of the working class are summed up in these two words: poverty and ignorance, ignorance and poverty. Now, in order to get out of this labyrinth, I see only one way: begin by educating women, because women are in charge of raising their children, male and female. . . .

Therefore it is up to you, workers, who are the victims of inequality in practice and of injustice—it is up to you to establish at last the reign of justice on earth and of absolute equality between men and women.

Give the world a great example, an example that will prove to your oppressors that it is by law that you wish to triumph and not by brute

---

[†]Why do workers go to the tavern? Egotism has struck the upper classes, those who rule, with complete blindness. They do not understand that their fortune, their happiness, and their security depend on the moral, intellectual, and material betterment of the working class. They abandon the worker to poverty and ignorance, reasoning according to the ancient maxim that the more brute-like the people are, the easier it is to muzzle them. All this was true before the *Declaration of the Rights of Man*. Since then it is a crassly ignorant anachronism, a grave mistake. Moreover, one should be at least consistent: if one believes that it is a good and wise policy to leave the poor in a brute condition, then why recriminate ceaselessly against their vices?

The rich accuse the workers of being lazy, debauched, drunken, and in order to support their accusations they say, "If the workers are poor, it is solely their own fault. Go to the . . . taverns, you will find them full of workers who are there to drink and waste their time." I believe that if the workers, instead of going to the tavern, assembled seven at a time (a number permitted by the September laws) in one room, to learn about their rights and consider what action to take in order to make them legally valid, the rich would be more unhappy than they are at seeing the taverns full.

In the present state of affairs the tavern is the worker's temple; it is the only place where he can go. He does not believe in the church, he understands nothing in the theater. That is why the taverns are always full. . . .

The taverns are not the cause of evil, but simply the effect. The cause of evil lies solely in the ignorance, the poverty, the brutalization into which the working class is plunged. . . .

force; nevertheless, you, seven, ten, fifteen million proletarians have this brute force at your disposal!

While claiming justice for yourselves, prove that you are just and impartial; proclaim, you strong men, men with bare arms, that you recognize the woman as your equal, and because of this claim, you recognize her equal right to the benefits of the Universal Union of Workingmen and Workingwomen.

Alexis de Tocqueville
THE JUNE DAYS

To the French workers the June 1848 revolt was against poverty and for a fairer distribution of property. Viewing this uprising as a threat to property and indeed to civilization, the rest of France rallied against the workers, who were crushed after several days of bitter street fighting. In his *Recollections* published posthumously in 1893, Alexis de Tocqueville (1805–1859), a leading statesman and political theorist, included a speech he made on January 29, 1848, before the French Chamber of Deputies, in which he warned the officials about the mood of the laboring poor.

. . . I am told that there is no danger because there are no riots; I am told that, because there is no visible disorder on the surface of society, there is no revolution at hand.

Gentlemen, permit me to say that I believe you are deceived. True, there is no actual disorder; but it has entered deeply into men's minds. See what is passing in the breasts of the working classes, who, I grant, are at present quiet. No doubt they are not disturbed by political passion, properly so-called, to the same extent that they have been; but can you not see that their passions, instead of political, have become social? Do you not see that there are gradually forming in their breasts opinions and ideas which are destined not only to upset this or that law, ministry, or even form of government, but society itself, until it totters upon the foundations on which it rests today? Do you not listen to what they say to themselves each day? Do you not hear them repeating unceasingly that all that is above them is incapable and unworthy of governing them; that the present distribution of goods throughout the world is unjust; that property rests on a foundation which is not an equitable foundation? And do you not realize that when such opinions take root, when they spread in an almost universal manner, when they sink deeply into the masses, they are bound to bring with them sooner or later, I know not when nor how, a most formidable revolution?

This, gentlemen, is my profound conviction: I believe that we are at this moment sleeping on a volcano. I am profoundly convinced of it. . . .

Later in his *Recollections*, de Tocqueville describes the second uprising in 1848, called the June Days.

I come at last to the insurrection of June, the most extensive and the most singular that has occurred in our history, and perhaps in any other: the most extensive, because, during four days, more than a hundred thousand men were engaged in it; the most singular, because the insurgents fought without a war-cry, without leaders, without flags, and yet with a marvellous harmony and an amount of military experience that astonished the oldest officers.

What distinguished it also, among all the events of this kind which have succeeded one another in France for sixty years, is that it did not aim at changing the form of government, but at altering the order of society. It was not, strictly speaking, a political struggle, in the sense which until then we had given to the word, but a combat of class against class, a sort of Servile War [slave uprising in ancient Rome]. It represented the facts of the Revolution of February in the same manner as the theories of Socialism represented its ideas; or rather it issued naturally from these ideas, as a son does from his mother. We behold in it nothing more than a blind and rude, but powerful, effort on the part of the workmen to escape from the necessities of their condition, which had been depicted to them as one of unlawful oppression, and to open up by main force a road towards that imaginary comfort with which they had been deluded. It was this mixture of greed and false theory which first gave birth to the insurrection and then made it so formidable. These poor people had been told that the wealth of the rich was in some way the produce of a theft practised upon themselves. They had been assured that the inequality of fortunes was as opposed to morality and the welfare of society as it was to nature. Prompted by their needs and their passions, many had believed this obscure and erroneous notion of right, which, mingled with brute force, imparted to the latter an energy, a tenacity and a power which it would never have possessed unaided.

It must also be observed that this formidable insurrection was not the enterprise of a certain number of conspirators, but the revolt of one whole section of the population against another. Women took part in it as well as men. While the latter fought, the former prepared and carried ammunition; and when at last the time had come to surrender, the women were the last to yield. These women went to battle with, as it were, a housewifely ardour: they looked to victory for the comfort of their husbands and the education of their children. . . .

As we know, it was the closing of the national workshops that occasioned the rising. Dreading to disband this formidable soldiery at one stroke, the Government had tried to disperse it by sending part of the workmen into the country. They refused to leave. On the 22nd of June, they marched through Paris in troops, singing in cadence, in a monotonous chant, "We won't be sent away, we won't be sent away. . . ."

. . . The spirit of insurrection circulated from one to the other of this immense class, and in each of its parts, as the blood does in the body; it filled the quarters where there was no fighting, as well as those which served as the scene of battle; it had penetrated into our houses, around, above, below us. The very places in which we thought ourselves the masters swarmed with domestic enemies; one might say that an atmosphere of civil war enveloped the whole of Paris, amid which, to whatever part we withdrew, we had to live. . . .

. . . It was easy to perceive through the multitude of contradictory reports that we had to do with the most universal, the best armed, and the most furious insurrection ever known in Paris. The national workshops and various revolutionary bands that had just been disbanded supplied it with trained and disciplined soldiers and with leaders. It was extending every moment, and it was difficult to believe that it would not end by being victorious, . . . all the great insurrections of the last sixty years had triumphed. . . .

Nevertheless, we succeeded in triumphing over this so formidable insurrection; nay more, it was just that which rendered it so terrible which saved us. . . . Had the revolt borne a less radical character and a less ferocious aspect, it is probable that the greater part of the middle class would have stayed at home; France would not have come to our aid; the National Assembly itself would perhaps have yielded, or at least a minority of its members would have advised it; and the energy of the whole body would have been greatly unnerved. But the insurrection was of such a nature that any understanding with it became at once impossible, and from the first it left us no alternative but to defeat it or to be destroyed ourselves.

REVIEW QUESTIONS

1. To what causes did Flora Tristan attribute the miseries of the working class in France? What remedies did she propose?
2. According to Alexis de Tocqueville, why did Parisian workers revolt in 1848?
3. How did the goals of Parisian workers who revolted in 1848 differ from those of members of Giuseppe Mazzini's Young Italy?
4. De Tocqueville observed that what distinguished this revolt was that it aimed to change the order of society, not the form of government. Explain.

CHAPTER 7

Thought and Culture in an Age of Science and Industry

A CARICATURE OF DARWIN. Darwin's theory of evolution created much controversy and aroused considerable bitterness. In this caricature, the ape-like Darwin, holding a mirror, is explaining his theory of evolution to a fellow ape. *(Hulton Archive/Getty Images)*

Romanticism dominated European art, literature, and music in the early nineteenth century. Stressing the feelings and the free expression of personality, the Romantic Movement was a reaction against the rationalism of the Enlightenment. In the middle decades of the century, realism and its close auxiliary naturalism supplanted romanticism as the chief norm of cultural expression. Rejecting religious, metaphysical, and romantic interpretations of reality, realists aspired to an exact and accurate portrayal of the external world and daily life. Realist and naturalist writers used the empirical approach: the careful collection, ordering, and interpretation of facts employed in science, which was advancing steadily in the nineteenth century. Among the most important scientific theories formulated was Charles Darwin's theory of evolution, which revolutionized conceptions of time and the origins of the human species.

The principal currents of political thought, Marxism and liberalism, also reacted against romantic, religious, and metaphysical interpretations of nature and society, focused on the empirical world, and strove for scientific accuracy. This emphasis on objective reality helped to stimulate a growing criticism of social ills, for despite unprecedented material progress, reality was often sordid, somber, and dehumanizing. In the last part of the century, reformers motivated by an expansive liberalism, revolutionary or evolutionary socialism, or a socially committed Christianity pressed for the alleviation of social injustice.

1 Realism in Literature

The middle decades of the nineteenth century were characterized by the growing importance of science and industrialization in European life. A movement known as positivism sought to apply the scientific method to the study of society. Rejecting theological and metaphysical theories as unscientific, positivists sought to arrive at the general laws that underlie society by carefully assembling and classifying data.

This stress on a rigorous observation of reality also characterized realism and naturalism, the dominant movements in art and literature. In several ways, realism differed from romanticism, the dominant cultural movement in the first half of the century. Romantics were concerned with the inner life—with feelings, intuition, and imagination. They sought escape from the city into natural beauty, and they venerated the past, particularly the Middle Ages, which they viewed as noble, idyllic, and good in contrast to the spiritually impoverished present. Realists, on the other hand, shifted attention away from individual human feelings to the external world, which they investigated with the meticulous care of the scientist. Preoccupied with reality as it actually is, realist writers and artists depicted ordinary people, including the poor and humble, in ordinary circumstances. With a careful eye for detail and in a matter-of-fact way devoid of romantic exuberance and exaggeration, realists described peasants, factory workers, laundresses, beggars, criminals, and prostitutes.

Realism quickly evolved into naturalism. Naturalist writers held that human behavior was determined by the social environment. They argued that certain social and economic conditions produced predictable traits in men and women and that cause and effect operated in society as well as in physical nature.

Vissarion Belinsky
THE POETRY OF REALITY

Vissarion Grigorevich Belinsky (1811–1848), a self-taught Russian intellectual concerned with moral and social issues, provided an early definition of realism.

Thus we have here another aspect of poetry, *realistic* poetry, the poetry of life, the poetry of reality, at last the true and genuine poetry of our time. Its distinct character consists in the fact that it is true to reality; it does not create life anew, but reproduces it, and, like a convex glass, mirrors in itself, from one point of view, life's diverse phenomena, extracting from them those that are necessary to create a full, vivid, and organically unified picture. The size and the limits of the contents of this picture are decisive in judging the greatness of the poetic work. In order to complete the characterization of that which I call *realistic* poetry, I add that its eternal hero, the unchanging object of poetic inspiration, is a human being, an individual, independent, acting freely, a symbol of the world—its final manifestation, the attempts to understand the curious riddle of himself, the final question of his own mind, the ultimate enigma of his own curious aspirations. The key to this riddle, the answer to this question, the resolution of this problem must be full *consciousness*, which is the mystery, the aim and the reason for his existence!

Is it surprising, after this, that this realistic trend in poetry, this close union of art with life has developed primarily in our time? Is it surprising that the distinct characteristic of the newest works of literature in general is a merciless frankness, that life appears in them as if in order to be put to shame, in all nakedness, in all its tremendous ugliness and in all its solemn beauty, as if it were dissected with an anatomist's knife? We demand not the ideal of life, but life as it is. Be it good or bad, we do not wish to adorn it, for we think that in poetic presentation it is equally beautiful in both cases precisely because it is true, and that where there is truth, there is poetry. . . .

[Realistic poetry] is the poetry of our time par excellence, more understandable and accessible to all, more in agreement with the spirit and needs of our time.

Henrik Ibsen
A DOLL'S HOUSE

Realism was not restricted to the novel alone. The leading realist playwright, Henrik Ibsen (1828–1906), a Norwegian, examined with clinical precision the commercial and professional classes, their personal ambitions, business practices, and family relationships. In a period of less than ten years, Ibsen wrote four realist "problem plays"—*Pillars of Society* (1877), *A Doll's House* (1879), *Ghosts* (1881), and *An Enemy of the People* (1882)—that drew attention to bourgeois pretensions, hypocrisy, and social conventions that thwart individual growth. Thus, Ibsen's characters are typically torn between their sense of duty to others and their own selfish wants. Although Ibsen wrote about profound social issues, he viewed himself as a dramatist relating a piece of reality and not a social reformer agitating for reform.

In *A Doll's House*, Ibsen took up a theme that shocked late-nineteenth century bourgeois audiences: a woman leaving her husband and children in search of self-realization. Nora Helmer resents being a submissive and dutiful wife to a husband who does not take her seriously, who treats her like a child, a doll.

In the following selection from *A Doll's House*, Nora tells her husband, Torvald, how she resents being treated like a child and why she is leaving him.

(She sits down at one side of the table.)

HELMER Nora—what is this?—this cold, set face?

NORA Sit down. It will take some time; I have a lot to talk over with you.

HELMER *(sits down at the opposite side of the table)* You alarm me, Nora!—and I don't understand you.

NORA No, that is just it. You don't understand me, and I have never understood you either—before to-night. No, you mustn't interrupt me. You must simply listen to what I say. Torvald, this is a settling of accounts.

HELMER What do you mean by that?

NORA *(after a short silence)* Isn't there one thing that strikes you as strange in our sitting here like this?

HELMER What is that?

NORA We have been married now eight years. Does it not occur to you that this is the first time we two, you and I, husband and wife, have had a serious conversation?

HELMER What do you mean by serious?

NORA In all these eight years—longer than that—from the very beginning of our acquaintance, we have never exchanged a word on any serious subject.

HELMER Was it likely that I would be continually and for ever telling you about worries that you could not help me to bear?

NORA I am not speaking about business matters. I say that we have never sat down in earnest together to try and get at the bottom of anything.

HELMER But, dearest Nora, would it have been any good to you?

NORA That is just it; you have never understood me. I have been greatly wronged, Torvald—first by papa and then by you.

HELMER What! By us two—by us two, who have loved you better than anyone else in the world?

NORA *(shaking her head)* You have never loved me. You have only thought it pleasant to be in love with me.

HELMER Nora, what do I hear you saying?

NORA It is perfectly true, Torvald. When I was at home with papa, he told me his opinion about everything, and so I had the same opinions; and if I differed from him I concealed the fact, because he would not have liked it. He called me his doll-child, and he played with me just as I used to play with my dolls. And when I came to live with you—

HELMER What sort of an expression is that to use about our marriage?

NORA *(undisturbed)* I mean that I was simply transferred from papa's hands into yours. You arranged everything according to your own taste, and so I got the same tastes as you—or else I pretended to, I am really not quite sure which—I think sometimes the one and sometimes the other. When I look back on it, it seems to me as if I had been living here like a poor woman—just from hand to mouth. I have existed merely to perform tricks for you, Torvald. But you would have it so. You and papa have committed a great sin against me. It is your fault that I have made nothing of my life.

HELMER How unreasonable and how ungrateful you are, Nora! Have you not been happy here?

NORA No. I have never been happy. I thought I was, but it has never really been so.

HELMER Not—not happy!

NORA No, only merry. And you have always been so kind to me. But our home has been nothing but a playroom. I have been your doll-wife, just as at home I was papa's doll-child; and here the children have been my dolls. I thought it great fun when you played with me, just as they thought it great fun when I played with them. That is what our marriage has been, Torvald.

HELMER There is some truth in what you say—exaggerated and strained as your view of it is. But for the future it shall be different. Playtime shall be over, and lesson-time shall begin.

NORA Whose lessons? Mine, or the children's?

HELMER Both yours and the children's, my darling Nora.

NORA Alas, Torvald, you are not the man to educate me into being a proper wife for you.

HELMER And you can say that!

NORA And I—how am I fitted to bring up the children?

HELMER Nora!

NORA Didn't you say so yourself a little while ago—that you dare not trust me to bring them up?

HELMER In a moment of anger! Why do you pay any heed to that?

NORA Indeed, you were perfectly right. I am not fit for the task. There is another task I must undertake first. I must try and educate myself—you are not the man to help me in that. I must do that for myself. And that is why I am going to leave you now.

HELMER *(springing up)* What do you say?

NORA I must stand quite alone, if I am to understand myself and everything about me. It is for that reason that I cannot remain with you any longer.

HELMER Nora! Nora!

NORA I am going away from here now, at once. I am sure Christine will take me in for the night—

HELMER You are out of your mind! I won't allow it! I forbid you!

NORA It is no use forbidding me anything any longer. I will take with me what belongs to myself. I will take nothing from you, either now or later.

HELMER What sort of madness is this!

NORA To-morrow I shall go home—I mean, to my old home. It will be easiest for me to find something to do there.

HELMER You blind, foolish woman!

NORA I must try and get some sense, Torvald.

HELMER To desert your home, your husband and your children! And you don't consider what people will say!

NORA I cannot consider that at all. I only know that it is necessary for me.

HELMER It's shocking. This is how you would neglect your most sacred duties.

NORA What do you consider my most sacred duties?

HELMER Do I need to tell you that? Are they not your duties to your husband and your children?

NORA I have other duties just as sacred.

HELMER That you have not. What duties could those be?

NORA Duties to myself.

HELMER Before all else, you are a wife and a mother.

NORA I don't believe that any longer. I believe that before all else I am a reasonable human being, just as you are—or, at all events, that I must try and become one. I know quite well, Torvald, that most people would think you right, and that views of that kind are to be found in books; but I can no longer content myself with what most people say, or with what is found in books. I must think over things for myself and get to understand them.

HELMER Can you not understand your place in your own home? Have you not a reliable guide in such matters as that?—have you no religion?

NORA I am afraid, Torvald, I do not exactly know what religion is.

HELMER What are you saying?

NORA I know nothing but what the clergyman said, when I went to be confirmed. He told us that religion was this, and that, and the other. When I am away from all this, and am alone, I will look into that matter too. I will see if what the clergyman said is true, or at all events if it is true for me.

HELMER This is unheard of in a girl of your age! But if religion cannot lead you aright, let me try and awaken your conscience. I suppose you have some moral sense? or—answer me— am I to think you have none?

NORA I assure you, Torvald, that is not an easy question to answer. I really don't know. The thing perplexes me altogether. I only know that you and I look at it in quite a different light. I am learning, too, that the law is quite another thing from what I supposed; but I find it impossible to convince myself that the law is right. According to it a woman has no right to spare her old dying father, or to save her husband's life. I can't believe that.

HELMER You talk like a child. You don't understand the conditions of the world in which you live.

NORA No, I don't. But now I am going to try. I am going to see if I can make out who is right, the world or I.

HELMER You are ill, Nora; you are delirious; I almost think you are out of your mind.

NORA I have never felt my mind so clear and certain as tonight.

HELMER And is it with a clear and certain mind that you forsake your husband and your children.

NORA Yes, it is.

HELMER Then there is only one possible explanation.

NORA What is that?

HELMER You do not love me any more.

NORA No, that is just it.

HELMER Nora!—and you can say that!

NORA It gives me great pain, Torvald, for you have always been so kind to me, but I cannot help it. I do not love you any more.

HELMER *(regaining his composure)* Is that a clear and certain conviction too?

NORA Yes, absolutely clear and certain. That is the reason I will not stay here any longer.

HELMER And can you tell me what I have done to forfeit your love?

NORA Yes, indeed I can. It was to-night, when the wonderful thing did not happen; then I saw you were not the man I had thought you.

HELMER Explain yourself better—I don't understand you.

When Nora was a young wife, Torvald became dangerously ill; doctors told her (but not him) that the only way to save her husband's life was to live in a warmer climate. Nora tried tears and entreaties with Torvald, saying that he ought to be kind to her by taking her on an extended trip to Italy, even if it meant taking a loan. Unaware of Nora's true intent—she wanted to save his life—Torvald would not hear of it. When she said her father provided the money, Torvald agreed. In reality, she borrowed the money by forging her dying father's name, something Torvald never knew. She continues to pay off the loan by carefully managing the funds alloted to her by Torvald for running the house, and Torvald does not know her secret. Recently promoted to a top position in the bank, Torvald fires Krogstad, who happened to be the person from whom Nora had borrowed the money. On news that he was fired, Krogstad delivers a letter to Torvald's home revealing the loan and the forgery. After reading the letter, Torvald hurls invectives at Nora: "miserable creature," "hypocrite," "liar," "criminal." "I shall not allow you to bring up the children; I dare not trust them to you."

NORA I have waited so patiently for eight years; for goodness knows, I knew very well that wonderful things don't happen every day. Then this horrible misfortune came upon me; and then I felt quite certain that the wonderful thing was going to happen at last. When Krogstad's letter was lying out there, never for a moment did I imagine that you would consent to accept this man's conditions. I was so absolutely certain that you would say to him: Publish the thing to the whole world. And when that was done—

HELMER Yes, what then—when I had exposed my wife to shame and disgrace?

NORA When that was done, I was so absolutely certain, you would come forward and take everything upon yourself, and say: I am the guilty one.

HELMER Nora—!

NORA You mean that I would never have accepted such a sacrifice on your part? No, of course not. But what would my assurances have been worth against yours? That was the wonderful thing which I hoped for and feared; and it was to prevent that, that I wanted to kill myself.

HELMER I would gladly work night and day for you, Nora—bear sorrow and want for your sake. But no man would sacrifice his honour for the one he loves.

NORA It is a thing hundreds of thousands of women have done.

HELMER Oh, you think and talk like a heedless child.

NORA Maybe. But you neither think nor talk like the man I could bind myself to. As soon as your fear was over—and it was not fear for what threatened me, but for what might happen to you—when the whole thing was past, as far as you were concerned it was exactly as if nothing at all had happened. Exactly as before, I was your little skylark, your doll, which you would in future treat with doubly gentle care, because it was so brittle and fragile. (*Getting up.*) Torvald—it was then it dawned upon me that for eight years I had been living here with a strange man, and had borne him three children—. Oh, I can't bear to think of it! I could tear myself into little bits!

HELMER (*sadly*) I see, I see. An abyss has opened between us—there is no denying it. But, Nora, would it not be possible to fill it up?

NORA As I am now, I am no wife for you.

HELMER I have it in me to become a different man.

NORA Perhaps—if your doll is taken away from you.

HELMER But to part!—to part from you! No, no. Nora, I can't understand that idea.

NORA (*going out to the right*) That makes it more certain that it must be done.

(*She comes back with her cloak and hat and a small bag which she puts on a chair by the table*)

HELMER Nora, Nora, not now! Wait till tomorrow.

NORA (*putting on her cloak*) I cannot spend the night in a strange man's room.

HELMER But can't we live here like brother and sister—?

NORA (*putting on her hat*) You know very well that would not last long. (*Puts the shawl round her.*) Good-bye, Torvald. I won't see the little ones. I know they are in better hands than mine. As I am now, I can be of no use to them.

HELMER But some day, Nora—some day?

NORA How can I tell? I have no idea what is going to become of me.

HELMER But you are my wife, whatever becomes of you.

NORA Listen, Torvald. I have heard that when a wife deserts her husband's house, as I am doing now, he is legally freed from all obligations towards her. In any case I set you free from all your obligations. You are not to feel yourself bound in the slightest way, any more than I shall. There must be perfect freedom on both sides. See, here is your ring back. Give me mine.

HELMER That too?

NORA That too.

HELMER Here it is.

NORA That's right. Now it is all over. I have put the keys here. The maids know all about everything in the house—better than I do. Tomorrow, after I have left her, Christine will come here and pack up my own things that I brought with me from home. I will have them sent after me.

HELMER All over! All over!—Nora, shall you never think of me again?

NORA I know I shall often think of you and the children and this house.

HELMER May I write to you, Nora?

NORA No—never. You must not do that.

HELMER But at least let me send you—

NORA Nothing—nothing—

HELMER Let me help you if you are in want.

NORA No. I can receive nothing from a stranger.

HELMER Nora—can I never be anything more than a stranger to you?

NORA *(taking her bag)* Ah, Torvald, the most wonderful thing of all would have to happen.

HELMER Tell me what that would be!

NORA Both you and I would have to be so changed that—Oh, Torvald, I don't believe any longer in wonderful things happening.

HELMER But I will believe in it. Tell me? So changed that—?

NORA That our life together would be a real wedlock. Good-bye.

> *(She goes out through the hall.)*

HELMER *(sinks down on a chair at the door and buries his face in his hands)* Nora! Nora! *(looks round, and rises)* Empty. She is gone. *(A hope flashes across his mind.)* The most wonderful thing of all—?

> *(The sound of a door shutting is heard from below.)*

REVIEW QUESTIONS

1. What did Vissarion Belinsky mean by realistic poetry?
2. What does *A Doll's House* tell you about middle-class life in the nineteenth century?
3. Do you agree with Nora's decision? Explain.

---

2 Theory of Evolution

In a century of outstanding scientific discoveries, none was more significant than the theory of evolution formulated by the English naturalist Charles Darwin (1809–1882). From December 1831 to 1836, Darwin had served as naturalist at sea on the *H.M.S. Beagle*, which surveyed parts of South America and some Pacific islands. He collected and classified many specimens of animal and plant life and from his investigations eventually drew several conclusions that startled the scientific community and enraged many members of the clergy.

Before Darwin's theory of evolution, most people adhered to the biblical account of creation found in Genesis, which said that God had created the universe, the various species of animal and plant life, and human beings, all in six days. The creation account also said that God had given each species of animal and plant a form that distinguished it from every other species. It was commonly held that the creation of the universe and of the first human beings had occurred some five or six thousand years earlier.

On the basis of his study, Darwin held that all life on earth had descended from earlier living forms; that human beings had evolved from lower, nonhuman species; and that the process had taken millions of years. Adopting the Malthusian idea that population reproduces faster than the food supply increases, Darwin held that within nature there is a continual struggle for existence. He said that the advantage lies with those living things that are stronger, faster, better camouflaged from their enemies, or better fitted in some way—such as adaptability—for survival than are other members of their species; those more fit to survive pass along the advantageous trait to offspring. This principle of *natural selection* explains why some members of a species survive and reproduce and why those less fit perish.

Charles Darwin
NATURAL SELECTION

According to Darwin, members of a species inherit variations that distinguish them from others in the species, and over many generations these variations become more pronounced. In time, a new variety of life evolves that can no longer breed with the species from which it descended. In this way, new species emerge and older ones die out. Human beings were also a product of natural selection, evolving from earlier, lower, nonhuman forms of life. In this first passage, from his autobiography, Darwin described his empirical method and his discovery of a general theory that coordinated and illuminated the data he found. Succeeding excerpts are from his *The Origin of Species* (1859) and *The Descent of Man* (1871).

DARWIN'S DESCRIPTION OF HIS METHOD AND DISCOVERY

From September 1854 I devoted my whole time to arranging my huge pile of notes, to observing, and to experimenting in relation to the transmutation of species. During the voyage of the *Beagle* I had been deeply impressed by discovering in the Pampean formation[1] great fossil animals covered with armour like that on the existing armadillos; secondly, by the manner in which closely allied animals replace one another in proceeding southwards over the Continent; and thirdly, by the South American character of most of the productions of the Galapagos archipelago,[2] and more especially by the manner in which they differ slightly on each island of the group; none of the islands appearing to be very ancient in a geological sense.

---

[1]The Pampean formation refers to the vast plain that stretches across Argentina, from the Atlantic Ocean to the foothills of the Andes Mountains.

[2]The Galapagos Islands, a Pacific archipelago 650 miles west of Ecuador, are noted for their unusual wildlife, which Darwin observed.

It was evident that such facts as these, as well as many others, could only be explained on the supposition that species gradually become modified; and the subject haunted me. But it was equally evident that neither the action of the surrounding conditions, nor the will of the organisms (especially in the case of plants) could account for the innumerable cases in which organisms of every kind are beautifully adapted to their habits of life—for instance, a woodpecker or a tree-frog to climb trees, or a seed for dispersal by hooks or plumes. I had always been much struck by such adaptations, and until these could be explained it seemed to me almost useless to endeavour to prove by indirect evidence that species have been modified.

After my return to England it appeared to me that by following the example of Lyell[3] in Geology, and by collecting all facts which bore in any way on the variation of animals and plants under domestication and nature, some light might perhaps be thrown on the whole subject. My first note-book was opened in July 1837. I worked on true Baconian principles,[4] and without any theory collected facts on a wholesale scale, more especially with respect to domesticated productions, by printed enquiries, by conversation with skilful breeders and gardeners, and by extensive reading. When I see the list of books of all kinds which I read and abstracted, including whole series of Journals and Transactions, I am surprised at my industry. I soon perceived that selection was the keystone of man's success in making useful races of animals and plants. But how selection could be applied to organisms living in a state of nature remained for some time a mystery to me.

In October 1838, that is, fifteen months after I had begun my systematic enquiry, I happened to read for amusement Malthus[5] on *Population*, and being well prepared to appreciate the struggle for existence which everywhere goes on from long-continued observation of the habits of animals and plants, it at once struck me that under these circumstances favourable variations would tend to be preserved and unfavourable ones to be destroyed. The result of this would be the formation of new species. Here, then, I had at last got a theory by which to work. . . .

It has sometimes been said that the success of *The Origin {of Species}* proved "that the subject was in the air," or "that men's minds were prepared for it." I do not think that this is strictly true, for I occasionally sounded not a few naturalists, and never happened to come across a single one who seemed to doubt about the permanence of species. Even Lyell and Hooker,[6] though they would listen with interest to me, never seemed to agree. I tried once or twice to explain to able men what I meant by Natural Selection, but signally failed. What I believe was strictly true is that innumerable well-observed facts were stored in the minds of naturalists ready to take their proper places as soon as any theory which would receive them was sufficiently explained. . . .

My *Descent of Man* was published in February 1871. As soon as I had become, in the year of 1837 or 1838, convinced that species were mutable productions, I could not avoid the belief that man must come under the same law.

In the following excerpt from *The Origin of Species* (1859), Darwin explained the struggle for existence and the principle of natural selection.

---

[3]Sir Charles Lyell (1797–1875) was a Scottish geologist whose work showed that the planet had evolved slowly over many ages. Like Lyell, Darwin sought to interpret natural history by observing processes still going on.
[4]"Baconian principles" refers to Sir Francis Bacon (1561–1626), one of the first to insist that new knowledge should be acquired through experimentation and the accumulation of data. (See page 39.)

[5]Thomas Malthus (1766–1834) was an English economist who maintained that population increases geometrically (2, 4, 8, 16, and so on) but the food supply increases arithmetically (1, 2, 3, 4, and so on). (See page 130.)
[6]Sir Joseph Dalton Hooker (1817–1911) was an English botanist who supported Darwin's ideas.

THE ORIGIN OF SPECIES

. . . Owing to this struggle [for existence], variations, however slight . . . , if they be in any degree profitable to the individuals of a species, in their infinitely complex relations to other organic beings and to their physical conditions of life, will tend to the preservation of such individuals, and will generally be inherited by the offspring. The offspring, also, will thus have a better chance of surviving, for, of the many individuals of any species which are periodically born, but a small number can survive. I have called this principle, by which each slight variation, if useful, is preserved, by the term Natural Selection, in order to mark its relation to man's power of selection. But the expression often used by Mr. Herbert Spencer[7] of the Survival of the Fittest is more accurate, and is sometimes equally convenient. . . .

A struggle for existence inevitably follows from the high rate at which all organic beings tend to increase. Every being, which during its natural lifetime produces several eggs or seeds, must suffer destruction during some period of its life, and during some season or occasional year, otherwise, on the principle of geometrical increase, its numbers would quickly become so inordinately great that no country could support the product. Hence, as more individuals are produced than can possibly survive, there must in every case be a struggle for existence, either one individual with another of the same species, or with the individuals of distinct species, or with the physical conditions of life. It is the doctrine of Malthus applied with manifold force to the whole animal and vegetable kingdoms; for in this case there can be no artificial increase of food, and no prudential restraint from marriage. Although some species may be now increasing, more or less rapidly, in numbers, all cannot do so, for the world would not hold them.

There is no exception to the rule that every organic being naturally increases at so high a rate, that, if not destroyed, the earth would soon be covered by the progeny of a single pair. Even slow-breeding man has doubled in twenty-five years, and at this rate, in less than a thousand years, there would literally not be standing-room for his progeny. . . . The elephant is reckoned the slowest breeder of all known animals, and I have taken some pains to estimate its probable minimum rate of natural increase; it will be safest to assume that it begins breeding when thirty years old, and goes on breeding till ninety years old, bringing forth six young in the interval, and surviving till one hundred years old; if this be so, after a period of from 740 to 750 years there would be nearly nineteen million elephants alive, descended from the first pair. . . .

. . . Can we doubt (remembering that many more individuals are born than can possibly survive) that individuals having any advantage, however slight, over others, would have the best chance of surviving and of procreating their kind? On the other hand, we may feel sure that any variation in the least degree injurious would be rigidly destroyed. This preservation of favourable individual differences and variations, and the destruction of those which are injurious, I have called Natural Selection, or the Survival of the Fittest. . . .

. . . Natural Selection acts solely through the preservation of variations in some way advantageous, which consequently endure. Owing to the high geometrical rate of increase of all organic beings, each area is already fully stocked with inhabitants; and it follows from this, that as the favoured forms increase in number, so, generally, will the less favoured decrease and become rare. . . .

From these several considerations I think it inevitably follows, that as new species in the course of time are formed through natural selection, others will become rarer and rarer, and finally extinct. The forms which stand in closest competition with those undergoing modification and improvement will naturally

---

[7]The British philosopher Herbert Spencer (1820–1903) coined the term *survival of the fittest*. (See page 191.)

suffer most. And we have seen in the chapter on the Struggle for Existence that it is the most closely-allied forms—varieties of the same species, and species of the same genus or of related genera—which, from having nearly the same structure, constitution, and habits, generally come into the severest competition with each other; consequently, each new variety or species, during the progress of its formation, will generally press hardest on its nearest kindred, and tend to exterminate them. We see the same process of extermination amongst our domesticated productions, through the selection of improved forms by man.

In *The Descent of Man* (1871), Darwin argued that human beings have evolved from lower forms of life.

THE DESCENT OF MAN

The main conclusion here arrived at, and now held by many naturalists who are well competent to form a sound judgment, is that man is descended from some less highly organised form. The grounds upon which this conclusion rests will never be shaken, for the close similarity between man and the lower animals in embryonic development, as well as in innumerable points of structure and constitution, both of high and of the most trifling importance,—the rudiments which he retains, and the abnormal reversions to which he is occasionally liable,—are facts which cannot be disputed. They have long been known, but until recently they told us nothing with respect to the origin of man. Now when viewed by the light of our knowledge of the whole organic world, their meaning is unmistakable. The great principle of evolution stands up clear and firm, when these groups of facts are considered in connection with others, such as the mutual affinities of the members of the same group, their geographical distribution in past and present times, and their geological succession. It is incredible that all these facts should speak falsely. He who is not content to look, like a savage, at the phenomena of nature as disconnected, cannot any longer believe that man is the work of a separate act of creation. He will be forced to admit that the close resemblance of the embryo of man to that, for instance, of a dog—the construction of his skull, limbs and whole frame on the same plan with that of other mammals, independently of the uses to which the parts may be put—the occasional reappearance of various structures, for instance of several muscles, which man does not normally possess, but which are common to the Quadrumana[8]—and a crowd of analogous facts—all point in the plainest manner to the conclusion that man is the co-descendant with other mammals of a common progenitor.

We have seen that man incessantly presents individual differences in all parts of his body and in his mental faculties. These differences or variations seem to be induced by the same general causes, and to obey the same laws as with the lower animals. In both cases similar laws of inheritance prevail. Man tends to increase at a greater rate than his means of subsistence; consequently he is occasionally subjected to a severe struggle for existence, and natural selection will have effected whatever lies within its scope. A succession of strongly-marked variations of a similar nature is by no means requisite; slight fluctuating differences in the individual suffice for the work of natural selection. . . .

Man may be excused for feeling some pride at having risen, though not through his own exertions, to the very summit of the organic scale; and the fact of his having thus risen, instead of having been aboriginally placed there, may give him hope for a still higher destiny in the distant future. But we are not here concerned with hopes or fears, only with the truth as far as our reason permits us to discover it; and I have given the evidence to the best of my ability.

---

[8]An order of mammals, Quadrumana includes all primates (monkeys, apes, and baboons) except human beings; the primates' hind and forefeet can be used as hands as they have opposable first digits.

We must, however, acknowledge, as it seems to me, that man with all his noble qualities, with sympathy which feels for the most debased, with benevolence which extends not only to other men but to the humblest living creature, with his god-like intellect which has penetrated into the movements and constitution of the solar system—with all these exalted powers—Man still bears in his bodily frame the indelible stamp of his lowly origin.

REVIEW QUESTIONS

1. How did Charles Darwin make use of Thomas Malthus's theory of population growth?
2. How did Darwin account for the extinction of old species and the emergence of new ones?
3. What did Darwin mean when he said that man "with his god-like intellect . . . still bears in his bodily frame the indelible stamp of his lowly origin"?

3 The Socialist Revolution

After completing a doctorate at the University of Jena in 1841, Karl Marx (1818–1883) edited a newspaper that was suppressed by the Prussian authorities for its radicalism and atheism. He left his native Rhineland for Paris, where he became friendly with Friedrich Engels. Expelled from France at the request of Prussia, Marx went to Brussels. In 1848, Marx and Engels produced for the Communist League the *Communist Manifesto*, advocating the violent overthrow of capitalism and the creation of a socialist society. Marx returned to Prussia and participated in a minor way in the Revolutions of 1848 in Germany. Expelled from Prussia in 1849, he went to England. He spent the rest of his life there, writing and agitating for the cause of socialism.

The *Communist Manifesto* presented a philosophy of history and a theory of society that Marx expanded upon in his later works, particularly *Capital* (1867). In the tradition of the Enlightenment, he maintained that history, like the operations of nature, was governed by scientific law. To understand the past and the present and to predict the essential outlines of the future, said Marx, one must concentrate on economic forces, on how goods are produced and how wealth is distributed. Marx's call for a working-class revolution against capitalism and for the making of a classless society established the ideology of twentieth-century Communist revolutionaries.

Karl Marx and Friedrich Engels
COMMUNIST MANIFESTO

In the opening section of the *Manifesto*, the basic premise of the Marxian philosophy of history is advanced: class conflict—the idea that the social order is divided into classes based on conflicting economic interests.

BOURGEOIS AND PROLETARIANS

The history of all hitherto existing society is the history of class struggles.

Freeman and slave, patrician and plebeian [aristocrat and commoner, in the ancient world], lord and serf, guild-master [master craftsman] and journeyman [who worked for a guild-master], in a word, oppressor and oppressed, stood in constant opposition to one another, carried on an uninterrupted, now hidden, now open fight, that each time ended, either in a revolutionary reconstitution of society at large, or in the common ruin of the contending classes.

In the earlier epochs of history we find almost everywhere a complicated arrangement of society into various orders, a manifold gradation of social rank. In ancient Rome we have patricians, knights, plebeians, slaves; in the Middle Ages, feudal lords, vassals [landowners pledged to lords], guild-masters, journeymen, apprentices, serfs; in almost all of these classes, again, subordinate gradations.

The modern bourgeois society that has sprouted from the ruins of feudal society, has not done away with class antagonisms. It has but established new forms of struggle in place of the old ones.

Our epoch, the epoch of the bourgeoisie [capitalist class], possesses, however, this distinctive feature; it has simplified the class antagonisms. Society as a whole is more and more splitting up into two great hostile camps, into two great classes directly facing each other: Bourgeoisie and Proletariat [industrial workers].

From the serfs of the middle ages sprang the chartered burghers of the earliest towns. From these burgesses the first elements of the bourgeoisie were developed.

The discovery of America, the rounding of the Cape, opened up fresh ground for the rising bourgeoisie. The East-Indian and Chinese markets, the colonization of America, trade with the colonies, the increase in the means of exchange and in commodities generally, gave to commerce, to navigation, to industry, an impulse never before known, and thereby, to the revolutionary element in the tottering feudal society, a rapid development.

The feudal system of industry, under which industrial production was monopolized by closed guilds, now no longer sufficed for the growing wants of the new market. The manufacturing system took its place. The guild-masters were pushed on one side by the manufacturing middle class; division of labor between the different corporate guilds vanished in the face of division of labor in each single workshop.

Meantime the markets kept ever growing, the demand ever rising. . . . Thereupon steam and machinery revolutionized industrial production. The place of manufacture was taken by the giant, Modern Industry, the place of the industrial middle class, by industrial millionaires, the leaders of whole industrial armies, the modern bourgeois.

Modern Industry has established the world's market, for which the discovery of America paved the way. This market has given an immense development to commerce, to navigation, to communication by land. This development has, in its turn, reacted on the extension of industry; and in proportion, as industry, commerce, navigation, railways extended, in the same proportion, the bourgeoisie developed, increased its capital, and pushed into the background every class handed down from the Middle Ages.

We see, therefore, how the modern bourgeoisie is itself the product of a long course of development, of a series of revolutions in the modes of production and of exchange.

Each step in the development of the bourgeoisie was accompanied by a corresponding political advance of that class. An oppressed class under the sway of the feudal nobility, an armed and self-governing association in the mediaeval commune [town], . . . the bourgeoisie has at last, since the establishment of Modern Industry and of the world's market, conquered for itself, in the modern representative State, exclusive political sway. The executive of the modern State is but a committee for managing the common affairs of the whole bourgeoisie.

The bourgeoisie, historically, has played a most revolutionary part.

The bourgeoisie, wherever it has got the upper hand, has put an end to all feudal, patriarchal, idyllic relations. It has pitilessly torn asunder the motley feudal ties that bound man to his "natural superiors," and has left remaining no other nexus [link] between man and man than naked self-interest, than callous "cash payment." It has drowned the most heavenly ecstasies of religious fervor, of chivalrous enthusiasm, . . . in the icy water of egotistical calculation. It has resolved personal worth into exchange value, and in place of the numberless indefeasible chartered freedoms, has set up that single, unconscionable freedom—Free Trade. In one word, for exploitation, veiled by religious and political illusions, it has substituted naked, shameless, direct, brutal exploitation. . . .

The bourgeoisie, states the *Manifesto*, has subjected nature's forces to human control to an unprecedented degree and has replaced feudal organization of agriculture (serfdom) and manufacturing (guild system) with capitalist free competition. But the capitalists cannot control these "gigantic means of production and exchange." Periodically, capitalist society is burdened by severe economic crises; capitalism is afflicted with overproduction— more goods are produced than the market will absorb. In all earlier epochs, which were afflicted with scarcity, the *Manifesto* declares, such a condition "would have seemed an absurdity." To deal with the crisis, the capitalists curtail production, thereby intensifying the poverty of the proletariat, who are without work. In capitalist society, the exploited worker suffers from physical poverty—a result of low wages—and spiritual poverty—a result of the monotony, regimentation, and impersonal character of the capitalist factory system. For the proletariat, work is not the satisfaction of a need but a repulsive means for survival. The products they help make bring them no satisfaction; they are alienated from their labor.

In proportion as the bourgeoisie, *i.e.*, capital, is developed, in the same proportion is the proletariat, the modern working class, developed—a class of laborers, who live only so long as they find work, and who find work only so long as their labor increases capital. These laborers, who must sell themselves piecemeal, are a commodity, like every other article of commerce, and are consequently exposed to all the vicissitudes of competition, to all the fluctuations of the market.

Owing to the extensive use of machinery and to division of labor, the work of the proletarians has lost all individual character, and, consequently, all charm for the workman. He becomes an appendage of the machine, and it is only the most simple, most monotonous, and most easily acquired knack, that is required of him. Hence, the cost of production of a workman is restricted, almost entirely, to the means of subsistence that he requires for his maintenance, and for the propagation of his race. But the price of a commodity, and therefore also of labor, is equal to its cost of production. In proportion, therefore, as the repulsiveness of the work increases, the wage decreases. Nay more, in proportion as the use of machinery and division of labor increases, in the same proportion the burden of toil also increases, whether by prolongation of the working hours, by increase of the work exacted in a given time, or by increased speed of the machinery, etc.

Modern industry has converted the little workshop of the patriarchal master into the great factory of the industrial capitalist. Masses of laborers, crowded into the factory, are organized like soldiers. As privates of the industrial army they are placed under the command of a perfect hierarchy of officers and sergeants. Not only are they slaves of the bourgeois class, and of the bourgeois state; they are daily and hourly enslaved by the machine, by the overlooker, and, above all, by the individual bourgeois manufacturer himself. The more openly this despotism proclaims gain to be its end and aim, the more petty, the more hateful and the more embittering it is.

The less the skill and exertion of strength implied in manual labor, in other words, the more modern industry develops, the more is the labor of men superseded by that of women. Differences of age and sex have no longer any distinctive social validity for the working class.

All are instruments of labor, more or less expensive to use, according to their age and sex.

No sooner has the laborer received his wages in cash, for the moment escaping exploitation by the manufacturer, than he is set upon by the other portions of the bourgeoisie, the landlord, the shop-keeper, the pawnbroker, etc. . . .

The exploited workers organize to defend their interests against the capitalist oppressors.

But with the development of industry the proletariat not only increases in number; it becomes concentrated in greater masses, its strength grows, and it feels that strength more. The various interests and conditions of life within the ranks of the proletariat are more and more equalized, in proportion as machinery obliterates all distinctions of labor and nearly everywhere reduces wages to the same low level. The growing competition among the bourgeois, and the resulting commercial crises, make the wages of the workers ever more fluctuating. The unceasing improvement of machinery, ever more rapidly developing, makes their livelihood more and more precarious: the collisions between individual workmen and individual bourgeois take more and more the character of collisions between two classes. Thereupon the workers begin to form combinations (trade unions) against the bourgeoisie; they club together in order to keep up the rate of wages; they found permanent associations in order to make provision beforehand for these occasional revolts. Here and there the contest breaks out into riots.

Now and then the workers are victorious, but only for a time. The real fruit of their battles lies, not in the immediate results, but in [their ever-expanding unity]. . . .

This organization of the proletarians into a class, and consequently into a political party, is continually being upset again by the competition between the workers themselves. But it ever rises up again, stronger, firmer, mightier. It compels legislative recognition of particular interests of the workers, by taking advantage of the divisions among the bourgeoisie itself. Thus the ten-hour bill[1] in England was carried. . . .

Increasingly, the proletariat, no longer feeling part of the old society, seeks to destroy it.

In the conditions of the proletariat, those of the old society at large are already virtually swamped. The proletarian is without property; his relation to his wife and children has no longer anything in common with the bourgeois family relations; modern industrial labor, modern subjection to capital, the same in England as in France, in America as in Germany, has stripped him of every trace of national character. Law, morality, religion, are to him so many bourgeois prejudices, behind which lurk in ambush just as many bourgeois interests.

All the preceding classes that got the upper hand sought to fortify their already acquired status by subjecting society at large to their conditions of appropriation. The proletarians cannot become masters of the productive forces of society, except by abolishing their own previous mode of appropriation, and thereby also every other previous mode of appropriation. They have nothing of their own to secure and to fortify; their mission is to destroy all previous securities for, and insurances of, individual property.

All previous historical movements were movements of minorities, or in the interest of minorities. The proletarian movement is the self-conscious, independent movement of the immense majority, in the interest of the immense majority. The proletariat, the lowest stratum of our present society, cannot stir, cannot raise itself up, without the whole superincumbent [overlying] strata of official society being [shattered].

Though not in substance, yet in form, the struggle of the proletariat with the bourgeoisie

---

[1]The Ten Hours Act (1847) provided a ten and a half hour day from 6 A.M. to 6 P.M., with an hour and a half for meals for women and children.

is at first a national struggle. The proletariat of each country must, of course, first of all settle matters with its own bourgeoisie.

In depicting the most general phases of the development of the proletariat, we traced the more or less veiled civil war, raging within existing society, up to the point where that war breaks out into open revolution, and where the violent overthrow of the bourgeoisie lays the foundation for the sway of the proletariat. . . .

The modern laborer . . . instead of rising with the progress of industry, sinks deeper and deeper below the conditions of existence of his own class. He becomes a pauper, and pauperism develops more rapidly than population and wealth. And here it becomes evident that the bourgeoisie is unfit any longer to be the ruling class in society and to impose its conditions of existence upon society as an overriding law. It is unfit to rule because it is incompetent to assure an existence to its slave within his slavery, because it cannot help letting him sink into such a state that it has to feed him instead of being fed by him. Society can no longer live under this bourgeoisie, in other words its existence is no longer compatible with society.

The essential condition for the existence and for the sway of the bourgeois class, is the formation and augmentation of capital; the condition for capital is wage-labor. Wage-labor rests exclusively on competition between the laborers. The advance of industry, whose involuntary promoter is the bourgeoisie, replaces the isolation of the laborers, due to competition, by their revolutionary combination, due to association. The development of modern industry, therefore, cuts from under its feet the very foundation on which the bourgeoisie produces and appropriates products. What the bourgeoisie therefore produces above all, are its own gravediggers. Its fall and the victory of the proletariat are equally inevitable. . . .

Communists, says the *Manifesto*, are the most advanced and determined members of working-class parties. Among the aims of the Communists are organization of the working class into a revolutionary party; overthrow

of bourgeois power and the assumption of political power by the proletariat; and an end to exploitation of one individual by another and the creation of a classless society. These aims will be achieved by the abolition of bourgeois private property (private ownership of the means of production) and the abolition of the bourgeoisie as a class.

The Communists, therefore, are on the one hand, practically, the most advanced and resolute section of the working class parties of every country, that section which pushes forward all others; on the other hand, theoretically, they have over the great mass of the proletariat the advantage of clearly understanding the line of march, the conditions, and the ultimate *general* results of the proletarian movement.

The immediate aim of the Communists is the same as that of all the other proletarian parties: formation of the proletariat into a class, overthrow of the bourgeois supremacy, conquest of political power by the proletariat. . . .

The distinguishing feature of Communism is not the abolition of property generally, but the abolition of bourgeois property. But modern bourgeois private property is the final and most complete expression of the system of producing and appropriating products, that is based on class antagonisms, on the exploitation of the many by the few.

In this sense the theory of the Communists may be summed up in the single sentence: Abolition of private property. . . .

One argument leveled against Communists by bourgeois critics, says the *Manifesto*, is that the destruction of the bourgeoisie would lead to the disappearance of bourgeois culture, which is "identical with the disappearance of all culture," and the loss of all moral and religious truths. Marx insists that these ethical and religious ideals lauded by the bourgeoisie are not universal truths at all but are common expressions of the ruling class at a particular stage in history.

That culture, the loss of which he [the bourgeois] laments, is for the enormous majority, a mere training to act as a machine.

But don't wrangle with us so long as you [the bourgeoisie] apply to our [the Communists'] intended abolition of bourgeois property, the standard of your bourgeois notions of freedom, culture, law, etc. Your very ideas are but the outgrowth of the conditions of your bourgeois production and bourgeois property, just as your jurisprudence is but the will of your class made into a law for all, a will, whose essential character and direction are determined by the economical conditions of existence of your class.

The selfish misconception that induces you to transform into eternal laws of nature and of reason, the social forms springing from your present mode of production and form of property—historical relations that rise and disappear in the progress of production—this misconception you share with every ruling class that has preceded you. What you see clearly in the case of ancient property, what you admit in the case of feudal property, you are of course forbidden to admit in the case of your own bourgeois form of property. . . .

The charges against Communism made from a religious, a philosophical, and, generally, from an ideological standpoint, are not deserving of serious examination.

Does it require deep intuition to comprehend that man's ideas, views, and conceptions, in one word, man's consciousness changes with every change in the conditions of his material existence, in his social relations and in his social life?

What else does the history of ideas prove than that intellectual production changes its character in proportion as material production is changed? The ruling ideas of each age have ever been the ideas of its ruling class. . . .

. . . The ideas of religious liberty and freedom of conscience merely gave expression to the sway of free competition within the domain of knowledge.

"Undoubtedly," it will be said, "religious, moral, philosophical, and juridical ideas have been modified in the course of historic development. But religion, morality, philosophy, political science, and law, constantly survived this change.

"There are besides, eternal truths, such as Freedom, Justice, etc., that are common to all states of society. But Communism abolishes eternal truths, it abolishes all religion and all morality, instead of constituting them on a new basis; it therefore acts as a contradiction to all past historical experience."

What does this accusation reduce itself to? The history of all past society has consisted in the development of class antagonisms, antagonisms that assumed different forms at different epochs.

But whatever form they may have taken, one fact is common to all past ages, *viz.*, the exploitation of one part of society by the other. No wonder, then, that the social consciousness of past ages, despite all the multiplicity and variety it displays, moves within certain common forms, or general ideas, which cannot completely vanish except with the total disappearance of class antagonisms.

The Communist revolution is the most radical rupture with traditional property relations; no wonder that its development involves the most radical rupture with traditional ideas.

Aroused and united by Communist intellectuals, says the *Manifesto*, the proletariat will wrest power from the bourgeoisie and overthrow the capitalist system that has oppressed them. In the new society, people will be fully free.

But let us have done with the bourgeois objections to Communism.

We have seen above that the first step in the revolution by the working class is to raise the proletariat to the position of the ruling class, to win the battle of democracy.

The proletariat will use its political supremacy to wrest, by degrees, all capital from the bourgeoisie; to centralize all instruments of production in the hands of the State, *i.e.*, of the proletariat organized as the ruling class; and to increase the total of productive forces as rapidly as possible. . . .

When, in the course of development, class distinctions have disappeared and all production has been concentrated in the hands of a vast association of the whole nation, the public power will lose its political character. Political power, properly so called, is merely the organized power of one class for oppressing another. If the proletariat during its contest with the bourgeoisie is compelled, by the force of circumstances, to organize itself as a class, if, by means of a revolution, it makes itself the ruling class, and, as such, sweeps away by force the old conditions of production, then it will, along with these conditions, have swept away the conditions for the existence of class antagonism, and of classes generally, and will thereby have abolished its own supremacy as a class.

In place of the old bourgeois society with its classes and class antagonisms we shall have an association in which the free development of each is the condition for the free development of all. . . .

The Communists disdain to conceal their views and aims. They openly declare that their ends can be attained only by the forcible overthrow of all existing social conditions. Let the ruling classes tremble at a communistic revolution. The proletarians have nothing to lose but their chains. They have a world to win.

Working men of all countries, unite!

REVIEW QUESTIONS

1. What do Karl Marx and Friedrich Engels mean by the term *class conflict*? What historical examples of class conflict are provided?
2. According to the *Manifesto*, what role has the state played in the class conflict?
3. How does the *Manifesto* describe the condition of the working class under capitalism?
4. According to the *Manifesto*, why is capitalism doomed? What conditions will bring about the end of capitalism?
5. "The ruling ideas of each age have ever been the ideas of its ruling class." What is meant by this statement? Do you agree or disagree? Explain.
6. Have Marx's predictions proven accurate? Explain your answer.

4 The Evolution of Liberalism

The principal concern of early nineteenth-century liberalism was protecting the rights of the individual against the demands of the state. For this reason, liberals advocated a constitution that limited the state's authority and a bill of rights that stipulated the citizen's basic freedoms. Believing that state interference in the economy endangered individual liberty and private property, liberals were strong advocates of laissez faire—leaving the market to its own devices. And convinced that the unpropertied and uneducated masses were not deeply committed to individual freedom, liberals approved property requirements for voting and office holding.

In the last part of the nineteenth century, however, liberalism changed substantially as many liberals came to support government reforms to deal with the problems created by unregulated industrialization. By the early twentieth century, liberalism—not without reservation and opposition on the part of some liberals—had evolved into social democracy, which maintains that government has an obligation to assist the needy.

L. T. Hobhouse
JUSTIFICATION FOR
STATE INTERVENTION

L. T. Hobhouse (1864–1929), an academic who also wrote for the *Manchester Guardian*, expressed these views in *Liberalism* (1911).

[It was conceived by an earlier liberalism] that, however deplorable the condition of the working classes might be, the right way of raising them was to trust to individual enterprise and possibly, according to some thinkers, to voluntary combination. By these means the efficiency of labour might be enhanced and its regular remuneration raised. By sternly withholding all external supports we should teach the working classes to stand alone, and if there were pain in the disciplinary process there was yet hope in the future. They would come by degrees to a position of economic independence in which they would be able to face the risks of life, not in reliance upon the State, but by the force of their own brains and the strength of their own right arms.

These views no longer command the same measure of assent. On all sides we find the State making active provision for the poorer classes and not by any means for the destitute alone. We find it educating the children, providing medical inspection, authorizing the feeding of the [needy] at the expense of the rate-payers, helping them to obtain employment through free Labour Exchanges, seeking to organize the labour market with a view to the mitigation of unemployment, and providing old age pensions for all whose incomes fall below thirteen shillings a week, without exacting any contribution. Now, in all this, we may well ask, is the State going forward blindly on the paths of broad and generous but unconsidered charity? Is it and can

it remain indifferent to the effect on individual initiative and personal or parental responsibility? Or may we suppose that the wiser heads are well aware of what they are about, have looked at the matter on all sides, and are guided by a reasonable conception of the duty of the State and the responsibilities of the individual? Are we, in fact—for this is really the question—seeking charity or justice?

We said above that it was the function of the State to secure the conditions upon which mind and character may develop themselves. Similarly we may say now that the function of the State is to secure conditions upon which its citizens are able to win by their own efforts all that is necessary to a full civic efficiency. It is not for the State to feed, house, or clothe them. It is for the State to take care that the economic conditions are such that the normal man who is not defective in mind or body or will can by useful labour feed, house, and clothe himself and his family. The "right to work" and the right to a "living wage" are just as valid as the rights of person or property. That is to say, they are integral conditions of a good social order. A society in which a single honest man of normal capacity is definitely unable to find the means of maintaining himself by useful work is to that extent suffering from malorganization. There is somewhere a defect in the social system, a hitch in the economic machine. Now, the individual workman cannot put the machine straight. He is the last person to have any say in the control of the market. It is not his fault if there is overproduction in his industry, or if a new and cheaper process has been introduced which makes his particular skill, perhaps the product of years of application, [obsolete] in the market. He does not direct or regulate industry. He is not responsible for its ups and downs, but he has to pay for them. That is why. it is not charity but justice for which he is asking. . . .

If this view of the duty of the State and the right of the workman is coming to prevail, it is owing partly to an enhanced sense of common responsibility, and partly to the teaching of experience. . . .

Herbert Spencer
THE MAN VERSUS THE STATE

Committed to a traditional laissez-faire policy, however, some liberals attacked state intervention as a threat to personal freedom and a betrayal of central liberal principles. In *The Man Versus the State* (1884), British philosopher Herbert Spencer (1820–1903) warned that increased government regulation would lead to socialism and slavery.

The extension of this policy . . . [of government legislation] fosters everywhere the tacit assumption that Government should step in whenever anything is not going right. "Surely you would not have this misery continue!" exclaims some one, if you hint . . . [an objection] to much that is now being said and done. Observe what is implied by this exclamation. It takes for granted . . . that every evil can be removed: the truth being that with the existing defects of human nature, many evils can only be thrust out of one place or form into another place or form—often being increased by the change. The exclamation also implies the unhesitating belief, here especially concerning us, that evils of all kinds should be dealt with by the State. . . . Obviously, the more numerous governmental interventions become, the more confirmed does this habit of thought grow, and the more loud and perpetual the demands for intervention.

Every extension of the regulative policy involves an addition to the regulative agents—a further growth of officialism and an increasing power of the organization formed of officials. . . .

. . . Moreover, every additional State-interference strengthens the tacit assumption that it is the duty of the State to deal with all evils and secure all benefits. Increasing power of a growing administrative organization is accompanied by decreasing power of the rest of the society to resist its further growth and control. . . .

"But why is this change described as 'the coming slavery'?" is a question which many will still ask. The reply is simple. All socialism involves slavery. . . .

Evidently then, the changes made, the changes in progress, and the changes urged, will carry us not only towards State-ownership of land and dwellings and means of communication, all to be administered and worked by State-agents, but towards State-usurpation of all industries: the private forms of which, disadvantaged more and more in competition with the State, which can arrange everything for its own convenience, will more and more die away, just as many voluntary schools have, in presence of Board-schools. And so will be brought about the desired ideal of the socialists. . . .

. . . It is a matter of common remark, often made when a marriage is impending, that those possessed by strong hopes habitually dwell on the promised pleasures and think nothing of the accompanying pains. A further exemplification

of this truth is supplied by these political en-
thusiasts and fanatical revolutionists. Impressed
with the miseries existing under our present social arrangements, and not regarding these miseries as caused by the ill-working of a human
nature but partially adapted to the social state,
they imagine them to be forthwith curable by
this or that rearrangement. Yet, even did their
plans succeed it could only be by substituting
one kind of evil for another. A little deliberate
thought would show that under their proposed
arrangements, their liberties must be surrendered in proportion as their material welfares
were cared for.

For no form of co-operation, small or great,
can be carried on without regulation, and an implied submission to the regulating agencies. . . .
. . . So that each [individual] would stand
toward the governing agency in the relation of
slave to master.

"But the governing agency would be a master
which he and others made and kept constantly
in check; and one which therefore would not
control him or others more than was needful for
the benefit of each and all."

To which reply the first rejoinder is that, even
if so, each member of the community as an individual would be a slave to the community as a
whole. Such a relation has habitually existed in
militant communities, even under quasi-popular
forms of government. In ancient Greece the accepted principle was that the citizen belonged
neither to himself nor to his family, but belonged
to his city—the city being with the Greek
equivalent to the community. And this doctrine,
proper to a state of constant warfare, is a doctrine
which socialism unawares re-introduces into a
state intended to be purely industrial. The services of each will belong to the aggregate of all;
and for these services, such returns will be given
as the authorities think proper. So that even if the
administration is of the beneficent kind intended
to be secured, slavery, however mild, must be the
outcome of the arrangement. . . .

The function of Liberalism in the past was
that of putting a limit to the powers of kings.
The function of true Liberalism in the future
will be that of putting a limit to the powers of
Parliaments.

REVIEW QUESTIONS

1. Why did L. T. Hobhouse believe that state intervention was needed to create
   "a good social order"?
2. What was Herbert Spencer's answer to the argument that government legislation
   is necessary to relieve human misery? Has history proven him correct?
3. What did Spencer mean by the dictum "All socialism involves slavery"?
4. According to Spencer, what was true liberalism? Compare his conception of
   liberalism with that of Hobhouse.

CHAPTER 8

Politics and Society, 1845–1914

CHILD LABOR. This illustration depicts children working in a brickyard in the English Midlands. An ongoing problem during the nineteenth century, child labor often evoked protests from reformers. *(HIP/Art Resource, NY)*

In the last half of the nineteenth century, the people of Europe, more numerous than ever and concentrated in ever-growing cities, interacted with each other in a busy exchange of goods, ideas, and services, which led to remarkable creativity in industry, science, and the arts. The physical sciences flourished; medical science advanced; the psychoanalytic method developed under Sigmund Freud. New technologies speeded communication and transportation, which intensified human contact and competition. Industrialization, promoted by capitalist enterprise, spread throughout Europe and the United States, raising the standard of living and advancing expectations among the poor for a better life. The new mobility and social interdependence provided greater opportunity for individual gain, but they also increased social tensions.

One source of tension arose from the growing demands among the lower classes for social justice and a share of political power; the misery of the poor and disenfranchised masses became a hot political issue. At the same time the agitation for women's rights mounted; women wanted to have rights equal to those of men in education and politics. Although women faced strenuous resistance with regard to suffrage, they continued to fight toward that goal. A third troublesome factor in European politics and society was anti-Semitism. Of long standing in European history, it became an active political force toward the end of the nineteenth century.

No country was more threatened by sociopolitical unrest than the Russian Empire. Contact with Western Europe convinced the tsarist government of the need to modernize their backward country and catch up with "the West," as Russians called the richer lands of Europe—a challenge beyond the resources of the tsarist regime. Increasing discontent among workers led to a revolution in 1905.

Despite the impressive achievements of European civilization and the domination of the globe by European states, the continent was becoming more and more deeply divided by the early 1900s. The competition for wealth and power heightened international rivalries. Nationalist ambitions, backed in most countries by popular support, and an arms race further worsened international relations. Although few people at the time recognized it, Europe's period of peace and security was ending. World War I, which broke out in 1914, was on the horizon.

1   The Lower Classes

The members of the upper and middle classes in European society looked down on "the lower classes"—industrial workers, domestic help, and peasants; and still further down, the street people, the mentally disturbed, the homeless, the unemployed, and vagrants; and at the bottom, the criminal underworld. These "lower classes" were most vulnerable to the vicissitudes of the business cycle and dependent on small and uncertain incomes; commonly they worked long hours under dehumanizing strain and were housed in urban slums under unsanitary conditions; they were hungry, illiterate, often reduced to outright destitution, and desperate to earn some money. In the slums of London's East End, one could see ragged men collect dog excrement for use in tanning leather; prostitution thrived.

In the economic progress of the nineteenth century, the overall material conditions of society improved remarkably, sharpening the social contrasts. Concerned people spoke of "two nations," the rich and the poor. The poor, however, were not entirely passive; workers began to rally, trying to improve their condition by political action, thereby scaring the upper classes into social awareness. At the same time, humanitarian concerns, often rising from religious inspiration, stirred some of the well-to-do. Toward the end of the nineteenth century, the misery of the poor caused lively public debate and heated political agitation.

Nikolaus Osterroth
THE YEARNING FOR SOCIAL JUSTICE

Nikolaus Osterroth (1875–1933), the son of a butcher, was a clay miner from the Palatinate, a region in Western Germany. His and his fellow miners' resentment at the deterioration of their working conditions undermined their traditional loyalty to their Catholic faith and prepared them for the appeal of the Social Democratic party, which, under the guidance of Marxist intellectuals, represented the interests of the German working class. Osterroth became a union and party organizer before World War I; after the war he played a part in the politics of the Weimar Republic.

This selection, taken from his autobiography published in 1920, describes in telling detail his transition from a docile clay miner to a Social Democratic agitator and organizer.

The hardest work is the rough cutting with the ax and cutting away the clumps from the seam. You can't take it for more than three hours because your hands get completely exhausted. So the shift is divided into four two-hour sections separated by breakfast, lunch, and the afternoon break. In his youth a miner's arms twitch from exhaustion even when he sleeps. . . .

. . . When there are a great number of people employed in a mine, then two tunnels on opposite sides of the shaft are worked, and one man works steadily at piling up the clumps. He also has to load the clumps onto wagons at the top of the shaft. The poor devil has to transport 800–1,000 wet, slippery clumps, each of which weighs 100 pounds. After years of this, his back gets all crooked and his arms get long like an ape's, so that he can scratch his knees without bending over.

For several hours every day the clumps are lifted up the shaft with a winch. In earlier days this work was usually done by women or girls.

It was a really murderous job and frequently resulted in premature births or great damage to the child-bearing organs of the women workers. After protracted pressure from the miners, the Bavarian Mining Law finally put an end to this disgraceful women's work. . . .

The clay-mining industry in Bavaria suffered hard times in the 1890s. The mine owners sought to reduce production costs at the expense of the workers, causing great friction.

MY FIRST ACQUAINTANCE WITH THE SOCIAL DEMOCRATS

The attempt to introduce . . . [wage cuts and] work rules created bad blood among the miners and stirred them to resistance, which at first found an outlet only in tavern debates.

When the mine owners stood by their plan . . . the miners turned to the priest, so that he might help them fight against this obvious injustice. But instead of standing by them, the priest preached that the employer was an authority appointed by God whom one had to obey. Humble obedience was the greatest virtue of subordinates. There had always been master and servant, and God had given the master the right to command his servant.

The workers could see what the priest was driving at, and they streamed from the church over to the tavern. There they reviled the priest in most unchristian language as one who, in exchange for the gift of a new church window from a mine owner, would preach patience to the workers instead of instilling humanity and righteousness in the mine owners. . . .

. . . [W]hen I heard with my own ears how the priest unambiguously sided against the workers instead of speaking to the conscience of the mine owners, I was angry and saw the priest above all as a Center party[1] man . . . groveling

to the upper classes and ready for any betrayal of the people; leading the people by the nose with religion; and always representing the "heretics" as the only danger. . . .

. . . And how did the priest use his influence? Instead of defending the rights of the oppressed, whose leadership he regarded as his monopoly, he preached submission and patience to the workers. He sat at the table of the rich and accepted the gifts that they had wrung from the poor, instead of reminding them that their actions were hardhearted and unchristian. Instead of saying to the mine owners, "Thou shalt love thy neighbor as thyself," he said to the exploited and raped workers, "You are servants, and servants you must remain; God wills it for your salvation."

A terrible storm raged through me. I doubted everything that up until then I had held as noble and good. . . .

On the last Sunday in April a leaflet was thrown through the open window while we were eating lunch. For a while it went unnoticed. After lunch I picked up the sheet of paper and glanced at the front and back sides, without reading the text. It was labeled, "To the Voters for the Reichstag!" and on the bottom of the back side it said, "The Social Democratic Reichstag Members." Now some life came into me. That was what I was looking for: a program, an authentic pronouncement of Social Democracy!

I began to read. Sentence by sentence there was an indictment against the government and the bourgeois parties, against armaments expenditures that had been driven to unbearable heights, against the insanely increasing debt burden of the Empire, against the excess of the new naval appropriations that oppressed the people, and against the plundering of the masses by tariffs and indirect taxes. And there was more: The stagnation of social welfare; the misery and lack of rights of the working class; the prison terms that the Emperor threatened, which would destroy the workers' right to organize! All that made an enormous, totally new impression on me.

---

[1]The Center party, representing the interests of the Catholic Church in Germany, generally followed a socially conservative course.

Suddenly I saw the world from the other side, from a side that up to now had been dark for me. . . . I was seized by a feeling of wild fury about the obvious injustice of a tax system that spared the ones who could best pay and plundered those who already despaired of life in their bitter misery.

But then I found something new that really gripped me: The Social Democratic leaflet not only criticized, it not only put its finger on the festering wounds and showed that the class character of society was the cause of the wrongs—no, it also produced a series of highly illuminating suggestions for the abolition of these wrongs. Numerous demands for the betterment of the condition of the people were made to the state. And then the leaflet turned to the voters, with a flaming appeal to them to make use of the universal suffrage, the greatest right of a citizen, in order to retaliate in the name of the people against a hostile government and treacherous parties.

He finds the people who had distributed the leaflet.

The leaflet affected me like a revelation. . . .

. . . [T]hey sat down again and for a whole hour they told me about the aspirations of Social Democracy and the growth of the young union movement. How heartily they laughed at the hopes I'd placed in the priest, and how convincingly and plainly they described how above all we workers lacked union organization. A union would bring together the weak uninfluential workers in order to counter the employers with the power of united action.

God, how clear and simple it all was! This new world of thought that gave the worker the weapons of self-awareness and self-consciousness was very different from the old world of priestly and economic authority where the worker was merely an object of domination and exploitation!

Once I'd gotten hold of these bringers of enlightenment I wouldn't let them go; I didn't have to be invited twice to help distribute

leaflets in the remaining two villages of the county. With the winged zeal of the newly converted, I leaped from house to house, taking three steps at a time and feeling lighter and happier than ever before in my life. My new friends liked my zeal. When we parted late in the evening, they gave me an "Erfurt Program"[2] and some newspapers, and promised that they would soon send me a package of pamphlets and newspapers. I spent almost the whole night studying the program, and I had the feeling that all these thoughts were etched into my brain with flamed writing.

The next day was the first of May. After a short, feverish sleep I awoke—for the first time as a Social Democrat. This was the day that the new work rules were to go into effect. . . .

On May Day—a holiday recently proclaimed by socialists to demonstrate workers' solidarity and their defiance of capitalism—Osterroth, inciting the workers to skip work, gives a speech.

At first I stammered and got confused when I saw the many curious people hanging on my every word. But soon the joyous shouts of agreement made me overcome all obstacles. I was amazed at myself, at how fast the new ideas from the article and the leaflet popped, one after another, into my mouth. And they were as new to my audience as to me. I discussed the purpose of our festival; I spoke of how our helplessness and powerlessness had emboldened our enemies, the mine owners, to impose the oppressive measures, the wage cuts, and the work rules, and to curtail our rights. I showed my comrades how impressive our unity was, and how it would help us further if we recognized the misery of our situation and got to know and value the means of improvement. I described how the workers were politically and

---

[2]Adopted in 1891, this was the official, Marxist-oriented program for the Social Democratic party.

economically exploited, deprived of their rights, duped, and deceived, and how deliverance from economic and political misery had to come from the working class itself. I described how the workers had to be unified and could not be allowed to fight among themselves for religious or political reasons. There were only two opposing sides that affected the workers very deeply and they were not "here the Catholics, there the non-Catholics"; rather, they were "here capital, there labor"—"here masters, there slaves"!

If we wanted to prevent the deterioration of our working conditions and fight for improvements, then we needed an organization that included all of us; and if we wanted to protest against political injustice and strive for healthier political conditions, then we had to vote for the Social Democratic candidate in the upcoming Reichstag election. Only the Social Democratic party dealt fairly with the workers, for it was the only workers' party that the upper classes fought against.

William Booth
IN DARKEST ENGLAND AND THE WAY OUT

The poor were not without compassionate friends. One of them was William Booth (1829–1912), the founder of the Salvation Army. Growing up poor himself, he was apprenticed to a pawnbroker while still a boy. At fifteen, under Methodist influence, he experienced a religious conversion, which eventually turned him into a Methodist minister; his wife and helpmate was one of the first Methodist woman preachers. Settled in London, he combined work at a pawnshop with ministering to the poor in the slums of London's East End. Booth and his wife devoted themselves to rescuing and rehabilitating the homeless, the unemployed, and the sinners of the urban underworld. In 1879 the organization that they had evolved officially became the Salvation Army. William Booth was its general; ordained ministers were its officers; the soldiers were men and women dedicated to saving others from the misery from which they themselves had escaped. All wore the Salvation Army's special uniform. The Salvation Army grew rapidly, spreading over the world. It now serves in seventy-seven countries, with over 300,000 soldiers in the United States.

In 1890 General Booth published *In Darkest England and the Way Out*, describing the misery of the poor and outlining his methods of achieving spiritual salvation through social service. In the opening two chapters, Booth outlined the extent of poverty in England at the height of its imperial glory. He begins by comparing England with journalist-explorer Henry Stanley's description of the brutality, slavery, and disease in "Darkest Africa."

WHY "DARKEST ENGLAND"?

This summer the attention of the civilised world has been arrested by the story which Mr. Stanley has told of "Darkest Africa" and his journeyings across the heart of the Lost Continent. . . .

It is a terrible picture, and one that has engraved itself deep on the heart of civilisation. But while brooding over the awful presentation of life as it exists in the vast African forest, it seemed to me only too vivid a picture of many parts of our own land. As there is a darkest Africa is there not also a darkest England? Civilisation, which can breed its own barbarians, does it not also breed its own pygmies? May we not find a parallel at our own doors, and discover within a stone's throw of our cathedrals and palaces similar horrors to those which Stanley has found existing in the great Equatorial forest?

The more the mind dwells upon the subject, the closer the analogy appears. The [Arab] ivory raiders who brutally traffic in the unfortunate denizens of the forest glades, what are they but the [exploiters] who flourish on the weakness of our poor? . . . As in Africa, it is all trees, trees, trees with no other world conceivable; so is it here—it is all vice and poverty and crime. To many the world is all slum, with the Workhouse as an intermediate purgatory before the grave. . . . Who can battle against the ten thousand million trees? Who can hope to make headway against the innumerable adverse conditions which doom the dweller in Darkest England to eternal and immutable misery?

. . . Talk about Danté's Hell, and all the horrors and cruelties of the torture-chamber of the lost! The man who walks with open eyes and with bleeding heart through the shambles of our civilisation needs no such fantastic images of the poet to teach him horror. Often and often, when I have seen the young and the poor and the helpless go down before my eyes into the morass, trampled underfoot by beasts of prey in human shape that haunt these regions, it seemed as if God were no longer in His world, but that in His stead reigned a fiend, merciless as Hell, ruthless as the grave. Hard it is, no doubt, to read in Stanley's pages of the slave-traders coldly arranging for the surprise of a village, the capture of the inhabitants, the massacre of those who resist, and the violation of all the women; but the stony streets of London, if they could but speak, would tell of tragedies as awful, of ruin as complete, of ravishments as horrible, as if we were in Central Africa; only the ghastly devastation is covered, corpse-like, with the artificialities and hypocrisies of modern civilisation.

The lot of a negress in the Equatorial Forest is not, perhaps, a very happy one, but is it so very much worse than that of many a pretty orphan girl in our Christian capital? . . . A young penniless girl, if she be pretty, is often hunted from pillar to post by her employers, confronted always by the alternative—Starve or Sin. And when once the poor girl has consented to buy the right to earn her living by the sacrifice of her virtue, then she is treated as a slave and an outcast by the very men who have ruined her. . . . [A]nd she is swept downward. . . .

The blood boils with impotent rage at the sight of these enormities, callously inflicted, and silently borne by these miserable victims. Nor is it only women who are the victims, although their fate is the most tragic. Those firms which reduce sweating [hard labor at low wages] to a fine art, who systematically and deliberately defraud the workman of his pay, who grind the faces of the poor, and who rob the widow and the orphan, and who for a pretence make great professions of public-spirit and philanthropy, those men nowadays are sent to Parliament to make laws for the people. The old prophets sent them to Hell—but we have changed all that. They send their victims to Hell, and are rewarded by all that wealth can do to make their lives comfortable. Read the House of Lords' Report on the Sweating System, and ask if any African slave system, making due allowance for the superior civilisation, and therefore sensitiveness, of the victims, reveals more misery.

Darkest England, like Darkest Africa, reeks with malaria. The foul and fetid breath of our slums is almost as poisonous as that of the African swamp. Fever is almost as chronic there as on the Equator. Every year thousands of children are killed off by what is called defects of our sanitary system. They are in reality starved and poisoned, and all that can be said is that, in many cases, it is better for them that they were taken away from the trouble to come.

Just as in Darkest Africa it is only a part of the evil and misery that comes from the superior race who invade the forest to enslave and massacre its miserable inhabitants, so with us, much of the misery of those whose lot we are considering arises from their own habits. Drunkenness and all manner of uncleanness, moral and physical, abound. Have you ever watched by the bedside of a man in delirium tremens [trembling and delusions brought on by alcohol abuse]? Multiply the sufferings of that one drunkard by the hundred thousand, and you have some idea of what scenes are being witnessed in all our great cities at this moment. . . . A population sodden with drink, steeped in vice, eaten up by every social and physical malady, these are the denizens of Darkest England amidst whom my life has been spent, and to whose rescue I would now summon all that is best in the manhood and womanhood of our land. . . .

. . . [T]he grimmest social problems of our time should be sternly faced, not with a view to the generation of profitless emotion, but with a view to its solution. . . .

Relying on the statistics of Charles Booth (no relation), William Booth concluded that three million people, one-tenth of the population, were pauperized and degraded.

THE SUBMERGED TENTH

What, then, is Darkest England? For whom do we claim that "urgency" which gives their case priority over that of all other sections of their countrymen and countrywomen? . . .

. . . The [people] in Darkest England, for whom I appeal, are (1) those who, having no capital or income of their own, would in a month be dead from sheer starvation were they exclusively dependent upon the money earned by their own work; and (2) those who by their utmost exertions are unable to attain the regulation allowance of food which the law prescribes as indispensable even for the worst criminals in our gaols.

I sorrowfully admit that it would be Utopian in our present social arrangements to dream of attaining for every honest Englishman a gaol standard of all the necessaries of life. Some time, perhaps, we may venture to hope that every honest worker on English soil will always be as warmly clad, as healthily housed, and as regularly fed as our criminal convicts—but that is not yet.

Neither is it possible to hope for many years to come that human beings generally will be as well cared for as horses. Mr. Carlyle long ago remarked that the four-footed worker has already got all that this two-handed one is clamouring for. . . .

What, then, is the standard towards which we may venture to aim with some prospect of realisation in our time? It is a very humble one, but if realised it would solve the worst problems of modern Society.

It is the standard of the London Cab Horse. . . .

The first question, then, which confronts us is, what are the dimensions of the Evil? How many of our fellow-men dwell in this Darkest England? How can we take the census of those who have fallen below the Cab Horse standard to which it is our aim to elevate the most wretched of our countrymen? . . .

Henry Mayhew
PROSTITUTION IN VICTORIAN LONDON

The destitute poor often turned to crime and prostitution for survival. In *London Labour and the London Poor*, published in 1862, Henry Mayhew (1812–1887), who had cultivated friendly contacts with London street people, including criminals and prostitutes, reported his findings with compassionate detachment. Practicing sociology with a human face, Mayhew pioneered oral history in hundreds of case studies. He hoped "to give the rich a more intimate knowledge of the sufferings and frequent heroism under those sufferings, of the poor—that it may . . . cause those who are in 'high places' and those of whom much is expected, to bestir themselves to improve the condition of a class of people whose misery, ignorance, and vice, amidst all the immense wealth and great knowledge of 'the first city in the world' is . . . a national disgrace. . . ." Below Mayhew records a young London prostitute's account of her squalid life.

STATEMENT OF A PROSTITUTE

The narrative which follows—that of a prostitute, sleeping in the low-lodging houses, where boys and girls are all huddled promiscuously together, discloses a system of depravity, atrocity, and enormity, which certainly cannot be paralleled in any nation, however barbarous, nor in any age, however "dark." The facts detailed, it will be seen, are gross enough to make us all blush for the land in which such scenes can be daily perpetrated. The circumstances, which it is impossible to publish, are of the most loathsome and revolting nature.

A good-looking girl of sixteen gave me the following awful statement:—

"I am an orphan. When I was ten I was sent to service as maid of all-work, in a small tradesman's family. It was a hard place, and my mistress used me very cruelly, beating me often. When I had been in place three weeks, my mother died; my father having died . . . years before. I stood my mistress's ill-treatment for about six months. She beat me with sticks as well as with her hands. I was black and blue, and at last I ran away. I got to Mrs.———, a low lodging-house. I didn't know before that there was such a place. I heard of it from some girls at the glasshouse (baths and washhouses), where I went for shelter. I went with them to have a halfpenny worth of coffee, and they took me to the lodging-house. I then had three shillings, and stayed about a month, and did nothing wrong, living on the three shillings and what I pawned my clothes for, as I got some pretty good things away with me. In the lodging-house I saw nothing but what was bad, and heard nothing but what was bad. I was laughed at, and was told to swear. They said, 'Look at her for a d———modest fool'—sometimes worse than that, until by degrees I got to be as bad as they were. During this time I used to see boys and girls from ten and twelve years old sleeping together, but understood nothing wrong. I had never heard of such places before I ran away. I can neither read nor write. My mother was a good woman, and I wish I'd had her to run away to. I saw things between almost children that I can't describe to you—very often I saw them, and that shocked me. At the month's end, when I was beat out, I met with a young man of fifteen—I myself was going on to twelve years old—and he persuaded me to take up with him. I stayed with him three months in the same lodging-house, living with him as his wife, though we were mere children, and being true to him. At the three months' end he was taken up for picking pockets, and got six months. I was sorry, for he was kind to me; though I was made ill through him; so I broke some windows in St. Paul's-churchyard to get into prison to get cured. I had a month in the Compter [debtors' prison], and came out well. I was scolded very much in the Compter, on account of the state I was in, being so young. I had 2s. 6d. [two shillings and sixpence] given to me when I came out, and was forced to go into the streets for a living. I continued walking the streets for three years, sometimes making a good deal of money, sometimes none, feasting one day and starving the next. The bigger girls could persuade me to do anything they liked with my money. I was never happy all the time, but I could get no character and could not get out of the life. I lodged all this time at a lodging-house in Kent-street. They were all thieves and bad girls. I have known between three and four dozen boys and girls sleep in one room. The beds were horrid filthy and full of vermin. There was very wicked carryings on. The boys, if any difference, was the worst. We lay packed on a full night, a dozen boys and girls squeedged into one bed. That was very often the case—some at the foot and some at the top—boys and girls all mixed. I can't go into all the particulars, but whatever could take place in words or acts between boys and girls did take place, and in the midst of the others. I am sorry to say I took part in these bad ways myself, but I wasn't so bad as some of the others. There was only a candle burning all night, but in summer it was light great part of the night. Some boys and girls slept without any clothes, and would dance about the room that way. I have seen them, and, wicked as I was, felt ashamed. I have seen two dozen capering about the room that way; some mere children, the boys generally the youngest. . . .

"There were no men or women present. There were often fights. The deputy never interfered. This is carried on just the same as ever to this day, and is the same every night. I have heard young girls shout out to one another how often they had been obliged to go to the hospital, or the infirmary, or the workhouse. There was a great deal of boasting about what the boys and girls had stolen during the day. I have known boys and girls change their 'partners,' just for a night. At three years' end I stole a piece of beef from a butcher. I did it to get into prison. I was sick of the life I was leading, and didn't know how to get out of it. I had a month for stealing. When I got out I passed two days and a night in the streets doing nothing wrong, and then went and threatened to break Messrs.————windows again. I did that to get into prison again; for when I lay quiet of a night in prison I thought things over, and considered what a shocking life I was leading, and how my health might be ruined completely, and I thought I would stick to prison rather than go back to such a life. I got six months for threatening. When I got out I broke a lamp

next morning for the same purpose, and had a fortnight. That was the last time I was in prison. I have since been leading the same life as I told you of for the three years, and lodging at the same houses, and seeing the same goings on. I hate such a life now more than ever. I am willing to do any work that I can in washing and cleaning. I can do a little at my needle. I could do hard work, for I have good health. I used to wash and clean in prison, and always behaved myself there. At the house where I am it is 3*d.* a night; but at Mrs.————'s it is 1*d.* and 2*d.* a night, and just the same goings on. Many a girl—nearly all of them—goes out into the streets from this penny and twopenny house, to get money for their favourite boys by prostitution. If the girl cannot get money she must steal something, or will be beaten by her 'chap' when she comes home. I have seen them beaten, often kicked and beaten until they were blind from bloodshot, and their teeth knocked out with kicks from boots as the girl lays on the ground. The boys, in their turn, are out thieving all day, and the lodging-house keeper will buy any stolen provisions of them, and sell them to the lodgers. I never saw the police in the house. If a boy comes to the house on a night without money or sawney [stolen cheese or bacon], or something to sell to the lodgers, a handkerchief or something of that kind, he is not admitted, but told very plainly, 'Go thieve it, then,' Girls are treated just the same. Any body may call in the daytime at this house and have a halfpenny worth of coffee and sit any length of time until evening. I have seen three dozen sitting there that way, all thieves and bad girls. There are no chairs, and only one form [bench] in front of the fire, on which a dozen can sit. The others sit on the floor all about the room, as near the fire as they can. Bad language goes on during the day, as I have told you it did during the night, and indecencies too, but nothing like so bad as at night. They talk about where there is good places to go and thieve. The missioners call sometimes, but they're laughed at often when they're talking, and always before the door's closed on them. If a decent girl goes there to get a ha'porth of coffee, seeing the board over the door, she is always shocked. Many a poor girl has been ruined in this house since I was, and boys have boasted about it. I never knew boy or girl do good, once get used there. Get used there, indeed, and you are life-ruined. I was an only child, and haven't a friend in the world.

I have heard several girls say how they would like to get out of the life, and out of the place. From those I know, I think the cruel parents and mistresses cause many to be driven there. One lodging-house keeper, Mrs.——, goes out dressed respectable, and pawns any stolen property, or sells it at public-houses."

REVIEW QUESTIONS

1. Describe the role of the Catholic priest in the discontent of Nikolaus Osterroth and the miners.
2. Describe how the ideas expressed in the Social Democrat pamphlet were seized by Osterroth and transformed his life.
3. What, according to William Booth, were the essential aspects of life in "Darkest England"? Why did he draw the comparison to "Darkest Africa"?
4. Do any of Booth's scathing criticisms apply to contemporary America?
5. How does the London prostitute's account of her life confirm the view that poverty was the underlying cause of prostitution? What circumstances prevented her from leaving the profession?

2 Feminism and Antifeminism

Inspired by the ideals of equality voiced in the Enlightenment and the French Revolution, women in nineteenth-century Europe and the United States began to demand equal rights, foremost the right to vote. In the United States, the women's suffrage movement held its first convention in 1848 in Seneca Falls, New York. The women adopted a Declaration of Principles that said in part: "We hold these truths to be self-evident: that all men and women are created equal." The struggle for equal rights and voting privileges continued, and by the end of the century, women were voting in a few state elections. Finally, in 1920, the Nineteenth Amendment gave women voting privileges throughout the United States.

In England, having failed to persuade Parliament in the mid-1860s to give them the vote, women organized reform societies, drew up petitions, and protested unfair treatment. The Women's Social and Political Union (WSPU), organized by Emmeline Pankhurst, employed militant tactics, which increased the hostility of their opponents.

During World War I, women worked in offices, factories, and service industries at jobs formerly held by men. Their wartime service made it clear that women played an essential role in the economic life of nations, and many political leaders argued for the extension of the vote to them. In 1918, British women over the age of thirty gained the vote, and in 1928, Parliament lowered the voting age for British women to twenty-one, the same as for men.

The first countries to permit women to vote were New Zealand in 1893 and Australia in 1902. In Europe, women were granted voting rights by stages, first for municipal elections, later for national ones. Finland extended voting rights to women in 1906; the other Scandinavian countries followed suit, but the majority of European countries did not allow women to vote until after World War I.

In their struggle for equal rights, women faced strong opposition. Opponents argued that feminist demands would threaten society by undermining marriage and the family. Thus in 1870, a member of the British House of Commons wondered "what would become, not merely of women's influence, but of her duties at home, her care of the household, her supervision of all those duties and surroundings which make a happy home . . . if we are to see women coming forward and taking part in the government of the country." This concern for the family was combined with a traditional biased view of woman's nature, as one writer for the *Saturday Review*, an English periodical, revealed:

> The power of reasoning is so small in women that they need [outside] help, and if they have not the guidance and check of a religious conscience, it is useless to expect from them self-control on abstract principles. They do not calculate consequences, and they are reckless when they once give way, hence they are to be kept straight only through their affections, the religious sentiment and a well educated moral sense.

John Stuart Mill
THE SUBJECTION OF WOMEN

John Stuart Mill (see page 158), a British philosopher and a liberal, championed women's rights. His interest in the subject was awakened by Harriet Taylor, a long-time friend and an ardent feminist, whom he married in 1851. Mill and Taylor had an intense intellectual companionship both before and after their marriage, and Taylor helped shape his ideas on the position of women in society and the urgent need for reform. In 1867, Mill, as a Member of Parliament, proposed that the suffrage be extended to women (the proposal was rejected by a vote of 194 to 74). In *The Subjection of Women* (1869), Mill argued that male dominance of women constituted a flagrant abuse of power. He maintained that female inequality, "a single relic of an old world of thought and practice exploded in everything else," violated the principle of individual rights and hindered the progress of humanity. Excerpts from Mill's classic in the history of feminism follow.

The object of this Essay is to explain, as clearly as I am able, the grounds of an opinion which I have held from the very earliest period when I had formed any opinions at all on social or political matters, and which, instead of being weakened or modified, has been constantly growing stronger by the progress of reflection and the experience of life: That the principle which regulates the existing social relations between the two sexes—the legal subordination of one sex to the other—is wrong in itself, and now one of the chief hindrances to human improvement;

and that it ought to be replaced by a principle of perfect equality, admitting no power or privilege on the one side, nor disability on the other. . . .

. . . The adoption of this system of inequality never was the result of deliberation, or forethought, or any social ideas, or any notion whatever of what conduced to the benefit of humanity or the good order of society. It arose simply from the fact that from the very earliest twilight of human society, every woman (owing to the value attached to her by men, combined with her inferiority in muscular strength) was found in a state of bondage to some man. . . .

But, it will be said, the rule of men over women differs from all these others in not being a rule of force: it is accepted voluntarily; women make no complaint, and are consenting parties to it. In the first place, a great number of women do not accept it. Ever since there have been women able to make their sentiments known by their writings (the only mode of publicity which society permits to them), an increasing number of them have recorded protests against their present social condition: and recently many thousands of them, headed by the most eminent women known to the public, have petitioned Parliament for their admission to the parliamentary suffrage. The claim of women to be educated as solidly, and in the same branches of knowledge, as men, is urged with growing intensity, and with a great prospect of success; while the demand for their admission into professions and occupations hitherto closed against them becomes every year more urgent. Though there are not in this country, as there are in the United States, periodical Conventions and an organized party to agitate for the Rights of Women, there is a numerous and active Society organized and managed by women, for the more limited object of obtaining the political franchise. Nor is it only in our own country and in America that women are beginning to protest, more or less collectively, against the disabilities under which they labour. France, and Italy, and Switzerland, and Russia now afford examples of the same thing. How many more women there are who silently cherish similar aspirations, no

one can possibly know; but there are abundant tokens how many *would* cherish them, were they not so strenuously taught to repress them as contrary to the proprieties of their sex. . . .

Men do not want solely the obedience of women, they want their sentiments. All men, except the most brutish, desire to have, in the woman most nearly connected with them, not a forced slave but a willing one; not a slave merely, but a favourite. They have therefore put everything in practice to enslave their minds. The masters of all other slaves rely, for maintaining obedience, on fear; either fear of themselves, or religious fears. The masters of women wanted more than simple obedience, and they turned the whole force of education to effect their purpose. All women are brought up from the very earliest years in the belief that their ideal of character is the very opposite to that of men; not self-will, and government by self-control, but submission, and yielding to the control of others. All the moralities tell them that it is the duty of women, and all the current sentimentalities that it is their nature, to live for others; to make complete abnegation of themselves, and to have no life but in their affections. And by their affections are meant the only ones they are allowed to have—those to the men with whom they are connected, or to the children who constitute an additional and indefeasible tie between them and a man. When we put together three things—first, the natural attraction between opposite sexes; secondly, the wife's entire dependence on the husband, every privilege or pleasure she has being either his gift, or depending entirely on his will; and lastly, that the principal object of human pursuit, consideration, and all objects of social ambition, can in general be sought or obtained by her only through him—it would be a miracle if the object of being attractive to men had not become the polar star of feminine education and formation of character. And, this great means of influence over the minds of women having been acquired, an instinct of selfishness made men avail themselves of it to the utmost as a means of holding women in subjection, by representing to them meekness, submissiveness, and resignation of all individual will into the hands of a man, as an essential part of sexual attractiveness. Can it be doubted that any of the other yokes which mankind have succeeded in breaking would have subsisted till now if the same means had existed, and had been as sedulously [diligently] used to bow down their minds to it?

Mill argues that women should be able to participate in political life and should not be barred from entering the professions.

On the other point which is involved in the just equality of women, their admissibility to all the functions and occupations hitherto retained as the monopoly of the stronger sex. . . . I believe that their disabilities [in occupation and civil life] elsewhere are only clung to in order to maintain their subordination in domestic life; because the generality of the male sex cannot yet tolerate the idea of living with an equal. Were it not for that, I think that almost every one, in the existing state of opinion in politics and political economy, would admit the injustice of excluding half the human race from the greater number of lucrative occupations, and from almost all high social functions; ordaining from their birth either that they are not, and cannot by any possibility become, fit for employments which are legally open to the stupidest and basest of the other sex, or else that however fit they may be, those employments shall be interdicted to them, in order to be preserved for the exclusive benefit of males. . . .

It will perhaps be sufficient if I confine myself, in the details of my argument, to functions of a public nature: since, if I am successful as to those, it probably will be readily granted that women should be admissible to all other occupations. . . . And here let me begin . . . [with] the suffrage, both parliamentary and municipal. . . .

. . . To have a voice in choosing those by whom one is to be governed, is a means of self-protection due to every one, though he were to remain for ever excluded from the function of governing. . . . Under whatever conditions, and within whatever limits, men are admitted to the

suffrage, there is not a shadow of justification for not admitting women under the same. The majority of the women of any class are not likely to differ in political opinion from the majority of the men of the same class, unless the question be one in which the interests of women, as such, are in some way involved; and if they are so, women require the suffrage, as their guarantee of just and equal consideration. . . .

With regard to the fitness of women, not only to participate in elections, but themselves to hold offices or practise professions involving important public responsibilities; I have already observed that this consideration is not essential to the practical question in dispute: since any woman, who succeeds in an open profession, proves by that very fact that she is qualified for it. And in the case of public offices, if the political system of the country is such as to exclude unfit men, it will equally exclude unfit women: while if it is not, there is no additional evil in the fact that the unfit persons whom it admits may be either women or men. . . .

. . . There is no country of Europe in which the ablest men have not frequently experienced, and keenly appreciated, the value of the advice and help of clever and experienced women of the world, in the attainment both of private and of public objects; and there are important matters of public administration to which few men are equally competent with such women; among others, the detailed control of expenditure. But what we are now discussing is not the need which society has of the services of women in public business, but the dull and hopeless life to which it so often condemns them, by forbidding them to exercise the practical abilities which many of them are conscious of, in any wider field than one which to some of them never was, and to others is no longer, open. If there is anything vitally important to the happiness of human beings, it is that they should relish their habitual pursuit [that is, they should be happy in their work]. This requisite of an enjoyable life is very imperfectly granted, or altogether denied, to a large part of mankind; and by its absence many a life is a failure, which is provided, in appearance, with every requisite of success.

Emmeline Pankhurst
"WHY WE ARE MILITANT"

Agitation in Great Britain for woman suffrage reached a peak during the turbulent years of parliamentary reform, 1909–1911. Under the leadership of Emmeline Pankhurst (1858–1928) and her daughter Christabel, women engaged in demonstrations, disrupted political meetings, and when dragged off to jail, resorted to passive resistance and hunger strikes. Some hunger strikers were subjected to the cruelty of force feeding. In 1913 Emmeline Pankhurst carried her appeal to the United States, where she delivered the speech that follows.

I know that in your minds there are questions like these; you are saying, "Woman Suffrage is sure to come; the emancipation of humanity is an evolutionary process, and how is it that some women, instead of trusting to that evolution, instead of educating the masses of people of their country, instead of educating their own sex to prepare them for citizenship, how is it that these militant women are using violence and upsetting the business arrangements of the country in their undue impatience to attain their end?"

Let me try to explain to you the situation. . . .

The extensions of the franchise to the men of my country have been preceded by very great violence, by something like a revolution, by something like civil war. In 1832, you know we were on the edge of a civil war and on the edge of revolution, and it was at the point of the sword—no, not at the point of the sword—it was after the practice of arson on so large a scale that half the city of Bristol was burned down in a single night, it was because more and greater violence and arson were feared that the Reform Bill of 1832 [which gave the vote to the middle class] was allowed to pass into law. In 1867, . . . rioting went on all over the country, and as the result of that rioting, as the result of that unrest, . . . as a result of the fear of more rioting and violence the Reform Act of 1867 [which gave workers the vote] was put upon the statute books.

In 1884 . . . rioting was threatened and feared, and so the agricultural labourers got the vote.

Meanwhile, during the '80's, women, like men, were asking for the franchise. Appeals, larger and more numerous than for any other reform, were presented in support of Woman's Suffrage. Meetings of the great corporations [group of principal officials in a town or city government], great town councils, and city councils, passed resolutions asking that women should have the vote. More meetings were held, and larger, for Woman Suffrage than were held for votes for men, and yet the women did not get it. Men got the vote because they were and would be violent. The women did not get it because they were constitutional and law-abiding. . . .

I believed, as many women still in England believe, that women could get their way in some mysterious manner, by purely peaceful methods. We have been so accustomed, we women, to accept one standard for men and another standard for women, that we have even applied that variation of standard to the injury of our political welfare.

Having had better opportunities of education, and having had some training in politics, having in political life come so near to the "superior" being as to see that he was not altogether such a fount of wisdom as they had supposed, that he had his human weaknesses as we had, the twentieth century women began to say to themselves, "Is it not time, since our methods have failed and the men's have succeeded, that we should take a leaf out of their political book?" . . .

Well, we in Great Britain, on the eve of the General Election of 1905, a mere handful of us—why, you could almost count us on the fingers of both hands—set out on the wonderful adventure of forcing the strongest Government of modern times to give the women the vote. . . .

The Suffrage movement was almost dead. The women had lost heart. You could not get a Suffrage meeting that was attended by members of the general public. . . .

Two women changed that in a twinkling of an eye at a great Liberal demonstration in Manchester, where a Liberal leader, Sir Edward Grey, was explaining the programme to be carried out during the Liberals' next turn of office. The two women put the fateful question, "When are you going to give votes to women?" and refused to sit down until they had been answered. These two women were sent to gaol, and from that day to this the women's movement, both militant and constitutional, has never looked back. We had little more than one moribund society for Woman Suffrage in those days. Now we have nearly 50 societies for Woman Suffrage, and they are large in membership, they are rich in money, and their ranks are swelling every day that passes. That is how militancy has put back the clock of Woman Suffrage in Great Britain. . . . I want to say here and now that the only justification for violence, the only justification for damage to property, the only justification for risk to the comfort of other human beings is the fact that you have tried all other available means and have failed to secure justice, and as a law-abiding person—and I am by nature a law-abiding person, as one hating violence, hating disorder—I want to say that from the moment we began our militant agitation to this day I have felt absolutely guiltless in this matter.

I tell you that in Great Britain there is no other way. . . .

Well, I say the time is long past when it became necessary for women to revolt in order to maintain their self respect in Great Britain. The women who are waging this war are women who would fight, if it were only for the idea of liberty—if it were only that they might be free citizens of a free country—I myself would fight for that idea alone. But we have, in addition to this love of freedom, intolerable grievances to redress. . . .

Those grievances are so pressing that, so far from it being a duty to be patient and to wait for evolution, in thinking of those grievances the idea of patience is intolerable. We feel that patience is something akin to crime when our patience involves continued suffering on the part of the oppressed.

We are fighting to get the power to alter bad laws; but some people say to us, "Go to the representatives in the House of Commons, point out to them that these laws are bad, and you will find them quite ready to alter them."

Ladies and gentlemen, there are women in my country who have spent long and useful lives trying to get reforms, and because of their voteless condition, they are unable even to get the ear of Members of Parliament, much less are they able to secure those reforms.

Our marriage and divorce laws are a disgrace to civilisation. I sometimes wonder, looking back from the serenity of past middle age, at the courage of women. I wonder that women have the courage to take upon themselves the responsibilities of marriage and motherhood when I see how little protection the law of my country affords them. I wonder that a woman will face the ordeal of childbirth with the knowledge that after she has risked her life to bring a child into the world she has absolutely no parental rights over the future of that child. Think what trust women have in men when a woman will marry a man, knowing, if she has knowledge of the law, that if that man is not all she in her love for him thinks him, he may even bring a strange woman into the house, bring his mistress into the house to live with her, and she cannot get legal relief from such a marriage as that. . . .

. . . [W]e realise how political power, how political influence, which would enable us to get better laws, would make it possible for thousands upon thousands of unhappy women to live happier lives. . . .

Take the industrial side of the question: have men's wages for a hard day's work ever been so low and inadequate as are women's wages today? Have men ever had to suffer from the laws, more injustice than women suffer? Is there a single reason which men have had for demanding liberty that does not also apply to women?

Why, if you were talking to the *men* of any other nation you would not hesitate to reply in the affirmative. There is not a man in this meeting who has not felt sympathy with the uprising of the men of other lands when suffering from intolerable tyranny, when deprived of all representative rights. You are full of sympathy with men in Russia. You are full of sympathy with nations that rise against the domination of the Turk. You are full of sympathy with all struggling people striving for independence. How is it, then, that some of you have nothing but ridicule and contempt and [condemnation] for women who are fighting for exactly the same thing?

All my life I have tried to understand why it is that men who value their citizenship as their dearest possession seem to think citizenship ridiculous when it is to be applied to the women of their race. And I find an explanation, and it is the only one I can think of. It came to me when I was in a prison cell, remembering how I had seen men laugh at the idea of women going to prison. Why they would confess they could not bear a cell door to be shut upon themselves for a single hour without asking to be let out. A thought came to me in my prison cell, and it was this: that to men women are not human beings like themselves. Some men think we are superhuman; they put us on pedestals; they revere us; they think we are too fine and too delicate to come down into the hurly-burly of life. Other men think us sub-human; they think we are a strange species unfortunately having to exist for the perpetuation of the race. They think that we are fit for drudgery, but that in

some strange way our minds are not like theirs, our love for great things is not like theirs, and so we are a sort of sub-human species.

We are neither superhuman nor are we sub-human. We are just human beings like yourselves.

Our hearts burn within us when we read the great mottoes which celebrate the liberty of your country; when we go to France and we read the words, liberty, fraternity and equality, don't you think that we appreciate the meaning of those words? And then when we wake to the knowledge that these things are not for us, they are only for our brothers, then there comes a sense of bitterness into the hearts of some women, and they say to themselves, "Will men never understand?" But so far as we in England are concerned, we have come to the conclusion that we are not going to leave men any illusions upon the question.

When we were patient, when we believed in argument and persuasion, they said, "You don't really want it because, if you did, you would do something unmistakable to show you were determined to have it." And then when we did something unmistakable they said, "You are behaving so badly that you show you are not fit for it."

Now, gentlemen, in your heart of hearts you do not believe that. You know perfectly well that there never was a thing worth having that was not worth fighting for. You know perfectly well that if the situation were reversed, if you had no constitutional rights and we had all of them, if you had the duty of paying and obeying and trying to look as pleasant, and we were the proud citizens who could decide our fate and yours, because we knew what was good for you better than you knew yourselves, you know perfectly well that you wouldn't stand it for a single day, and you would be perfectly justified in rebelling against such intolerable conditions.

The Goncourt Brothers
ON FEMALE INFERIORITY

The brothers Edmund (1822–1896) and Jules (1830–1870) Goncourt were French writers who produced in partnership novels, plays, and art and literary criticism. Starting in December 1851, they kept a journal in which they recorded, often insightfully, the doings of Parisian cultural and social life. In the following entries the Goncourts reveal an extreme bias against women. Even if these sentiments were not shared by all intellectuals, they do show the traditional prejudices confronting French feminists.

13 October, 1855

A conversation about woman, after a couple of tankards of beer at Binding's. Woman is an evil, stupid animal unless she is educated and civilized to a high degree. She is incapable of dreaming, thinking, or loving. Poetry in a woman is never natural but always a product of education. Only the woman of the world is a woman; the rest are females.

Inferiority of the feminine mind to the masculine mind. All the physical beauty, all the strength, and all the development of a woman is concentrated in and as it were directed towards the central and lower parts of the body: the pelvis, the buttocks, the thighs; the beauty of a man is to be found in the upper, nobler parts, the pectoral muscles, the broad shoulders, the high forehead. Venus has a narrow forehead. Dürer's *Three Graces* have flat heads at the back and little shoulders; only their hips are big and beautiful. As regards the inferiority of the feminine mind, consider the self-assurance of a woman, even when she is only a girl, which allows her to be extremely witty with nothing but a little vivacity and a touch of spontaneity. Only man is endowed with the modesty and timidity which woman lacks and which she uses only as weapons.

Woman: the most beautiful and most admirable of laying machines.

21 May, 1857

Men like ourselves need a woman of little breeding and education who is nothing but gaiety and natural wit, because a woman of that sort can charm and please us like an agreeable animal to which we may become quite attached. But if a mistress has acquired a veneer of breeding, art, or literature, and tries to talk to us on an equal footing about our thoughts and our feeling for beauty; if she wants to be a companion and partner in the cultivation of our tastes or the writing of our books, then she becomes for us as unbearable as a piano out of tune—and very soon an object of dislike.

Almroth E. Wright
THE UNEXPURGATED CASE AGAINST WOMAN SUFFRAGE

Sir Almroth Wright (1861–1947) was an eminent physician and one of the founders of modern immunology. He was also a thinker who attempted to construct "a system of Logic which searches for Truth," as he put it.

Wright's opposition to giving women the vote was expressed in letters to *The Times* of London and in a slender book, *The Unexpurgated Case Against Woman Suffrage* (1913). In the extracts below, he describes how the disabilities of women make female suffrage impossible, at one point dismissing the suffrage movement as the product of "sex-hostility" caused by the excess population of women without hope of marrying. All told, he found that women's suffrage would be a recipe for social disaster, resulting in unacceptable demands for economic and intellectual equality.

The primordial argument against giving woman the vote is that that vote would not represent physical force.

Now it is by physical force alone and by prestige—which represents physical force in the background—that a nation protects itself against foreign interference, upholds its rule over subject populations, and enforces its own laws. And nothing could in the end more certainly lead to war and revolt than the decline of the military spirit and loss of prestige which would inevitably follow if man admitted woman into political co-partnership. . . .

[A] virile and imperial race will not brook any attempt at forcible control by women. Again, no military foreign nation or native race would ever believe in the stamina and firmness of purpose of any nation that submitted even to the semblance of such control. . . .

The woman voter would be pernicious to the State not only because she could not back her vote by physical force, but also by reason of her intellectual defects.

Woman's mind . . . arrives at conclusions on incomplete evidence; has a very imperfect sense of proportion; accepts the congenial as true, and rejects the uncongenial as false; takes the imaginary which is desired for reality, and treats the undesired reality which is out of sight as non-existent—building up for itself in this way, when biased by predilections and aversions, a very unreal picture of the external world.

The explanation of this is to be found in all the physiological attachments of woman's mind: in the fact that mental images are in her over-intimately linked up with emotional reflex responses; that yielding to such reflex responses gives gratification; that intellectual analysis and suspense of judgment involve an inhibition of reflex responses which is felt as neural distress; that precipitate judgment brings relief from this physiological strain; and that woman looks upon her mind not as an implement for the pursuit of truth, but as an instrument for providing her with creature comforts in the form of agreeable mental images. . . .

In further illustration of what has been said above, it may be pointed out that woman, even intelligent woman, nurses all sorts of misconceptions about herself. She, for instance, is constantly picturing to herself that she can as a worker lay claim to the same all-round efficiency as a man—forgetting that woman is notoriously unadapted to tasks in which severe physical hardships have to be confronted; and that hardly any one would, if other alternative offered, employ a woman in any work which imposed upon her a combined physical and mental strain, or in any work where emergencies might have to be faced. . . .

Yet a third point has to come into consideration in connexion with the woman voter. This is, that she would be pernicious to the State also by virtue of her defective moral equipment. . . .

It is only a very exceptional woman who would, when put to her election between the claims of a narrow and domestic and a wider or public morality, subordinate the former to the latter.

In ordinary life, at any rate, one finds her following in such a case the suggestions of domestic—I had almost called it animal—morality.

It would be difficult to find any one who would trust a woman to be just to the rights of others in the case where the material interests of her children, or of a devoted husband, were involved. And even to consider the question of being in such a case intellectually just to any one who came into competition with personal belongings like husband and child would, of course, lie quite beyond the moral horizon of ordinary woman. . . . In this matter one would not be very far from the truth if one alleged that there are no good women, but only women who have lived under the influence of good men. . . .

In countries, such as England, where an excess female population [of three million] has made economic difficulties for woman, and where the severe sexual restrictions, which here obtain, have bred in her sex-hostility, the suffrage movement has as its avowed ulterior object the abrogation of all distinctions which depend upon sex; and the achievement of the economic independence of woman.

To secure this economic independence every post, occupation, and Government service is to be thrown open to woman; she is to receive everywhere the same wages as man; male and female are to work side by side; and they are indiscriminately to be put in command the one over the other. Furthermore, legal rights are to be secured to the wife over her husband's property and earnings. The programme is, in fact, to give to woman an economic independence out of the earnings and taxes of man.

Nor does feminist ambition stop short here. It demands that women shall be included in every advisory committee, every governing board, every jury, every judicial bench, every electorate, every parliament, and every ministerial cabinet; further, that every masculine foundation, university, school of learning, academy, trade union, professional corporation, and scientific society shall be converted into an epicene institution [including both male and female]—until we shall have everywhere one vast cock-and-hen show.

The proposal to bring man and woman together everywhere into extremely intimate relationships raises very grave questions. It brings up, first, the question of sexual complications; secondly, the question as to whether the tradition of modesty and reticence between the sexes is to be definitely sacrificed; and, most important of all, the question as to whether [bringing men and women together] would place obstacles in the way of intellectual work. . . .

The matter cannot so lightly be disposed of. It will be necessary for us to find out whether really intimate association with woman on the purely intellectual plane is realisable. And if it is, in fact, unrealisable, it will be necessary to consider whether it is the exclusion of women from masculine corporations; or the perpetual attempt of women to force their way into these, which would deserve to be characterised as *selfish*. . .

What we have to ask is whether—even if we leave out of regard the whole system of attractions or, as the case may be, repulsions which comes into operation when the sexes are thrown together—purely intellectual intercourse between man and the typical unselected woman is not barred by the intellectual immoralities and limitations which appear to be secondary sexual characters of woman. . . .

Wherever we look we find aversion to compulsory intellectual co-operation with woman.

We see it in the sullen attitude which the ordinary male student takes up towards the presence of women students in his classes. We see it in the fact that the older English universities, which have conceded everything else to women, have made a strong stand against making them actual members of the university; for this would impose them on men as intellectual associates. Again we see the aversion in the opposition to the admission of women to the bar.

But we need not look so far afield. Practically every man feels that there is in woman—patent, or hidden away—an element of unreason which, when you come upon it, summarily puts an end to purely intellectual intercourse. One may reflect, for example, upon the way the woman's suffrage controversy has been conducted.

But the feminist will want to argue. She will—taking it as always for granted that woman has a right to all that men's hands or brains have fashioned—argue that it is very important for the intellectual development of woman that she should have exactly the same opportunities as man. And she will, scouting the idea of any differences between the intelligences of man and woman, discourse to you of their intimate affinity. . . .

From these general questions, which affect only the woman with intellectual aspirations, we pass to consider what would be the effect of feminism upon the rank and file of women if it made of these co-partners with man in work. They would suffer, not only because woman's physiological disabilities and the restrictions which arise out of her sex place her at a great disadvantage when she has to enter into competition with man, but also because under feminism man would be less and less disposed to take off woman's shoulders a part of her burden.

And there can be no dispute that the most valuable financial asset of the ordinary woman is the possibility that a man may be willing—and may, if only woman is disposed to fulfil her part of the bargain, be not only willing but anxious—to support her, and to secure for her, if he can, a measure of that freedom which comes from the possession of money.

In view of this every one who has a real fellow-feeling for woman, and who is concerned for her material welfare, as a father is concerned for his daughter's, will above everything else desire to nurture and encourage in man the sentiment of chivalry, and in woman that disposition of mind that makes chivalry possible.

And the woman workers who have to fight the battle of life for themselves would indirectly profit from this fostering of chivalry; for those women who are supported by men do not compete in the limited labour market which is open to the woman worker.

From every point of view, therefore, except perhaps that of the exceptional woman who would be able to hold her own against masculine competition—and men always issue informal letters of [admission] to such an exceptional woman—the woman suffrage which leads up to feminism would be a social disaster.

REVIEW QUESTIONS

1. In John Stuart Mill's view, what was the ultimate origin of the subjection of women?
2. According to Mill, what character qualities did men seek to instill in women? Why, according to Mill's argument, should women have the right to participate in politics and public affairs on equal terms with men?
3. Why did Emmeline Pankhurst think that violence was justified in fighting for women's rights?
4. Why, according to her, did men, who valued their citizenship as their dearest possession, feel it was ridiculous to grant it to women?
5. In what ways did the Goncourt brothers consider women inferior?
6. Why did Sir Almroth Wright think that women voters would be pernicious to the state?
7. In Wright's view, how were feminist reforms disadvantageous to women?

3 German Racial Nationalism

German nationalists were especially attracted to racist doctrines. Racist thinkers held that race was the key to history and that not only physical features, but also moral, aesthetic, and intellectual qualities distinguished one race from another. In their view, a race retained its vigor and achieved greatness when it preserved its purity; intermarriage between races was contamination that would result in genetic, cultural, and military decline. Unlike liberals, who held that anyone who accepted German law was a member of the German nation, German racist thinkers argued that a person's nationality was a function of his or her "racial soul" or "blood." On the basis of this new conception of nationality, racists argued that Jews, no matter how many centuries their ancestors had dwelt in Germany, could never think and feel like Germans and should be deprived of citizenship. Like their Nazi successors, nineteenth-century German racists claimed that the German race was purer than, and therefore superior to, all other races; its superiority was revealed in such physical characteristics as blond hair, blue eyes, and fair skin—all signs of inner qualities lacking in other races.

Houston Stewart Chamberlain
THE IMPORTANCE OF RACE

German racist thinkers embraced the ideas of Houston Stewart Chamberlain (1855–1927), an Englishman whose devotion to Germanism led him to adopt German citizenship. In *Foundations of the Nineteenth Century* (1899), Chamberlain attempted to assert in scientific fashion that races differed not only physically but also morally, spiritually, and intellectually and that the struggle between races was the driving force of history. He held that the Germans, descendants of the ancient Aryans (see page 217), were physically superior and bearers of a higher culture. He attributed Rome's decline to the dilution of its racial qualities through miscegenation. The blond, blue-eyed, long-skulled Germans, possessing the strongest strain of Aryan blood and distinguished by an inner spiritual depth, were the true shapers and guardians of high civilization.

Chamberlain's book was enormously popular in Germany. Nationalist organizations frequently cited it. Kaiser Wilhelm II called *Foundations* a "hymn to Germanism" and read it to his children. "Next to the national liberal historians like Heinrich von Treitschke and Heinrich von Sybel," concludes German historian Fritz Fischer, "Houston Stewart Chamberlain had the greatest influence upon the spiritual life of Wilhelmine Germany."

Chamberlain's racist and anti-Semitic views make him a spiritual forerunner of Nazism, and he was praised as such by Alfred Rosenberg, the leading Nazi racial theorist in the early days of Hitler's movement. Josef Goebbels, the Nazi propagandist, hailed Chamberlain as a "pathbreaker" and "pioneer" after meeting him in 1926. Excerpts from Chamberlain's work follow.

Nothing is so convincing as the consciousness of the possession of Race. The man who belongs to a distinct, pure race, never loses the sense of it. . . . Race lifts a man above himself: it endows him with extraordinary—I might almost say supernatural—powers, so entirely does it distinguish him from the individual who springs from the chaotic jumble of peoples drawn from all parts of the world: and should this man of pure origin be perchance gifted above his fellows, then the fact of Race strengthens and elevates him on every hand, and he becomes a genius towering over the rest of mankind, not because he has been thrown upon the earth like a flaming meteor by a freak of nature, but because he soars heavenward like some strong and stately tree, nourished by thousands and thousands of roots—no solitary individual, but the living sum of untold souls striving for the same goal. . . .

. . . As far back as our glance can reach, we see human beings, we see that they differ essentially in their gifts and that some show more vigorous powers of growth than others. Only one thing can be asserted without leaving the basis of historical observation: a high state of excellence is only attained gradually and under particular circumstances, it is only forced activity that can bring it about; under other circumstances it may completely degenerate. The struggle which means destruction for the fundamentally weak race steels the strong; the same struggle, moreover, by eliminating the weaker elements, tends still further to strengthen the strong. Around the childhood of great races, as we observe, even in the case of the metaphysical Indians, the storm of war always rages. . . .

. . . Only quite definite, limited mixtures of blood contribute towards the ennoblement of a race, or, it may be, the origin of a new one. Here again the clearest and least ambiguous examples are furnished by animal breeding. The mixture of blood must be strictly limited as regards time, and it must, in addition, be appropriate; not all and any crossings, but only definite ones can form the basis of ennoblement. By time-limitation I mean that the influx of new blood must take place as quickly as possible and then

cease; continual crossing ruins the stongest race. To take an extreme example, the most famous pack of greyhounds in England was crossed once only with bulldogs, whereby it gained in courage and endurance, but further experiments prove that when such a crossing is continued, the characters of both races disappear and quite characterless mongrels remain behind. . . .

. . . Marius and Sulla had, by murdering the flower of the genuine Roman youth, dammed the source of noble blood and at the same time, by the freeing of slaves, brought into the nation perfect floods of African and Asiatic blood, thus transforming Rome into . . . the trysting-place of all the mongrels of the world. . . .

Let us attempt a glance into the depths of the soul. What are the specific intellectual and moral characteristics of this Germanic race? Certain anthropologists would fain teach us that all races are equally gifted; we point to history and answer: that is a lie! The races of mankind are markedly different in the nature and also in the extent of their gifts, and the Germanic races belong to the most highly gifted group, the group usually termed Aryan. . . .

The civilisation and culture, which radiating from Northern Europe, to-day dominate (though in very varying degrees) a considerable part of the world, are the work of Teutonism; what is not Teutonic consists either of alien elements not yet exorcised, which were formerly forcibly introduced and still, like baneful germs, circulate in the blood, or of alien wares sailing, to the disadvantage of our work and further development, under the Teutonic flag, under Teutonic protection and privilege, and they will continue to sail thus, until we send these pirate ships to the bottom. This work of Teutonism is beyond question the greatest that has hitherto been accomplished by man. . . . As the youngest of races, we Teutons could profit by the achievements of former ones; but this is no proof of a universal progress of humanity, but solely of the pre-eminent capabilities of a definite human species, capabilities which have been proved to be gradually weakened by influx of non-Teutonic blood.

Pan-German League
"THERE ARE DOMINANT RACES AND SUBORDINATE RACES"

Organized in 1894, the ultranationalist and imperialist Pan-German League called for German expansion both in Europe and overseas. It often expressed blatantly Social Darwinist and racist views as illustrated in the following article, which appeared in 1913 in the league's principal publication.

"The historical view as to the biological evolution of races tells us that there are dominant races and subordinate races. Political history is nothing more than the history of the struggles between the dominant races. Conquest in particular is always a function of the dominant races. . . .

"Where now in all the world does it stand written that conquering races are under obligations to grant after an interval political rights to the conquered? Is not the practice of political rights an advantage which biologically belongs to the dominant races? . . . In my opinion, the rights of men are, first, personal freedom; secondly, the right of free expression of opinion—as well as freedom of the press; . . . and, finally, the right to work, in case one is without means. . . .

"In like manner there is the school question. The man with political rights sets up schools, and the speech used in the instruction is his speech. . . . The purpose must be to crush the [individuality of the] conquered people and its political and lingual existence. . . .

"The conquerors are acting only according to biological principles if they suppress alien languages and undertake to destroy strange popular customs. . . [. Only the conquering race must be populous, so that it can overrun the territory it has won. Nations that are populous are, moreover, the only nations which have a moral claim to conquest, for it is wrong that in one country there should be overpopulation while close at hand—and at the same time on better soil—a less numerous population stretches its limbs at ease.

[As to the inferior races:] "From political life they are to be excluded. They are eligible only to positions of a non-political character, to commercial commissions, chambers of commerce, etc. . . . The principal thing for the conqueror is the outspoken will to rule and the will to destroy the political and national life of the conquered. . . ."

REVIEW QUESTIONS

1. Why were many Germans attracted to Chamberlain's racial theories?
2. Why is Chamberlain regarded as a spiritual forerunner of Hitler?
3. Why is an ideology based on biological racism, as in the case of the Pan-Germanic League, particularly dangerous?

4 Anti-Semitism: Regression to the Irrational

Anti-Semitism, a European phenomenon of long standing, rose to new prominence in the late nineteenth century. Formerly segregated by law into ghettoes, Jews, under the aegis of the Enlightenment and the French Revolution, had gained legal equality in most European lands. In the nineteenth century, Jews participated in the economic and cultural progress of the times and often achieved distinction in business, the professions, and the arts and sciences. However, driven by irrational fears and mythical conceptions that had survived from the Middle Ages, many people regarded Jews as a dangerous race of international conspirators and foreign intruders who threatened their nations.

Throughout the nineteenth century, anti-Semitic outrages occurred in many European lands. Russian anti-Semitism assumed a particularly violent form in the infamous pogroms—murderous mob attacks on Jews—occasionally abetted by government officials. Even in highly civilized France, anti-Semitism proved a powerful force. At the time of the Dreyfus Affair (see page 220), Catholic and nationalist zealots demanded that Jews be deprived of their civil rights. In Germany, anti-Semitism became associated with the ideological defense of a distinctive German culture, the volkish thought popular in the last part of the nineteenth century. After the foundation of the German Empire in 1871, the pace of economic and cultural change quickened, and with it the cultural disorientation that fanned anti-Semitism. Volkish thinkers, who valued traditional Germany—the landscape, the peasant, and the village—associated Jews with the changes brought about by rapid industrialization and modernization. Compounding the problem was the influx into Germany of Jewish immigrants from the Russian Empire, who were searching for a better life and brought with them their own distinctive culture and religion, which many Germans found offensive. Nationalists and conservatives used anti-Semitism in an effort to gain a mass following.

Racial-nationalist considerations were the decisive force behind modern anti-Semitism. Racists said that the Jews were a wicked race of Asiatics, condemned by their genes; they differed physically, intellectually, and spiritually from Europeans who were descendants of ancient Aryans. The Aryans emerged some 4,000 years ago, probably between the Caspian Sea and the Hindu Kush Mountains. Intermingling with others, the Aryans lost whatever identity as a people they might have had. After discovering similarities between core European languages (Greek, Latin, German) and ancient Persian and ancient Sanskrit (the language of the conquerors of India), nineteenth-century scholars believed that these languages all stemmed from a common tongue spoken by the Aryans. From there, some leaped to the conclusion that the Aryans constituted a distinct race endowed with superior racial qualities.

Houston Stewart Chamberlain (see previous section) pitted Aryans and Jews against each other in a struggle of world historical importance. As agents of a spiritually empty capitalism and divisive liberalism, the Jews, said Chamberlain, were the opposite of the idealistic, heroic, and faithful Germans. Chamberlain denied that Jesus was a Jew, hinting that he was of Aryan stock, and held that the goal of the Jew was "to put his foot upon the neck of all the nations of the world and be lord and possessor of the whole earth." Racial anti-Semitism became a powerful force in European intellectual life, especially in Germany. It was the seedbed of Hitler's movement.

Hermann Ahlwardt
THE SEMITIC VERSUS
THE TEUTONIC RACE

In the following reading, Hermann Ahlwardt (1846–1914), an anti-Semitic member of the Reichstag and author of *The Desperate Struggle Between Aryan and Jew*, addresses the chamber on March 6, 1895, with a plea to close Germany's borders to Jewish immigrants. His speech reflects the anti-Semitic rhetoric popular among German conservatives before World War I. The material in parentheses is by Paul W. Massing, translator and editor.

It is certainly true that there are Jews in our country of whom nothing adverse can be said. Nevertheless, the Jews as a whole must be considered harmful, for the racial traits of this people are of a kind that in the long run do not agree with the racial traits of the Teutons. Every Jew who at this very moment has not as yet transgressed is likely to do so at some future time under given circumstances because his racial characteristics drive him on in that direction. . . .

My political friends, do not hold the view that we fight the Jews because of their religion. . . . We would not dream of waging a political struggle against anyone because of his religion. . . . We hold the view that the Jews are a different race, a different people with entirely different character traits.

Experience in all fields of nature shows that innate racial characteristics which have been acquired by the race in the course of many thousands of years are the strongest and most enduring factors that exist, and that therefore we can rid ourselves of the characteristics of

our race no more than can the Jews. One need not fight the Jew individually, and we are not doing that, by the way. But, when countless specimens prove the existence of certain racial characteristics and when these characteristics are such as to make impossible a common life, well, then I believe that we who are natives here, who have tilled the soil and defended it against all enemies—that we have a duty to take a stand against the Jews who are of a quite different nature.

We Teutons are rooted in the cultural soil of labor. . . . The Jews do not believe in the culture of labor, they do not want to create values themselves, but want to appropriate, without working, the values which others have created; that is the cardinal difference that guides us in all our considerations. . . .

Herr Deputy Rickert[2] here has just expounded how few Jews we have altogether and that their number is steadily declining. Well, gentlemen,

_____
[1]Teutons refers to the quintessential Germans. The name comes from a German tribe that once defeated a Roman army.

_____
[2]Heinrich Rickert, a leader of the Progressives and an outspoken opponent of anti-Semitism, had pointed out that the Jews constituted only 1.29 percent of the population of Prussia. What enraged the German Right was that the Jews accounted for 9.58 percent of the university students in Prussia.

why don't you go to the main business centers and see for yourselves whether the percentages indicated by Herr Rickert prevail there too. Why don't you walk along the Leipzigerstrasse (in Berlin) or the Zeil in Frankfurt and have a look at the shops? Wherever there are opportunities to make money, the Jews have established themselves, but not in order to work—no, they let others work for them and take what the others have produced by their labor.

Deputy Hasse . . . has committed the grave mistake of putting the Jews and other peoples on the same level, and that is the worst mistake that we could possibly make.

The Jews have an attitude toward us which differs totally from that of other peoples. It is one thing when a Pole, a Russian, a Frenchman, a Dane immigrates to our country, and quite another thing when a Jew settles here. . . . Once our (Polish, etc.) guests have lived here for ten, twenty years, they come to resemble us. For they have stood with us on the same cultural soil of labor. . . . After thirty, forty years they have become Germans and their grandchildren would be indistinguishable from us except for the strange-sounding names they still bear. The Jews have lived here for 700, 800 years, but have they become Germans? Have they placed themselves on the cultural soil of labor? They never even dreamed of such a thing; as soon as they arrived, they started to cheat and they have been doing that ever since they have been in Germany. . . .

The Jews should not be admitted, whether or not there is overpopulation, for they do not belong to a productive race, they are exploiters, parasites. . . .

(Answering Rickert's arguments that . . . it would be a shame if fifty million Germans were afraid of a few Jews, Ahlwardt continued:) . . .

Herr Rickert, who is just as tall as I am, is afraid of one single cholera bacillus—well, gentlemen, the Jews are just that, cholera bacilli!

Gentlemen, the crux of the matter is Jewry's capacity for contagion and exploitation. . . . How many thousands of Germans have perished as a result of this Jewish exploitation, how many may have hanged themselves, shot themselves,

drowned themselves, how many may have ended by the wayside as tramps in America or drawn their last breath in the gutter, all of them people who had worked industriously on the soil their fathers had acquired, perhaps in hundreds of years of hard work. . . . Don't you feel any pity for those countless Germans? Are they to perish unsung? Ah, why were they foolish enough to let themselves be cheated? But the Germans are by no means so foolish, they are far more intelligent than the Jews. All inventions, all great ideas come from the Germans and not from the Jews. No, I shall tell you the national difference: The German is fundamentally trusting, his heart is full of loyalty and confidence. The Jew gains this confidence, only to betray it at the proper moment, ruining and pauperizing the German. This abuse of confidence on the part of the Jews is their main weapon. And these Jewish scoundrels are to be defended here! Is there no one to think of all those hundreds of thousands, nor of those millions of workers whose wages grow smaller and smaller because Jewish competition brings the prices down? One always hears: you must be humane toward the Jews. The humanitarianism of our century . . . is our curse. Why aren't you for once humane toward the oppressed? You'd better exterminate those beasts of prey and you'd better start by not letting any more of them into our country. . . .

(Taking issue with the liberals' argument of Jewish achievements in the arts, Ahlwardt declared:)

Art in my opinion is the capacity for expressing one's innermost feelings in such a way as to arouse the same feelings in the other person. Now the Jewish world of emotions (*Gefühlswelt*) and the Teutonic world of emotions are two quite different things. German art can express only German feelings; Jewish art only Jewish feelings. Because Jewry has been thrusting itself forward everywhere, it has also thrust itself forward in the field of art and therefore the art that is now in the foreground is Jewish art. Nowadays the head of a family must be very careful when he decides to take his family to the theater lest his Teutonic feelings be outraged by the infamous Jewish art that has spread everywhere.

The Jew is no German. If you say, the Jew was born in Germany, he was nursed by a German wetnurse, he abides by German laws, he has to serve as a soldier—and what kind of a soldier at that! let's not talk about it—he fulfills all his obligations, he pays his taxes—then I say that all this is not the crucial factor with regard to his nationality; the crucial factor is the race from which he stems. Permit me to make a rather trite comparison which I have already used elsewhere in my speeches: a horse that is born in a cowshed is far from being a cow.

A Jew who was born in Germany does not thereby become a German; he is still a Jew. Therefore it is imperative that we realize that Jewish racial characteristics differ so greatly from ours that a common life of Jews and Germans under the same laws is quite impossible because the Germans will perish. . . .

. . . I beg you from the bottom of my heart not to take this matter* lightly but as a very serious thing. It is a question of life and death for our people. . . .

We wouldn't think of going as far as have the Austrian anti-Semites in the Federal Council (*Reichsrat*) and to move that a bounty be paid for every Jew shot or to decree that he who kills a Jew shall inherit his property. We have no such intention. We shall not go as far as that. What we want is a clear and reasonable separation of the Jews from the Germans. An immediate prerequisite is that we slam the door and see to it that no more of them get in.[†]

---

*Prohibition of Jewish immigration.
[†]At the end of the debate a vote was taken, with 218 representatives present. Of these, 51 voted for, 167 against the motion.

THE DREYFUS AFFAIR: THE HENRY MEMORIAL

In 1894, on the basis of forged evidence in which army officers were complicit, Captain Alfred Dreyfus, the first Jewish officer to be appointed to the French general staff, was convicted of selling secrets to Germany and sentenced to prison for life on Devil's Island, the forbidding penal colony in South America. After five years of what amounted to solitary confinement, Dreyfus was granted a second trial. Again found guilty, but with extenuating circumstances, he was sentenced to ten years' detention. Finally, after a new inquiry, Dreyfus was vindicated and restored to the army.

The Dreyfus Affair tore France apart. The Right—nationalists, clergy, the army, royalists, and conservatives—believing that the honor of the army was at stake, insisted on Dreyfus' guilt despite the mounting evidence that he was framed. A torrent of anti-Semitic venom was unleashed and "Death to the Jews" became a rallying cry of the French Right.

Major Hubert-Joseph Henry, who had forged documents implicating Dreyfus, committed suicide when the forgery was discovered. The Right hailed Lieutenant Colonel Henry (he had been promoted posthumously) as a martyr who gave his life "for the honor of the army and the good of the country." Édouard Drumont's paper *La Libre Parole*, which had engaged in vile anti-Semitic invectives during the crisis, raised money for a memorial fund for Henry's widow. Donors to the fund often vented their hatred of Jews, as the following examples from a list of donors published in 1898–1899 illustrate.

A rural priest, who offers up the most ardent prayers for the extermination of the two enemies of France: the Jew and the Freemason. 5 fr.

A teacher, sworn enemy of stateless people. 1.50 fr.

A teacher from the Jura, who does not fail to tell his students that Jews and their friends are the vampires of France. 1 fr.

A future medical student, already sharpening his scalpels to dissect the Maccabee Dreyfus, bored through by a dozen bullets of a firing squad. 0.25 fr.

A group of policemen who would be very happy to thump hard and fast on Dreyfusards and filthy Yids, while, *by command and under pain of dismissal*, they are compelled to protect these rogues. 12.50 fr.

A royalist widow who misses the old bygone days when Jews were kept in their place. 2 fr.

A widow, who raises her son for God and France and in hatred of Freemasons and Jews. 0.15 fr.

A woman with great admiration for Drumont, who would like to see him govern France with the power of a king or emperor. 0.15 fr.

Sabatier (Madame Achille). Saint Joan of Arc, patron of our Sweet France, deliver us from the Jews! 20 fr.

H. L., brother of an infantry lieutenant, for [French President] Felix Faure when he kills as many kikes as rabbits. 0.50 fr.

XXXX. Finding not enough Jews to massacre, I propose cutting them in two, in order to get twice as many. 0.50 fr.

When will the alarm bell sound to rid France of the evil Yids? 1 fr.

A lieutenant of the colonial infantry. For the shame of the Jews and the triumph of honest men. 3 fr.

L. M., ex-second lieutenant of the 159th infantry. Long live France! Down with the kikes and freemasons who insult the army! 5 fr.

An administrative officer, in retirement. For the expulsion of the Yids. 5 fr.

A superior officer who would be delighted to see France in the hands of the French. 5 fr.

A section of officers from a frontier fortress who await with impatience the order to try new cannon and new explosives on the 100,000 Jews [there were not more than 75,000 French Jews, half of them in Paris] who poison the country. 25 fr.

A veteran of 1870, who considers the Jews the ten plagues of Egypt reunited. 2 fr.

Galey (Abbot), for the defense of the eternal law against the Puritan quackery and Judeo-Huguenot swindling. 5 fr.

THE KISHINEV POGROM, 1903

Between 1881 and 1921 there were three large-scale waves of pogroms (mob attacks against Jews) in Russia. The civil and military authorities generally made no attempt to stop the murderous rampages and, at times, provided support. The worst of the pogroms occurred during the Civil War that followed the

Bolshevik Revolution of 1917; some 60,000 Jews were slaughtered, particularly in the Ukraine, long a hotbed of anti-Semitism.

None of the numerous anti-Semitic outbreaks against Russian Jews in the years before World War I had a greater impact than that of the Kishinev pogrom, in southwestern Russia, in 1903. Its exceptional brutalities left a deep mark on Jewish consciousness. In 1903 almost half of Kishinev's population was Jewish; having achieved success in commerce and petty industry, Jews were the mainstay of the city's prosperity. This condition aroused the anti-Semitic feelings of their neighbors, already predisposed to hatred of Jews by a deeply embedded Christian bias.

After the assassination of Tsar Alexander II in 1881, the anti-Semitism of the Russian government gained ground. With influential support, a journalist named Pavolski Krushevan founded a newspaper in 1897 called *The Bessarabian*, which stirred up anti-Semitic sentiment. He accused the Jews of exploiting the Christian population, and worse, of ritual murder. In the course of five years, Krushevan stepped up his agitation, printing lurid stories designed to incite popular violence against Jews. He and his like-minded associates brought public indignation to the boiling point in the spring of 1903. Calling for "a bloody reckoning with the Jews," he prepared the attack for April 6. It was Easter Sunday for the Christians and part of the Passover week for the Jews. The details of what happened in Kishinev on April 6 and 7 are taken from a report entitled *Die Judenpogrome in Russland* (The Jewish Pogroms in Russia), prepared by a Zionist organization in London and published in Germany in 1910.

Sunday morning the weather cleared. The Jews were celebrating the last two days of Passover. Not anticipating trouble, they put on their holiday clothes and went to the synagogue. . . .

. . . Suddenly at about 3 P.M. a crowd of men appeared on the square Novyi Bazar, all dressed in red shirts. The men howled like madmen, incessantly shouting: "Death to the Jews. Beat the Jews." In front of the Moscow Tavern the crowd of some hundred split into 24 groups of 10–15 men each. There and then the systematic destruction, pillaging, and robbing of Jewish houses and shops began. At first they threw stones in great quantity and force, breaking windows and shutters. Then they tore open doors and windows, breaking into the Jewish houses and living quarters, smashing whatever furniture and equipment they found. The Jews had to hand over to the robbers their jewelry, money, and whatever other valuables they possessed. If they offered the slightest resistance, they were beaten over the head with pieces of their broken furniture. The storerooms were ransacked with special fury. The goods were either carried away or thrown on the street and destroyed. A large crowd of Christians followed the rioters, members of the intelligentsia, officials, students in the theological school, and others. . . .

At 5 P.M. the first Jew was murdered. The robbers stormed a trolley car with a Jewish passenger on board, shouting "Throw out the Jew." The Jew was pushed out and from all sides beaten on his head until his skull cracked and his brains spilled out. At first the sight of a dead Jew seemed to momentarily scare the bandits, but when they saw that the police did not care, they dispersed in all directions, shouting "Kill the Jews!"

On those streets where the pillaging took place Jews had to give up all attempts at self-defense. . . . But on the square Novyi Bazar the Jewish butchers gathered to defend themselves and their families. They bravely fought back and chased away the attackers, who were as cowardly as they were wild. Then the police came and arrested the Jews.

That was the final signal for the organizers of the mob. Until 10 P.M. the unleashed passions were vented in plunder, robbery, and destruction. Seven other murders took place. . . .

The Jews spent the night from Sunday to Monday in indescribable fear, yet hoping that the terror might be over.

During that night the leaders of the pogrom prepared further attacks, as in war. First the gangs which during the previous evening had arrived from the countryside were equipped with weapons. All weapons were of the same kind: axes, iron bars, and clubs, all strong enough to break doors and shutters, and even metal cabinets and safes. All men wore the same outfit: the red workshirts were worn by all members of the rabble, by peasants, workers, petty bourgeois, even seminary students and police. The second systematic action was the marking of all Jewish houses by the committee organizing the pogrom. During the night all Jewish houses and shops were painted with white chalk. Next came the organization of a permanent information and communication network among the various gangs. Several bicyclists were engaged, who subsequently played an important role. The bicyclists were high school students, theological students, and officials. The organization covered more than the city of Kishinev. Messengers were sent out to the nearest villages inviting the peasants: "Come to the city and help plunder the Jews. Bring big bags." Around 3 A.M. the preparations were finished. The signal for the attack was given.

The terror that now followed can hardly be described—orgies of loathsome savagery, bloodthirsty brutishness, and devilish lechery claimed their victims. Forty-nine Jews were murdered in Kishinev. When one hears about the excess of horror, one recognizes that only a few victims were lucky enough to die a simple death. Most of them had to suffer a variety of unbelievable abuse and repulsive torture unusual even among barbarians.

From 3 A.M. to 8 P.M. on Monday the gangs raged through the ruins and rubble which they themselves had piled up. They plundered, robbed, destroyed Jewish property, stole it, burned it, devastated it. They chased, slew, raped, and martyred the Jews. Representatives of all layers of the population took part in this witches' sabbath; soldiers, policemen, officials, and priests; children and women; peasants, workers, and vagabonds.

Major streets resounded with the terrifying roar of murdering gangs and the heart rending cries of the unfortunate victims. . . . The storerooms and shops were robbed, as on the previous day, down to the last item. . . . In the Jewish houses, the gangs burst into the living quarters with murderous howls, demanding all money and valuables. . . . If, however, the Jews could offer nothing or did not respond quickly enough, or if the gangsters were in a murderous mood, the men were knocked down, badly wounded, or killed. The women were raped one after the other in front of their men and children. They tore the arms and legs off the children, or broke them; some children were carried to the top floor and thrown out of the window. . . .

Early Monday morning a Jewish deputation hurried to the Governor of the province to plead for protection. He answered that he could do nothing, since he had no orders from St. Petersburg [the capital]. At the same time he refused to accept private telegrams from St. Petersburg. The vain appeal of the Jews to the governor was followed by a catastrophic worsening of their fate. The gangs henceforth could count on the patronage of the highest authority. . . .

In ever-rising fury the robbery, murder, and desecration continued. Jews had their heads hacked off. Towels were soaked in their blood and then waved like red flags. The murderers wrote with Jewish blood on white flags in large letters: "Death to the Jews!" They slit open the bodies of men and women, ripped out their guts and filled the hollows with leathers. They jumped on the corpses and danced, roaring, and drunk with vodka—men and women of "the best society." Officials and policemen laughed at the spectacle and joined in the fun. They beat pregnant women on their stomachs until they bled to death. . . .

They cut off the breasts of women after raping them. . . . Nails were driven into Chaja Sarah Phonarji's nostrils until they penetrated her skull. They hacked off the upper jaw of David Chariton, with all his teeth and his upper lip. Another man, Jechiel Selzer, had his ears pulled off before being beaten on the head until he became insane. . . .

These are some of the inhumanities committed during the pogrom. They are certified as true by eyewitnesses and the testimony of Christian physicians and Russian newspapers, which had passed through the most anti-Semitic and despotic censorship.

The synagogues were stormed and plundered with special spite. In one synagogue the gabai [sexton] braved death in front of the holy ark holding the Torah. Dressed in the *tales* [prayer shawl] and with the *tephalin* [phylacteries] on his forehead, he prepared for the onslaught of the murderers in order to protect the sacred scroll. He was cut down in the foulest manner. Then they tore, here and elsewhere, the Torah from the holy ark and cut the parchment into small scraps (Christian children later sold them on the streets for a few kopeks as mementos of Kishinev). After that the mobsters demolished, here as elsewhere, the synagogue's interior.

The barbarism of these scenes was so shattering that no less than 13 Jews went out of their minds. . . .

It would be unjust and ungrateful not to mention those Christians who in those days of mad brutality proved themselves true human beings and illustrious exceptions. They deserve to be remembered with special esteem because they were so few. . . .

Theodor Herzl
THE JEWISH STATE

Theodor Herzl (1860–1904) was raised in a comfortable Jewish middle-class home. Moving from Budapest, where he was born, to Vienna, the capital of the Austro-Hungarian Empire, he started to practice law, but soon turned to journalism, writing from Paris for the leading Vienna newspaper. A keen observer of the contemporary scene, he vigorously agitated for the ideal of an independent Jewish state. It was not a new idea but one whose time had come. Nationalist ferment was rising everywhere, often combined with virulent anti-Semitism. Under the circumstances, Herzl argued, security for Jews could be guaranteed only by a separate national state for Jews, preferably in Palestine.

In 1896 he published his program in a book, *Der Judenstaat* (The Jewish State), in which he envisaged a glorious future for an independent Jewish state harmoniously cooperating with the local population. In the following year he presided over the first Congress of Zionist Organizations held in Basel (Switzerland), attended mostly by Jews from Central and Eastern Europe. In its program the congress called for "a publicly guaranteed homeland for the Jewish people in the land of Israel." Subsequently, Herzl negotiated with the German emperor, the British government, and the sultan of the Ottoman Empire (of which Palestine was a part) for diplomatic support. In 1901 the Jewish National Fund was created to help settlers purchase land in Palestine. At his death, Herzl firmly expected a Jewish state to arise sometime in the future. The following excerpts from his book express the main points in his plea for a Jewish state.

We are a people—one people.

We have honestly endeavored everywhere to merge ourselves in the social life of surrounding communities and to preserve the faith of our fathers. We are not permitted to do so. In vain are we loyal patriots, our loyalty in some places running to extremes; in vain do we make the same sacrifices of life and property as our fellow-citizens; in vain do we strive to increase the fame of our native land in science and art, or her wealth by trade and commerce. In countries where we have lived for centuries we are still cried down as strangers, and often by those whose ancestors were not yet domiciled in the land where Jews had already had experience of suffering. . . . I think we shall not be left in peace.

Oppression and persecution cannot exterminate us. No nation on earth has survived such struggles and sufferings as we have gone through. Jew-baiting has merely stripped off our weaklings; the strong among us were invariably true to their race when persecution broke out against them. . . .

. . . [O]ld prejudices against us still lie deep in the hearts of the people. He who would have proofs of this need only listen to the people where they speak with frankness and simplicity: proverb and fairy-tale are both Anti-Semitic. . . .

No one can deny the gravity of the situation of the Jews. Wherever they live in perceptible numbers, they are more or less persecuted. Their equality before the law, granted by statute, has become practically a dead letter. They are debarred from filling even moderately high positions, either in the army, or in any public or private capacity. And attempts are made to thrust them out of business also: "Don't buy from Jews!"

Attacks in Parliaments, in assemblies, in the press, in the pulpit, in the street, on journeys—for example, their exclusion from certain hotels—even in places of recreation, become daily more numerous. The forms of persecutions varying according to the countries and social circles in which they occur. In Russia, imposts are levied on Jewish villages; in Rumania, a few persons are put to death; in Germany, they get a good beating occasionally; in Austria, Anti-Semites exercise terrorism over all public life; in Algeria, there are travelling agitators; in Paris, the Jews are shut out of the so-called best social circles and excluded from clubs. Shades of anti-Jewish feeling are innumerable. But this is not to be an attempt to make out a doleful category of Jewish hardships.

I do not intend to arouse sympathetic emotions on our behalf. That would be a foolish, futile, and undignified proceeding. I shall content myself with putting the following questions to the Jews: Is it not true that, in countries where we live in perceptible numbers, the position of Jewish lawyers, doctors, technicians, teachers, and employees of all descriptions becomes daily more intolerable? Is it not true, that the Jewish middle classes are seriously threatened? Is it not true, that the passions of the mob are incited against our wealthy people? Is it not true, that our poor endure greater sufferings than any other proletariat? I think that this external pressure makes itself felt everywhere. In our economically upper classes it causes discomfort, in our middle classes continual and grave anxieties, in our lower classes absolute despair.

Everything tends, in fact, to one and the same conclusion, which is clearly enunciated in that classic Berlin phrase: *"Juden Raus!"* (Out with the Jews!)

I shall now put the Question in the briefest possible form: Are we to "get out" now and where to?

Or, may we yet remain? And, how long?

Let us first settle the point of staying where we are. Can we hope for better days, can we possess our souls in patience, can we wait in pious res-ignation till the princes and peoples of this earth are more mercifully disposed towards us? I say that we cannot hope for a change in the current of feeling. . . . The nations in whose midst Jews live are all either covertly or openly Anti-Semitic. . . .

. . . We might perhaps be able to merge our-selves entirely into surrounding races, if these were to leave us in peace for a period of two gen-erations. But they will not leave us in peace. For a little period they manage to tolerate us, and then their hostility breaks out again and again. . . .

Thus, whether we like it or not, we are now, and shall henceforth remain, a historic group with unmistakable characteristics common to us all.

We are one people—our enemies have made us one without our consent, as repeatedly hap-pens in history. Distress binds us together, and, thus united, we suddenly discover our strength. Yes, we are strong enough to form a State, and, indeed, a model State. We possess all human and material resources necessary for the purpose. . . .

Let the sovereignty be granted us over a por-tion of the globe large enough to satisfy the rightful requirements of a nation; the rest we shall manage for ourselves.

The creation of a new State is neither ridiculous nor impossible. We have in our day witnessed the process in connection with nations which were not largely members of the middle class, but poorer, less educated, and consequently weaker than ourselves. . . .

Palestine is our ever-memorable historic home. The very name of Palestine would attract our people with a force of marvellous potency. If His Majesty the Sultan were to give us Palestine, we could in return undertake to regulate the whole finances of Turkey. We should there form a portion of a rampart of Europe against Asia, an outpost of civilization as opposed to barbarism. We should as a neutral State remain in contact with all Europe, which would have to guarantee our existence. The sanctuaries of Christendom would be safeguarded by assigning to them an extra-territorial status such as is well-known to the law of nations. We should form a guard of honor about these sanctuaries, answering for the fulfillment of this duty with our existence. This guard of honor would be the great symbol of the solution of the Jewish Question after eighteen centuries of Jewish suffering.

REVIEW QUESTIONS

1. What, according to Hermann Ahlwardt, were the racial characteristics of Jews? What, in contrast, were the racial characteristics of Germans?
2. What, said Ahlwardt, would be the ultimate result if Jewish immigration into Germany were not stopped?
3. How did Ahlwardt's anti-Semitism differ from traditional Christian anti-Semitism?
4. Do you see any common threads in the anti-Semitic sentiments voiced by the donors to the Henry Memorial?
5. What social groups in Kishinev took part in the attack on the Jews? What does the pogrom reveal about human nature? What role did government officials play?
6. Why did Theodor Herzl believe that the creation of a Jewish state was the only solution to the Jewish question?

CHAPTER 9
European Imperialism

PREMPAH, chief of the Ashanti tribe, disregarded treaties he signed with the British and faced military defeat. Here, he and his mother submit to the authority of the British governor of the Gold Coast (now Ghana) in 1896. *(Hulton Archive/Getty Images)*

Overseas territorial expansion has been part of European history since the fifteenth century. Portuguese and Spaniards explored maritime routes around Africa to India and East Asia; they crossed the Atlantic to the Western Hemisphere, soon followed by the English, Dutch, and French. All began to establish overseas colonies as bases for their ships and traders. Acquisition of colonies became part of the European power struggle. It was based on Europe's rapid progress in science, technology, economic skills, and political organization, enriched by ready assimilation of useful achievements from around the world. No people could match Western Europe's power resources.

The Europeans established a hold in India, East Asia, and coastal Africa; they populated North America with their immigrants and gained control over South America. In the late eighteenth century the English extended their seapower into the Pacific Ocean, claiming Australia and New Zealand. After achieving independence the United States too felt the expansionist urge, ultimately stretching from the Atlantic to the Pacific. In the nineteenth century the Spaniards and Portuguese in South America set up their own independent states; the Western Hemisphere became an extension of the European state system.

In the late nineteenth century, industrial growth and worldwide trade created among Europeans a new global competition for empire. The search for vital raw materials, markets, and investments intensified economic outreach, leading to ruthless exploitation and domination. The expenses of imperialism, usually greater than its economic benefits, were justified by rising nationalism, which fueled the quest for overseas possessions. What counted by the end of the century, as the traditional European rivalries expanded around the world, was global power; overseas possessions enhanced national prestige. Britain, thanks to its seapower, emerged as the colonial giant, claiming India as the core of the British Empire and provoking imitation by other ambitious European countries. Envious of the British Empire, other states did not want to be left behind.

Thus started a frantic race to occupy the last unclaimed parts of the world. The European powers began a "scramble for Africa." The Russians pressed into the Near East and Central Asia. Anti-foreign Japan, pried open to Western influence by the U.S. Commodore Matthew Perry in 1854, quickly westernized itself without impairing its cultural continuity, a unique case in history; catching the imperialist fever, Japan looked toward neighboring China for possible conquests. In 1898 the United States moved across the Pacific, occupying Hawaii and the Philippines. In 1900, responding to the Boxer Rebellion, a massive outburst in China of anti-foreign violence, the major European powers plus the United States and Japan expanded their rule in that country, greatly limiting the power of its government and inflicting a ruinous blow to its age-old pride. In the Age of Imperialism the world had essentially fallen under European—or now more generally "Western"—domination.

Obviously, the imperialist impact varied, depending on local conditions. Because of its geographical obstacles (dense tropical rainforests, savannahs, and deserts) sub-Saharan Africa was penetrated by the Europeans only late in the nineteenth century, carved up by England, France, Germany, and Belgium, each imposing its own boundaries regardless of local loyalties. Once established, the imperialists began to dominate their helpless subjects; all resistance was ruthlessly suppressed with the aid of indigenous soldiers. Convinced of their superiority, the imperialists often viewed Africans with disdain, dismissing their culture as barbaric. Indigenous ways, uncomprehended and generally repulsive to Europeans, provided a profound challenge to Western attitudes. Their reactions ranged from Social Darwinist racism (see page 234) to a patronizing conviction that they were obliged to civilize their subjects according to their own values. In Africa especially Christian missionaries played an important role in this effort, at considerable personal risk; because of tropical diseases and lack of medical care their death rate was painfully high. Only gradually, and sometimes with the missionaries' help, did the imperialist masters begin to open their minds to their subjects culture, even then never questioning their own superiority. Extending the benefits of imperial rule over "primitive" people was a source of deep patriotic pride.

The European masters never appreciated the devastating effects of their domination upon indigenous life and traditions in African and Asian lands. All peoples were now subject to profound cultural disorientation. Their customary ways were discredited as inferior, while the Western ways remained alien and perplexing. The cultural gap between indigenous and Western life became a source of much misery and violence. In Africa the Europeans encountered the sharpest cultural contrasts with their own ways, while in India the British confronted a high civilization that lacked political power. Here too the British imperialists faced a difficult task in elevating their subjects to their own standards. Everywhere the clash between indigenous and Western ways continues to the present day.

The imperialists generally imposed their Western culture upon all other cultures, thereby also disseminating their own ideals of freedom and self-determination. After World War I these ideals began to impress the educated minority, as in India. After World War II all colonial countries struggled toward independence. Thus imperialism gave rise to the present unprecedented age of intense global interaction, in which all peoples, to a lesser or greater degree, have to adjust to each other largely on Western, now simply called "modern," terms.

1 The Spirit of British Imperialism

In 1872 the British statesman Benjamin Disraeli (1804–1881) delivered a famous speech at the Crystal Palace in London that posed a crucial choice for his country: it was either insignificance in world affairs or imperial power with prosperity and global prestige. His speech was soon followed by an outburst of speeches, lectures, and books in which imperialists made claims for British worldwide superiority buttressed by arguments drawn from racist and Social Darwinist convictions popular at the time. Although public opinion was divided, these ideas, illustrated in the following three readings, found a receptive audience.

Cecil Rhodes
CONFESSION OF FAITH

One ardent supporter of British expansion was Cecil Rhodes (1853–1902). Raised in a parsonage north of London, Rhodes went to southern Africa at the age of seventeen for his health and to join his brother. Within two years he had established himself in the diamond industry. In the 1870s, he divided his time between Africa and studying at Oxford University. While at Oxford he was inspired by Disraeli's Crystal Palace speech and the views of the prominent Oxford professor John Ruskin (1819–1900), who urged England "to found colonies as fast and as far as she is able, formed of the most energetic and worthiest of men." In this spirit Rhodes wrote, for his own satisfaction, a "Confession of Faith." Composed in 1877, when he was twenty-four years old, it offered a vision of racist expansionism popular before the First World War. It was not published in his lifetime.

His faith propelled him into political and financial prominence in South Africa. In 1889 he became head of the British South African Company, whose territory, twice as large as England, was named Rhodesia six years later (it was renamed Zimbabwe in 1980). He controlled 90 percent of the world's diamond production and a large share of South Africa's gold fields. Never regarding wealth as an end in itself—he endowed the Rhodes Scholarships at Oxford—he sought to extend British influence in East Africa and around the world.

In 1890 he was named prime minister of the British Cape Colony, where government forces were heavily involved in conflict with the original Dutch settlers, the Boers. Driven north by the British, the Boers had set up their own state. Rhodes died during the Boer War (1899–1902), which put the Boers under British rule.

Excerpts follow from the "Confession of Faith" of 1877, included in the appendix of John E. Flint's biography of Cecil Rhodes. Flint reproduced the document "in its original form without any editing of spelling or punctuation."

It often strikes a man to inquire what is the chief good in life; to one the thought comes that it is a happy marriage, to another great wealth, and as each seizes on his idea, for that he more or less works for the rest of his existence. To myself thinking over the same question the wish came to render myself useful to my country. I then asked myself how could I and after reviewing the various methods I have felt that at the present day we are actually limiting our children and perhaps bringing into the world half the human beings we might owing to the lack of country for them to inhabit that if we had retained America there would at this moment be millions more of English living. I contend that we are the finest race in the world and that the more of the world we inhabit the better it is for the human race. Just fancy those parts that are at present inhabited by the most despicable specimens of human beings what an alteration there would be if they were brought under Anglo-Saxon influence, look again at the extra employment a new country added to our dominions gives. I contend that every acre added to our territory means in the future birth to some more of the English race who otherwise would not be brought into existence. Added to this the absorption of the greater portion of the world under our rule simply means the end of all wars. . . .

The idea gleaming and dancing before ones eyes like a will-of-the-wisp at last frames itself into a plan. Why should we not form a secret society with but one object the furtherance of the British Empire and the bringing of the whole uncivilised world under British rule for the recovery of the United States for the making the Anglo-Saxon race but one Empire. What a dream, but yet it is probable, it is possible. I once heard it argued by a fellow in my own college, I am sorry to own it by an Englishman, that it was a good thing for us that we have lost the United States. There are some subjects on which there can be no arguments, and to an Englishman this is one of them, but even from an American's point of view just picture what they have lost, look at their government, are not the frauds that yearly come before the public view a disgrace to any country and especially their's which is the finest in the world. Would they have occurred had they remained under English rule great as they have become how infinitely greater they would have been with the softening and elevating influences of English rule, think of those countless 000's [thousands] of Englishmen that during the last 100 years would have crossed the Atlantic and settled and populated the United States. Would they have not made without any prejudice a finer country of it than the low class Irish and German emigrants? All this we have lost and that country loses owing to whom? Owing to two or three ignorant pigheaded statesmen of the last century, at their door lies the blame. Do you ever feel mad? do you ever feel murderous. I think I do with those men. I bring facts to prove my assertion. Does an English father when his sons wish to emigrate ever think of suggesting emigration to a country under another flag, never—it would seem a disgrace to suggest such a thing I think that we all think that poverty is better under our own flag than wealth under a foreign one.

Put your mind into another train of thought. Fancy Australia discovered and colonised under the French flag. . . . We learn from having lost to cling to what we possess. We know the size of the world we know the total extent. Africa is still lying ready for us it is our duty to take it. It is our duty to seize every opportunity of acquiring more territory and we should keep this one idea steadily before our eyes that more territory simply means more of the Anglo-Saxon race more of the best the most human, most honourable race the world possesses.

To forward such a scheme what a splendid help a secret society would be a society not openly acknowledged but who would work in secret for such an object.

I contend that there are at the present moment numbers of the ablest men in the world who would devote their whole lives to it. . . .

What has been the main cause of the success of the Romish Church? The fact that every enthusiast, call it if you like every madman finds employment in it. Let us form the same kind of society a Church for the extension of the British Empire. A society which should have its members in every part of the British Empire working with one object and one idea. . . .

(In every Colonial legislature the Society should attempt to have its members prepared at all times to vote or speak and advocate the closer union of England and the colonies, to crush all disloyalty and every movement for the severance of our Empire. The Society should inspire and even own portions of the press for the press rules the mind of the people. The Society should always be searching for members who might by their position in the world by their energies or character forward the object but the ballot and test for admittance should be severe). . . .[1]

For fear that death might cut me off before the time for attempting its development I leave all my worldly goods in trust to S. G. Shippard and the Secretary for the Colonies at the time of my death to try to form such a Society with such an object.

---

[1]It is not clear why Rhodes placed this paragraph in parentheses.

Joseph Chamberlain
THE BRITISH EMPIRE: COLONIAL COMMERCE AND "THE WHITE MAN'S BURDEN"

British imperialists like Joseph Chamberlain (1836–1914) argued that the welfare of Britain depended upon the preservation and extension of the empire, for colonies fostered trade and served as a source of raw materials. In addition, Chamberlain asserted that the British Empire had a sacred duty to carry civilization, Christianity, and British law to the "backward" peoples of Africa and Asia. As a leading statesman, Chamberlain made many speeches, both in Parliament and before local political groups, that endorsed imperialist ventures. Excerpts from these speeches, later collected and published under the title *Foreign and Colonial Speeches* (1897), follow.

June 10, 1896

. . . The Empire, to parody a celebrated expression, is commerce. It was created by commerce, it is founded on commerce, and it could not exist a day without commerce. (Cheers.) . . . The fact is, history teaches us that no nation has ever achieved real greatness without the aid of commerce, and the greatness of no nation has survived the decay of its trade. Well, then, gentlemen, we have reason to be proud of our commerce and to be resolved to guard it from attack. (Cheers.) . . .

March 31, 1897

. . . We have suffered much in this country from depression of trade. We know how many of our fellow-subjects are at this moment unemployed. Is there any man in his senses who believes that the crowded population of these islands could exist for a single day if we were to cut adrift from us the great dependencies which now look to us for protection and assistance, and which are the natural markets for our trade? (Cheers.) The area of the United Kingdom is only 120,000 miles; the area of the British Empire is over 9,000,000 square miles, of which nearly 500,000 are to be found in the portion of Africa with which we have been dealing. If tomorrow it were possible, as some people apparently desire, to reduce by a stroke of the pen the British Empire to the dimensions of the United Kingdom, half at least of our population would be starved (cheers). . . .

January 22, 1894

We must look this matter in the face, and must recognise that in order that we may have more employment to give we must create more demand. (Hear, hear.) Give me the demand for more goods and then I will undertake to give plenty of employment in making the goods; and the only thing, in my opinion, that the Government can do in order to meet this great difficulty that we are considering, is so to arrange its policy that every inducement shall be given to the demand; that new markets shall be created, and that old markets shall be effectually developed. (Cheers.) . . . I am convinced that it is a necessity as well as a duty for us to uphold the dominion and empire which we now possess. (Loud cheers.) . . . I would never lose the hold which we now have over our great Indian dependency—(hear, hear)—by far the greatest and most valuable of all the customers we have or ever shall have in this country. For the same reasons I approve of the continued occupation of Egypt; and for the same reasons I have urged upon this Government, and upon previous Governments, the necessity for using every legitimate opportunity to extend our influence and control in that great African continent which is now being opened up to civilisation and to commerce; and, lastly, it is for the same reasons that I hold that our navy should be strengthened—(loud cheers)—until its supremacy is so assured that we cannot be shaken in any of the possessions which we hold or may hold hereafter.

Believe me, if in any one of the places to which I have referred any change took place which deprived us of that control and influence of which I have been speaking, the first to suffer would be the working-men of this country. Then, indeed, we should see a distress which would not be temporary, but which would be chronic, and we should find that England was entirely unable to support the enormous population which is now maintained by the aid of her foreign trade. If the working-men of this country understand, as I believe they do—I am one of those who have had good reason through my life to rely upon their intelligence and shrewdness—if they understand their own interests, they will never lend any countenance to the doctrines of those politicians who never lose an opportunity of pouring contempt and abuse upon the brave Englishmen, who, even at this moment, in all parts of the world are carving out new dominions for Britain, and are opening up fresh markets for British commerce, and laying out fresh fields for British labour. (Applause.) . . .

March 31, 1897

. . . We feel now that our rule over these territories can only be justified if we can show that it adds to the happiness and prosperity of the people—(cheers)—and I maintain that our rule does, and has, brought security and peace and comparative prosperity to countries that never knew these blessings before. (Cheers.)

In carrying out this work of civilisation we are fulfilling what I believe to be our national mission, and we are finding scope for the exercise of those faculties and qualities which have made of us a great governing race. (Cheers.) I do not say that our success has been perfect in every case, I do not say that all our methods have been beyond reproach; but I do say that in almost every instance in which the rule of the Queen has been established and the great *Pax Britannica*[1] has been enforced, there has come with it greater security to life and property, and a material improvement in the condition of the bulk of the population. (Cheers.) No doubt, in the first instance, when

---

[1] *Pax Britannica* means "British Peace" in the tradition of the *Pax Romana*—the peace, stability, and prosperity that characterized the Roman Empire at its height in the first two centuries A.D.

these conquests have been made, there has been bloodshed, there has been loss of life among the native populations, loss of still more precious lives among those who have been sent out to bring these countries into some kind of disciplined order, but it must be remembered that this is the condition of the mission we have to fulfil. . . .

. . . You cannot have omelettes without breaking eggs; you cannot destroy the practices of barbarism, of slavery, of superstition, which for centuries have desolated the interior of Africa, without the use of force; but if you will fairly contrast the gain to humanity with the price which we are bound to pay for it, I think you may well rejoice in the result of such expeditions as those which have recently been conducted with such signal success—(cheers)—in Nyassaland, Ashanti, Benin, and

Nupé [regions in Africa]—expeditions which may have, and indeed have, cost valuable lives, but as to which we may rest assured that for one life lost a hundred will be gained, and the cause of civilisation and the prosperity of the people will in the long run be eminently advanced. (Cheers.) But no doubt such a state of things, such a mission as I have described, involve heavy responsibility. . . . and it is a gigantic task that we have undertaken when we have determined to wield the sceptre of empire. Great is the task, great is the responsibility, but great is the honour—(cheers); and I am convinced that the conscience and the spirit of the country will rise to the height of its obligations, and that we shall have the strength to fulfil the mission which our history and our national character have imposed upon us. (Cheers.)

Karl Pearson
SOCIAL DARWINISM: IMPERIALISM
JUSTIFIED BY NATURE

In the last part of the nineteenth century, the spirit of expansionism was buttressed by application of Darwin's theory of evolution to human society. Theorists called Social Darwinists argued that nations and races, like the species of animals, were locked in a struggle for existence in which only the fittest survived and deserved to survive. British and American imperialists employed the language of Social Darwinism to promote and justify Anglo-Saxon expansion and domination of other peoples. Social Darwinist ideas spread to Germany, which was inspired by the examples of British and American expansion. In a lecture given in 1900 and titled "National Life from the Standpoint of Science," Karl Pearson (1857–1936), a British professor of mathematics, expressed the beliefs of Social Darwinists.

What I have said about bad stock seems to me to hold for the lower races of man. How many centuries, how many thousands of years, have the Kaffir [a tribe in southern Africa] or the negro held large districts in Africa undisturbed by the white man? Yet their intertribal struggles have not yet produced a civilization in the least comparable with the Aryan[1] [Western European]. Educate and

nurture them as you will, I do not believe that you will succeed in modifying the stock. History shows me one way, and one way only, in which a high state of civilization has been produced, namely, the struggle of race with race, and the survival of the physically and mentally fitter race. . . .

in the region from the Caspian Sea to the Hindu Kush Mountains. Around 2000 B.C., some Aryan-speaking people migrated to Europe and India. Nineteenth-century racialist thinkers held that Europeans, descendants of the ancient Aryans, were racially superior to other peoples.

---

[1]Most European languages derive from the Aryan language spoken by people who lived thousands of years ago

. . . Let us suppose we could prevent the white man, if we liked, from going to lands of which the agricultural and mineral resources are not worked to the full; then I should say a thousand times better for him that he should not go than that he should settle down and live alongside the inferior race. The only healthy alternative is that he should go and completely drive out the inferior race. That is practically what the white man has done in North America. . . . But I venture to say that no man calmly judging will wish either that the whites had never gone to America, or would desire that whites and Red Indians were to-day living alongside each other as negro and white in the Southern States, as Kaffir and European in South Africa, still less that they had mixed their blood as Spaniard and Indian in South America. . . . I venture to assert, then, that the struggle for existence between white and red man, painful and even terrible as it was in its details, has given us a good far outbalancing its immediate evil. In place of the red man, contributing practically nothing to the work and thought of the world, we have a great nation, mistress of many arts, and able, with its youthful imagination and fresh, untrammelled impulses, to contribute much to the common stock of civilized man. . . .

But America is but one case in which we have to mark a masterful human progress following an inter-racial struggle. The Australian nation is another case of great civilization supplanting a lower race unable to work to the full the land and its resources. . . . The struggle means suffering, intense suffering, while it is in progress; but that struggle and that suffering have been the stages by which the white man has reached his present stage of development, and they account for the fact that he no longer lives in caves and feeds on roots and nuts. This dependence of progress on the survival of the fitter race, terribly black as it may seem to some of you, gives the struggle for existence its redeeming features; it is the fiery crucible out of which comes the finer metal. You may hope for a time when the sword shall be turned into the ploughshare, when American and German and English traders shall no longer compete in the markets of the world for their raw material and for their food supply, when the white man and the dark shall share the soil between them, and each till it as he lists [pleases]. But, believe me, when that day comes mankind will no longer progress; there will be nothing to check the fertility of inferior stock; the relentless law of heredity will not be controlled and guided by natural selection. Man will stagnate. . . .

The . . . great function of science in national life . . . is to show us what national life means, and how the nation is a vast organism subject . . . to the great forces of evolution. . . . There is a struggle of race against race and of nation against nation. In the early days of that struggle it was a blind, unconscious struggle of barbaric tribes. At the present day, in the case of the civilized white man, it has become more and more the conscious, carefully directed attempt of the nation to fit itself to a continuously changing environment. The nation has to foresee how and where the struggle will be carried on; the maintenance of national position is becoming more and more a conscious preparation for changing conditions, an insight into the needs of coming environments. . . .

. . . If a nation is to maintain its position in this struggle, it must be fully provided with trained brains in every department of national activity, from the government to the factory, and have, if possible, a *reserve of brain and physique* to fall back upon in times of national crisis. . . .

You will see that my view—and I think it may be called the scientific view of a nation—is that of an organized whole, kept up to a high pitch of internal efficiency by insuring that its numbers are substantially recruited from the better stocks, and kept up to a high pitch of external efficiency by contest, chiefly by way of war with inferior races, and with equal races by the struggle for trade-routes and for the sources of raw material and of food supply. This is the natural history view of mankind, and I do not think you can in its main features subvert it. . . .

. . . Is it not a fact that the daily bread of our millions of workers depends on their having somebody to work for? that if we give up the contest for trade-routes and for free markets and for waste lands, we indirectly give up our food-supply? Is it not a fact that our strength depends on these and upon our colonies, and that our colonies have been won by the ejection of inferior races, and are maintained against equal races only by respect for the present power of our empire? . . .

. . . We find that the law of the survival of the fitter is true of mankind, but that the struggle is that of the [social] animal. A community not knit together by strong social instincts, by sympathy between man and man, and class and class, cannot face the external contest, the competition with other nations, by peace or by war, for the raw material of production and for its food supply. This struggle of tribe with tribe, and nation with nation, may have its mournful side; but we see as a result of it the gradual progress of mankind to higher intellectual and physical efficiency. It is idle to condemn it; we can only see that it exists and recognise what we have gained by it—civilization and social sympathy. But while the statesman has to watch this external struggle, . . . he must be very cautious that the nation is not silently rotting at its core. He must insure that the fertility of the inferior stocks is checked, and that of the superior stocks encouraged; he must regard with suspicion anything that tempts the physically and mentally fitter men and women to remain childless. . . .

. . . The path of progress is strewn with the wrecks of nations; traces are everywhere to be seen of the hecatombs [slaughtered remains] of inferior races, and of victims who found not the narrow way to perfection. Yet these dead people are, in very truth, the stepping stones on which mankind has arisen to the higher intellectual and deeper emotional life of today.

REVIEW QUESTIONS

1. What nationalistic views were expressed in Cecil Rhodes' "Confession of Faith"?
2. What role did the concept of race—the English or Anglo-Saxon—play in the arguments of Rhodes? Compare his views with those advanced by Hermann Ahlwardt on page 218.
3. How did Chamberlain define the national mission of the "great governing race"? What were the economic benefits of that mission?
4. How did Karl Pearson define the difference between inferior and superior races?
5. What measures did Pearson advocate for keeping a nation such as Britain at its highest potential?

2 European Rule in Africa

Africa, the world's second largest continent after Asia, posed a special challenge to European imperialists who penetrated its tropical depths. While its territories north of the Sahara desert had long been integrated into Mediterranean and Mideastern life, in sub-Saharan Africa the Europeans encountered harrowing conditions as nowhere else in the world. They were repelled by the debilitating climate, impenetrable rainforests, deadly diseases, the great variety of black-skinned peoples and their strange customs. Seen through European eyes, Africans were illiterate heathen barbarians, still trading in helpless slaves among themselves and with Arabs, decades after Western countries had banned slave trading in Africa.

Cultural differences conditioned by African geography and climate constituted an immense divide between Europeans and Africans. The profound inequality in military and political power provided the sharpest contrast. Africans lived mostly in small communities divided by over one thousand languages; a few large states like Mali and "Songai" had grown up under Muslim influence but had collapsed by the sixteenth century. Cut off from developments in the Far East and Western Europe that had long stimulated science, technology, and political power, sub-Saharan Africans, divided among themselves, helplessly faced the Europeans, who were equipped with superior weapons and backed up by powerful states. Inevitably, they fell victim to European imperialism. By the late nineteenth century Europeans had acquired sufficient resources, including medicines against tropical diseases, to explore the interior and establish their rule. Sub-Saharan Africa now became the focus of rivalry among England, France, and Germany; even the king of Belgium claimed a share in the much publicized "scramble for Africa."

At times the European conquerors proceeded with unrestrained brutality, proclaiming in the language of Social Darwinism that the "inferior" races of Africa had to be sacrificed to "progress."

Cecil Rhodes and Lo Bengula
"I HAD SIGNED AWAY THE MINERAL RIGHTS OF MY WHOLE COUNTRY"

A good example of how colonial expansion in Africa proceeded is furnished by Cecil Rhodes's dealings with Lo Bengula, king of Matabeleland, Mashonaland, and adjacent territories (now Zimbabwe). In his "Confession of Faith" of 1877 Rhodes had included hope for poor Africans: "just fancy those parts [of the world] that are at present inhabited by the most despicable specimens of human beings, what an alternative there would be if they were brought under Anglo-Saxon influence." Eleven years later, eager to expand his business, he arranged through three of his agents a contract with Lo Bengula, giving his agents "the complete and inclusive charge" of all the metals and minerals in the king's lands. In return, he pledged a financial subsidy and delivery of weapons. The illiterate Lo Bengula put his mark to the contract that follows.

Know all men by these presents, that whereas Charles Dunell Rudd, of Kimberley; Rochfort Maguire, of London; and Francis Robert Thompson, of Kimberley, have covenanted and agreed . . . to pay me . . . the sum of one hundred pounds sterling, British currency, on the first day of every lunar month: and further, to deliver at my royal kraal [village] one thousand Martini-Henry breech-loading rifles, together with one hundred thousand rounds of suitable ball cartridges . . . and further to deliver on the Zambesi River a steamboat with guns suitable for defensive purposes, or in lieu of the said steamboat, should I [so] elect, to pay to me the sum of five hundred pounds sterling, British currency. On the execution of these presents, I, Lo Bengula, King of Matabeleland, Mashonaland, and other adjoining territories . . . do hereby grant and assign unto the said grantees . . . the complete and exclusive charge over all metals and minerals situated and contained in my kingdoms . . . together with full power to do all things that they may deem necessary to win and procure the same, and to hold, collect, and enjoy the profits and revenues, if any, derivable from the said metals and minerals, subject to the aforesaid payment; and whereas I have been much molested of late by divers persons seeking and desiring to obtain grants and concessions of land and mining rights in my territories, I do hereby authorize the said grantees . . . to exclude from my kingdom . . . all persons seeking land, metals, minerals, or mining rights therein, and I do hereby undertake to render them all such needful assistance as they may from time to time require for the exclusion of such persons, and to grant no concessions of land or mining rights . . . without their consent and concurrence. . . . This given under my hand this thirtieth day of October, in the year of our Lord 1888, at my royal kraal.

> Lo Bengula X his mark
> C. D. Rudd
> Rochfort Maguire
> F. R. Thompson

When the terms of the contract became known among Lo Bengula's subjects, they protested that their ruler had been tricked. After having his fears confirmed by friendly British missionaries, Lo Bengula executed his Head Counsellor and sent a mission to Queen Victoria. After an unsatisfactory response, he sent a formal protest on April 23, 1889. This pathetic appeal from the untutored African ruler had no effect on the course of events. He was told by the Queen's Advisor that it was "impossible for him to exclude white men." The Advisor said that the Queen had made inquiries as to the persons concerned and was satisfied that they "may be trusted to carry out the working for gold in the chief's country without molesting his people, or in any way interfering with their kraals [villages], gardens [cultivated fields], or cattle." Thus Rhodes made Lo Bengula's territories his personal domain and part of the British Empire.

Following is Lo Bengula's futile appeal to Queen Victoria.

Some time ago a party of men came to my country, the principal one appearing to be a man called Rudd. They asked me for a place to dig for gold, and said they would give me certain things for the right to do so. I told them to bring what they could give and I would show them what I would give. A document was written and presented to me for signature. I asked what it contained, and was told that in it were my words and the words of those men. I put my hand to it. About three months afterwards I heard from other sources that I had given by that document the right to all the minerals of my country. I called a meeting of my *Indunas* [counsellors], and also of the white men and demanded a copy of the document. It was proved to me that I had signed away the mineral rights of my whole country to Rudd and his friends. I have since had a meeting of my *Indunas* and they will not recognise the paper, as it contains neither my words nor the words of those who got it. . . . I write to you that you may know the truth about this thing.

Edmund Morel
THE BLACK MAN'S BURDEN

E.D. Morel (1873–1924) was an English author and journalist with a keen sense of moral responsibility, who was especially concerned with the colonial exploitation of Africa. The most extreme abuses of the nineteenth century took place in the

Congo Free State established in 1885 under the personal rule of King Leopold II of Belgium. By 1904 the king's ruthless methods of enriching himself while destroying the native population had become a scandal widely publicized in England and the United States. Morel took a leading part in denouncing the selfish exploiters of the Congo System. As a result, in 1908 Leopold II was forced to turn over his colonial domain to the Belgian government, which initiated more humane policies.

After World War I, Morel, moved by "the desolation and misery into which Europe was plunged," foresaw a new era heralding the birth of "an international conscience in regard to Africa." In 1920 he published his book, *The Black Man's Burden: The White Man in Africa from the Fifteenth Century to World War I.* While recognizing the accomplishments of Europeans in Africa, "many of them worthy of admiration," he was foremost concerned with the immense suffering Europe had inflicted upon the peoples of that continent, pleading that "Africa is really helpless against the material goods of the white man, as embodied in the trinity of imperialism, capitalistic-exploitation, and militarism." He wanted to make the public aware of the evils that were still perpetrated in many African regions. As a left-wing intellectual and a Member of Parliament for the Labour Party, he thus helped to set off an anti-colonial tide of compassion for the African people. The following passages are selected from Morel's description of the Congo System.

The Congo Free State—known since August, 1908, as the Belgian Congo—is roughly one million square miles in extent. When Stanley discovered the course of the Congo and observed its densely-populated river banks, he formed the, doubtless very much exaggerated, estimate that the total population amounted to forty millions. In the years that followed, when the country had been explored in every direction by travellers of divers nationalities, estimates varied between twenty and thirty millions. No estimate fell below twenty millions. In 1911 an official census was taken. It was not published in Belgium, but was reported in one of the British Consular dispatches. *It revealed that only eight and a half million people were left.* The Congo system lasted for the best part of twenty years. The loss of life can never be known with even approximate exactitude. But data, extending over successive periods, are procurable in respect of a number of regions, and a careful study of these suggests that a figure of ten million victims would be a very conservative estimate.

. . . It is very difficult for anyone who has not experienced in his person the sensations of the tropical African forest to realise the tremendous handicaps which man has to contend against whose lot is cast beneath its sombre shades; the extent to which nature, there seen in her most titanic and ruthless moods, presses upon man; the intellectual disabilities against which man must needs constantly struggle not to sink to the level of the brute; the incessant combat to preserve life and secure nourishment. Communities living in this environment who prove themselves capable of systematic agriculture and of industry; who are found to be possessed of keen commercial instincts; who are quick at learning, deft at working iron and copper, able to weave cloths of real artistic design; these are communities full of promise in which the divine spark burns brightly. To destroy these activities; to reduce all the varied, and picturesque, and stimulating episodes in savage life to a dull routine of endless toil for uncomprehended ends; to dislocate social ties and disrupt social institutions; to stifle nascent desires and crush mental development; to graft upon primitive passions the annihilating evils of scientific slavery, and the bestial imaginings of civilized man, unrestrained by convention or law; in fine, to kill the soul in a people—this is a crime which transcends physical murder. And this crime it was, which, for twenty dreadful years, white men perpetrated upon the Congo natives. . . .

From 1891 until 1912, the paramount object of European rule in the Congo was the pillaging of its natural wealth to enrich private interests in Belgium. To achieve this end a specific, well-defined System was thought out in Brussels and applied on the Congo. . . .

The Policy was quite simple. Native rights in land were deemed to be confined to the actual sites of the town or village, and the areas under food cultivation around them. Beyond those areas no such rights would be admitted. The land was "vacant," *i.e.,* without owners. Consequently the "State" was owner. The "State" was Leopold II., not in his capacity of constitutional Monarch of Belgium, but as Sovereign of the "Congo Free State." Native rights in nine-tenths of the Congo territory being thus declared non-existent, it followed that the native population had no proprietary right in the plants and trees growing upon that territory, and which yielded rubber, resins, oils, dyes, etc.: no right, in short, to anything animal, vegetable, or mineral which the land contained. In making use of the produce of the land, either for internal or external trade or internal industry and social requirements, the native population would thus obviously be making use of that which did not belong to it, but which belonged to the "State," *i.e.,* Leopold II. It followed logically that any third person—European or other—acquiring, or attempting to acquire, such produce from the native population by purchase, in exchange for corresponding goods or services, would be guilty of robbery, or attempted robbery, of "State property." A "State" required revenue. Revenue implied taxation. The only articles in the Congo territory capable of producing revenue were the ivory, the rubber, the resinous gums and oils; which had become the property of the "State." The only medium through which these articles could be gathered, prepared and exported

to Europe—where they would be sold and converted into revenue—was native labour. Native labour would be called upon to furnish those articles in the name of "taxation."

. . . Regulations were issued forbidding the natives to sell rubber or ivory to European merchants, and threatening the latter with prosecution if they bought these articles from the natives. In the second place, every official in the country had to be made a partner in the business of getting rubber and ivory out of the natives in the guise of "taxation." Circulars, which remained secret for many years, were sent out, to the effect that the paramount duty of Officials was to make their districts yield the greatest possible quantity of these articles; promotion would be reckoned on that basis. As a further stimulus to "energetic action" a system of sliding-scale bonuses was elaborated, whereby the less the native was "paid" for his *labour* in producing theses articles of "taxation," *i.e.,* the lower the outlay in obtaining them, the higher was the Official's commission. . . . "Concessionaire" Companies were created to which the King farmed out a large proportion of the total territory, retaining half the shares in each venture. These privileges were granted to business men, bankers, and others with whom the King thought it necessary to compound. They floated their companies on the stock exchange. The shares rose rapidly. . . .

These various measures at the European end were comparatively easy. The problem of dealing with the natives themselves was more complex. A native army was the pre-requisite. The five years . . . [from 1886 to 1891] were employed in raising the nucleus of a force of 5,000. It was successively increased to nearly 20,000 apart from the many thousands of "irregulars" employed by the Concessionaire Companies. This force was amply sufficient for the purpose, for a single native soldier armed with a rifle and with a plentiful supply of ball cartridge can terrorise a whole village. The same system of promotion and reward would apply to the native soldier as to the Official—the more rubber from the village, the greater the prospect of having a completely free hand to loot and rape. A systematic warfare upon the women and children would prove an excellent means of pressure. They would be converted into "hostages" for the good behaviour, in rubber collecting, of the men. "Hostage houses" would become an institution in the Congo. But in certain parts of the Congo the rubber vine did not grow. This peculiarity of nature was, in one way, all to the good. For the army of Officials and native soldiers, with their wives, and concubines, and camp-followers generally, required feeding. The non-rubber producing districts should feed them. Fishing tribes would be "taxed" in fish; agricultural tribes in foodstuffs. In this case, too, the women and children would answer for the men. Frequent military expeditions would probably be an unfortunate necessity. Such expeditions would demand in every case hundreds of carriers for the transport of loads, ammunition, and general impedimenta. Here, again, was an excellent school in which this idle people could learn the dignity of labour. The whole territory would thus become a busy hive of human activities, continuously and usefully engaged for the benefit of the "owners" of the soil thousands of miles away, and their crowned Head, whose intention, proclaimed on repeated occasions to an admiring world, was the "moral and material regeneration" of the natives of the Congo.

Such was the Leopoldian "System," briefly epitomised. It was conceived by a master brain.

Richard Meinertzhagen
AN EMBATTLED COLONIAL OFFICER IN EAST AFRICA

Richard Meinertzhagen (1878–1967) was stationed as a young soldier in Kenya from 1902 to 1906, serving on the raw frontier of British imperialism. Living under great hardships in the African wilderness, exposed to poisoned arrows, his sensibilities outraged by the practices of people the colonial conquerors called "niggers" and "savages," he participated in imposing British rule on the rebellious Nandi tribe. In his spare time he enjoyed shooting wild animals, while also appreciating as an ornithologist the exotic birds he observed. The entries in his diary reprinted below provide insight into the harrowing experiences and the anguish of an isolated young Englishman facing the strains of colonial service, where Western and indigenous ways clashed more sharply than anywhere else in the world.

August 20, 1902

News came in this evening that a policeman had been murdered by a village only a mile or so from the station, as a protest against the white men. . . . At midnight I sent a reliable native to the offending village to ascertain what was happening. He returned at 3 A.M. this morning, saying all the neighbouring villages had joined forces with the offending village and were at the moment conducting an orgy round the dead policeman's body, which had been badly mutilated. A council of war had been held by the natives and they had decided to march on Fort Hall at dawn. So we marched out of the station at 3.30 A.M., crossed the Mathyoia and reached our destination half an hour before dawn. The village had bonfires burning and the Wakikuyu were dancing round them in all their war-paint. It was really rather a weird sight. The alarm was given by a native who tried to break through our rather thin cordon. He refused to stop when challenged and was shot down. There was then a rush from the village into the surrounding bush, and we killed about 17 niggers. Two policemen and one of my men were killed. I narrowly escaped a spear which whizzed past my head. Then the fun began. We at once burned the village and captured the sheep and goats. After that we systematically cleared the valley in which the village was situated, burned all the huts, and killed a few more niggers, who finally gave up the fight and cleared off, but not till 3 more of our men had been killed.

At 3 P.M. we returned to Fort Hall and told the chiefs who had assembled to meet us that they were to go out to the village at once, get into touch with the local chief, bring him in, and generally spread the news that our anger was by no means appeased. They returned just before dark with a deputation from the village, saying their chief was killed and they begged for mercy. McClean [a fellow official] fined them 50 head of cattle, at the same time intimating that half would be remitted if the murderers of the policeman were produced. This they promised to do tomorrow. We have told them that we are quite prepared to continue tomorrow what we began today, and I think they are impressed. Such nonsense as attacking the station is completely driven from their stupid heads. So order once more reigns in Kenya District.

September 8, 1902

I have performed a most unpleasant duty today. I made a night march to the village at the edge of forest where the white settler had been so brutally murdered the day before yesterday. Though the war drums were sounding throughout the night we reached the village without incident and surrounded it. By the light of fires we could see savages dancing in the village, and our guides assured me that they were dancing round the mutilated body of the white man.

I gave orders that every living thing except children should be killed without mercy. I hated the work and was anxious to get through with it. So soon as we could see to shoot we closed in. Several of the men tried to break out but were immediately shot. I then assaulted the place before any defence could be prepared. Every soul was either shot or bayoneted, and I am happy to say that no children were in the village. They, with the younger women, had already been removed by the villagers to the forest. We burned all the huts and razed the banana plantations to the ground.

In the open space in the centre of the village was a sight which horrified me—a naked white man pegged out on his back, mutilated and disembowelled, his body used as a latrine by all and sundry who passed by. We washed his corpse in a stream and buried him just outside the village. The whole of this affair took so short a time that the sun was barely up before we beat a retreat to our main camp.

My drastic action on this occasion haunted me for many years, and even now I am not sure whether I was right. My reason for killing all adults, including women, was that the latter had been the main instigators of not only the murder but the method of death, and it was the women who had befouled the corpse after death.

November 23, 1902

Meanwhile a Land Office under my friend Barton Wright has been started with a view to parcelling out land to settlers. Eliot thinks there is a great future for East Africa, transforming it into a huge white farming and stock area. Perhaps that is correct, but sooner or later it must lead to a clash between black and white. I cannot see millions of educated Africans—as there will be in a hundred years' time—submitting tamely to white domination. After all, it is an African country, and they will demand domination. Then blood will be spilled, and I have little doubt about the eventual outcome.

January 12, 1904

The authorities give no help. The administrative officers, with few exceptions, seem to dislike their country being mapped by soldiers. In fact the soldier is not in favour in British East Africa. This is largely due to the low class of man who is appointed to administrative appointments. Few of them have had any education, and many of them do not pretend to be members of the educated class. One can neither read nor write. This is not surprising when one realises that no examination is required to enter the local Civil Service. Sir Clement Hill, who recently visited the colony on behalf of the Foreign Office, remarked that "so long as Civil Servants were enlisted from the gutter" we could not expect a high standard of administration. When such men are given unlimited power over uneducated and simple-minded natives it is not extraordinary that they should abuse their powers, suffer from megalomania and regard themselves as little tin gods.

February 19, 1904

Before this expedition started I issued an order to my company and to the Masai Levies [African soldiers in the pay of the British authorities] that if any man was guilty of killing women or children he would be shot. My men are mere savages in the laws and customs of war, and the Masai are bloodthirsty villains to whom the killing of women and children means nothing.

Today we had occasion to rush a small village in which some of the enemy were concealed and from which they were firing arrows at the column. I quickly formed up 10 of my men and 30 Masai and rushed the place. The enemy ran, and we killed 4 of them. I formed up this party some 150 yards on the other side of the village before moving on, and then heard a woman shriek from the village, which I had presumed empty. I ran back to the village, where I saw two of my men and three Masai in the act of dragging a woman from a hut, and the body of a small boy on the ground, one of the Levies being in the act of withdrawing his spear from the little body. Another levy was leading a small girl by the hand and was about to knock her on the head with his knobkerrie [a short club with a knob at the end]. I yelled to him to stay

his hand, but I suppose his blood was up, for he paid no attention to me and killed the child. Meanwhile one of my own men bayoneted the woman within 30 yards of me. Putting up my rifle I shot the man dead and then his companion, who I think contemplated having a pot shot at me. The Levies bolted, but I bagged them all three before they were clear of the village.

July 27, 1904

On reading through the first part of this record I am shocked by the account of taking human life and the constant slaughter of big game. I do not pretend to excuse it, but perhaps I may explain it. I have no belief in the sanctity of human life or in the dignity of the human race. Human life has never been sacred; nor has man, except in a few exceptional cases, been dignified. Moreover, in Kenya fifty years ago, when stationed with 100 soldiers amid an African population of some 300,000, in cases of emergency where local government was threatened we had to act, and act quickly. To do nothing in an emergency is to do something definitely wrong, and talking comes under the category of "nothing." There was no telegraph or telephone, no motor cars or wireless, and action was imperative for safety. Thank God there was no time or opportunity for talks, conferences and discussions.

I also regarded discipline in my company as paramount, more important when dealing with coloured troops than with one's own countrymen. What may appear to have been outrageous and cruel conduct on my part was an insistence on strict discipline—the obedience of orders. I have seen so many coloured troops rendered useless by inefficient discipline.

September 15, 1905

Living isolated in a savage country, rarely speaking my own language, and surrounded by a population whose civilisation is on a much lower plane than my own are conditions to which I have indeed grown accustomed, but which do not improve on acquaintance unless one lowers one's own plane to that of the savage, when perhaps one might be contented. Isolation from my family, whose formative effect has been considerable on my character, is dreary and might of itself account for unwholesome ideas and gloomy thoughts. I seem to have received a heavy sowing of unhappiness and depression, which seems to thrive in the isolated conditions which I now experience. . . .

Normally I am healthy-minded, but the worries and conditions of the past few months have been too much for me. All men are not affected in the same way. Others with greater strength of character than myself might suffer little from moral and intellectual starvation. To others, natural history or some object of unceasing pursuit is an effective barrier against complete isolation. But my experience shows me that it is but a small percentage of white men whose characters do not in one way or another undergo a subtle process of deterioration when they are compelled to live for any length of time among savage races and under such conditions as exist in tropical climates. It is hard to resist the savagery of Africa when one falls under its spell. One soon reverts to one's ancestral character, both mind and temperament becoming brutalised. I have seen so much of it out here and I have myself felt the magnetic power of the African climate drawing me lower and lower to the level of a savage. This is a condition which is accentuated by worry or mental depression, and which has to be combated with all the force in one's power. My love of home and my family, the dread of being eventually overcome by savage Africa, the horror of losing one's veneer of western civilisation and cutting adrift from all one holds good—these are the forces which

help me to fight the temptation to drift down to the temporary luxury of the civilisation of the savage.

March 17, 1906

My 5 years are up this year, and I must decide whether or not to revert to my regiment. I think I had better go back, for if I were to remain out here much longer I should get less and less anxious ever to go back to my British regiment, and that I know I would in the end regret. But I admit I am a bit tired of this sort of life. It is too solitary for any length of time. Niggers are rather getting on my nerves, the climate is making me feel depressed, and altogether I feel I want a change. I want to be more with my own folk than with these savages. . . .

March 20, 1906

Natives are queer creatures and hold still queerer ideas. No European can fully understand the working of the black mind. Their morals, ideals and principles are all based on quite different models from ours, and it frequently happens that some trivial and unnoticed incident gives them an impression which the European would never discern.

It is hard to put oneself in their place, as I try to do. A white man is so essentially different in every respect, and unless one is master of their language, manners and customs, only attainable after many years' residence in their country, it is a risky boast to imagine that one understands them. By doing so one arrives at wrong conclusions, which is worse than having an empty mind on the subject.

GERMAN BRUTALITY IN SOUTHWEST AFRICA: EXTERMINATING THE HERERO

In the 1880s Germany gained control over what became German Southwest Africa (modern day Namibia). Hoping to profit from farming, cattle raising, and mining, Germans settled the new colony. The German settlers brutalized the native Herero people, exploiting their labor and flogging, murdering, and raping with impunity. "The missionary says that we are children of God like our white brothers," said a Herero to a German settler, "but just look at us. Dogs, slaves, worse than the baboons on the rocks. . . . That is how you treat us." In 1904, the Hereros attacked isolated German farms, torturing and killing settlers. Kaiser Wilhelm dispatched an army from Germany commanded by Lothar von Trotha to crush the rebellion. The German army drove the Hereros into the desert of Sandveld, beyond the colony's border and sealed off water holes; von Trotha then ordered his soldiers to kill Hereros, including women and children, still remaining on German territory, and German patrols in the desert made a sport of hunting down and killing Herero stragglers dying of thirst and starvation. Prisoners were herded into forced labor camps where more than half died of malnutrition and mistreatment and women were subjected to constant rape. Those Hereros who managed to survive the desert found asylum in British-controlled Bechuanaland. Between 1904 and 1907, 65,000 of the 80,000 Hereros perished in what some call the first genocide of the twentieth century. In the first part of this selection, a leader of German settlers explicitly reveals his racist attitude, shared by most of the settlers, toward the Herero.

The decision to colonize in South Africa means nothing else than that the Native tribes must withdraw from the lands on which they have pastured *their* cattle and so let the *White man* pasture *his* cattle on these self-same lands. If the moral right of this standpoint is questioned, the answer is that for people of the culture standard of the South African Natives, the loss of their free national barbarism and the development of a class of workers in the service of and dependent on the Whites is primarily a law of existence in the highest degree. For a people, as for an individual, an existence appears to be justified in the degree that it is useful in the progress of general development. By no argument in the world can it be shown that the preservation of any degree of national independence, national prosperity and political organisation by the races of South West Africa would be of greater or even of equal advantage for the development of mankind in general or the German people in particular than that these races should be made serviceable in the enjoyment of their former territories by the White races.

. . . I followed their [trail] and found numerous wells which presented a terrifying sight. Cattle which had died of thirst lay scattered around the wells. These cattle had reached the wells but there had not been enough time to water them. The Herero fled ahead of us into the Sandveld. Again and again this terrible scene kept repeating itself. With feverish energy the men had worked at opening the wells, however the water became ever sparser, and wells evermore rare. They fled from one well to the next and lost virtually all their cattle and a large number of their people. The people shrunk into small remnants who continually fell into our hands, sections of the people escaped now and later through the Sandveld into English territory [present-day Botswana]. It was a policy which was equally gruesome as senseless, to hammer the people so much, we could have still saved many of them and their rich herds, if we had pardoned and taken them up again, they had been punished enough. I suggested this to General von Trotha but he wanted their total extermination.

A German officer described the results of von Trotha's policy.

Following is the proclamation that von Trotha read to his officers in October 1904 calling for the annihilation of the Herero.

I the great General of the German troops send this letter to the Herero people.

The Herero are no longer German subjects. They have murdered and stolen, they have cut off the ears, noses and other body parts of wounded soldiers, now out of cowardice they no longer wish to fight. I say to the people anyone who delivers a captain will receive 1000 Mark, whoever delivers Samuel will receive 5000 Mark. The Herero people must however leave the land. If the populace does not do this I will force them with the *Groot Rohr* [cannon]. Within the German borders every Herero, with or without a gun, with or without cattle, will be shot. I will no longer accept women and children, I will drive them back to their people or I will let them be shot at.

These are my words to the Herero people.

The great General of the mighty German Kaiser.

The following day von Trotha revealed further the implications of his proclamation.

Now I have to ask myself *how* to end the war with the Hereros. The views of the Governor and also a few old Africa hands on the one hand, and my views on the other, differ completely. They first wanted to negotiate for some time already and regard the Herero nation as necessary labour material for the future development of the country. I believe that the [Herero] nation as such should be annihilated, or, if this was not possible by tactical measures, have to be expelled from the country by operative means and further detailed treatment. This will be possible if the water-holes from Grootfontein to Gobabis are occupied. The constant movement of our troops will enable us to find the small groups of the nation who have moved back westwards and destroy them gradually. . . .

My intimate knowledge of many central African tribes (Bantu and others) has everywhere convinced me of the necessity that the Negro does not respect treaties but only brute force. . . .

I find it most appropriate that the nation perishes instead of infecting our soldiers and diminishing their supplies of water and food. Apart from that, mildness on my side would only be interpreted as weakness by the other side. They have to perish in the Sandveld or try to cross the Bechuanaland border.

A German missionary described the brutalization of Herero prisoners of war.

"When [. . .] [I] arrived in Swakopmund in 1905 there were very few Herero present. Shortly thereafter vast transports of prisoners of war arrived. They were placed behind double rows of barbed wire fencing, which surrounded all the buildings of the harbour department quarters, and housed in miserable structures constructed out of simple sacking and planks, in such a manner that in one structure 30–50 people were forced to stay without distinction as to age and sex. From early morning until late at night, on weekdays as well as on Sundays and holidays, they had to work under the clubs of brutal overseers until they broke down. Added to this the food was extremely scarce: the rice without any necessary additions was not enough to support their bodies, already weakened by life in the field [as refugees] and used to the hot sun of the interior, from the cold and the exertion without rest of all their powers in the prison conditions of Swakopmund. Like cattle hundreds were driven to death and like cattle they were buried. This opinion may appear hard or exaggerated, lots changed and became milder during the course of the imprisonment [. . .] but the chronicles are not permitted to suppress that such a remorseless brutality, randy sensuality, and brutish overlordship was to be found amongst the troops and civilians here that a full description is hardly possible."

REVIEW QUESTIONS

1. How did Cecil Rhodes gain control over the riches in Lo Bengula's land? Did his method match the good intentions expressed in his "Confession of Faith" (see page 230)?
2. What were the effects of King Leopold's rule over the Congo people? How did he establish the "Leopoldian System"?
3. Describe Richard Meinertzhagen's attitude toward the Africans he encountered.
4. What was Meinertzhagen's attitude toward colonial service in East Africa? Did he change his attitude during his four years there?
5. How did German settlers regard the Herero?
6. What was General von Trotha's policy toward the Hereros? How did he justify the policy?

---

3   Chinese Resentment of Western Imperialism

By the end of the nineteenth century European powers had carved out spheres of influence in China. The Chinese were compelled to make humiliating trade and railway concessions to the imperialists. Resentment of foreign domination drew people to a secret religious society, the Society of Righteous and Harmonious Fists, so-called because its members engaged in the martial arts and rigorous calisthenics that, they believed, gave them supernatural power, including resistance to bullets. The Boxers were convinced that driving the "foreign devils" from China would improve the poor harvests and renew commitment to ancient Chinese traditions now threatened by foreign ways.

THE BOXER REBELLION

In 1900, the Boxers roamed the countryside burning churches and foreign residences and slaughtering missionaries and Chinese Christians; in June, the Boxers converged on Beijing. Western diplomats, their families and staff, and Chinese Christians sought refuge in the Legation quarters and a Roman Catholic cathedral. For almost two months the defenders, a small military force enhanced by the besieged civilians, withstood attacks until rescued by a multinational force.

The Western armies looted the capital and later compelled the imperial government to pay a high indemnity and agree to the stationing of Western troops in the capital. The following wall posters reveal the Boxers' anti-Western and anti-Christian outlook.

"EXTERMINATE ALL FOREIGN DEVILS"

The will of heaven is that the telegraph wires be first cut, then the railways torn up and then shall the foreign devils be decapitated. On that day shall the hour of their calamities come. The time for rain to fall is yet far off, and all on account of these devils.

I thereby make known these commands to all you righteous folk that ye may strive with one accord to exterminate all foreign devils and to turn aside the path of heaven.

"CHINA YET REGARDS THEM AS BARBARIANS"

Foreign devils have come with their teaching, and converts to Christianity, Roman Catholic and Protestant, have become numerous. These (churches) have attracted all the greedy and grasping as converts, and to an unlimited degree they have practiced oppression, until every good official has been corrupted and has become their servant. So telegraphs and railways have been established, foreign rifles and guns have been manufactured. Locomotives, balloons, and electric lamps the foreign devils think excellent. Though they ride in sedans unbefitting their rank, China yet regards them as barbarians. The Volunteer Associated Fists will burn down the foreign houses and restore the temples. Foreign goods of every kind they will destroy. They will destroy the evil demons and establish right teaching. The purpose of heaven is fixed and a clean sweep is to be made. Within three years all will be accomplished.

"YOU'LL SEE THE DEVIL'S EYES/ ARE ALL A SHINING BLUE"

Divinely aided Boxers,
United-in-Righteousness Corps
Arose because the Devils
Messed up the Empire of yore.

They proselytize their sect,
And believe in only one God,
The spirits and their own ancestors
Are not even given a nod.

Their men are all immoral;
Their women truly vile.
For the Devils it's mother-son sex
That serves as the breeding style.

And if you don't believe me,
Then have a careful view:

You'll see the Devils' eyes
Are all a shining blue.

No rain comes from Heaven.
The earth is parched and dry.
And all because the churches
Have bottled up the sky.

The gods are very angry.
The spirits seek revenge.
En masse they come from Heaven
To teach the Way to men.

The Way is not a heresy;
It's not the White Lotus Sect.
The chants and spells we utter,
Follow mantras, true and correct.

Raise up the yellow charm,
Bow to the incense glow.
Invite the gods and spirits
Down from the mountain grotto.

Spirits emerge from the grottos;
Gods come down from the hills,
Possessing the bodies of men,
Transmitting their boxing skills.

When their martial and magic techniques
Are all learned by each one of you,
Suppressing the Foreign Devils
Will not be a tough thing to do.

Rip up the railroad tracks!
Pull down the telegraph lines!
Quickly! Hurry up! Smash them—
The boats and the steamship combines.

The mighty nation of France
Quivers in abject fear,
While from England, America, Russia
And from Germany nought do we hear.

When at last all the Foreign Devils
Are expelled to the very last man,
The Great Qing, united, together,
Will bring peace to this our land.

REVIEW QUESTIONS

1. What reasons did the Boxers give for hating the West?
2. What were their demands?

4 Imperialism Debated

Imperialist ventures aroused considerable debate. Advocates of overseas empires often argued in moral terms—Europeans were bringing the advantages of a higher civilization to African and Asian lands, many of which were steeped in barbarism. Rejecting this position, opponents of imperialism maintained that colonial ventures were motivated by capitalist greed and resulted in exploitation and bloodshed.

The Edinburgh Review
"WE . . . CAN RESTORE ORDER WHERE THERE IS CHAOS, AND FERTILITY WHERE THERE IS STERILITY"

The author of the following article published in 1907 in *The Edinburgh Review* praises imperialist powers for serving as "the missionaries of civilization."

[L]et us in the first place say boldly that the modern European movement of expansion is not purely, nor even primarily, a colonising movement. It is not a movement merely in favour of annexing territory, of opening up new countries, of settling on the soil and bringing backwoods and prairies under cultivation. It is much more a movement towards organising, directing and controlling where organisation, direction and control are needed and are lacking. What pushes us on in Egypt, and France on in Morocco, is not so much the lust of dominion and desire for acquiring fresh possessions, as the sense that we, England or France, can restore order where there is chaos, and fertility where there is sterility. Our Cromers and Willcockses and Garstins* act not from narrowly selfish motives of personal or even national aggrandisement. They act because they are charged with certain ideas and capacities which, in the sphere where they are called upon to work, are precisely the ideas and capacities of which there is most urgent need. The triumph of Lord Cromer has been the triumph of certain principles of good government and administration, the triumph of continuity, consistency, strength of purpose and honesty, in a land where society was falling to pieces for the lack of these things. The triumph of Sir W. Willcocks and Sir W. Garstin has been the triumph of practical science and skill in a region where there existed wonderful opportunities for their display, and where they were entirely ignored. But at the same time these ideas of government and these applications of science not only are not the especial property of our Cromers and Willcockses and Garstins, but they are not the especial property of the English nation. They are not individual, and they are not national; but neither are they universal or world-wide. The idea of a Government and administration honestly devoted to the welfare of

*Evelyn Baring, 1st Earl of Cromer (1814–1917), British Consul-General in Egypt from 1883 to 1907. Sir William Willcocks (1852–1932) and Sir William Garstin (1849–1925) were instrumental in the design and construction of the First Aswan Dam in Egypt. Built between 1898 and 1902, the dam was valuable for flood control and irrigation.

society, which has proved such a blessing to the Egyptian people, the idea of a scientific knowledge and skill applied to the practical affairs of life, which has so marvellously extended the productivity of the Nile Valley, are in truth European ideas. They are ideas which the Western races have spent centuries in testing, analysing and perfecting, and they in fact constitute the main elements in what we call in the lump European civilisation.

Europe had absorbed these political and scientific ideas until she was full to bursting with them when the greatly increased facilities in locomotion resulting from her own practical science brought her into contact with regions where these ideas had never been heard of, and where life in consequence was lived under conditions of anarchy, with none of its possibilities realised and resources developed. The result of this contact has been a lively recognition on the part of Europe of the field for effective action thus opened to her, and an overmastering desire to bring her political and scientific ideas to bear on these new scenes of social anarchy and wasted opportunity. Nothing is easier than, in the way this desire has been carried out, to see only shallow and selfish motives at work; but there could be no more infallible proof of intellectual inferiority and second-rateness than is implied in . . . such explanations. Under the selfish rivalries and jealousies which are apt to distort and colour a national application of European ideas there has always been the deeper motive at work, the consciousness of possessing the powers and the knowledge most needed and which could be most favourably exercised. This deeper European motive has been stronger than the selfish national motive. We have profited by the work we have done in India, and shall profit perhaps by the work we are doing in Egypt. France has on the whole profited by the work she has done in Algeria and Tunisia, and will probably profit some day by the work that awaits her in Morocco. But the work was not done for the profit, nevertheless. It was done on the same impulse as prompts any man of firm will and strong purpose to intervene on the side of order

amidst anarchy, or as prompts a man who knows how a thing should be done to instruct those who do not know and are making a bungle of it. It was done, in a word, because those who did it, no matter what others may have thought, or what they may have thought themselves, were acting, not on behalf of England or on behalf of France, but on behalf of European ideas and European science. If the reader doubts this, let him ask himself with what thoughts Englishmen receive the news of barrages and dams built on the Nile, of deserts fertilised and a peasantry emancipated. Is it the case that our thoughts turn primarily to the chances of national benefits and advantages; or is it not rather true that we should still be proud of our work in Egypt even if we were out of pocket by it, and that no part of Lord Cromer's policy has been more generally approved than that which was directed to thwarting the selfish aims of those who saw in the new improvements a chance of money-making? . . .

Most of us, probably, are ready enough to admit our own disinterestedness. We are no greedy landgrabbers, but the apostles of an idea, the missionaries of Western civilisation. We make that claim for ourselves, and we make it also for those with whom we are in friendship and sympathy. We make it for France. France, introducing order into chaos, transforming a pirates' den into a beautiful and prosperous city, and reviving by her wells and springs the date palms of a thousand perishing oases, is also a missionary of Western civilisation. Her action, like ours, is to be accounted for, not by selfish and sordid motives, but by an appreciation of the great opportunities that have been set before her for bringing European ideas and European science to bear upon regions which most need their influence. But will anyone venture to make this claim on behalf of England and France, but to deny its application to Germany? Germany's share in European civilisation is equal to England's share or France's. Germany, as much as England or France, believes in and lives by the great political and scientific ideals which have inspired that civilisation; and, this being so, is it not evident that if, or rather when, she builds her new railway she too will be actuated by the desire which we have described as lying at the root of the modern European movement of expansion, the desire to introduce order into chaos, to cultivate and develop natural resources, to apply, in a word, Western ideas to the conditions of life where they are most needed? Whether the new railway will ever profit her much it is impossible to say, but whether it does or not, it will not have been undertaken mainly for mere profit. It will have been undertaken mainly because the anarchy and ignorance of Asia Minor and Mesopotamia are a perpetual challenge to the ideas and capacities of which Germany is full. To deny this, to insist on seeing in Germany's Turkish policy nothing but an exhibition of national selfishness, is to lay ourselves palpably open to that very charge of intellectual inferiority and second-rateness which we recognise as the basis of similar charges brought against us.

John Atkinson Hobson
AN EARLY CRITIQUE OF IMPERIALISM

One of the early English critics of imperialism was the social reformer and economist John Atkinson Hobson (1858–1940). Hobson's primary interest was social reform, and he turned to economics to try to solve the problem of poverty. Like Rhodes, he was influenced by Ruskin's ideas, but his interpretation of them led him to a diametrically opposed view of colonialism. As an economist, he argued that the unequal distribution of income made capitalism unproductive and unstable. It could not maintain itself except through investing in less developed countries on an increasing scale, thus fostering colonial expansion. Lenin, leader of the Russian Revolution, later adopted this thesis. Hobson's stress upon the economic causes of imperialism has been disputed by some historians who see the desire for national power and glory as a far more important cause. Hobson attacked imperialism in the following passages from his book *Imperialism* (1902).

. . . The decades of Imperialism have been prolific in wars; most of these wars have been directly motivated by aggression of white races upon "lower races," and have issued in the forcible seizure of territory. Every one of the steps of expansion in Africa, Asia, and the Pacific has been accompanied by bloodshed; each imperialist Power keeps an increasing army available for foreign service; rectification of frontiers, punitive expeditions, and other euphemisms for war are in incessant progress. The *pax Britannica*, always an impudent falsehood, has become of recent years a grotesque monster of hypocrisy; along our Indian frontiers, in West Africa, in the Soudan, in Uganda, in Rhodesia fighting has been well-nigh incessant. Although the great imperialist Powers have kept their hands off one another, save where the rising empire of the United States has found its opportunity in the falling empire of Spain, the self-restraint has been costly and precarious. Peace as a national policy is antagonised not merely by war, but by militarism, an even graver injury. Apart from the enmity of France and Germany, the main cause of the vast armaments which are draining the resources of most European countries is their conflicting interests in territorial and commercial expansion. Where thirty years ago there existed one sensitive spot in our relations with France, or Germany, or Russia, there are a dozen now; diplomatic strains are of almost monthly occurrence between Powers with African or Chinese interests, and the chiefly business nature of the national antagonisms renders them more dangerous, inasmuch as the policy of Governments passes more under the influence of distinctively financial juntos [cliques]. . . .

Our economic analysis has disclosed the fact that it is only the interests of competing cliques of business men—investors, contractors, export manufacturers, and certain professional classes—that are antagonistic; that these cliques, usurping the authority and voice of the people, use the public resources to push their private businesses, and spend the blood and money of the people in this vast and disastrous military game, feigning national antagonisms which have no basis in reality. It is not to the interest of the British people, either as producers of wealth or as tax-payers, to risk a war with Russia and France in order to join Japan in preventing Russia from seizing [K]orea; but it may serve the interests of a group of commercial politicians to promote this dangerous policy. The South African war [the Boer War, 1899–1902], openly fomented by gold speculators for their private purposes, will rank in history as a leading case of this usurpation of nationalism. . . .

. . . So long as this competitive expansion for territory and foreign markets is permitted to misrepresent itself as "national policy" the antagonism of interests seems real, and the peoples must sweat and bleed and toil to keep up an ever more expensive machinery of war. . . .

. . . The industrial and financial forces of Imperialism, operating through the party, the press, the church, the school, mould public opinion and public policy by the false idealisation of those primitive lusts of struggle, domination, and acquisitiveness which have survived throughout the eras of peaceful industrial order and whose stimulation is needed once again for the work of imperial aggression, expansion, and the forceful exploitation of lower races. For these business politicians biology and sociology weave thin convenient theories of a race struggle for the subjugation of the inferior peoples in order that we, the Anglo-Saxon, may take their lands and live upon their labours; while economics buttresses the argument by representing our work in conquering and ruling them as our share in the division of labour among nations, and history devises reasons why the lessons of past empire do not apply to ours, while social ethics paints the motive of "Imperialism" as the desire to bear the "burden" of educating and elevating races of "children." Thus are the "cultured" or semi-cultured classes indoctrinated with the intellectual and moral grandeur of Imperialism. For the masses there is a cruder appeal to hero-worship and sensational glory, adventure and the sporting spirit: current history falsified in coarse flaring colours, for the direct stimulation of the combative instincts. But while various methods are employed, some delicate and indirect, others coarse and flamboyant, the operation everywhere resolves itself into an incitation and direction of the brute lusts of human domination which are everywhere latent in civilised humanity, for the pursuance of a policy fraught with material gain to a minority of co-operative vested interests which usurp the title of the commonwealth. . . .

. . . The presence of a scattering of white officials, missionaries, traders, mining or plantation overseers, a dominant male caste with little knowledge of or sympathy for the institutions of the people, is ill-calculated to give to these lower races even such gains as Western civilisation might be capable of giving.

The condition of the white rulers of these lower races is distinctively parasitic; they live upon these natives, their chief work being that of organising native labour for their support. The normal state of such a country is one in which the most fertile lands and the mineral resources are owned by white aliens and worked by natives under their direction, primarily for their gain: they do not identify themselves with the interests of the nation or its people, but remain an alien body of sojourners, a "parasite" upon the carcass of its "host," destined to extract wealth from the country and retire to consume it at home. All the hard manual or other severe routine work is done by natives. . . .

Nowhere under such conditions is the theory of white government as a trust for civilisation made valid; nowhere is there any provision to secure the predominance of the interests, either of the world at large or of the governed people, over those of the encroaching nation, or more commonly a section of that nation. The relations subsisting between the superior and the inferior nations, commonly established by pure force, and resting on that basis, are such as preclude the genuine sympathy essential to the operation of the best civilising influences, and usually resolve themselves into the maintenance of external good order so as to forward the profitable development of certain natural resources of the land, under "forced" native labour, primarily for the benefit of white traders and investors, and secondarily for the benefit of the world of white Western consumers.

This failure to justify by results the forcible rule over alien peoples is attributable to no special defect of the British or other modern European nations. It is inherent in the nature of such domination. . . .

REVIEW QUESTIONS

1. According to the author of the article in *The Edinburgh Review*, what specific benefits did Europeans bring to their overseas possessions?
2. Why, in Hobson's opinion, was the *pax Britannica* an "impudent falsehood"?
3. One ideal of imperialism was to spread civilizing influences among native populations. How did Hobson interpret this sense of mission?

CHAPTER 10

Modern Consciousness

EDVARD MUNCH (1863–1944), THE SCREAM, 1893. The dark forces of emotional torment and sexual aberration fill the canvases of Norwegian Postimpressionist Edvard Munch. *(Digital Image © The Museum of Modern Art/Licensed by SCALA/Art Resource, NY © 2012 The Much Museum/The Munch-Ellingsen Group/ Artist's Rights Society (ARS), New York)*

The closing decades of the nineteenth century and the opening of the twentieth witnessed a crisis in Western thought. Rejecting the Enlightenment belief in the essential rationality of human beings, thinkers such as Friedrich Nietzsche and Sigmund Freud stressed the immense power of the nonrational in individual and social life. They held that subconscious drives, impulses, and instincts lay at the core of human nature, that people were moved more by religious-mythic images and symbols than by logical thought, that feelings determine human conduct more than reason does. This new image of the individual led to unsettling conclusions. If human beings are not fundamentally rational, then what are the prospects of resolving the immense problems of modern industrial civilization? Although most thinkers shared the Enlightenment's visions of humanity's future progress, doubters were also heard.

At the same time that Nietzsche, Freud, and other thinkers were breaking with the Enlightenment view of human nature and society, artists and writers were rebelling against traditional forms of artistic and literary expression that had governed European cultural life since the Renaissance. Rejecting both classical and realist models, they subordinated form and objective reality to the inner life—to feelings, imagination, and the creative process. These avant-garde writers and artists found new and creative ways to express those explosive forces within the human psyche that increasingly had become the subject of contemporary thinkers. Their experimentations produced a great cultural revolution called *modernism*, which still profoundly influences the arts. Like Freud, modernist artists and writers probed beyond surface appearances for a more profound reality—impulses, instincts, and drives—hidden in the human psyche. Artists like Pablo Picasso and writers like James Joyce and Franz Kafka exhibited a growing fascination with the nonrational—with dreams, fantasies, sexual conflicts, and guilt, with tortured, fragmented, and dislocated inner lives. In the process, they rejected traditional aesthetic standards established during the Renaissance and the Enlightenment and experimented with new forms of artistic and literary representation.

These developments in thought and culture produced insights into human nature and society and opened up new possibilities in art and literature. But such changes also contributed to the disorientation and insecurity that characterized the twentieth century.

1   The Futility of Reason and the Power of the Will

The outlook of the Enlightenment, which stressed science, political freedom, the rational reform of society, and the certainty of progress, was the dominant intellectual current in the late nineteenth century. However, in the closing decades of the century, several thinkers challenged and rejected the Enlightenment outlook. In particular, they maintained that people are not fundamentally rational, that below surface rationality lie impulses, instincts, and drives that constitute a deeper reality.

A powerful attack on the rational-scientific tradition of the Enlightenment came from Fyodor Dostoyevsky (1821–1881), a Russian novelist and essayist whose masterpieces include *Crime and Punishment* (1866), *The Idiot* (1868), and *The Brothers Karamazov* (1879–1880).

Fyodor Dostoyevsky
NOTES FROM UNDERGROUND

In *Notes from Underground* (1864), Dostoyevsky attacked thinkers who enshrined science and believed that reason governs human behavior. He rejected the notion that once these laws were understood, people could create (as socialists in fact tried to do) utopian communities in which society would be rationally planned and organized to promote human betterment. The narrator in the novel, called the Underground Man, rebels against the efforts of rationalists, positivists, liberals, and socialists to define human nature according to universal principles and to reform society so as to promote greater happiness and security. For the Underground Man, there are no objective truths; there are only individuals with subjective desires and unpredictable, irrepressible wills.

Dostoyevsky maintained that human beings cannot be defined by reason alone—human nature is too dynamic, too diversified, too volcanic to be schematized and programmed by the theoretical mind. He urged a new definition of human beings, one that would affirm each person's individuality and subjectivity and encompass the total personality—feelings and will as well as reason.

In the first part of *Notes from Underground*, the Underground Man addresses an imaginary audience. In a long monologue, he expresses a revulsion for the liberal-rationalist assertion that with increased enlightenment, people would "become good and noble," that they would realize it was to their advantage to pursue "prosperity, wealth, [political] freedom, peace." The Underground Man argues that the individual's principal concern is not happiness or security but a free and unfettered will.

. . . Oh, tell me, who first declared, who first proclaimed, that man only does nasty things because he does not know his own real interests; and that if he were enlightened, if his eyes were opened to his real normal interests, man would at once cease to do nasty things, would at once become good and noble because, being enlightened and understanding his real advantage, he would see his own advantage in the good and nothing else, and we all know that not a single man can knowingly act to his own disadvantage. Consequently, so to say, he would begin doing good through necessity. Oh, the babe! Oh, the pure, innocent child! Why, in the first place, when in all these thousands of years has there ever been a time when man has acted only for his own advantage? What is to be done with the millions of facts that bear witness that men, *knowingly*, that is, fully understanding their real advantages, have left them in the background and have rushed headlong on another path, to risk, to chance, compelled to this course by nobody and by nothing, but, as it were, precisely because they did not want the beaten track, and stubbornly, wilfully, went off on another difficult, absurd way seeking it almost in the darkness. After all, it means that this stubbornness and willfulness were more pleasant to them than any advantage. Advantage! What is advantage? And will you take it upon yourself to define with perfect accuracy in exactly what the advantage of man consists of? And what if it so happens that a man's advantage *sometimes* not only may, but even must, consist exactly in his desiring under certain conditions what is harmful to himself and not what is advantageous. . . . After all, you, [imaginary] gentlemen, so far as I know, have taken your whole register of human advantages from the average of statistical figures and scientific-economic formulas. After all, your advantages are prosperity, wealth, freedom, peace—and so on, and so on. So that a man who, for instance, would openly and knowingly oppose that whole list would, to your thinking, and indeed to mine too, of course, be an obscurantist [one who prevents enlightenment] or an absolute madman, would he not? But, after all, here is something amazing: why does it happen that all these statisticians, sages and lovers of humanity, when they calculate human advantages invariably leave one out? . . .

. . . The fact is, gentlemen, it seems that something that is dearer to almost every man than his greatest advantages must really exist, or (not to be illogical) there is one most advantageous advantage (the very one omitted of which we spoke just now) which is more important and more advantageous than all other advantages, for which, if necessary, a man is ready to act in opposition to all laws, that is, in opposition to reason, honor, peace, prosperity—in short, in opposition to all those wonderful and useful things if only he can attain that fundamental, most advantageous advantage which is dearer to him than all. . . .

. . . Why, one may choose what is contrary to one's own interests, and sometimes one

positively ought (that is my idea). One's own free unfettered choice, one's own fancy, however wild it may be, one's own fancy worked up at times to frenzy—why that is that very "most advantageous advantage" which we have overlooked, which comes under no classification and through which all systems and theories are continually being sent to the devil. And how do these sages know that man must necessarily need a rationally advantageous choice? What man needs is simply *independent* choice, whatever that independence may cost and wherever it may lead. Well, choice, after all, the devil only knows. . . .

Life is more than reasoning, more than "simply extracting square roots," declares the Underground Man. The will, which is "a manifestation of all life," is more precious than reason. Simply to have their own way, human beings will do something stupid, self-destructive, irrational. Reason constitutes only a small part of the human personality.

. . . You see, gentlemen, reason, gentlemen, is an excellent thing, there is no disputing that, but reason is only reason and can only satisfy man's rational faculty, while will is a manifestation of all life, that is, of all human life including reason as well as all impulses. And although our life, in this manifestation of it, is often worthless, yet it is life nevertheless and not simply extracting square roots. After all, here I, for instance, quite naturally want to live, in order to satisfy all my faculties for life, and not simply my rational faculty, that is, not simply onetwentieth of all my faculties for life. What does reason know? Reason only knows what it has succeeded in learning (some things it will perhaps never learn; while this is nevertheless no comfort, why not say so frankly?) and human nature acts as a whole, with everything that is in it, consciously or unconsciously, and, even if it goes wrong, it lives. I suspect, gentlemen, that you are looking at me with compassion; you repeat to me that an enlightened and developed man, such, in short, as the future man will be, cannot knowingly desire anything disadvantageous to himself, that this can be proved mathematically. I thoroughly agree, it really can—by mathematics. But I repeat for the hundredth time, there is one case, one only, when man may purposely, consciously, desire what is injurious to himself, what is stupid, very stupid—simply in order *to have the right* to desire for himself even what is very stupid and not to be bound by an obligation to desire only what is rational. After all, this very stupid thing, after all, this caprice of ours, may really be more advantageous for us, gentlemen, than anything else on earth, especially in some cases. And in particular it may be more advantageous than any advantages even when it does us obvious harm, and contradicts the soundest conclusions of our reason about our advantage—because in any case it preserves for us what is most precious and most important— that is, our personality, our individuality. Some, you see, maintain that this really is the most precious thing for man; desire can, of course, if it desires, be in agreement with reason; particularly if it does not abuse this practice but does so in moderation, it is both useful and sometimes even praiseworthy. But very often, and even most often, desire completely and stubbornly opposes reason, and . . . and . . . and do you know that that, too, is useful and sometimes even praiseworthy?

To intellectuals who want to "cure men of their old habits and reform their will in accordance with science and common sense," the Underground Man asks: Is it possible or even desirable to reform human beings? Perhaps they prefer uncertainty and caprice, chaos and destruction, or just living in their own way. How else do they preserve their uniqueness?

. . . In short, one may say anything about the history of the world—anything that might enter the most disordered imagination. The only thing one cannot say is that it is rational. The very word sticks in one's throat. And, indeed, this is even the kind of thing that continually happens. After all, there are continually turning up in life moral and rational people, sages, and lovers of humanity, who make it their goal for life to live as morally and rationally as possible, to be, so to speak, a light to their neighbors, simply in order to show them that it is really possible to live morally and rationally in this world. And so what? We all know that those very people sooner or later toward the end of their lives have been false to themselves, playing some trick, often a most indecent one. Now I ask you: What can one expect from man since he is a creature endowed with such strange qualities? Shower upon him every earthly blessing, drown him in bliss so that nothing but bubbles would dance on the surface of his bliss, as on a sea; give him such economic prosperity that he would have nothing else to do but sleep, eat cakes and busy himself with ensuring the continuation of world history and even then man, out of sheer ingratitude, sheer libel, would play you some loathsome trick. He would even risk his cakes and would deliberately desire the most fatal rubbish, the most uneconomical absurdity, simply to introduce into all this positive rationality his fatal fantastic element. It is just his fantastic dreams, his vulgar folly, that he will desire to retain, simply in order to prove to himself (as though that were so necessary) that men still are men and not piano keys, which even if played by the laws of nature themselves threaten to be controlled so completely that soon one will be able to desire nothing but by the calendar. And, after all, that is not all: even if man really were nothing but a piano key, even if this were proved to him by natural science and mathematics, even then he would not become reasonable, but would purposely do something perverse out of sheer ingratitude, simply to have his own way. And if he does not find any means he will devise destruction and chaos, will devise sufferings of all sorts, and will thereby have his own way. He will launch a curse upon the world . . . [to] convince himself that he is a man and not a piano key! If you say that all this, too, can be calculated and tabulated, chaos and darkness and curses, so that the mere possibility of calculating it all beforehand would stop it all, and reason would reassert itself—then man would purposely go mad in order to be rid of reason and have his own way! I believe in that, I vouch for it, because, after all, the whole work of man seems really to consist in nothing but proving to himself continually that he is a man and not an organ stop. It may be at the cost of his skin! But he has proved it; he may become a caveman, but he will have proved it. And after that can one help sinning, rejoicing that it has not yet come, and that desire still depends on the devil knows what! . . .

. . . Gentlemen, I am tormented by questions; answer them for me. Now you, for instance, want to cure men of their old habits and reform their will in accordance with science and common sense. But how do you know, not only that it is possible, but also that it is *desirable*, to reform man in that way? And what leads you to the conclusion that it is so *necessary* to reform man's desires? In short, how do you know that such a reformation will really be advantageous to man? And go to the heart of the matter, why are you *so sure* of your conviction that not to act against his real normal advantages guaranteed by the conclusions of reason and arithmetic is

always advantageous for man and must be a law for all mankind? . . .

And why are you so firmly, so triumphantly convinced that only the normal and the positive—in short, only prosperity—is to the advantage of man? Is not reason mistaken about advantage? After all, perhaps man likes something besides prosperity? Perhaps he likes suffering just as much? Perhaps suffering is just as great an advantage to him as prosperity? Man is sometimes fearfully, passionately in love with suffering and that is a fact. There is no need to appeal to universal history to prove that; only ask yourself, if only you are a man and have lived at all. As far as my own personal opinion is concerned, to care only for prosperity seems to me somehow even ill-bred. Whether it's good or bad, it is sometimes very pleasant to smash things, too. After all, I do not really insist on suffering or on prosperity either. I insist on my caprice, and its being guaranteed to me when necessary. Suffering would be out of place in vaudevilles, for instance; I know that. In the crystal palace [utopia] it is even unthinkable; suffering means doubt, means negation, and what would be the good of a crystal palace if there could be any doubt about it? And yet I am sure man will never renounce real suffering, that is, destruction and chaos.

REVIEW QUESTIONS

1. Why did Fyodor Dostoyevsky believe that people will act in opposition to their own interests?
2. How did Dostoyevsky regard intellectuals who sought to "cure men of their old habits and reform their will in accordance with science and common sense"?
3. What did Dostoyevsky mean when he said that "the whole work of man seems really to consist in nothing but proving to himself continually that he is a man and not an organ stop"?
4. What role did reason play in Dostoyevsky's view of human nature and society?

2   The Overman and the Will to Power

Few modern thinkers have aroused more controversy than the German philosopher Friedrich Nietzsche (1844–1900). Although scholars pay tribute to
Nietzsche's originality and genius, they are often in sharp disagreement over the
meaning and influence of his work. Nietzsche was a relentless critic of modern
society. He attacked democracy, universal suffrage, equality, and socialism for
suppressing a higher type of human existence. Nietzsche was also critical of the
Western rational tradition. The theoretical outlook, the excessive intellectualizing
of philosophers, he said, smothers the will, thereby stifling creativity and nobility;
reason also falsifies life through the claim that it allows apprehension of universal
truth, for no such truth exists. Nietzsche was not opposed to the critical use of the
intellect, but like the romantics, he focused on the immense vitality of the emotions. He also held that life is a senseless flux devoid of any overarching purpose.
There are no moral values revealed by God. Indeed, Nietzsche proclaimed that
God is dead. Nor are values and certainties woven into the fabric of nature that
can be apprehended by reason—the "natural rights of man," for example. All the
values taught by Christian and bourgeois thinkers are without foundation, said
Nietzsche. There is only naked man living in a godless and absurd world.

Nietzsche called for the emergence of the *overman* or *superman*, a higher
type of man who asserts his will, gives order to chaotic passions, makes great
demands on himself, and lives life with a fierce joy. The overman aspires to self-
perfection. Without fear or guilt, he creates his own values and defines his own
life. In this way, he overcomes nihilism—the belief that there is nothing of ultimate value. It is such rare individuals, the highest specimens of humanity, that
concern Nietzsche, not the herdlike masses.

The overman grasps the central reality of human existence—that people
instinctively, uncompromisingly, ceaselessly, strive for power. The will to
exert power is the determining factor in domestic politics, personal relations, and
international affairs. Life is a contest in which the enhancement of power is the
ultimate purpose of our actions; it brings supreme enjoyment: "the love of power
is the demon of men. Let them have everything—health, food, a place to live,
entertainment—they are and remain unhappy and low-spirited: for the demon
waits and waits and will be satisfied. Take everything from them and satisfy this
and they are almost happy—as happy as men and demons can be."

Friedrich Nietzsche
THE WILL TO POWER
AND *THE ANTICHRIST*

Two of Nietzsche's works—*The Will to Power* and *The Antichrist*—are
represented in the following readings. First published in 1901, one year after
Nietzsche's death, *The Will to Power* consists of the author's notes written in the

years 1883 to 1888. The following passages from this work show Nietzsche's contempt for democracy and socialism and proclaim the will to power.

THE WILL TO POWER
720 (1886–1887)

The most fearful and fundamental desire in man, his drive for power—this drive is called "freedom"—must be held in check the longest. This is why ethics . . . has hitherto aimed at holding the desire for power in check: it disparages the tyrannical individual and with its glorification of social welfare and patriotism emphasizes the power-instinct of the herd.

728 (March–June 1888)

. . . A society that definitely and *instinctively* gives up war and conquest is in decline: it is ripe for democracy and the rule of shopkeepers— In most cases, to be sure, assurances of peace are merely narcotics.

751 (March–June 1888)

"The will to power" is so hated in democratic ages that their entire psychology seems directed toward belittling and defaming it. . . .

752 (1884)

. . . Democracy represents the disbelief in great human beings and an elite society: "Everyone is equal to everyone else." "At bottom we are one and all self-seeking cattle and mob."

753 (1885)

I am opposed to 1. socialism, because it dreams quite naively of "the good, true, and beautiful" and of "equal rights" (—anarchism also desires the same ideal, but in a more brutal fashion); 2. parliamentary government and the press, because these are the means by which the herd animal becomes master.

762 (1885)

European democracy represents a release of forces only to a very small degree. It is above all a release of laziness, of weariness, of *weakness*.

765 (Jan.–Fall 1888)

. . . Another Christian concept, no less crazy, has passed even more deeply into the tissue of modernity: the concept of the "equality of souls before God." This concept furnishes the prototype of all theories of equal rights: mankind was first taught to stammer the proposition of equality in a religious context, and only later was it made into morality: no wonder that man ended by taking it seriously, taking it practically!— that is to say, politically, democratically, socialistically, in the spirit of the pessimism of indignation.

854 (1884)

In the age of *suffrage universel*, i.e., when everyone may sit in judgment on everyone and everything, I feel impelled to reestablish *order of rank*.

855 (Spring–Fall 1887)

What determines rank, sets off rank, is only quanta of power, and nothing else.

857 (Jan.–Fall 1888)

I distinguish between a type of ascending life and another type of decay, disintegration, weakness. Is it credible that the question of the relative rank of these two types still needs to be posed?

858 (Nov. 1887–March 1888)

What determines your rank is the quantum of power you are: the rest is cowardice.

861 (1884)

A declaration of war on the masses by *higher men* is needed! Everywhere the mediocre are combining in order to make themselves master! Everything that makes soft and effeminate, that serves the ends of the "people" or the "feminine," works in favor of *suffrage universel*, i.e., the dominion of *inferior* men. But we should take reprisal and bring this whole affair (which in Europe commenced with Christianity) to light and to the bar of judgment.

862 (1884)

A doctrine is needed powerful enough to work as a breeding agent: strengthening the strong, paralyzing and destructive for the world-weary.

The annihilation of the decaying races. Decay of Europe.—The annihilation of slavish evaluations.—Dominion over the earth as a means of producing a higher type.—The annihilation of the tartuffery [hypocrisy] called "morality." . . . The annihilation of *suffrage universel*; i.e., the system through which the lowest natures prescribe themselves as laws for the higher.—The annihilation of mediocrity and its acceptance. (The onesided, individuals—peoples; to strive for fullness of nature through the pairing of opposites: race mixture to this end).—The new courage—no *a priori* [innate and universal] truths (such truths were sought by those accustomed to faith!), but a *free* subordination to a ruling idea that has its time: e.g., time as a property of space, etc.

870 (1884)

The root of all evil: that the slavish morality of meekness, chastity, selflessness, absolute obedience, has triumphed—ruling natures were thus condemned (1) to hypocrisy, (2) to torments of conscience—creative natures felt like rebels against God, uncertain and inhibited by eternal values. . . .

In summa: the best things have been slandered because the weak or the immoderate swine have cast a bad light on them—and the best men have remained hidden—and have often misunderstood themselves.

874 (1884)

The degeneration of the rulers and the ruling classes has been the cause of the greatest mischief in history! Without the Roman Caesars and Roman society, the insanity of Christianity would never have come to power.

When lesser men begin to doubt whether higher men exist, then the danger is great! And one ends by discovering that there is *virtue* also among the lowly and subjugated, the poor in spirit, and that *before God* men are equal—which has so far been the . . . [height] of nonsense on earth! For ultimately, the higher men measured themselves according to the standard of virtue of slaves—found they were "proud," etc., found all their higher qualities reprehensible.

997 (1884)

I teach: that there are higher and lower men, and that a single individual can under certain circumstances justify the existence of whole millennia—that is, a full, rich, great, whole human being in relation to countless incomplete fragmentary men.

998 (1884)

The highest men live beyond the rulers, freed from all bonds; and in the rulers they have their instruments.

999 (1884)

Order of rank: He who *determines* values and directs the will of millennia by giving direction to the highest natures is the *highest* man.

1001 (1884)

Not "mankind" but *overman* is the goal!

1067 (1885)

. . . *This world is the will to power—and nothing besides!* And you yourselves are also this will to power—and nothing besides!

Nietzsche regarded Christianity as a life-denying religion that appeals to the masses. Fearful and resentful of their betters, he said, the masses espouse a faith that preaches equality and compassion. He maintained that Christianity has "waged a war to the death against (the) higher type of man." The following passages are from *The Antichrist*, written in 1888.

THE ANTICHRIST

2. What is good?—All that heightens the feeling of power, the will to power, power itself in man.

What is bad?—All that proceeds from weakness.

What is happiness?—The feeling that power *increases*—that a resistance is overcome.

Not contentment, but more power; *not* peace at all, but war; *not* virtue, but proficiency (virtue in the Renaissance style, *virtù*, virtue free of moralic acid).

The weak and ill-constituted shall perish: first principle of *our* philanthropy. And one shall help them to do so.

What is more harmful than any vice?—Active sympathy for the ill-constituted and weak—Christianity. . . .

3. The problem I raise here is not what ought to succeed mankind in the sequence of species (—the human being is an *end*—): but what type of human being one ought to *breed*, ought to *will*, as more valuable, more worthy of life, more certain of the future.

This more valuable type has existed often enough already: but as a lucky accident, as an exception, never as *willed*. He has rather been the most feared, he has hitherto been virtually *the* thing to be feared—and out of fear the reverse type has been willed, bred, *achieved*: the domestic animal, the herd animal, the sick animal man—the Christian. . . .

5. One should not embellish or dress up Christianity: it has waged *a war to the death* against this *higher* type of man, it has excommunicated all the fundamental instincts of this type, it has distilled evil, the *Evil One*, out of these instincts—the strong human being as the type of reprehensibility, as the "outcast." Christianity has taken the side of everything weak, base, ill-constituted, it has made an ideal out of *opposition* to the preservative instincts of strong life; it has depraved the reason even of the intellectually strongest natures by teaching men to feel the supreme values of intellectuality as sinful, as misleading, as *temptations*. The most

deplorable example: the depraving of Pascal,[1] who believed his reason had been depraved by original sin while it had only been depraved by his Christianity! . . .

7. Christianity is called the religion of *pity*.—Pity stands in antithesis to the tonic emotions which enhance the energy of the feeling of life: it has a depressive effect. One loses force when one pities. . . .

15. In Christianity neither morality nor religion come into contact with reality at any point. Nothing but imaginary *causes* ("God," "soul," "ego," "spirit," "free will"—or "unfree will"): nothing but imaginary *effects* ("sin," "redemption," "grace," "punishment," "forgiveness of sins"). . . .

18. The Christian conception of God—God as God of the sick, God as spider, God as spirit—is one of the most corrupt conceptions of God arrived at on earth: perhaps it even represents the low-water mark in the descending development of the God type. God degenerated to the *contradiction of life*, instead of being its transfiguration and eternal *Yes!* In God a declaration of hostility towards life, nature, the will to life! God the formula for every calumny of "this world," for every lie about "the next world"! In God, nothingness deified, the will to nothingness sanctified! . . .

21. In Christianity the instincts of the subjugated and oppressed come into the foreground: it is the lowest classes which seek their salvation in it. . . .

43. The poison of the doctrine "*equal* rights for all"—this has been more thoroughly sowed by Christianity than by anything else; from the most secret recesses of base instincts, Christianity has waged a war to the death against every feeling of reverence and distance between man and man, against, that is, the *precondition* of every elevation, every increase in culture—it has forged out of the [resentment] of the masses its *chief weapon* against *us*, against everything noble, joyful, high-spirited on earth,

---

[1]Blaise Pascal (1623–1662) was a French mathematician, philosopher, and eloquent defender of the Christian faith.

against our happiness on earth. . . . "Immortality" granted to every Peter and Paul has been the greatest and most malicious outrage on *noble* mankind ever committed.—*And* let us not underestimate the fatality that has crept out of Christianity even into politics! No one any longer possesses today the courage to claim special privileges or the right to rule, the courage to feel a sense of reverence towards himself and towards his equals—the courage for a *pathos of distance*. . . . Our politics is *morbid* from this lack of courage!—The aristocratic outlook has been undermined most deeply by the lie of equality of souls; and if the belief in the "prerogative of the majority" makes revolutions and *will continue to make them*—it is Christianity, let there be no doubt about it, *Christian* value judgement which translates every revolution into mere blood and crime! Christianity is a revolt of everything that crawls along the ground directed against that which is *elevated*: the Gospel of the "lowly" *makes* low. . . .

REVIEW QUESTIONS

1. Do you agree with Friedrich Nietzsche that the pursuit of power is a human being's most elemental desire?
2. Why did Nietzsche attack democracy and socialism? How do you respond to his attack?
3. What were Nietzsche's criticisms of Christianity? How do you respond to this attack?
4. How does Nietzsche's philosophy stand in relation to the Enlightenment?

3　The Unconscious

After graduating from medical school in Vienna, Sigmund Freud (1856–1939), the founder of psychoanalysis, specialized in the treatment of nervous disorders. By encouraging his patients to speak to him about their troubles, Freud was able to probe deeper into their minds. These investigations led him to conclude that childhood fears and experiences, often sexual in nature, accounted for neuroses—hysteria, anxiety, depression, obsessions, and so on. So threatening and painful were these childhood emotions and experiences that his patients banished them from conscious memory to the realm of the unconscious. To understand and treat neurotic behavior, Freud said it is necessary to look behind overt symptoms and bring to the surface emotionally charged experiences and fears—childhood traumas—that lie buried in the unconscious. Freud probed the unconscious by urging his patients to say whatever came to their minds. This procedure, called free association, rests on the premise that spontaneous and uninhibited talk reveals a person's underlying preoccupations, his or her inner world. A second avenue to the unconscious is the analysis of dreams; an individual's dreams, said Freud, reveal his or her secret wishes.

Sigmund Freud
A NOTE ON THE UNCONSCIOUS IN PSYCHOANALYSIS AND *CIVILIZATION AND ITS DISCONTENTS*

Readings from two works of Freud are included: *A Note on the Unconscious in Psychoanalysis* (1912) and *Civilization and Its Discontents* (1930). Freud's scientific investigation of psychic development led him to conclude that powerful mental processes hidden from consciousness govern human behavior more than reason does. His exploration of the unconscious produced a new image of the human being that has had a profound impact on twentieth-century thought and beyond. In the following excerpt from *A Note on the Unconscious in Psychoanalysis*, Freud defined the term *unconscious*.

A NOTE ON THE UNCONSCIOUS IN PSYCHOANALYSIS

I wish to expound in a few words and as plainly as possible what the term "unconscious" has come to mean in psychoanalysis and in psychoanalysis alone. . . .

. . . The well-known experiment, . . . of the "post-hypnotic suggestion" teaches us to insist upon the importance of the distinction between *conscious* and *unconscious* and seems to increase its value.

In this experiment, as performed by Bernheim,[1] a person is put into a hypnotic state and is subsequently aroused. While he was in the hypnotic state, under the influence of the physician, he was ordered to execute a certain action at a certain fixed moment after his awakening, say half an hour later. He awakes, and seems fully conscious and in his ordinary condition; he has no recollection of his hypnotic state, and yet at the prearranged moment there rushes into his mind the impulse to do such and such a thing, and he does it consciously, though not knowing why. It seems impossible to give any other description of the phenomenon than to say that the order has been present in the mind of the person in a condition of latency, or had been present unconsciously,

until the given moment came, and then had become conscious. But not the whole of it emerged into consciousness: only the conception of the act to be executed. All the other ideas associated with this conception—the order, the influence of the physician, the recollection of the hypnotic state, remained unconscious even then. . . .

The mind of the hysterical patient is full of active yet unconscious ideas; all her symptoms proceed from such ideas. It is in fact the most striking character of the hysterical mind to be ruled by them. If the hysterical woman vomits, she may do so from the idea of being pregnant. She has, however, no knowledge of this idea, although it can easily be detected in her mind, and made conscious to her, by one of the technical procedures of psychoanalysis. If she is executing the jerks and movements constituting her "fit," she does not even consciously represent to herself the intended actions, and she may perceive those actions with the detached feelings of an onlooker. Nevertheless analysis will show that she was acting her part in the dramatic reproduction of some incident in her life, the memory of which was unconsciously active during the attack. The same preponderance of active unconscious ideas is revealed by analysis as the essential fact in the psychology of all other forms of neurosis. . . .

. . . The term *unconscious* . . . designates . . . ideas with a certain dynamic character, ideas keeping apart from consciousness in spite of their intensity and activity.

---

[1]Hippolyte Bernheim (1840–1919), a French physician, used hypnosis in the treatment of his patients and published a successful book on the subject.

In the tradition of the Enlightenment philosophes, Freud valued reason and science, but he did not share the philosophes' confidence in human goodness and humanity's capacity for future progress. In *Civilization and Its Discontents* (1930), Freud posited the frightening theory that human beings are driven by an inherent aggressiveness that threatens civilized life—that civilization is fighting a losing battle with our aggressive instincts. Although Freud's pessimism was no doubt influenced by the tragedy of World War I, many ideas expressed in *Civilization and Its Discontents* derived from views that he had formulated decades earlier.

CIVILIZATION AND ITS DISCONTENTS

The element of truth behind all this, which people are so ready to disavow, is that men are not gentle creatures who want to be loved, and who at most can defend themselves if they are attacked; they are, on the contrary, creatures among whose instinctual endowments is to be reckoned a powerful share of aggressiveness. As a result, their neighbour is for them not only a potential helper or sexual object, but also someone who tempts them to satisfy their aggressiveness on him, to exploit his capacity for work without compensation, to use him sexually without his consent, to seize his possessions, to humiliate him, to cause him pain, to torture and to kill him. *Homo homini lupus*. [Man is wolf to man.] Who, in the face of all his experience of life and of history, will have the courage to dispute this assertion? As a rule this cruel aggressiveness waits for some provocation or puts itself at the service of some other purpose, whose goal might also have been reached by milder measures. In circumstances that are favourable to it, when the mental counterforces which ordinarily inhibit it are out of action, it also manifests itself spontaneously and reveals man as a savage beast to whom consideration towards his own kind is something alien. Anyone who calls to mind the atrocities committed during the racial migrations or the invasions of the Huns, or by the people known as Mongols under Jenghiz Khan and Tamerlane, or at the capture of Jerusalem by the pious Crusaders, or even, indeed, the horrors of the recent World War—anyone who calls these things to mind will have to bow humbly before the truth of this view.

The existence of this inclination to aggression, which we can detect in ourselves and justly assume to be present in others, is the factor which disturbs our relations with our neighbour and which forces civilization into such a high expenditure [of energy]. In consequence of this primary mutual hostility of human beings, civilized society is perpetually threatened with disintegration. The interest of work in common would not hold it together; instinctual passions are stronger than reasonable interests. Civilization has to use its utmost efforts in order to set limits to man's aggressive instincts and to hold the manifestations of them in check by psychical reaction-formations. Hence, therefore, the use of methods intended to incite people into identifications and aim-inhibited relationships of love, hence the restriction upon sexual life, and hence too the ideal's commandment to love one's neighbour as oneself—a commandment which is really justified by the fact that nothing else runs so strongly counter to the original nature of man. In spite of every effort, these endeavours of civilization have not so far achieved very much. It hopes to prevent the crudest excesses of brutal violence by itself assuming the right to use violence against criminals, but the law is not able to lay hold of the more cautious and refined manifestations of human aggressiveness. The time comes when each one of us has to give up as illusions the expectations which, in his youth, he pinned upon his fellowmen, and when he may learn how much difficulty and pain has been added to his life by their ill-will. At the same time, it would be unfair to reproach civilization with trying to eliminate strife and competition from human activity. These things are undoubtedly indispensable. But opposition is not necessarily enmity; it is merely misused and made an *occasion* for enmity.

The communists believe that they have found the path to deliverance from our evils. According to them, man is wholly good and is well-disposed to his neighbour; but the institution of private property has corrupted his nature. The ownership of private wealth gives the individual power, and with it the temptation to ill-treat his neighbour; while the man who is excluded from possession is bound to rebel in hostility against his oppressor. If private property were abolished, all wealth held in common, and everyone allowed to share in the enjoyment of it, ill-will and hostility would disappear among men. Since everyone's needs would be satisfied, no one would have any reason to regard another as his enemy; all would willingly undertake the work that was necessary. I have no concern with any economic criticisms of the communist system. . . . But I am able to recognize that the psychological premises on which the system is based are an untenable illusion. In abolishing private property we deprive the human love of aggression of one of its instruments, certainly a strong one, though certainly not the strongest; but we have in no way altered the differences in power and influence which are misused by aggressiveness, nor have we altered anything in its nature. Aggressiveness was not created by property. It reigned almost without limit in primitive times, when property was still very scanty, and

it already shows itself in the nursery almost before property has given up its primal, anal form; it forms the basis of every relation of affection and love among people (with the single exception, perhaps, of the mother's relation to her male child). If we do away with personal rights over material wealth, there still remains prerogative in the field of sexual relationships, which is bound to become the source of the strongest dislike and the most violent hostility among men who in other respects are on an equal footing. If we were to remove this factor, too, by allowing complete freedom of sexual life and thus abolishing the family, the germ-cell of civilization, we cannot, it is true, easily foresee what new paths the development of civilization could take; but one thing we can expect, and that is that this indestructible feature of human nature will follow it there.

It is clearly not easy for men to give up the satisfaction of this inclination to aggression. They do not feel comfortable without it. . . .

If civilization imposes such great sacrifices not only on man's sexuality but on his aggressivity, we can understand better why it is hard for him to be happy in that civilization. . . .

In all that follows I adopt the standpoint, therefore, that the inclination to aggression is an original, self-subsisting instinctual disposition in man, and I return to my view that it constitutes the greatest impediment to civilization.

REVIEW QUESTIONS

1. What was Sigmund Freud's definition of the *unconscious*? What examples of the power of the unconscious did he provide?
2. Compare and contrast the approaches of Freud and Nietzsche to the nonrational.
3. What did Freud consider the "greatest impediment to civilization"? Why?
4. How did Freud react to the Marxist view that private property is the source of evil?
5. Compare Freud's view of human nature and reason to that of Enlightenment philosophes.

4   The Political Potential of the Irrational

The new insights into the irrational side of human nature and the growing assault on reason had immense implications for political life. In succeeding decades, these currents of irrationalism would be ideologized and politicized by unscrupulous demagogues, who sought to mobilize and manipulate the masses. The popularity after World War I of Fascist movements, which openly denigrated reason and exalted race, blood, action, and will, demonstrated the naiveté of nineteenth-century liberals, who believed that reason had triumphed in human affairs.

Among the late nineteenth- and early twentieth-century social theorists who focused on the implications of the nonrational for political life was Gustave Le Bon. Twentieth-century dictators would employ his insights into groups and mass psychology for the purpose of gaining and maintaining power.

Gustave Le Bon
MASS PSYCHOLOGY

Gustave Le Bon (1841–1931), a French social psychologist with strong conservative leanings, examined mass psychology as demonstrated in crowd behavior, a phenomenon of considerable importance in an age of accelerating industrialization and democratization. "The substitution of the unconscious action of crowds for the conscious activity of individuals is one of the principal characteristics of the present age," Le Bon declared in the preface to *The Crowd* (1895), excerpts from which follow.

Thousands of isolated individuals may acquire at certain moments, and under the influence of certain violent emotions—such, for example, as a great national event—the characteristics of a psychological crowd. . . .

The most striking peculiarity presented by a psychological crowd is the following: Whoever be the individuals that compose it, however like or unlike be their mode of life, their occupations, their character, or their intelligence, the fact that they have been transformed into a crowd puts them in possession of a sort of collective mind which makes them feel, think, and act in a manner quite different from that in which each individual of them would feel, think, and act were he in a state of isolation. . . .

To obtain [an understanding of crowds] it is necessary in the first place to call to mind the truth established by modern psychology, that unconscious phenomena play an altogether preponderating part not only in organic life, but also in the operations of the intelligence. The conscious life of the mind is of small importance in comparison with its unconscious life. . . . Behind the avowed causes of our acts there undoubtedly lie secret causes that we do not avow, but behind these secret causes there are many others more secret still which we ourselves ignore. The greater part of our daily actions are the result of hidden motives which escape our observation. . . .

. . . In the collective mind the intellectual aptitudes of the individuals, and in consequence their individuality, are weakened . . . and the unconscious qualities obtain the upper hand. . . .

. . . In a crowd every sentiment and act is contagious, and contagious to such a degree that an individual readily sacrifices his personal interest to the collective interest. This is an aptitude very contrary to his nature, and of which a man is scarcely capable, except when he [is] part of a crowd. . . .

. . . [An] individual [immersed] for some length of time in a crowd in action soon finds himself . . . in a special state, which much resembles the state of fascination in which the hypnotised individual finds himself in the hands of the hypnotiser. The activity of the brain being paralysed in the case of the hypnotised subject, the latter becomes the slave of all the unconscious activities of his spinal cord, which the hypnotiser directs at will. The conscious personality has entirely vanished; will and discernment are lost. All feelings and thoughts are bent in the direction determined by the hypnotiser.

Such also is approximately the state of the individual forming part of a psychological crowd. He is no longer conscious of his acts. In his case, as in the case of the hypnotised subject, at the same time that certain faculties are destroyed, others may be brought to a high degree of exaltation. Under the influence of a suggestion, he will undertake the accomplishment of certain acts with irresistible impetuosity. . . . He is no longer himself, but has become an automaton who has ceased to be guided by his will.

Moreover, by the mere fact that he forms part of an organised crowd, a man descends several rungs in the ladder of civilisation. Isolated, he may be a cultivated individual; in a crowd, he is a barbarian—that is, a creature acting by instinct. He possesses the spontaneity, the violence, the ferocity, and also the enthusiasm and heroism of primitive beings, whom he further tends to resemble by the facility with which he allows himself to be impressed by words and images—which would be entirely without action on each of the isolated individuals composing the crowd—and to be induced to commit acts contrary to his most obvious interests and his best-known habits. . . .

In consequence, a crowd perpetually hovering on the borderland of unconsciousness, readily yielding to all suggestions, having all the violence of feeling peculiar to beings who cannot appeal to the influence of reason, deprived of all critical faculty, cannot be otherwise than excessively credulous. The improbable does not exist for a crowd, and it is necessary to bear this circumstance well in mind to understand the facility with which are created and propagated the most improbable legends and stories. . . . A crowd thinks in images, and the image itself immediately calls up a series of other images, having no logical connection with the first. . . . Our reason shows us the incoherence there is in these images, but a crowd is almost blind to this truth, and confuses with the real event what the deforming action of its imagination has superimposed thereon. A crowd scarcely distinguishes between the subjective and the objective. It accepts as real the images evoked in its mind. . . .

Whatever be the ideas suggested to crowds they can only exercise effective influence on condition that they assume a very absolute, uncompromising, and simple shape. They present themselves then in the guise of images, and are only accessible to the masses under this form. These imagelike ideas are not connected by any logical bond of analogy or succession. . . .

. . . A chain of logical argumentation is totally incomprehensible to crowds, and for this reason it is permissible to say that they do not reason or that they reason falsely and are not to be influenced by reasoning. . . . An orator in intimate communication with a crowd can evoke images by which it will be seduced. . . .

. . . [The] powerlessness of crowds to reason aright prevents them displaying any trace of the critical spirit, prevents them, that is, from being capable of discerning truth from error, or of forming a precise judgment on any matter. Judgments accepted by crowds are merely judgments forced upon them and never judgments adopted after discussion. . . .

. . . Crowds are to some extent in the position of the sleeper whose reason, suspended for the time being, allows the arousing in his mind of images of extreme intensity which would quickly be dissipated could they be submitted to the action of reflection. Crowds, being incapable both of reflection and of reasoning, are devoid of the notion of improbability; and it is to be noted that in a general way it is the most improbable things that are the most striking.

This is why it happens that it is always the marvellous and legendary side of events that more specially strike crowds. . . .

Crowds being only capable of thinking in images are only to be impressed by images. It is only images that terrify or attract them and become motives of action. . . .

How is the imagination of crowds to be impressed?. . . [The] feat is never to be achieved by attempting to work upon the intelligence or reasoning faculty, that is to say, by way of demonstration. . . .

Whatever strikes the imagination of crowds presents itself under the shape of a startling and very clear image, freed from all accessory explanation . . . examples in point are a great victory, a great miracle, a great crime, or a great hope. Things must be laid before the crowd as a whole, and their genesis must never be indicated. A hundred petty crimes or petty accidents will not strike the imagination of crowds in the least, whereas a single great crime or a single great accident will profoundly impress them. . . .

When [the convictions of crowds] are closely examined, whether at epochs marked by fervent religious faith, or by great political upheavals such as those of the last century, it is apparent that they always assume a peculiar form which I cannot better define than by giving it the name of a religious sentiment. . . .

A person is not religious solely when he worships a divinity, but when he puts all the resources of his mind, the complete submission of his will, and the whole-souled ardour of fanaticism at the service of a cause or an individual who becomes the goal and guide of his thoughts and actions.

Intolerance and fanaticism are the necessary accompaniments of the religious sentiment. . . .

All founders of religious or political creeds have established them solely because they were successful in inspiring crowds with those fanatical sentiments which have as result that men find their happiness in worship and obedience and are ready to lay down their lives for their idol. This has been the case at all epochs. . . .

We have already shown that crowds are not to be influenced by reasoning, and can only comprehend rough-and-ready associations of ideas. The orators who know how to make an impression upon them always appeal in consequence to their sentiments and never to their reason. The laws of logic have no action on crowds. To bring home conviction to crowds it is necessary first of all to thoroughly comprehend the sentiments by which they are animated, to pretend to share these sentiments. . . .

As soon as a certain number of living beings are gathered together, whether they be animals or men, they place themselves instinctively under the authority of a chief.

In the case of human crowds the chief is often nothing more than a ringleader or agitator, but as such he plays a considerable part. His will is the nucleus around which the opinions of the crowd are grouped and attain to identity. . . . A crowd is a servile flock that is incapable of ever doing without a master.

The leader has most often started as one of the led. He has himself been hypnotised by the idea, whose apostle he has since become. It has taken possession of him to such a degree that everything outside it vanishes, and that every contrary opinion appears to him an error or a superstition. An example in point is Robespierre, hypnotised by the philosophical ideas of Rousseau, and employing the methods of the Inquisition to propagate them.

The leaders we speak of are more frequently men of action than thinkers. . . . The multitude is always ready to listen to the strong-willed man, who knows how to impose himself upon it. Men gathered in a crowd lose all force of will, and turn instinctively to the person who possesses the quality they lack. . . .

When . . . it is proposed to imbue the mind of a crowd with ideas and beliefs . . . the leaders have recourse to different expedients. The principal of them are three in number and clearly defined—affirmation, repetition, and contagion. . . .

Affirmation pure and simple, kept free of all reasoning and all proof, is one of the surest means of making an idea enter the mind of crowds. The conciser an affirmation is, the more destitute of every appearance of proof and demonstration, the more weight it carries. . . .

Affirmation, however, has no real influence unless it be constantly repeated, and so far as possible in the same terms. It was Napoleon, I believe, who said that there is only one figure in rhetoric of serious importance, namely, repetition. The thing affirmed comes by repetition to fix itself in the mind in such a way that it is accepted in the end as a demonstrated truth.

The influence of repetition on crowds is comprehensible when the power is seen which it exercises on the most enlightened minds. This power is due to the fact that the repeated statement is embedded in the long run in those profound regions of our unconscious selves in which the motives of our actions are forged. At the end of a certain time we have forgotten who is the author of the repeated assertion, and we finish by believing it.

When an affirmation has been sufficiently repeated and there is unanimity in this repetition . . . what is called a current of opinion is formed and the powerful mechanism of contagion intervenes. Ideas, sentiments, emotions, and beliefs possess in crowds a contagious power as intense as that of microbes.

REVIEW QUESTIONS

1. According to Gustave Le Bon, how are individuals transformed once they become part of a crowd? How does the leader sway the crowd?
2. Point out instances in recent and contemporary history that support Le Bon's insights.

---

5 Modern Art and the Questioning of Western Values

New trends in art that emerged during the late nineteenth and the early twentieth centuries resulted in modern art. Beginning with the postimpressionists of the 1880s and 1890s (such as Paul Cézanne, Paul Gauguin, and Vincent van Gogh), artists began to turn away from standards that had ruled art since the Renaissance, increasingly repudiating the idea of depicting an object as it appears to the eye. Then, in the years just prior to World War I, several artists, including Henri Matisse and Wassily Kandinsky, further obscured the physical world from their paintings and expressed their private inner experiences. But it was Pablo Picasso's *The Young Ladies of Avignon* (1907), the first cubist painting, that broke all of the established rules. These innovators repudiated Western aesthetic standards that were based on the conviction that the universe embodied an inherent mathematical order. Modernist artists acknowledged no objective reality; reality is what the viewer perceives it to be through the prism of the imagination. An abstract form will reveal a deeper reality than will a depiction of physical reality.

Although these innovators questioned Western artistic standards, they did not repudiate Enlightenment values. But many artists and literary figures who followed them regarded the Enlightenment belief in human goodness, reason, and the progress of humanity as expressions of naive optimism. Three movements in particular—futurism, Dada, and surrealism—manifest this loss of faith in Western values. Futurism, launched prior to World War I, glorified the irrational and abhorred what it considered to be the cultural decadence of the West. "The Great War," World War I, led to art and literary movements that intensified this critique of Western values. Dada, which came into existence during the war, embraced nihilism and a contempt for Europe's moral and intellectual values. Following the war, surrealism focused on the importance of the unconscious to reach a higher reality. Surrealists stressed fantasy and made use of Freudian insights and symbols as they sought to reproduce the raw state of the unconscious and to arrive at truths beyond reason's grasp.

Filippo Tommaso Marinetti
MANIFESTO OF FUTURISM

On February 20, 1909, the Paris newspaper *Le Figaro* published a manifesto by the Italian poet Filippo Tommaso Marinetti (1876–1944), proclaiming the emergence of a new literary movement called futurism. The movement appealed to young Italian artists and writers who were repulsed by bourgeois materialism and by what they considered to be Italy's political weakness and cultural decadence. The most prominent futurist artists—Umberto Coccioni, Carlo Carrá, and Luigi Russolo—sought to depict the dynamism—the speed and power—of modern urban life and modern industry. The historical significance of futurist artists and poets lay less in the aesthetic merit of their works (which in some cases was considerable) and more in their rejection of the Western liberal-humanist tradition and their espousal of action and the primordial. To this extent they were symptomatic of a mindset that welcomed World War I and embraced Fascism after the war. Marinetti himself was a staunch Italian nationalist who served Mussolini's Fascist state. Excerpted below is the *Manifesto of Futurism* written by Marinetti in 1909.

1. We intend to sing the love of danger, the habit of energy and fearlessness.
2. Courage, audacity, and revolt will be essential elements of our poetry.
3. Up to now literature has exalted a pensive immobility, ecstasy, and sleep. We intend to exalt aggressive action, a feverish insomnia, the racer's stride, the mortal leap, the punch and the slap.
4. We say that the world's magnificence has been enriched by a new beauty; the beauty of speed. A racing car whose hood is adorned with great pipes, like serpents of explosive breath—a roaring car that seems to ride on grapeshot—is more beautiful than the *Victory of Samothrace*.

5. We want to hymn the man at the wheel, who hurls the lance of his spirit across the Earth, along the circle of its orbit.
6. The poet must spend himself with ardor, splendor, and generosity, to swell the enthusiastic fervor of the primordial elements.
7. Except in struggle, there is no more beauty. No work without an aggressive character can be a masterpiece. Poetry must be conceived as a violent attack on unknown forces, to reduce and prostate them before man.
8. We stand on the last promontory of the centuries. . . . Why should we look back, when what we want is to break down the mysterious doors of the Impossible? Time and Space died yesterday. We already live

in the absolute, because we have created eternal omnipresent speed.

9. We will glorify war—the world's only hygiene—militarism, patriotism, the destructive gesture of freedom-bringers, beautiful ideas worth dying for, and scorn for woman.

10. We will destroy the museums, libraries, academies of every kind, will fight moralism, feminism, every opportunistic or utilitarian cowardice.

11. We will sing of great crowds excited by work, by pleasure, and by riot; we will sing of the multicolored polyphonic tides of revolution in the modern capitals; we will sing of the vibrant nightly fervor of arsenals and shipyards blazing with violent electric moons; greedy railway stations that devour smoke-plumed serpents; factories hung on clouds by the crooked lines of their smoke; bridges that stride the rivers like giant gymnasts, flashing in the sun with a glitter of knives; adventurous steamers that sniff the horizon; deep-chested locomotives whose wheels paw the tracks like the hooves of enormous steel horses bridled by tubing; and the sleek flight of planes whose propellers chatter in the wind like banners and seem to cheer like an enthusiastic crowd.

It is from Italy that we launch through the world this violently upsetting, incendiary manifesto of ours. With it, today, we establish Futurism because we want to free this land from its smelly gangrene of professors, archaeologists, ciceroni, and antiquarians. For too long has Italy been a dealer in secondhand clothes. We mean to free her from the numberless museums that cover her like so many graveyards.

Museums: cemeteries! . . . Identical, surely, in the sinister promiscuity of so many bodies unknown to one another. Museums: public dormitories where one lies forever beside hated or unknown beings. Museums: absurd [slaughterhouses] of painters and sculptors ferociously [weakening] each other with color-blows and line-blows, the length of the fought-over walls!

That one should make an annual pilgrimage, just as one goes to the graveyard on All Souls' Day—that I grant. That once a year one should leave a floral tribute beneath the *Gioconda* {Mona Lisa}, I grant you that. . . . But I don't admit that our sorrows, our fragile courage, our morbid restlessness should be given a daily conducted tour through the museums. Why poison ourselves? Why rot?

And what is there to see in an old picture except the laborious contortions of an artist throwing himself against the barriers that thwart his desire to express his dream completely? . . . Admiring an old picture is the same as pouring our sensibility into a funerary urn instead of hurling it far off, in violent spasms of action and creation.

Do you, then, wish to waste all your best powers in this eternal and futile worship of the past, from which you emerge fatally exhausted, shrunken, beaten down?

In truth I tell you that daily visits to museums, libraries, and academies (cemeteries of empty exertion, calvaries of crucified dreams, registries of aborted beginnings!) is, for artists, as damaging as the prolonged supervision by parents of certain young people drunk with their talent and their ambitious wills. When the future is barred to them, the admirable past may be a solace for the ills of the moribund, the sickly, the prisoner. . . . But we want no part of it, the past, we the young and strong *Futurists!*

So let them come, the gay incendiaries with charred fingers! Here they are! . . . Come on! set fire to the library shelves! Turn aside the canals to flood the museums! . . . Oh, the joy of seeing the glorious old canvases bobbing adrift on those waters, discolored and shredded! . . . Take up your pickaxes, your axes and hammers, and wreck, wreck the venerable cities, pitilessly!

The oldest of us is thirty: so we have at least a decade for finishing our work. When we are forty, other younger and stronger men will probably throw us in the wastebasket like useless manuscripts—we want it to happen!

They will come against us, our successors, will come from far away, from every quarter, dancing to the winged cadence of their first songs, flexing the hooked claws of predators, sniffing doglike at the academy doors the strong odor of our decaying minds, which already will have been promised to the literary catacombs.

But we won't be there. . . . At last they'll find us—one winter's night—in open country, beneath a sad roof drummed by a monotonous rain. They'll see us crouched beside our trembling airplanes in the act of warming our hands at the poor little blaze that our books of today will give out when they take fire from the flight of our images.

They'll storm around us, panting with scorn and anguish, and all of them, exasperated by our proud daring, will hurtle to kill us, driven by hatred: the more implacable it is, the more their hearts will be drunk with love and admiration for us.

Injustice, strong and sane, will break out radiantly in their eyes.

Art, in fact, can be nothing but violence, cruelty, and injustice.

The oldest of us is thirty: even so we have already scattered treasures, a thousand treasures of force, love, courage, astuteness, and raw will power; have thrown them impatiently away, with fury, carelessly, unhesitatingly, breathless and unresting. . . . Look at us! We are still untired! Our hearts know no weariness because they are fed with fire, hatred, and speed! . . . Does that amaze you? It should, because you can never remember having lived! Erect on the summit of the world, once again we hurl our defiance at the stars!

You have objections?—Enough! Enough! We know them . . . we've understood! . . . Our fine deceitful intelligence tells us that we are the revival and extension of our ancestors—perhaps! . . . If only it were so!—But who cares? We don't want to understand! . . . Woe to anyone who says those infamous words to us again!

Lift up your heads!

Erect on the summit of the world, once again we hurl defiance to the stars!

REVIEW QUESTION

1. What was the futurists' view of the past? Of the future? Of art? How did these views express the irrational?

CHAPTER 11

World War I

CELEBRATING THE BEGINNING OF WORLD WAR I. For many people, the declaration of war was a cause for celebration. Few Europeans realized what a horror the war would turn out to be. *(Sueddeutsche Zeitung Photo/The Image Works)*

To many Europeans, the opening years of the twentieth century seemed full of promise. Advances in science and technology, the rising standard of living, the expansion of education, and the absence of wars between the Great Powers since the Franco-Prussian War (1870–1871) all contributed to a general feeling of optimism. Yet these accomplishments hid disruptive forces that were propelling Europe toward a cataclysm. On June 28, 1914, Archduke Francis Ferdinand, heir to the throne of Austria-Hungary, was assassinated by Gavrilo Princip, a young Serbian nationalist (and Austrian subject), at Sarajevo in the Austrian province of Bosnia, inhabited largely by South Slavs. The assassination triggered those explosive forces that lay below the surface of European life, and six weeks later, Europe was engulfed in a general war that altered the course of Western civilization.

Belligerent, irrational, and extreme nationalism was a principal cause of World War I. Placing their country above everything, nationalists in various countries fomented hatred of other nationalities and called for the expansion of their nation's borders—attitudes that fostered belligerence in foreign relations. Wedded to nationalism was a militaristic view that regarded war as heroic and as the highest expression of individual and national life.

Yet Europe might have avoided the world war had the nations not been divided into hostile alliance systems. By 1907, the Triple Alliance of Germany, Austria-Hungary, and Italy confronted the loosely organized Triple Entente of France, Russia, and Great Britain. What German chancellor Otto von Bismarck said in 1879 was just as true in 1914: "The great powers of our time are like travellers, unknown to one another, whom chance has brought together in a carriage. They watch each other, and when one of them puts his hand into his pocket, his neighbor gets ready his own revolver in order to be able to fire the first shot."

A danger inherent in an alliance is that a country, knowing that it has the support of allies, may pursue an aggressive foreign policy and may be less likely to compromise during a crisis; also, a war between two states may well draw in the other allied powers. These dangers materialized in 1914.

In the diplomatic furor of July and early August 1914, following the assassination of Francis Ferdinand, several patterns emerged. Austria-Hungary, a multinational empire dominated by Germans and Hungarians, feared the nationalist aspirations of its Slavic minorities. The nationalist yearnings of neighboring Serbia aggravated Austria-Hungary's problems, for the Serbs, a South Slav people, wanted to create a Greater Serbia by uniting with South Slavs of Austria-Hungary. If Slavic nationalism gained in intensity, the Austro-Hungarian (or Hapsburg) Empire would be broken into states based on nationality. Austria-Hungary decided to use the assassination as justification for crushing Serbia.

The system of alliances escalated the tensions between Austria-Hungary and Serbia into a general European war. Germany saw itself threatened by the Triple Entente (a conviction based more on paranoia than on objective fact) and regarded Austria-Hungary as its only reliable ally. Holding that at all costs its ally must be kept strong, German officials supported Austria-Hungary's decision to crush Serbia. Fearing that Germany and Austria-Hungary aimed to extend their power into southeastern Europe, Russia would not permit the destruction of Serbia. With the support of France, Russia began to mobilize, and when it moved to full mobilization, Germany declared war. As German battle plans, drawn up years before, called for a war with both France and Russia, France was drawn into the conflict; Germany's invasion of neutral Belgium brought Great Britain into the war.

Most European statesmen and military men believed the war would be over in a few months. Virtually no one anticipated that it would last more than four years and that the casualties would number in the millions.

World War I was a turning point in Western history. In Russia, it led to the downfall of the tsarist autocracy and the rise of the Soviet state. The war created unsettling conditions that led to the emergence of Fascist movements in Italy and Germany, and it shattered, perhaps forever, the Enlightenment belief in the inevitable and perpetual progress of Western civilization.

1 Militarism

Historians regard a surging militarism as an underlying cause of World War I. One sign of militarism was the rapid increase in expenditures for armaments in the years prior to 1914. Between 1910 and 1914, both Austria-Hungary and Germany, for example, doubled their military budgets. The arms race intensified suspicion among the Great Powers. A second danger was the increased power of the military in policymaking, particularly in Austria-Hungary and Germany. In the crisis following the assassination, generals tended to press for a military solution. The few dissenting voices raised against militarism were all but drowned out in this martial atmosphere.

Heinrich von Treitschke
THE GREATNESS OF WAR

Coupled with the military's influence on state decisions was a romantic glorification of the nation and war, an attitude shared by both the elite and the masses. Although militarism generally pervaded Europe, it was particularly strong in

Germany. In the following reading from *Politics* (1899–1900), the influential German historian Heinrich von Treitschke (1834–1896) glorified warfare.

. . . One must say with the greatest determination: War is for an afflicted people the only remedy. When the State exclaims: My very existence is at stake! then social self-seeking must disappear and all party hatred be silent. The individual must forget his own *ego* and feel himself a member of the whole, he must recognize how negligible is his life compared with the good of the whole. Therein lies the greatness of war that the little man completely vanishes before the great thought of the State. The sacrifice of nationalities for one another is nowhere invested with such beauty as in war. At such a time the corn is separated from the chaff. All who lived through 1870 will understand the saying of Niebuhr[1] with regard to the year 1813, that he then experienced the "bliss of sharing with all his fellow citizens, with the scholar and the ignorant, the one common feeling—no man who enjoyed this experience will to his dying day forget how loving, friendly and strong he felt."

It is indeed political idealism which fosters war, whereas materialism rejects it. What a

perversion of morality to want to banish heroism from human life. The heroes of a people are the personalities who fill the youthful souls with delight and enthusiasm, and amongst authors we as boys and youths admire most those whose words sound like a flourish of trumpets. He who cannot take pleasure therein, is too cowardly to take up arms himself for his fatherland. All appeal to Christianity in this matter is perverted. The Bible states expressly that the man in authority shall wield the sword; it states likewise that: "Greater love hath no man than this that he giveth his life for his friend." Those who preach the nonsense about everlasting peace do not understand the life of the Aryan race, the Aryans are before all brave. They have always been men enough to protect by the sword what they had won by the intellect. . . .

To the historian who lives in the realms of the Will, it is quite clear that the furtherance of an everlasting peace is fundamentally reactionary. He sees that to banish war from history would be to banish all progress and becoming. It is only the periods of exhaustion, weariness and mental stagnation that have dallied with the dream of everlasting peace. . . . The living God will see to it that war returns again and again as a terrible medicine for humanity.

---

[1]Barthold G. Niebuhr (1776–1831) was a Prussian historian. The passage refers to the German War of Liberation against Napoleon, which German patriots regarded as a glorious episode in their national history.

Friedrich von Bernhardi
GERMANY AND THE NEXT WAR

Friedrich von Bernhardi (1849–1930), a German general and influential military writer, considered war "a biological necessity of the first importance." The following excerpt comes from his work *Germany and the Next War* (1911), which was immensely popular in his country.

. . . War is a biological necessity of the first importance, a regulative element in the life of mankind which cannot be dispensed with, since without it an unhealthy development will follow, which excludes every advancement of the race, and therefore all real civilization. "War is the father of all things." The sages of antiquity long before Darwin recognized this.

The struggle for existence is, in the life of Nature, the basis of all healthy development. . . . The law of the stronger holds good everywhere. Those forms survive which are able to procure themselves the most favourable conditions of life, and to assert themselves in the universal economy of Nature. The weaker succumb. . . .

Struggle is, therefore, a universal law of Nature, and the instinct of self-preservation which leads to struggle is acknowledged to be a natural condition of existence.

Strong, healthy, and flourishing nations increase in numbers. From a given moment they require a continual expansion of their frontiers, they require new territory for the accommodation of their surplus population. Since almost every part of the globe is inhabited, new territory must, as a rule, be obtained at the cost of its possessors—that is to say, by conquest, which thus becomes a law of necessity.

The right of conquest is universally acknowledged.

. . . Vast territories inhabited by uncivilized masses are occupied by more highly civilized States, and made subject to their rule. Higher civilization and the correspondingly greater power are the foundations of the right to annexation. . . .

Lastly, in all times the right of conquest by war has been admitted. It may be that a growing people cannot win colonies from civilized races, and yet the State wishes to retain the surplus population which the mother-country can no longer feed. Then the only course left is to acquire the necessary territory by war. Thus the instinct of self-preservation leads inevitably to war, and the conquest of foreign soil. It is not the possessor, but the victor, who then has the right. . . .

In such cases might gives the right to occupy or to conquer. Might is at once the supreme right, and the dispute as to what is right is decided by the arbitrament of war. War gives a biologically just decision, since its decisions rest on the very nature of things. . . .

The knowledge, therefore, that war depends on biological laws leads to the conclusion that every attempt to exclude it from international relations must be demonstrably untenable.

Henri Massis and Alfred de Tarde
THE YOUNG PEOPLE OF TODAY

War fever was not limited to Germany. A few years prior to the war, two French journalists, Henri Massis and Alfred de Tarde, undertook a survey of Parisian students enrolled at various elite educational institutions. The survey, which first appeared as a newspaper article in 1912 and then as a book in 1913, seemed to demonstrate that many young French males between the ages of eighteen and twenty-five had abandoned the Enlightenment humanitarianism of the older generation for a militant Catholicism, fervent nationalism, and romantic militarism. Excerpts from the survey follow.

The sentiment which underlies all these youthful attitudes, which unanimously accords with the deepest tendencies in their thought, is that of patriotic faith. That they are possessed of this sentiment is unequivocal and undeniable. Optimism, that state of mind which defines the attitude of these young people, manifests itself from the outset in the confidence which they place in the future of France: there they find their first motive for acting, the one which determines and directs all their activity.

The young men of today have read the word of their destiny in this French soul, which dictates to them a clear and imperious duty. . . .

Consider something even more significant. Students of advanced rhetoric in Paris, that is, the most cultivated elite among young people, declare that they find in warfare an aesthetic ideal of energy and strength. They believe that "France needs heroism in order to live." "Such is the faith," comments Monsieur Tourolle, "which consumes modern youth."

How many times in the last two years have we heard this repeated: "Better war than this eternal waiting!" There is no bitterness in this avowal, but rather a secret hope. . . .

War! The word has taken on a sudden glamour. It is a youthful word, wholly new, adorned with that seduction which the eternal bellicose instinct has revived in the hearts of men. These young men impute to it all beauty with which they are in love and of which they have been deprived by ordinary life. Above all, war, in their eyes, is the occasion for the most noble of human virtues, those which they exalt above all others: energy, mastery, and sacrifice for a cause which transcends ourselves. With William James, they believe that life "would become odious if it offered neither risks nor rewards for the courageous man."

A professor of philosophy at the Lycée Henri IV confided to us: "I once spoke about war to my pupils. I explained to them that there were unjust wars, undertaken out of anger, and that it was necessary to justify the bellicose sentiment. Well, the class obviously did not follow me; they rejected that distinction."

Read this passage from a letter written to us by a young student of rhetoric, Alsatian in origin. "The existence that we lead does not satisfy us completely because, even if we possess all the elements of a good life, we cannot organize them in a practical, immediate deed that would take us, body and soul, and hurl us outside of ourselves. One event only will permit that deed—war; and hence we desire it. It is in the life of the camps, it is around the fire that we will experience the supreme expansion of those French powers that are within us. Our intellect will no longer be troubled in the face of the unknowable, since it will be able to concentrate itself entirely on a present duty from which uncertainty and hesitation are excluded."

Above all, perhaps, how can one ignore the success that accounts of our colonialists have had among the young intellectuals under consideration here? The expeditions of Moll, Lenfant, and Baratier arouse their enthusiasm; they search in their own unperilous existences for a moral equivalent to these bold destinies; they attempt to transpose this intrepid valor into their inner lives.

Some go further: their studies completed, they satisfy their taste for action in colonial adventures. It is not enough for them to learn history: they are making it. A young student from the Normale, Monsieur Klipfell, who received his teaching degree in literature in July of 1912, requested to be assigned to active service in Morocco, as a member of the Expeditionary Corps. We can cite many a similar example. One thinks of Jacques Violet, a twenty-year-old officer, who died so gloriously at Ksar-Teuchan, in Adrar: he was killed at the head of his men, at the moment of victory, in a grove of palm trees; among his belongings, they found a pair of white gloves and a copy of *Servitude and Military Grandeur;*[1] it was thus that he went into combat. . . .

For such young men, fired by patriotic faith and the cult of military virtues, only the occasion for heroism is lacking.

---

[1]Alfred-Victor de Vigny (1797–1863) wrote *Servitude and Military Grandeur* (1835), a combination of his memoirs and short stories. The work glorified martial values and the supreme good of service to God and country, even unto death.

REVIEW QUESTIONS

1. Why did Heinrich von Treitschke regard war as a far more desirable condition than peace?
2. According to Treitschke, what is the individual's highest responsibility?
3. According to Treitschke, what function does the hero serve in national life?
4. What conclusions did Friedrich von Bernhardi draw from his premise that war was "a biological necessity"?
5. Why were French students so attracted to war?

---

2 Pan-Serbism: Nationalism and Terrorism

The conspiracy to assassinate Archduke Francis Ferdinand was organized by a secret Serbian society called Union or Death, more popularly known as the Black Hand. Founded in 1911, the Black Hand aspired to create a Greater Serbia by uniting with their kinsmen, the South Slavs dwelling in Austria-Hungary. Thus, Austrian officials regarded the aspirations of Pan-Serbs as a significant threat to the Hapsburg Empire.

THE BLACK HAND

In 1914, the Black Hand had some 2,500 members, most of them army officers. The society indoctrinated members with a fanatic nationalism and trained them in terrorist methods. The initiation ceremony, designed to strengthen a new member's commitment to the cause and to foster obedience to the society's leaders, had the appearance of a sacred rite. The candidate entered a dark room in which a table stood covered with a black cloth; resting on the table were a dagger, a revolver, and a crucifix. When the candidate declared his readiness to take the oath of allegiance, a masked member of the society's elite entered the room and stood in silence. After the initiate pronounced the oath, the masked man shook his hand and departed without uttering a word. Excerpts of the Black Hand's bylaws, including the oath of allegiance, follow.

BY-LAWS OF THE ORGANIZATION UNION OR DEATH

Article 1. This organization is created for the purpose of realizing the national ideal: the union of all Serbs. Membership is open to every Serb, without distinction of sex, religion, or place of birth, and to all those who are sincerely devoted to this cause.

Article 2. This organization prefers terrorist action to intellectual propaganda, and for this reason it must remain absolutely secret.

Article 3. The organization bears the name *Ujedinjenje ili Smirt* (Union or Death).

Article 4. To fulfill its purpose, the organization will do the following:

1. Exercise influence on government circles, on the various social classes, and on the entire social life of the kingdom of Serbia, which is considered the Piedmont[1] of the Serbian nation;
2. Organize revolutionary action in all territories inhabited by Serbs;
3. Beyond the frontiers of Serbia, fight with all means the enemies of the Serbian national idea;
4. Maintain amicable relations with all states, peoples, organizations, and individuals who support Serbia and the Serbian element;
5. Assist those nations and organizations that are fighting for their own national liberation and unification. . . .

Article 24. Every member has a duty to recruit new members, but the member shall guarantee with his life those whom he introduces into the organization.

Article 25. Members of the organization are forbidden to know each other personally. Only members of the central committee are known to each other.

Article 26. In the organization itself, the members are designated by numbers. Only the central committee in Belgrade knows their names.

Article 27. Members of the organization must obey absolutely the commands given to them by their superiors.

Article 28. Each member has a duty to communicate to the central committee at Belgrade all information that may be of interest to the organization.

Article 29. The interests of the organization stand above all other interests.

Article 30. On entering the organization, each member must know that he loses his own personality, that he can expect neither personal glory nor personal profit, material or moral. Consequently, any member who endeavors to exploit the organization for personal, social, or party motives, will be punished. If by his acts he harms the organization itself, his punishment will be death.

Article 31. Those who enter the organization may never leave it, and no one has the authority to accept a member's resignation.

Article 32. Each member must aid the organization, with weekly contributions. If need be, the organization may procure funds through coercion. . . .

Article 33. When the central committee of Belgrade pronounces a death sentence the only thing that matters is that the execution is carried out unfailingly. The method of execution is of little importance.

Article 34. The organization's seal is composed as follows. On the center of the seal a powerful arm holds in its hand an unfurled flag. On the flag, as a coat of arms, are a skull and crossed bones; by the side of the flag are a knife, a bomb and poison. Around, in a circle, are inscribed the following words reading from left to right: "Unification or Death," and at the base "The Supreme Central Directorate."

Article 35. On joining the organization, the recruit takes the following oath:

"I (name), in becoming a member of the organization, 'Unification or Death,' do swear by the sun that shines on me, by the earth that nourishes me, by God, by the blood of my ancestors, on my honor and my life that from this moment until my death, I shall be faithful to the regulations of the organization and that I will be prepared to make any sacrifice for it. I swear before God, on my honor and on my life, that I shall carry with me to the grave the organization's secrets. May God condemn me and my comrades judge me if I violate or do not respect, consciously or not, my oath."

Article 36. These regulations come into force immediately.

Article 37. These regulations must not be changed.

Belgrade, 9 May 1911.

---

[1]The Piedmont was the Italian state that served as the nucleus for the unification of Italy.

REVIEW QUESTIONS

1. How did Union or Death seek to accomplish its goal of uniting all Serbs?
2. What type of people do you think were attracted to the objectives and methods of the Black Hand?

---

3 War as Celebration: The Mood in European Capitals

An outpouring of patriotism greeted the proclamation of war. Huge crowds thronged the avenues and squares of capital cities to express their devotion to their nations and their willingness to bear arms. Many Europeans regarded war as a sacred moment that held the promise of adventure and an escape from a humdrum and purposeless daily existence. Going to war seemed to satisfy a yearning to surrender oneself to a noble cause: the greatness of the nation. The image of the nation united in a spirit of fraternity and self-sacrifice was immensely appealing.

Roland Doregelès
PARIS: "THAT FABULOUS DAY"

In "After Fifty Years," Roland Doregelès (1886–1973), a distinguished French writer, recalls the mood in Paris at the outbreak of the war.

"It's come!* It's posted at the district mayor's office," a passerby shouted to me as he ran.

I reached the Rue Drouot in one leap and shouldered through the mob that already filled the courtyard to approach the fascinating white sheet pasted to the door. I read the message at a glance, then reread it slowly, word for word, to convince myself that it was true:

THE FIRST DAY OF
MOBILIZATION WILL BE
SUNDAY, AUGUST 2

Only three lines, written hastily by a hand that trembled. It was an announcement to a million and a half Frenchmen.

The people who had read it moved away, stunned, while others crowded in, but this silent numbness did not last. Suddenly a heroic wind lifted their heads. What? War, was it? Well, then, let's go! Without any signal, the "Marseillaise" poured from thousands of throats, sheafs of flags appeared at windows, and howling processions rolled out on the boulevards. Each column brandished a placard: ALSACE VOLUNTEERS, JEWISH VOLUNTEERS, POLISH VOLUNTEERS. They hailed one another above the bravos of the crowd, and this human torrent, swelling at every corner, moved on to circle around the Place de la Concorde, before the statue of Strasbourg banked with flowers, then flowed toward the Place de la République, where mobs from Belleville and the Faubourg St. Antoine yelled themselves hoarse on the refrain from

---

*Translated from the French by Sally Abeles.

the great days, *"Aux armes, citoyens!"* (To arms, citizens!) But this time it was better than a song.

To gather the news for my paper, I ran around the city in every direction. At the Cours la Reine I saw the fabled cuirassiers [cavalry] in their horsetail plumes march by, and at the Rue La Fayette footsoldiers in battle garb with women throwing flowers and kisses to them. In a marshaling yard I saw guns being loaded, their long, thin barrels twined around with branches and laurel leaves, while troops in red breeches piled gaily into delivery vans they were scrawling with challenges and caricatures. Young and old, civilians and military men burned with the same excitement. It was like a Brotherhood Day.

Dead tired but still exhilarated, I got back to *L'Homme libre* and burst into the office of Georges Clemenceau, our chief.[†]

"What is Paris saying?" he asked me.

"It's singing, sir!"

"Then everything will be all right. . . ."

His old patriot's heart was not wrong; no cloud marred that fabulous day. . . .

Less than twenty-four hours later, seeing their old dreams of peace crumble [socialist workers] would stream out into the boulevards . . . [but] they would break into the "Marseillaise," not the "Internationale"; they would cry, "To Berlin!," not "Down with war!"

 socialists

What did they have to defend, these black-nailed patriots? Not even a shack, an acre to till,

indeed hardly a patch of ground reserved at the Pantin Cemetery; yet they would depart, like their rivals of yesterday, a heroic song on their lips and a flower in their guns. No more poor or rich, proletarians or bourgeois, right-wingers or militant leftists; there were only Frenchmen.

Beginning the next day, thousands of men eager to fight would jostle one another outside recruiting offices, waiting to join up. Men who could have stayed home, with their wives and children or an imploring mama. But no. The word "duty" had a meaning for them, and the word "country" had regained its splendor.

I close my eyes, and they appear to me, those volunteers on the great day; then I see them again in the old kepi [military cap] or blue helmet, shouting, "Here!" when somebody called for men for a raid, or hurling themselves into an attack with fixed bayonets, and I wonder, and I question their bloody [ghosts].

Tell me, comrades in eternal silence, would you have besieged the enlistment offices with the same enthusiasm, would you have fought such a courageous fight had you known that fifty years later those men in gray knit caps or steel helmets you were ordered to kill would no longer be enemies and that we would have to open our arms to them? Wouldn't the heroic "Let's go!" you shouted as you cleared the parapets have stuck in your throats? Deep in the grave where you dwell, don't you regret your sacrifice? "Why did we fight? Why did we let ourselves get killed?" This is the murmur of a million and a half voices rising from the bowels of the earth, and we, the survivors, do not know what to answer.

[†]*L'Homme libre* (The Free Man) was but one of several periodicals Clemenceau founded and directed during his long political career.—Tr.

Stefan Zweig
VIENNA: "THE RUSHING FEELING OF FRATERNITY"

Some intellectuals viewed the war as a way of regenerating the nation; nobility and fraternity would triumph over life's petty concerns. In the following reading, Stefan Zweig (1881–1942), a prominent Austrian literary figure, recalled the scene in Vienna, the capital of the Austro-Hungarian Empire, at the outbreak of World War I. This passage comes from Zweig's autobiography, *The World of Yesterday*, written in 1941.

The next morning I was in Austria. In every station placards had been put up announcing general mobilization. The trains were filled with fresh recruits, banners were flying, music sounded, and in Vienna I found the entire city in a tumult. The first shock at the news of war—the war that no one, people or government, had wanted—the war which had slipped, much against their will, out of the clumsy hands of the diplomats who had been bluffing and toying with it, had suddenly been transformed into enthusiasm. There were parades in the street, flags, ribbons, and music burst forth everywhere, young recruits were marching triumphantly, their faces lighting up at the cheering—they, the John Does and Richard Roes who usually go unnoticed and uncelebrated.

And to be truthful, I must acknowledge that there was a majestic, rapturous, and even seductive something in this first outbreak of the people from which one could escape only with difficulty. And in spite of all my hatred and aversion for war, I should not like to have missed the memory of those first days. As never before, thousands and hundreds of thousands felt what they should have felt in peace time, that they belonged together. A city of two million, a country of nearly fifty million, in that hour felt that they were participating in world history, in a moment which would never recur, and that each one was called upon to cast his infinitesimal self into the glowing mass, there to be purified of all selfishness. All differences of class, rank, and language were flooded over at that moment by the rushing feeling of fraternity. Strangers spoke to one another in the streets, people who had avoided each other for years shook hands, everywhere one saw excited faces. Each individual experienced an exaltation of his ego, he was no longer the isolated person of former times, he had been incorporated into the mass, he was part of the people, and

his person, his hitherto unnoticed person, had been given meaning. The petty mail clerk, who ordinarily sorted letters early and late, who sorted constantly, who sorted from Monday until Saturday without interruption; the clerk, the cobbler, had suddenly achieved a romantic possibility in life: he could become a hero, and everyone who wore a uniform was already being cheered by the women, and greeted beforehand with this romantic appellation by those who had to remain behind. They acknowledged the unknown power which had lifted them out of their everyday existence. Even mothers with their grief, and women with their fears, were ashamed to manifest their quite natural emotions in the face of this first transformation. But it is quite possible that a deeper, more secret power was at work in this frenzy. So deeply, so quickly did the tide break over humanity that, foaming over the surface, it churned up the depths, the subconscious primitive instincts of the human animal—that which Freud so meaningfully calls "the revulsion from culture," the desire to break out of the conventional bourgeois world of codes and statutes, and to permit the primitive instincts of the blood to rage at will. It is also possible that these powers of darkness had their share in the wild frenzy into which everything was thrown—self-sacrifice and alcohol, the spirit of adventure and the spirit of pure faith, the old magic of flags and patriotic slogans, that mysterious frenzy of the millions which can hardly be described in words, but which, for the moment, gave a wild and almost rapturous impetus to the greatest crime of our time. . . .

. . . What did the great mass know of war in 1914, after nearly half a century of peace? They did not know war, they had hardly given it a thought. It had become legendary, and distance had made it seem romantic and heroic. They still saw it in the perspective of their school readers and of paintings in museums; brilliant cavalry attacks in glittering uniforms, the fatal shot always straight through the heart, the entire campaign a resounding march of victory— "We'll be home at Christmas," the recruits shouted laughingly to their mothers in August of 1914. Who in the villages and the cities of Austria remembered "real" war? A few ancients at best, who in 1866 had fought against Prussia, which was now their ally. But what a quick, bloodless far-off war that had been, a campaign that had ended in three weeks with few victims

and before it had well started! A rapid excursion into the romantic, a wild, manly adventure— that is how the war of 1914 was painted in the imagination of the simple man, and the young people were honestly afraid that they might miss this most wonderful and exciting experience of their lives; that is why they hurried and thronged to the colors, and that is why they shouted and sang in the trains that carried them to the slaughter; wildly and feverishly the red wave of blood coursed through the veins of the entire nation.

Philipp Scheidemann
BERLIN: "THE HOUR WE YEARNED FOR"

Philipp Scheidemann (1865–1939), one of the founding fathers of the Weimar Republic, described Berlin's martial mood in his memoirs, published in 1929.

At express speed I had returned to Berlin. Everywhere a word could be heard the conversation was of war and rumours of war. There was only one topic of conversation—war. The supporters of war seemed to be in a great majority. Were these pugnacious fellows, young and old, bereft of their senses? Were they so ignorant of the horrors of war? . . . Vast crowds of demonstrators paraded. . . . Schoolboys and students were there in their thousands; their bearded seniors, with their Iron Crosses of 1870–71 on their breasts, were there too in huge numbers.

Treitschke and Bernhardi[1] (to say nothing of the National Liberal beer-swilling heroes) seemed to have multiplied a thousandfold. Patriotic demonstrations had an intoxicating effect and excited the war-mongers to excess. "A call like the voice of thunder." Cheers! "In triumph we will smite

France to the ground." "All hail to thee in victor's crown." Cheers! Hurrah!

The counter-demonstrations immediately organized by the Berlin Social Democrats were imposing, and certainly more disciplined than the Jingo [extremely nationalistic] processions, but could not outdo the shouts of the fire-eaters. "Good luck to him who cares for truth and right. Stand firmly round the flag." "Long live peace!" "Socialists, close up your ranks." The Socialist International cheer. The patriots were sometimes silenced by the Proletarians; then they came out on top again. This choral contest . . . went on for days.

"It is the hour we yearned for—our friends know that," so the Pan-German[2] papers shouted, that had for years been shouting for war.

---

[1]Both Heinrich von Treitschke and General von Bernhardi glorified war (see pages 277–278).

[2]The Pan-German League, whose membership included professors, schoolteachers, journalists, lawyers, and aristocrats, spread nationalist and racial theories and glorified war as an expression of national vitality (see page 216).

The *Post*, conducted by von Stumm, the Independent Conservative leader and big Industrial, had thus moaned in all its columns in 1900, at the fortieth celebration of the Franco-German War: "Another forty years of peace would be a national misfortune for Germany." Now these firebrands saw the seeds they had planted ripening. Perhaps in the heads of many who had been called upon to make every effort to keep the peace Bernhardi's words, that "the preservation of peace can and never shall be the aim of politics," had done mischief. These words are infernally like the secret instructions given by Baron von Holstein to the German delegates to the first Peace Conference at The Hague:

"For the State there is no higher aim than the preservation of its own interests; among the Great Powers these will not necessarily coincide with the maintenance of peace, but rather with the hostile policy of enemies and rivals."

Bertrand Russell
LONDON: "AVERAGE MEN AND WOMEN WERE DELIGHTED AT THE PROSPECT OF WAR"

Bertrand Russell (1872–1970), the distinguished mathematician and philosopher, was dismayed by the war fever that gripped English men and women. During the war Russell was fined and imprisoned for his pacifistic activities. The following account is from his autobiography published in 1968.

During the hot days at the end of July, I was at Cambridge, discussing the situation with all and sundry. I found it impossible to believe that Europe would be so mad as to plunge into war, but I was persuaded that, if there was war, England would be involved. I felt strongly that England ought to remain neutral, and I collected the signatures of a large number of professors and Fellows to a statement which appeared in the *Manchester Guardian* to that effect. The day war was declared, almost all of them changed their minds. . . . I spent the evening walking round the streets, especially in the neighbourhood of Trafalgar Square, noticing cheering crowds, and making myself sensitive to the emotions of passers-by. During this and the following days I discovered to my amazement that average men and women were delighted at the prospect of war. I had fondly imagined what most pacifists contended, that wars were forced upon a reluctant population by despotic and Machiavellian governments. . . .

The first days of the war were to me utterly amazing. My best friends, such as the Whiteheads, were savagely warlike. Men like J. L. Hammond, who had been writing for years against participation in a European war, were swept off their feet by [Germany's invasion of] Belgium.

Meanwhile, I was living at the highest possible emotional tension. Although I did not foresee anything like the full disaster of the war, I foresaw a great deal more than most people did. The prospect filled me with horror, but what filled me with even more horror was the fact that the anticipation of carnage was delightful to something like ninety per cent of the population. I had to revise my views on human nature. At that time I was wholly ignorant of psychoanalysis, but I arrived for myself at a view of human passions not unlike that of the psychoanalysts. I arrived at this view in an endeavour to understand popular feeling about the War. I had supposed until that time that it was quite common for parents to love their children, but the War persuaded me that it is a rare exception. I had supposed that most people liked money better than almost anything else, but I discovered that they like destruction even better. I had supposed that intellectuals frequently loved truth, but I found here again that not ten per cent of them prefer truth to popularity. . . .

. . . As a lover of truth, the national propaganda of all the belligerent nations sickened me. As a lover of civilization, the return to barbarism appalled me. As a man of thwarted parental feeling, the massacre of the young wrung my heart. I hardly supposed that much good would come of opposing the War, but I felt that for the honour of human nature those who were not swept off their feet should show that they stood firm.

On August 15, 1914, the London *Nation* published a letter written by Russell, part of which follows.

. . . Those who saw the London crowds, during the nights leading up to the Declaration of War saw a whole population, hitherto peaceable and humane, precipitated in a few days down the steep slope to primitive barbarism, letting loose, in a moment, the instincts of hatred and blood lust against which the whole fabric of society has been raised. "Patriots" in all countries acclaim this brutal orgy as a noble determination to vindicate the right; reason and mercy are swept away in one great flood of hatred; dim abstractions of unimaginable wickedness—Germany to us and the French, Russia to the Germans—conceal the simple fact that the enemy are men, like ourselves, neither better nor worse—men who love their homes and the sunshine, and all the simple pleasures of common lives.

REVIEW QUESTIONS

1. Why was war welcomed as a positive event by so many different peoples?
2. Do you think human beings are aggressive by nature? Explain your answer.
3. Why did the events of July and August 1914 cause Bertrand Russell to revise his views of human nature? Do you agree with his assessment?

4 Trench Warfare

In 1914 the young men of European nations marched off to war believing that they were embarking on a glorious and chivalrous adventure. They were eager to serve their country, to demonstrate personal valor, and to experience life at its most intense moments. But in the trenches, where unseen enemies fired machine guns and artillery that killed indiscriminately and relentlessly, this romantic illusion about combat disintegrated.

Erich Maria Remarque
ALL QUIET ON THE WESTERN FRONT

The following reading is taken from Erich Maria Remarque's novel *All Quiet on the Western Front* (1929), the most famous literary work to emerge from World War I. A veteran of the trenches himself, Remarque (1898–1970) graphically described the slaughter that robbed Europe of its young men. His narrator is a young German soldier.

We wake up in the middle of the night. The earth booms. Heavy fire is falling on us. We crouch into corners. We distinguish shells of every calibre.

Each man lays hold of his things and looks again every minute to reassure himself that they are still there. The dug-out heaves, the night roars and flashes. We look at each other in the momentary flashes of light, and with pale faces and pressed lips shake our heads.

Every man is aware of the heavy shells tearing down the parapet, rooting up the embankment and demolishing the upper layers of concrete. When a shell lands in the trench we note how the hollow, furious blast is like a blow from the paw of a raging beast of prey. Already by morning a few of the recruits are green and vomiting. They are too inexperienced. . . .

The bombardment does not diminish. It is falling in the rear too. As far as one can see spout fountains of mud and iron. A wide belt is being raked.

The attack does not come, but the bombardment continues. We are gradually benumbed. Hardly a man speaks. We cannot make ourselves understood.

Our trench is almost gone. At many places it is only eighteen inches high, it is broken by holes, and craters, and mountains of earth. A shell lands square in front of our post. At once it is dark. We are buried and must dig ourselves out. . . .

Towards morning, while it is still dark, there is some excitement. Through the entrance rushes in a swarm of fleeing rats that try to storm the walls. Torches light up the confusion. Everyone yells and curses and slaughters.

The madness and despair of many hours unloads itself in this outburst. Faces are distorted, arms strike out, the beasts scream; we just stop in time to avoid attacking one another. . . .

Suddenly it howls and flashes terrifically, the dug-out cracks in all its joints under a direct hit, fortunately only a light one that the concrete blocks are able to withstand. It rings metallically, the walls reel, rifles, helmets, earth, mud, and dust fly everywhere. Sulphur fumes pour in.

If we were in one of those light dug-outs that they have been building lately instead of this deeper one, none of us would be alive.

But the effect is bad enough even so. The recruit starts to rave again and two others follow suit. One jumps up and rushes out, we have trouble with the other two. I start after the one who escapes and wonder whether to shoot him in the leg—then it shrieks again, I fling myself down and when I stand up the wall of the trench is plastered with smoking splinters, lumps of flesh, and bits of uniform. I scramble back.

The first recruit seems actually to have gone insane. He butts his head against the wall like a goat. We must try to-night to take him to the rear. Meanwhile we bind him, but in such a way that in case of attack he can be released at once. . . .

Suddenly the nearer explosions cease. The shelling continues but it has lifted and falls behind us, our trench is free. We seize the hand-grenades, pitch them out in front of the dug-out and jump after them. The bombardment has stopped and a heavy barrage now falls behind us. The attack has come.

No one would believe that in this howling waste there could still be men; but steel helmets now appear on all sides out of the trench, and fifty yards from us a machine-gun is already in position and barking.

The wire entanglements are torn to pieces. Yet they offer some obstacle. We see the storm-troops coming. Our artillery opens fire. Machine-guns rattle, rifles crack. The charge works its way across. Haie and Kropp begin with the hand-grenades. They throw as fast as they can, others pass them, the handles with the strings already pulled. Haie throws seventy-five yards, Kropp sixty, it has been measured, the distance is important. The enemy as they run cannot do much before they are within forty yards.

We recognize the smooth distorted faces, the helmets: they are French. They have already suffered heavily when they reach the remnants of the barbed wire entanglements. A whole line has gone down before our machine-guns; then we have a lot of stoppages and they come nearer.

I see one of them, his face upturned, fall into a wire cradle. His body collapses, his hands remain suspended as though he were praying. Then his body drops clean away and only his hands with the stumps of his arms, shot off, now hang in the wire.

The moment we are about to retreat three faces rise up from the ground in front of us. Under one of the helmets a dark pointed beard and two eyes that are fastened on me. I raise my hand, but I cannot throw into those strange eyes; for one mad moment the whole slaughter whirls like a circus round me, and these two eyes alone are motionless; then the head rises up, a hand, a movement, and my hand-grenade flies through the air and into him.

We make for the rear, pull wire cradles into the trench and leave bombs behind us with the strings pulled, which ensures us a fiery retreat. The machine-guns are already firing from the next position.

We have become wild beasts. We do not fight, we defend ourselves against annihilation. It is not against men that we fling our bombs,

what do we know of men in this moment when Death is hunting us down—now, for the first time in three days we can see his face, now for the first time in three days we can oppose him; we feel a mad anger. No longer do we lie helpless, waiting on the scaffold, we can destroy and kill, to save ourselves, to save ourselves and to be revenged.

We crouch behind every corner, behind every barrier of barbed wire, and hurl heaps of explosives at the feet of the advancing enemy before we run. The blast of the hand-grenades impinges powerfully on our arms and legs; crouching like cats we run on, overwhelmed by this wave that bears us along, that fills us with ferocity, turns us into thugs, into murderers, into God only knows what devils; this wave that multiplies our strength with fear and madness and greed of life, seeking and fighting for nothing but our deliverance. If your own father came over with them you would not hesitate to fling a bomb at him.

The forward trenches have been abandoned. Are they still trenches? They are blown to pieces, annihilated—there are only broken bits of trenches, holes linked by cracks, nests of craters, that is all. But the enemy's casualties increase. They did not count on so much resistance.

———

It is nearly noon. The sun blazes hotly, the sweat stings in our eyes, we wipe it off on our sleeves and often blood with it. At last we reach a trench that is in a somewhat better condition. It is manned and ready for the counter-attack, it receives us. Our guns open in full blast and cut off the enemy attack.

The lines behind us stop. They can advance no farther. The attack is crushed by our artillery. We watch. The fire lifts a hundred yards and we break forward. Beside me a lance-corporal has his head torn off. He runs a few steps more while the blood spouts from his neck like a fountain.

It does not come quite to hand-to-hand fighting; they are driven back. We arrive once again at our shattered trench and pass on beyond it. . . .

We have lost all feeling for one another. We can hardly control ourselves when our glance lights on the form of some other man. We are insensible, dead men, who through some trick, some dreadful magic, are still able to run and to kill.

A young Frenchman lags behind, he is overtaken, he puts up his hands, in one he still holds his revolver—does he mean to shoot or to give himself up!—a blow from a spade cleaves through his face. A second sees it and tries to run farther; a bayonet jabs into his back. He leaps in the air, his arms thrown wide, his mouth wide open, yelling; he staggers, in his back the bayonet quivers. A third throws away his rifle, cowers down with his hands before his eyes. He is left behind with a few other prisoners to carry off the wounded.

Suddenly in the pursuit we reach the enemy line.

We are so close on the heels of our retreating enemies that we reach it almost at the same time as they. In this way we suffer few casualties. A machine-gun barks, but is silenced with a bomb. Nevertheless, the couple of seconds has sufficed to give us five stomach wounds. With the butt of his rifle Kat smashes to pulp the face of one of the unwounded machine-gunners. We bayonet the others before they have time to get out their bombs. Then thirstily we drink the water they have for cooling the gun.

Everywhere wire-cutters are snapping, planks are thrown across the entanglements, we jump through the narrow entrances into the trenches. Haie strikes his spade into the neck of a gigantic Frenchman and throws the first hand-grenade; we duck behind a breastwork for a few seconds, then the straight bit of trench ahead of us is empty. The next throw whizzes obliquely over the corner and clears a passage; as we run past we toss handfuls down into the dug-outs, the earth shudders, it crashes, smokes and groans, we stumble over slippery lumps of flesh, over yielding bodies; I fall into an open belly on which lies a clean, new officer's cap.

The fight ceases. We lose touch with the enemy. We cannot stay here long but must retire under cover of our artillery to our own position. No sooner do we know this than we dive into the nearest dug-outs, and with the utmost haste seize on whatever provisions we can see, especially the tins of corned beef and butter, before we clear out.

We get back pretty well. There is no further attack by the enemy. We lie for an hour panting and resting before anyone speaks. We are so completely played out that in spite of our great hunger we do not think of the provisions. Then gradually we become something like men again.

Siegfried Sassoon
"BASE DETAILS"

Front-line soldiers often looked with contempt on generals who, from a safe distance, ordered massive assaults against enemy lines protected by barbed wire and machine guns. Such attacks could cost the lives of tens of thousands of soldiers in just a few days. Siegfried Sassoon (1886–1967), a British poet who served at the front for much of the war and earned a Military Cross for bravery, showed his disdain for coldhearted officers in the following poem, composed in 1917.

If I were fierce, and bald, and short of breath,
   I'd live with scarlet Majors at the Base,
And speed glum heroes up the line to death.
    You'd see me with my puffy petulant face,
Guzzling and gulping in the best hotel,
    Reading the Roll of Honour. "Poor young
      chap,"

I'd say—"I used to know his father well;
   Yes, we've lost heavily in this last
   scrap."
And when the war is done and youth stone
   dead,
I'd toddle safely home and die—in bed.

Wilfred Owen
"DISABLED"

Wilfred Owen (1893–1918), another British poet, volunteered for duty in 1915. At the Battle of the Somme he sustained shell shock, and he was sent to a hospital in Britain. In 1918 he returned to the front and was awarded the Military Cross; he died one week before the Armistice. In the following poem, "Disabled," Owen portrays the enduring misery of war.

He sat in a wheeled chair, waiting for dark,
And shivered in his ghastly suit of gray,
Legless, sewn short at elbow. Through the park
Voices of boys rang saddening like a hymn,
Voices of play and pleasure after day,
Till gathering sleep mothered them from him.

About this time Town used to swing so gay
When glow-lamps budded in the light blue trees,
And girls glanced lovelier as the air grew dim,—
In the old times, before he threw away his
   knees. . . .

He asked to join. He didn't have to beg;
Smiling they wrote his lie: aged nineteen years.
Germans he scarcely thought of; all their guilt,
And Austria's, did not move him. And no fears
Of Fear came yet. He thought of jeweled hilts

For daggers in plaid socks; of smart salutes;
And care of arms; and leave; and pay arrears;
Esprit de corps,[1] and hints for young recruits.
And soon, he was drafted out with drums
   and cheers. . . .

Now, he will spend a few sick years in
   Institutes,
And do what things the rules consider wise,
And take whatever pity they may dole.
Tonight he noticed how the women's eyes
Passed from him to the strong men that were
   whole.
How cold and late it is! Why don't they come
And put him into bed? Why don't they come?

---

[1]*Esprit de corps*: group spirit.

REVIEW QUESTIONS

1. In Erich Maria Remarque's account, how did the soldiers in the trenches react to artillery bombardment?
2. What ordeal did the attacking soldiers encounter as they neared the enemy trenches?
3. What were the feelings of the soldiers as they engaged the attackers?
4. Which line(s) in either Siegfried Sassoon or Wilfred Owen's poem do you consider the most powerful?

5 Women at War

In order to release men for military service, women in England, France, and Germany responded to their countries' wartime needs and replaced men in all branches of civilian life. They took jobs in munitions factories, worked on farms, were trained for commercial work and in the nursing service. They drove ambulances, mail trucks, and buses. They worked as laboratory assistants, plumbers' helpers, and bank clerks. By performing effectively in jobs formerly occupied by men, women demonstrated that they had an essential role to play in their countries' economic life. By the end of the war, little opposition remained to granting women political rights.

Naomi Loughnan
GENTEEL WOMEN IN THE FACTORIES

Naomi Loughnan was one of millions of women who replaced men in all branches of civilian life, in allied and enemy countries alike, during World War I. She was a young, upper-middle-class woman who lived with her family in London and had never had to work for her living. In her job in a munitions plant, she had to adjust to close association with women from the London slums, to hostel life, and to twelve-hour shifts doing heavy and sometimes dangerous work. The chief motivation for British women of her class was their desire to aid the war effort, not the opportunity to earn substantial wages.

We little thought when we first put on our overalls and caps and enlisted in the Munition Army how much more inspiring our life was to be than we had dared to hope. Though we munition workers sacrifice our ease we gain a life worth living. Our long days are filled with interest, and with the zest of doing work for our country in the grand cause of Freedom. As we handle the weapons of war we are learning great lessons of life. In the busy, noisy workshops we come face to face with every kind of class, and each one of these classes has something to learn from the others. Our muscles may be aching, and the brightness fading a little from our eyes, but our minds are expanding, our very souls are growing stronger. And excellent, too, is the discipline for our bodies, though we do not always recognize this. . . .

The day is long, the atmosphere is breathed and rebreathed, and the oil smells. Our hands are black with warm, thick oozings from the machines, which coat the work and, incidentally, the workers. We regard our horrible, begrimed members [limbs] with disgust and secret pride. . . .

. . . The genteel among us wear gloves. We vie with each other in finding the most up-to-date grease-removers, just as we used to vie about hats. Our hands are not alone in suffering from dirt. . . . [D]ust-clouds, filled with unwelcome life, find a resting-place in our lungs and noses.

The work is hard. It may be, perhaps, from sheer lifting and carrying and weighing, or merely because of those long dragging hours that keep us sitting on little stools in front of whirring, clattering machines that are all too easy to work. We wish sometimes they were not quite so "fool-proof," for monotony is painful.

Or life may appear hard to us by reason of those same creeping hours spent on our feet, up and down, to and fro, and up and down again, hour after hour, until something altogether queer takes place in the muscles of our legs. But we go on. . . . It is amazing what we can do when there is no way of escape but desertion. . . .

. . . The first thing that strikes the newcomer, as the shop door opens, is the great wall of noise that seems to rise and confront one like a tangible substance. The crashing, tearing, rattling whirr of machinery is deafening. And yet, though this may seem almost impossible, the workers get so accustomed to it after a little time that they do not notice it until it stops. . . .

The twelve-hour shift at night, though taking greater toll of nerve and energy, has distinct charms of its own. . . . The first hours seem to go more quickly than the corresponding ones on day work, until at last two o'clock is reached. Then begins a hand-to-hand struggle with Morpheus [Greek god of dreams]. . . . A stern sense of duty, growing feebler as the moments pass, is our only weapon of defence, whereas the crafty god has a veritable armoury of leaden eyelids, weakening pulses, sleep-weighted heads, and slackening wills. He even leads the foremen away to their offices and softens the hearts of languid over-lookers. Some of us succumb, but there are those among us who will not give in. An unbecoming greyness alters our faces, however young and fresh by day, a strange wilting process that steals all youth and beauty from us—until the morning. . . .

Engineering mankind is possessed of the unshakable opinion that no woman can have the mechanical sense. If one of us asks humbly why such and such an alteration is not made to prevent this or that drawback to a machine, she is told, with a superior smile, that a man has worked her machine before her for years, and that therefore if there were any improvement possible it would have been made. As long as we do exactly what we are told and do not attempt to use our brains, we give entire satisfaction, and are treated as nice, good children. Any swerving from the easy path prepared for us by our males

arouses the most scathing contempt in their manly bosoms. The exceptions are as delightful to meet as they are rare. Women have, however, proved that their entry into the munition world has increased the output. Employers who forget things personal in their patriotic desire for large results are enthusiastic over the success of women in the shops. But their workmen have to be handled with the utmost tenderness and caution lest they should actually imagine it was being suggested that women could do their work equally well, given equal conditions of training—at least where muscle is not the driving force. This undercurrent of jealousy rises to the surface rather often, but as a general rule the men behave with much kindness, and are ready to help with muscle and advice whenever called upon. If eyes are very bright and hair inclined to curl, the muscle and advice do not even wait for a call.

The coming of the mixed classes of women into the factory is slowly but surely having an educative effect upon the men. "Language" is almost unconsciously becoming subdued. There are fiery exceptions who make our hair stand up on end under our close-fitting caps, but a sharp rebuke or a look of horror will often [straighten out] the most truculent. He will at the moment, perhaps, sneer at the "blooming milksop fools of women," but he will be more careful next time. It is grievous to hear the girls also swearing and using disgusting language. Shoulder to shoulder with the children of the slums, the upper classes are having their eyes prised open at last to the awful conditions among which their sisters have dwelt. Foul language, immorality, and many other evils are but the natural outcome of overcrowding and bitter poverty. If some of us, still blind and ignorant of our responsibilities, shrink horrified and repelled from the rougher set, the compliment is returned with open derision and ribald laughter. There is something, too, about the prim prudery of the "genteel" that tickles the East-Ender's [a lower-class person] sharp wit. On the other hand, attempts at friendliness from the more understanding are treated with the utmost suspicion, though once that suspicion is overcome and friendship is established, it is unshakable. Our working hours are highly flavoured by our neighbours' treatment of ourselves and of each other. Laughter, anger, acute confusion, and laughter again, are constantly changing our immediate outlook on life. Sometimes disgust will overcome us, but we are learning with painful clarity that the fault is not theirs whose actions disgust us, but must be placed to the discredit of those other classes who have allowed the continued existence of conditions which generate the things from which we shrink appalled. . . .

Whatever sacrifice we make of wearied bodies, brains dulled by interminable night-shifts, of roughened hands, and faces robbed of their soft curves, it is, after all, so small a thing. We live in safety, we have shelter, and food whenever necessary, and we are even earning quite a lot of money. What is ours beside the great sacrifice? Men in their prime, on the verge of ambition realized, surrounded by the benefits won by their earlier struggles, are offering up their very lives. And those boys with Life, all glorious and untried, spread before them at their feet, are turning a smiling face to Death.

Magda Trott
OPPOSITION TO FEMALE EMPLOYMENT

In the second year of the war a German woman described the hostility faced by women in the work force.

With the outbreak of war men were drawn away from the management of numerous organizations and, gradually, the lack of experienced personnel made itself felt. Women working in offices were therefore urged not to waste the opportunities offered them by the war, and to continue their education so that they would be prepared to take on the position once held by a male colleague, should the occasion arise.

Such occasions have indeed arisen much sooner than anticipated. The demand for educated women has risen phenomenally during the six months since the war began. Women have been employed in banks, in large commercial businesses, in urban offices—everywhere, in fact, where up till now only men had been employed. They are to be tested in order to see whether they can perform with equal success.

All those who were certain that women would be completely successful substitutes for men were painfully disappointed to discover that many women who had worked for years in a firm and were invited to step up to a higher level,

now that the men were absent, suddenly handed in their resignations. An enquiry revealed that, especially in recent days, these notices were coming with great frequency and, strange as it may seem, applied mostly to women who had been working in the same company from four to seven years and had now been offered a better and even better-paid job. They said "no" and since there was no possibility for them to remain in their old jobs, they resigned.

The enemies of women's employment were delighted. Here was their proof that women are incapable of holding down responsible positions. Female workers were quite successful as clerks, stenographers, and typists, in fact, in all those positions that require no independent activity—but as soon as more serious duties were demanded of them, they failed.

Naturally, we enquired of these women why they had given up so quickly, and then the truth of the matter became plain. All women were quite ready, if with some trepidation, to accept the new positions, particularly since the boss made it clear that one of the gentlemen would carefully explain the new assignments to them. Certainly the work was almost entirely new to the young ladies since till now they had only been concerned with their stenography, their books, and so forth. However, they entered their new duties with enthusiasm.

But even on the first day it was noticeable that not everything would proceed as had been supposed. Male colleagues looked askance at the "intruder" who dared to usurp the position and bread of a colleague now fighting for the Fatherland, and who would, it was fervently hoped, return in good health. Moreover, the lady who came as a substitute received exactly half of the salary of the gentleman colleague who had previously occupied the same position. A dangerous implication, since if the lady made good, the boss might continue to draw on female personnel; the saving on salaries would clearly be substantial. It became essential to use all means to show the boss that female help was no substitute for men's work, and a united male front was organized.

It was hardly surprising that all the lady's questions were answered quite vaguely. If she asked again or even a third time, irritated remarks were passed concerning her inadequacy in comprehension, and very soon the male teacher lost patience. Naturally, most of his colleagues supported him and the lady found it difficult, if not impossible, to receive any instruction and was finally forced to resign.

This is what happened in most known cases. We must, however, also admit that occasionally the fault does lie with the lady, who simply did not have sufficient preparation to fill a difficult position. There may be male colleagues who would gladly share information with women; however, these women are unable to understand, because they have too little business experience. In order to prevent this sort of thing, we would counsel all women who are seeking a position in which they hope to advance, to educate themselves as much as possible. All those women who were forced to leave their jobs of long standing might not have been obliged to do so, had they been more concerned in previous years with understanding the overall nature of the business in which they were employed. Their colleagues would surely and generously have answered their questions and given them valuable advice, which would have offered them an overview and thereby avoided the total ignorance with which they entered these advanced positions when they were offered. At least they would have had an inkling and saved themselves the questions that betrayed their great ignorance to their colleagues. They might even have found their way through all the confusion and succeeded in the new position.

Therefore, once again: all you women who want to advance yourselves and create an independent existence, use this time of war as a learning experience and keep your eyes open.

REVIEW QUESTIONS

1. How was Naomi Loughnan's life transformed by her job as a munitions worker?
2. What insights into gender and class distinctions at the time of World War I does Loughnan provide?
3. Why, according to Magda Trott, did German women have difficulty gaining acceptance in the work force?

6 The Paris Peace Conference

The most terrible war the world had experienced ended in November 1918; in January 1919, representatives of the victorious powers assembled in Paris to draw up a peace settlement. The principal figures at the Paris Peace Conference were Woodrow Wilson (1856–1924), president of the United States; David Lloyd George (1863–1945), prime minister of Great Britain; Georges Clemenceau (1841–1929), premier of France; and Vittorio Orlando (1860–1952), premier of Italy. Disillusioned intellectuals and the war-weary masses turned to Wilson as the prince of peace who would fashion a new and better world.

Woodrow Wilson
THE IDEALISTIC VIEW

Wilson sought a peace of justice and reconciliation, one based on democratic and Christian ideals, as the following excerpts from his speeches illustrate.

(May 26, 1917)

We are fighting for the liberty, the self-government, and the undictated development of all peoples, and every feature of the settlement that concludes this war must be conceived and executed for that purpose. Wrongs must first be righted and then adequate safeguards must be created to prevent their being committed again. . . .

. . . No people must be forced under sovereignty under which it does not wish to live. No territory must change hands except for the purpose of securing those who inhabit it a fair chance of life and liberty. No indemnities must be insisted on except those that constitute payment for manifest wrongs done. No readjustments of power must be made except such as will tend to secure the future peace of the world and the future welfare and happiness of its peoples.

And then the free peoples of the world must draw together in some common covenant, some genuine and practical co-öperation that will in effect combine their force to secure peace and justice in the dealings of nations with one another.

The following are excerpts from the Fourteen Points, the plan for peace that Wilson announced on January 8, 1918.

IV. Adequate guarantees given and taken that national armaments will be reduced to the lowest point consistent with domestic safety.

V. A free, open-minded, and absolutely impartial adjustment of all colonial claims, based upon a strict observance of the principle that in determining all such questions of sovereignty the interests of the populations concerned must have equal weight with the equitable claims of the government whose title is to be determined. . . .

VIII. All French territory should be freed and the invaded portions restored, and the wrong done to France by Prussia in 1871 in the matter of Alsace-Lorraine, which has unsettled the peace of the world for nearly fifty years, should be righted, in order that peace may once more be made secure in the interest of all.

IX. A readjustment of the frontiers of Italy should be effected along clearly recognizable lines of nationality.

X. The peoples of Austria-Hungary, whose place among the nations we wish to see safeguarded and assured, should be accorded the freest opportunity of autonomous development. . . .

XII. The Turkish portions of the present Ottoman Empire should be assured a secure sovereignty, but the other nationalities which are now under Turkish rule should be assured an undoubted security of life and an absolutely unmolested opportunity of autonomous development, and the Dardanelles should be permanently opened as a free passage to the ships and commerce of all nations under international guarantees.

XIII. An independent Polish state should be erected which should include the territories inhabited by indisputably Polish populations, which should be assured a free and secure access to the sea, and whose political and economic independence and territorial integrity should be guaranteed by international covenant.

XIV. A general association of nations must be formed under specific covenants for the purpose of affording mutual guarantees of political independence and territorial integrity to great and small states alike.

————

(February 11, 1918)

. . . The principles to be applied [in the peace settlement] are these:

First, that each part of the final settlement must be based upon the essential justice of that particular case and upon such adjustments as are most likely to bring a peace that will be permanent;

Second, that peoples and provinces are not to be bartered about from sovereignty to sovereignty as if they were mere chattels and pawns in a game, even the great game, now forever discredited, of the balance of power; but that

Third, every territorial settlement involved in this war must be made in the interest and for the benefit of the populations concerned, and not as a part of any mere adjustment or compromise of claims amongst rival states; and

Fourth, that all well-defined national aspiration shall be accorded the utmost satisfaction that can be accorded them without introducing new or perpetuating old elements of discord and antagonism that would be likely in time to break the peace of Europe and consequently of the world.

————

(April 6, 1918)

. . . We are ready, whenever the final reckoning is made, to be just to the German people, deal fairly with the German power, as with all others. There can be no difference between peoples in the final judgment, if it is indeed to be a righteous judgment. To propose anything but justice, even-handed and dispassionate justice, to Germany at any time, whatever the outcome of the war, would be to renounce and dishonor our own cause. For we ask nothing that we are not willing to accord.

————

(December 16, 1918)

. . . The war through which we have just passed has illustrated in a way which never can be forgotten the extraordinary wrongs which can be perpetrated by arbitrary and irresponsible power.

It is not possible to secure the happiness and prosperity of the world, to establish an enduring peace, unless the repetition of such wrongs is rendered impossible. This has indeed been a people's war. It has been waged against absolutism and militarism, and these enemies of liberty must from this time forth be shut out from the possibility of working their cruel will upon mankind.

————

(January 3, 1919)

. . . Our task at Paris is to organize the friendship of the world, to see to it that all the moral forces that make for right and justice and liberty are united and are given a vital organization to which the peoples of the world will readily and gladly respond. In other words, our task is no less colossal than this, to set up a new international psychology, to have a new atmosphere.

———

(January 25, 1919)

. . . We are . . . here to see that every people in the world shall choose its own masters and govern its own destinies, not as we wish, but as it wishes. We are here to see, in short, that the very foundations of this war are swept away.

Those foundations were the private choice of small coteries of civil rulers and military staffs. Those foundations were the aggression of great powers upon the small. Those foundations were the holding together of empires of unwilling subjects by the duress of arms. Those foundations were the power of small bodies of men to work their will upon mankind and use them as pawns in a game. And nothing less than the emancipation of the world from these things will accomplish peace.

Georges Clemenceau
FRENCH DEMANDS FOR SECURITY AND REVENGE

Wilson's promised new world clashed with French demands for security and revenge. Almost all the fighting on the war's Western Front had taken place in France; its industries and farmlands lay in ruins, and many of its young men had perished. France had been invaded by Germany in 1870 as well as in 1914, so the French believed that only by crippling Germany could they gain security. Premier Georges Clemenceau, who was called "the Tiger," dismissed Wilson's vision of a new world as mere noble sentiment divorced from reality, and he fought tenaciously to gain security for France. Clemenceau's profound hatred and mistrust of Germany are revealed in his book *Grandeur and Misery of Victory* (1930), written a decade after the Paris Peace Conference.

For the catastrophe of 1914 the Germans are responsible. Only a professional liar would deny this. . . .

What after all is this war, prepared, undertaken, and waged by the German people, who flung aside every scruple of conscience to let it loose, hoping for a peace of enslavement under the yoke of a militarism destructive of all human dignity? It is simply the continuance, the recrudescence, of those never-ending acts of violence by which the first savage tribes carried out their depredations with all the resources of barbarism. The means improve with the ages. The ends remain the same. . . .

Germany, in this matter, was unfortunate enough to allow herself (in spite of her skill at dissimulation) to be betrayed into an excess of candour by her characteristic tendency to go to extremes. *Deutschland über alles. Germany above everything!* That, and nothing less, is what she asks, and when once her demand is satisfied she will let you enjoy a peace under the yoke. Not only does she make no secret of her aim, but the intolerable arrogance of the German aristocracy, the servile good nature of the intellectual and the scholar, the gross vanity of the most competent leaders in industry, and the wide-spread influence of a violent popular poetry conspire to shatter throughout the world all the time-honoured traditions of individual, as well as international, dignity. . . .

On November 11, 1918, the fighting ceased.

It is not I who will dispute the German soldier's qualities of endurance. But he had been promised a *fresh and frolicsome war*, and for four years he had been pinned down between the anvil and the hammer. . . . Our defeat would have resulted in a relapse of human civilization into violence and bloodshed. . . .

Outrages against human civilization are in the long run defeated by their own excess, and thus I discern in the peculiar mentality of the German soldier, with his *"Deutschland über alles,"* the cause of the premature exhaustion that brought him to beg for an armistice before the French soldier, who was fighting for his independence. . . .

And what is this "Germanic civilization," this monstrous explosion of the will to power, which threatens openly to do away entirely with the diversities established by many evolutions, to set in their place the implacable mastery of a race whose lordly part would be to substitute itself, by force of arms, for all national developments? We need only read [General Friedrich von] Bernhardi's famous pamphlet *Our Future*, in which it is alleged that Germany sums up within herself, as the historian Treitschke asserts, the greatest manifestation of human supremacy, and finds herself condemned, by her very greatness, either to absorb all nations in herself or to return to nothingness. . . . Ought we not all to feel menaced in our very vitals by this mad doctrine of universal Germanic supremacy over England, France, America, and every other country? . . .

What document more suitable to reveal the direction of "German culture" than the famous manifesto of the ninety-three super-intellectuals of Germany,[1] issued to justify the bloodiest and the least excusable of military aggressions against the great centres of civilization? At the moment . . . violated Belgium lay beneath the heel of the malefactor (October 1914) . . . [and German troops were] razing . . . great historical buildings to the ground [and] burning

down . . . libraries. It would need a whole book to tell of the infamous treatment inflicted upon noncombatants, to reckon up those who were shot down, or put to death, or deported, or condemned to forced labour. . . .

Well, this was the hour chosen by German intellectuals to make themselves heard. Let all the nations give ear! . . .

. . . Their learning made of them merely Germans better than all others qualified to formulate, on their own account, the extravagances of Germanic arrogance. The only difference is that they speak louder than the common people, those docile automatons. The fact is that they really believe themselves to be the representatives of a privileged *"culture"* that sets them above the errors of the human race, and confers on them the prerogative of a superior power. . . .

The whole document is nothing but denials without the support of a single proof. *"It is not true* that Germany wanted the War." [Kaiser] William II had for years been *"mocked at by his adversaries of today on account of his unshakable love of peace."* They neglect to tell us whence they got this lie. They forget that from 1871 till 1914 we received from Germany a series of war threats in the course of which Queen Victoria and also the Czar had to intervene with the *Kaiser* direct for the maintenance of peace.

I have already recalled how our German intellectuals account for the violation of the Belgian frontier:

> It is not true that we criminally violated Belgian neutrality. It can be proved that France and England had made up their minds to violate it. It can be proved that Belgium was willing. It would have been suicide not to forestall them. . . .

. . . And when a great chemist such as Ostwald tells us, with his colleagues, that our struggle *"against the so-called German militarism"* is really directed *"against German culture,"* we must remember that *this same savant published a history of chemistry* IN WHICH THE NAME OF [eighteenth-century French chemist Antoine] LAVOISIER WAS NOT MENTIONED.

---

[1]Shortly after the outbreak of war, ninety-three leading German scholars and scientists addressed a letter to the world, defending Germany's actions.

The "intellectuals" take their place in public opinion as the most ardent propagandists of the thesis which makes Germany the very model of the *"chosen people."* The same Professor Ostwald had already written, *"Germany has reached a higher stage of civilization than the other peoples, and the result of the War will be an organization of Europe under German leadership."* Professor Haeckel had demanded *the conquest of London, the division of Belgium between Germany and Holland, the annexation of North-east France, of Poland, the Baltic Provinces, the Congo, and a great part of the English colonies.* Professor Lasson went further still:

> We are morally and intellectually superior to all men. We are peerless. So too are our organizations and our institutions. *Germany is the most perfect creation known in history,* and the Imperial Chancellor, Herr von Bethmann-Hollweg, is *the most eminent of living men.*

Ordinary laymen who talked in this strain would be taken off to some safe asylum. Coming from duly hallmarked professors, such statements explain all German warfare by alleging that Germany's destiny is universal domination, and that for this very reason she is bound either to disappear altogether or to exercise violence on all nations with a view to their own betterment....

May I further recall, since we have to emphasize the point, that on September 17, 1914, Erzberger, the well-known German statesman, an eminent member of the Catholic Party, wrote to the Minister of War, General von Falkenhayn,

"We must not worry about committing an offence against the rights of nations nor about violating the laws of humanity. Such feelings today are of secondary importance." A month later, on October 21, 1914, he wrote in *Der Tag*, *"If a way was found of entirely wiping out the whole of London it would be more humane to employ it* than to allow the blood of A SINGLE GERMAN SOLDIER to be shed on the battlefield!"....

... General von Bernhardi himself, the best pupil, as I have already said, of the historian Treitschke, whose ideas are law in Germany, has just preached the doctrine of "World power or Downfall" at us. So there is nothing left for other nations, as a way of salvation, but to be conquered by Germany....

I have sometimes penetrated into the sacred cave of the Germanic cult, which is, as every one knows, the *Bierhaus* [beer hall]. A great aisle of massive humanity where there accumulate, amid the fumes of tobacco and beer, the popular rumblings of a nationalism upheld by the sonorous brasses blaring to the heavens the supreme voice of Germany, *"Deutschland über alles!"* Men, women, and children, all petrified in reverence before the divine stoneware pot, brows furrowed with irrepressible power, eyes lost in a dream of infinity, mouths twisted by the intensity of will-power, drink in long draughts the celestial hope of vague expectations. These only remain to be realized presently when the chief marked out by Destiny shall have given the word. There you have the ultimate framework of an old but childish race.

REVIEW QUESTIONS

1. What principles did Woodrow Wilson want to serve as the basis of the peace settlement?
2. According to Wilson, what were the principal reasons for the outbreak of war in 1914?
3. What accusations did Georges Clemenceau make against the German national character? What contrasts did he draw between the Germans and the French?
4. How did Clemenceau respond to the manifesto of the German intellectuals?
5. Why, more than a decade after the war, did Clemenceau believe that Germany should still be feared?

7   The Bolshevik Revolution

In March 1917, in the middle of World War I, Russians were demoralized. The army, poorly trained, inadequately equipped, and incompetently led, had suffered staggering losses; everywhere soldiers were deserting. Food shortages and low wages drove workers to desperation; the loss of fathers and sons at the front embittered peasants. Discontent was keenest in Petrograd, where on March 9, two hundred thousand striking workers shouting "Down with autocracy!" packed the streets. After some bloodshed, government troops refused to fire on them. Faced with a broad and debilitating crisis—violence and anarchy in the capital, breakdown of transport, uncertain food and fuel supplies, and general disorder—Tsar Nicholas II was forced to turn over authority to a provisional government, thereby ending three centuries of tsarist rule under the Romanov dynasty.

The Provisional Government, after July 1917 guided by Aleksandr Kerensky (1881–1970), sought to transform Russia into a Western-style liberal state, but the government failed to comprehend the urgency with which the Russian peasants wanted the landlords' land, and soldiers and the masses wanted peace. Resentment spiraled. Kerensky's increasing unpopularity and the magnitude of popular unrest seemed to the Bolsheviks' leader, Vladimir Ilyich Lenin (1870–1924), then in hiding, to offer the long-expected opportunity for the Bolsheviks to seize power and bring about a socialist revolution.

Army Intelligence Report
THE BREAKDOWN OF MILITARY DISCIPLINE

By the summer of 1917 demoralized Russian soldiers were deserting in large numbers. The following excerpts, drawn from an army intelligence report of October 1917, reveal the breakdown in military discipline.

Northern front.—The situation in the army has not changed and may be described as a complete lack of confidence in the officers and the higher commanding personnel. The belief is growing among the soldiers that they cannot be punished for what they do. . . . The influence of Bolshevik ideas is spreading very rapidly. To this must be added a general weariness, an irritability, and a desire for peace at any price.

Any attempt on the part of the officers to regulate the life of the army . . . is looked upon by the soldiers as counter-revolution. . . .

. . . Considerable numbers of soldiers . . . feigning sickness are leaving the front for the hospital. . . .

12th Army.— . . . The press of the political parties is no longer influencing the soldier masses. Again and again one hears the orders of the Provisional Government severely criticized.

The committee of the 95th Regiment . . . declared Kerensky a traitor. . . .

Apart from the Bolshevik not a single [political] movement has any popularity. Those who read moderate newspapers are looked upon as [followers of the] "bourgeoisie" and "counter-revolutionists." An intensive agitation is being conducted in favor of an immediate cessation of military operations on all fronts. Whenever a whole regiment or battalion refuses to carry out a military order, the fact is immediately made known to other parts of the army through special agitators. . . .

Western front. — . . . Because of general war weariness, bad nourishment, mistrust of officers, etc., there has developed an intense defeatist agitation accompanied by refusals to carry out orders, threats to the commanding personnel, and attempts to fraternize with Germans. Everywhere one hears voices calling for immediate peace, because, they say, no one will stay in the trenches during the winter. . . . There is a deep-rooted conviction among the rank and file that fraternization with the enemy is a sure way of attaining peace. . . .

[Bolshevik] newspapers . . . openly advocate the immediate cessation of war, the transfer of political and military power to the proletariat, the immediate socialization of land, and a merciless struggle against capitalists and the bourgeoisie. Their method of argument is quite simple and comprehensible to the masses. It runs as follows: All the ministers of the Provisional Government are subservient to the bourgeoisie and are counter-revolutionists; they continue to wage war to please the Allied and the Russian capitalists; the government introduced the death penalty with the view of exterminating the soldiers, workers, and peasants. . . .

Among the phenomena indicative of tendencies in the life in the rear of the Western front are the recent disturbances at the replacement depot in Gomel. On October 1 over eight thousand soldiers who were to be transferred to the front demanded to be sent home instead. . . . Incited by agitators they stormed the armory, took some fifteen hundred suits of winter equipment, and assaulted the Assistant Commissar and a member of the front committee. Similar events . . . have taken place in Smolensk. . . .

Southwestern front. — . . . Defeatist agitation is increasing and the disintegration of the army is in full swing. The Bolshevik wave is growing steadily, owing to general disintegration in the rear, the absence of strong power, and the lack of supplies and equipment. The dominant theme of conversation is peace at any price and under any condition. Every order, no matter what its source, is met with hostility. . . .

The guard-cavalry corps of the 2d Army passed a resolution of no confidence in the majority of officers. The soldiers are engaging in organized armed invasions of the surrounding country estates, plundering provisions . . . of which there is a scarcity in the army. Not a thing can be done to counteract this restlessness . . . as there is no force which could be relied upon in any attempt to enforce order. The activity of the courts is paralyzed because of the hostile attitude of the soldiers. . . .

The following general conclusions may be drawn from the reports of the commissars: The approaching winter campaign has accelerated the disintegration of the army and increased the longing for peace. It is necessary to leave nothing undone which might supply the soldiers with food, shoes, and winter clothing; to see that the army is reduced in numbers; to improve the discipline in the reserve regiments. Otherwise the ranks will be filled with such material as will lead to the complete demoralization and destruction of the army. . . .

[The rest of the report deals with the Rumanian and Caucasian fronts, describing similar conditions.]

V. I. Lenin
THE CALL TO POWER

On November 6 (October 24 by the old-style calendar then in use in Russia),
Lenin urged immediate action, as the following document reveals.

. . . The situation is critical in the extreme. In fact it is now absolutely clear that to delay the uprising would be fatal.

With all my might I urge comrades to realise that everything now hangs by a thread; that we are confronted by problems which are not to be solved by conferences or congresses (even congresses of Soviets), but exclusively by peoples, by the masses, by the struggle of the armed people. The bourgeois onslaught of the Kornilovites [followers of General Kornilov, who tried to establish a military dictatorship] show that we must not wait. We must at all costs, this very evening, this very night, arrest the government, having first disarmed the officer cadets (defeating them, if they resist), and so on.

We must not wait! We may lose everything!

Who must take power?

That is not important at present. Let the Revolutionary Military Committee [Bolshevik organization working within the army and navy] do it, or "some other institution" which will declare that it will relinquish power only to the true representatives of the interests of the people, the interests of the army (the immediate proposal of peace), the interests of the peasants (the land to be taken immediately and private property abolished), the interests of the starving.

All districts, all regiments, all forces must be mobilised at once and must immediately send their delegations to the Revolutionary Military Committee and to the Central Committee of the Bolsheviks [governing organization of the Bolshevik party] with the insistent demand that under no circumstances should power be left in the hands of Kerensky and Co. . . . not under any circumstances; the matter must be decided without fail this very evening, or this very night.

History will not forgive revolutionaries for procrastinating when they could be victorious today (and they certainly will be victorious today), while they risk losing much tomorrow, in fact, they risk losing everything.

If we seize power today, we seize it not in opposition to the Soviets but on their behalf.

The seizure of power is the business of the uprising; its political purpose will become clear after the seizure. . . .

. . . It would be an infinite crime on the part of the revolutionaries were they to let the chance slip, knowing that the *salvation of the revolution*, the offer of peace, the salvation of Petrograd, salvation from famine, the transfer of the land to the peasants depend upon them.

The government is tottering. It must be *given the death-blow* at all costs.

To delay action is fatal.

REVIEW QUESTIONS

1. What caused the breakdown of military discipline in the Russian ranks in 1917?
2. What promises did V. I. Lenin hold out to his supporters should the revolution succeed?
3. How would you define, from the evidence here offered, a revolutionary situation? What factors create it?

8 The War and European Consciousness

World War I caused many intellectuals to have grave doubts about the Enlightenment tradition and the future of Western civilization. More than ever the belief in human goodness, reason, and the progress of humanity seemed an illusion. Despite its many accomplishments, intellectuals contended that Western civilization was flawed and perishable.

Paul Valéry
DISILLUSIONMENT

Shortly after World War I, Paul Valéry (1871–1945), a prominent French writer, expressed the mood of disillusion that gripped many intellectuals. The first reading was written in 1919; the second reading is from a 1922 speech. Both were published in *Variety*, a collection of some of Valéry's works.

We modern civilizations have learned to recognize that we are mortal like the others.

We had heard tell of whole worlds vanished, of empires foundered with all their men and all their engines, sunk to the inexplorable depths of the centuries with their gods and laws, their academies and their pure and applied sciences, their grammars, dictionaries, classics, romantics, symbolists, their critics and the critics of their critics. We knew that all the apparent earth is made of ashes, and that ashes have a meaning. We perceived, through the misty bulk of history, the phantoms of huge vessels once laden with riches and learning. We could not count them. But these wrecks, after all, were no concern of ours.

Elam, Nineveh, Babylon were vague and splendid names; the total ruin of these worlds, for us, meant as little as did their existence. But *France, England, Russia* . . . these names, too, are splendid. . . . And now we see that the abyss of history is deep enough to bury all the world. We feel that a civilization is fragile as a life. The circumstances which will send the works of [John] Keats [English poet] and the works of [Charles] Baudelaire [French poet] to join those

of Menander[1] are not at all inconceivable; they are found in the daily papers.

The following passage is from an address that Valéry delivered at the University of Zurich on November 15, 1922.

The storm has died away, and still we are restless, uneasy, as if the storm were about to break. Almost all the affairs of men remain in a terrible uncertainty. We think of what has disappeared, we are almost destroyed by what has been destroyed; we do not know what will be born, and we fear the future, not without reason. We hope vaguely, we dread precisely; our fears are infinitely more precise than our hopes; we confess that the charm of life is behind us, abundance is behind us, but doubt and disorder are in us and with us. There is no thinking man, however shrewd or learned he may be, who can hope to dominate this anxiety, to escape from

---

[1]Menander was an ancient Greek poet whose works were lost until fragments were found in Egypt at the end of the nineteenth century.

this impression of darkness, to measure the probable duration of this period when the vital relations of humanity are disturbed profoundly.

We are a very unfortunate generation, whose lot has been to see the moment of our passage through life coincide with the arrival of great and terrifying events, the echo of which will resound through all our lives.

One can say that all the fundamentals of the world have been affected by the war, or more exactly, by the circumstances of the war; something deeper has been worn away than the renewable parts of the machine. You know how greatly the general economic situation has been disturbed, and the polity of states, and the very life of the individual; you are familiar with the universal discomfort, hesitation, apprehension. *But among all these injured things is the Mind.* The Mind has indeed been cruelly wounded; its complaint is heard in the hearts of intellectual man; it passes a mournful judgment on itself. It doubts itself profoundly.

Erich Maria Remarque
THE LOST GENERATION

In Erich Maria Remarque's *All Quiet on the Western Front*, a wounded German soldier reflects on the war and his future. He sees himself as part of a lost generation. (See also page 289.)

Gradually a few of us are allowed to get up. And I am given crutches to hobble around on. But I do not make much use of them; I cannot bear Albert's gaze as I move about the room. His eyes always follow me with such a strange look. So I sometimes escape to the corridor;—there I can move about more freely.

On the next floor below are the abdominal and spine cases, head wounds and double amputations. On the right side of the wing are the jaw wounds, gas cases, nose, ear, and neck wounds. On the left the blind and the lung wounds, pelvis wounds, wounds in the joints, wounds in the kidneys, wounds in the testicles, wounds in the intestines. Here a man realizes for the first time in how many places a man can get hit.

Two fellows die of tetanus. Their skin turns pale, their limbs stiffen, at last only their eyes live—stubbornly. Many of the wounded have their shattered limbs hanging free in the air from a gallows; underneath the wound a basin is placed into which drips the pus. Every two or three hours the vessel is emptied. Other men lie in stretching bandages with heavy weights hanging from the end of the bed. I see intestine wounds that are constantly full of excreta. The surgeon's clerk shows me X-ray photographs of completely smashed hip-bones, knees, and shoulders.

A man cannot realize that above such shattered bodies there are still human faces in which life goes its daily round. And this is only one hospital, one single station; there are hundreds of thousands in Germany, hundreds of thousands in France, hundreds of thousands in Russia. How senseless is everything that can ever be written, done, or thought, when such things are possible. It must be all lies and of no account when the culture of a thousand years could not prevent this stream of blood being poured out, these torture-chambers in their hundreds of thousands. A hospital alone shows what war is.

I am young, I am twenty years old; yet I know nothing of life but despair, death, fear, and fatuous superficiality cast over an abyss of sorrow. I see how peoples are set against one another, and in silence, unknowingly, foolishly, obediently, innocently slay one another. I see that the keenest brains of the world invent weapons and words to make it yet more refined and enduring. And all men of my age, here and over there, throughout the whole world see these things; all my generation is experiencing these things with me. What would our fathers do if we suddenly stood up and came before them and proffered our account? What do they expect of us if a time ever comes when the war is over? Through the years our business has been killing;—it was our first calling in life. Our knowledge of life is limited to death. What will happen afterwards? And what shall come out of us?

Ernst von Salomon
BRUTALIZATION OF THE INDIVIDUAL

The war also produced a fascination with violence, one that persisted after peace was declared. Many returned veterans, their whole being enveloped by the war, continued to yearn for the excitement of battle and the fellowship of the trenches. Brutalized by the war, these men became ideal recruits for Fascist parties that relished violence and sought the destruction of the liberal state.

Immediately after the war ended, thousands of soldiers and adventurers joined the Free Corps—volunteer brigades that defended Germany's eastern borders against encroachments by the new states of Poland, Latvia, and Estonia, and fought Communist revolutionaries. Many of these freebooters later became members of Hitler's movement. Ernst von Salomon, a leading spokesman of the Free Corps movement, was a sixteen-year-old student in Berlin when the defeated German army marched home. In the passage that follows, taken from his book *Die Geächteten* (The Outlaws), published in 1930, he describes the soldiers who "will always carry the trenches in their blood."

The soldiers walked quickly, pressed closely to each other. Suddenly the first four came into sight, looking lifeless. They had stony, rigid faces. . . .

Then came the others. Their eyes lay deep in dark, gray, sharp-edged hollows under the shadow of their helmets. They looked neither right nor left, but straight ahead, as if under the power of a terrifying target in front of them; as if they peered from a mud hole or a trench over torn-up earth. In front of them lay emptiness. They spoke not a word. . . .

O God, how these men looked, as they came nearer—those utterly exhausted, immobile faces under their steel helmets, those bony limbs, those ragged dusty uniforms! And around them an infinite void. It was as if they had drawn a magic circle around themselves, in which dangerous forces, invisible to outsiders, worked their secret spell. Did they still carry in their minds the madness of a thousand battles compressed into whirling visions, as they carried in their uniforms the dirt and the dust of shell-torn fields? The sight was unbearable. They marched like envoys of death, of dread, of the most deadly and solitary coldness. And here was their homeland, warmth, and happiness. Why were they so silent? Why did they not smile?

. . . When I saw these deadly determined faces, these faces as hard as if hacked out of wood, these eyes that glanced past the onlookers, unresponsive, hostile—yes, hostile indeed—then I knew—it suddenly came over me in a fright—that everything had been utterly different from what we had thought, all of us who stood here watching. . . . What did we know about these men? About the war in the trenches? About our soldiers? Oh God, it was terrible: What we had been told was all untrue. We had been told lies. These were not our beloved heroes, the protectors of our homes—these were men who did not belong to us, gathered here to meet them. They did not want to belong to us; they came from other worlds with other laws and other friendships. And all of a sudden everything that I had hoped and wished for, that had inspired me, turned shallow and empty. . . . What an abysmal error it had been to believe for four years that these men belonged to us. Now that misunderstanding vanished. . . .

Then I suddenly understood. These were not workers, peasants, students; no, these were not mechanics, white-collar employees, business-men, officials—these were soldiers. . . . These were men who had responded to the secret call of blood, of spirit, volunteers one way or the other, men who had experienced exacting comradeship and the things behind things— who had found a home in war, a fatherland, a community, and a nation. . . .

The homeland belonged to them; the nation belonged to them. What we had blab-bered like marketwomen, they had actually lived. . . . The trenches were their home, their fatherland, their nation. And they had never used these words; they never believed in them; they believed in themselves. The war held them in its grip and dominated them; the war will never discharge them; they will never return home; they will always carry the trenches in their blood, the closeness of death, the dread, the intoxication, the iron. And sud-denly they were to become peaceful citizens, set again in solid every-day routines? Never! That would mean a counterfeit that was bound to fail. The war is over; the warriors are still marching, . . . dissatisfied when they are de-mobilized, explosive when they stay together. The war had not given them answers; it had achieved no decision. The soldiers continue to march. . . .

Appeals were posted on the street corners for volunteer units to defend Germany's eastern borders. The day after the troops marched into our town, I volunteered. I was accepted and outfitted. Now I too was a soldier.

Sigmund Freud
A LEGACY OF EMBITTERMENT

In a 1915 essay, "Thoughts for the Times on War and Death," Sigmund Freud (see page 264) said that World War I's fury would shatter the bonds of a common European civilization and engulf Europeans in hatred for years to come. He reflects in the following passage on the singular destructiveness of World War I and its uniqueness in world history to date.

We cannot but feel that no event has ever destroyed so much that is precious in the com-mon possessions of humanity, confused so many of the clearest intelligences, or so thoroughly debased what is highest. Science herself has lost her passionless impartiality; her deeply embittered servants seek for weapons from her with which to contribute towards the struggle with the enemy. Anthropologists feel driven to declare him [the enemy] inferior and degener-ate, psychiatrists issue a diagnosis of his disease of mind or spirit. . . .

We had expected the great world-dominating nations of white race upon whom the leadership of the human species has fallen, who were known to have world-wide interests as their concern, to whose creative powers were due not only our technical advances towards the control of nature but the artistic and scientific standards of civilization—we had expected these peoples to succeed in discovering another way of settling misunderstandings and conflicts of interest. Within each of these nations high norms of moral conduct were laid down for the individual, to which his manner of life was bound to conform if he desired to take part in a civilized community. . . .

Relying on this unity among the civilized peoples, countless men and women have exchanged their native home for a foreign one, and made their existence dependent on the intercommunications between friendly nations. Moreover anyone who was not by stress of circumstance confined to one spot could create for himself out of all the advantages and attractions of these civilized countries a new and wider fatherland, in which he could move about without hindrance or suspicion. In this way he enjoyed the blue sea and the grey; the beauty of snow-covered mountains and of green meadow lands; the magic of northern forests and the splendour of southern vegetation; the mood evoked by landscapes that recall great historical events, and the silence of untouched nature. This new fatherland was a museum for him, too, filled with all the treasures which the artists of civilized humanity had in the successive centuries created and left behind. As he wandered from one gallery to another in this museum, he could recognize with impartial appreciation what varied types of perfection a mixture of blood, the course of history, and the special quality of their mother-earth had produced among his compatriots in this wider sense. Here he would find cool, inflexible energy developed to the highest point; there, the graceful art of beautifying existence; elsewhere the feeling for orderliness and law, or others among the qualities which have made mankind the lords of the earth.

Nor must we forget that each of these citizens of the civilized world had created for himself a "Parnassus" and a "School of Athens" [that is,

a center of high culture and learning] of his own. From among the great thinkers, writers and artists of all nations he had chosen those to whom he considered he owed the best of what he had been able to achieve in enjoyment and understanding of life, and he had venerated them along with the immortal ancients as well as with the familiar masters of his own tongue. None of these great men had seemed to him foreign because they spoke another language—neither the incomparable explorer of human passions, nor the intoxicated worshipper of beauty, nor the powerful and menacing prophet, nor the subtle satirist; and he never reproached himself on that account for being a renegade towards his own nation and his beloved mother-tongue.

The enjoyment of this common civilization was disturbed from time to time by warning voices, which declared that old traditional differences made wars inevitable, even among the members of a community such as this. We refused to believe it; but if such a war were to happen, how did we picture it? . . . [W]e pictured it as a chivalrous passage of arms, which would limit itself to establishing the superiority of one side in the struggle, while as far as possible avoiding acute suffering that could contribute nothing to the decision, and granting complete immunity for the wounded who had to withdraw from the contest, as well as for the doctors and nurses who devoted themselves to their recovery. There would, of course, be the utmost consideration for the non-combatant classes of the population—for women who take no part in war-work, and for the children who, when they are grown up, should become on both sides one another's friends and helpers. And again, all the international undertakings and institutions in which the common civilization of peace-time had been embodied would be maintained.

Even a war like this would have produced enough horror and suffering; but it would not have interrupted the development of ethical relations between the collective individuals of mankind—the peoples and states.

Then the war in which we had refused to believe broke out, and it brought—disillusionment.

Not only is it more bloody and more destructive than any war of other days, because of the enormously increased perfection of weapons of attack and defence; it is at least as cruel, as embittered, as implacable as any that has preceded it. It disregards all the restrictions known as International Law, which in peace-time the states had bound themselves to observe; it ignores the prerogatives of the wounded and the medical service, the distinction between civil and military sections of the population, the claims of private property. It tramples in blind fury on all that comes in its way, as though there were to be no future and no peace among men after it is over. It cuts all the common bonds between the contending peoples, and threatens to leave a legacy of embitterment that will make any renewal of those bonds impossible for a long time to come.

REVIEW QUESTIONS

1. What did Paul Valéry mean in saying that the mind of Europe doubted itself profoundly?
2. Why do you think many veterans felt that they were part of a lost generation?
3. What reasons can you think of why many Germans were attracted to paramilitary organizations immediately after the war?
4. How did Sigmund Freud describe the prevailing mood in Europe just prior to the war? How did the war alter this mood and create a "legacy of embitterment"?

CHAPTER 12

Era of Totalitarianism

HITLER AT A 1934 NAZI RALLY. Carefully orchestrated to show the irresistible might of the Nazi movement, the Nuremberg rallies were among the greatest theatrical performances of the twentieth century. *(Corbis)*

Following World War I, Fascist movements arose in Italy, Germany, and many other European countries. Although these movements differed—each a product of separate national histories and the outlook of its leader—they shared a hatred of liberalism, democracy, and communism; a commitment to aggressive nationalism; and a glorification of the party leader. Fascist leaders cleverly utilized myths, rituals, and pageantry to mobilize and manipulate the masses.

Several conditions fostered the rise of Fascism. One factor was the fear of Communism among the middle and upper classes. Inspired by the success of the Bolsheviks in Russia, Communists in other lands were calling for the establishment of Soviet-style republics. Increasingly afraid of a Communist takeover, industrialists, landowners, government officials, army leaders, professionals, and shopkeepers were attracted to Fascist movements that promised to protect their nations from this threat. A second factor contributing to the growth of Fascism was the disillusionment of World War I veterans and the mood of violence bred by the war. The thousands of veterans facing unemployment and poverty made ideal recruits for Fascist parties that glorified combat and organized private armies. A third contributing factor was the inability of democratic parliamentary governments to cope with the problems that burdened postwar Europe. Having lost confidence in the procedures and values of democracy, many people joined Fascist movements that promised strong leadership, an end to party conflicts, and a unified national will.

Fascism's appeal to nationalist feelings also drew people into the movement. In a sense, Fascism expressed the aggressive racial nationalism that had emerged in the late nineteenth century. Fascists saw themselves as dedicated idealists engaged in a heroic struggle to rescue their nations from domestic and foreign enemies; they aspired to regain lands lost by their countries in World War I or to acquire lands denied them by the Paris Peace Conference.

Fascists glorified instinct, will, and blood as the true forces of life; they openly attacked the ideals of reason, liberty, and equality—the legacies of the Enlightenment and the French Revolution. At the center of German Fascism (National Socialism or Nazism) was a bizarre racial mythology that preached the superiority of the German race and the inferiority of others, particularly Jews and Slavs.

Benito Mussolini, founder of the Italian Fascist Party, came to power in 1922. Although he established a one-party state, he was less successful than Adolf Hitler, the leader of the German National Socialists, in controlling the state and the minds of the people. After gaining power as chancellor of the German government in 1933, Hitler moved to establish a totalitarian state.

In the 1930s, the term *totalitarianism* was used to describe the Fascist regime in Italy, the National Socialist regime in Germany, and the communist regime in the Soviet Union. To a degree that far exceeds the ancient tyrannies and early modern autocratic states, these dictatorships aspired to and, with varying degrees of success, attained control over the individual's consciousness and behavior and all phases of political, social, and cultural life. To many people it seemed that a crises-riddled democracy was dying and that the future belonged to these dynamic totalitarian movements.

Totalitarianism was a twentieth-century phenomenon, for such all-embracing control over the individual and society could have been achieved only in an age of modern ideology, technology, and bureaucracy. The ideological aims and social and economic policies of Hitler and Stalin differed fundamentally. However, both Communist Russia and Nazi Germany shared the totalitarian goal of monolithic unity and total domination, and both employed similar methods to achieve it. Mussolini's Italy is more accurately called authoritarian, for the party-state either did not intend to control all phases of life or lacked the means to do so. Moreover, Mussolini hesitated to use the ruthless methods that Hitler and Stalin employed so readily.

Striving for total unity, control, and obedience, the totalitarian dictatorship is the antithesis of liberal democracy. It abolishes all competing political parties, suppresses individual liberty, eliminates or regulates private institutions, and utilizes the modern state's bureaucracy and technology to impose its ideology and enforce its commands. The party-state determines what people should believe—what values they should hold. There is no room for individual thinking, private moral judgment, or individual conscience. The individual possesses no natural rights that the state must respect.

Unlike previous dictatorial regimes, the dictatorships of both the Left and the Right sought to legitimize their rule by gaining the masses' approval. They claimed that their governments were higher and truer expressions of the people's will. The Soviet and Nazi dictatorships established their rule in the name of the people—the German Volk or the Soviet proletariat.

A distinctive feature of totalitarianism is the overriding importance of the leader, who is seen as infallible and invincible. The masses' slavish adulation of the leader and their uncritical acceptance of the dogma that the leader or the party is always right promote loyalty, dedication, and obedience and distort rational thinking.

Totalitarian leaders want more than power for its own sake; in the last analysis, they seek to transform the world according to an all-embracing ideology, a set of convictions and beliefs, which, says Hannah Arendt, "pretend[s] to know the mysteries of the whole historical process—the secrets of the past, the intricacies of the present, the uncertainties of the future." The ideology constitutes a higher and exclusive truth, based on a law of history, and it contains a dazzling vision of the future—a secular New Jerusalem—that strengthens the will of the faithful and attracts converts.

Like a religion, the totalitarian ideology provides its adherents with beliefs that make society and history intelligible, that explain all of existence in an emotionally gratifying way. Again like a religion, it creates true believers, who feel that they are participating in a great cause—a heroic fight against evil—that gives meaning to their lives.

Not only did the totalitarian religion-ideology supply followers with a cause that claimed absolute goodness; it also provided a Devil. For the Soviets, the source of evil and the cause of all the people's hardships were the degenerate capitalists, the traitorous Trotskyites, or the saboteurs and foreign agents, who impeded the realization of the socialist society. For the Nazis, the Devil was the conspirator Jew. These "evil" ones must be eliminated in order to realize the totalitarian movement's vision of the future. Thus, totalitarian regimes liquidate large segments of the population designated as "enemies of the people." Historical necessity or a higher purpose demands and justifies their liquidation. The appeal to historical necessity has all the power of a great myth. Presented as a world-historical struggle between the forces of good and the forces of evil, the myth incites fanaticism and numbs the conscience. Seemingly decent people engage in terrible acts of brutality with no remorse, convinced that they are waging a righteous war.

Unlike earlier autocratic regimes, the totalitarian dictatorship is not satisfied with its subjects' outward obedience; it demands the masses' unconditional loyalty and enthusiastic support. It strives to control the inner person: to shape thoughts, feelings, and attitudes in accordance with the party ideology, which becomes an official creed. It seeks to create a "new man," one who dedicates himself body and soul to the party and its ideology. Such unquestioning, faithful subjects can be manipulated by the party.

The totalitarian dictatorship deliberately politicizes all areas of human activity. Ideology pervades works of literature, history, philosophy, art, and even science. It dominates the school curriculum and influences everyday speech and social relations. The state is concerned with everything its citizens do: there is no distinction between public and private life, and every institution comes under the party-state's authority. If voluntary support for the regime cannot be generated by indoctrination, then the state unhesitatingly resorts to terror and violence to compel obedience.

1   Modernize or Perish

Joseph Stalin (1879–1953) was the Communist leader who made the Soviet Union into a superpower. He was born Iosif Vissarionovich Dzhugashvili in Trans-Caucasus Georgia. A rebel from childhood, he was one of Lenin's favored professional revolutionaries, trained in the tough schools of underground agitation, tsarist prisons, and Siberian exile. Unscrupulous, energetic, and endowed with a keen nose for the realities of power within the party and the country as a whole, Stalin surpassed his political rivals in strength of will and organizational astuteness. After he was appointed secretary-general of the Communist party (then considered a minor post) in 1922, he concentrated on building, amid the disorganization caused by war, revolution, and civil war, an effective party organization adapted to the temper of the Russian people. With this structure's help, he established himself as Lenin's successor. Stalin, more powerful and more ruthless than Lenin, was determined to force his country to overcome the economic and political weakness that had led to defeat and ruin in 1917. After Lenin's death, Stalin preached the "Leninist style of work," which combined "Russian revolutionary sweep" with "American efficiency."

Joseph Stalin
THE HARD LINE

Firmly entrenched in power by 1929, Stalin started a second revolution (called the Stalin revolution), mobilizing at top speed the economic potential of the country, however limited the human and material resources available, whatever the obstacles, and whatever the human price. The alternative, he was sure, was foreign domination that would totally destroy his country's independence. In this spirit, he addressed a gathering of industrial managers in 1931, talking to them not in Marxist-Leninist jargon, but in terms of hard-line Russian nationalism.

It is sometimes asked whether it is not possible to slow down the tempo a bit, to put a check on the movement. No, comrades, it is not possible! The tempo must not be reduced! On the contrary, we must increase it as much as is within our powers and possibilities. This is dictated to us by our obligations to the workers and peasants of the U.S.S.R. This is dictated to us by our obligations to the working class of the whole world.

To slacken the tempo would mean falling behind. And those who fall behind get beaten. But we do not want to be beaten. No, we refuse to be beaten! One feature of the history of old Russia was the continual beatings she suffered for falling behind, for her backwardness. She was beaten by the Mongol Khans. She was beaten by the Turkish beys. She was beaten by the Swedish feudal lords. She was beaten by the Polish and Lithuanian gentry. She was beaten by the British and French capitalists. She was beaten by the Japanese barons. All beat her—for

her backwardness: for military backwardness, for cultural backwardness, for political backwardness, for industrial backwardness, for agricultural backwardness. She was beaten because to do so was profitable and could be done with impunity. Do you remember the words of the pre-revolutionary poet [Nikolai Nekrassov]: "You are poor and abundant, mighty and impotent, Mother Russia." These words of the old poet were well learned by those gentlemen. They beat her, saying: "You are abundant," so one can enrich oneself at your expense. They beat her, saying: "You are poor and impotent," so you can be beaten and plundered with impunity. Such is the law of the exploiters—to beat the backward and the weak. It is the jungle law of capitalism. You are backward, you are weak—therefore you are wrong; hence, you can be beaten and enslaved. You are mighty—therefore you are right; hence, we must be wary of you.

That is why we must no longer lag behind.

In the past we had no fatherland, nor could we have one. But now that we have overthrown capitalism and power is in the hands of the working class, we have a fatherland, and we will defend its independence. Do you want our socialist fatherland to be beaten and to lose its independence? If you do not want this you must put an end to its backwardness in the shortest possible time and develop genuine Bolshevik tempo in building up its socialist system of economy. There is no other way. That is why Lenin said during the October Revolution: "Either perish, or overtake and outstrip the advanced capitalist countries."

We are fifty or a hundred years behind the advanced countries. We must make good this distance in ten years. Either we do it, or they crush us.

This is what our obligations to the workers and peasants of the U.S.S.R. dictate to us.

REVIEW QUESTIONS

1. Why did Joseph Stalin argue that the tempo of industrialization could not be slowed down?
2. How important is the idea of "fatherland" to Stalin?

---

2   Forced Collectivization

The forced collectivization of agriculture from 1929 to 1933 was an integral part of the Stalin revolution. His argument in favor of it was simple: an economy divided against itself cannot stand—planned industrial mobilization was incompatible with small-scale private agriculture in the traditional manner. Collectivization meant combining many small peasant holdings into a single large unit run in theory by the peasants (now called collective farmers), but run in practice by the collective farm chairman and guided by the government's Five-Year Plan, which was designed to industrialize the country rapidly.

Collectivization, not surprisingly, met with fierce resistance, especially from the more successful peasants called kulaks, who were averse to surrendering their private plots and their freedom in running their households. Their resistance therefore had to be broken, and the Communist Party fomented a rural class struggle, seeking help from the poorer peasants. Sometimes, however, even the poorest peasants sided with the local kulaks. Under these conditions, Stalin did not shrink from unleashing violence in the countryside aimed at the "liquidation of the kulaks as a class." For Stalin the collectivization drive meant an all-out war on what was for him the citadel of backwardness: the peasant tradition and rebelliousness so prominent under the tsars.

Lev Kopelev
TERROR IN THE COUNTRYSIDE

The liquidation of the kulaks began in late 1929, extending through the length and breadth of the country during the winter. The confiscation of kulak property, the deportations, and the killing rose to a brutal climax in the following spring and continued for another two years, by which time the bulk of the private farms had been eliminated. By some estimates, almost five million people were liquidated. Some were driven from their huts, deprived of all possessions, and left destitute in the dead of winter; the men were sent to forced labor and their families left abandoned. Others killed themselves or were killed outright, sometimes in pitched battles involving a whole village—men, women, and children.

The upheaval destroyed agricultural production in these years; farm animals died or were killed in huge numbers; fields lay barren. In 1932 and 1933, famine stalked the south and southeast, killing additional millions. The vast tragedy caused by collectivization did not deter Stalin from pursuing his goals: the establishment of state farms run like factories and the subordination of the rebellious and willful peasantry to state authority.

Here a militant participant in the collectivization drive, Lev Kopelev, recalls some of his experiences. These passages are from his memoirs published in 1978. Kopelev (1912–1997), raised in a Ukrainian middle-class Jewish family, evolved from a youthful Stalinist into a tolerant, gentle person in later years. After trying to keep Russian soldiers from raping and pillaging in German territory in 1945, he was given a ten-year sentence for antistate crimes. Subsequently out of favor because of his literary protests against the inhumanities of the Soviet system, he was exiled from the Soviet Union to West Germany in 1980.

The grain front! Stalin said the struggle for grain was the struggle for socialism. I was convinced that we were warriors on an invisible front, fighting against kulak sabotage for the grain which was needed by the country, by the five-year plan. Above all, for the grain, but also for the souls of these peasants who were mired in unconscientiousness, in ignorance, who succumbed to enemy agitation, who did not understand the great truth of communism. . . .

The highest measure of coercion on the hardcore holdouts was "undisputed confiscation."

A team consisting of several young kolkhozniks [collective farmers] and members of the village soviet . . . would search the hut, barn, yard, and take away all the stores of seed, lead away the cow, the horse, the pigs.

In some cases they would be merciful and leave some potatoes, peas, corn for feeding the family. But the stricter ones would make a clean sweep. They would take not only the food and livestock, but also "all valuables and surpluses of clothing," including icons in their frames, samovars, painted carpets and even metal kitchen utensils which might be silver. And any money they found stashed away. Special instructions ordered the removal of gold, silver and currency. . . .

Several times Volodya and I were present at such plundering raids. We even took part: we were entrusted to draw up inventories of the confiscated goods. . . . The women howled hysterically, clinging to the bags.

"Oy, that's the last thing we have! That was for the children's kasha [cereal]! Honest to God, the children will starve!"

They wailed, falling on their trunks:

"Oy, that's a keepsake from my dead mama! People, come to my aid, this is my trousseau, never e'en put on!"

I heard the children echoing them with screams, choking, coughing with screams. And I saw the looks of the men: frightened, pleading, hateful, dully impassive, extinguished with despair or flaring up with half-mad, daring ferocity.

"Take it. Take it away. Take everything away. There's still a pot of borscht on the stove. It's plain, got no meat. But still it's got beets, taters 'n' cabbage. And it's salted! Better take it, comrade citizens! Here, hang on, I'll take off my shoes. They're patched and re-patched, but maybe they'll have some use for the proletariat, for our dear Soviet power."

It was excruciating to see and hear all this. And even worse to take part in it. . . . And I persuaded myself, explained to myself. I mustn't give in to debilitating pity. We were realizing historical necessity. We were performing our revolutionary duty. We were obtaining grain for the socialist fatherland. For the five-year plan. . . .

I have always remembered the winter of the last grain collections, the weeks of the great famine. And I have always told about it. But I did not begin to write it down until many years later. . . .

How could all this have happened?

Who was guilty of the famine which destroyed millions of lives?

How could I have participated in it? . . .

We were raised as the fanatical [believers] of a new creed, the only true *religion* of scientific socialism. The party became our church militant, bequeathing to all mankind eternal salvation, eternal peace and the bliss of an earthly paradise. It victoriously surmounted all other churches, schisms and heresies. The works of

Marx, Engels and Lenin were accepted as holy writ, and Stalin was the infallible high priest.

. . . Stalin was the most perspicacious, the most wise (at that time they hadn't yet started calling him "great" and "brilliant"). He said: "The struggle for grain is the struggle for socialism." And we believed him unconditionally. And later we believed that unconditional collectivization was unavoidable if we were to overcome the capriciousness and uncertainty of the market and the backwardness of individual farming, to guarantee a steady supply of grain, milk and meat to the cities. And also if we were to reeducate millions of peasants, those petty landowners and hence potential bourgeoisie, potential kulaks, to transform them into laborers with a social conscience, to liberate them from "the idiocy of country life," from ignorance and prejudice, and to accustom them to culture, to all the boons of socialism. . . .

In the following passage Kopelev reflects, even more searchingly, on his own motivation and state of mind as a participant in Stalin's collectivization drive.

With the rest of my generation I firmly believed that the ends justified the means. Our great goal was the universal triumph of Communism, and for the sake of that goal everything was permissible—to lie, to steal, to destroy hundreds of thousands and even millions of people, all those who were hindering our work or could hinder it, everyone who stood in the way. And to hesitate or doubt about all this was to give in to "intellectual squeamishness" and "stupid liberalism," the attributes of people who "could not see the forest for the trees."

That was how I had reasoned, and everyone like me, even when I did have my doubts, when I saw what "total collectivization" meant—how . . . mercilessly they stripped the peasants in the winter of 1932–33. I took part in this myself, scouring the countryside, searching for hidden grain, testing the earth with an iron rod for loose spots that might lead to buried grain. With the others, I emptied out the old folks' storage chests, stopping my ears to the children's crying and the women's wails. For I was convinced that I was accomplishing the great and necessary transformation of the countryside; that in the days to come the people who lived there would be better off for it; that their distress and suffering were a result of their own ignorance or the machinations of the class enemy; that those who sent me—and I myself—knew better than the peasants how they should live, what they should sow and when they should plow.

In the terrible spring of 1933 I saw people dying from hunger. I saw women and children with distended bellies, turning blue, still breathing but with vacant, lifeless eyes. And corpses—corpses in ragged sheepskin coats and cheap felt boots; corpses in peasant huts, in the melting snow of old Vologda, under the bridges of Kharkov. . . . I saw all this and did not go out of my mind or commit suicide. Nor did I curse those who had sent me to take away the peasants' grain in the winter, and in the spring to persuade the barely walking, skeleton-thin or sickly-swollen people to go into the fields in order to "fulfill the Bolshevik sowing plan in shock-worker style."

Nor did I lose my faith. As before, I believed because I wanted to believe. Thus from time

immemorial men have believed when possessed by a desire to serve powers and values above and beyond humanity: gods, emperors, states; ideals of virtue, freedom, nation, race, class, party. . . .

Any single-minded attempt to realize these ideals exacts its toll of human sacrifice. In the name of the noblest visions promising eternal happiness to their descendants, such men bring merciless ruin on their contemporaries. Bestowing paradise on the dead, they maim and destroy the living. They become unprincipled liars and unrelenting executioners, all the while seeing themselves as virtuous and honorable militants—convinced that if they are forced into villainy, it is for the sake of future good, and that if they have to lie, it is in the name of eternal truths.

. . . That was how we thought and acted—we, the fanatical disciples of the all-saving ideals of Communism. When we saw the base and cruel acts that were committed in the name of our exalted notions of good, and when we ourselves took part in those actions, what we feared most was to lose our heads, fall into doubt or heresy and forfeit our unbounded faith. . . . The concepts of conscience, honor, humaneness we dismissed as idealistic prejudices, "intellectual" or "bourgeois," and hence, perverse.

REVIEW QUESTIONS

1. How would you characterize the motivation of the young Lev Kopelev and his associates in carrying out the collectivization of agriculture?
2. How, in retrospect, did Kopelev explain his role in the collectivization drive?

3 Famine in Ukraine

The suffering caused by Stalin's collectivization drive was most cruel in Ukraine, where famine killed approximately seven million people, many of whom had already endured extreme abuse and persecution. In order to buy industrial equipment abroad so that industrialization could proceed on target, the Soviet Union had to export food, as much of it as possible and for prices disastrously lowered by the Great Depression. Let the peasants in the Ukrainian breadbasket perish so that the country could grow strong! Moreover, Stalin relished the opportunity to punish the Ukrainians for opposing the Bolsheviks during the civil war and resisting collectivization. Through rigid social control, he hoped to crush nationalist sentiments among the Ukrainians.

Miron Dolot
EXECUTION BY HUNGER

Miron Dolot witnessed the horrors of state-induced famine in Ukraine and later emigrated to the West. In *Execution by Hunger: The Hidden Holocaust* (1985), excerpted below, Dolot recounts his experiences.

The year 1932 witnessed the last battle of collectivization: the battle for bread, or to be more specific, for the crop of 1932. On the one side was the Communist government; on the other, the starving farmers. The government forces resorted to any means in getting as many agricultural products from the countryside as possible, without regard to the consequences. The farmers, already on the verge of starvation, desperately tried to keep what food they had left, and, in spite of government efforts to the contrary, tried to stay alive. . . .

The long and cold winter of 1931–1932 was slowly giving way to spring. . . .

Around this time the plight of the villagers became desperate. This was the memorable spring of 1932 when the famine broke out, and the first deaths from hunger began to occur. I remember the endless procession of beggars on roads and paths, going from house to house. They were in different stages of starvation, dirty and ragged. With outstretched hands, they begged for food, any food: a potato, a beet, or at least a kernel of corn. Those were the first victims of starvation: destitute men and women; poor widows and orphaned children who had no chance of surviving the terrible ordeal.

Some starving farmers still tried to earn their food by doing chores in or outside the village. One could see these sullen, emaciated men walking from house to house with an ax, or a shovel, in search of work. Perhaps someone might hire them to dig up the garden, or chop some firewood. They would do it for a couple of potatoes. But not many of us had a couple of potatoes to spare.

Crowds of starving wretches could be seen scattered all over the potato fields. They were looking for potatoes left over from last year's harvest. No matter what shape the potatoes were in, whether frozen or rotten, they were still edible. Others were roaming the forest in search of food; the riverbanks were crowded too; there was much new greenery around: young shoots of reed or other river plants. One might catch something, anything, in the water to eat.

But the majority of those who looked for help would go to the cities as they used to do before. It was always easier to find some work there, either gardening, cleaning backyards, or sweeping streets. But now, times had changed. It was illegal to hire farmers for any work. The purpose of the prohibition was twofold: it was done not only to stop the flow of labor from the collective farms, but also, and primarily, to prevent the farmers from receiving food rations in the cities. . . .

By this time our village was in economic ruin. Poverty was universal. We had never been rich, it is true, but economically, we had always been completely self-sufficient and had never gone hungry for so long. Now starving, we were facing the spring of 1932 with great anxiety for there was no hope of relief from the outside. Deaths from starvation became daily occurrences. There was always some burial in the village cemetery. One could see strange funeral processions: children pulling homemade handwagons with the bodies of their dead parents in them or the parents carting the bodies of their children. There were no coffins; no burial ceremonies performed by priests. The bodies of the starved were just deposited in a large common grave, one upon the other; that was all there was to it. . . .

Looking back to those events now, it seems to me that I lived in some kind of a wicked fantasy world. All the events which I witnessed and experienced then and which I am now describing, seem unreal to me because of their cruelty and unspeakable horror. It is simply too difficult to associate all those happenings with real life in a normal human society. . . .

The battle for the Ukrainian wheat crop of 1932 started almost two months before the harvest.

At the end of May, some strangers appeared in our village, and little by little, we began finding out who they were. The Party had mobilized 112,000 of its most active and reliable members in order to organize a speedy harvest of the new crop, and to secure its swift and smooth requisitioning and final delivery to the State. Soon these members became known to us as the Hundred Thousanders, or just Thousanders. There were nine of them in our village. . . . In no time at all, these new Thousanders took over our entire village like tyrants, imposing their wills and their demands upon us. . . .

Comrade Thousander's announcement that in 1932 we had to deliver the same quota of grain as in 1931 was a hard blow to us. We simply could not fulfill his demands. The 1932 grain quota was not based on the actual amount of grain sown, cultivated, and harvested; it was based upon an unrealistic government plan. . . .

Faced with starvation, the villagers tried everything possible to save themselves and their families. Some of them started eating dogs and cats. Others went hunting for birds: crows, magpies, swallows, sparrows, storks, and even nightingales. One could see starving villagers searching in the bushes along the river for birds' nests or looking for crabs and other small crustaceans in the water. Even their hard shells, though not edible, were cooked and the broth consumed as nourishment. One could see crowds of famished villagers combing the woods in search of roots or mushrooms and berries. Some tried to catch small forest animals.

Driven by hunger, people ate everything and anything: even food that had already rotted—potatoes, beets, and other root vegetables that pigs normally refused to eat. They even ate weeds, the leaves and bark of trees, insects, frogs, and snails. Nor did they shy away from eating the meat of diseased horses and cattle. Often that meat was already decaying and those who ate it died of food poisoning. . . .

One morning in late January 1933, while it was still dark, Mother and I set out along the main street through the center of the village for the county town. We followed the street to the main road which led straight into the town. . . .

Soon, however, as we slowly made our way through the snow toward the village center, graphic evidence of starvation became visible. We noticed a black object which, from afar, looked like a snow-covered tree stump. As we came near, however, we saw that it was the body of a dead man. Frozen limbs protruding from under the snow gave the body the appearance of some grotesque creature. I bent down and cleared the snow off the face. It was Ulas, our elderly neighbor whom we had last seen about a month ago.

A few steps further, we saw another frozen body. It was the corpse of a woman. As I brushed away the snow, horror made my blood turn cold: under her ragged coat, clutched tightly to her bosom with her stiff hands, was the frozen little body of her baby.

We finally left our village behind and stepped onto the open road which led to the county seat. However, another ghostly panorama now opened in front of us. Everywhere we looked dead and frozen bodies lay by the sides of the road. To our right were bodies of those villagers who apparently had tried to reach the town in search of work and food. Weakened by starvation, they were unable to make it and ended up lying or falling down by the roadside, never to rise again. The gentle snow mercifully covered their bodies with its white blanket.

One could easily imagine the fate of those people whose bodies were lying to our left. They most probably were returning from the county town, without having accomplished anything. They had tramped many kilometers in vain, only to be refused a job and a chance to stay alive. They were returning home empty-handed. Death caught up with them as they trudged homeward, resigned to dying in their village.

The wide open kolhosp[1] fields, stretching for kilometers on both sides of the main road, looked like a battlefield after a great war. Littering the fields were the bodies of the starving farmers who had been combing the potato fields over and over again in the hope of finding at least a fragment of a potato that might have been overlooked or left over from the last harvest. They died where they collapsed in their endless search for food. Some of those frozen corpses must have been lying out there for months. Nobody seemed to be in a hurry to cart them away and bury them. . . .

. . . Dmytro had never returned home after he had been taken to the county center.[2] His young wife Solomia was left alone with their daughter. She had gone to work in the collective farm, taking her little child with her. As the wife of a banished man, she too was considered an "enemy of the people," and her child was refused admission to the nursery. Later, Solomia was expelled from the collective farm, and thus forced to seek a job in the city. That was impossible, however, because she could not show a certificate of release from the collective farm. She found herself trapped in the circle of the Communist death ring. She had to return to her village.

When winter came, Solomia went from house to house, willing to work for just a piece of bread. She was too proud to beg. People were sympathetic and helped her as much as they could. However, as the famine worsened, and the villagers were no longer able to help her, she was not seen on her rounds any more.

We found the front door of Solomia's house open, but the entrance was blocked with snowdrifts, and it was hard to get inside. When we finally reached the living room, we saw a pitiful sight: Solomia was hanging from the ceiling in the middle of the room. She was dressed in her Ukrainian national costume, and at her breast hung a large cross. It was obvious that she had made preparations before committing suicide. Her hair was combed neatly in two braids hanging over her shoulders.

Frightened, we ran to fetch Mother. We helped her take down Solomia's frozen body, and laid it on a bench, and covered it with a handmade blanket. It was only after we finished doing this that we noticed the dead body of her little daughter. The child was lying in a wooden tub in the corner under the icons, clean and dressed in her best clothes. Her little hands were folded across her chest.

On the table was a note:

Dear Neighbors:

Please bury our bodies properly. I have to leave you, dear neighbors. I can bear this life no longer. There is no food in the house, and there is no sense in living without my little daughter who starved to death, or my husband. If you ever see Dmytro, tell him about us. He will understand our plight, and he will forgive me. Please tell him that I died peacefully, thinking about him and our dear daughter.

I love you, my dear neighbors, and I wish with all my heart that you somehow recover from this disaster. Forgive me for troubling you. Thank you for everything you have done for me.

Solomia.

---

[1]The Ukrainian term for collective farm.
[2]Dmytro, a neighbor and distant relative of the author, had been jailed after punching a collective farm official who accused him of sabotage.

After reading the note, we stood there for a while, motionless and forlorn. Our mother tried to suppress the sound of her weeping, pressing the corner of her head scarf to her lips. Mykola gazed at the corpses in disbelief.

In my imagination I was recreating the agony of their dying: the child's hunger cries, and then the death convulsions of its exhausted little body.

How great must have been the sufferings of the mother. She had to listen helplessly to the pleas of her child for food, while she herself was near starvation. She must have felt great relief, I thought, when she saw her little daughter breathing for the last time. Then, in my imagination, I saw the mother attending to her lifeless child: dressing her in the best and cleanest clothing she had, praying on her knees near the body, and finally kissing her for the last time before her own suicide. . . .

Toward the end of March, the famine struck us with full force. Life in the village had sunk to its lowest level, an almost animallike struggle for survival of the fittest.

The village ceased to exist as a coherent community. The inhabitants who still managed to stay alive shut themselves within the walls of their houses. People became too weak even to step outside their doors. Each house became an entity in itself. Visits became a rarity. All doors were bolted and barred against any possible intruders. Even between immediate neighbors, there was little, if any, communication, and people ceased caring about one another.

In fact, they avoided each other. Friends and even relatives became strangers. Mothers abandoned their children, and brother turned away from brother. . . .

One must consider the inexorable pressure of hunger under which a person can completely become bereft of his or her senses and sink to an absolute animallike level. That happened to many of our villagers. The more resistant ones who kept on living with minimal or no food at all for some time, felt no more of the initial hunger pangs. They either lapsed into comas, or existed in a semicomatose, lethargic stupor. But some reacted differently. They became like madmen. They lost all traces of compassion, honor, and morality. They suffered from hallucinations of food, of something to bite into and chew, to satisfy the gnawing pains of their empty stomachs. Intolerable cravings assailed them; they were ready to sink their teeth into anything, even into their own hands and arms, or into the flesh of others.

The first rumors of actual cannibalism were related to the mysterious and sudden disappearances of people in the village. . . .

As the cases of missing persons grew in number, an arrest was made which shook us to our souls. A woman was taken into custody, charged with killing her two children.

Another woman was found dead, her neck contorted in a crudely made noose. The neighbors who discovered the tragedy also found the reason for it. The flesh of the woman's three-year-old daughter was found in the oven.

REVIEW QUESTION

1. Describe the different ways people in Ukraine responded to the famine.

4 Soviet Indoctrination

Pressed by the necessity to transform their country into a modern state, the communist leaders used every opportunity to force the population to adopt the attitudes and motivation necessary to effect such a transformation. Education, from nursery school to university, provided special opportunities to mold attitudes. The Soviet regime made impressive gains in promoting education among its diverse people; it also used education to foster dedication to hard work, disciplined social cooperation, and pride in the nation. For a backward country that, as Lenin had said, must "either perish or overtake and outstrip the advanced capitalist countries," such changes were considered essential, even though they were contrary to traditional Russian attitudes. To ensure their implementation, the Soviet regime employed terror and indoctrination.

During the Stalin era, artists and writers were compelled to promote the ideals of the Stalin revolution. In the style of "socialist realism," their heroes were factory workers and farmers who labored tirelessly and enthusiastically to build a new society. Even romance served a political purpose. Novelists wrote love stories following limited, prosaic themes. For example, a young girl might lose her heart to a coworker who is a leader in the Communist youth organization and who outproduces his comrades at his job; as the newly married couple is needed at the factory, they choose to forgo a honeymoon.

A. O. Avdienko
THE CULT OF STALIN

Among a people so deeply divided by ethnicity and petty localism and limited by a pervasive narrowness of perspective, building countrywide unity and consensus was a crucial challenge for the government. In the Russian past the worship of saints and the veneration of the tsar had served that purpose. The political mobilization of the masses during the revolution required an intensification of that tradition. It led to the "cult of personality," the deliberate fixation of individual dedication and loyalty on the all-powerful leader, whose personality exemplified the challenge of extraordinary times. The following selection, written in 1936, illustrates by what emotional bonds the individual was tied to Stalin, and through Stalin to the prodigious transformation of Russian state and society that he was attempting.

Thank you, Stalin. Thank you because I am joyful. Thank you because I am well. No matter how old I become, I shall never forget how we received Stalin two days ago. Centuries will pass, and the generations still to come will regard us as the happiest of mortals, as the most fortunate of men, because we lived in the century of centuries, because we were privileged to see Stalin, our inspired leader. Yes, and we regard ourselves as the happiest of mortals because we are the contemporaries of a man who never had an equal in world history.

The men of all ages will call on thy name, which is strong, beautiful, wise and marvellous. Thy name is engraved on every factory, every machine, every place on the earth, and in the hearts of all men.

Every time I have found myself in his presence I have been subjugated by his strength, his charm, his grandeur. I have experienced a great desire to sing, to cry out, to shout with joy and happiness. And now see me—me!—on the same platform where the Great Stalin stood a year ago. In what country, in what part of the world could such a thing happen.

I write books. I am an author. All thanks to thee, O great educator, Stalin. I love a young woman with a renewed love and shall perpetuate myself in my children—all thanks to thee, great educator, Stalin. I shall be eternally happy and joyous, all thanks to thee, great educator, Stalin. Everything belongs to thee, chief of our great country. And when the woman I love presents me with a child the first word it shall utter will be: Stalin.

O great Stalin, O leader of the peoples,
Thou who broughtest man to birth.
Thou who fructifiest the earth,
Thou who restorest the centuries,
Thou who makest bloom the spring,
Thou who makest vibrate the musical
   chords . . .
Thou, splendour of my spring, O Thou,
Sun reflected by millions of hearts . . .

Yevgeny Yevtushenko
LITERATURE AS PROPAGANDA

After Stalin's death in 1953, Soviet intellectuals breathed more freely, and they protested against the rigid Stalinist controls. In the following extract from his *Precocious Autobiography* (1963), Russian poet Yevgeny Yevtushenko (b. 1933) looks back to the raw days of intellectual repression under Stalin.

Blankly smiling workers and collective farmers looked out from the covers of books. Almost every novel and short story had a happy ending. Painters more and more often took as their subject state banquets, weddings, solemn public meetings, and parades.

The apotheosis of this trend was a movie which in its grand finale showed thousands of collective farmers having a gargantuan feast against the background of a new power station.

Recently I had a talk with its producer, a gifted and intelligent man.

"How could you produce such a film?" I asked. "It is true that I also once wrote verses in that vein, but I was still wet behind the ears, whereas you were adult and mature."

The producer smiled a sad smile. "You know, the strangest thing to me is that I was absolutely sincere. I thought all this was a necessary part of building communism. And then I believed Stalin."

So when we talk about "the cult of personality," we should not be too hasty in accusing all those who, one way or another, were involved in it, debasing themselves with their flattery. There were of course sycophants [servile flatterers] who used the situation for their own ends. But that many people connected with the arts sang Stalin's praises was often not vice but tragedy.

How was it possible for even gifted and intelligent people to be deceived?

To begin with, Stalin was a strong and vivid personality. When he wanted to, Stalin knew how to charm people. He charmed Gorky and Barbusse. In 1937, the cruelest year of the purges, he managed to charm that tough and experienced observer, Lion Feuchtwanger.[1]

In the second place, in the minds of the Soviet people, Stalin's name was indissolubly linked with Lenin's. Stalin knew how popular Lenin was and saw to it that history was rewritten in such a way as to make his own relations with Lenin seem much more friendly than they had been in fact. The rewriting was so thorough that perhaps Stalin himself believed his own version in the end.

There can be no doubt of Stalin's love for Lenin. His speech on Lenin's death, beginning with the words, "In leaving us, Comrade Lenin has bequeathed . . ." reads like a poem in prose. He wanted to stand as Lenin's heir not only in other people's eyes, but in his own eyes too. He deceived himself as well as the others. Even [Boris] Pasternak put the two names side by side:

> Laughter in the village,
> Voice behind the plow,
> Lenin and Stalin,
> And these verses now . . .

In reality, however, Stalin distorted Lenin's ideas, because to Lenin—and this was the whole meaning of his work—communism was to serve man, whereas under Stalin it appeared that man served communism.

Stalin's theory that people were the little cogwheels of communism was put into practice and with horrifying results. . . . Russian poets, who had produced some fine works during the war, turned dull again. If a good poem did appear now and then, it was likely to be about the war—this was simpler to write about.

Poets visited factories and construction sites but wrote more about machines than about the men who made them work. If machines could read, they might have found such poems interesting. Human beings did not.

The size of a printing was not determined by demand but by the poet's official standing. As a result bookstores were cluttered up with books of poetry which no one wanted. . . . A simple, touching poem by the young poet Vanshenkin, about a boy's first love, caused almost a sensation against this background of industrial-agricultural verse. Vinokurov's first poems, handsomely disheveled among the general sleekness, were avidly seized upon—they had human warmth. But the general situation was unchanged. Poetry remained unpopular. The older poets were silent, and when they did break their silence, it was even worse. The generation of poets that had been spawned by the war and that had raised so many hopes had petered out. Life in peacetime turned out to be more complicated than life at the front. Two of the greatest Russian poets, Zabolotsky and Smelyakov, were in concentration camps. The young poet Mandel (Korzhavin) had been deported. I don't know if Mandel's name will be remembered in the history of Russian poets but it will certainly be remembered in the history of Russian social thought.

He was the only poet who openly wrote and recited verses against Stalin while Stalin was alive. That he recited them seems to be what saved his life, for the authorities evidently thought him insane. In one poem he wrote of Stalin:

> There in Moscow, in whirling darkness,
> Wrapped in his military coat,
> Not understanding Pasternak,
> A hard and cruel man stared at the snow.

. . . Now that ten years have gone by, I realize that Stalin's greatest crime was not the arrests and the shootings he ordered. His greatest crime was the corruption of the human spirit.

---

[1]Gorky was a prominent Russian writer; Barbusse and Feuchtwanger were well-known Western European writers.

REVIEW QUESTIONS

1. In light of the A. O. Avdienko reading, how would you say Communists were supposed to feel about Stalin?
2. What were Yevgeny Yevtushenko's reasons for denouncing Stalin?
3. What do you think Yevtushenko meant by the "corruption of the human spirit" under Stalin?

---

5 Stalin's Terror

The victims of Stalin's terror number in the many millions. Stalin had no qualms about sacrificing multitudes of people to build up the Soviet Union's strength and to make it a powerful factor in world politics. In addition, he felt entitled to settle his own private scores as well as national ones against secessionist Ukrainians. The Soviet government's first acknowledgment of Stalin's terror was made by Khrushchev.

Nikita S. Khrushchev
KHRUSHCHEV'S SECRET SPEECH

Nikita Khrushchev (1894–1971), first secretary of the Communist party (1953–1964) and premier of the Soviet Union (1958–1964), delivered a famous speech to an unofficial, closed session of the twentieth Party Congress on February 25, 1956. Although the speech was considered confidential, it was soon leaked to outsiders. While safeguarding the moral authority of Lenin, Khrushchev attacked Stalin, who had died three years earlier, revealing some of the crimes committed by him and his closest associates in the 1930s. The following passages from the speech draw on evidence collected by a special commission of inquiry.

We have to consider seriously and analyze correctly this matter [the crimes of the Stalin era] in order that we may preclude any possibility of a repetition in any form whatever of what took place during the life of Stalin, who absolutely did not tolerate collegiality in leadership and in work, and who practiced brutal violence, not only toward everything which opposed him, but also toward that which seemed to his capricious and despotic character, contrary to his concepts.

Stalin acted not through persuasion, explanation, and patient co-operation with people, but by imposing his concepts and demanding absolute submission to his opinion. Whoever opposed this concept or tried to prove his viewpoint, and the correctness of his position, was doomed to removal from the leading collective and to subsequent moral and physical annihilation. This was especially true during the period following the XVIIth Party Congress [1934], when many prominent Party leaders and rank-and-file Party workers, honest and dedicated to the cause of Communism, fell victim to Stalin's despotism. . . .

Stalin originated the concept "enemy of the people." This term automatically rendered it unnecessary that the ideological errors of a man or men engaged in a controversy be proven; this term made possible the usage of the most cruel repression, violating all norms of revolutionary legality, against anyone who in any way disagreed with Stalin, against those who were only suspected of hostile intent, against those who had bad reputations. This concept, "enemy of the people," actually eliminated the possibility of any kind of ideological fight or the making of one's views known on this or that issue, even those of a practical character. In the main, and in actuality, the only proof of guilt used, against all norms of current legal science, was the "confession" of the accused himself; and, as subsequent probing proved, "confessions" were acquired through physical pressures against the accused.

This led to glaring violations of revolutionary legality, and to the fact that many entirely innocent persons, who in the past had defended the Party line, became victims. . . .

The Commission [of Inquiry] has become acquainted with a large quantity of materials in the NKVD [secret police, forerunner to the KGB] archives and with other documents and has established many facts pertaining to the fabrication of cases against Communists, to false accusations, to glaring abuses of socialist legality—which resulted in the death of innocent people. It became apparent that many Party, Soviet and economic activists who were branded in 1937–1938 as "enemies" were actually never enemies, spies, wreckers, etc., but were always honest Communists; they were only so stigmatized, and often, no longer able to bear barbaric tortures, they charged themselves (at the order of the investigative judges—falsifiers) with all kinds of grave and unlikely crimes. . . .

Lenin used severe methods only in the most necessary cases, when the exploiting classes were still in existence and were vigorously opposing the revolution, when the struggle for survival was decidedly assuming the sharpest forms, even including a civil war.

Stalin, on the other hand, used extreme methods and mass repressions at a time when the revolution was already victorious, when the Soviet state was strengthened, when the exploiting classes were already liquidated and Socialist relations were rooted solidly in all phases of national economy, when our Party was politically consolidated and had strengthened itself both numerically and ideologically. It is clear that here Stalin showed in a whole series of cases his intolerance, his brutality and his abuse of power. Instead of proving his political correctness and mobilizing the masses, he often chose the path of repression and physical annihilation, not only against actual enemies, but also against individuals who had not committed any crimes against the Party and the Soviet government. . . .

An example of vile provocation, of odious falsification and of criminal violation of revolutionary legality is the case of the former candidate for the Central Committee Political Bureau, one of the most eminent workers of the Party and of the Soviet government, Comrade Eikhe, who was a Party member since 1905. *(Commotion in the hall.)*

Comrade Eikhe was arrested on April 29, 1938, on the basis of slanderous materials, without the sanction of the Prosecutor of the USSR, which was finally received 15 months after the arrest.

Investigation of Eikhe's case was made in a manner which most brutally violated Soviet legality and was accompanied by willfulness and falsification.

Eikhe was forced under torture to sign ahead of time a protocol of his confession prepared by the investigative judges, in which he and several other eminent Party workers were accused of anti-Soviet activity.

On October 1, 1939, Eikhe sent his declaration to Stalin in which he categorically denied his guilt and asked for an examination of his case. In the declaration he wrote: "There is no more bitter misery than to sit in the jail of a government for which I have always fought."

A second declaration of Eikhe has been preserved which he sent to Stalin on October 27, 1939; in it he cited facts very convincingly and countered the slanderous accusations made against him, arguing that his provocatory accusation was on the one hand the work of real Trotskyites whose arrests he had sanctioned as First Secretary of the West Siberian Krai [local] Party Committee and who conspired in order to take revenge on him, and, on the other hand, the result of the base falsification of materials by the investigative judges. . . .

It would appear that such an important declaration was worth an examination by the Central Committee. This, however, was not done and the declaration was transmitted to Beria [head of the NKVD] while the terrible maltreatment of the Political Bureau candidate, Comrade Eikhe, continued.

On February 2, 1940, Eikhe was brought before the court. Here he did not confess any guilt and said as follows:

In all the so-called confessions of mine there is not one letter written by me with the exception of my signatures under the protocols which were forced from me. I have made my confession under pressure from the investigative judge who from the time of my arrest tormented me. After that I began to write all this nonsense. . . . The most important thing for me is to tell the court, the Party and Stalin that I am not guilty. I have never been guilty of any conspiracy. I will die believing in the truth of Party policy as I have believed in it during my whole life.

On February 4 Eikhe was shot. (*Indignation in the hall.*)

Lev Razgon
TRUE STORIES

"Corrective labor" was part of Stalin's efforts to terrorize the peoples of the Soviet Union into compliance with his plan to modernize the country's economy and society. All those accused of disloyalty to the party and not killed outright ended up in one of the *gulags. Gulag* is the Russian term for the Soviet forced-labor camps, scattered, like islands in an archipelago, over the entire Soviet Union. The inhabitants of that archipelago were the *zeks*, as the political prisoners were called. Their labor served a double purpose. It was designed as punishment for their alleged crimes and as a means of obtaining vital raw materials—including lumber and minerals—from areas too inhospitable for, or outright hostile to, regular labor. Forced labor also built the canal linking the Leningrad area with the White Sea in the far north.

In 1988, Lev Razgon, a survivor of Stalin's camps, published an account of his experiences, which appeared in English under the title *True Stories* in 1997. Razgon was a journalist who married the daughter of a high-ranking member of the Soviet secret police. Gaining access to the Soviet elite, in 1934 he attended the Seventeenth Party Congress. In 1937, his father-in-law was arrested for "counter-revolutionary" activities, along with many family friends; the following year the police came for Razgon and his wife. She perished in a transit prison en route to a northern camp, and Razgon spent the next seven years in a labor camp. Released in 1945, he was confined to various provincial towns, but in 1949 was rearrested and returned to the camps. Finally, he was released again in 1956 after Stalin's death.

Over the years Razgon began to write down his prison experiences for his desk drawer, with the specific intent of preserving the memory of fellow prisoners who did not survive. As the Soviet Union began to crumble, Razgon was able to publish his stories. The following extracts from *True Stories* reveal the brutality and irrationality of the Soviet prison system under Stalin. In the first selection, Razgon reproduces a discussion he had with a former prison guard, whom he met by chance in a hospital ward in 1977. The guard described to Razgon his role as an executioner of political prisoners.

THE ROUTINE OF EXECUTION

"It was like this. In the morning we'd hand everything over to the new shift and go into the guardhouse. We'd collect our weapons, and then and there they'd give us each a shot glass of vodka. After that we'd take the list and go round with the senior warder to pick them up from the cells and take them out to the truck."

"What kind of truck?"

"A closed van. Six of them and four of us in each one."

"How many trucks would leave at the same time?"

"Three or four."

"Did they know where they were going? Did someone read them their death sentence before, or what?"

"No, no sentences were announced. No one even spoke, just, 'Come out, then straight ahead, into the van—fast!'"

"Were they in handcuffs?"

"No, we didn't have any."

"How did they behave, once they were in the van?"

"The men, well, they kept quiet. But the women would start crying, they'd say: 'What are you doing, we're not guilty of anything, comrades, what are you doing?' and things like that."

"They used to take men and women together?"

"No, always separately."

"Were the women young? Were there a lot of them?"

"Not so many, about two vanloads a week. No very young ones but there were some about twenty-five or thirty. Most were older, and some even elderly."

"Did you drive them far?"

"Twelve kilometers or so, to the hill. The Distant Hill, it was called. There were hills all around and that's where we unloaded them."

"So you would unload them, and then tell them their sentence?"

"What was there to tell them?! No, we yelled, 'Out! Stand still!' They scrambled down and there was already a trench dug in front of them. They clambered down, clung together and right away we got to work. . . ."

"They didn't make any noise?"

"Some didn't, others began shouting, 'We're Communists, we are being wrongly executed,' that type of thing. But the women would only cry and cling to each other. So we just got on with it. . . ."

"Did you have a doctor with you?"

"What for? We would shoot them, and those still wriggling got another bullet and then we were off back to the van. The work team from the Dalag camps was already nearby, waiting."

"What work team was that?"

"There was a team of criminal inmates from Dalag who lived in a separate compound. They were the trusties[1] at Bikin and they also had to dig and fill in the pits. As soon as we left they would fill in that pit and dig a new one for the next day. When they finished their work, they went back to the compound. They got time off their sentence for it and were well fed. It was easy work, not like felling timber."

---

[1]Trusties were convicts regarded as trustworthy, who were given special duties and privileges.

"And what about you?"

"We would arrive back at the camp, hand in our weapons at the guardhouse and then we could have as much to drink as we wanted. The others used to lap it up—it didn't cost them a kopeck. I always had my shot, went off to the canteen for a hot meal, and then back to sleep in the barracks."

"And did you sleep well? Didn't you feel bad or anything?"

"Why should I?"

"Well, that you had just killed other people. Didn't you feel sorry for them?"

"No, not at all. I didn't give it a thought. No, I slept well and then I'd go for a walk outside the camp. There's some beautiful places around there. Boring, though, with no women."

"Were any of you married?"

"No, they didn't take married men. Of course, the bosses made out all right. There were some real lookers on the Dalag work team! Your head would spin! Cooks, dishwashers, floor cleaners— the bosses had them all. We went without. It was better not to even think about it. . . ."

"Grigory Ivanovich, did you know that the people you were shooting were not guilty at all, that they hadn't done anything wrong?"

"Well, we didn't think about that then. Later, yes. We were summoned to the procurators [officials] and they asked us questions. They explained that those had been innocent people. There had been mistakes, they said, and—what was the word?—excesses. But they told us that it was nothing to do with us, we were not guilty of anything."

"Well, I understand, then you were under orders and you shot people. But when you learned that you had been killing men and women who were not guilty at all, didn't your conscience begin to bother you?"

"Conscience? No, Naum'ich, it didn't bother me. I never think about all that now, and when I do remember something. . . . no, nothing at all, as if nothing had happened. You know, I've become so soft-hearted that one look at an old man suffering today and I feel so much pity

that I even cry sometimes. But those ones, no, I'm not sorry for them. Not at all, it's just like they never existed. . . ."

The "special operation" at Bikin existed for almost three years. Well, two and a half, to be more exact. It also probably had its holidays and weekends—perhaps no one was shot on Sundays, May Day, Revolution Day and the Day of the Soviet Constitution. Even so, that means that it functioned for a total of 770 days. Every morning on each of those days four trucks set out from Bikin compound for the Distant Hill. Six people in each truck, a total of 24. It took 25–30 minutes for them to reach the waiting pit. The "special operation" thus disposed of 15,000 to 18,000 people during its existence. Yet it was of a standard design, just like any transit camp. The well-tried, well-planned machinery operated without interruption, functioning regularly and efficiently, filling the ready-made pits with bodies—in the hills of the Far East, in the Siberian forests, and in the glades of the Tambov woods or the Meshchera nature reserve. They existed everywhere, yet nothing remains of them now. There are no terrible museums as there are today at Auschwitz [in Poland], or at Mauthausen in Austria. There are no solemn and funereal memorials like those that testify to the Nazi atrocities at . . . Lidice [and other European cities and towns].[2] Thousands of unnamed graves, in which there lie mingled the bones of hundreds of thousands of victims, have now been overgrown by bushes, thick luxuriant grass and young new forest. Not exactly the same as the Germans, it must be admitted. The men and women were buried separately

---

[2]After Czech resistance fighters assassinated Richard Heydrich, Chief of the Security Police, the Germans took savage revenge on the little Czech village of Lidice. They massacred all the men and deported the women and children to concentration camps (some children with suitable "Aryan features" were sent to live with German families and to be reared as Germans). The Nazis then burned, dynamited, and levelled the village.

here. Our regime made sure that even at that point no moral laxity might occur.

And the murderers? They are still alive.

. . . There were a great many, of course, who took part in these shootings. There were yet more, however, who never made the regular journey to the Distant Hill or the other killing grounds. Only in bourgeois society are the procurator and others obliged to attend an execution. Under our regime, thank God, that was not necessary. There were many, many more involved in these murders than those who simply pulled the trigger. For them a university degree, often in the "humanities," was more common than the rudimentary education of the Niyazovs [the former guard Razgon questioned]. They drafted the instructions and decisions; they signed beneath the words "agreed," "confirmed," "to be sentenced to . . ." Today they are all retired and most of them receive large individual pensions. They sit in the squares and enjoy watching the children play. They go to concerts and are moved by the music. We meet them when we attend a meeting, visit friends, or find ourselves sitting at the same table, celebrating with our common acquaintances. They are alive, and there are many of them.

COLLECTIVE GUILT

In the most general terms, paragraph 17 [of the Soviet criminal code] said that each member of a criminal group (and membership in that group was expressed by knowledge of its existence and failure to report it) was responsible not only for his own individual criminal deeds but also for the deeds of the criminal group as a whole and for each of its individual members, taken separately. It did not matter that the individual in question might not know the other members of the group, might be unaware what they were up to, and might not have any idea at all what the group he belonged to was doing. The purpose of the "doctrine of complicity" was to alleviate the exhausting labors of the interrogators. Undoubtedly, however, it also lightened

the burden of those under investigation. The techniques of cross-examination became far simpler. Several dozen people were linked together in a group and then one of them, the weakest, was beaten almost to death in order to obtain confessions of espionage, sabotage, subversion and, of course, attempts on the life of "one of the leaders of the Party and the government." The others could be more gently treated, only requiring beating until they admitted they knew the individual who had given a "complete and full confession." Then the same crimes, in accordance with paragraph 17, were automatically attributed to them as well. What this sounded like during a court hearing I can describe from the words of a man I came to know in the camps.

Yefim Shatalov was a very high-ranking manager and for years he headed the State Cement Administration. Why they needed to send him to prison, God only knows! He had no political interests or involvements and did not wish to have any, since he was always prepared to serve his immediate superior faithfully and truthfully, and was unquestionably loyal to his ultimate chief, Comrade Stalin. Furthermore, he was incredibly circumspect and every step he took was protected by an entire system of safety measures. When he was baldly accused of sabotage he conducted himself so aggressively in court that the judge, in panic, deferred the hearing of his case. Some time after, Shatalov was presented with a new charge sheet and within an hour he was summoned to appear before a new sitting of the Military Tribunal. The chairman now was Ulrich himself. For the defendant Vasya Ulrich was an old, dear and kind acquaintance. For many years they had always sat at the same table at the Party elite's sanatorium, The Pines; they went for walks together, shared a drink or two, and exchanged men's jokes. Evidently the chairman was observing the old principles that justice must be rapid, fair and clement in his conduct of this hearing. What follows includes almost everything that was said, as recalled by Yefim Shatalov.

ULRICH (in a business-like, quiet, and jaded voice): Defendant! you have read the charge sheet? Do you recognize your guilt?

SHATALOV (with all the force of his love and loyalty to the judge): No! I am not guilty in any respect!

ULRICH: Did you know that there was a counter-revolutionary Right-Trotskyist organization in the People's Commissariat of Heavy Industry?

SHATALOV (throwing up his arms): I had no idea whatsoever. I had no suspicion there was such a hostile gang of saboteurs and terrorists there.

ULRICH (gazing with affectionate attention at his former drinking companion): You were not in prison during the last trial of the Right-Trotskyist center, were you?

SHATALOV: No, I was not.

ULRICH: You were reading the newspapers then?

SHATALOV (slowly, trying to grasp the purpose of such a strange question): I did. . . .

ULRICH: So you read Pyatakov's testimony that there was a counter-revolutionary organization in the People's Commissariat of Heavy Industry?

SHATALOV (uncertainly): Of course, of course.

ULRICH (triumphantly): Well, there we are! So you knew there was a counter-revolutionary organization in the People's Commissariat of Heavy Industry. (Turning to the secretary of the court.) Write down: the defendant acknowledges that he knew about the existence of Pyatakov's organization. . . .

SHATALOV (shouts passionately, stuttering from horror): But it was from the newspapers, the newspapers, that I learnt there was an organization there!

ULRICH (calm and satisfied): But to the court it is not important where you found out. You knew! (Hurriedly, like a priest at a poorly-paid funeral.) Any questions? No. You want to say a last word? No need for repetition, we've heard it already! (Nodding right and left at his assessors.) I pronounce sentence. Mmmh . . . 15 years . . .

I shall not insist that this trial strictly met the requirement for fairness. Yet compared to others it was clement, leaving Shatalov among the living. And it was indisputably rapid. Evidently the speed was typical. In the late 1950s I attended a memorial evening at the Museum of the Revolution for Kosarev, the 1930s Komsomol leader executed by Stalin. The head of the Central Committee administrative department told me that Khrushchev had entrusted him to re-examine Kosarev's case: "The hearing began at 11.00 a.m.," read the record of the trial, "and ended at 11.10 a.m."

THE HEARTLESS BUREAUCRACY

Auntie Pasha, a kindly middle-aged woman, washed the floors in the camp office. She pitied the office workers because they were so helpless and impractical: and she darned and sewed patches on the trousers and quilt jackets of the "trusties" who were not yet privileged to wear first-hand clothing. The story of her life was simple. Auntie Pasha came from Zlatoust in the Urals. Her husband, a furnace man, died during an accident at work and she was left with two teenage sons. Their life was predictably hard. Someone taught Auntie Pasha to go to Chelyabinsk to buy stockings and then sell them (naturally, at a suitably higher price) in Zlatoust where they were not to be found. The rest was recorded in the charge sheet and the sentence passed by the court. "For the purposes of speculation" she had "obtained 72 pairs of knitted stockings in Chelyabinsk which she then tried to resell at the market in Zlatoust." Auntie Pasha was reported, arrested, tried and sentenced to seven years imprisonment with confiscation of all her property. The children were taken in by acquaintances and, besides, they were almost old enough to take up any profession at the trade school. Five years passed, the war began, and Auntie Pasha's boys had reached the age when they could defend the Motherland. So off they went to fight. First Auntie Pasha was informed that her younger son had been killed. Staying behind in the office at night to wash the floors, she moaned and beat her head against the table.

Then one evening she came up to me with a glassy-eyed expression and handed over a thick package which she had been given in Records and Distribution. This contained several medical reports and the decisions of various commissions. To these was added a letter to Auntie Pasha from the hospital administrator. It concerned her elder son. He had been severely wounded and was in the hospital. The doctors had done all within their power and he was, as they put it in his medical history, "fit, to all intents and purposes"—apart, that is, from having lost both arms and one leg. He could be discharged from the hospital if there was some close relation to look after him. Evidently the son had explained where she was because the administrator advised the mother of this wounded soldier to send an appeal to the USSR Procurator General's Office, including the enclosed documents, after which they would release her and she could come and fetch him.

"Manuilich, dear heart," Auntie Pasha said, starting to cry, "You write for me."

So I wrote, and very persuasively. I attached all the documents and handed in the letter. Two or three months passed, and each day I reassured Auntie Pasha: they received a great many such appeals, I told her, and it would take time to process her release. I described in detail the lengthy procedures as her application passed from one level to another. Auntie Pasha wept, but believed me and each day I gave her paper on which to write her son a letter.

One day I went into Records and Distribution myself. A great pile of mail lay on the table, already sorted out to be handed over, or its contents communicated, to the prisoners. Auntie Pasha's surname caught my eye. I picked up the flimsy sheet of headed paper from the USSR Procurator General's Office and read it through. A public procurator of a certain rank or class informed Auntie Pasha that her application had been examined and her request for early release turned down because there were "no grounds." I carefully placed the single sheet on the table and went out onto the verandah, terrified that I might suddenly meet Auntie Pasha. . . . Everywhere, in the barracks and in the office, there were people I did not want to see. I ran to the latrines and there, clinging to the stinking walls, started to shake uncontrollably. Only two times in my prison life did this happen. Why was I crying? Then I understood: I felt ashamed, terribly ashamed, before Auntie Pasha.

She had already served five years for 72 pairs of stockings. She had given the state her two sons. Now, there it was, there were "no grounds.". . .

REVIEW QUESTIONS

1. Why was Nikita Khrushchev careful to distinguish Stalin from Lenin?
2. What charges against Stalin did Khrushchev highlight in his speech?
3. What image of Stalin did Khrushchev draw?
4. From a reading of these passages from Lev Razgon's book, what do you think motivated the behavior of Stalin's bureaucrats who committed these terrible crimes?

6 The Rise of Italian Fascism

Benito Mussolini (1883–1945) started his political life as a socialist and in 1912 was appointed editor of *Avanti*, the leading socialist newspaper. During World War I, Mussolini was expelled from the Socialist Party for advocating Italy's entry into the conflict. Immediately after the war, he organized the Fascist Party. Exploiting labor unrest, fear of Communism, and thwarted nationalist hopes, Mussolini gained followers among veterans and the middle class. Powerful industrialists and landowners, viewing the Fascists as a bulwark against Communism, helped to finance the young movement. An opportunist, Mussolini organized a march on Rome in 1922 to bring down the government. King Victor Emmanuel, fearful of civil war, appointed the Fascist leader prime minister. Had Italian liberals and the king taken a firm stand, the government could have easily crushed the 20,000 lightly armed marchers.

Benito Mussolini
FASCIST DOCTRINES

Ten years after he seized power, Mussolini, assisted by philosopher Giovanni Gentile (1875–1944), contributed an article to the *Italian Encyclopedia* in which he discussed Fascist political and social doctrines. In this piece, Mussolini lauded violence as a positive experience; attacked Marxism for denying idealism by subjecting human beings to economic laws and for dividing the nation into warring classes; and denounced liberal democracy for promoting individual selfishness at the expense of the national community and for being unable to solve the nation's problems. The Fascist state, he said, required unity and power, not individual freedom. The following excerpts are from Mussolini's article.

. . . Above all, Fascism, the more it considers and observes the future and the development of humanity quite apart from political considerations of the moment, believes neither in the possibility nor the utility of perpetual peace. It thus repudiates the doctrine of Pacifism— born of a renunciation of the struggle and an act of cowardice in the face of sacrifice. War alone brings up to its highest tension all human energy and puts the stamp of nobility upon the peoples who have the courage to meet it. All other trials are substitutes, which never really put men into the position where they have to make the great decision—the alternative of life or death. Thus a doctrine which is founded upon this harmful postulate of peace is hostile to Fascism. And thus hostile to the spirit of Fascism, though accepted for what use they can be in dealing with particular political situations, are all the international leagues and societies which, as history will show, can be scattered to the winds when once strong national feeling is aroused by any motive—sentimental, ideal, or practical. This anti-pacifist spirit is carried by Fascism even into the life of the individual; the proud motto of the *Squadrista*, "Me ne frego" [It doesn't matter], written on the bandage of the wound, is an act of philosophy not only stoic, the summary of a doctrine not only political—it is the education to combat, the acceptation of the risks which combat implies, and a new way of life for Italy. Thus the Fascist accepts life and loves it, knowing nothing of and despising suicide: he rather conceives of life as duty and struggle and conquest, life which should be high and full, lived for oneself, but above all for others—those who are at hand and those who are far distant, contemporaries, and those who will come after. . . .

. . . Fascism [is] the complete opposite of . . . Marxian Socialism, the materialist conception of history; according to which the history of human civilization can be explained simply through the conflict of interests among the various social groups and by the change and development in the means and instruments of production. That the changes in the economic field—new discoveries of raw materials, new methods of working them, and the inventions of science—have their importance no one can deny; but that these factors are sufficient to explain the history of humanity excluding all others is an absurd delusion. Fascism, now and always, believes in holiness and in heroism; that is to say, in actions influenced by no economic motive, direct or indirect. And if the economic conception of history be denied, according to which theory men are no more than puppets, carried to and fro by the waves of chance, while the real directing forces are quite out of their control, it follows that the existence of an unchangeable and unchanging class-war is also denied—the natural progeny of the economic conception of history. And above all Fascism denies that class-war can be the preponderant force in the transformation of society. . . .

After Socialism, Fascism combats the whole complex system of democratic ideology, and repudiates it, whether in its theoretical premises or in its practical application. Fascism denies that the majority, by the simple fact that it is a majority, can direct human society; it denies that numbers alone can govern by means of a periodical consultation, and it affirms the immutable, beneficial, and fruitful inequality of mankind, which can never be permanently leveled through the mere operation of a mechanical process such as universal suffrage. . . .

. . . Fascism denies, in democracy, the absurd conventional untruth of political equality dressed out in the garb of collective irresponsibility, and the myth of "happiness" and indefinite progress. . . .

. . . Given that the nineteenth century was the century of Socialism, of Liberalism, and of Democracy, it does not necessarily follow that the twentieth century must also be a century of Socialism, Liberalism, and Democracy: political doctrines pass, but humanity remains; and it may rather be expected that this will be a century of authority, . . . a century of Fascism. For if the nineteenth century was a century of individualism (Liberalism always signifying individualism) it may be expected that this will be the century of collectivism, and hence the century of the State. . . .

The foundation of Fascism is the conception of the State, its character, its duty, and its aim. Fascism conceives of the State as an absolute, in comparison with which all individuals or groups are relative, only to be conceived of in their relation to the State. The conception of the Liberal State is not that of a directing force, guiding the play and development, both material and spiritual, of a collective body, but merely a force limited to the function of recording results: on the other hand, the Fascist State is itself conscious and has itself a will and a personality—thus it may be called the "ethic" State. . . .

. . . The Fascist State organizes the nation, but leaves a sufficient margin of liberty to the individual; the latter is deprived of all useless and possibly harmful freedom, but retains what is essential; the deciding power in this question cannot be the individual, but the State alone. . . .

. . . For Fascism, the growth of empire, that is to say the expansion of the nation, is an essential manifestation of vitality, and its opposite a sign of decadence. Peoples which are rising, or rising again after a period of decadence, are always imperialist; any renunciation is a sign of decay and of death. Fascism is the doctrine best adapted to represent the tendencies and the aspirations of a people, like the people of Italy, who are rising again after many centuries of abasement and foreign servitude. But empire demands discipline, the coordination of all forces and a deeply felt sense of duty and sacrifice: this fact explains many aspects of the practical working of the régime, the character of many forces in the State, and the necessarily severe measures which must be taken against those who would oppose this spontaneous and inevitable movement of Italy in the twentieth century, and would oppose it by recalling the outworn ideology of the nineteenth century—repudiated wheresoever there has been the courage to undertake great experiments of social and political transformation; for never before has the nation stood more in need of authority, of direction, and of order. If every age has its own characteristic doctrine, there are a thousand signs which point to Fascism as the characteristic doctrine of our time. For if a doctrine must be a living thing, this is proved by the fact that Fascism has created a living faith; and that this faith is very powerful in the minds of men is demonstrated by those who have suffered and died for it.

REVIEW QUESTIONS

1. Why did Benito Mussolini consider Pacifism to be the enemy of Fascism?
2. Why did Mussolini attack Marxism?
3. How did Mussolini view majority rule and equality?
4. What relationship did Mussolini see between the individual and the state?

7 The Great Depression

The Great Depression started in the United States in 1929 and quickly spread throughout the world. In the 1920s, hundreds of thousands of Americans had bought stock on credit; this buying spree sent stock prices soaring well beyond what the stocks were actually worth. In late October 1929, the stock market was hit by a wave of panic selling; prices plummeted. Within a few weeks, the value of stocks listed on the New York Stock Exchange fell by some $26 billion. A terrible chain reaction followed. Businesses cut production and fired their employees; farmers unable to meet mortgage payments lost their land; banks that had made poor investments closed down. American investors withdrew the capital they had invested in Europe, causing European banks and businesses to fail. Throughout the world, trade declined and unemployment soared.

Max Cohen
I WAS ONE OF THE UNEMPLOYED

Mounting unemployment reinforced a sense of hopelessness in the British and cast a pall over Great Britain. Despite the economic slump of the 1920s and the Great Depression, the country remained politically stable, a testament to the strength of its parliamentary tradition. Neither the Communists nor the newly formed British Union of Fascists gained mass support. Not until Britain began to rearm did unemployment decline significantly.

Max Cohen was a twenty-year-old cabinetmaker when he lost his job in 1931 and joined over three million unemployed workers in Great Britain. His firsthand account of privation, hunger, and loss of self-respect was published in 1945. In the following selection he describes the psychological wounds suffered by the unemployed.

Many people cannot understand why so many unemployed become, if not out-and-out nervous wrecks, then at least gloomy shadows of their former selves, walking phantoms of worry and dejection. Some people take it upon themselves to "cheer the unemployed up," "make them look on the bright side of life," and so on.

"Tut, tut, my dear fellow," they say, kindly and well-meaningly, "there is no need for you to get downhearted. Every cloud has a silver lining . . . the darkest hour is before the dawn," and similar amiable platitudes.

These people forget, do not know, cannot know, the multifarious sources of worry that can afflict an out-of-work. Unemployment brings into being many diverse sources of worry which become so intermingled and interlocked that their cumulative effect is well-nigh intolerable.

These worries are not merely financial—though of course financial worries are at the root of the whole problem. When a man has been out-of-work for any length of time, he begins to worry about his past, his present, and above all about his future. He worries about himself and about his wife and his children and his parents; in short, about himself and his dependants.

He worries about the Labour Exchange[1]; about how long it will be before his present parlous financial condition gives way to a worse. He worries because he has too much time on his hands, and he worries because nearly all the more pleasant ways of passing his time are barred to him. He worries about his clothes, because they are shabby; and he worries because

soon, willy-nilly, he will have to get new ones for himself and his family, and he does not know where the money for them is coming from.

And above all, more bitter than gall is the fact that day after day, despite search after search, application after application, work is denied to him. In the vast edifice of our civilisation there is no useful work to be given to him—work that will at one and the same time enable him to be an equal with his fellow-men, and provide him with the necessities of life and peace of mind.

It may be thought that unemployed single men or women will not be so affected by worry as those unemployed who are married and have children. What must be kept clear, however, is that it is not the fact of marriage and children that is the basic cause of worry to the unemployed. The basic cause of worry is the fact of unemployment. Single men and women are just as much worried by unemployment as married people, with the additional fact that they are often living on their own and have no one with whom to share their more secret and agonising worries. Moreover, young people need that interchange of experience between the sexes known as "romance." Too often unemployment makes a romantic social life impossible; where it comes into being in spite of unemployment it is starved and stultified and poisoned, owing to the lack of the elementary material basis to keep it alive and healthy.

What is astonishing is not that there are some unemployed men and women who are nervous wrecks and psychopathic cases (the medical statistics on this question would surprise many people), but that there are not many more.

---

[1]The Labour Exchange is a government office where unemployment compensation is paid out.

It is, however, not the least crime of the present social system that there are today, at this very moment, thousands upon thousands of people who are suffering what can be literally described as excruciating mental tortures. They suffer in this way not because they are congenitally more neurotic than the average, but solely and simply because anarchic social forces have uprooted them, and undermined their social, economic, and therefore psychological stability.

Psychological suffering or instability does not necessarily reveal itself openly to the casual observer. There are far more cases of abnormal psychology signing on at the Labour Exchanges than are apparent on the surface, because relatively few are really noticeable. Nevertheless, those who, by reason of their more unbearable existence on the dole,[2] combined with the lesser stability of the temperament, have become somewhat abnormal, are generally those who talk loudest and most vociferously in the queues. They argue vehemently about things that don't matter, and are often very aggrieved and angry over things that are not of very great importance.

Cases of people who have become abnormal because of the intolerable harshness of their economic existence are more noticeable among "down-and-outs" than among others—though whether it is psychological abnormality that has made them down-and-out, or the fact of being down-and-out that has created a psychological instability, is a moot point. Neither conclusion reflects a very flattering light on the present social system. . . .

I myself could not continue living alone for months under intolerable conditions without being affected not merely physically, but mentally. These mental effects could be divided into two kinds. The first was more or less gradual and cumulative in its results. The second was sudden in its onslaught, though more temporary in character.

The first of these effects has been more or less indicated, in passing, in what has been told

previously. It consisted of the slow but sure change in my attitude to the world and to myself. It took the form of a lack of self-confidence and an absence of self-respect; a tacit assumption of inferiority to nearly everyone, and an innate certainty that I was not, and never would be, a useful member of society. These unspoken and unconsidered feelings increased and became part of my intellectual make-up in geometrical proportion to the length of my unemployment.

Distressing though these feelings were, particularly when they reached consciousness and were accompanied by depression and pessimism, they were as nothing compared to that which came later. Privation and frustration gave birth to a distress of mind which went beyond reasoning and control.

I had felt for some time vague moods of uneasiness and depression. Then an incident took place which at one stroke catapulted me into a state in which morbidness began to play an ever-increasing rôle.

One day as I stood waiting in the queue at the Labour Exchange, the thought came to me that it was fantastic to be standing waiting so long in a queue just in order to sign one's name. I agreed with myself that it was fantastic, though I felt too tired to reason why it should be more fantastic than anything else. The thought recurred to me: "It's fantastic!" Again the thought recurred, insistently: "It's fantastic!" Suddenly everything seemed fantastic—the whole complex of civilisation, with its underfed and under-clothed unemployed, its idle, sybaritic [luxury loving] upper strata, its teeming millions of earnest workers by hand and brain, so essentially naïve and innocent in the way they tolerated the drones in their beehive—it was all fantastic.

The feeling became more intense: "It's fantastic!", still more intense. "It's fantastic!" I began to be alarmed. ("All right, no need to be excited about it! Calm down.") It was unreal—everything was unreal. I could not shake off a nightmarish sense that it was all unreal; everything was unreal: the Labour Exchange was unreal; the clerks were unreal; the notices were

---

[2]The "dole" was unemployment compensation.

unreal; the crowd was unreal; I was unreal. Terror smote me like a blow. My heart began to pound. What—what was all this about, anyway? ("Keep a grip on yourself, man! What's up with you?") Unreal . . . unreal . . . unreal. . . .

Sweat stood out on my forehead. Where am I? What's happening? ("Keep a grip on yourself, man!") . . . A grey mist was descending before my eyes. There was a sinister roar in my ears. The walls of the Labour Exchange seemed to crowd around me, threatening to shut me tightly in narrow confines. The crowd clamoured from far away. I was weak, my knees were as water, the blood was perceptibly draining from my face, "Am I going to faint?" The thought boomed in the huge, hollow emptiness of my brain. . . .

After this incident an unwelcome visitor began to insinuate himself gradually but persistently into my being. At first he was unnoticed. When I became aware of his presence I tried to dismiss him with increasing anger. Then perforce I accepted his presence. Then I became his slave, and the thought of banishing him from me became as the thought of some unattainable hope. The name of this visitor?—his name was Fear.

I began to be vaguely afraid of different things for brief periods. Then I became more definitely afraid of more things for longer times. Eventually I lived under a menacing cloud of fear that darkened my whole existence.

I became unreasonably afraid of things innocuous in themselves. I began to be afraid of being afraid. Life and its manifestations became transformed into subject-matter for fear. I began after a time subconsciously to approach things from the standpoint of whether they would make me afraid or not. . . .

Ordinary fear sometimes acts as a stimulant. It has a certain dread excitement which is sometimes a spur to action, even to heroism. But this unreasoning and uncontrollable emotion brought with it no such possibilities. There was no immediately obvious cause for it, no objective happenings or surroundings to which it could be immediately traced. It was a hellish brew, compounded of crushing despair, an abysmal sinking of the heart, and a mental distress so acute as to be well-nigh indistinguishable from physical pain.

I grew to an attitude of life that was entirely morbid. I sank deeper and deeper into a vortex of fear, depression, despair.

Heinrich Hauser
"With Germany's Unemployed"

The following article excerpted from the periodical *Die Tat* [The Deed] describes the loss of dignity suffered by the unemployed wandering Germany's roads and taking shelter in municipal lodging houses. The author, a German writer, experienced conditions in a public shelter firsthand. Conditions in 1932 as described in the article radicalized millions of Germans, particularly young people, and led them to embrace Hitler's leadership.

An almost unbroken chain of homeless men extends the whole length of the great Hamburg-Berlin highway.

There are so many of them moving in both directions, impelled by the wind or making their way against it, that they could shout a message from Hamburg to Berlin by word of mouth.

It is the same scene for the entire two hundred miles, and the same scene repeats itself between Hamburg and Bremen, between Bremen and

Kassel, between Kassel and Würzburg, between Würtzburg and Munich. All the highways in Germany over which I traveled this year presented the same aspects. . . .

. . . Most of the hikers paid no attention to me. They walked separately or in small groups, with their eyes on the ground. And they had the queer, stumbling gait of barefooted people, for their shoes were slung over their shoulders. Some of them were guild members,—carpenters with embroidered wallets, knee breeches, and broad felt hats; milkmen with striped red shirts, and bricklayers with tall black hats,—but they were in a minority. Far more numerous were those whom one could assign to no special profession or craft—unskilled young people, for the most part, who had been unable to find a place for themselves in any city or town in Germany, and who had never had a job and never expected to have one. There was something else that had never been seen before—whole families that had piled all their goods into baby carriages and wheelbarrows that they were pushing along as they plodded forward in dumb despair. It was a whole nation on the march.

I saw them—and this was the strongest impression that the year 1932 left with me—I saw them, gathered into groups of fifty or a hundred men, attacking fields of potatoes. I saw them digging up the potatoes and throwing them into sacks while the farmer who owned the field watched them in despair and the local policeman looked on gloomily from the distance. I saw them staggering toward the lights of the city as night fell, with their sacks on their backs. What did it remind me of? Of the War, of the worst periods of starvation in 1917 and 1918, but even then people paid for the potatoes. . . .

I saw that the individual can know what is happening only by personal experience. I know what it is to be a tramp. I know what cold and hunger are. I know what it is to spend the night outdoors or behind the thin walls of a shack through which the wind whistles. I have slept in holes such as hunters hide in, in hayricks, under bridges, against the warm walls of boiler houses, under cattle shelters in pastures,

on a heap of fir-tree boughs in the forest. But there are two things that I have only recently experienced—begging and spending the night in a municipal lodging house.

I entered the huge Berlin municipal lodging house in a northern quarter of the city. . . .

. . . There was an entrance arched by a brick vaulting, and a watchman sat in a little wooden sentry box. His white coat made him look like a doctor. We stood waiting in the corridor. Heavy steam rose from the men's clothes. Some of them sat down on the floor, pulled off their shoes, and unwound the rags that were bound around their feet. More people were constantly pouring in the door, and we stood closely packed together. Then another door opened. The crowd pushed forward, and people began forcing their way almost eagerly through this door, for it was warm in there. Without knowing it I had already caught the rhythm of the municipal lodging house. It means waiting, waiting, standing around, and then suddenly jumping up.

We now stand in a long hall, down the length of which runs a bar dividing the hall into a narrow and a wide space. All the light is on the narrow side. There under yellow lamps that hang from the ceiling on long wires sit men in white smocks. We arrange ourselves in long lines, each leading up to one of these men, and the mill begins to grind. . . .

. . . As the line passes in single file the official does not look up at each new person to appear. He only looks at the paper that is handed to him. These papers are for the most part invalid cards or unemployment certificates. The very fact that the official does not look up robs the homeless applicant of self-respect, although he may look too beaten down to feel any. . . .

. . . Now it is my turn and the questions and answers flow as smoothly as if I were an old hand. But finally I am asked, "Have you ever been here before?"

"No."

"No?" The question reverberates through the whole room. The clerk refuses to believe me and looks through his card catalogue. But no, my name is not there. The clerk thinks this strange, for he cannot have made a mistake, and the terrible thing that one notices in all these clerks is that they expect you to lie. They do not believe what you say. They do not regard you as a human being but as an infection, something foul that one keeps at a distance. He goes on. "How did you come here from Hamburg?"

"By truck."

"Where have you spent the last three nights?"

I lie coolly.

"Have you begged?"

I feel a warm blush spreading over my face. It is welling up from the bourgeois world that I have come from. "No."

A course peal of laughter rises from the line, and a loud, piercing voice grips me as if someone had seized me by the throat: "Never mind. The day will come, comrade, when there's nothing else to do." And the line breaks into laughter again, the bitterest laughter I have ever heard, the laughter of damnation and despair. . . .

Again the crowd pushes back in the kind of rhythm that is so typical of a lodging house, and we are all herded into the undressing room. It is like all the other rooms except that it is divided by benches and shelves like a fourth-class railway carriage. I cling to the man who spoke to me. He is a Saxon with a friendly manner and he has noticed that I am a stranger here. A certain sensitiveness, an almost perverse, spiritual alertness makes me like him very much.

Out of a big iron chest each of us takes a coat hanger that would serve admirably to hit somebody over the head with. As we undress the room becomes filled with the heavy breath of poverty. We are so close together that we brush against each other every time we move. Anyone who has been a soldier, anyone who has been to a public bath is perfectly accustomed to the look of naked bodies. But I have never seen anything quite so repulsive as all these hundreds of withered human frames. For in the homeless army the majority are men who have already been defeated in the struggle of life, the crippled, old, and sick. There is no repulsive disease of which traces are not to be seen here. There is no form of mutilation or degeneracy that is not

represented, and the naked bodies of the old men are in a disgusting state of decline. . . .

It is superfluous to describe what follows. Towels are handed out by the same methods described above. Then nightgowns—long, sack-like affairs made of plain unbleached cotton but freshly washed. Then slippers. All at once a new sound goes up from the moving mass that has been walking silently on bare feet. The shuffling and rattling of the hard soles of the slippers ring through the corridor.

Distribution of spoons, distribution of enameledware bowls with the words "Property of the City of Berlin" written on their sides. Then the meal itself. A big kettle is carried in. Men with yellow smocks have brought it and men with yellow smocks ladle out the food. These men, too, are homeless and they have been expressly picked by the establishment and given free food and lodging and a little pocket money in exchange for their work about the house.

Where have I seen this kind of food distribution before? In a prison that I once helped to guard in the winter of 1919 during the German civil war. There was the same hunger then, the same trembling, anxious expectation of rations. Now the men are standing in a long row, dressed in their plain nightshirts that reach to the ground, and the noise of their shuffling feet is like the noise of big wild animals walking up and down the stone floor of their cages before feeding time. The men lean far over the kettle so that the warm steam from the food envelops them and they hold out their bowls as if begging and whisper to the attendant. "Give me a real helping. Give me a little more." A piece of bread is handed out with every bowl.

My next recollection is sitting at table in another room on a crowded bench that is like a seat in a fourth-class railway carriage. Hundreds of hungry mouths make an enormous noise eating their food. The men sit bent over their food like animals who feel that someone is going to take it away from them. They hold their bowl with their left arm part way around it, so that nobody can take it away, and they also protect it with their other elbow and with their head and mouth, while they move the spoon as fast as they can between their mouth and the bowl. . . .

We shuffle into the sleeping room, where each bed has a number painted in big letters on the wall over it. You must find the number that you have around your neck, and there is your bed, your home for one night. It stands in a row with fifty others and across the room there are fifty more in a row. . . .

I curl up in a ball for a few minutes and then see that the Saxon is lying the same way, curled up in the next bed. We look at each other with eyes that understand everything . . .

. . . Only a few people, very few, move around at all. The others lie awake and still, staring at their blankets, wrapped up in themselves but not sleeping. Only an almost soldierly sense of comradeship, an inner self-control engendered by the presence of so many people, prevents the despair that is written on all these faces from expressing itself. The few who are moving about do so with the tormenting consciousness of men who merely want to kill time. They do not believe in what they are doing.

Going to sleep means passing into the unconscious, eliminating the intelligence. And one can read deeply into a man's life by watching the way he goes to sleep. For we have not always slept in municipal lodgings. There are men among us who still move as if they were in a bourgeois bedchamber. . . .

. . . The air is poisoned with the breath of men who have stuffed too much food into empty stomachs. There is also a sickening smell of lysol. It seems completely terrible to me, and I am not merely pitying myself. It is painful just to look at the scene. Life is no longer human here. Today, when I am experiencing this for the first time, I think that I should prefer to do away with myself, to take gas, to jump into the river, or leap from some high place, if I were ever reduced to such straits that I had to live here in the lodging house. But I have had too much experience not to mistrust even myself. If I ever were reduced so low, would I really come to such a decision? I do not know. Animals die, plants wither, but men always go on living.

REVIEW QUESTION

1. Both Max Cohen and Heinrich Hauser offer astute insights into the psychological impact on those victimized by unemployment. Provide some examples.

8 The Rise of Nazism

Many extreme racist-nationalist and paramilitary organizations sprang up in postwar Germany. Adolf Hitler (1889–1945), a veteran of World War I, joined one of these organizations, which became known as the National Socialist German Worker's Party (commonly called the Nazi party). Hitler's uncanny insight into the state of mind of postwar Germans, along with his extraordinary oratorical gifts, enabled him to gain control of the party. Had it not been for the Great Depression that began in late 1929, the National Socialists might have remained a relatively small and insignificant party, a minor irritant outside the mainstream of German politics. In 1928 the Nazis had 810,000 votes; in 1930, during the Depression, their share of votes soared to 6,400,000. To many Germans, the Depression was final evidence that the Weimar Republic had failed.

Adolf Hitler
MEIN KAMPF

In the "Beer Hall Putsch" of November 1923, Hitler attempted to overthrow the state government in Bavaria as the first step in bringing down the Weimar Republic. But the Nazis quickly scattered when the Bavarian police opened fire. Hitler was arrested and sentenced to five years' imprisonment—he served only nine months. While in prison, Hitler wrote *Mein Kampf (My Struggle)* (1925–1926), in which he presented his views. The book came to be regarded as an authoritative expression of the Nazi world-view and served as a kind of sacred writing for the Nazi movement.

Hitler's thought—a patchwork of nineteenth-century anti-Semitic, Volkish, Social Darwinist, and anti-Marxist ideas—contrasted sharply with the core values of both the Judeo-Christian and the Enlightenment traditions. Central to Hitler's world-view was racial mythology: a heroic Germanic race that was descended from the ancient Aryans, who once swept across Europe, and was battling for survival against racial inferiors. In the following passages excerpted from *Mein Kampf*, Hitler presents his views of race, of propaganda, and of National Socialist territorial goals.

THE PRIMACY OF RACE

Nature does not want a pairing of weaker individuals with stronger ones; it wants even less a mating of a higher race with a weaker one. Otherwise its routine labors of promoting a higher breed lasting perhaps over hundreds of thousands of years would be wiped out.

History offers much evidence for this process. It proves with terrifying clarity that any genetic mixture of Aryan blood with people of a lower quality undermines the culturally superior people. The population of North America consists to a large extent of Germanic elements, which have mixed very little with inferior people of color. Central and South America shows a different humanity and culture; here Latin immigrants mixed with the aborigines, sometimes on a large scale. This example alone allows a clear recognition of the effects of racial mixtures. Remaining racially pure the Germans of North America rose to be masters of their continent; they will remain masters as long as they do not defile their blood.

The result of mixing races in short is: a) lowering the cultural level of the higher race;

b) physical and spiritual retrogression and thus the beginning of a slow but progressive decline.

To promote such a development means no less than committing sin against the will of the eternal creator. . . .

Everything that we admire on earth—science, technology, invention—is the creative product of only a few people, and perhaps originally of only *one* race; our whole culture depends upon them. If they perish, the beauties of the earth will be buried. . . .

All great cultures of the past perished because the original creative race was destroyed by the poisoning of its blood.

Such collapse always happened because people forgot that all cultures depend on human beings. In order to preserve a given culture it is necessary to preserve the human beings who created it. Cultural preservation in this world is tied to the iron law of necessity and the right to victory of the stronger and better. . . .

If we divide humanity into three categories: into founders of culture, bearers of culture, and destroyers of culture, the Aryan would undoubtedly rate first. He established the foundations and walls of all human progress. . . .

The mixing of blood and the resulting lowering of racial cohesion is the sole reason why cultures perish. People do not perish by defeat in war, but by losing the power of resistance inherent in pure blood.

All that is not pure race in this world is chaff. . . .

A state which in the age of racial poisoning dedicates itself to the cultivation of its best racial elements will one day become master of the world.

Modern anti-Semitism was a powerful legacy of the Middle Ages and the unsettling changes brought about by rapid industrialization; it was linked to racist doctrines that asserted the Jews were inherently wicked and bore dangerous racial qualities. Hitler grasped the political potential of anti-Semitism: by concentrating all evil in one enemy, he could provide non-Jews with an emotionally satisfying explanation for all their misfortunes and thus manipulate and unify the German people.

ANTI-SEMITISM

The Jew offers the most powerful contrast to the Aryan. . . . Despite all their seemingly intellectual qualities the Jewish people are without true culture, and especially without a culture of their own. What Jews seem to possess as culture is the property of others, for the most part corrupted in their hands.

In judging the Jewish position in regard to human culture, we have to keep in mind their essential characteristics. There never was—and still is no—Jewish art. The Jewish people made no original contribution to the two queen goddesses of all arts: architecture and music. What they have contributed is bowdlerization or spiritual theft. Which proves that Jews lack the very qualities distinguishing creative and culturally blessed races. . . .

The first and biggest lie of Jews is that Jewishness is not a matter of race but of religion, from which inevitably follow even more lies. One of them refers to the language of Jews. It is not a means of expressing their thoughts, but

of hiding them. While speaking French a Jew thinks Jewish, and while he cobbles together some German verse, he merely expresses the mentality of his people.

As long as the Jew is not master of other peoples, he must for better or worse speak their languages. Yet as soon as the others have become his servants, then all should learn a universal language (Esperanto for instance), so that by these means the Jews can rule more easily. . . .

For hours the blackhaired Jewish boy lies in wait, with satanic joy on his face, for the unsuspecting girl whom he disgraces with his blood and thereby robs her from her people. He tries by all means possible to destroy the racial foundations of the people he wants to subjugate.

But a people of pure race conscious of its blood can never be enslaved by the Jew; he remains forever a ruler of bastards.

Thus he systematically attempts to lower racial purity by racially poisoning individuals.

In politics he begins to replace the idea of democracy with the idea of the dictatorship of the proletariat.

He found his weapon in the organized Marxist masses, which avoid democracy and instead help him to subjugate and govern people dictatorially with his brutal fists.

Systematically he works toward a double revolution, in economics and politics.

With the help of his international contacts he enmeshes people who effectively resist his attacks from within in a net of external enemies whom he incites to war, and, if necessary, goes on to unfurling the red flag of revolution over the battlefield.

He batters the national economies until the ruined state enterprises are privatized and subject to his financial control.

In politics he refuses to give the state the means for its self-preservation, destroys the bases of any national self-determination and defense, wipes out the faith in leadership, denigrates the historic past, and pulls everything truly great into the gutter.

In cultural affairs he pollutes art, literature, theatre, befuddles national sentiment, subverts all concepts of beauty and grandeur, of nobleness and goodness, and reduces people to their lowest nature.

Religion is made ridiculous, custom and morals are declared outdated, until the last props of national character in the battle for survival have collapsed. . . .

Thus the Jew is the big rabble-rouser for the complete destruction of Germany. Wherever in the world we read about attacks on Germany, Jews are the source, just as in peace and during the war the newspapers of both the Jewish stock market and the Marxists systematically incited hatred against Germany. Country after country gave up its neutrality and joined the world war coalition in disregard of the true interest of the people.

Jewish thinking in all this is clear. The Bolshevization of Germany, i.e., the destruction of the German national people-oriented intelligentsia and thereby the exploitation of German labor under the yoke of Jewish global finance are but the prelude for the expansion of the Jewish tendency to conquer the world. As so often in history, Germany is the turning point in this mighty struggle. If our people and our state become the victims of blood-thirsty and money-thirsty Jewish tyrants, the whole world will be enmeshed in the tentacles of this octopus. If, however, Germany liberates itself from this yoke, we can be sure that the greatest threat to all humanity has been broken. . . .

Hitler was a master propagandist and advanced his ideas on propaganda techniques in *Mein Kampf*. He mocked the learned and book-oriented German liberals and socialists who he felt were entirely unsuited for modern mass politics. The successful leader, he said, must win over the masses through the use of simple ideas and images, constantly repeated, to control the mind by evoking primitive feelings. Hitler contended that mass meetings were the most effective means of winning followers. What counted most at these demonstrations, he said, was will power, strength, and unflagging determination radiating from the speaker to every single individual in the crowd.

PROPAGANDA AND MASS RALLIES

The task of propaganda does not lie in the scientific training of individuals, but in directing the masses toward certain facts, events, necessities, etc., whose significance is to be brought to their attention.

The essential skill consists in doing this so well that you convince people about the reality of a fact, about the necessity of an event, about the correctness of something necessary, etc. . . . You always have to appeal to the emotions and far less to the so-called intellect. . . .

The art of propaganda lies in sensing the emotional temper of the broad masses, so that you, in psychologically effective form, can catch their attention and move their hearts. . . .

The attention span of the masses is very short, their understanding limited; they easily forget. For that reason all effective propaganda has to concentrate on very few points and drive them home through simple slogans, until even the simplest can grasp what you have in mind. As soon as you give up this principle and become too complex, you will lose your effectiveness, because the masses cannot digest and retain what you have offered. You thereby weaken your case and in the end lose it altogether.

The larger the scope of your case, the more psychologically correct must be the method of your presentation. . . .

The task of propaganda lies not in weighing right and wrong, but in driving home your own point of view. You cannot objectively explore the facts that favor others and present them in doctrinaire sincerity to the masses. You have to push relentlessly your own case. . . .

Even the most brilliant propaganda will not produce the desired results unless it follows this fundamental rule: You must stick to limiting yourself to essentials and repeat them endlessly. Persistence on this point, as in so many other cases in the world, is the first and most important precondition for success. . . .

Propaganda does not exist to furnish interesting diversions to blasé young dandies, but to convince above all the masses. In their clumsiness they always require a long lead before they are ready to take notice. Only by thousandfold repetition will the simplest concepts stick in their memories.

No variation of your presentation should change the content of your propaganda; you always have to come to the same conclusion. You may want to highlight your slogans from various sides, but at the end you always have to reaffirm it. Only consistent and uniform propaganda will succeed. . . .

Every advertisement, whether in business or politics, derives its success from its persistence and uniformity. . . .

The mass meeting is . . . necessary because an incipient supporter of a new political movement will feel lonely and anxiously isolated. He needs at the start a sense of a larger community which among most people produces vitality and courage. The same man as member of a military company or battalion and surrounded by his comrades will more lightheartedly join an attack than if he were all by himself. In a crowd he feels more sheltered, even if reality were a thousandfold against him.

The sense of community in a mass demonstration not only empowers the individual, but also promotes an esprit de corps. The person who in his business or workshop is the first to represent a new political creed is likely to be exposed to heavy discrimination. He needs the reassurance that comes from the conviction of being a member and a fighter in a large comprehensive organization. The sense of this organization comes first to him in a mass demonstration. When he for the first time goes from a petty workshop or from a large factory, where he feels insignificant, to a mass demonstration surrounded by thousands and thousands of like-minded fellows—when he as a seeker is gripped by the intoxicating surge of enthusiasm among three or four thousand others—when the visible success and the consensus of thousands of others prove the correctness of his new political creed and for the first time arouse doubts about his previous political convictions—then he submits to the miraculous influence of what we call "mass suggestion." The will,

the yearning, and also the power of thousands of fellow citizens now fill every individual. The man who full of doubts and uncertain enters such a gathering, leaves it inwardly strengthened; he has become a member of a community. . . .

Hitler was an extreme nationalist who wanted a reawakened, racially united Germany to expand eastward at the expense of the Slavs, whom he viewed as racially inferior.

LEBENSRAUM

A people gains its freedom of existence only by occupying a sufficiently large space on earth. . . .

If the National Socialist movement really wants to achieve a hallowed mission in history for our people, it must, in painful awareness of its position in the world, boldly and methodically fight against the aimlessness and incapacity which have hitherto guided the foreign policy of the German people. It must then, without respect for "tradition" and prejudice, find the courage to rally the German people to a forceful advance on the road which leads from their present cramped living space to new territories. In this manner they will be liberated from the danger of perishing or being enslaved in service to others.

The National Socialist movement must try to end the disproportion between our numerous population and its limited living space, the source of our food as well as the base of our power—between our historic past and the hopelessness of our present impotence. . . .

The demand for restoring the boundaries of 1914 is a political nonsense with consequences so huge as to make it appear a crime—quite apart from the fact that our pre-war boundaries were anything but logical. They neither united all people of German nationality nor served strategic-political necessity. . . .

In the light of this fact we National Socialists must resolutely stick to our foreign policy goals, namely *to secure for the German people the territorial base to which they are entitled.* This is the only goal which before God and our German posterity justifies shedding our blood. . . .

Just as our forebears did not receive the soil on which we live as a gift from heaven—they had to risk their lives for it—so in future we will not secure the living space for our people by divine grace, but by the might of the victorious sword.

However much all of us recognize the necessity of a reckoning with France, it would remain ineffectual if we thereby limited the scope of our foreign policy. It makes sense only if we consider it as a rear-guard action for expanding our living space elsewhere in Europe. . . .

If we speak today about gaining territory in Europe, we think primarily of Russia and its border states. . . .

Kurt G. W. Ludecke
THE DEMAGOGIC ORATOR

Nazi popularity grew partly due to Hitler's power as an orator to play on the dissatisfactions of postwar Germans with the Weimar Republic. In the following selection from *I Knew Hitler—The Story of a Nazi Who Escaped the Blood Purge* (1937), Kurt G. W. Ludecke, an early supporter of Hitler who later broke with the Nazis, describes Hitler's ability to mesmerize his audience.

. . . [W]hen the Nazis marched into the Koenigsplatz with banners flying, their bands playing stirring German marches, they were greeted with tremendous cheers. An excited, expectant crowd was now filling the beautiful square to the last inch and overflowing into surrounding streets. They were well over a hundred thousand. . . . I was close enough to see Hitler's face, watch every change in his expression, hear every word he said.

When the man stepped forward on the platform, there was almost no applause. He stood silent for a moment. Then he began to speak, quietly and ingratiatingly at first. Before long his voice had risen to a hoarse shriek that gave an extraordinary effect of an intensity of feeling. There were many high-pitched, rasping notes. . . .

Critically I studied this slight, pale man, his brown hair parted on one side and falling again and again over his sweating brow. Threatening and beseeching, with small, pleading hands and flaming, steel-blue eyes, he had the look of a fanatic.

Presently my critical faculty was swept away. Leaning from the tribune as if he were trying to impel his inner self into the consciousness of all these thousands, he was holding the masses, and me with them, under a hypnotic spell by the sheer force of his conviction.

He urged the revival of German honor and manhood with a blast of words that seemed to cleanse. "Bavaria is now the most German land in Germany!" he shouted, to roaring applause. Then, plunging into sarcasm, he indicted the leaders in Berlin as "November Criminals," daring to put into words thoughts that Germans were now almost afraid to think and certainly to voice.

It was clear that Hitler was feeling the exaltation of the emotional response now surging up toward him from his thousands of hearers.

His voice rising to passionate climaxes, he finished his speech with an anthem of hate against the "Novemberlings" and a pledge of undying love for the Fatherland. "Germany must be free!" was his final defiant slogan. Then two last words that were like the sting of a lash:

"Deutschland Erwache!"

Awake, Germany! There was thunderous applause. then the masses took a solemn oath "to save Germany in Bavaria from Bolshevism."

I do not know how to describe the emotions that swept over me as I heard this man. His words were like a scourge. When he spoke of the disgrace of Germany, I felt ready to spring on any enemy. His appeal to German manhood was like a call to arms, the gospel he preached a sacred truth. He seemed another Luther. I forgot everything but the man; then, glancing round, I saw that his magnetism was holding these thousands as one.

Of course I was ripe for this experience. I was a man of thirty-two, weary of disgust and disillusionment, a wanderer seeking a cause; a patriot without a channel for his patriotism, a yearner after the heroic without a hero.

The intense will of the man, the passion of his sincerity seemed to flow from him into me. I experienced an exaltation that could be likened only to religious conversion.

I felt sure that no one who had heard Hitler that afternoon could doubt that he was the man of destiny, the vitalizing force in the future of Germany. The masses who had streamed into the Koenigsplatz with a stern sense of national humiliation seemed to be going forth renewed.

The bands struck up, the thousands began to move away. I knew my search was ended. I had found myself, my leader, and my cause.

Thomas Mann
"AN APPEAL TO REASON"

In 1931, two years before Hitler took power, the internationally prominent German author Thomas Mann (1875–1955) wrote an article entitled "An Appeal to Reason," in which he discussed the crisis in the European soul that gave rise to Fascism. He saw National Socialism and the extreme nationalism it espoused as a rejection of the Western rational tradition and as a regression to primitive and barbaric modes of behavior. Some excerpts from Mann's article follow.

. . . The economic decline of the middle classes was accompanied—or even preceded—by a feeling which amounted to an intellectual prophecy and critique of the age: the sense that here was a crisis which heralded the end of the bourgeois epoch that came in with the French revolution and the notions appertaining to it. There was proclaimed a new mental attitude for all mankind, which should have nothing to do with bourgeois principles such as freedom, justice, culture, optimism, faith in progress. As art, it gave vent to expressionistic soul-shrieks; as philosophy it repudiated . . . reason, and the . . . ideological conceptions of bygone decades; it expressed itself as an irrationalistic throwback, placing the conception *life* at the centre of thought, and raised on its standard the powers of the unconscious, the dynamic, the darkly creative, which alone were life-giving. Mind,

quite simply the intellectual, it put under a taboo as destructive of life, while it set up for homage as the true inwardness of life . . . the darkness of the soul, the holy procreative underworld. Much of this nature-religion, by its very essence inclining to the orgiastic and to . . . [frenzied] excess, has gone into the nationalism of our day, making of it something quite different from the nationalism of the nineteenth century, with its bourgeois, strongly cosmopolitan and humanitarian cast. It is distinguished in its character as a nature-cult, precisely by its absolute unrestraint, its orgiastic, radically anti-humane, frenziedly dynamic character. . . .

. . . And there is even more: there are other intellectual elements come to strengthen this national-social political movement—a certain ideology, a Nordic creed, a Germanistic romanticism, from philological, academic, professorial spheres. It addresses the Germany of 1930 in a highflown wishy-washy jargon full of mystical good feeling, with hyphenated prefixes like race- and folk- and fellowship-, and lends to the movement a . . . fanatical cult-barbarism, . . . dangerous and estranging, with . . . power to clog and stultify the brain. . . .

Fed, then, by such intellectual and pseudo-intellectual currents as these, the movement which we sum up under the name of national-socialism and which has displayed such a power of enlisting recruits to its banner, mingles with the mighty wave—a wave of anomalous barbarism, of primitive popular vulgarity—that sweeps over the world today, assailing the nerves of mankind with wild, bewildering, stimulating, intoxicating sensations. . . . Humanity seems to have run like boys let out of school away from the humanitarian, idealistic nineteenth century, from whose morality—if we can speak at all of morality in this connection—our time represents a wide and wild reaction. Everything is possible, everything permitted as a weapon against human decency; if we have got rid of the idea of freedom as a relic of the bourgeois state of mind, as though an idea so bound up with all European feeling, upon which Europe has been founded, for which she has made such sacrifices, could ever be utterly lost—it comes back again, this cast-off conception, in a guise suited to the time: as demoralization, as a mockery of all human authority, as a free rein to instincts, as the emancipation of brutality, the dictatorship of force. . . . In all this violence demonstrates itself, and demonstrates nothing but violence, and even that is unnecessary, for all other considerations are fallen away, man does not any longer believe in them, and so the road is free to vulgarity without restraint.

This fantastic state of mind, of a humanity that has outrun its ideas, is matched by a political scene in the grotesque style, with Salvation Army methods, hallelujahs and bell-ringing and dervishlike repetition of monotonous catchwords, until everybody foams at the mouth. Fanaticism turns into a means of salvation, enthusiasm into epileptic ecstasy, politics becomes an opiate for the masses, . . . and reason veils her face.

REVIEW QUESTIONS

1. How did Adolf Hitler account for cultural greatness? Cultural decline?
2. What comparisons did Hitler draw between Aryans and Jews?
3. What kind of evidence did Hitler offer for his anti-Semitic arguments?
4. Theodor Mommsen, a nineteenth-century German historian, said that anti-Semites do not listen to "logic and ethical arguments. . . . They listen only to their own envy and hatred, to the meanest instincts." Discuss this statement.
5. What insights did Hitler have into mass psychology and propaganda?
6. What foreign policy goals did Hitler have for Germany? How did he expect them to be achieved?
7. How did Hitler mesmerize his audience?
8. According to Thomas Mann, what new mental attitude emerged that heralded the end of the bourgeois age?
9. How did Mann view extreme nationalism and National Socialism?
10. What did Mann mean by "politics becomes an opiate for the masses"?

9   The Leader-State

Adolf Hitler came to power by legal means, appointed chancellor by President Paul von Hindenburg on January 30, 1933, according to the constitution of the Weimar Republic. Thereafter, however, he proceeded to dismantle the legal structure of the Weimar system and replace it with an inflexible dictatorship that revolved around his person. Quickly reacting to the popular confusion caused by the suspicious Reichstag fire, Hitler issued a decree on February 28 that suspended all guarantees of civil and individual freedom. In March, the Reichstag adopted the Enabling Act, which vested all legislative powers in his hands. Then Hitler proceeded to destroy the autonomy of the federal states, dissolve the trade unions, outlaw other political parties, and end freedom of the press. By the time he eliminated party rivals in a blood purge on June 30, 1934, the consolidation of power was complete. Meanwhile, much of Germany's public and institutional life fell under Nazi Party control in a process known as the *Gleichschaltung*, or coordination. The Third Reich was organized as a leader-state, in which Hitler the *Führer* (leader) embodied and expressed the real will of the German people, commanded the supreme loyalty of the nation, and had unlimited authority.

Ernst Rudolf Huber
"THE AUTHORITY OF THE FÜHRER IS . . . ALL-INCLUSIVE AND UNLIMITED"

In *Verfassungsrecht des grossdeutschen Reiches* (Constitutional Law of the Greater German Reich) (1939), legal scholar Ernst Rudolf Huber (1903–1990) offered a classic explication of the basic principles of National Socialism. The following excerpts from that work describe the nature of Hitler's political authority.

The Führer-Reich of the [German] people is founded on the recognition that the true will of the people cannot be disclosed through parliamentary votes and plebiscites but that the will of the people in its pure and uncorrupted form can only be expressed through the Führer. Thus a distinction must be drawn between the supposed will of the people in a parliamentary democracy, which merely reflects the conflict of the various social interests, and the true will of the people in the Führer-state, in which the collective will of the real political unit is manifested. . . .

It would be impossible for a law to be introduced and acted upon in the Reichstag which had not originated with the Führer or, at least,

received his approval. The procedure is similar to that of the plebiscite: The lawgiving power does not rest in the Reichstag; it merely proclaims through its decision its agreement with the will of the Führer, who is the lawgiver of the German people.

The Führer unites in himself all the sovereign authority of the Reich; all public authority in the state as well as in the movement is derived from the authority of the Führer. We must speak not of the state's authority but of the Führer's authority if we wish to designate the character of the political authority within the Reich correctly. The state does not hold political authority as an impersonal unit but receives it from the Führer as the executor of the national will. The authority of the Führer is complete and all-embracing; it unites in itself all the means of political direction; it extends into all fields of national life; it embraces the entire people, which is bound to the Führer in loyalty and obedience. The authority of the Führer is not limited by checks and controls, by special autonomous bodies or individual rights, but it is free and independent, all-inclusive and unlimited. It is not, however, self-seeking or arbitrary and its ties are within itself. It is derived from the people; that is, it is entrusted to the Führer by the people. It exists for the people and has its justification in the people; it is free of all outward ties because it is in its innermost nature firmly bound up with the fate, the welfare, the mission, and the honor of the people.

REVIEW QUESTION

1. Point out several ways that Ernst Rudolf Huber's views represent a rejection of the Western liberal-democratic tradition.

---

10 The Nazification of Culture and Society

The Nazis aspired to more than political power; they also wanted to have the German people view the world in accordance with National Socialist ideology. Toward this end, the Nazis strictly regulated cultural life. Believing that the struggle of racial forces occupied the center of world history, Nazi ideologists tried to strengthen the racial consciousness of the German people. Numerous courses in "race science" introduced in schools and universities emphasized the superiority of the Nordic soul as well as the worthlessness of Jews and their threat to the nation.

Jakob Graf
HEREDITY AND RACIAL BIOLOGY FOR STUDENTS

The following assignments from a textbook entitled *Heredity and Racial Biology for Students* (1935) show how young people were indoctrinated with racist teachings.

HOW WE CAN LEARN TO RECOGNIZE A PERSON'S RACE
Assignments

1. Summarize the spiritual characteristics of the individual races.

2. Collect from stories, essays, and poems examples of ethnological illustrations. Underline those terms which describe the type and mode of the expression of the soul.

3. What are the expressions, gestures, and movements which allow us to make conclusions as to the attitude of the racial soul?

4. Determine also the physical features which go hand in hand with the specific racial soul characteristics of the individual figures.

5. Try to discover the intrinsic nature of the racial soul through the characters in stories and poetical works in terms of their inner attitude. Apply this mode of observation to persons in your own environment.

6. Collect propaganda posters and caricatures for your race book and arrange them according to a racial scheme. What image of beauty is emphasized by the artist (a) in posters publicizing sports and travel? (b) in publicity for cosmetics? How are hunters, mountain climbers, and shepherds drawn?

7. Collect from illustrated magazines, newspapers, etc., pictures of great scholars, statesmen, artists, and others who distinguish themselves by their special accomplishments (for example, in economic life, politics, sports). Determine the preponderant race and admixture, according

to physical characteristics. Repeat this exercise with the pictures of great men of all nations and times.

8. When viewing monuments, busts, etc., be sure to pay attention to the race of the person portrayed with respect to figure, bearing, and physical characteristics. Try to harmonize these determinations with the features of the racial soul.

9. Observe people whose special racial features have drawn your attention, also with respect to their bearing when moving or when speaking. Observe their expressions and gestures.

10. Observe the Jew: his way of walking, his bearing, gestures, and movements when talking.

11. What strikes you about the way a Jew talks and sings?

Louis P. Lochner
BOOK BURNING

The anti-intellectualism of the Nazis was demonstrated on May 10, 1933, when the principal German student body organized students for a book-burning festival. In university towns, students consigned to the flames books that were considered a threat to the Germanic spirit, many of them written by prominent Jewish authors. Louis P. Lochner (1887–1975), head of the Associated Press Bureau in Berlin, provided an eyewitness account of the scene in the German capital in *The Goebbels Diaries 1942–43* (1948).

The whole civilized world was shocked when on the evening of May 10, 1933, the books of authors displeasing to the Nazis, including even those of our own Helen Keller, were solemnly burned on the immense Franz Joseph Platz between the University of Berlin and the State Opera on Unter den Linden. I was a witness to the scene.

All afternoon Nazi raiding parties had gone into public and private libraries, throwing onto the streets such books as Dr. [Joseph] Goebbels [Nazi Propaganda Minister] in his supreme wisdom had decided were unfit for Nazi Germany. From the streets Nazi columns of beerhall

fighters had picked up these discarded volumes and taken them to the square above referred to.

Here the heap grew higher and higher, and every few minutes another howling mob arrived, adding more books to the impressive pyre. Then, as night fell, students from the university, mobilized by the little doctor, performed veritable Indian dances and incantations as the flames began to soar skyward.

When the orgy was at its height, a cavalcade of cars drove into sight. It was the Propaganda Minister himself, accompanied by his bodyguard and a number of fellow torch bearers of the new Nazi *Kultur.*

"Fellow students, German men and women!" he said as he stepped before a microphone for all Germany to hear him. "The age of extreme Jewish intellectualism has now ended, and the success of the German revolution has again given the right of way to the German spirit." . . .

"You are doing the right thing in committing the evil spirit of the past to the flames at this late hour of the night. It is a strong, great, and symbolic act—an act that is to bear witness before all the world to the fact that the spiritual foundation of the November Republic has disappeared. From the ashes there will rise the phoenix of the spirit." . . .

"The past is lying in flames. The future will rise from the flames within our own hearts. . . . Brightened by these flames our vow shall be: The Reich and the Nation and our Fuehrer Adolf Hitler: *Heil! Heil! Heil!*"

The few foreign correspondents who had taken the trouble to view this "symbolic act" were stunned. What had happened to the "Land of Thinkers and Poets?" they wondered.

Joseph Roth
"THE AUTO-DA-FÉ OF THE MIND"

Joseph Roth (1894–1939) was born to Jewish parents in the Austro-Hungarian Empire. He became a distinguished journalist in Berlin during the short-lived Weimar Republic. Until 1933, when the rise of the Nazis forced him into exile, he worked uninterruptedly for major newspapers and wrote many novels, of which *The Radetzky March*, set in the Austro-Hungarian Empire, is the best known. Already in exile in Paris when the book burnings in Germany took place, Roth reflected on what the burning of those books meant for German cultural life. He described German-Jewish writers as having "fallen on the intellect's field of honor. All of them, in the eyes of the German murderer and arsonist, share a common fault: *their Jewish blood and their European intellect*." The book burning, he declared, threatened European civilization. The following excerpts are from an essay he wrote immediately after the Nazi outrage. The term auto-da-fé in its title refers to the public burning of heretics in Spain during the Spanish Inquisition. Many of the heretics were forcibly converted Jews whom the Inquisition believed to be secretly practicing Judaism.

Very few observers anywhere in the world seem to have understood what the Third Reich's burning of books, the expulsion of Jewish writers, and all its other crazy assaults on the intellect actually mean. The technical apotheosis of the barbarians, the terrible march of the mechanized orangutans, armed with hand grenades, poison gas, ammonia, and nitroglycerine, with gas masks and airplanes, the return of the spiritual (if not the actual) descendants of the Cimbri and Teutoni[1]—all this means far more than the threatened and terrorized world seems to realize: It must be understood. Let me say it loud and clear: The European mind is capitulating. It is capitulating out of weakness, out of sloth, out of apathy, out of lack of imagination (it will be the task of some future generation

---

[1]The Cimbri and Teutoni were Germanic tribes who ravaged Europe in the second century B.C.

to establish the reasons for this disgraceful capitulation).

Now, as the smoke of our burned books rises into the sky, we German writers of Jewish descent must acknowledge above all that we have been defeated. Let us, who were fighting on the front line, under the banner of the European mind, let us fulfill the noblest duty of the defeated warrior: Let us concede our defeat.

Yes, we have been beaten. . . . We are proud of our defeat. We stood in the front row of the defenders of Europe, and we were the first to be defeated. Our comrades "of Aryan descent" can still hope to be pardoned (always assuming that they will be prepared to make some concession to the language of Goebbels and Göring). There is even a chance that the vandals of the Third Reich will try to exploit such "Aryan" writers of great renown as Thomas Mann and Gerhart Hauptmann (currently persecuted) for a while, in order to trick mankind into believing that National Socialism has some respect for the human spirit. But we writers of Jewish descent are, thank God, safe from any temptation to take the side of the barbarians in any way. We are the only representatives of Europe who are debarred from returning to Germany. Even if there were in our ranks a traitor, who, from personal ambition, stupidity, and blindness, wanted to conclude a shameful peace with the destroyers of Europe—he couldn't do it! That "Asiatic" and "Oriental" blood which the current wielders of power in the German Reich hold against us will quite certainly not permit us to desert from the noble ranks of the European army. God himself—and we are proud of the fact—will not allow us to betray Europe, Christendom, and Judaism. God is with the vanquished, not with the victors! At a time when His Holiness, the infallible Pope of Christendom, is concluding a peace agreement, a Concordat, with the enemies of Christ, when the Protestants are establishing a "German church" and censoring the Bible, we descendants of the old Jews, the forefathers of European culture, are the only legitimate German representatives of that culture. Thanks to inscrutable divine wisdom, we are physically incapable of betraying it to the heathen civilization of poison gases, to the ammonia-breathing Germanic war god. . . .

It would be true to say that, from about 1900, German cultural life was largely defined, if not dominated by this "top class" of German Jews. To be fair, what they did was not wholly bad. Even their errors were sometimes salutary. In the whole of that large kingdom with a population of sixty million, among all those industrialists, there was—individual exceptions aside—no class that was actively interested in art and intellect. As far as the Prussian Junkers[2] are concerned, the civilized world will know that they were just about able to read and write. One of their representatives, President Hindenburg,[3] openly admitted *that he had never read a book in his life.* And, incidentally, it was this icon, ancient from early youth, that the workers, Social Democrats, journalists, artists, and Jews worshipped during the war, and that the German people (workers, Jews, journalists, artists, Social Democrats, and the rest of them) then reelected president. Is a people that elects as its president an icon that has never read a book all that far away from burning books itself? And are the Jewish writers, scholars, and philosophers who voted for Hindenburg really entitled to complain about the bonfire in which our thoughts are consumed?

As for the industrialists—their minds were taken up by iron and steel, by guns and "Big Berthas"; they were smelting the modern version of "Siegfried's sword." The big businesspeople were producing the cheap junk labeled "Made in Germany" with which they flooded an unhappy world. *Only the German Jews (doctors, lawyers, tradesmen, department store owners, artisans, or manufacturers) were interested in books, theater, museums, music.* Even if they were occasionally guilty of bad taste, it remains a fact that

[2]Prussian Junkers were aristocratic landowners who provided the army's leadership.
[3]President Hindenburg (1847–1934) was a general in World War I and president of the Weimar Republic from 1925 until his death.

there was no one else in the whole of Germany capable of pointing out and correcting their errors. The magazines and newspapers were edited by Jews, managed by Jews, read by Jews! A swarm of intellectual Jewish critics and reviewers discovered and promoted numerous "pure Aryan" poets, writers, and actors! Does there exist—now that theater and literature have been "cleansed"—a single outstanding actor or writer who was not recognized and praised at a time when reviewing and public opinion were in the hands of Jews? I challenge the Third Reich to come up with a single example of a gifted "pure Aryan" poet, actor, or musician who was kept down by the Jews and emancipated by Herr Goebbels! It's only the feeblest dilettantes who flourish in the swastika's shadow, in the bloody glow cast by the ash heaps in which we are consumed. . . .

The threatened and terrorized world must understand that the arrival on the scene of Corporal Hitler does not mark the beginning of any new chapter in the history of anti-Semitism: Far from it! What the arsonists tell us is true, though not in the way they intended: This Third Reich is only the beginning of the end! By destroying Jews they are persecuting Christ. For the first time the Jews are not being murdered for crucifying Christ but for having produced him from their midst. If the books of Jewish or supposed Jewish authors are burned, what is really set fire to is the Book of Books: the Bible. If Jewish judges and attorneys are expelled or locked up, it represents a symbolic assault on law and justice.

REVIEW QUESTIONS

1. What was Jakob Graf's purpose in teaching students how to recognize a person's race?
2. Why do you think the Nazis made the burning of books a public event? Why does book burning have such potent symbolism?
3. What lessons did Roth draw from the book burning?

11   Persecution of the Jews

The Nazis deprived Jews of their German citizenship and instituted many anti-Jewish measures designed to make them outcasts. Thousands of Jewish doctors, lawyers, musicians, artists, and professors were barred from practicing their professions, and Jewish members of the civil service were dismissed. A series of laws tightened the screws of humiliation and persecution. Marriages or sexual encounters between Germans and Jews were forbidden. Universities, schools, restaurants, pharmacies, hospitals, theaters, museums, and athletic fields were gradually closed to Jews.

In November 1938, using as a pretext the assassination of a German official in Paris by a seventeen-year-old Jewish youth whose family had been mistreated by the Nazis, the Nazis organized an extensive pogrom. Nazi gangs murdered scores of Jews and burned and looted thousands of Jewish businesses, homes, and synagogues all over Germany—an event that became known as Night of the Broken Glass (*Kristallnacht*). Thirty thousand Jews were thrown into concentration camps. The Reich then imposed on the Jewish community a fine of one billion marks. By the outbreak of the war in September 1939, approximately one-half of Germany's six hundred thousand Jews had fled the country. Those who stayed behind would fall victim to the last stage of the Nazi anti-Jewish campaign—the Final Solution.

Hertha Nathorff
A GERMAN-JEWISH DOCTOR'S DIARY

Hertha Nathorff, niece of Albert Einstein, practiced medicine in Berlin. In her diary, she recorded the constant abuse and humiliation inflicted on Jews as a result of Nazi anti-Semitic policies. Dr. Nathorff managed to leave Germany in 1939 before the outbreak of war. Following are excerpts from her diary.

1 April 1933

Jewish Boycott.

This day is engraved in my heart in flames. To think that such things are still possible in the twentieth century. In front of all Jewish shops, lawyers' offices, doctors' surgeries and flats there are young boys with signs saying, "Don't buy from Jews," "Don't go to Jewish doctors," "Anybody who buys from Jews is a traitor," "Jews are the incarnation of lies and deceit." Doctors' signs on the walls of houses are soiled, and sometimes damaged, and people have looked on, gawping in silence. They must have forgotten to stick anything over my sign. I think I would have reacted violently. It was afternoon before one of these boys visited me at home and asked: "Is this a Jewish business?" "This isn't a business at all; it's a doctor's surgery," I said. "Are you sick?" After these ironic words the youth disappeared without posting anybody in front of my door. Of course some patients who had appointments did not turn up. One woman rang to say that of course she couldn't come today, and I said that it would be better if she didn't come any more at all. For my own part, I shopped deliberately in places where such pickets were posted. One of them wanted to stop me going into a little soap shop, but I pushed him to one side, saying, "I'll spend my money where I want." Why doesn't everybody do that? That would soon settle the boycott. But people are a cowardly lot, as I know only too well.

In the evening we were with friends at the Hohenzollerndamm, three couples, all doctors. They were all quite depressed. One of the company, Emil, the optimist, tried to convince us: "It'll all be over in a few days." They don't understand my anger when I say, "They should strike us dead instead. It would be more humane than the psychological death they have in mind. . . ." But my instincts have always proved right.

25 April 1933

A letter from Charlottenburg municipal authorities: "You are requested to cease your activity as senior doctor at the women's advice centre!" Full stop.

Thrown out then—full stop. My poor women, whose hands will they fall into now? I've run that place for five years, expanded it and made it well known, and now? It's all over. I have to repeat it again and again, in order to be able to grasp it.

30 August 1933

Back from holidays in southern Germany. How tense the atmosphere is there. The situation is completely changed in my home town, where everyone knows everyone else.

My family have lived in that small town for two hundred years, looked up to, respected and now. . . . My old father said to me in passing that he no longer goes to his local [pub]. Mother got rather worked up because nobody knows how to greet her properly any more.

A friend of my sister's, a lawyer's wife, comes to visit only in the evenings after dark, until my sister suggests she doesn't bother coming at all. The Catholics are beside themselves with fear and dread. Where will it all end?

2 October 1934

I have just come from the H. mental asylum. They rang to ask if I would come. A patient had arrived during the night who was calling for me. She had been picked up on the street, in front of a hospital. They thought she was drunk, the way she was behaving, talking, crying in the street, and giving away her possessions to passers-by. Then she was brought to the asylum. Did I know her? A young colleague who is not allowed to practise. Her licence has been taken away. A love affair with an Aryan colleague suddenly came to an end. Then she tried to work as a nurse, and it proved too much for her soul, for her intellect. As a result she had gone mad.

30 November 1934

I have been to southern Germany. My dear father was seriously ill. The things I had to do to get the doctor treating him—it would be unprofessional to comment on his medical ability— to agree to send him for a consultation with the capable specialist in Ulm! "One can't consult a Jewish doctor!" He would rather treat the patient wrongly and badly! He should be grateful that he can get an Aryan doctor to come at all. There is no Jewish doctor left in the small town, and the other Nazi doctor does not treat Jews. It's almost like the camps where they have imprisoned innocent people. "If one happens to be a Jew, one is either healthy or dead!"

One of the Catholic nurses looking after Father told me: "Frau Doktor, we needn't fear hell any more. The devil is already abroad in the world."

30 December 1934

Three more suicides by people who could no longer stand the continuing defamation and spite.

The boy is afraid to go on the ice rink. Yesterday Jewish children were chased away and beaten up.

9 October 1935

I met my former secretary today. She fixed me sharply with her short-sighted eyes, and then turned away. I was so nauseated I spat into my handkerchief. She was once a patient of mine. Later I met her in the street. Her boyfriend had left her and she was out of work and without money. I took her on, trained her for years and employed her in my clinic until the last day. Now she has changed so much that she can no longer greet me; me, who rescued her from the gutter!

I never go anywhere any more. I am so well known through my profession and my position; why should I make trouble for myself and for others? I'm happy to be at home in peace.

4 December 1935

Miss G. in the surgery, completely broken. She knows nothing of Jews and Jewry. Suddenly they've dug up her Jewish grandmother! She is no longer allowed to work as an artist, and she must give up her boyfriend, a senior officer. She wants something "to end it all." She can only groan pitifully, "I can't go on living." What can I do? I can no longer help my patients, it's a living death for me.

5 August 1938

There was a telephone call as we were sitting at the table with guests. I went to the telephone myself. A colleague, S., who asks: "Have you been listening to the radio?" "No," I say, "what's happened now?" The colleague, usually so calm, says with a trembling, angry voice: "What you always said would happen. They're taking away our licenses, we are no longer allowed to practise—it's just been on the radio." "On the radio." This is how we learn that they are taking away from us what we earned through years of study, what we were taught by eminent professors, famous universities. . . . All I could think at that moment

was: "And now I have to tell my husband." How I went calmly back to the dining table, drew the meal to a close, and told my guests, "It's nothing much," I don't know; I know only that I sat at the desk, my hands clenched and said to my husband: "It's over—over—over." He went to get a paper, and it had already been reported. This is how we Jewish doctors learnt of our death sentence. In the clinic they are all in a state of complete despair.

Marta Appel
MEMOIRS OF A GERMAN-JEWISH WOMAN

Marta Appel and her husband, Dr. Ernst Appel, a rabbi in the city of Dortmund, fled Germany in 1937. In 1940–1941, while in the United States, she wrote her memoirs, which described conditions in Dortmund after the Nazis took power.

The children had been advised not to come to school on April 1, 1933, the day of the boycott. Even the principal of the school thought Jewish children's lives were no longer safe. One night they placed big signs on every store or house owned by Jewish people. In front of our temple, on every square and corner, billboards were scoffing at us. Everywhere, and on all occasions, we read and heard that we were vermin and had caused the ruin of the German people. No Jewish store was closed on that day, none was willing to show fear in the face of the boycott. The only building which did not open its door as usual, since it was Saturday, was the temple. We did not want this holy place desecrated by any trouble.

I even went downtown that day to see what was going on in the city. There was no cheering crowd as the Nazis had expected, no running and smashing of Jewish businesses. I heard only words of anger and disapproval. People were massed before the Jewish stores to watch the Nazi guards who were posted there to prevent

anyone from entering to buy. And there were many courageous enough to enter, although they were called rude names by the Nazi guards, and their pictures were taken to show them as enemies of the German people in the daily papers. . . .

Our gentile friends and neighbors, even people whom we had scarcely known before, came to assure us of their friendship and to tell us that these horrors could not last very long. But after some months of a regime of terror, fidelity and friendship had lost their meaning, and fear and treachery had replaced them. For the sake of our gentile friends, we turned our heads so as not to greet them in the streets, for we did not want to bring upon them the danger of imprisonment for being considered a friend of Jews.

With each day of the Nazi regime, the abyss between us and our fellow citizens grew larger. Friends whom we had loved for years did not know us anymore. They suddenly saw that we were different from themselves. Of course we were different, since we were bearing the stigma of

Nazi hatred, since we were hunted like deer. Through the prominent position of my husband we were in constant danger. Often we were warned to stay away from home. We were no longer safe, wherever we went.

How much our life changed in those days! Often it seemed to me I could not bear it any longer, but thinking of my children, I knew we had to be strong to make it easier for them. From then on I hated to go out, since on every corner I saw signs that the Jews were the misfortune of the people. . . .

In the evenings we sat at home at the radio listening fearfully to all the new and outrageous restrictions and laws which almost daily brought further suffering to Jewish people. . . .

Since I had lived in Dortmund, I had met every four weeks with a group of women, all of whom were born in Metz, my beloved home city. We all had been pupils or teachers in the same high school. After the Nazis came, I was afraid to go to the meetings. I did not want the presence of a Jewess to bring any trouble, since we always met publicly in a café. One day on the street, I met one of my old teachers, and with tears in her eyes she begged me: "Come again to us; we miss you; we feel ashamed that you must think we do not want you anymore. Not one of us has changed in her feeling toward you." She tried to convince me that they were still my friends, and tried to take away my doubts. I decided to go to the next meeting. It was a hard decision, and I had not slept the night before. I was afraid for my gentile friends. For nothing in the world did I wish to bring them trouble by my attendance, and I was also afraid for myself. I knew I would watch them, noticing the slightest expression of embarrassment in their eyes when I came. I knew they could not deceive me; I would be aware of every change in their voices. Would they be afraid to talk to me?

It was not necessary for me to read their eyes or listen to the change in their voices. The empty table in the little alcove which always had been reserved for us spoke the clearest language. It was even unnecessary for the waiter to come and say that a lady phoned that morning not to reserve the table thereafter. I could not blame them. Why should they risk losing a position only to prove to me that we still had friends in Germany?

I, personally, did not mind all those disappointments, but when my children had to face them, and were not spared being offended everywhere, my heart was filled with anguish. It required a great deal of inner strength, of love and harmony among the Jewish families, to make our children strong enough to bear all that persecution and hatred. . . . My heart was broken when I saw tears in my younger child's eyes when she had been sent home from school while all the others had been taken to a show or some other pleasure. . . .

Almost every lesson began to be a torture for Jewish children. There was not one subject anymore which was not used to bring up the Jewish question. And in the presence of Jewish children the teachers denounced all the Jews, without exception, as scoundrels and as the most destructive force in every country where they were living. My children were not permitted to leave the room during such a talk; they were compelled to stay and to listen; they had to feel all the other children's eyes looking and staring at them, the examples of an outcast race.

Every day they had to face another degrading and offensive incident. As Mother's Day came near, the children were practicing songs at school to celebrate that day. Every year on that occasion the whole school gathered in a joint festival. It was the day before when my girls were ordered to see the music teacher. "You have to be present for the festival," the teacher told them, "but since you are Jewish, you are not allowed to join in the songs." "Why can't we sing?" my children protested with tears in their eyes. "We have a mother too, and we wish to sing for her." But it seemed the teacher did not want to understand the children's feelings. Curtly she rebuked their protest. "I know you have a mother," she said haughtily, "but she is only a Jewish mother." At that the girls had no reply; there was no use to speak any longer to the teacher, but seldom had they been so much disturbed as when they came from school that day, when someone had tried to condemn their mother. . . .

One day, for the first time in a long while, I saw my children coming back from school with shining eyes, laughing and giggling together. Most of the classes had been gathered that morning in the big hall, since an official of the new *Rasseamt*, the office of races, had come to give a talk about the differences of races. "I asked the teacher if I could go home," my daughter was saying, "but she told me she had orders not to dismiss anyone. You may imagine it was an awful talk. He said that there are two groups of races, a high group and a low one. The high and upper race that was destined to rule the world was the Teutonic, the German race, while one of the lowest races was the Jewish race. And then, Mommy, he looked around and asked one of the girls to come to him." The children again began to giggle about their experience. "First we did not know," my girl continued, "what he intended, and we were very afraid when he picked out Eva. Then he began, and he was pointing at Eva, 'Look here, the small head of this girl, her long forehead, her very blue eyes, and blond hair,' and he was lifting one of her long blond braids. 'And look,' he said, 'at her tall and slender figure. These are

the unequivocal marks of a pure and unmixed Teutonic race.' Mommy, you should have heard how at this moment all the girls burst into laughter. Even Eva could not help laughing. Then from all sides of the hall there was shouting, 'She is a Jewess!' You should have seen the officer's face! I guess he was lucky that the principal got up so quickly and, with a sign to the pupils, stopped the laughing and shouting and dismissed the man, thanking him for his interesting and very enlightening talk. At that we began again to laugh, but he stopped us immediately. Oh, I was so glad that the teacher had not dismissed me and I was there to hear it."

When my husband came home, they told him and enjoyed it again and again. And we were thankful to know that they still had not completely forgotten how to laugh and to act like happy children.

"If only I could take my children out of here!" That thought was occupying my mind more and more. I no longer hoped for any change as did my husband. Besides, even a changed Germany could not make me forget that all our friends, the whole nation, had abandoned us in our need. It was no longer the same country for me. Everything had changed, not people alone—the city, the forest, the river—the whole country looked different in my eyes.

David H. Buffum
NIGHT OF THE BROKEN GLASS (*KRISTALLNACHT*)

The Nazi press depicted the terrible events of *Kristallnacht*—the burning and vandalizing of thousands of Jewish synagogues, homes, and businesses throughout Germany and the killing and maiming of Jews—as a "spontaneous wave of righteous indignation" directed at enemies of Germany. The violence was planned and coordinated by the Nazi government. While many Germans were horrified by the destruction of property and the abuse inflicted on helpless people, often neighbors and respected merchants, there were others who rejoiced at the Jews' misfortune. The following account of the vicious onslaught in Leipzig was prepared by David H. Buffum, the American consul.

At 3 A.M. November 10, 1938 was unleashed a barrage of Nazi ferocity as had had no equal hitherto in Germany, or very likely anywhere else in the world since savagery, if ever. Jewish dwellings were smashed into and contents demolished or looted. In one of the Jewish sections an eighteen year old boy was hurled from a three story window to land with both legs broken on a street littered with burning beds and other household furniture and effects from his family's and other apartments. This information was supplied by an attending physician. It is reported from another quarter that among domestic effects thrown out of a Jewish dwelling, a small dog descended four flights to a broken spine on a cluttered street. Although apparently centered in poor districts, the raid was not confined to the humble classes. One apartment of exceptionally refined occupants known to this office, was violently ransacked, presumably in a search for valuables that was not in vain, and one of the marauders thrust a cane through a priceless medieval painting portraying a biblical scene. Another apartment of the same category is known to have been turned upside down in the frenzied course of whatever the invaders were after. Reported loss of looting of cash, silver, jewelry, and otherwise easily convertible articles, have been frequent.

Jewish shop windows by the hundreds were systematically and wantonly smashed throughout the entire city at a loss estimated at several millions of marks. There are reports that substantial losses have been sustained on the famous Leipzig "Bruhl," as many of the shop windows at the time of the demolition were filled with costly furs that were seized before the windows could be boarded up. In proportion to the general destruction of real estate, however, losses of goods are felt to have been relatively small. The spectators who viewed the wreckage when daylight had arrived were mostly in such a bewildered mood, that there was no danger of impulsive acts, and the perpetrators probably were too busy in carrying out their schedule to take off a whole lot of time for personal profit. At all events, the main streets of the city were a positive litter of shattered plate glass. According to reliable testimony, the debacle was executed by S. S. men and Storm Troopers not in uniform, each group having been provided with hammers, axes, crowbars and incendiary bombs.

Three synagogues in Leipzig were fired simultaneously by incendiary bombs and all sacred objects and records desecrated or destroyed, in most instances hurled through the windows and burned in the streets. No attempts whatsoever were made to quench the fires, functions of the fire brigade having been confined to playing water on adjoining buildings. All of the synagogues were irreparably gutted by flames, and the walls of the two that are in the close proximity of the consulate are now being razed. The blackened frames have been centers of attraction during the past week of terror for eloquently silent and bewildered crowds. One of the largest clothing stores in the heart of the city was destroyed by flames from incendiary bombs, only the charred walls and gutted roof having been left standing. As was the case with the synagogues, no attempts on the part of the fire brigade were made to extinguish the fire, although apparently there was a certain amount of apprehension for adjacent property, for the walls of a coffee house next door were covered with asbestos and sprayed by the doughty firemen. It is extremely difficult to believe, but the owners of the clothing store were actually charged with setting the fire and on that basis were dragged from their beds at 6 A.M. and clapped into prison.

Tactics which closely approached the ghoulish took place at the Jewish cemetery where the temple was fired together with a building occupied by caretakers, tombstones uprooted and graves violated. Eye witnesses considered reliable report that ten corpses were left unburied at this cemetery for a week's time because all grave diggers and cemetery attendants had been arrested.

Ferocious as was the violation of property, the most hideous phase of the so-called "spontaneous" action, has been the wholesale arrest and transportation to concentration camps of male

German Jews between the ages of sixteen and sixty, as well as Jewish men without citizenship. This has been taking place daily since the night of horror. This office has no way of accurately checking the numbers of such arrests, but there is very little question that they have gone into several thousands in Leipzig alone. Having demolished dwellings and hurled most of the moveable effects to the streets, the insatiably sadistic perpetrators threw many of the trembling inmates into a small stream that flows through the Zoological Park, commanding horrified spectators to spit at them, defile them with mud and jeer at their plight. The latter incident has been repeatedly corroborated by German witnesses who were nauseated in telling the tale. The slightest manifestation of sympathy evoked a positive fury on the part of the perpetrators, and the crowd was powerless to do anything but turn horror-stricken eyes from the scene of abuse, or leave the vicinity. These tactics were carried out the entire morning of November 10th without police intervention and they were applied to men, women and children.

There is much evidence of physical violence, including several deaths. At least half a dozen cases have been personally observed, victims with bloody, badly bruised faces having fled to this office, believing that as refugees their desire to emigrate could be expedited here. As a matter of fact this consulate has been a bedlam of humanity for the past ten days, most of these visitors being desperate women, as their husbands and sons had been taken off to concentration camps.

Similarly violent procedure was applied throughout this consular district, the amount of havoc wrought depending upon the number of Jewish establishments or persons involved. It is understood that in many of the smaller communities even more relentless methods were employed than was the case in the cities. Reports have been received from Weissenfels to the effect that the few Jewish families there are experiencing great difficulty in purchasing food. It is reported that three Aryan professors of the University of Jena have been arrested and taken off to concentration camps because they had voiced disapproval of this insidious drive against mankind.

REVIEW QUESTIONS

1. How did Hertha Nathorff react to the Nazi boycott of Jewish doctors?
2. What effect did the Nazi boycott of Jews in Dortmund have on Marta Appel, her family, and her friends?
3. What evidence does David H. Buffum provide to show that many Germans did not approve of the events of *Kristallnacht*?

12 The Anguish of the Intellectuals

A somber mood gripped European intellectuals in the postwar period. The memory of World War I and the hypernationalism behind it, the rise of totalitarianism, and the Great Depression caused intellectuals to have grave doubts about the nature and destiny of Western civilization. To many European liberals, it seemed that the sun was setting on the Enlightenment tradition, that the ideals of reason and freedom, already gravely weakened by World War I, could not endure the threats posed by resurgent chauvinism, economic collapse, and totalitarian ideologies.

Johan Huizinga
IN THE SHADOW OF TOMORROW

Dutch historian Johan Huizinga (1872–1945) wrote that European civilization was at the breaking point in his book *In the Shadow of Tomorrow* (1936).

We are living in a demented world. And we know it. It would not come as a surprise to anyone if tomorrow the madness gave way to a frenzy which would leave our poor Europe in a state of distracted stupor, with engines still turning and flags streaming in the breeze, but with the spirit gone.

Everywhere there are doubts as to the solidity of our social structure, vague fears of the imminent future, a feeling that our civilization is on the way to ruin. They are not merely the shapeless anxieties which beset us in the small hours of the night when the flame of life burns low. They are considered expectations founded on observation and judgment of an overwhelming multitude of facts. How to avoid the recognition that almost all things which once seemed sacred and immutable have now become unsettled, truth and humanity, justice and reason? We see forms of government no longer capable of functioning, production systems on the verge of collapse, social forces gone wild with power. The roaring engine of this tremendous time seems to be heading for a breakdown. . . .

If, then, this civilization is to be saved, if it is not to be submerged by centuries of barbarism but to secure the treasures of its inheritance on new and more stable foundations, there is indeed need for those now living fully to realise how far the decay has already progressed.

It is but a little while since the apprehension of impending doom and of a progressive deterioration of civilization has become general. For the majority of men it is the economic crisis with its direct material effects (most of us being more sensitive in body than in spirit), which has first prepared the soil for thoughts and sentiments of this nature. Obviously those whose occupation it is to deal systematically and critically with problems of human society and civilization, philosophers and sociologists, have long ago realised that all was not well with our vaunted modern civilization. They have recognised from the outset that the economic dislocation is only one aspect of a transformation-process of much wider import.

The first ten years of this century have known little if anything in the way of fears and apprehensions regarding the future of our civilization. Friction and threats, shocks and dangers, there were then as ever. But except for the revolution menace which Marxism had hung over the world, they did not appear as evils threatening mankind with ruin. . . .

To-day, however, the sense of living in the midst of a violent crisis of civilization, threatening complete collapse, has spread far and wide. Oswald Spengler's *Untergang des Abendlandes*[1] has been the alarm signal for untold numbers the world over. This is not to say that all those who have read Spengler's famous work have become converts to his views. But it has jolted them out of their unreasoning faith in the providential nature of Progress and familiarised them with the idea of a decline of existing civilization and culture in our own time. Unperturbed optimism is at present only possible for those who through lack of insight fail to realise what is ailing civilization, having themselves been affected by the disease, and for those who in their social or political creed of salvation think to have the key to the hidden treasure-room of earthly weal from which to scatter on humanity the blessings of the civilization to come. . . .

---

[1]Oswald Spengler was the author of *Untergang des Abendlandes* (*The Decline of the West;* volume 1, 1918; volume 2, 1922), which maintained that Western civilization was dying.

How naïve the glad and confident hope of a century ago, that the advance of science and the general extension of education assured the progressive perfection of society, seems to us today! Who can still seriously believe that the translation of scientific triumphs into still more marvelous technical achievements is enough to save civilization, or that the eradication of illiteracy means the end of barbarism! Modern society, with its intensive development and mechanisation, indeed looks very different from the dream vision of Progress! . . .

Delusion and misconception flourish everywhere. More than ever men seem to be slaves to a word, a motto, to kill one another with, to silence one another in the most literal sense. The world is filled with hate and misunderstanding. There is no way of measuring how great the percentage of the deluded is and whether it is greater than formerly, but delusion and folly have more power to harm and speak with greater authority. For the shallow, semi-educated person the beneficial restraints of respect for tradition, form and cult are gradually falling away. Worst of all is that widely prevalent indifference to truth which reaches its peak in the open advocacy of the political lie.

Barbarisation sets in when, in an old culture which once, in the course of many centuries, had raised itself to purity and clarity of thought and understanding, the vapours of the magic and fantastic rise up again from the seething brew of passions to cloud the understanding: when the *muthos* [myth] supplants the *logos* [reason].

Again and again the new creed of the heroic will to power, with its exaltation of life over understanding, is seen to embody the very tendencies which to the believer in the Spirit spell the drift towards barbarism. For the "life-philosophy" does exactly this: it extols *muthos* over *logos*. To the prophets of the life-philosophy barbarism has no deprecatory implications. The term itself loses its meaning. The new rulers desire nothing else. . . .

. . . Against all that seems to presage decline and ruin, contemporary humanity, except for a few fatalists, for once unanimously [asserts] the energetic declaration . . . we *will* not perish. This world of ours is, with all its misery, too fine to allow it to sink into a night of human degradation and blindness of the spirit. . . . This heirloom of centuries called Western civilization has been entrusted to us to pass it on to coming generations, preserved, safeguarded, if possible enriched and improved, if it must be, impoverished, but at any rate as pure as it is in our power to keep it.

Nicolas Berdyaev
MODERN IDEOLOGIES AT VARIANCE WITH CHRISTIANITY

To Nicolas Berdyaev, a Russian Christian philosopher who fled the Soviet Union, Communism and Nazism were modern forms of idolatry in opposition to the core values of Christianity. Nationalism, he said, "dehumanizes ethics" and provokes hatred among peoples; Nazi racism, which demonizes Jews because of their genes, is "unworthy of a Christian." Only by a return to Christian piety, maintained Berdyaev, can we overcome the "collective demoniac possession" that is destroying European civilization. By Christian piety, he meant an active struggle for human dignity and social justice. Berdyaev expressed these views in *The Fate of Man in the Modern World* (1935), which is excerpted below.

We are witnessing the process of dehumanization in all phases of culture and of social life. Above all, moral consciousness is being dehumanized. Man has ceased to be the supreme value: he has ceased to have any value at all. The youth of the whole world, communist, fascist, national-socialist or those simply carried away by technics . . . this youth is not only anti-humanistic in its attitudes, but often anti-human. . . .

. . . A bestial cruelty toward man is characteristic of our age, and this is more astonishing since it is displayed at the very peak of human refinement, where modern conceptions of sympathy, it would seem, have made impossible the old, barbaric forms of cruelty. Bestialism is something quite different from the old, natural, healthy barbarism; it is barbarism within a refined civilization. Here the atavistic, barbaric instincts are filtered through the prism of civilization, and hence they have a pathological character. . . . The bestialism of our time is a continuation of the war, it has poisoned mankind with the blood of war. The morals of war-time have become those of "peaceful" life, which is actually the continuation of war, a war of all against all. According to this morality, everything is permissible: man may be used in any way desired for the attainment of inhuman or anti-human aims. Bestialism is a denial of the value of the human person, of every human personality; it is a denial of all sympathy with the fate of any man. The new humanism is closing: this is inescapable.

We are entering an inhuman world, a world of inhumanness, inhuman not merely in fact, but in principle as well. Inhumanity has begun to be presented as something noble, surrounded with an aureole of heroism. Over against man there rises a class or a race, a deified collective or state. Modern nationalism bears marks of bestial inhumanity. No longer is every man held to be a man, a value, the image and likeness of God. For often even Christianity is interpreted inhumanly. The "Aryan paragraph" offered to German Christians is the project for a new form of inhumanity in Christianity. . . .

. . . The new world which is taking form is moved by other values than the value of man or of human personality, or the value of truth: it is moved by such values as power, technics, race-purity, nationality, the state, the class, the collective. The will to justice is overcome by the will to power. . . .

. . . National passion is tearing the world and threatening the destruction of European culture. This is one more proof of the strength of atavism [primitivism] in human society, of how much stronger than the conscious is the subconcious, of how superficial has been the humanizing process of past centuries. . . . [M]odern Nationalism means the dehumanization and bestialization of human societies. It is a reversion from the category of culture and history to that of zoology. . . .

. . . The results of the Christian-humanistic process of unifying humanity seem to be disappearing. We are witnessing the paganization of Christian society. Nationalism is polytheism: it is incompatible with monotheism.

This process of paganization takes shocking forms in Germany, which wishes no longer to be a Christian nation, has exchanged the swastika for the cross and demands of Christians that they should renounce the very fundamentals of the Christian revelation and the Christian faith, and cast aside the moral teaching of the Gospels. . . .

Nationalism turns nationality into a supreme and absolute value to which all life is subordinated. This is idolatry. The nation replaces God. Thus Nationalism cannot but come into conflict with Christian universalism, with the Christian revelation that there is neither Greek nor Jew, and that every man has absolute value. Nationalism uses everything as its own instrument, as an instrument of national power and prosperity. . . .

. . . Nationalism has no Christian roots and it is always in conflict with Christianity. . . .

. . . Nationalism involves not only love of one's own, but hatred of other nations, and hatred is usually a stronger motive than love. Nationalism preaches either seclusion, isolation, blindness to other nations and culture, self-satisfaction and particularism, or else expansion at the expense of others, conquest, subjection, imperialism. And in both cases it denies Christian conscience, contraverts the principle and the habits of the brotherhood of man. Nationalism is in complete contradiction to a personal ethic; it denies the supreme value of human personality. Modern Nationalism dehumanizes ethics, it demands of man that he renounce humanity. It is all one and the same process, in Communism as in Nationalism. Man's inner world is completely at the mercy of collectivism, national or social. . . .

[R]acialism . . . has no basis at all in Christianity. The mere consideration of the "Aryan paragraph" is unworthy of a Christian, although it is now demanded of Christians in Germany. Racialist anti-Semitism inevitably leads to anti-Christianity, as we see in Germany today. That Germano-Aryan Christianity now being promoted is a denial of the Gospels and of Christ Himself. The ancient religious conflict between Christianity and Judaism, a real conflict by the way, has taken such a turn in our difficult and uncertain times, that militant anti-Judaism turns out to be anti-Christianity. Truly Christian anti-Judaism is directed, not against the Bible or the Old Testament, but against the Talmudic-rabbinic Judaism which developed after the Jews' refusal to accept Christ. But when religious anti-Judaism becomes racialist anti-Semitism, it inevitably turns into anti-Christianity, for the human origins of Christianity are Hebrew. . . . [I]t is impossible, it is forbidden, for a true Christian to be a racialist and to hate the Jews. . . .

. . . According to the race theory there is no hope of salvation, whatever: if you were born a Jew or a negro, no change of consciousness or belief or conviction can save you, you are doomed. A Jew may become a Christian: that does him no good. Even if he becomes a national-socialist, he cannot be saved.

REVIEW QUESTIONS

1. What contrasts did Johan Huizinga draw between Europe at the turn of the century and the Europe of his day?
2. According to Nicolas Berdyaev, how is nationalism contradictory to Christian values?

CHAPTER 13

World War II

THE NAZIS HERDED THE JEWS OF POLAND into walled ghettos where they were starved, beaten and humiliated prior to being deported to death camps. This picture from 1943 shows Jews being rounded up, probably for deportation and the gas chambers. *(Hulton Deutsch Collection/Historical/Corbis)*

From the early days of his political career, Hitler dreamed of forging a vast German empire in Central and Eastern Europe. He believed that only by waging a war of conquest against Russia could the German nation gain the living space and security it required and, as a superior race, deserved. War was an essential component of National Socialist ideology; it also accorded with Hitler's temperament. For the former corporal from the trenches, the Great War had never ended. Hitler aspired to political power because he wanted to mobilize the material and human resources of the German nation for war and conquest. Whereas historians may debate the question of responsibility for World War I, few would disagree with French historian Pierre Renouvin that World War II was Hitler's war:

> It appears to be an almost incontrovertible fact that the Second World War was brought on by the actions of the Hitler government, that these actions were the expression of a policy laid down well in advance in *Mein Kampf*, and that this war could have been averted up until the last moment if the German government had so wished.

Western statesmen had sufficient warning that Hitler was a threat to peace and the essential values of Western civilization, but they failed to rally their people and take a stand until Germany had greatly increased its capacity to wage aggressive war.

World War II was the most destructive war in history. Estimates of the number of dead range as high as fifty million, including twenty-five million Russians, who sacrificed more than the other participants in both population and material resources. The consciousness of Europe, already profoundly damaged by World War I, was again grievously wounded. Nazi racial theories showed that even in an age of sophisticated science the mind remains attracted to irrational beliefs and mythical imagery. Nazi atrocities proved that people will torture and kill with religious zeal and machine-like indifference. The Nazi assault on reason and freedom demonstrated anew the precariousness of Western civilization. This assault would forever cast doubt on the Enlightenment conception of human goodness, secular rationality, and the progress of civilization through advances in science and technology.

1 Prescient Observers of Nazi Germany

After Hitler took power in January 1933, many Western officials hoped that his radicalism would be tamed by the responsibilities of leadership. Moreover, these officials either never read *Mein Kampf* or did not take it seriously. But there were also astute observers who, within months after Hitler became chancellor, warned that Nazi Germany constituted a threat to the European peace. They maintained that Hitler, who believed that a Darwinian struggle for existence governed relations between nations and races, would eventually launch a war in order to realize the territorial aims of Nazi ideology.

Horace Rumbold
"PACIFISM IS THE DEADLIEST OF SINS"

On April 26, 1933, Horace Rumbold (1869–1941), Britain's ambassador to Germany, sent the following dispatch to London. It is clear that Rumbold had read and correctly assessed the meaning of *Mein Kampf.*

The outlook for Europe is far from peaceful if the speeches of Nazi leaders, especially of the Chancellor, are borne in mind. The Chancellor's account of his political career in *Mein Kampf* contains not only the principles which have guided him during the last fourteen years, but explains how he arrived at these fundamental principles. Stripped of the verbiage in which he has clothed it, Hitler's thesis is extremely simple. He starts with the assertions that man is a fighting animal, therefore the nation is, he concludes, a fighting unit, being a community of fighters. Any living organism which ceases to fight for its existence is, he asserts, doomed to extinction. A country or a race which ceases to fight is equally doomed. The fighting capacity of a race depends on its purity. Hence the necessity for ridding it of foreign impurities. The Jewish race, owing to its universality, is of necessity pacifist and internationalist. Pacifism is the deadliest sin, for pacifism means the surrender of the race in the fight for existence. The first duty of every country is, therefore, to nationalise the masses; intelligence is of secondary importance in the case of the individual; will and determination are of higher importance. The individual who is born to command is more valuable than countless thousands of subordinate natures. Only brute force can ensure the survival of the race. Hence the necessity for military forms. The race must fight; a race

that rests must rust and perish. The German race, had it been united in time, would now be master of the globe today. The new Reich must gather within its fold all the scattered German elements in Europe. A race which has suffered defeat can be rescued by restoring its self-confidence. Above all things, the army must be taught to believe in its own invincibility. To restore the German nation again, it is only necessary to convince the people that the recovery of freedom by force of arms is a possibility.

Hitler describes at great length in his turgid style the task which the new Germany must therefore set itself. Intellectualism is undesirable. The ultimate aim of education is to produce a German who can be converted with the minimum of training into a soldier. The idea that there is something reprehensible in chauvinism is entirely mistaken. Indeed, the greatest upheavals in history would have been unthinkable had it not been for the driving force of fanatical and hysterical passions. Nothing could have been effected by the *bourgeois* virtues of peace and order. The world is now moving towards such an upheaval, and the new (German) State must see to it that the race is ready for the last and greatest decisions on this earth (p. 475, 17th edition of *Mein Kampf*). Again and again he proclaims that fanatical conviction and uncompromising resolution are indispensable qualities in a leader.

The climax of education is military service (p. 476). A man may be a living lexicon, but unless he is a soldier he will fail in the great crises of life. . . . An army is indispensable to ensure the maintenance and expansion of the race. The recovery of lost provinces has never been effected by protest and without the use of force. To forge the necessary weapons is the task of the internal political leaders of the people.

. . . Germany's lost provinces cannot be gained by solemn appeals to Heaven or by pious hopes in the League of Nations, but only by force of arms (p. 708). Germany must not repeat the mistake of fighting all her enemies at once. She must single out the most dangerous in turn and attack him with all her forces. . . . It is the business of the Government to implant in the people feelings of manly courage and passionate hatred. The world will only cease to be anti-German when Germany recovers equality of rights and resumes her place in the sun. . . .

Still more disquieting is the fact that though Germany remains nominally a member of the League of Nations the official policy of the country so far as it has been translated into action or expounded by members of the Government is fundamentally hostile to the principles on which the League is founded. Not only is it a crime to preach pacificism or condemn militarism but it is equally objectionable to preach international understanding, and while politicians and writers who have been guilty of the one have actually been arrested and incarcerated, those guilty of the other have at any rate been removed from public life and of course from official employment. . . .

[Germany has] to rearm on land, and, as Herr Hitler explains in his memoirs, they have to lull their adversaries into such a state of coma that they will allow themselves to be engaged one by one. It may seem astonishing that the Chancellor should express himself so frankly, but it must be noted that his book was written in 1925, when his prospects of reaching power were so remote that he could afford to be candid. He would probably be glad to suppress every copy extant today. Since he assumed office, Herr Hitler has been as cautious and discreet as he was formerly blunt and frank. He declares that he is anxious that peace should be maintained for a ten-year period. What he probably means can be more accurately expressed by the [following] formula: Germany needs peace until she has recovered such strength that no country can challenge her without serious and irksome preparations. I fear that it would be misleading to base any hopes on a return to sanity or a serious modification of the views of the Chancellor and his entourage.

George S. Messersmith
"THE NAZIS WERE AFTER . . .
UNLIMITED TERRITORIAL EXPANSION"

Two months after Rumbold's dispatch, George S. Messersmith, American consul general at Berlin, reported to the State Department on the "dangerous situation" developing in Germany. Appointed minister to Austria in 1934, he continued to warn that the Nazis were serious about expanding Germany's territory.

CONSUL GENERAL MESSERSMITH'S REPORT FROM BERLIN

The United States Consul General at Berlin, George S. Messersmith, who had been at that post since 1930, reported frequently to the Department of State during this period on the menace inherent in the Nazi regime. Mr. Messersmith expressed the view, in a letter of June 26, 1933 to Under Secretary of State Phillips, that the United States must be exceedingly careful in its dealings with Germany as long as the existing Government was in power, as that Government had no spokesmen who could really be depended upon and those who held the highest positions were "capable of actions which really outlaw them from ordinary intercourse." He reported that some of the men who were running the German Government were "psychopathic cases"; that others were in a state of exaltation and in a frame of mind that knew no reason; and that those men in the party and in responsible positions who were really worthwhile were powerless because they had to follow the orders of superiors who were suffering from the "abnormal psychology" prevailing in Germany. "There is a real revolution here and a dangerous situation," he said.

Consul General Messersmith reported further that a martial spirit was being developed in Germany; that everywhere people were seen drilling, including children from the age of five or six to persons well into middle age; that a psychology was being developed that the whole world was against Germany, which was defenseless before the world; that people were being trained against gas and airplane attacks; and that the idea of war from neighboring countries was constantly harped upon. He emphasized that Germany was headed in directions which could only carry ruin to it and create a situation "dangerous to world peace." He said we must recognize that while Germany at that time wanted peace, it was by no means a peaceful country or one looking forward to a long period of peace; that the German Government and its adherents desired peace ardently for the time being because they needed peace to carry through the changes in Germany which they wanted to bring about. What they wanted to do was to make Germany "the most capable instrument of war that there has ever existed."

Consul General Messersmith reported from Berlin five months later, in a letter of November 23, 1933 to Under Secretary Phillips, that the military spirit in Germany was constantly growing and that innumerable measures were being taken to develop the German people into a hardy, sturdy race which would "be able to meet all comers." He said that the leaders of Germany had no desire for peace unless it was a peace in complete compliance with German ambitions; that Hitler and his associates really wanted peace for the moment, but only to have a chance to prepare for the use of force if it were found essential; and that they were preparing their way so carefully that the German people would be with them when they wanted to use force and when they felt that they had the "necessary means to carry through their objects." . . .

Mr. Messersmith, who had been appointed Minister to Austria in 1934, continued to send to the Department of State reports on the situation in Germany. In February 1935 he reported that the Nazis had their eyes on Memel, Alsace-Lorraine, and the eastern frontier; that they nourished just as strongly the hope to get the Ukraine for the surplus German population; that Austria was a definite objective; and that absorption or hegemony over the whole of southeastern Europe was a definite policy. A few weeks later he reported a conversation with William E. Dodd, United States Ambassador to Germany, in which they had agreed that no faith whatsoever could be placed in the Nazi regime and its promises, that what the Nazis were after was "unlimited territorial expansion," and that there was probably in existence a German-Japanese understanding, if not an alliance.

REVIEW QUESTIONS

1. According to Rumbold, what was the basic thesis underlying Hitler's political philosophy?
2. Why, according to Rumbold, did Hitler want to maintain peace for a ten-year period? How did the events of the 1930s prove Rumbold's assertions correct?
3. What indications did George Messersmith have that Germany was preparing for war?

---

2 Remilitarization of the Rhineland

In the Locarno Pact (1925), Germany, France, and Belgium agreed not to change their existing borders, which meant, in effect, that Germany had accepted both the return of Alsace and Lorraine to France and the demilitarization of the Rhineland—two provisions of the Treaty of Versailles. On March 7, 1936, Hitler marched troops into the Rhineland, violating both the Versailles Treaty and the Locarno Pact. German generals had cautioned Hitler that such a move would provoke a French invasion of Germany and reoccupation of the Rhineland, which the German army still in the first stages of rearmament could not repulse. But Hitler gambled that France and Britain, lacking the will to fight, would take no action. He had assessed the Anglo-French mood correctly. British statesmen in particular championed a policy of appeasement: giving in to Hitler in the hope that Europe would not be dragged through another world war.

William L. Shirer
BERLIN DIARY

Immediately after the German army occupied the demilitarized zone, Hitler addressed the Reichstag. William L. Shirer, an American correspondent in Germany, witnessed the speech and recorded his observations, reproduced below, in his diary.

The Reichstag, more tense then I have ever felt it (apparently the hand-picked deputies on the main floor had not yet been told what had happened, though they knew something was afoot), began promptly at noon. The French, British, Belgian, and Polish ambassadors were absent, but the Italians were there and Dodd. General von Blomberg, the War Minister, sitting with the Cabinet on the left side of the stage, was as white as a sheet and fumbled the top of the bench nervously with his fingers. I have never seen him in such a state. Hitler began with a long harangue which he has often given before, but never tires of repeating, about the injustices of the Versailles Treaty and the peacefulness of Germans. Then his voice, which had been low and hoarse at the beginning, rose to a shrill, hysterical scream as he raged against Bolshevism.

"I will not have the gruesome Communist international dictatorship of hate descend upon the German people! This destructive Asiatic *Weltanschauung* strikes at all values! I tremble for Europe at the thought of what would happen should this destructive Asiatic conception of life, this chaos of the Bolshevist revolution, prove successful!" (Wild applause.)

Then, in a more reasoned voice, his argument that France's pact with Russia had invalidated the Locarno Treaty. A slight pause and:

"Germany no longer feels bound by the Locarno Treaty. In the interest of the primitive rights of its people to the security of their frontier and the safeguarding of their defence, the German Government has re-established, as from today, the absolute and unrestricted sovereignty of the Reich in the demilitarized zone!"

Now the six hundred deputies, personal appointees all of Hitler, little men with big bodies and bulging necks and cropped hair and pouched bellies and brown uniforms and heavy boots, little men of clay in his fine hands, leap to their feet like automatons, their right arms upstretched in the Nazi salute, and scream *"Heil's,"* the first two or three wildly, the next twenty-five in unison, like a college yell. Hitler raises his hand for silence. It comes slowly. Slowly the automatons sit down. Hitler now has them in his claws. He appears to sense it. He says in a deep, resonant voice: "Men of the German Reichstag!" The silence is utter.

"In this historic hour, when in the Reich's western provinces German troops are at this minute marching into their future peace-time garrisons, we all unite in two sacred vows."

He can go no further. It is news to this hysterical "parliamentary" mob that German soldiers are already on the move into the Rhineland. All the militarism in their German blood surges to their heads. They spring, yelling and crying, to their feet. The audience in the galleries does the same, all except a few diplomats and about fifty of us correspondents. Their hands are raised in slavish salute, their faces now contorted with hysteria, their mouths wide open, shouting, shouting, their eyes, burning with fanaticism, glued on the new god, the Messiah. The Messiah plays his role superbly. His head lowered as if in all humbleness, he waits patiently for silence. Then, his voice still low, but choking with emotion, utters the two vows:

"First, we swear to yield to no force whatever in the restoration of the honour of our people,

preferring to succumb with honour to the severest hardships rather than to capitulate. Secondly, we pledge that now, more than ever, we shall strive for an understanding between European peoples, especially for one with our western neighbour nations. . . . We have no territorial demands to make in Europe! . . . Germany will never break the peace."

It was a long time before the cheering stopped. Down in the lobby the deputies were still under the magic spell, gushing over one another. A few generals made their way out. Behind their smiles, however, you could not help detecting a nervousness.

Shirer recorded that Hitler "staked all on the success of his move and cannot survive if the French humiliate him" by taking action. The following day he made this entry in his diary.

Hitler has got away with it! France is not marching. Instead it is appealing to the League! No wonder the faces of Hitler and Göring and Blomberg and Fritsch were all smiles this noon as they sat in the royal box at the State Opera and for the second time in two years celebrated in a most military fashion Heroes Memorial Day, which is supposed to mark the memory of the two million Germans slain in the last war.

Oh, the stupidity (or is it paralysis?) of the French! I learned today on absolute authority that the German troops which marched into the demilitarized zone of the Rhineland yesterday had strict orders to beat a hasty retreat if the French army opposed them in any way. They were not prepared or equipped to fight a regular army. That probably explains Blomberg's white face yesterday. Apparently Fritsch (commander-in-chief of the Reichswehr) and most of the generals opposed the move, but Blomberg, who has a blind faith in the Führer and his judgment, talked them into it. It may be that Fritsch, who loves neither Hitler nor the Nazi regime, consented to go along on the theory that if the coup failed, that would be the end of Hitler; if it succeeded, then one of his main military problems was solved.

REVIEW QUESTIONS

1. What did William L. Shirer think of the Nazis?
2. Why was Shirer critical of French policy?

---

3 The Anschluss, March 1938

One of Hitler's aims was the incorporation of Austria into the Third Reich. The Treaty of Versailles had expressly prohibited the union of the two countries, but in *Mein Kampf*, Hitler had insisted that an Anschluss was necessary for German *Lebensraum* (living space). In February 1938, under intense pressure from Hitler, Austrian Chancellor Kurt von Schuschnigg promised to accept Austrian Nazis in his cabinet and agreed to closer relations with Germany. Austrian independence was slipping away, and increasingly, Austrian Nazis undermined Schuschnigg's authority. Seeking to gain his people's support, Schuschnigg made plans for a plebiscite on the issue of preserving Austrian independence. An enraged Hitler ordered his generals to draw up plans for an invasion of Austria. Hitler then demanded Schuschnigg's resignation and the formation of a new government headed by Arthur Seyss-Inquart, an Austrian Nazi.

Believing that Austria was not worth a war, Britain and France informed the embattled chancellor that they would not help in the event of a German invasion. Schuschnigg then resigned, and Austrian Nazis began to take control of the government. Under the pretext of preventing violence, Hitler ordered his troops to cross into Austria, and on March 13, 1938, Austrian leaders declared that Austria was a province of the German Reich.

The Anschluss was supported by many Austrians: Nazis and their sympathizers, average people who hoped it would bring improved material conditions, and opportunists who had their eyes set on social and economic advancement by working with the Nazis. Even many opponents of the Nazis felt that Austrian unity with Germany was fated to be accomplished, even as they lamented that it meant incorporation into Hitler's regime.

In the first days after the Anschluss, anti-Nazis, particularly Social Democrats, were incarcerated; a wave of dissidents, politicians, and intellectuals fled the country; and Jews were subjected to torment and humiliation. Austrian Nazis, often with the approval of their fellow citizens, plundered Jewish shops, pulled elderly Orthodox Jews around by their beards, and made Jews scour pro-Schuschnigg slogans off the streets with toothbrushes or their bare hands. One eyewitness recalled years later: "I saw in the crowd a well-dressed woman . . . holding up a little girl, a blond lovely little girl with these curls, so that the girl could see better how a . . . Nazi Storm Trooper kicked an old Jew who fell down because he wasn't allowed to kneel. He had to scrub and just bend down sort of, and he fell and he kicked him. And they all laughed and she laughed as well—it was wonderful entertainment—and that shook me."

Stefan Zweig
THE WORLD OF YESTERDAY

One of modern German-speaking Europe's most important authors, Stefan Zweig (see page 284) was born into a well-to-do Viennese Jewish household, came of age during the waning years of the monarchy, and witnessed both the devastation of World War I and the chaos of the interwar years. A passionate European and a convinced Austrian patriot, Zweig was disgusted by national chauvinisms, particularly the virulent German nationalism clearly discernible in Austria after the collapse of the Habsburg monarchy. His *World of Yesterday* (1943) both laments the loss of European cosmopolitanism and offers biting criticism of the inability, or unwillingness, of many Austrians to come to terms with the violent intolerance in their own society and the spreading danger of Nazism. Zweig's despair was all-consuming; he took his own life in South American exile, unable to reconcile himself to the changes in his beloved Europe and his Austrian homeland.

In the following selection from his autobiography, Zweig describes the orgy of hate that engulfed Vienna immediately after the Anschluss.

I thought that I had foreboded all the terror that would come to pass when Hitler's dream of hate would come true and he would triumphantly occupy Vienna, the city which had turned him off, poor and a failure, in his youth. But how timid, how petty, how lamentable my imagination, all human imagination, in the light of the inhumanity which discharged itself on that March 13, 1938, that day when Austria and Europe with it fell prey to sheer violence! The mask was off. The other States having plainly shown their fear, there was no further need to check moral inhibitions or to employ hypocritical pretexts about "Marxists" having to be politically liquidated. Who cared for England, France, for the whole world! Now there was no longer mere robbery and theft, but every private lust for revenge was given free rein. University professors were obliged to scrub the streets with their naked hands, pious white-bearded Jews were dragged into the synagogue by hooting youths and forced to do knee-exercises and to shout "Heil Hitler" in chorus. Innocent people in the streets were trapped like rabbits and herded off to clean the latrines in the S. A. barracks. All the sickly, unclean fantasies of hate that had been conceived in many orgiastic nights found raging expression in bright daylight. Breaking into homes and tearing earrings from trembling women may well have happened in the looting of cities, hundreds of years ago during medieval wars; what was new, however, was the shameless delight in public tortures, in spiritual martyrization, in the refinements of humiliation. All this has been recorded not by one but by thousands who suffered it; and a more peaceful day—not one already morally fatigued as ours is—will shudder to read what a single hate-crazed man perpetrated in that city of culture in the twentieth century. For amidst his military and political victories Hitler's most diabolic triumph was that he succeeded through progressive excesses in blunting every sense of law and order. Before this "New Order," the murder of a single man without legal process and without apparent reason would have shocked the world; torture was considered unthinkable in the twentieth century, expropriations were known by the old names, theft and robbery. But now after successive [murderous] nights the daily mortal tortures in the S. A. prisons and behind barbed wire, what did a single injustice or earthly suffering signify? In 1938, after Austria, our universe had become accustomed to inhumanity, to lawlessness, and brutality as never in centuries before. In a former day the occurrences in unhappy Vienna alone would have been sufficient to cause international proscription, but in 1938 the world conscience was silent or merely muttered surlily before it forgot and forgave.

Those days, marked by daily cries for help from the homeland when one knew close friends to be kidnapped and humiliated and one trembled helplessly for every loved one, were among the most terrible of my life. These times have so perverted our hearts that I am not ashamed to say that I was not shocked and did not mourn upon learning of the death of my mother in Vienna; on the contrary, I even felt something like composure in the knowledge that she was now safe from suffering and danger. Eighty-four years old, almost completely deaf, she occupied rooms in our old home and thus could not, even under the new "Aryan" code, be evicted for the time being and we had hoped somehow to get her abroad after a while. One of the first Viennese ordinances had hit her hard. At her advanced age she was a little shaky on her legs and was accustomed, when on her daily laborious walk, to rest on a bench in the Ringstrasse or in the park, every five or ten minutes. Hitler had not been master of the city for a week when the bestial order forbidding Jews to sit on public benches was issued—one of those orders obviously thought up only for the sadistic purpose of malicious torture. There was logic and reason in robbing Jews for with the booty from factories, the home furnishings, the villas, and the jobs compulsorily vacated they could feather their followers' nests, reward their satellites; after all, Goering's picture-gallery owes its splendor mainly to this generously exercised practice. But to deny an aged woman or an exhausted old man a few minutes on a park bench to catch his breath—this remained reserved to the twentieth century and to the man whom millions worshipped as the greatest in our day.

Fortunately, my mother was spared suffering such brutality and humiliation for long. She died a few months after the occupation of Vienna and I cannot forbear to write about an episode in connection with her passing; it seems important to me to record just such details for a time in which such things will again seem impossible.

One morning the eighty-four-year-old woman suddenly lost consciousness. The doctor who was called declared that she could hardly live through the night and engaged a nurse, a woman of about forty, to attend her deathbed. Neither my brother nor I, her only children, was there nor could we have come back, because a return to the deathbed of a mother would have been counted a misdeed by the representatives of German culture. A cousin of ours undertook to spend the night in the apartment so that at least one of the family might be present at her death. He was then a man of sixty, and in poor health; in fact he too died about a year later. As he was uncovering his bed in an adjoining room the nurse appeared and declared her regret that because of the new National-Socialist laws it was impossible for her to stay overnight with the dying woman. To her credit be it said that she was rather shamefaced about it. My cousin being a Jew and she a woman under fifty, she was not permitted to spend a night under the same roof with him, even at a deathbed, because according to the [vile Nazi] mentality, it must be a Jew's first thought to practice race defilement upon her. Of course the regulation was extremely embarrassing, but she would have to obey the law. So my sixty-year-old cousin had to leave the house in the evening so that the nurse could stay with my dying mother; it will be intelligible, then, why I considered her almost lucky not to have to live on among such people.

REVIEW QUESTIONS

1. What was the underlying purpose of the various anti-Jewish ordinances in Vienna that Stefan Zweig refers to? How might they have paved the way for even harsher actions?
2. Zweig accurately predicted that people in "a more peaceful day" would later "shudder to read what a single hate-crazed man perpetrated in that city of culture in the twentieth century." Why do you think so many of Zweig's contemporaries failed to feel the same dismay and horror as these events unfolded?

---

4   The Munich Agreement

Hitler sought power to build a great German empire in Europe, a goal that he revealed in *Mein Kampf.* In 1935, Hitler declared that Germany was no longer bound by the Versailles Treaty and would restore military conscription. Germany remilitarized the Rhineland in 1936 and incorporated Austria into the Third Reich in 1938. Although these actions violated the Versailles Treaty, Britain and France offered no resistance.

In 1938, Hitler also threatened war if Czechoslovakia did not cede to Germany the Sudetenland with its large German population—of the 3.5 million people living in the Czech Sudetenland, some 2.8 million were Germans. In September 1938, Hitler met with other European leaders at Munich. Prime Minister Neville Chamberlain (1869–1940) of Great Britain and Prime Minister Édouard Daladier (1884–1970) of France agreed to Hitler's demands, despite France's mutual assistance pact with Czechoslovakia and the Czechs' expressed determination to resist the dismemberment of their country. Both Chamberlain and Daladier were praised by their compatriots for ensuring, as Chamberlain said, "peace in our time."

Neville Chamberlain
IN DEFENSE OF APPEASEMENT

Britain and France pursued a policy of appeasement—giving in to Germany in the hope that a satisfied Hitler would not drag Europe into another war. Appeasement expressed the widespread British desire to heal the wounds of World War I and to correct what many British officials regarded as the injustices of the Versailles Treaty. Some officials, lauding Hitler's anticommunism, regarded a powerful Germany as a bulwark against the Soviet Union. Britain's lack of military preparedness was another compelling reason for not resisting Hitler. On September 27, 1938, when negotiations between Hitler and Chamberlain reached a tense moment, the British prime minister addressed his nation. Excerpts of this speech and of another before the House of Commons, which appeared in his *In Search of Peace* (1939), follow.

First of all I must say something to those who have written to my wife or myself in these last weeks to tell us of their gratitude for my efforts and to assure us of their prayers for my success. Most of these letters have come from women— mothers or sisters of our own countrymen. But there are countless others besides—from France, from Belgium, from Italy, even from Germany, and it has been heartbreaking to read of the growing anxiety they reveal and their intense relief when they thought, too soon, that the danger of war was past.

If I felt my responsibility heavy before, to read such letters has made it seem almost overwhelming. How horrible, fantastic, incredible it is that we should be digging trenches and trying on gas masks here because of a quarrel in a far-away country between people of whom we know nothing. It seems still more impossible that a quarrel which has already been settled in principle should be the subject of war.

I can well understand the reasons why the Czech Government have felt unable to accept the terms which have been put before them in the German memorandum. Yet I believe after my talks with Herr Hitler that, if only time were allowed, it ought to be possible for the arrangements for transferring the territory that the Czech Government has agreed to give to Germany to be settled by agreement under conditions which would assure fair treatment to the population concerned. . . .

However much we may sympathise with a small nation confronted by a big and powerful neighbour, we cannot in all circumstances undertake to involve the whole British Empire in war simply on her account. If we have to fight it must be on larger issues than that. I am myself a man of peace to the depths of my soul. Armed conflict between nations is a nightmare to me; but if I were convinced that any nation had made up its mind to dominate the world by fear of its force, I should feel that it must be resisted. Under such a domination life for people who believe in liberty would not be worth living; but war is a fearful thing, and we must be very clear, before we embark on it, that it is really

the great issues that are at stake, and that the call to risk everything in their defence, when all the consequences are weighed, is irresistible.

For the present I ask you to await as calmly as you can the events of the next few days. As long as war has not begun, there is always hope that it may be prevented, and you know that I am going to work for peace to the last moment. Good night. . . .

On October 6, 1938, in a speech to Britain's House of Commons, Chamberlain defended the Munich agreement signed on September 30.

Since I first went to Berchtesgaden [to confer with Hitler in Germany] more than 20,000 letters and telegrams have come to No. 10, Downing Street [British prime minister's residence]. Of course, I have only been able to look at a tiny fraction of them, but I have seen enough to know that the people who wrote did not feel that they had such a cause for which to fight, if they were asked to go to war in order that the Sudeten Germans might not join the Reich. That is how they are feeling. That is my answer to those who say that we should have told Germany weeks ago that, if her army crossed the border of Czechoslovakia, we should be at war with her. We had no treaty obligations and no legal obligations to Czechoslovakia and if we had said that, we feel that we should have received no support from the people of this country. . . .

. . . When we were convinced, as we became convinced, that nothing any longer would keep the Sudetenland within the Czechoslovakian State, we urged the Czech Government as strongly as we could to agree to the cession of territory, and to agree promptly. The Czech Government, through the wisdom and courage of President Benes, accepted the advice of the French Government and ourselves. It was a hard decision for anyone who loved his country to take, but to accuse us of having by that advice betrayed the Czechoslovakian State is simply preposterous. What we did was to save her from annihilation and give her a chance of new life as a new State, which involves the loss of territory and fortifications, but may perhaps enable her to enjoy in the future and develop a national existence under a neutrality and security comparable to that which we see in Switzerland today. Therefore, I think the Government deserve the approval of this House for their conduct of affairs in this recent crisis which has saved Czechoslovakia from destruction and Europe from Armageddon.

Does the experience of the Great War and of the years that followed it give us reasonable hope that, if some new war started, that would end war any more than the last one did? . . .

One good thing, at any rate, has come out of this emergency through which we have passed. It has thrown a vivid light upon our preparations for defence, on their strength and on their weakness. I should not think we were doing our duty if we had not already ordered that a prompt and thorough inquiry should be made to cover the whole of our preparations, military and civil, in order to see, in the light of what has happened during these hectic days, what further steps may be necessary to make good our deficiencies in the shortest possible time.

Winston Churchill
"A DISASTER OF THE FIRST MAGNITUDE"

On October 5, 1938, Britain's elder statesman Winston Churchill (1874–1965) delivered a speech in the House of Commons attacking the Munich Agreement and British policy toward Nazi Germany.

. . . I will begin by saying what everybody would like to ignore or forget but which must nevertheless be stated, namely, that we have sustained a total and unmitigated defeat, and that France has suffered even more than we have. . . .

. . . And I will say this, that I believe the Czechs, left to themselves and told they were going to get no help from the Western Powers, would have been able to make better terms than they have got—they could hardly have worse—after all this tremendous perturbation. . . .

. . . I have always held the view that the maintenance of peace depends upon the accumulation of deterrents against the aggressor, coupled with a sincere effort to redress grievances. . . . After [Hitler's] seizure of Austria in March . . . I ventured to appeal to the Government . . . to give a pledge that in conjunction with France

and other Powers they would guarantee the security of Czechoslovakia while the Sudeten-Deutsch question was being examined either by a League of Nations Commission or some other impartial body, and I still believe that if that course had been followed events would not have fallen into this disastrous state. . . .

France and Great Britain together, especially if they had maintained a close contact with Russia, which certainly was not done, would have been able in those days in the summer, when they had the prestige, to influence many of the smaller States of Europe, and I believe they could have determined the attitude of Poland. Such a combination, prepared at a time when the German dictator was not deeply and irrevocably committed to his new adventure, would, I believe, have given strength to all those forces in Germany which resisted this departure, this new design. They were varying forces, those of a military character which declared that Germany was not ready to undertake a world war, and all that mass of moderate opinion and popular opinion which dreaded war, and some elements of which still have some influence upon the German Government. Such action would have given strength to all that intense desire for peace which the helpless German masses share with their British and French fellow men. . . .

. . . I do not think it is fair to charge those who wished to see this course followed, and followed consistently and resolutely, with having wished for an immediate war. Between submission and immediate war there was this third alternative, which gave a hope not only of peace but of justice. It is quite true that such a policy in order to succeed demanded that Britain should declare straight out and a long time beforehand that she would, with others, join to defend Czechoslovakia against an unprovoked aggression. His Majesty's Government refused to give that guarantee when it would have saved the situation. . . .

All is over. Silent, mournful, abandoned, broken, Czechoslovakia recedes into the darkness. She has suffered in every respect by her association with the Western democracies and with the League of Nations, of which she has always been an obedient servant. She has suffered in particular from her association with France, under whose guidance and policy she has been actuated for so long. . . .

We in this country, as in other Liberal and democratic countries, have a perfect right to exalt the principle of self-determination, but it comes ill out of the mouths of those in totalitarian States who deny even the smallest element of toleration to every section and creed within their bounds. . . .

What is the remaining position of Czechoslovakia? Not only are they politically mutilated, but, economically and financially, they are in complete confusion. Their banking, their railway arrangements, are severed and broken, their industries are curtailed, and the movement of their population is most cruel. The Sudeten miners, who are all Czechs and whose families have lived in that area for centuries, must now flee into an area where there are hardly any mines left for them to work. It is a tragedy which has occurred. . . .

I venture to think that in future the Czechoslovak State cannot be maintained as an independent entity. You will find that in a period of time which may be measured by years, but may be measured only by months, Czechoslovakia will be engulfed in the Nazi régime. Perhaps they may join it in despair or in revenge. At any rate, that story is over and told. But we cannot consider the abandonment and ruin of Czechoslovakia in the light only of what happened only last month. It is the most grievous consequence which we have yet experienced of what we have done and of what we have left undone in the last five years—five years of futile good intention, five years of eager search for the line of least resistance, five years of uninterrupted retreat of British power, five years of neglect of our air defences. Those are the features which I stand here to declare and which marked an improvident stewardship for which Great Britain and France have dearly to pay. We have been reduced in those five years from a position of security so overwhelming and so unchallengeable that we never cared to think about it. We have been reduced from a position where the very word "war" was considered one which would be used only by persons qualifying for a lunatic asylum. We have been reduced from a position of safety and power—power to do good, power to be generous to a beaten foe, power to make terms with Germany, power to give her proper redress for her grievances, power to stop her arming if we chose, power to take any step in strength or mercy or justice which we thought right—reduced in five years from a position safe and unchallenged to where we stand now.

When I think of the fair hopes of a long peace which still lay before Europe at the beginning of 1933 when Herr Hitler first obtained power, and of all the opportunities of arresting the growth of the Nazi power which have been thrown away, when I think of the immense combinations and resources which have been neglected or squandered, I cannot believe that a parallel exists in the whole course of history. So far as this country is concerned the responsibility must rest with those who have the undisputed control of our political affairs. They neither prevented Germany from rearming, nor did they rearm ourselves in time. . . . They neglected to make alliances and combinations which might have repaired previous errors, and thus they left us in the hour of trial without adequate national defence or effective international security. . . .

We are in the presence of a disaster of the first magnitude which has befallen Great Britain and France. Do not let us blind ourselves to that. It must now be accepted that all the countries of Central and Eastern Europe will make the best terms they can with the triumphant Nazi Power. The system of alliances in Central Europe upon which France has relied for her safety has been swept away, and I can see no means by which it can be reconstituted. . . .

. . . If the Nazi dictator should choose to look westward, as he may, bitterly will France and England regret the loss of that fine army of ancient Bohemia [Czechoslovakia] which was estimated last week to require not fewer than 30 German divisions for its destruction. . . .

. . . Many people, no doubt, honestly believe that they are only giving away the interests of Czechoslovakia, whereas I fear we shall find that we have deeply compromised, and perhaps fatally endangered, the safety and even the independence of Great Britain and France. . . . [T]here can never be friendship between the British democracy and the Nazi Power, that Power which spurns Christian ethics, which cheers its onward course by a barbarous paganism, which vaunts the spirit of aggression and conquest, which derives strength and perverted pleasure from persecution, and uses, as we have seen, with pitiless brutality the threat of murderous force. That Power cannot ever be the trusted friend of the British democracy. . . .

. . . [O]ur loyal, brave people . . . should know the truth. They should know that there has been gross neglect and deficiency in our defences; they should know that we have sustained a defeat without a war, the consequences of which will travel far with us along our road; they should know that we have passed an awful milestone in our history, when the whole equilibrium of Europe has been deranged, and that the terrible words have for the time being been pronounced against the Western democracies:

Thou art weighed in the balance and found wanting.

And do not suppose that this is the end. This is only the beginning of the reckoning. This is only the first sip, the first foretaste of a bitter cup which will be proffered to us year by year unless by a supreme recovery of moral health and martial vigour, we arise again and take our stand for freedom as in the olden time.

REVIEW QUESTIONS

1. In Neville Chamberlain's view, how did the British people regard a war with Germany over the Sudetenland?
2. How did Chamberlain respond to the accusation that Britain and France had betrayed Czechoslovakia?
3. What did Chamberlain consider to be the "one good thing" to come out of the Sudetenland crisis?
4. Why did Winston Churchill believe that "there [could] never be friendship between the British democracy and the Nazi Power"?
5. Why did Churchill believe that the Munich agreement was "a disaster of the first magnitude" for Britain and France?
6. What policy toward Nazi Germany did Churchill advocate?

5 World War II Begins

After Czechoslovakia, Hitler turned to Poland. In the middle of June 1939, the army presented him with a battle plan for an invasion of Poland, and on August 22, Hitler informed his leading generals that war with Poland was necessary. The following day, Nazi Germany signed a nonaggression pact with Communist Russia, which blocked Britain and France from duplicating their World War I alliance against Germany. The Nazi–Soviet Pact was the green light for an attack on Poland. At dawn on September 1, German forces, striking with coordinated speed and power, invaded Poland, starting World War II.

Adolf Hitler
"POLAND WILL BE DEPOPULATED AND SETTLED WITH GERMANS"

An American journalist was given a copy of Hitler's speech to his generals at the August 22 conference. Probably the supplier was an official close to Admiral Canaris, an opponent of Hitler who had attended the conference. The journalist then gave it to the British ambassador. The speech is reproduced below.

Decision to attack Poland was arrived at in spring. Originally there was fear that because of the political constellation we would have to strike at the same time against England, France, Russia and Poland. This risk too we should have had to take. Göring had demonstrated to us that his Four-Year Plan is a failure and that we are at the end of our strength, if we do not achieve victory in a coming war.

Since the autumn of 1938 and since I have realised that Japan will not go with us unconditionally and that Mussolini is endangered by that nitwit of a King and the treacherous scoundrel of a Crown Prince, I decided to go with Stalin. After all there are only three great statesmen in the world, Stalin, I and Mussolini. Mussolini is the weakest, for he has been able to break the power neither of the crown nor of the Church. Stalin and I are the only ones who visualise the future. So in a few weeks hence I shall stretch out my hand to Stalin at the common German-Russian frontier and with him undertake to re-distribute the world.

Our strength lies in our quickness and in our brutality; Genghis Khan has sent millions of women and children into death knowingly and with a light heart. History sees in him only the great founder of States. As to what the weak Western European civilisation asserts about me, that is of no account. I have given the command and I shall shoot everyone who utters one word of criticism, for the goal to be obtained in the war is not that of reaching certain lines but of physically demolishing the opponent. And so for the present only in the East I have put my death-head formations[1] in place with the command relentlessly and without compassion to

---

[1]The S.S. Death's Head formations were principally employed in peacetime in guarding concentration camps. When war started they became part of the Waffen SS combat units.

send into death many women and children of Polish origin and language. Only thus we can gain the living space that we need. Who after all is today speaking about the destruction of the Armenians?

Colonel-General von Brauchitsch has promised me to bring the war against Poland to a close within a few weeks. Had he reported to me that he needs two years or even only one year, I should not have given the command to march and should have allied myself temporarily with England instead of Russia for we cannot conduct a long war. To be sure a new situation has arisen. I experienced those poor worms Daladier and Chamberlain in Munich. They will be too cowardly to attack. They won't go beyond a blockade. Against that we have our autarchy and the Russian raw materials.

Poland will be depopulated and settled with Germans. My pact with the Poles was merely conceived of as a gaining of time. As for the rest, gentlemen, the fate of Russia will be exactly the same as I am now going through with in the case of Poland. After Stalin's death—he is a very sick man—we will break the Soviet Union. Then there will begin the dawn of the German rule of the earth. . . .

The opportunity is as favourable as never before. I have but one worry, namely that Chamberlain or some other such pig of a fellow ("Saukerl") will come at the last moment with proposals or with ratting ("Umfall"). He will fly down the stairs, even if I shall personally have to trample on his belly in the eyes of the photographers.

No, it is too late for this. The attack upon and the destruction of Poland begins Saturday[2]

early. I shall let a few companies in Polish uniform attack in Upper Silesia or in the Protectorate. Whether the world believes it is quite indifferent ("Scheissegal"). The world believes only in success.

For you, gentlemen, fame and honour are beginning as they have not since centuries. Be hard, be without mercy, act more quickly and brutally than the others. The citizens of Western Europe must tremble with horror. That is the most human way of conducting a war. For it scares the others off.

The new method of conducting war corresponds to the new drawing of the frontiers. A war extending from Reval, Lublin, Kaschau to the mouth of the Danube. The rest will be given to the Russians. Ribbentrop has orders to make every offer and to accept every demand. In the West I reserve to myself the right to determine the strategically best line. Here one will be able to work with Protectorate regions, such as Holland, Belgium and French Lorraine.

And now, on to the enemy, in Warsaw we will celebrate our reunion.

The speech was received with enthusiasm. Göring jumped on a table, thanked bloodthirstily and made bloodthirsty promises. He danced like a wild man. The few that had misgivings remained quiet. (Here a line of the memorandum is missing in order no doubt to protect the source of information.)[3]

During the meal which followed Hitler said he must act this year as he was not likely to live very long. His successor however would no longer be able to carry this out. Besides, the situation would be a hopeless one in two years at the most.

---

[2]August 26.

[3]This sentence in parentheses forms part of the original typescript.

REVIEW QUESTIONS

1. What were the decisive reasons that led Hitler to launch the war against Poland?
2. What type of warfare did Hitler want his generals to wage?

6 The Fall of France

On May 10, 1940, Hitler launched his offensive in the west with an invasion of neutral Belgium, Holland, and Luxembourg. French troops rushed to Belgium to prevent a breakthrough, but the greater menace lay to the south, on the French frontier. Meeting almost no resistance, German Panzer divisions had moved through the narrow mountain passes of Luxembourg and the dense Forest of the Ardennes in southern Belgium. On May 12, German units were on French soil near Sedan. Thinking that the Forest of the Ardennes could not be penetrated by a major German force, the French had only lightly fortified the western extension of the Maginot Line, the immense fortifications designed to hold back a German invasion.

The battle for France turned into a rout. Whole French divisions were cut off or in retreat. On June 10, Mussolini also declared war on France. With authority breaking down and resistance dying, the French cabinet appealed for an armistice, which was signed on June 22 in the same railway car in which Germany had agreed to the armistice ending World War I.

Several reasons explain the collapse of France. France had somewhat fewer planes, particularly bombers, than Germany, but, what is still a mystery, many French planes never left the airfields. And because French airfields lacked early warning systems and sufficient antiaircraft guns, many were destroyed on the ground. Nor did French High Command deploy their airforce properly. Unlike the Germans, the French were not proponents of a tactical airforce in close support of infantry and tanks. As for tanks the French had as many as the Germans, and some were superior. Nor was German manpower overwhelming. France met disaster largely because its military leaders, unlike the Germans, had not mastered the psychology and technology of motorized warfare. "The French commanders, trained in the slow-motion methods of 1918, were mentally unfitted to cope with Panzer pace, and it produced a spreading paralysis among them," says British military expert Sir Basil Liddell Hart. One also senses a loss of will among the French people: a consequence of internal political disputes dividing the nation, poor leadership, the years of appeasement and lost opportunities, and German propaganda, which depicted Nazism as irresistible and the Führer as a man of destiny. It was France's darkest hour.

Heinz Guderian
"FRENCH LEADERSHIP . . . COULD NOT GRASP THE SIGNIFICANCE OF THE TANK IN MOBILE WARFARE"

After the war, General Heinz Guderian (1888–1954), whose Panzer divisions formed the vanguard of the attack through the Ardennes into France, analyzed the reasons for France's collapse in *Panzer Leader* (1952).

The First World War on the Western Front, after being for a short time a war of movement, soon settled down to positional warfare. No massing of war material, on no matter how vast a scale, had succeeded in getting the armies moving again until, in November 1916, the enemy's tanks appeared on the battlefield. With their armour plating, their tracks, their guns and their machine-guns, they succeeded in carrying their crews, alive and capable of fighting, through artillery barrages and wire entanglements, over trench systems and shell craters, into the centre of the German lines. The power of the offensive had come back into its own.

The true importance of tanks was proved by the fact that the Versailles Treaty forbade Germany the possession or construction of armoured vehicles, tanks or any similar equipment which might be employed in war, under pain of punishment.

So our enemies regarded the tank as a decisive weapon which we must not be allowed to have. I therefore decided carefully to study the history of this decisive weapon and to follow its future development. For someone observing tank theory from afar, unburdened by tradition, there were lessons to be learned in the employment, organisation and construction of armour and of armoured units that went beyond the doctrines then accepted abroad. After years of hard struggle, I had succeeded in putting my theories into practice before the other armies had arrived at the same conclusions. The advance we had made in the organisation and employment of tanks was the primary factor on which my belief in our forthcoming success was based. Even in 1940 this belief was shared by scarcely anybody in the German Army.

A profound study of the First World War had given me considerable insight into the psychology of the combatants. I already, from personal experience, knew a considerable amount about our own army. I had also formed certain opinions about our Western adversaries which the events of 1940 were to prove correct. Despite the tank weapons to which our enemies owed in large measure their 1918 victory, they were preoccupied with the concepts of positional warfare.

France possessed the strongest land army in Western Europe. France possessed the numerically strongest tank force in Western Europe.

The combined Anglo-French forces in the West in May 1940 consisted of some 4,000 armoured vehicles: the German Army at that time had 2,800, including armoured reconnaissance cars, and when the attack was launched only 2,200 of these were available for the operation. We thus faced superiority in numbers, to which was added the fact that the French tanks were superior to the German ones both in armour and in gun-calibre, though admittedly inferior in control facilities and in speed. Despite possessing the strongest forces for mobile warfare the French had also built the strongest line of fortifications in the world, the Maginot Line. Why was the money spent on the construction of those fortifications not used for the modernisation and strengthening of France's mobile forces?

The proposals of de Gaulle, Daladier and others along these lines had been ignored. From this it must be concluded that the highest French leadership either would not or could not grasp the significance of the tank in mobile warfare. In any case all the manoeuvres and large-scale exercises of which I had heard led to the conclusion that the French command wanted its troops to be trained in such a way that careful movement and planned measures for attack or for defence could be based on definite, pre-arranged circumstances. They wanted a complete picture of the enemy's order of battle and intentions before deciding on any undertaking. Once the decision was taken it would be carried out according to plan, one might almost say methodically, not only during the approach march and the deployment of troops, but also during the artillery preparation and the launching of the attack or the construction of the defence as the case might be. This mania for planned control, in which nothing should be left to chance, led to the organisation of the armoured forces within the army in a form that would destroy the general scheme, that is to say their assignment in detail to the infantry divisions. Only a fraction of the French armour was organised for operational employment.

So far as the French were concerned the German leadership could safely rely on the defence of France being systematically based on fortifications and carried out according to a rigid doctrine: this doctrine was the result of the lessons that the French had learned from the First World War, their experience of positional warfare, of the high value they attached to fire power, and of their underestimation of movement.

These French strategic and tactical principles, well known to us in 1940 and the exact contrary of my own theories of warfare, were the second factor on which my belief in victory was founded.

By the spring of 1940 we Germans had gained a clear picture of the enemy's dispositions, and of his fortifications. We knew that somewhere between Montmédy and Sedan the Maginot Line changed from being very strong indeed to being rather weaker. We called the fortifications from Sedan to the Channel "the prolonged Maginot Line." We knew about the locations and, usually, about the strength of the Belgian and Dutch fortifications. They all faced only towards Germany.

While the Maginot Line was thinly held, the mass of the French army together with the British Expeditionary Force was assembled in Flanders, between the Meuse and the English Channel, facing northeast; the Belgian and Dutch troops, on the other hand, were deployed to defend their frontiers against an attack from the east.

From their order of battle it was plain that the enemy expected the Germans to attempt the Schlieffen Plan once again, and that they intended to bring the bulk of the allied armies

against this anticipated outflanking movement through Holland and Belgium. A sufficient safeguard of the hinge of their proposed advance into Belgium by reserve units—in the area, say, of Charleville and Verdun—was not apparent. It seemed that the French High Command did not regard any alternative to the old Schlieffen Plan as even conceivable.

Our knowledge of the enemy's order of battle and of his predictable reactions at the beginning of the German advance was the third factor that contributed to my belief in victory.

In addition there were a number of other aspects in our general evaluation of the enemy which, though of less reliability, were still worth taking into consideration.

We knew and respected the French soldier from the First World War as a brave and tough fighter who had defended his country with stubborn energy. We did not doubt that he would show the same spirit this time. But so far as the French leaders were concerned, we were amazed that they had not taken advantage of their favourable situation during the autumn of 1939 to attack, while the bulk of the German forces, including the entire armoured force, was engaged in Poland. Their reasons for such restraint were at the time hard to see. We could only guess. Be that as it may, the caution shown by the French leaders led us to believe that our adversaries hoped somehow to avoid a serious clash of arms. The rather inactive behavior of the French during the winter of 1939–40 seemed to indicate a limited enthusiasm for the war on their part.

From all this I concluded that a determined and forcibly led attack by strong armoured forces through Sedan and Amiens, with the Atlantic coast as its objective, would hit the enemy deep in the flank of his forces advancing into Belgium; I did not think that he disposed of sufficient reserves to parry this thrust; and I therefore believed it had a great chance of succeeding and, if the initial success were fully exploited, might lead to the cutting off of all the main enemy forces moving up into Belgium.

REVIEW QUESTIONS

1. According to Heinz Guderian, why was it an error for French military strategy to rely so heavily on the Maginot Line?
2. How did World War I demonstrate the importance of tanks in modern warfare?
3. What mistaken lessons did the French draw from their experience in World War I?

---

7 The Battle of Britain

Hitler expected that after his stunning victories in the West, Britain would make peace. The British, however, continued to reject Hitler's overtures, for they envisioned a bleak future if Nazi Germany dominated the Continent. With Britain unwilling to come to terms, Hitler proceeded in earnest with invasion plans. A successful crossing of the English Channel and the establishment of beachheads on the English coast depended on control of the skies. In early August 1940, the Luftwaffe began massive attacks on British air and naval installations. Virtually every day during the Battle of Britain, hundreds of planes fought in the sky above Britain as British pilots rose to the challenge. On September 15, the Royal Air Force (RAF) shot down sixty aircraft; two days later Hitler postponed the invasion of Britain "until further notice." The development of radar by British scientists, the skill and courage of British fighter pilots, and the inability of Germany to make up its losses in planes saved Britain in its struggle for survival. With the invasion of Britain called off, the Luftwaffe concentrated on bombing English cities, industrial centers, and ports. Almost every night for months, the inhabitants of London sought shelter in subways and cellars to escape German bombs, while British planes rose time after time to make the Luftwaffe pay the price. British morale never broke during the "Blitz."

Winston Churchill
"BLOOD, TOIL, TEARS, AND SWEAT"

Churchill, at the age of sixty-six, proved to be an undaunted leader, sharing the perils faced by all and able by example and by speeches to rally British morale. When he first addressed Parliament as prime minister on May 13, 1940, he left no doubt about the grim realities that lay ahead. Excerpts from his speeches in 1940 follow.

May 13, 1940

I would say to the House, as I said to those who have joined this Government: "I have nothing to offer but blood, toil, tears, and sweat." We have before us an ordeal of the most grievous kind. We have before us many, many long months of struggle and suffering. You ask: "What is our policy?" I will say: "It is to wage war by sea, land, and air with all our might, and with all the strength that God can give us; to wage war against a monstrous tyranny, never surpassed in the dark lamentable catalogue of human crime." That is our policy.

You ask: "What is our aim?" I can answer in one word: "Victory!" Victory at all costs, victory in spite of all terror, victory however long and hard the road may be; for without victory there is no survival.

When Churchill spoke next, on May 19, the Dutch had surrendered to the Germans, and the French and British armies were in retreat. Still, Churchill promised that "conquer we shall."

May 19, 1940

This is one of the most awe-striking periods in the long history of France and Britain. It is also beyond doubt the most sublime. Side by side, unaided except by their kith and kin in the great Dominions and by the wide Empires which rest beneath their shield—side by side, the British and French peoples have advanced to rescue not only Europe but mankind from the foulest and most soul-destroying tyranny which has ever darkened and stained the pages of history. Behind them—behind us—behind the armies and fleets of Britain and France—gather a group of shattered states and bludgeoned races: the Czechs, the Poles, the Norwegians, the Danes, the Dutch, the Belgians—upon all of whom the long night of barbarism will descend unbroken even by a star of hope, unless we conquer, as conquer we must; as conquer we shall.

By early June the Belgians had surrendered to the Germans, and the last units of the British Expeditionary Force in France had been evacuated from Dunkirk; the French armies were in full flight. Again Churchill spoke out in defiance of events across the Channel.

June 4, 1940

We shall not flag or fail. We shall go on to the end. We shall fight in France, we shall fight on the seas and oceans, we shall fight with growing confidence and growing strength in the air. We shall defend our island, whatever the cost may be. We shall fight on the beaches, we shall fight on the landing-grounds, we shall fight in the fields and in the streets, we shall fight in the hills. We shall never surrender; and even if, which I do not for a moment believe, this island or a large part of it were subjugated and starving, then our Empire beyond the seas, armed and guarded by the British Fleet, would carry on the struggle, until, in God's good time, the New World, with all its power and might, steps forth to the rescue and liberation of the Old.

By June 18 the battle of France was lost; on June 22 France surrendered. Now Britain itself was under siege. Churchill again found the right words to sustain his people:

June 18, 1940

What General [Maxime] Weygand [commander of the French army] called the Battle of France is over. . . . The Battle of Britain is about to begin. Upon this battle depends the survival of Christian civilization. Upon it depends our own British life and the long continuity of our institutions and our Empire. The whole fury and might of the enemy must very soon be turned upon us. Hitler knows that he will have to break us in this island or lose the war.

If we can stand up to him, all Europe may be free and the life of the world may move forward into broad sunlit uplands. But if we fail, then the whole world, including the United States, including all that we have known and cared for, will sink into the abyss of a new Dark Age made more sinister and perhaps more prolonged by the lights of a perverted science.

Let us therefore brace ourselves to our duty and so bear ourselves that if the British Empire and Commonwealth last for a thousand years, men will still say, "This was their finest hour."

While the Battle of Britain raged, Churchill lauded the courage of British airmen who rose to the challenge.

August 20, 1940

The gratitude of every home in our island, in our Empire, and indeed throughout the world, except in the abodes of the guilty, goes out to the British airmen who, undaunted by odds, unwearied in their constant challenge and mortal danger, are turning the tide of world war by their prowess and by their devotion. Never in the field of human conflict was so much owed by so many to so few. All hearts go out to the fighter pilots whose brilliant actions we see with our own eyes day after day.

REVIEW QUESTIONS

1. According to Winston Churchill, what would a Nazi victory mean for Europe?
2. On whose help did Churchill ultimately count for the liberation of Europe?
3. Both Hitler and Churchill were gifted orators. Compare their styles.

---

8 Nazi Propaganda: For Volk, Führer, and Fatherland

After World War II, Germans maintained that the Wehrmacht (the German army) was an apolitical professional fighting force that remained free of Nazi ideology and was uninvolved in criminal acts perpetrated by Heinrich Himmler's SS, the elite units responsible for the extermination of Jews. It is now known that units of the German army assisted the SS in the rounding up of Jews and at times participated in mass murder. Recently historians have also argued that the regular army, far from being apolitical, was imbued with Nazi ideology, and that many German officers and soldiers, succumbing to Nazi indoctrination, viewed the war, particularly on the Eastern Front, as a titanic struggle against evil and subhuman Jewish-led Bolsheviks who threatened the very existence of the German Volk.

THE INDOCTRINATION OF THE GERMAN SOLDIER

The following excerpts from German army propaganda and letters written by soldiers show how Nazi ideology influenced ordinary German troops. The first is a news-sheet published by the High Command of the Armed Forces in the spring of 1940, and distributed to all army units, which expressed quasi-religious fervor for the Führer.

THE FÜHRER AS SAVIOR

Behind the battle of annihilation of May 1940 stands in lone greatness the name of the Führer.

All that has been accomplished since he has taken the fate of our people into his strong hands!

... He gave the people back its unity, smashed the parties and destroyed the hydra of the organizations ... he decontaminated the body of our people from the Jewish subversion, created a stock-proud, race-conscious *Volk*, which had overcome the racial death of diminishing births and was granted renewed [abundance of childbirths] as a carrier of the great future of the Fatherland. He subdued the terrible plight of unemployment and granted to millions of people who had already despaired of the *Volk* a new belief in the *Volksgemeinschaft* [community of the people] and happiness in a new Fatherland. ...

His genius, in which the whole strength of Germandom is embodied with ancient powers, has animated the souls of 80,000,000 Germans, has filled them with strength and will, with the storm and stress {*Sturm und Drang*} of a renewed young people; and, himself the first soldier of Germany, he has entered the name of the German soldier into the book of immortality.

All this we were allowed to experience. Our great duty in this year of decision is that we do not accept it as observers, but that we, enchanted, and with all the passion of which we are capable, sacrifice ourselves to this Führer and strive to be worthy of the historical epoch molded by a heaven-storming will.

This same religious devotion to Hitler and Nazi ideology was expressed in literature given to company commanders to assist them in indoctrinating their troops.

Only the Führer could carry out what had not been achieved for a thousand years. ... [He has] brought together all the German stock ... for the struggle for freedom and living space ...

[and] directed all his thoughts and efforts toward the National Socialist education of the *Volk*, the inner cohesion of the state, the armament and offensive capability of the Wehrmacht. ... When the German Eastern Armies fought an unparalleled battle during the winter of 1941–42 in the snow and ice of the Russian winter, he said: "Any weakling can put up with victories. Only the strong can stand firm in battles of destiny. But heaven gives the ultimate and highest prize only to those who are capable of withstanding battles of destiny." In the difficult winter of 1942–43 the strength of the Führer was demonstrated once more, when ... he called upon the German *Volk* at the front and in the homeland to stand firm and make the supreme effort. The Führer ... clearly sees the goal ahead: a strong German Reich as the power of order in Europe and a firm root of the German *Lebensraum*. This goal will be achieved if the whole *Volk* remains loyal to him even in difficult times and as long as we soldiers do our duty.

Such words were not without their impact on German soldiers. In November 1940, one soldier expressed his feelings about Hitler in a letter home.

The last words of the Führer's radio address are over and a new strength streams through our veins. It is as if he spoke to each individual, to everyone of us, as if he wanted to give everyone new strength. With loyalty and a sense of duty, we must fight for our principles and endure to the end. Our Führer represents our united German Fatherland. ... What we do for him, we do for all of you; what we sacrifice in foreign lands, we sacrifice for our loved ones. When the Führer speaks on these festive occasions, I feel deep in my soul that you at home also feel that we must be ready to make all sacrifices. ... German victory is as certain as our love for each other. Just as we believe in our love, so we believe in our final victory and in the future of our people and our Fatherland.

Similar sentiments were voiced by a private in a letter to his brother.

The Führer has grown into the greatest figure of the century, in his hand lies the destiny of the world and of culturally-perceptive humanity. May his pure sword strike down the Satanic monster. Yes, the blows are still hard, but the horror will be forced into the shadows through the inexorable Need, through the command which derives from our National Socialist idea. This [battle] is for a new ideology, a new belief, a new life! I am glad that I can participate, even if as a tiny cog, in this war of light against darkness.

BOLSHEVIKS AND JEWS AS DEVILS

German propaganda described Jews and Russian communists in racial and religious terms, calling them a morally depraved form of humanity in the service of Satan. A tract from SS headquarters illustrates the mythical nature of Nazi ideology.

Just as night rises up against the day, just as light and darkness are eternal enemies, so the greatest enemy of world-dominating man is man himself. The sub-man—that creature which looks as though biologically it were of absolutely the same kind, endowed by Nature with hands, feet and a sort of brain, with eyes and mouth—is nevertheless a totally different, a fearful creature, is only an attempt at a human being, with a quasi-human face, yet in mind and spirit lower than any animal. Inside this being a cruel chaos of wild, unchecked passions: a nameless will to destruction, the most primitive lusts, the most undisguised vileness. A sub-man—nothing else! . . . Never has the sub-man granted peace, never has he permitted rest. . . . To preserve himself he needed mud, he needed hell, but not the sun. And this underworld of sub-men found its leader: the eternal Jew!

The news-sheet distributed to regular army units used similar language.

Anyone who has ever looked at the face of a red commissar knows what the Bolsheviks are like. Here there is no need for theoretical expressions. We would insult the animals if we described these mostly Jewish men as beasts. They are the embodiment of the Satanic and insane hatred against the whole of noble humanity. The shape of these commissars reveals to us the rebellion of the *Untermenschen* [sub-men] against noble blood. The masses, whom they have sent to their deaths [in this war against Germany] by making use of all means at their disposal such as ice-cold terror and insane incitement, would have brought an end to all meaningful life, had this eruption not been dammed at the last moment.

In October 1941, Walter von Reichenau, commander of the sixth army, appealed to his men in the language of Nazi racial ideology.

The essential goal of the campaign against the Jewish-Bolshevik system is the complete destruction of its power instruments and the eradication of the Asiatic influence on the European cultural sphere. . . . Therefore the soldier must have *complete* understanding for the necessity of the harsh, but just atonement of Jewish subhumanity.

In November 1941, General von Manstein, commander of the eleventh army, used much the same language.

Since 22 June the German *Volk* is in the midst of a battle for life and death against the Bolshevik system. This battle is conducted against the Soviet army not only in a conventional manner according to the rules of European warfare. . . .

Judaism constitutes the mediator between the enemy in the rear and the still fighting remnants of the Red Army and the Red leadership. It has a stronger hold than in Europe on all key positions of the political leadership and administration, it occupies commerce and trade and further forms cells for all the disturbances and possible rebellions.

The Jewish-Bolshevik system must be eradicated once and for all. Never again may it interfere in our European living space.

The German soldier is therefore not only charged with the task of destroying the power instrument of this system. He marches forth also as a carrier of a racial conception and as an avenger of all the atrocities which have been committed against him and the German people.

The soldier must show understanding for the harsh atonement of Judaism, the spiritual carrier of the Bolshevik terror.

And in that same month, Colonel-General Hoth also interpreted the war as a struggle between racial superiors and inferiors.

It has become increasingly clear to us this summer, that here in the East spiritually unbridgeable conceptions are fighting each other: German sense of honor and race, and a soldierly tradition of many centuries, against an Asiatic mode of thinking and primitive instincts,

whipped up by a small number of mostly Jewish intellectuals: fear of the knout [whip used for flogging], disregard of moral values, levelling down, throwing away of one's worthless life.

More than ever we are filled with the thought of a new era, in which the strength of the German people's racial superiority and achievements entrust it with the leadership of Europe. We clearly recognize our mission to save European culture from the advancing Asiatic barbarism. We now know that we have to fight against an incensed and tough opponent. This battle can only end with the destruction of one or the other; a compromise is out of the question.

The front-line soldier was affected by ideological propaganda.

I have received the "Stürmer" [a notoriously anti-Semitic newspaper] now for the third time. It makes me happy with all my heart. . . . You could not have made me happier. . . . I recognized the Jewish poison in our people long ago; how far it might have gone with us, this we see only now in this campaign. What the Jewish-regime has done in Russia, we see every day, and even the last doubters are cured here in view of the facts. We must and we will liberate the world from this plague, this is why the German soldier protects the Eastern Front, and we shall not return before we have uprooted all evil and destroyed the center of the Jewish-Bolshevik "world-do-gooders."

REVIEW QUESTIONS

1. How did Nazi propaganda depict Hitler? Germans? Jews? Russians?
2. Why was such propaganda effective?

9 Stalingrad: A Turning Point

In July 1942, the Germans resumed their advance into the U.S.S.R. begun the previous summer, seeking to conquer Stalingrad, a vital transportation center located on the Volga River. Germans and Russians battled with dogged ferocity over every part of the city; 99 percent of Stalingrad was reduced to rubble. A Russian counteroffensive in November trapped the German Sixth Army. Realizing that the Sixth Army, exhausted and short of weapons, ammunition, food, and medical supplies, faced annihilation, German generals pleaded in vain with Hitler to permit withdrawal before the Russians closed the ring. On February 2, 1943, the remnants of the Sixth Army surrendered. More than a million people—Russian civilians and soldiers, Germans and their Italian, Hungarian, and Romanian allies—perished in the epic struggle for Stalingrad. The Russian victory was a major turning point in the war.

William Hoffman
DIARY OF A GERMAN SOLDIER

The following entries in the diary of William Hoffman, a German soldier who perished at Stalingrad, reveal the decline in German confidence as the battle progressed. While the German army was penetrating deeply into Russia, he believed that victory was not far away and dreamed of returning home with medals. Then the terrible struggles in Stalingrad made him curse the war.

Today, after we'd had a bath, the company commander told us that if our future operations are as successful, we'll soon reach the Volga, take Stalingrad and then the war will inevitably soon be over. Perhaps we'll be home by Christmas.

July 29 1942. . . . The company commander says the Russian troops are completely broken, and cannot hold out any longer. To reach the Volga and take Stalingrad is not so difficult for us. The Führer knows where the Russians' weak point is. Victory is not far away. . . .

August 2. . . . What great spaces the Soviets occupy, what rich fields there are to be had here after the war's over! Only let's get it over with quickly. I believe that the Führer will carry the thing through to a successful end.

August 10. . . . The Führer's orders were read out to us. He expects victory of us. We are all convinced that they can't stop us.

August 12. We are advancing towards Stalingrad along the railway line. Yesterday Russian "katyushi" [small rocket launchers] and then tanks halted our regiment. "The Russians are throwing in their last forces," Captain Werner explained to me. Large-scale help is coming up for us, and the Russians will be beaten.

This morning outstanding soldiers were presented with decorations. . . . Will I really go back to Elsa without a decoration? I believe that for Stalingrad the Führer will decorate even me. . . .

August 23. Splendid news—north of Stalingrad our troops have reached the Volga and captured part of the city. The Russians have two alternatives, either to flee across the Volga or give themselves up. Our company's interpreter has interrogated a captured Russian officer. He was wounded, but asserted that the Russians would fight for Stalingrad to the last round. Something incomprehensible is, in fact, going on. In the north our troops capture a part of Stalingrad and reach the Volga, but in the south the doomed divisions are continuing to resist bitterly. Fanaticism. . . .

August 27. A continuous cannonade on all sides. We are slowly advancing. Less than twenty miles to go to Stalingrad. In the daytime we can see the smoke of fires, at night-time the bright glow. They say that the city is on fire; on the Führer's orders our Luftwaffe [air force] has sent it up in flames. That's what the Russians need, to stop them from resisting. . . .

September 4. We are being sent northward along the front towards Stalingrad. We marched all night and by dawn had reached Voroponovo Station. We can already see the smoking town. It's a happy thought that the end of the war is getting nearer. That's what everyone is saying. If only the days and nights would pass more quickly. . . .

September 5. Our regiment has been ordered to attack Sadovaya station—that's nearly in Stalingrad. Are the Russians really thinking of holding out in the city itself? We had no peace all night from the Russian artillery and aeroplanes. Lots of wounded are being brought by. God protect me. . . .

September 8. Two days of non-stop fighting. The Russians are defending themselves with insane stubbornness. Our regiment has lost

many men from the "katyushi," which belch out terrible fire. I have been sent to work at battalion H.Q. It must be mother's prayers that have taken me away from the company's trenches. . . .

September 11. Our battalion is fighting in the suburbs of Stalingrad. We can already see the Volga; firing is going on all the time. Wherever you look is fire and flames. . . . Russian cannon and machine-guns are firing out of the burning city. Fanatics. . . .

September 13. An unlucky number. This morning "katyushi" attacks caused the company heavy losses: twenty-seven dead and fifty wounded. The Russians are fighting desperately like wild beasts, don't give themselves up, but come up close and then throw grenades. Lieutenant Kraus was killed yesterday, and there is no company commander.

September 16. Our battalion, plus tanks, is attacking the [grain storage] elevator, from which smoke is pouring—the grain in it is burning, the Russians seem to have set light to it themselves. Barbarism. The battalion is suffering heavy losses. There are not more than sixty men left in each company. The elevator is occupied not by men but by devils that no flames or bullets can destroy.

September 18. Fighting is going on inside the elevator. The Russians inside are condemned men; the battalion commander says: "The commissars have ordered those men to die in the elevator."

If all the buildings of Stalingrad are defended like this then none of our soldiers will get back to Germany. I had a letter from Elsa today. She's expecting me home when victory's won.

September 20. The battle for the elevator is still going on. The Russians are firing on all sides. We stay in our cellar; you can't go out into the street. Sergeant-Major Nuschke was killed today running across a street. Poor fellow, he's got three children.

September 22. Russian resistance in the elevator has been broken. Our troops are advancing towards the Volga. . . .

. . . Our old soldiers have never experienced such bitter fighting before.

September 26. Our regiment is involved in constant heavy fighting. After the elevator was taken the Russians continued to defend themselves just as stubbornly. You don't see them at all, they have established themselves in houses and cellars and are firing on all sides, including from our rear—barbarians, they use gangster methods.

In the blocks captured two days ago Russian soldiers appeared from somewhere or other and fighting has flared up with fresh vigour. Our men are being killed not only in the firing line, but in the rear, in buildings we have already occupied.

The Russians have stopped surrendering at all. If we take any prisoners it's because they are hopelessly wounded, and can't move by themselves. Stalingrad is hell. Those who are merely wounded are lucky; they will doubtless be at home and celebrate victory with their families. . . .

September 28. Our regiment, and the whole division, are today celebrating victory. Together with our tank crews we have taken the southern part of the city and reached the Volga. We paid dearly for our victory. In three weeks we have occupied about five and a half square miles. The commander has congratulated us on our victory. . . .

October 3. After marching through the night we have established ourselves in a shrub-covered gully. We are apparently going to attack the factories, the chimneys of which we can see clearly. Behind them is the Volga. We have entered a new area. It was night but we saw many crosses

with our helmets on top. Have we really lost so many men? Damn this Stalingrad!

October 4. Our regiment is attacking the Barrikady settlement. A lot of Russian tommy-gunners have appeared. Where are they bringing them from?

October 5. Our battalion has gone into the attack four times, and got stopped each time. Russian snipers hit anyone who shows himself carelessly from behind shelter.

October 10. The Russians are so close to us that our planes cannot bomb them. We are preparing for a decisive attack. The Führer has ordered the whole of Stalingrad to be taken as rapidly as possible.

October 14. It has been fantastic since morning: our aeroplanes and artillery have been hammering the Russian positions for hours on end; everything in sight is being blotted from the face of the earth. . . .

October 22. Our regiment has failed to break into the factory. We have lost many men; every time you move you have to jump over bodies. You can scarcely breathe in the daytime: there is nowhere and no one to remove the bodies, so they are left there to rot. Who would have thought three months ago that instead of the joy of victory we would have to endure such sacrifice and torture, the end of which is nowhere in sight? . . .

The soldiers are calling Stalingrad the mass grave of the Wehrmacht [German army]. There are very few men left in the companies. We have been told we are soon going to be withdrawn to be brought back up to strength.

October 27. Our troops have captured the whole of the Barrikady factory, but we cannot break through to the Volga. The Russians are not men, but some kind of cast-iron creatures; they never get tired and are not afraid of fire. We are absolutely exhausted; our regiment now has barely the strength of a company. The Russian artillery at the other side of the Volga won't let you lift your head. . . .

October 28. Every soldier sees himself as a condemned man. The only hope is to be wounded and taken back to the rear. . . .

November 3. In the last few days our battalion has several times tried to attack the Russian positions, . . . to no avail. On this sector also the Russians won't let you lift your head. There have been a number of cases of self-inflicted wounds and malingering among the men. Every day I write two or three reports about them.

November 10. A letter from Elsa today. Everyone expects us home for Christmas. In Germany everyone believes we already hold Stalingrad. How wrong they are. If they could only see what Stalingrad has done to our army.

November 18. Our attack with tanks yesterday had no success. After our attack the field was littered with dead.

November 21. The Russians have gone over to the offensive along the whole front. Fierce fighting is going on. So, there it is—the Volga, victory and soon home to our families! We shall obviously be seeing them next in the other world.

November 29. We are encircled. It was announced this morning that the Führer has said: "The army can trust me to do everything necessary to ensure supplies and rapidly break the encirclement."

December 3. We are on hunger rations and waiting for the rescue that the Führer promised.

I send letters home, but there is no reply.

December 7. Rations have been cut to such an extent that the soldiers are suffering terribly from hunger; they are issuing one loaf of stale bread for five men.

December 11. Three questions are obsessing every soldier and officer: When will the Russians stop firing and let us sleep in peace, if only for one night? How and with what are we going to fill our empty stomachs, which, apart from $3^{1}/_{2}$-7 ozs of bread, receive virtually nothing at all? And when will Hitler take any decisive steps to free our armies from encirclement?

December 14. Everybody is racked with hunger. Frozen potatoes are the best meal, but to get them out of the ice-covered ground under fire from Russian bullets is not so easy.

December 18. The officers today told the soldiers to be prepared for action. General Manstein is approaching Stalingrad from the south with strong forces. This news brought hope to the soldiers' hearts. God, let it be!

December 21. We are waiting for the order, but for some reason or other it has been a long time coming. Can it be that it is not true about Manstein? This is worse than any torture.

December 23. Still no orders. It was all a bluff with Manstein. Or has he been defeated at the approaches to Stalingrad?

December 25. The Russian radio has announced the defeat of Manstein. Ahead of us is either death or captivity.

December 26. The horses have already been eaten. I would eat a cat; they say its meat is also tasty. The soldiers look like corpses or lunatics, looking for something to put in their mouths. They no longer take cover from Russian shells; they haven't the strength to walk, run away and hide. A curse on this war! . . .

Anton Kuzmich Dragan
A SOVIET VETERAN RECALLS

Anton Kuzmich Dragan, a Russian soldier, describes the vicious street fighting
in Stalingrad during late September 1942.

"The Germans had cut us off from our neighbours. The supply of ammunition had been cut off; every bullet was worth its weight in gold. I gave the order to economize on ammunition, to collect the cartridge-pouches of the dead and all captured weapons. In the evening the enemy again tried to break our resistance, coming up close to our positions. As our numbers grew smaller, we shortened our line of defence. We began to move back slowly towards the Volga, drawing the enemy after us, and the ground we occupied was invariably too small for the Germans to be able easily to use artillery and aircraft.

"We moved back, occupying one building after another, turning them into strongholds. A soldier would crawl out of an occupied position only when the ground was on fire under him and his clothes were smouldering. During the day the Germans managed to occupy only two blocks.

"At the crossroads of Krasnopiterskaya and Komsomolskaya Streets we occupied a three-storey building on the corner. This was a good position from which to fire on all comers and it became our last defence. I ordered all entrances to be barricaded, and windows and embrasures to be adapted so that we could fire through them with all our remaining weapons.

"At a narrow window of the semi-basement we placed the heavy machine-gun with our emergency supply of ammunition—the last belt of cartridges. I had decided to use it at the most critical moment.

"Two groups, six in each, went up to the third floor and the garret. Their job was to break down walls, and prepare lumps of stone and beams to throw at the Germans when they came up close. A place for the seriously wounded was set aside in the basement. Our garrison consisted of forty men. Difficult days began. Attack after attack broke unendingly like waves against us. After each attack was beaten off we felt it was impossible to hold off the onslaught any longer, but when the Germans launched a fresh attack, we managed to find means and strength. This lasted five days and nights.

"The basement was full of wounded; only twelve men were still able to fight. There was no water. All we had left in the way of food was a few pounds of scorched grain; the Germans decided to beat us with starvation. Their attacks stopped, but they kept up the fire from their heavy-calibre machine-guns all the time.

"We did not think about escape, but only about how to sell our lives most dearly—we had no other way out. . . .

"The Germans attacked again. I ran upstairs with my men and could see their thin, blackened and strained faces, the bandages on their wounds, dirty and clotted with blood, their guns held firmly in their hands. There was no fear in their eyes. Lyuba Nesterenko, a nurse, was dying, with blood flowing from a wound in her chest. She had a bandage in her hand. Before she died she wanted to help to bind someone's wound, but she failed. . . .

"The German attack was beaten off. In the silence that gathered around us we could hear the bitter fighting going on for Mameyev Kurgan and in the factory area of the city.

"How could we help the men defending the city? How could we divert from over there even a part of the enemy forces, which had stopped attacking our building?

"We decided to raise a red flag over the building, so that the Nazis would not think we had given up. But we had no red material. Understanding what we wanted to do, one of the men who was severely wounded took off his bloody vest and, after wiping the blood off his wound with it, handed it over to me.

"The Germans shouted through a megaphone: 'Russians! Surrender! You'll die just the same!'

"At that moment a red flag rose over our building.

"'Bark, you dogs! We've still got a long time to live!' shouted my orderly, Kozhushko.

"We beat off the next attack with stones, firing occasionally and throwing our last grenades. Suddenly from behind a blank wall, from the rear, came the grind of a tank's caterpillar tracks. We had no anti-tank grenades. All we had left was one anti-tank rifle with three rounds. I handed this rifle to an anti-tank man, Berdyshev, and sent him out through the back to fire at the tank point-blank. But before he could get into position he was captured by German tommy-gunners. What Berdyshev told the Germans I don't know, but I can guess that he led them up the garden path, because an hour later they started to attack at precisely that point where I had put my machine-gun with its emergency belt of cartridges.

"This time, reckoning that we had run out of ammunition, they came impudently out of their shelter, standing up and shouting. They came down the street in a column.

"I put the last belt in the heavy machine-gun at the semi-basement window and sent the whole of the 250 bullets into the yelling, dirty-grey Nazi mob. I was wounded in the hand but did not leave go of the machine-gun. Heaps of bodies littered the ground. The Germans still alive ran for cover in panic. An hour later they led our anti-tank rifleman on to a heap of ruins and shot him in front of our eyes, for having shown them the way to my machine-gun.

"There were no more attacks. An avalanche of shells fell on the building. The Germans stormed at us with every possible kind of weapon. We couldn't raise our heads.

"Again we heard the ominous sound of tanks. From behind a neighbouring block stocky German tanks began to crawl out. This, clearly, was the end. The guardsmen said goodbye to one another. With a dagger my orderly scratched on a brick wall: 'Rodimtsev's guardsmen fought and died for their country here.' The battalion's documents and a map case containing the Party and Komsomol cards of the defenders of the building had been put in a hole in a corner of the basement. The first salvo shattered the silence. There were a series of blows, and the building rocked and collapsed. How much later it was when I opened my eyes, I don't know. It was dark. The air was full of acrid brickdust. I could hear muffled groans around me. Kozhushko, the orderly, was pulling at me:

"'You're alive. . . .'

"On the floor of the basement lay a number of other stunned and injured soldiers. We had been buried alive under the ruins of the three-storey building. We could scarcely breathe. We had no thought for food or water—it was air that had become most important for survival. I spoke to the soldiers:

"'Men! We did not flinch in battle, we fought even when resistance seemed impossible, and we have to get out of this tomb so that we can live and avenge the death of our comrades!'

"Even in pitch darkness you can see somebody else's face, feel other people close to you.

"With great difficulty we began to pick our way out of the tomb. We worked in silence, our bodies covered with cold, clammy sweat, our badly-bound wounds ached, our teeth were covered with brickdust, it became more and more difficult to breathe, but there were no groans or complaints.

"A few hours later, through the hole we had made, we could see the stars and breathe the fresh September air.

"Utterly exhausted, the men crowded round the hole, greedily gulping in the autumn air. Soon the opening was wide enough for a man to crawl through. Kozhushko, being only relatively slightly injured, went off to reconnoitre. An hour later he came back and reported:

"'Comrade Lieutenant, there are Germans all round us; along the Volga they are mining the bank; there are German patrols nearby. . . .'

"We took the decision to fight our way through to our own lines."

REVIEW QUESTIONS

1. What were the expectations of William Hoffman as he marched with the German army in July and August? How did he view Hitler and the war?
2. How did the hard fighting at Stalingrad alter Hoffman's conception of the war and his attitude toward the Russians?
3. What does Anton Kuzmich Dragan's account reveal about the resolve of the Russian soldiers at Stalingrad?

10 The Holocaust

Over conquered Europe the Nazis imposed a "New Order" marked by exploitation, torture, and mass murder. The Germans took some 5.5 million Russian prisoners of war, of whom more than 3.5 million perished; many of these prisoners were deliberately starved to death. The Germans imprisoned and executed many Polish intellectuals and priests and slaughtered vast numbers of Roma (Gypsies). Using the modern state's organizational capacities and the instruments of modern technology, the Nazis murdered six million Jews, including one and a half million children—two-thirds of the Jewish population of Europe. Gripped by the mythical, perverted world-view of Nazism, the SS, Hitler's elite guard, carried out these murders with dedication and idealism; they believed that they were exterminating subhumans who threatened the German nation.

Hermann Graebe
SLAUGHTER OF JEWS IN UKRAINE

While the regular German army penetrated deeply into Russia, special SS units, the *Einsatzgruppen*, rounded up Jews for mass executions. Aided by Ukrainian, Lithuanian, and Latvian auxiliaries, and contingents from the Romanian army, the Einsatzgruppen massacred 1 to 1.4 million Jews. Hermann Graebe, a German construction engineer, saw such a mass slaughter in Dubno in Ukraine. He gave a sworn affidavit before the Nuremberg tribunal, a court at which the Allies tried Nazi war criminals after the end of World War II.

Graebe had joined the Nazi party in 1931 but later renounced his membership, and during the war he rescued Jews from the SS. Graebe was the only
German citizen to volunteer to testify at the Nuremberg trials, an act that earned
him the enmity of his compatriots. Socially ostracized, Graebe emigrated to the
United States, where he died in 1986 at the age of eighty-five.

On October 5, 1942, when I visited the building office at Dubno, my foreman told me that in the vicinity of the site, Jews from Dubno had been shot in three large pits, each about 30 metres long and 3 metres deep. About 1,500 persons had been killed daily. All the 5,000 Jews who had still been living in Dubno before the pogrom were to be liquidated. As the shooting had taken place in his presence, he was still much upset.

Thereupon, I drove to the site accompanied by my foreman and saw near it great mounds of earth, about 30 metres long and 2 metres high. Several trucks stood in front of the mounds. Armed Ukrainian militia drove the people off the trucks under the supervision of an S.S. man. The militiamen acted as guards on the trucks and drove them to and from the pit. All these people had the regulation yellow patches on the front and back of their clothes, and thus could be recognized as Jews.

My foreman and I went directly to the pits. Nobody bothered us. Now I heard rifle shots in quick succession from behind one of the earth mounds. The people who had got off the trucks—men, women and children of all ages—had to undress upon the orders of an S.S. man, who carried a riding or dog whip. They had to put down their clothes in fixed places, sorted according to shoes, top clothing and undercloth-ing. I saw a heap of shoes of about 800 to 1,000 pairs, great piles of underlinen and clothing.

Without screaming or weeping, these people undressed, stood around in family groups, kissed each other, said farewells, and waited for a sign from another S.S. man, who stood near the pit, also with a whip in his hand. During the fifteen minutes that I stood near I heard no complaint or plea for mercy. I watched a fam-ily of about eight persons, a man and a woman

both about fifty with their children of about one, eight and ten, and two grown-up daugh-ters of about twenty to twenty-nine. An old woman with snow-white hair was holding the one-year-old child in her arms and singing to it and tickling it. The child was cooing with de-light. The couple were looking on with tears in their eyes. The father was holding the hand of a boy about ten years old and speaking to him softly; the boy was fighting his tears. The father pointed to the sky, stroked his head, and seemed to explain something to him.

At that moment the S.S. man at the pit shouted something to his comrade. The latter counted off about twenty persons and instructed them to go behind the earth mound. Among them was the family which I have mentioned. I well remember a girl, slim and with black hair, who, as she passed close to me, pointed to her-self and said "23." I walked around the mound and found myself confronted by a tremendous grave. People were closely wedged together and lying on top of each other so that only their heads were visible. Nearly all had blood running over their shoulders from their heads. Some of the people shot were still moving. Some were lifting their arms and turning their heads to show that they were still alive. The pit was already two-thirds full. I estimated that it already contained about 1,000 people.

I looked for the man who did the shooting. He was an S.S. man, who sat at the edge of the narrow end of the pit, his feet dangling into the pit. He had a tommy-gun on his knees and was smoking a cigarette. The people, completely naked, went down some steps which were cut in the clay wall of the pit and clambered over the heads of the people lying there, to the place to which the S.S. man directed them. They lay down in front of the dead or injured people; some caressed those who were still alive and spoke to them in a low voice.

Then I heard a series of shots. I looked into the pit and saw that the bodies were twitching or the heads lying motionless on top of the bodies which lay before them. Blood was running from their necks. I was surprised that I was not ordered away, but I saw that there were two or three postmen in uniform nearby. The next batch was approaching already. They went down into the pit, lined themselves up against the previous victims and were shot.

When I walked back round the mound, I noticed another truckload of people which had just arrived. This time it included sick and infirm persons. An old, very thin woman with terribly thin legs was undressed by others who were already naked, while two people held her up. The woman appeared to be paralyzed. The naked people carried the woman around the mound. I left with my foreman and drove in my car back to Dubno.

On the morning of the next day, when I again visited the site, I saw about thirty naked people lying near the pit—about 30 to 50 metres away from it. Some of them were still alive; they looked straight in front of them with a fixed stare and seemed to notice neither the chilliness of the morning nor the workers of my firm who stood around. A girl of about twenty spoke to me and asked me to give her clothes and help her escape. At that moment we heard a fast car approach and I noticed that it was an S.S. detail. I moved away to my site. Ten minutes later we heard shots from the vicinity of the pit. The Jews alive had been ordered to throw the corpses into the pit, then they had themselves to lie down in it to be shot in the neck.

Rudolf Hoess
COMMANDANT OF AUSCHWITZ

To speed up the "final solution of the Jewish problem," the SS established death camps in Poland. Jews from all over Europe were crammed into cattle cars and shipped to these camps to be gassed or worked to death. At Auschwitz, the most notorious of the concentration camps, the SS used five gas chambers to kill as many as 9,000 people a day. Special squads of prisoners, called *Sonderkommandos*, were forced to pick over the corpses for gold teeth, jewelry, and anything else of value for the German war effort. Some 1.3 million Jews perished at Auschwitz. In the following passage from *Commandant of Auschwitz*, Rudolf Hoess (1900–1947), who commanded the camp and was executed by Poland after the war, recalled the murder process when he was in a Polish prison.

In the spring of 1942 the first transports of Jews, all earmarked for extermination, arrived from Upper Silesia.

They were taken from the detraining platform to the "cottage"—to bunker I—across the meadows where later building site II was located. The transport was conducted by Aumeier and Palitzsch and some of the block leaders. They talked with the Jews about general topics, inquiring concerning their qualifications and trades, with a view to misleading them. On arrival at the "cottage," they were told to undress. At first they went calmly into the rooms where they were supposed to be disinfected.

But some of them showed signs of alarm, and spoke of death by suffocation and of annihilation. A sort of panic set in at once. Immediately all the Jews still outside were pushed into the chambers, and the doors were screwed shut. With subsequent transports the difficult individuals were picked out early and most carefully supervised. At the first signs of unrest, those responsible were unobtrusively led behind the building and killed with a small-caliber gun, that was inaudible to the others. The presence and calm behavior of the Special Detachment [of *Sonderkommandos*] served to reassure those who were worried or who suspected what was about to happen. A further calming effect was obtained by members of the Special Detachment accompanying them into the rooms and remaining with them until the last moment, while an SS man also stood in the doorway until the end.

It was most important that the whole business of arriving and undressing should take place in an atmosphere of the greatest possible calm. People reluctant to take off their clothes had to be helped by those of their companions who had already undressed, or by men of the Special Detachment.

The refractory ones were calmed down and encouraged to undress. The prisoners of the Special Detachment also saw to it that the process of undressing was carried out quickly, so that the victims would have little time to wonder what was happening. . . .

Many of the women hid their babies among the piles of clothing. The men of the Special Detachment were particularly on the lookout for this, and would speak words of encouragement to the woman until they had persuaded her to take the child with her. The women believed that the disinfectant might be bad for their smaller children, hence their efforts to conceal them.

The smaller children usually cried because of the strangeness of being undressed in this fashion, but when their mothers or members of the Special Detachment comforted them, they became calm and entered the gas chambers, playing or joking with one another and carrying their toys.

I noticed that women who either guessed or knew what awaited them nevertheless found the courage to joke with the children to encourage them, despite the mortal terror visible in their own eyes.

One woman approached me as she walked past and, pointing to her four children who were manfully helping the smallest ones over the rough ground, whispered:

"How can you bring yourself to kill such beautiful, darling children? Have you no heart at all?"

One old man, as he passed by me, hissed:

"Germany will pay a heavy penance for this mass murder of the Jews."

His eyes glowed with hatred as he said this. Nevertheless he walked calmly into the gas chamber, without worrying about the others.

One young woman caught my attention particularly as she ran busily hither and thither, helping the smallest children and the old women to undress. During the selection she had had two small children with her, and her agitated behavior and appearance had brought her to my notice at once. She did not look in the least like a Jewess. Now her children were no longer with her. She waited until the end, helping the women who were not undressed and who had several children with them, encouraging them and calming the children. She went with the very last ones into the gas chamber. Standing in the doorway, she said:

"I knew all the time that we were being brought to Auschwitz to be gassed. When the selection took place I avoided being put with the able-bodied ones, as I wished to look after the children. I wanted to go through it all, fully conscious of what was happening. I hope that it will be quick. Goodbye!"

From time to time women would suddenly give the most terrible shrieks while undressing, or tear their hair, or scream like maniacs. These were immediately led away behind the building and shot in the back of the neck with a small-caliber weapon.

It sometimes happened that, as the men of the Special Detachment left the gas chamber, the women would suddenly realize what was happening, and would call down every imaginable curse upon our heads.

I remember, too, a woman who tried to throw her children out of the gas chamber, just as the door was closing. Weeping, she called out:

"At least let my precious children live."

There were many such shattering scenes, which affected all who witnessed them.

During the spring of 1942 hundreds of vigorous men and women walked all unsuspecting to their death in the gas chambers, under the blossom-laden fruit trees of the "cottage" orchard. This picture of death in the midst of life remains with me to this day.

The process of selection, which took place on the unloading platforms, was in itself rich in incident.

The breaking up of families, and the separation of the men from the women and children, caused much agitation and spread anxiety throughout the whole transport. This was increased by the further separation from the others of those capable of work. Families wished at all costs to remain together. Those who had been selected ran back to rejoin their relations. Mothers with children tried to join their husbands, or old people attempted to find those of their children who had been selected for work, and who had been led away.

Often the confusion was so great that the selections had to be begun all over again. The limited area of standing room did not permit better sorting arrangements. All attempts to pacify these agitated mobs were useless. It was often necessary to use force to restore order.

As I have already frequently said, the Jews have strongly developed family feelings. They stick together like limpets. . . .

Then the bodies had to be taken from the gas chambers, and after the gold teeth had been extracted, and the hair cut off, they had to be dragged to the pits or to the crematoria. Then the fires in the pits had to be stoked, the surplus fat drained off, and the mountain of burning corpses constantly turned over so that the draught might fan the flames. . . .

It happened repeatedly that Jews of the Special Detachment would come upon the bodies of close relatives among the corpses, and even among the living as they entered the gas chambers. They were obviously affected by this, but it never led to any incident.[1]

----

[1] On October 7, 1944, the *Sonderkommandos* attacked the SS. Some SS guards were killed, and one crematorium was burned. Most of the prisoners who escaped were caught and killed.

Y. Pfeffer
CONCENTRATION CAMP LIFE
AND DEATH

Jews not immediately selected for extermination faced a living death in the concentration camp, which also included non-Jewish inmates, many of them opponents of the Nazi regime. The SS, who ran the camps, took sadistic pleasure in humiliating and brutalizing their helpless Jewish victims. In 1946, Y. Pfeffer, a Jewish survivor of Majdanek concentration camp in Poland, described the world created by the SS and Nazi ideology.

You get up at 3 A.M. You have to dress quickly, and make the "bed" so that it looks like a matchbox. For the slightest irregularity in bed-making the punishment was 25 lashes, after which it was impossible to lie or sit for a whole month.

Everyone had to leave the barracks immediately. Outside it is still dark—or else the moon is shining. People are trembling because of lack of sleep and the cold. In order to warm up a bit, groups of ten to twenty people stand together, back to back so as to rub against each other.

There was what was called a wash-room, where everyone in the camp was supposed to wash—there were only a few faucets—and we were 4,500 people in that section (no. 3). Of course there was neither soap nor towel or even a handkerchief, so that washing was theoretical rather than practical. . . . In one day, a person there [be]came a lowly person indeed.

At 5 A.M. we used to get half a litre of black, bitter coffee. That was all we got for what was called "breakfast." At 6 A.M.—a headcount (*Appell* in German). We all had to stand at attention, in fives, according to the barracks, of which there were 22 in each section. We stood there until the SS men had satisfied their game-playing instincts by "humorous" orders to take off and put on caps. Then they received their report, and counted us. After the headcount—work.

We went in groups—some to build railway tracks or a road, some to the quarries to carry stones or coal, some to take out manure, or for potato-digging, latrine-cleaning, barracks—or sewer—repairs. All this took place inside the camp enclosure. During work the SS men beat up the prisoners mercilessly, inhumanly and for no reason.

They were like wild beasts and, having found their victim, ordered him to present his backside, and beat him with a stick or a whip, usually until the stick broke.

The victim screamed only after the first blows, afterwards he fell unconscious and the SS man then kicked at the ribs, the face, at the most sensitive parts of a man's body, and then, finally convinced that the victim was at the end of his strength, he ordered another Jew to pour one pail of water after the other over the beaten person until he woke and got up.

A favorite sport of the SS men was to make a "boxing sack" out of a Jew. This was done in the following way: Two Jews were stood up, one being forced to hold the other by the collar, and an SS man trained giving him a knock-out. Of course, after the first blow, the poor victim was likely to fall, and this was prevented by the other Jew holding him up. After the fat, Hitlerite murderer had "trained" in this way for 15 minutes, and only after the poor victim was completely shattered, covered in blood, his teeth knocked out, his nose broken, his eyes hit, they released him and ordered a doctor to treat his wounds. That was their way of taking care and being generous.

Another customary SS habit was to kick a Jew with a heavy boot. The Jew was forced to stand to attention, and all the while the SS man kicked him until he broke some bones. People who stood near enough to such a victim, often heard the breaking of the bones. The pain was so terrible that people, having undergone that treatment, died in agony.

Apart from the SS men there were other expert hangmen. These were the so-called Capos. The name was an abbreviation for "barracks police." The Capos were German criminals who were also camp inmates. However, although they belonged to "us," they were privileged. They had a special, better barracks of their own, they had better food, better, almost normal clothes, they wore special red or green riding pants, high leather boots, and fulfilled the functions of camp guards. They were worse even than the SS men. One of them, older than the others and the worst murderer of them all, when he descended on a victim, would not revive him later with water but would choke him to death. Once, this murderer caught a boy of 13 (in the presence of his father) and hit his head so that the poor child died instantly. This "camp elder" later boasted in front of his peers, with a smile on his beast's face and with pride, that he managed to kill a Jew with one blow.

In each section stood a gallows. For being late for the headcount, or similar crimes, the "camp elder" hanged the offenders.

Work was actually unproductive, and its purpose was exhaustion and torture.

At 12 noon there was a break for a meal. Standing in line, we received half a litre of soup each. Usually it was cabbage soup, or some other watery liquid, without fats, tasteless. That was lunch. It was eaten—in all weather—under the open sky, never in the barracks. No spoons were allowed, though wooden spoons lay on each bunk—probably for show, for Red Cross committees. One had to drink the soup out of the bowl and lick it like a dog.

From 1 P.M. till 6 P.M. there was work again. I must emphasize that if we were lucky we got a 12 o'clock meal. There were "days of punishment"—when lunch was given together with the evening meal, and it was cold and sour, so that our stomach was empty for a whole day.

Afternoon work was the same: blows, and blows again. Until 6 P.M.

At 6 there was the evening headcount. Again we were forced to stand at attention. Counting, receiving the report. Usually we were left standing at attention for an hour or two, while some prisoners were called up for "punishment parade"—they were those who in the Germans' eyes had transgressed in some way during the day, or had not been punctilious in their performance. They were stripped naked publicly, laid out on specially constructed benches, and whipped with 25 or 50 lashes.

The brutal beating and the heart-rending cries—all this the prisoners had to watch and hear.

REVIEW QUESTIONS

1. What do the accounts of Hermann Graebe, Rudolf Hoess, and Y. Pfeffer reveal about the capacity of people to inflict oppression? How did the SS view their victims?
2. What do these accounts reveal about the ways in which people respond to overwhelmingly hopeless oppression?

11　Resistance

Each occupied country had its collaborators who welcomed the demise of democracy, saw Hitler as Europe's best defense against Communism, and profited from the sale of war material. Each country also produced a resistance movement that grew stronger as Nazi barbarism became more visible and prospects of a German defeat more likely. The Nazis retaliated by torturing and executing captured resistance fighters and killing hostages—generally, fifty for every German killed.

In Western Europe, the resistance rescued downed Allied airmen, radioed military intelligence to Britain, and sabotaged German installations. Norwegians blew up the German stock of heavy water needed for atomic research. The Danish underground sabotaged railways and smuggled into neutral Sweden almost all of Denmark's eight thousand Jews just before they were to be deported to the death camps. The Greek resistance blew up a vital viaduct, interrupting the movement of supplies to German troops in North Africa. After the Allies landed on the coast of France in June 1944, the French resistance delayed the movement of German reinforcements and liberated sections of the country. Belgian resistance fighters captured the vital port of Antwerp.

The Polish resistance, numbering nearly 400,000 at its height, reported on German troop movements and interfered with supplies destined for the Eastern Front. In August 1944, with Soviet forces approaching Warsaw, the Poles staged a full-scale revolt against the German occupiers. The Poles appealed to the Soviets, camped ten miles away, for help. Thinking about a future Russian-dominated Poland, the Soviets did not move. After sixty-three days of street fighting, remnants of the Polish underground surrendered, and the Germans destroyed what was left of Warsaw.

Russian partisans numbered several hundred thousand men and women. Operating behind the German lines, they sabotaged railways, destroyed trucks, and killed thousands of German soldiers in hit-and-run attacks.

The mountains and forests of Yugoslavia provided excellent terrain for guerrilla warfare. The leading Yugoslav resistance army was headed by Josip Broz (1892–1980), better known as Tito. Moscow-trained, intelligent, and courageous, Tito organized the partisans into a disciplined fighting force, which tied down a huge German army and ultimately liberated the country from German rule.

Jews participated in the resistance movements in all countries and were particularly prominent in the French resistance. Specifically Jewish resistance organizations emerged in Eastern Europe, but they suffered from shattering hardships. They had virtually no access to weapons. Poles, Ukrainians, Lithuanians, and other peoples of Eastern Europe with a long history of anti-Semitism gave little or no support to Jewish resisters—at times, even denounced them to the Nazis, or killed them. For centuries, European Jews had dealt with persecution by complying with their oppressors, and they had unlearned the habit of armed resistance that their ancestors had demonstrated against the Romans. The Germans responded to acts of resistance with savage reprisals against other Jews, creating a moral dilemma for any Jew who considered taking up arms. Nevertheless, revolts did take place in the ghettos and concentration camps. In the spring of 1943, the surviving Jews of the Warsaw ghetto, armed only with a few guns and homemade bombs, fought the Germans for several weeks.

Italy and German also had resistance movements. After the Allies landed in Italy in 1943, bands of Italian partisans helped to liberate Italy from Fascism and the German occupation. In Germany, army officers plotted to assassinate the Führer. On July 20, 1944, Colonel Claus von Stauffenberg planted a bomb at a staff conference attended by Hitler, but the Führer escaped serious injury. In retaliation, some five thousand suspected anti-Nazis were tortured and executed in exceptionally barbarous fashion.

Albert Camus
"I AM FIGHTING YOU BECAUSE YOUR LOGIC IS AS CRIMINAL AS YOUR HEART"

Reared and educated in French-ruled Algeria, Albert Camus (1908–1960) gained an instant reputation in 1942 with the publication of *The Stranger*, a short novel, and "The Myth of Sisyphus," a philosophical essay. For Camus, neither religion nor philosophy provides a sure basis for human values; neither can tell us with certainty what is right or wrong. Ultimately existence has no higher meaning, and the universe is indifferent to us.

While serving in the French Resistance, he wrote letters to an imaginary German friend, which were published clandestinely during the German occupation. These letters, said Camus years later, "had a purpose, which was to throw some light on the blind battle we were then waging and thereby to make our battle more effective." In the following letter, written in July 1944, Camus reveals an attitude that pervades his writings: a moralistic humanism that promotes fraternity and dignity and offers a worthwhile response to the absurdity of the human condition.

Now the moment of your defeat is approaching. I am writing you from a city known throughout the world which is now preparing against you a celebration of freedom. . . .

. . . I want to tell you how it is possible that, though so similar, we should be enemies today, how I might have stood beside you and why all is over between us now.

For a long time we both thought that this world had no ultimate meaning and that consequently we were cheated. I still think so in a way. But I came to different conclusions from the ones you used to talk about, which, for so many years now, you have been trying to introduce into history. I tell myself now that if I had really followed your reasoning, I ought to approve what you are doing. And this is so serious that I must stop and consider it, during this summer night so full of promises for us and of threats for you.

You never believed in the meaning of this world, and you therefore deduced the idea that everything was equivalent and that good and evil could be defined according to one's wishes. You supposed that in the absence of any human or divine code the only values were those of the animal world—in other words, violence and cunning. Hence you concluded that man was negligible and that his soul could be killed, that in the maddest of histories the only pursuit for the individual was the adventure of power and his only morality, the realism of conquests. And, to tell the truth, I, believing I thought as you did, saw no valid argument to answer you except a fierce love of justice which, after all, seemed to me as unreasonable as the most sudden passion.

Where lay the difference? Simply that you readily accepted despair and I never yielded to it. Simply that you saw the injustice of our condition to the point of being willing to add to it, whereas it seemed to me that man must exalt justice in order to fight against eternal injustice, create happiness in order to protest against the universe of unhappiness. Because you turned your despair into intoxication, because you freed yourself from it by making a principle of it, you were willing to destroy man's works and to fight him in order to add to his basic misery. Meanwhile, refusing to accept that despair and that tortured world, I merely wanted men to rediscover their solidarity in order to wage war against their revolting fate.

As you see, from the same principle we derived quite different codes, because along the way you gave up the lucid view and considered it more convenient (you would have said a matter of indifference) for another to do your thinking for you and for millions of Germans. Because you were tired of fighting heaven, you relaxed in that exhausting adventure in which you had to mutilate souls and destroy the world. In short, you chose injustice and sided with the gods. Your logic was merely apparent.

I, on the contrary, chose justice in order to remain faithful to the world. I continue to believe that this world has no ultimate meaning.

But I know that something in it has a meaning and that is man, because he is the only creature to insist on having one. This world has at least the truth of man, and our task is to provide its justifications against fate itself. And it has no justification but man; hence he must be saved if we want to save the idea we have of life. With your scornful smile you will ask me: what do you mean by saving man? And with all my being I shout to you that I mean not mutilating him and yet giving a chance to the justice that man alone can conceive.

At present everything must be obvious to you; you know that we are enemies. You are the man of injustice, and there is nothing in the world that my heart loathes so much. But now I know the reasons for what was once merely a passion. I am fighting you because your logic is as criminal as your heart. And in the horror you have lavished upon us for four years, your reason plays as large a part as your instinct. This is why my condemnation will be sweeping; you are already dead as far as I am concerned. But at the very moment when I am judging your horrible behavior, I shall remember that you and we started out from the same solitude, that you and we, with all Europe, are caught in the same tragedy of the intelligence. And, despite yourselves, I shall still apply to you the name of man. In order to keep faith with ourselves, we are obliged to respect in you what you do not respect in others. For a long time that was your great advantage since you kill more easily than we do. And to the very end of time that will be the advantage of those who resemble you. But to the very end of time, we, who do not resemble you, shall have to bear witness so that mankind, despite its worst errors, may have its justification and its proof of innocence.

This is why, at the end of this combat, from the heart of this city that has come to resemble hell, despite all the tortures inflicted on our people, despite our disfigured dead and our villages peopled with orphans, I can tell you that at the very moment when we are going to destroy you without pity, we still feel no hatred for you. And even if tomorrow, like so many others, we had to die, we should still be without hatred. We cannot guarantee that we shall not be afraid; we shall simply try to be reasonable. But we can guarantee that we shall not hate anything. And we have come to terms with the only thing in the world I could loathe today, I assure you, and we want to destroy you in your power without mutilating you in your soul.

As for the advantage you had over us, you see that you continue to have it. But it likewise constitutes our superiority. And it is what makes this night easy for me. Our strength lies in thinking as you do about the essence of the world, in rejecting no aspect of the drama that is ours. But at the same time we have saved the idea of man at the end of this disaster of the intelligence, and that idea gives us the undying courage to believe in a rebirth. To be sure, the accusation we make against the world is not mitigated by this. We paid so dear for this new knowledge that our condition continues to seem desperate to us. Hundreds of thousands of men assassinated at dawn, the terrible walls of prisons, the soil of Europe reeking with millions of corpses of its sons—it took all that to pay for the acquisition of two or three slight distinctions which may have no other value than to help some among us to die more nobly. Yes, that is heart-breaking. But we have to prove that we do not deserve so much injustice. This is the task we have set ourselves; it will begin tomorrow. In this night of Europe filled with the breath of summer, millions of men, armed or unarmed, are getting ready for the fight. The dawn about to break will mark your final defeat. I know that heaven, which was indifferent to your horrible victories, will be equally indifferent to your just defeat. Even now I expect nothing from heaven. But we shall at least have helped save man from the solitude to which you wanted to relegate him. Because you scorned such faith in mankind, you are the men who, by thousands, are going to die solitary. Now, I can say farewell to you.

July 1944

Hans and Sophie Scholl
THE WHITE ROSE

In February 1943, Hans Scholl, aged twenty-five, a medical student, and his twenty-two-year-old sister, Sophie Scholl, who was studying biology and philosophy, were executed by the Nazis for high treason. The Scholls belonged to the White Rose, a small group of idealistic students at the University of Munich that urged passive resistance to the National Socialist regime. The White Rose hoped that if more Germans were aware of the Nazi regime's inhumane character they would withdraw their loyalty.

The Scholls had once been enthusiastic members of the Hitler Youth, but over the years they grew increasingly disillusioned with Nazism. Their outlook was shaped by their anti-Nazi father, by a commitment to the German humanist tradition best represented by Schiller and Goethe, and by Kurt Huber, a professor of philosophy and psychology at their university, who spoke to trusted students of a duty "to enlighten those Germans who are still unaware of the evil intentions of our government." Hans was also swayed by the persecution of Jews he had witnessed when he was in transport through Poland to the Russian front.

On walls in Munich, the Scholls painted signs: "Down with Hitler" and "Freedom." Stowing their anti-Nazi leaflets in luggage, the students traveled by railroad to several German cities to drop them off.

On February 18, 1943, Hans and Sophie were spotted dropping leaflets in the university by the building superintendent, who reported them to the Gestapo. On February 23, Hans, Sophie, and Christoph Probst, also a medical student, were executed. Several days before she died, Sophie stated: "What does my death matter if through us thousands of people will be stirred to action and awakened?" Han's last words, "Long live freedom," echoed through the prison. Kurt Huber and other members of the group were executed on July 13, 1943.

The following excerpts come from the White Rose's leaflets.

[SECOND LEAFLET]

We do not want to discuss here the question of the Jews, nor do we want in this leaflet to compose a defense or apology. No, only by way of example do we want to cite the fact that since the conquest of Poland *three hundred thousand* Jews have been murdered in this country in the most bestial way. Here we see the most frightful crime against human dignity, a crime that is unparalleled in the whole of history. For Jews, too, are human beings—no matter what position we take with respect to the Jewish question—and a crime of this dimension has been perpetrated against human beings. Someone may say that the Jews deserved their fate. This assertion would be a monstrous impertinence; but let us assume that someone said this—what position has he then taken toward the fact that the entire Polish aristocratic youth is being annihilated? (May God grant that this program has not fully achieved its aim as yet!) All male offspring of the houses of the nobility between the ages of fifteen and twenty were transported to concentration camps in Germany and sentenced to forced labor, and all girls of this age group were sent to Norway, into the bordellos of the SS! Why tell you these things, since you are fully aware of them—or if not of these, then of other equally grave crimes committed by this frightful sub-humanity? Because here we touch on a problem which involves us deeply and forces us all to take thought. Why do the German people behave so apathetically in the face of all these abominable crimes, crimes so unworthy of the human race? Hardly anyone thinks about that. It is accepted as fact and put out of mind. The German people slumber on in their dull, stupid sleep and encourage these Fascist criminals; they give them the opportunity to carry on their depredations; and of course they do so. Is this a sign that the Germans are brutalized in their simplest human feelings, that no chord within them cries out at the sight of such deeds, that they have sunk into a fatal consciencelessness from which they will never, never awake? It seems to be so, and will certainly be so, if the German does not at last start up out of his stupor, if he does not protest wherever and whenever he can against this clique of criminals, if he shows no sympathy for these hundreds of thousands of victims. He must evidence not only sympathy; no, much more: a sense of *complicity* in guilt. For through his apathetic behavior he gives these evil men the opportunity to act as they do; he tolerates this "government" which has taken upon itself such an infinitely great burden of guilt; indeed, he himself is to blame for the fact that it came about at all! Each man wants to be exonerated of a guilt of this kind, each one continues on his way with the most placid, the calmest conscience. But he cannot be exonerated; he is *guilty, guilty, guilty!* It is not too late, however, to do away with this most reprehensible of all miscarriages of government, so as to avoid being burdened with even greater guilt. Now, when in recent years our eyes have been opened, when we know exactly who our adversary is, it is high time to root out, this brown horde. Up until the outbreak of the war the larger part of the German people was blinded; the Nazis did not show themselves in their true aspect. But now, now that we have

recognized them for what they are, it must be the sole and first duty, the holiest duty of every German to destroy these beasts. . . .

Please make as many copies as possible of this leaflet and distribute them.

[THIRD LEAFLET]

. . . Every individual human being has a claim to a useful and just state, a state which secures the freedom of the individual as well as the good of the whole. For, according to God's will, man is intended to pursue his natural goal, his earthly happiness, in self-reliance and self-chosen activity, freely and independently within the community of life and work of the nation.

But our present "state" is the dictatorship of evil. "Oh, we've known that for a long time," I hear you object, "and it isn't necessary to bring that to our attention again." But, I ask you, if you know that, why do you not bestir yourselves, why do you allow these men who are in power to rob you step by step, openly and in secret, of one domain of your rights after another, until one day nothing, nothing at all will be left but a mechanized state system presided over by criminals and drunks? Is your spirit already so crushed by abuse that you forget it is your right—or rather, your *moral duty*—to eliminate this system? But if a man no longer can summon the strength to demand his right, then it is absolutely certain that he will perish. . . .

. . . At *all* points we must oppose National Socialism, wherever it is open to attack. We must soon bring this monster of a state to an end. A victory of Fascist Germany in this war would have immeasurable, frightful consequences. The military victory over Bolshevism dare not become the primary concern of the Germans. The defeat of the Nazis must *unconditionally* be the first order of business. . . .

And now every convinced opponent of National Socialism must ask himself how he can fight against the present "state" in the most effective way, how he can strike it the most telling blows. Through passive resistance, without a doubt. We cannot provide each man with the blueprint for his acts, we can only suggest them in general terms, and he alone will find the way of achieving this end:

Sabotage in armament plants and war industries, sabotage at all gatherings, rallies, public ceremonies, and organizations of the National Socialist Party. Obstruction of the smooth functioning of the war machine (a machine for war that goes on solely to shore up and perpetuate the National Socialist Party and its dictatorship). *Sabotage* in all the areas of science and scholarship which further the continuation of the war—whether in universities, technical schools, laboratories, research institutes, or technical bureaus. *Sabotage* in all cultural institutions which could potentially enhance the "prestige" of the Fascists among the people. *Sabotage* in all branches of the arts which have even the slightest dependence on National Socialism or render it service. *Sabotage* in all publications, all newspapers, that are in the pay of the "government" and that defend its ideology and aid in disseminating the brown lie. Do not give a penny to public drives. . . . Do not contribute to the collections of metal, textiles, and the like. Try to convince all your acquaintances, including those in the lower social classes, of the senselessness of continuing, of the hopelessness of this war; of

our spiritual and economic enslavement at the hands of the National Socialists; of the destruction of all moral and religious values; and urge them to *passive resistance*! . . .

Please duplicate and distribute!

[FOURTH LEAFLET]

Every word that comes from Hitler's mouth is a lie. When he says peace, he means war, and when he blasphemously uses the name of the Almighty, he means the power of evil, the fallen angel, Satan. His mouth is the foul-smelling maw of Hell, and his might is at bottom accursed. True, we must conduct the struggle against the National Socialist terrorist state with rational means; but whoever today still doubts the reality, the existence of demonic powers, has failed by a wide margin to understand the metaphysical background of this war. Behind the concrete, the visible events, behind all objective, logical considerations, we find the irrational element: the struggle against the demon, against the servants of the Antichrist. . . .

. . . Has God not given you the strength, the will to fight? We *must* attack evil where it is strongest, and it is strongest in the power of Hitler.

Marek Edelman
THE GHETTO FIGHTS, THE WARSAW GHETTO UPRISING, 1943

Three million Jews lived in Poland at the time of the Nazi invasion in 1939. In 1940, the Nazis began herding Jews from all over the country into densely packed ghettos—six or seven to a room in Warsaw—located in a number of cities. There the Jews worked as slave laborers for the German war effort. Many died of beatings, shootings, disease, and starvation before being transported to death camps. The largest of the ghettos was in Warsaw, the Polish capital, where 450,000 Jews were confined behind a ten-foot wall, sealing them off from the rest of the Polish population—the "Aryan side." The Germans killed anyone they found trying to escape from the ghetto, including starving children desperate to smuggle food in from beyond the wall. Between July and October 1942 the Germans deported some 300,000 Jews in freight cars from the Warsaw Ghetto to be gassed in the death camp at Treblinka.

By the beginning of 1943, a remnant of 60,000 Jews remained in the Warsaw Ghetto. Jewish underground organizations now resolved to resist the final deportations to the gas chambers. They knew they had no chance to succeed; their hope was stated in the Jewish Resistance Organization's (ZOB) "Manifesto to the Poles": "We, as well as you, are burning with the desire to punish the enemy for all his crimes, with a desire for vengeance. It is a fight for our freedom, as well as yours; for our human dignity and national honour, as well as yours." Armed with a few pistols, rifles, automatic firearms, and several hundred homemade bottled explosives, the insurgents battled the German troops, and their Ukrainian and Latvian auxiliaries from April 19 to May 16. From their hiding places in buildings, the Jews rained grenades and bullets on Nazi patrols. Unable to dislodge the Jews from their positions, the Nazis block-by-block systematically set fire to and blew up the buildings in the ghetto. In this ghastly inferno, the Jewish partisans continued their desperate struggle until resistance was no longer possible. Some 14,000 Jews perished in the uprising, many of them were burned alive or perished from smoke inhalation. The Germans rounded up surviving Jews, executing large numbers on the spot, and transporting the remaining mainly to Treblinka where most were exterminated. A few Jews escaped to the "Aryan side" through the sewers and continued their struggle in the forests. Some were imprisoned in a concentration camp in the ghetto and, when liberated by Polish forces in the second Warsaw Uprising the following year, fought alongside their fellow Poles (see next selection). News of the Jewish revolt in the Warsaw Ghetto quickly spread throughout Poland and occupied Europe, inspiring Jews and non-Jews to resist their Nazi overlords.

The following selection is from *The Ghetto Fights*, first published in Warsaw in 1945. The author, Marek Edelman who died in 2009, was the last surviving leader of the Warsaw Ghetto Uprising. After the war Edelman became a prominent cardiologist; in the 1980s he was a leading supporter of Solidarity, the independent trade union movement that helped bring down the Communist regime.

Finally, the Germans decided to liquidate the Warsaw Ghetto completely, regardless of cost. On 19 April, 1943, at 2 AM, the first messages concerning the German's approach arrived from our outermost observation posts. These reports made it clear that German gendarmes, aided by Polish 'navy-blue' policemen, were encircling the outer Ghetto walls at 30-yard intervals. An emergency alarm to all our battle groups was immediately ordered, and at 2.15 AM, that is 15 minutes later, all the groups were already at their battle stations. We also informed the entire population of the imminent danger, and most of the Ghetto inhabitants moved instantly to previously prepared shelters and hide-outs in the cellars and attics of buildings. A deathly silence enveloped the Ghetto. The ZOB was on the alert.

At 4 AM the Germans, in groups of threes, fours, or fives, so as not to arouse the ZOB's or the population's suspicion, began penetrating into the 'inter-Ghetto' areas. Here they formed into platoons and companies. At seven o'clock motorised detachments, including a number of tanks and armoured vehicles, entered the

Ghetto. Artillery pieces were placed outside the walls. Now the SS men were ready to attack. In closed formations, stepping haughtily and loudly, they marched into the seemingly dead streets of the Central Ghetto. Their triumph appeared to be complete. It looked as if this superbly equipped modern army had scared off the handful of bravado-drunk men. . . .

But no, they did not scare us and we were not taken by surprise. We were only awaiting an opportune moment. Such a moment presently arrived. The Germans chose the intersection at Mila and Zamenhofa Streets for their bivouac area, and battle groups barricaded at the four corners of the street opened concentric fire on them. Strange projectiles began exploding everywhere (the hand grenades of our own make), the lone machine pistol sent shots through the air now and then (ammunition had to be conserved carefully), rifles started firing a bit further away. Such was the beginning.

The Germans attempted a retreat, but their path was cut. German dead soon littered the street. The remainder tried to find cover in the neighbouring stores and house entrances, but this shelter proved insufficient. The 'glorious' SS, therefore, called tanks into action under the cover of which the remaining men of two companies were to commence a 'victorious' retreat. But even the tanks seemed to be affected by the Germans' bad luck. The first was burned out by one of our incendiary bottles, the rest did not approach our positions. The fate of the Germans caught in the Mila Street-Zamenhofa Street trap was settled. Not a single German left this area alive. . . .

Simultaneously, fights were going on at the intersection of Nalewki and Gesia Streets. Two battle groups kept the Germans from entering the Ghetto area at this point. The fighting lasted more than seven hours. The Germans found some mattresses and used them as cover, but the partisans' well-aimed fire forced them to several successive withdrawals. German blood flooded the street. German ambulances continuously transported their wounded to the small square near the Community buildings. Here the wounded lay in rows on the sidewalk awaiting their turn to be admitted to the hospital. At the corner of Gesia Street a German air liaison observation post signalled the partisans' positions and the required bombing targets to the planes. But from the air as well as on the ground the partisans appeared to be invincible. The Gesia Street-Nalewki Street battle ended in the complete withdrawal of the Germans. . . .

The following day there was silence until 2 PM. At that time the Germans, again in closed formation, arrived at the brushmakers' gate. They did not suspect that at that very moment an observer lifted an electric plug. A German factory guard walked toward the gate wanting to open it. At precisely the same moment the plug was placed in the socket and a mine, waiting for the Germans for a long time, exploded under the SS men's feet. Over one hundred SS men were killed in the explosion. The rest, fired on by the partisans, withdrew. . . .

The Germans tried again. They attempted to enter the Ghetto at several other points, and everywhere they encountered determined opposition. Every house was a fortress. . . .

The partisans' stand was so determined that the Germans were finally forced to abandon all ordinary fighting methods and to try new, apparently infallible tactics. Their new idea was to set fire to the entire brushmakers' block from the outside, on all sides simultaneously. In an instant fires were raging over the entire block, black smoke choked one's throat, burned one's eyes. The partisans, naturally, did not intend to be burnt alive in the flames. We decided to gamble for our lives and attempt to reach the Central Ghetto area regardless of consequences. . . .

The flames cling to our clothes, which now start smouldering. The pavement melts under our feet into a black, gooey substance. Broken glass, littering every inch of the streets, is transformed into a sticky liquid in which our feet are caught. Our soles begin to burn from the heat of the stone pavement. One after another we stagger through the conflagration. From house to house, from courtyard to courtyard, with no air to breathe, with a hundred hammers clanging in our heads, with burning rafters continuously falling over us, we finally reach the end of the area under fire. We feel lucky just to stand here, to be out of the inferno. . . .

The omnipotent flames were now able to accomplish what the Germans could not do. Thousands of people perished in the conflagration. The stench of burning bodies was everywhere. Charred corpses lay around on balconies, in window recesses, on unburned steps. The flames chased the people out from their shelters, made them leave the previously prepared safe hideouts in attics and cellars. Thousands staggered about in the courtyards where they were easy prey for the Germans who imprisoned them or killed them outright. Tired beyond all endurance, they would fall asleep in driveways, entrances, standing, sitting, lying and were caught asleep by a passing German's bullet. Nobody would even notice that an old man sleeping in a corner would never again wake up, that a mother feeding her baby had been cold and dead for three days, that a baby's crying and sucking was futile since its mother's arms were cold and her breast dead. Hundreds committed suicide jumping from fourth or fifth stories of apartment houses. Mothers would thus save their children from terrible death in flames. The Polish population saw these scenes from Sto Jerska Street and from Krasinskich Square. . . .

The Germans now tried to locate all inhabited shelters by means of sensitive sound-detecting devices and police dogs. On 3 May they located the shelter on 30 Franciszkanska Street, where the operation base of those of our groups who had formerly forced their way from the brushmakers' area was at the time located. Here one of the most brilliant battles was fought. The fighting lasted for two days and half of all our men were killed in its course. . . .

On 8 May detachments of Germans and Ukrainians surrounded the Headquarters of the ZOB Command. The fighting lasted two hours, and when the Germans convinced themselves that they would be unable to take the bunker by storm, they tossed in a gas-bomb. Whoever survived the German bullets, whoever was not gassed, committed suicide, for it was quite clear that from here there was no way out, and nobody even considered being taken alive by the Germans. Jurek Wilner called upon all partisans to commit suicide together. Lutek Rotblat shot his mother, his sister, then himself. Ruth fired at herself seven times.

Thus 80 per cent of the remaining partisans perished, among them the ZOB Commander, Mordchaj Anilewicz.

At night the remnants, who had miraculously escaped death, joined the remaining few of the brushmakers' detachments now deployed at 22 Franciszkanska Street.

That very same night two of our liaison men (S Ratajzer—'Kazik', and Franek) arrived from the 'Aryan side'.

Ten days previously the ZOB Command had dispatched Kazik and Zygmunt Frydrych to our representative on the 'Aryan side', Icchak Cukierman ('Antek'), to arrange the withdrawal of the fighting groups through the sewer mains. Now these liaison men arrived. . . .

All night we walked through the sewers, crawling through numerous entanglements built by the Germans for just such an emergency. The entrance traps were buried under heaps of rubble, the throughways booby-trapped with hand-grenades exploding at a touch. Every once in a while the Germans would let gas into the mains. In similar conditions, in a sewer 28 inches high, where it was impossible to stand up straight and where the water reached our lips, we waited 48 hours for the time to get out. Every minute someone else lost consciousness.

Thirst was the worst handicap. Some even drank the thick slimy sewer water. Every second seemed like months.

On 10 May, at 10 AM, two trucks halted at the trap door on the Prosta Street-Twarda Street intersection. In broad daylight, with almost no cover whatsoever (the promised Home Army cover failed and only three of our liaison men and Comrade Krzaczek—a People's Army representative specially detailed for this assignment—patrolled the street), the trap door opened and one after another, with the stunned crowd looking on, armed Jews appeared from the depths of the dark hole (at this time the sight of *any* Jew was already a sensational occurrence). Not all were able to get out. Violently, heavily the trap-door snapped shut, the trucks took off at full speed.

Two battle groups remained in the Ghetto. We were in contact with them until the middle of June. From then on every trace of them disappeared.

Those who had gone over to the 'Aryan side' continued the partisan fight in the woods. The majority perished eventually. The small group that was still alive at the time took an active part in the 1944 Warsaw Uprising as the 'ZOB Group'.

Tadeusz Bor-Komorowski
THE WARSAW RISING, 1944

Nazi policy toward defeated Poland was especially harsh. To counter this brutality and maintain their national identity, the Poles created an underground, alternative society. Perhaps their most notable institution was the Home Army, an amalgamation of all of the resistance units in Poland. With 380,000 members at its height, the Home Army represented the fourth-largest Allied army, after the Soviet, United States, and British. It carried out numerous intelligence and guerrilla operations against the German occupiers while awaiting the proper moment for a general revolt. That moment seemed to have arrived in the summer of 1944. Nazi armies were in flight throughout Europe, and the Red Army stood just across the Vistula. Fearful of Stalin's intention to install a puppet government in Poland after the war, the Home Army decided to take matters into its own hands and rid Warsaw of the Nazis, in effect declaring themselves masters in their own house.

The Warsaw Uprising began August 1, 1944. In the opening days of the battle, the Home Army, which numbered about 50,000 fighters, defeated the Germans in several bloody skirmishes, and the citizens of Warsaw were jubilant when the Polish national flag was unfurled. Several other partisan groups and volunteers, including Jews in hiding on the "Aryan side" and recently freed by Polish insurgents from a concentration camp standing in the ruins of the Warsaw Ghetto, fought with the Home Army. Reinforced German troops counterattacked, and, true to Heinrich Himmler's orders, special murder squads went house to house massacring some 40,000 civilians, including women and children in the Wola district alone. Despite these and other German atrocities—using civilians as human shields for tanks and killing outright captured insurgents—the Poles continued their heroic resistance. However, defying the expectations of the insurgents' leaders, the Red Army provided no support. Seeing an opportunity to rid himself of political opponents, Stalin prevented Soviet troops from assisting the Poles. Shortages of food, water, and ammunition and the great loss of life—some 2,000 a day were perishing—forced the capitulation of the Home Army on October 2, 1944. An enraged Hitler ordered the total destruction of the city, particularly its historic religious and cultural centers. The Nazis evacuated the remainder of Warsaw's population and then street by street special detonation squads reduced the once beautiful Polish capital to rubble and ruins. It is estimated that more than 200,000 Poles died in the Uprising and many survivors were sent to concentration camps; some 25,000 Germans were also killed.

After the war, the Communist leadership imposed by Stalin deported to Siberia or executed many of the leaders of the Uprising and until the demise of Communism in Poland, it was prohibited to honor the insurgents. Today the Poles commemorate the 63-day Uprising as a symbol of national pride and inspiration.

Tadeusz Bor-Komorowski was one of the organizers of the Home Army and, from 1943 until its disbandment late in 1944, its commander. His history of this underground military organization, *The Secret Army,* appeared in 1950. The following excerpts from that work provide a thumbnail sketch of the Warsaw Rising.

. . . Warsaw by now was fully aware that the battle would not pass it by. The hope that it would be fought for the dignity, freedom, and sovereignty of the Polish nation gave the inhabitants a strength of spirit capable of the greatest valour and sacrifice. The general lust of revenge for the years of tragedy and humiliation suffered under the Germans was overwhelming and practically impossible to check. The whole town was waiting breathlessly for a call to arms, and the vast majority of the population would have considered a passive attitude as a betrayal of the Polish cause. . . .

Having decided to fight, we faced a situation without precedent in the carrying out of full mobilisation in a town occupied by an enemy. For the first time a revolution was worked out as a military operation, according to a prearranged plan. Our strength amounted to nearly 40,000 Underground soldiers and about 4,200 women. The majority were workers, railwaymen, artisans, students and clerks in factories, railways and offices. These men had to be informed verbally of the place, date and hour to muster. It was only after many rehearsals and thanks to a continuously improved system of warning that we achieved the rate at which an order given by me reached the lower ranks in two hours. This enabled us to decide the rising no more than twenty-four hours before it was to start. But the task of informing 40,000 men, of giving them the code word and fixing hours and places of assembly was not the whole work. There was also liaison between the fighting groups to be established. Commanders of all ranks had to be constantly furnished with information and orders, and thousands of

instructions had to be distributed throughout the city. All these tasks were carried out by girl messengers. From dawn till dusk they covered the length and breadth of the city, climbed numberless stairs and repeated orders and reports, mostly by word of mouth. . . .

. . . Thirty minutes before zero hour, all preparations were completed. The soldiers brought out their arms and put on white-and-red armbands, the first open sign of a Polish army on Polish soil since the occupation. For five years they had all awaited this moment. Now the last seconds seemed an eternity. At five o'clock they would cease to be an underground resistance movement and would become once more Regular soldiers fighting in the open.

At exactly five o'clock thousands of windows flashed as they were flung open. From all sides a hail of bullets struck passing Germans, riddling their buildings and their marching formations. In the twinkling of an eye, the remaining civilians disappeared from the streets. From the entrances of houses, our men streamed out and rushed to the attack. In fifteen minutes an entire city of a million inhabitants was engulfed in the fight. . . .

My first message to the soldiers in the capital read:

Soldiers of the capital!

I have to-day issued the order which you desire, for open warfare against Poland's age-old enemy, the German invader. After nearly five years of ceaseless and determined struggle, carried on in secret, you stand to-day openly with arms in hand, to restore freedom to our country and to mete out fitting punishment to the German criminals for the terror and crimes committed by them in Polish soil.

Bor.

Commander-in-Chief, Home Army.

. . . People in the streets reacted with shouts and applause at the sight of the Polish eagle or the uniform which they had not seen for five years and when they saw German prisoners or captured arms. In this case, a window was flung open and a loud-speaker started up the song "Warszawianka," the Polish revolutionary song composed 114 years before. Everyone in the street, whether passing by or busy at the barricades, stood to attention and joined in the song. I was deeply affected by the fervour of the crowd. I think those moments were my happiest of the whole war. Unfortunately, they were short-lived.

On my return to the Kammler Factory, I found reports awaiting me on the incredible bestialities being practised by the Germans on civilians. This cruelty affected all the civilians in districts and buildings still in German hands. At the beginning, the Germans had set fire to most of the houses in these districts. The city was covered by a smoky glow. In many cases the inhabitants were not allowed to leave their houses or else not given sufficient time to do so. Thousands of people were burned alive. . . .

. . . Actually, there was not a single place in Warsaw which was out of range of artillery fire, incendiaries and mines, or grenades and bombs. Raid followed raid in such quick succession that from dawn to dusk the whole city lived in a state of continual alert. Every day, in nearly every street, more houses fell victim to the Luftwaffe. . . .

Meanwhile, the prolongation of the fight in the city forced us to more intensive use of the sewers for communication purposes. These dark, underground tunnels, mysterious and forbidding, stretching for miles, were the scene of a human effort of the greatest self-sacrifice—an effort to link up the torn shreds of fighting Warsaw so that all our isolated battles could form one whole and united operation fought in common. The network of sewers carried water and sewage to the Vistula. Built sixty years before, they formed a complicated labyrinth under the houses and streets of the city.

They had previously been used when fighting was going on in the Ghetto, which the Germans had surrounded by a wall and a cordon of police. By this route food, arms and ammunition had been smuggled in. Special organisations were formed at the time and provided with a suitable means of transport to ensure the supply of food for the Jewish population over a period of several months. Handcarts on rubber wheels, built to a width which would allow them to be pushed along the tunnels, were used. During the massacre of the Ghetto, many young Jews managed to flee by the same route.

When the Ghetto had been liquidated and destroyed, the sewers were forgotten, but now that our present fight was continuing, we were obliged once more to use these underground lines of communication. . . .

The tunnels were pitch dark, because for security reasons lights were either severely restricted or completely banned. The acrid air was asphyxiating and brought tears to the eyes. The size of passages varied. The smallest which could be negotiated were 3 feet high and 2 wide. Sharp debris, such as broken glass, strewed the semicircular floor of the passages, making hand support impossible when crawling. The most superficial scratch would have caused septicæmia. Two sticks had to be used as supports and progress was made in short jumps, rather like the motion of a kangaroo. It was extremely tiring and slow. To give an example, one of the routes leading from Stare Miasto to the centre of the city through one of the narrowest tunnels took as long as nine hours to negotiate, although the distance was no more than a mile. To advance along a narrow passage of this sort in pitch darkness, with mud up to the shoulders, often caused stark terror. I knew many men, in no way lacking courage, who would never have hesitated to attack enemy tanks with a bottle of petrol, who nevertheless lost their nerve and were overcome by complete exhaustion after only a few hundred yards in one of these narrow passages. The feeling of panic was increased by the difficulty of breathing in the fœtid atmosphere and by the fact that it was impossible to turn round. If an immovable obstacle was encountered, the only course was to back out.

Great help was given to the traffic now moving along the sewers by women's units. The women who volunteered for it were known as *Kanalarki* (*kanal,* in Polish, is a sewer). They carried messages and orders, reconnoitred new passages and removed obstacles.

In September the tunnels became the route of withdrawal for units being evacuated from overrun positions. Even wounded were transported underground, a proof of the greatest self-sacrifice and devotion on the part of the soldiers who refused to allow their officers and comrades to be left to fall into enemy hands. . . .

REVIEW QUESTION

1. What motivated Albert Camus to resist the Nazis? The Scholls? The Fighters in the Warsaw Ghetto? The Polish Home Army?

12 D-Day, June 6, 1944

On June 6, 1944, the Allied forces launched their invasion of Nazi-occupied France. The invasion, called Operation Overlord, had been planned with meticulous care. Under the supreme command of General Dwight D. Eisenhower (1890–1969), the Allies organized the biggest amphibious operation of the war. It involved 5,000 ships of all kinds, 11,000 aircraft, and 2 million soldiers, 1.5 million of them Americans, all equipped with the latest military gear. Two artificial harbors and several oil pipelines stood ready to supply the troops once the invasion was under way.

Historical Division, War Department
OMAHA BEACHHEAD

Allied control of the air was an important factor in the success of D-Day. A second factor was the fact that the Germans were caught by surprise. Although expecting an invasion, they did not believe that it would take place in the Normandy area of France, and they dismissed June 6 as a possible date because weather conditions were unfavorable.

Ultimately the invasion's success depended on what happened during the first few hours. If the Allies had failed to secure beachheads, the operation would have ended in disaster. As the following reading illustrates, some of the hardest fighting took place on Omaha Beach, which was attacked by the Americans. The extract, published in 1945, comes from a study prepared in the field by the 2nd Information and Historical Service attached to the First Army, and by the Historical Section, European Theater of Operations.

As expected, few of the LCVP's and LCA's [amphibious landing craft] carrying assault infantry were able to make dry landings. Most of them grounded on sandbars 50 to 100 yards out, and in some cases the water was neck deep. Under fire as they came within a quarter-mile of the shore, the infantry met their worst experiences of the day and suffered their heaviest casualties just after touchdown. Small-arms fire, mortars, and artillery concentrated on the landing area, but the worst hazard was produced by converging fires from automatic weapons. Survivors from some craft report hearing the fire beat on the ramps before they were lowered, and then seeing the hail of bullets whip the surf just in front of the lowered ramps. Some men dove under water or went over the side to escape the beaten zone of the machine guns. Stiff, weakened from seasickness, and often heavily loaded, the debarking troops had little chance of moving fast in water that was knee deep or higher, and their progress was made more difficult by uneven footing in the runnels crossing the tidal flat. Many men were exhausted before they reached shore, where they faced 200 yards or more of open sand to cross before reaching cover at the sea wall or shingle bank. Most men who reached that cover made it by walking, and under increasing enemy fire. Troops who stopped to organize, rest, or take shelter behind obstacles or tanks merely prolonged their difficulties and suffered heavier losses. . . .

Perhaps the worst area on the beach was Dog Green, directly in front of strongpoints guarding the Vierville draw [gully] and under heavy flanking fire from emplacements to the west, near Pointe de la Percée. Company A of the 116th was due to land on this sector with Company C of the 2d Rangers on its right flank, and both units came in on their targets. One of the six LCA's carrying Company A foundered about a thousand yards off shore, and passing Rangers saw men jumping overboard and being dragged down by their loads. At H+6[1] minutes the remaining craft grounded in water 4 to 6 feet

deep, about 30 yards short of the outward band of obstacles. Starting off the craft in three files, center file first and the flank files peeling right and left, the men were enveloped in accurate and intense fire from automatic weapons. Order was quickly lost as the troops attempted to dive under water or dropped over the sides into surf over their heads. Mortar fire scored four direct hits on one LCA, which "disintegrated." Casualties were suffered all the way to the sand, but when the survivors got there, some found they could not hold and came back into the water for cover, while others took refuge behind the nearest obstacles. Remnants of one boat team on the right flank organized a small firing line on the first yards of sand, in full exposure to the enemy. In short order every officer of the company, including Capt. Taylor N. Fellers, was a casualty, and most of the sergeants were killed or wounded. The leaderless men gave up any attempt to move forward and confined their efforts to saving the wounded, many of whom drowned in the rising tide. Some troops were later able to make the sea wall by staying in the edge of the water and going up the beach with the tide. Fifteen minutes after landing, Company A was out of action for the day. Estimates of its casualties range as high as two-thirds. . . .

As headquarters groups arrived from 0730 on, they found much the same picture at whatever sector they landed. Along 6,000 yards of beach, behind sea wall or shingle embankment, elements of the assault force were immobilized in what might well appear to be hopeless confusion. As a result of mislandings, many companies were so scattered that they could not be organized as tactical units. At some places, notably in front of the German strongpoints guarding draws, losses in officers and noncommissioned officers were so high that remnants of units were practically leaderless. . . .

There was, definitely, a problem of morale. The survivors of the beach crossing, many of whom were experiencing their first enemy fire, had seen heavy losses among their comrades or in neighboring units. No action could be fought in circumstances more calculated

---

[1]H indicates the start of an operation.

to heighten the moral effects of such losses. Behind them, the tide was drowning wounded men who had been cut down on the sands and was carrying bodies ashore just below the shingle. Disasters to the later landing waves were still occurring, to remind of the potency of enemy fire. . . .

At 0800, German observers on the bluff sizing up the grim picture below them might well have felt that the invasion was stopped at the edge of the water. Actually, at three or four places on the four-mile beachfront, U.S. troops were already breaking through the shallow crust of enemy defenses.

The outstanding fact about these first two hours of action is that despite heavy casualties, loss of equipment, disorganization, and all the other discouraging features of the landings, the assault troops did not stay pinned down behind the sea wall and embankment. At half-a-dozen or more points on the long stretch, they found the necessary drive to leave their cover and move out over the open beach flat toward the bluffs. Prevented by circumstance of mislandings from using carefully rehearsed tactics, they improvised assault methods to deal with what defenses they found before them. In nearly every case where advance was attempted, it carried through the enemy beach defenses. . . .

Various factors, some of them difficult to evaluate, played a part in the success of these advances. . . . But the decisive factor was leadership. Wherever an advance was made, it depended on the presence of some few individuals, officers and noncommissioned officers, who inspired, encouraged, or bullied their men forward, often by making the first forward moves. On Easy Red a lieutenant and a wounded sergeant of divisional engineers stood up under fire and walked over to inspect the wire obstacles just beyond the embankment. The lieutenant came back and, hands on hips, looked down disgustedly at the men lying behind the shingle bank. "Are you going to lay there and get killed, or get up and do something about it?" Nobody stirred, so the sergeant and the officer got the materials and blew the wire. On the same sector, where a group advancing across the flat was held up by a marshy area suspected of being mined, it was a lieutenant of engineers who crawled ahead through the mud on his belly, probing for mines with a hunting knife in the absence of other equipment. When remnants of an isolated boat section of Company B, 116th Infantry, were stopped by fire from a well-concealed emplacement, the lieutenant in charge went after it single-handed. In trying to grenade the rifle pit he was hit by three rifle bullets and eight grenade fragments, including some from his own grenade. He turned his map and compass over to a sergeant and ordered his group to press on inland. . . .

. . . Col. George A. Taylor arrived in the second section at 0815 and found plenty to do on the beach. Men were still hugging the embankment, disorganized, and suffering casualties from mortar and artillery fire. Colonel Taylor summed up the situation in terse phrase: "Two kinds of people are staying on this beach, the dead and those who are going to die—now let's get the hell out of here." Small groups of men were collected without regard to units, put under charge of the nearest non-commissioned officer, and sent on through the wire and across the flat, while engineers worked hard to widen gaps in the wire and to mark lanes through the minefields.

REVIEW QUESTIONS

1. What difficulties did Allied troops face while attempting the amphibious landing at Omaha Beach? Why were casualties so heavy?
2. According to the Historical Division study, many of the Allied soldiers at Omaha Beach were experiencing their first enemy fire. How did the officers who survived manage to rally these shaken and demoralized soldiers?

13 The End of the Third Reich

In January 1945, the Russians launched a major offensive, which ultimately brought them into Berlin. In February, American and British forces were battling the Germans in the Rhineland, and in March they crossed the Rhine into the interior of Germany. In April, the Russians encircled Berlin. After heavy artillery and rocket-launchers inflicted severe damage on the besieged city, Russian infantry attacked and engaged in vicious street fighting. From his underground bunker near the chancellery in Berlin, a physically exhausted and emotionally unhinged Hitler engaged in wild fantasies about new German victories.

The last weeks of the war were chaotic and murderous. Many German soldiers fought desperately against the invaders of the Fatherland, particularly the Russians, who had been depicted by Nazi propaganda as Asiatic barbarians. SS crews, still loyal to Hitler and National Socialism, hunted down and executed reluctant fighters as a warning to others. The misery of the Jews never abated. As the Russians neared the concentration camps, the SS marched the inmates into the German interior. It was a death march, for many of them, already human skeletons, could not endure the long trek, the weather, and the brutality of guards who shot stragglers.

Nerin E. Gun
THE LIBERATION OF DACHAU

In the closing weeks of the war, the Allies liberated German concentration camps, revealing the full horror of Nazi atrocities to a shocked world. On April 29, 1945, American soldiers entered Dachau. One of the liberated prisoners was Nerin E. Gun, a Turkish Catholic journalist, who had been imprisoned by the Nazis during the war for his reports about the Warsaw Ghetto and his prediction that the German armies would meet defeat in Russia. Gun described the liberation of Dachau in *The Day of the Americans* (1966), from which the following selection is taken.

The first wave of Americans had been followed by a second, which must have broken into the camp either through the crematorium or through the marshaling-yard, where the boxcars loaded with thousands of corpses had been parked. For, as soon as they saw the SS men standing there with their hands on their heads, these Americans, without any other semblance of trial, without even saying a warning word, turned their fire on them. Most of the inmates applauded this summary justice, and those who had been able to get over the ditch rushed out to strip the corpses of the Germans. Some even hacked their feet off, the more quickly to be able to get their boots. . . .

The detachment under the command of the American major had not come directly to the [entrance]. It had made a detour by way of the marshaling yard, where the convoys of deportees normally arrived and departed. There they found some fifty-odd cattle cars parked on the tracks. The cars were not empty.

"At first sight," said [Lieutenant Colonel Will] Cowling, "they seemed to be filled with rags, discarded clothing. Then we caught sight of hands, stiff fingers, faces. . . ."

The train was full of corpses, piled one on the other, 2,310 of them, to be exact. The train had come from Birkenau, and the dead were Hungarian and Polish Jews, children among them. Their journey had lasted perhaps thirty or forty days. They had died of hunger, of thirst, of suffocation, of being crushed, or of being beaten by the guards. There were even evidences of cannibalism. They were all practically dead when they arrived at Dachau Station. The SS men did not take the trouble to unload them. They simply decided to stand guard and shoot down any with enough strength left to emerge from the cattle cars. The corpses were strewn everywhere—on the rails, the steps, the platforms.

The men of the 45th Division had just made contact with the 42nd, here in the station. They too found themselves unable to breathe at what they saw. One soldier yelled: "Look, Bud, it's moving!" He pointed to something in motion among the cadavers. A louse-infested prisoner was crawling like a worm, trying to attract attention. He was the only survivor.

"I never saw anything like it in my life," said Lieutenant Harold Mayer. "Every one of my men became raving mad. We turned off toward the east, going around the compound, without even taking the trouble to reconnoiter first. We were out to avenge them." . . .

The ire of the men of the First Battalion, 157th Regiment, was to mount even higher as they got closer to the Lager [camp] of the deportees. The dead were everywhere—in the ditches, along the side streets, in the garden before a small building with chimneys—and there was a huge mountain of corpses inside the yard of this building, which they now understood to be the crematorium. And finally there was the ultimate horror—the infernal sight of those thousands and thousands of living skeletons, screaming like banshees, on the other side of the placid poplars.

When some of the SS men on the watchtowers started to shoot into the mobs of prisoners, the Americans threw all caution to the winds. They opened fire on the towers with healthy salvos. The SS men promptly came down the ladders, their hands reaching high. But now the American GI saw red. He shot the Germans down with a telling blast, and to make doubly sure sent a final shot into their fallen bodies. Then the hunt started for any other Germans in SS uniforms. Within a quarter of an hour there was not a single one of the Hitler henchmen alive within the camp.

In the SS refectory, one soldier had been killed while eating a plate of beans. He still held a spoonful in his hand. At the signal center, the SS man in charge of the switchboard was slumped over his panel, blood running down to the receiver, the busy signal from Munich still ringing in his unheeding ear. At the power plant, the SS foreman had been beaten to death with shovels by a Polish prisoner and his Czech assistant. After that, they had been able to cut the high-voltage current from the barbed-wire fences around the camp.

Margaret Freyer
THE FIRE-BOMBING OF DRESDEN

In an attempt to shatter German morale and to support the Russians who were advancing west into Germany, in early 1945 the Allies planned to mass bomb several large cities in East Germany. They believed that such attacks, particularly if they destroyed railyards, would hinder the movement of German reinforcements to the Russian front. On February 13–14, Allied planes dropped tons of high explosive bombs and incendiaries packed with highly combustible chemicals on the relatively defenseless city of Dresden. The bombings created a firestorm that turned the city into an inferno. A landmark cultural center, famous for its splendid architecture, and devastated some 30,000 inhabitants, many of them refugees fleeing the advancing Russians, perished, and thousands of others suffered horrific wounds.

The massive destruction of Dresden has aroused a historical controversy regarding the morality of terror bombing civilians. The German Far Right has maintained that the firebombings of German cities, particularly Dresden, were war crimes that equalled or exceeded what the Nazis had done, and that the Allied leadership should be labeled war criminals. And some British and American commentators have called the bombing a criminal act. Dresden, they argue, was of no military importance and with the war nearly won its destruction was totally unnecessary. Defenders of the raid point out that Dresden was a major railway junction that could be used for transporting troops to fight the Russians, its factories produced military gunsights, radar equipment, gas masks and parts for the German air force, and fuses for anti-aircraft shells, and that, with the Germans offering strong resistance on both fronts, there was no certainty that the war would end shortly. Moreover, Allied bombing of German cities was the price Germany paid for initiating this policy of destroying civilian targets—Guernica (1937) during the Spanish Civil War, Warsaw (1939), Rotterdam (1940), London (1940), Stalingrad (1942)—in order to terrorize the population.

Margaret Freyer (born 1920), who barely escaped being sent to a concentration camp by the Gestapo for telling political jokes, took shelter in a cellar during the first wave of the attack. During a lull in the bombing, she left the damaged building and went to her friend Ceci's apartment. When the sirens sounded again, she and Ceci, thirty nine other women, and Ceci's husband fled to the building's cellar. In the following excerpt, Freyer describes the horror of the fire-bombing.

Out of here—nothing but out! Three women went up the stairs in front of us, only to come rushing down again, wringing their hands. 'We can't get out of here! Everything outside is burning!' they cried. Cenci and I went up to make sure. It was true.

Then we tried the 'Breakthrough' which had been installed in each cellar, so people could exit from one cellar to the other. But here we met only thick smoke which made it impossible to breathe.

So we went upstairs. The back door, which opened on to the back yard and was made partly of glass, was completely on fire. It would have been madness to touch it. And at the front entrance, flames a metre and a half high came licking at short intervals into the hall.

In spite of this, it was clear that we could not stay in the building unless we wanted to suffocate. . . .

I made a last attempt to convince everyone in the cellar to leave, because they would suffocate if they did not; but they didn't want to. And so I left alone—and all the people in that cellar suffocated. Most died down there, but three women were found outside the door, amongst them Cenci. I cried bitterly when I found out that I was the only one who had escaped from that cellar.

I stood by the entrance and waited until no flames came licking in, then I quickly slipped through and out into the street. . . .

A witches' cauldron was waiting for me out there: no street, only rubble nearly a metre high, glass, girders, stones, craters. I tried to get rid of the sparks by constantly patting them off my coat. It was useless. I stopped doing it, stumbled, and someone behind me called out: 'Take your coat off, it's started to burn.' In the pervading extreme heat I hadn't even noticed. I took off the coat and dropped it.

Next to me a woman was screaming continually: 'My den's burning down, my den's burning down,' and dancing in the street. As I go on, I can still hear her screaming but I don't see her again. I run, I stumble, anywhere. I don't even know where I am any more, I've lost all sense of direction because all I can see is three steps ahead.

Suddenly I fall into a big hole—a bomb crater, about six metres wide and two metres deep, and I end up down there lying on top of three women. I shake them by their clothes and start to scream at them, telling them that they must get out of here—but they don't move any more. I believe I was severely shocked by this incident; I seemed to have lost all emotional feeling. Quickly, I climbed across the women, pulled my suitcase after me, and crawled on all fours out of the crater.

To my left I suddenly see a woman. I can see her to this day and shall never forget it. She carries a bundle in her arms. It is a baby. She runs, she falls, and the child flies in an arc into the fire. It's only my eyes which take this in; I myself feel nothing. The woman remains lying on the ground, completely still. Why? What for? I don't know, I just stumble on. The fire-storm is incredible, there are calls for help and screams from somewhere but all around is one single inferno. I hold another wet handkerchief in front of my mouth, my hands and my face are burning; it feels as if the skin is hanging down in strips. . . .

In front of me is something that might be a street, filled with a hellish rain of sparks which look like enormous rings of fire when they hit the ground. I have no choice. I must go through. I press another wet handkerchief to my mouth and almost get through, but I fall and am convinced that I cannot go on. It's hot.

Hot! My hands are burning like fire. I just drop my suitcase, I am past caring, and too weak. At least, there's nothing to lug around with me any more.

I stumbled on towards where it was dark. Suddenly, I saw people again, right in front of me. They scream and gesticulate with their hands, and then—to my utter horror and amazement—I see how one after the other they simply seem to let themselves drop to the ground. I had a feeling that they were being shot, but my mind could not understand what was really happening. Today I know that these unfortunate people were the victims of lack of oxygen. They fainted and then burnt to cinders. I fall then, stumbling over a fallen woman and as I lie right next to her I see how her clothes are burning away. Insane fear grips me and from then on I repeat one simple sentence to myself continuously: 'I don't want to burn to death—no, no burning—I don't want to burn!' Once more I fall down and feel that I am not going to be able to get up again, but the fear of being burnt pulls me to my feet. Crawling, stumbling, my last handkerchief pressed to my mouth . . . I do not know how many people I fell over. I knew only one feeling: that I must not burn. . . .

I try once more to get up on my feet, but I can only manage to crawl forward on all fours. I can still feel my body, I know I'm still alive. Suddenly, I'm standing up, but there's something wrong, everything seems so far away and I can't hear or see properly any more. As I found out later, like all the others, I was suffering from lack of oxygen. I must have stumbled forwards roughly ten paces when I all at once inhaled fresh air.

[The next day I searched for my fiancé] amongst the dead, because hardly any living beings were to be seen anywhere. What I saw is so horrific that I shall hardly be able to describe it. Dead, dead, dead everywhere. Some completely black like charcoal. Others completely untouched, lying as if they were asleep. Women in aprons, women with children sitting in the trams as if they had just nodded off. Many women, many young girls, many small children, soldiers who were only identifiable as such by the metal buckles on their belts, almost all of them naked. Some clinging to each other in groups as if they were clawing at each other.

From some of the debris poked arms, heads, legs, shattered skulls. The static water-tanks were filled up to the top with dead human beings, with large pieces of masonry lying on top of that again. Most people looked as if they had been inflated, with large yellow and brown stains on their bodies. People whose clothes were still glowing . . . I think I was incapable of absorbing the meaning of this cruelty any more, for there were also so many little babies, terribly mutilated; and all the people lying so close together that it looked as if someone had put them down there, street by street, deliberately.

I then went through the Grosser Garten and there is one thing I did realise. I was aware that I had constantly to brush hands away from me, hands which belonged to people who wanted me to take them with me, hands which clung to me. But I was much too weak to lift anyone up.

Joseph Goebbels
"THE MORALE OF THE GERMAN PEOPLE, BOTH AT HOME AND AT THE FRONT, IS SINKING EVER LOWER"

In his diary, Joseph Goebbels (1897–1945), the cynical and sinister head of the propaganda ministry, recorded his impressions of Germany in the last weeks of the war. The following selections from his diary show Goebbels' concern with German morale, particularly as affected by devastating air raids.

March 8 {1945}

During the last 24 hours the air war has again raged over Reich territory with devastating effect. It was the turn of Magdeburg and even more of Dessau. The greater part of Dessau is a sheet of flame and totally destroyed; yet another German city which has been largely flattened. In addition reports coming in from towns recently attacked, Chemnitz in particular, make one's hair grow grey. Yet once more it is frightful that we have no defence worth mentioning with which to oppose the enemy air war.

The Party Chancellery is now planning a special operation to raise the troops' morale. . . . Evidence of demoralization is now to be seen. . . . Desertions have reached a considerable level. . . . Again and again one hears that the enemy air bombardment is at the bottom of it all. It is understandable that a people which has been subjected for years to the fire-effect of a weapon against which it has no defence, should gradually lose its courage.

March 12

The morale of the German people, both at home and at the front, is sinking ever lower. The Reich propaganda agencies are complaining very noticeably about this. The people thinks that it is facing a perfectly hopeless situation in this war. Criticism of our war strategy does not now stop short even of the Führer himself. . . . It must always be pointed out, however, that the present level of morale must not be confused with definite defeatism. The people will continue to do their duty and the front-line soldier will defend himself as far as he has a possibility of doing so. These possibilities are becoming increasingly limited, however, primarily owing to the enemy's air superiority. The air terror which rages uninterruptedly over German home territory makes people thoroughly despondent. One feels so impotent against it that no one can now see a way out of the dilemma. The total paralysis of transport in West Germany also contributes to the mood of increasing pessimism among the German people.

March 13

. . . [P]eople in Eisenhower's headquarters are clear that they still face a titanic struggle in the West. They declare that on both sides war is being waged without mercy and that there is no question whatsoever of the German Wehrmacht yielding. Above all people in Eisenhower's headquarters are deeply impressed by the fact that all German prisoners of war still have faith in victory and—as they explicitly state—believe in Hitler with well-nigh mystical fanaticism. . . .

The Jews are re-emerging. Their spokesman is the well known notorious Leopold Schwarzschild [former newspaper editor, who had emigrated to America]; he is now arguing in the American press that under no circumstances should Germany be given lenient treatment. Anyone in a position to do so should kill these Jews off like rats. In Germany, thank God, we have already done a fairly complete job. I trust that the world will take its cue from this.

March 16

Mail received testifies to a deep-seated lethargy throughout the German people degenerating almost into hopelessness. There is very sharp criticism of the Luftwaffe but also of the entire national leadership. The latter is accused of being over-ambitious in its policy and strategy, of having been negligent in its conduct of the war, particularly in the air, and this is given as the main reason for our misfortunes.

March 21

The number killed in air raids up to December inclusive is reported as 353,000—a horrifying figure which becomes even more terrible when one adds the 457,000 wounded. This is a war within a war, sometimes more frightful than the war at the front. The homeless are simply innumerable. The air war has turned the Reich into one great heap of ruins. In the last 24 hours a further crazy series of air raids has been reported, particularly on the west of the Reich.

March 23

The letters I receive evince profound apathy and resignation. All refer quite openly to the leadership crisis. All the letter-writers show marked aversion to Göring, Ley and Ribbentrop.[1] Unfortunately even the Führer is now more frequently referred to in critical terms. I get off somewhat more lightly in the letters I receive but that must not be over-estimated. Everything must be looked at relatively. I think that my work too is no longer being totally effective today. A fateful development seems to me to be that now neither the Führer in person nor the National-Socialist concept nor the National-Socialist movement are immune from criticism. Many Party members, moreover, are now beginning to waver. All our set-backs are unanimously ascribed to Anglo-American air superiority.

March 26

As we know, the Americans succeeded in taking our Saar front in rear. The Army fighting on the Siegfried Line was withdrawn too late and largely fell into enemy hands. The troops' morale was correspondingly low. That of the civil population was even worse; in many places people opposed the troops and placed obstacles in the way of the defence. To a great extent the tank barriers constructed in the hinterland were captured by the enemy without a fight. I [blame] Slesina [head of the propaganda office

---

[1]Reichsmarschall Hermann Göring headed the German airforce. Robert Ley headed the Nazi German Labor Front. Joachim von Ribbentrop was the Nazi foreign minister from 1938 to 1945.

in Westmark] with the fact that not a single symbol of resistance has emerged in the West, like Breslau or Königsberg, for instance, in the East. His explanation is that people in the West have been so worn down by the months and years of enemy air raids that they prefer an end to this horror rather than an endless horror.

March 29

The military situation in the West is characterised mainly by sinking morale both among the civil population and among the troops. This loss of morale implies great danger for us since a people and an army no longer prepared to fight cannot be saved, however great the reinforcements in men and weapons. In Siegburg, for instance, a women's demonstration took place outside the Town Hall demanding the laying down of arms and capitulation.

March 30

As far as morale is concerned, I am firmly convinced that, now that the Führer has removed from me the impediment of the Reich Press Officer, I can get going again. I shall very quickly purge the Press Section of refractory and defeatist elements and can now carry on propaganda against the West which will be in no way inferior to that against the East. Anti-Anglo-American propaganda is now the order of the day. Only if we can demonstrate to our people that Anglo-American intentions towards them are no different from those of the Bolshevists will they adopt a different attitude to the enemy in the West. If we succeeded in stiffening the German people against the bolshevists and instilling hatred into them, why should we not succeed in doing so against the Anglo-Americans!

Marie Neumann
"WE'RE IN THE HANDS OF A MOB, NOT SOLDIERS, AND THEY'RE ALL DRUNK OUT OF THEIR MINDS"

As Russian troops advanced into Germany, many terrified German civilians fled westward, and not without reason. The invading Russians, seeking vengeance for the misery and ruin the Nazis had inflicted on their homeland and kinfolk, committed numerous atrocities against the conquered enemy. It quickly became official Soviet policy to prevent the perpetration of such personal acts of revenge and mayhem.

Marie Neumann of Baerwalde in Pomerania was one of the victims of this "terrible revenge." She put her nightmare in writing in 1948. Thirty years later, after reading *Nemesis at Potsdam* by Alfred-Maurice de Zayas, she sent the author her story. Following an exchange of letters and two personal visits, de Zayas was convinced she was telling the truth and later incorporated her testimony into a book about the postwar fate of Germans in Eastern Europe. Frau Neumann eventually left the Soviet zone of occupation and began a new life in West Germany. Unlike many others, she survived the acts of cruelty carried out against her and her family, described in the following passages from her 1948 account.

. . . My sister was on one side of the house with her seven-year-old daughter, and I was on the other side with her two other children and my husband. Someone had pressed a burning candle into his hand. My sister and I were raped again and again. The beasts lined up for us. During this time one of the military policemen held the door shut. I saw this because I was finally left alone before my sister was. Once she and her daughter both screamed in a most unnatural way, so that I thought they were being killed; and I wanted to go over to them when the policeman standing guard burst into our room and knocked my husband to the ground with his rifle. My niece Ilschen was crying and threw herself on my husband while the boy and I held the policeman's arm crying loudly, otherwise he would probably have killed my husband.

When we were finally granted a little peace and my husband had regained his senses, my sister came over to us and begged my husband to help her, asking, "Karl, what's going to happen to us?" My husband said, "I can't help any of you; we're in the hands of a mob, not soldiers, and they're all drunk out of their minds." I said, "Karl has to hide himself or they'll beat him to death; they've already beaten him half to death." My husband agreed with me and wanted to hide, but Grete held him back and begged him to think of her poor children. My husband then answered: "Grete, I just can't help anybody, but I'll stay with you; all we can do is hide, all of us, out in the hayloft." No sooner said than done. But just as we were climbing up into the loft, three men appeared; since there was snow outside, they had seen our tracks. We had to climb down; the two little girls were kissed and their mother raped again. She and her children cried so that it broke my heart. She cried out desperately: "O God, O God, why is this happening?" The men left, and my husband said: "They're going to kill me, they're going to kill all of you, and what they'll do to the children you can well imagine." My husband said that hiding now made no sense, we don't have any time to do it. I said: "Everybody get up there. I'll lock all the doors and they'll have to break

them down first," hoping that it would give us the time to hide ourselves. But I had forgotten in the excitement that the yard gates had been broken down already because we had been closing them whenever we could. We had just gotten into the loft when there came a howling and yelling of rabble in our yard, shooting like crazy into the ground, and then they came after us. It had gotten dark in the meantime and they had flashlights. They were civilians and some military wearing cornered hats with pompoms. What happened next I can barely write down, the pen sticks in my hand. They hanged us all in that hayloft, from the rafters, except for the children. The mob strangled them by hand with a rope.

Later I was told by the people who had taken shelter in the Hackbarth family's cellar on Polziner Street that they had heard our unnatural screams, even down in the cellar; but no one had the courage to come for us, they were all fighting for their own lives at the time. I came to on the floor, lying next to my loved ones. I didn't know yet what had happened to them, although I had a good idea, it was the details I lacked. Because I was first thrown to the floor when the mob caught us, hit on the head and raped, after which I was hanged. I had lost consciousness immediately. Later I heard voices. I was lying on the floor, four men kneeling around me. They said, "Frau komm," and when I tried to stand, I fell down at once. Later I found myself in the yard being held up by two men. They took me inside and laid me on a bed. One of the four men, a civilian, a Pole, stayed by me and asked: "Frau, who did?" I said: "The Russians." Then he hit me and said: "Russians, good soldiers. German SS, pigs, hang women and children." I fell into a fit of crying; it was impossible to stop. Then the other three came back in, but when they saw me, they left my apartment. Shortly thereafter a Russian came in carrying a whip, constantly yelling at me. Apparently he wanted me to be still, but I just couldn't. So he hit me once with the whip, then kept hitting the side of the bed. When that didn't work, he gave up and left my house. Then I heard voices in front of the house and got more scared than I was ever before or since. Seized by a cold panic I ran out to the little creek next to our garden, where the geese used to swim. I wanted to drown myself and tried for a long time until I was faint. But even that didn't bring my life to an end.

How I got through all this I don't know to this day. In any case someone had hauled me out of the creek. When I regained my senses I made my way to Fraulein Bauch's room on the ground floor of Schmechel's, the shopkeeper. Dear God how I was freezing because there were no windows or doors left in the place, and my clothes were wet; it was the night of March 4th to 5th and there was still snow and ice about. After a while I saw there was a bed in the room, so I laid down thinking I was alone in the place. But I quickly saw that someone had been sitting at the table and was now standing up, coming over to my bed, and, oh no, it was a Russian. Suddenly my whole miserable plight came before my eyes. I cried again and begged him if he wouldn't please shoot me. He shined a flashlight into my face, took off his coat and showed me his medals, saying that he was a first lieutenant and that I need not be afraid. He took a hand towel down from the wall and began to rub me dry. When he saw my throat, he asked: "Who did?" I said, "the Russians." "Yes, yes," he said, "Was the Bolsheviks, but now not Bolsheviks, now White Russians; White Russians good." He then took his bayonet and cut off my panties, whereupon I again was ready to die, for I didn't know what to expect anymore. He rubbed my legs dry; but I was still freezing and didn't know what I should do if I had frostbite. But then he took off my wedding ring and put it in his pocket. He asked me where my husband was, and then raped me in spite of my miserable condition. Afterwards he promised to send me to a German doctor. I was happy about that, but then I remembered there were no more German doctors in our area.

Shortly after he left four 18- to 20-year-old Russians appeared. Totally drunk, they pulled me out of bed and raped me in an unnatural way. In my condition I wasn't able to do more and fell beside the bed, so they kicked me with their boots, getting me just in the worst spot. I fainted again. When I came to, I crawled back into the bed. Then two more such bums showed up, but they left me alone as I was more dead than alive. I learned back then how much a human being can endure; I couldn't talk, couldn't cry, couldn't even utter a sound. They hit me a bit, which didn't matter to me since I couldn't feel anything, and then left me alone. I fell asleep out of sheer exhaustion.

When I awoke very early next morning, I realized again where I was. I quickly noticed an open wardrobe door, and inside was a dress. There was also a shirt and some underwear. So even though the things were much too small, I put them on; what was left of my clothes was still wet. I had to put the dress on leaving the back unfastened, to make it fit. There were no stockings to be found; mine had been wound up so tight they were like bones. Then I was visited by the Russians again. First one who apparently thought the room was empty, because when he saw me in bed, he left the room immediately. He came back with three more men; that first one wanted to hit me, but the officer wouldn't let him. So the first man pointed to the Hitler portrait on the wall which was full of bullet holes, and he said I was a Hitler Fascist. I said, "No! This isn't my house." He said, "Come! Go your house!" I had to walk ahead of them to my house and must have been a pretty sight. When I got there I saw a truck parked in front, and Russian soldiers were loading my slaughtered livestock into a car. The soldiers almost laughed themselves to death when they saw me. They indicated to their officer, their fingers tapping their heads, that I was probably crazy, and when four female soldiers appeared, they wanted to shoot me. But the officer didn't permit it. He asked about my neck, and I said, "Russian soldiers; my husband, sister, children, too." When he heard the word children, he was shocked. I asked him to come to the barn with me but he didn't want to, and I wasn't allowed to go back either. So I asked to go to the commandant.

He agreed at once with that and sent a soldier with me. But when we got to the corner by Kollatz, he indicated to me that I should continue along Neustettiner Street by myself. There were several men already in the marketplace, clearing things away. When I got to the butcher, Albert Nass's place, a Russian soldier told me to go in: Commander's Headquarters.

Inside the courtyard. . . .

[A] Russian soldier said, "German woman! Stairs there, go up." I was immediately made a prisoner for my effort, locked into a room with others.

When evening arrived, it was hell itself. One woman after another in our group was hauled out. The shoemaker's wife, Frau Graf, who was in her last month of pregnancy, was taken, also a woman from Wusterhausen, and the Peters' daughter Frau Schmidt. They were driven away by some soldier. The women screamed as they were being forced into the car, and the prisoners' room was full of screaming. Our nerves were raw. Then we heard the motor revving up, the Russians shone searchlights into the room through the window, so bright that several women screamed out that they were using flame throwers against us. The children cried miserably; it was horrible. Toward morning the women came back. Two came into the room and collapsed; the other woman was raped once more by the door before they let her in. They came to get me once during the night. I was taken into the slaughterhouse and assaulted on a feather bed right on the soil. When I came to, my neighbor Herr Held was crying over me. My neck had swollen so much over the past hours that I had trouble moving my mouth, and I was spitting blood.

Adolf Hitler
POLITICAL TESTAMENT

On April 30, 1945, with the Russians only blocks away, Hitler took his own life. In his political testament, which is printed below, he again resorted to his delusions and pathological obsessions, blaming the war on Jews.

More than thirty years have now passed since I in 1914 made my modest contribution as a volunteer in the first world-war that was forced upon the Reich.

In these three decades I have been actuated solely by love and loyalty to my people in all my thoughts, acts, and life. They gave me the strength to make the most difficult decisions which have ever confronted mortal man. I have spent my time, my working strength, and my health in these three decades.

It is untrue that I or anyone else in Germany wanted the war in 1939. It was desired and instigated exclusively by those international statesmen who were either of Jewish descent or worked for Jewish interests. I have made too many offers for the control and limitation of armaments, which posterity will not for all time be able to disregard for the responsibility for the outbreak of this war to be laid on me. I have further never wished that after the first fatal world war a second against England, or even against America, should break out. Centuries will pass away, but out of the ruins of our towns and monuments the hatred against those finally responsible whom we have to thank for everything, International Jewry and its helpers, will grow.

Three days before the outbreak of the German-Polish war I again proposed to the British ambassador in Berlin a solution to the German-Polish problem—similar to that in the case of the Saar district, under international control. This offer also cannot be denied. It was only rejected because the leading circles in English politics wanted the war, partly on account of the business hoped for and partly under influence of propaganda organized by international Jewry.

I also made it quite plain that, if the nations of Europe are again to be regarded as mere shares to be bought and sold by these international conspirators in money and finance, then that race, Jewry, which is the real criminal of this murderous struggle, will be saddled with the responsibility. I further left no one in doubt that this time not only would millions of children of Europe's Aryan peoples die of hunger, not only would millions of grown men suffer death, and not only hundreds of thousands of women and children be burnt and bombed to death in the towns, without the real criminal having to atone for this guilt, even if by more humane means.

After six years of war, which in spite of all set-backs, will go down one day in history as the most glorious and valiant demonstration of a nation's life purpose, I cannot forsake the city which is the capital of this Reich. As the forces are too small to make any further stand against the enemy attack at this place and our resistance is gradually being weakened by men who are as deluded as they are lacking in initiative, I should like, by remaining in this town, to share my fate with those, the millions of others, who have also taken upon themselves to do so. Moreover I do not wish to fall into the hands of an enemy who requires a new spectacle organized by the Jews for the amusement of their hysterical masses.

I have decided therefore to remain in Berlin and there of my own free will to choose death at the moment when I believe the position of the Fuehrer and Chancellor itself can no longer be held.

I die with a happy heart, aware of the immeasurable deeds and achievements of our soldiers at the front, our women at home, the achievements of our farmers and workers and the work, unique in history, of our youth who bear my name.

That from the bottom of my heart I express my thanks to you all, is just as self-evident as my wish that you should, because of that, on no account give up the struggle, but rather continue it against the enemies of the Fatherland, no matter where, true to the creed of the great Clausewitz.[1] From the sacrifice of our soldiers and from my own unity with them unto death, will in any case spring up in the history of Germany, the seed of a radiant renaissance of the National-Socialist movement and thus of the realization of a true community of nations.

Many of the most courageous men and women have decided to unite their lives with mine until the very last. I have begged and finally ordered them not to do this, but to take part in the further battle of the Nation. I beg the heads of the Armies, the Navy and the Air Force to strengthen by all possible means the spirit of resistance of our soldiers in the National-Socialist sense, with special reference to the fact that also I myself, as founder and creator of this movement, have preferred death to cowardly abdication or even capitulation.

May it, at some future time, become part of the code of honour of the German officer—as is already the case in our Navy—that the surrender of a district or of a town is impossible, and that above all the leaders here must march ahead as shining examples, faithfully fulfilling their duty unto death.

Before my death I expel the former Reichsmarschall Hermann Goering from the party and deprive him of all rights which he may enjoy by virtue of the decree of June 29th, 1941, and also by virtue of my statement in the Reichstag on September 1st, 1939, I appoint in his place Grossadmiral Doenitz, President of the Reich and Supreme Commander of the Armed Forces.

Before my death I expel the former Reichsfuehrer-SS and Minister of the Interior, Heinrich

---

[1]Karl von Clausewitz (1780–1831), a Prussian general whose classic treatise *On War* greatly influenced military strategy and tactics in the nineteenth and twentieth centuries.

Himmler, from the party and from all offices of State. In his stead I appoint Gauleiter Karl Hanke as Reichsfuehrer-SS and Chief of the German Police, and Gauleiter Paul Giesler as Reich Minister of the Interior.

Goering and Himmler, quite apart from their disloyalty to my person, have done immeasurable harm to the country and the whole nation by secret negotiations with the enemy, which they conducted without my knowledge and against my wishes, and by illegally attempting to seize power in the State for themselves.

In order to give the German people a government composed of honourable men,—a government which will fulfill its pledge to continue the war by every means—I appoint the following members of the new Cabinet as leaders of the nation:

President of the Reich: Doenitz.

Chancellor of the Reich: Dr. Goebbels.

Party Minister: Bormann. . . .

Several other appointees are listed; then the text resumes.

Although a number of these men, such as Martin Bormann, Dr. Goebbels, etc., together with their wives, have joined me of their own free will and did not wish to leave the capital of the Reich under any circumstances, but were willing to per-

ish with me here, I must nevertheless ask them to obey my request, and in this case set the interests of the nation above their own feelings. By their work and loyalty as comrades they will be just as close to me after death, as I hope that my spirit will linger among them and always go with them. Let them be hard, but never unjust, above all let them never allow fear to influence their actions, and set the honour of the nation above everything in the world. Finally, let them be conscious of the fact that our task, that of continuing the building of a National Socialist State, represents the work of the coming centuries, which places every single person under an obligation always to serve the common interest and to subordinate his own advantage to this end. I demand of all Germans, all National Socialists, men, women and all the men of the Armed Forces, that they be faithful and obedient unto death to the new government and its President.

Above all I charge the leaders of the nation and those under them to scrupulous observance of the laws of race and to merciless opposition to the universal poisoner of all peoples, international Jewry.

Given in Berlin, this 29th day of April 1945. 4:00 A.M.

Adolf Hitler.

Witnessed by

Dr. Josef Fuhr.   Wilhelm Buergdorf.

Martin Bormann.   Hans Krebs.

REVIEW QUESTIONS

1. According to Nerin E. Gun, how did the American soldiers react when they discovered conditions at Dachau?
2. What do you think was the reaction of Germans to the mass bombings of their cities and towns?
3. What signs did Joseph Goebbels remark on as evidence of sinking German morale? What did he consider the primary reason for this failure of nerve?
4. What do atrocities such as those described by Marie Neumann reveal about the nature of warfare? Do you think it is possible to wage war without awakening barbaric instincts in soldiers? Explain why or why not.
5. Compare Hitler's final testament with his speech to his generals in 1939 (see page 383). How had his views and expectations changed by the end of the war?

14 The Defeat of Japan

By the spring of 1942, the Japanese had conquered the coast of China, Indochina (Vietnam), Thailand, Burma, Malaya, the Dutch East Indies (Indonesia), and several Pacific islands, including the Philippines. But in June 1942 Japan suffered a major reversal at Midway when American carrier-based planes destroyed 4 aircraft carriers and 322 Japanese planes. American forces then attacked strategic islands held by Japan. American troops had to battle their way up beaches and through tropical jungles tenaciously defended by Japanese soldiers who believed that death was preferable to the disgrace of surrender. By early 1945 Japan's navy had been decimated and key islands lost. American submarines blockaded Japanese ports, greatly reducing the food supply, and American planes regularly bombed Japanese cities causing great damage and loss of life. With little chance of victory, Japan hoped to engage the United States in a war of attrition that would inflict many casualties on the Americans, thereby making them reluctant to invade the Japanese mainland and more amenable to a negotiated settlement that would permit Japan to retain parts of its empire. This is how they envisioned the forthcoming American invasion of the island of Okinawa located only 340 miles from mainland Japan.

Hiromichi Yahara
THE BATTLE FOR OKINAWA

Okinawa was the site of one of the bloodiest conflicts of the war. The Japanese had constructed a network of underground fortresses that withstood bombardment by American fighter-bombers and naval guns. Massed attacks by kamikaze pilots who deliberately crashed their planes into American ships resulted in many casualties. Several factors contributed to the American victory. Finding gaps that Japanese fire did not reach, small groups of soldiers moved forward and knocked out Japanese firing positions one at a time. Using fire hoses, special squads doused caves harboring Japanese troops with fuel and then set them afire. And unwise Japanese counterattacks fell prey to immense American firepower, causing the death of some of their best units.

In the following selection, from *The Battle of Okinawa* Colonel Hiromichi Yahara, a senior staff officer at Okinawa and one of a small percentage of Japanese combatants to survive the conflict, describes the last days of the battle.

On Sunday, June 17, a message from General Simon Buckner, the enemy commander, to General Ushijima came to our headquarters cave:

The forces under your command have fought bravely and well. Your infantry tactics have

merited the respect of your opponents in the battle for Okinawa.

Like myself you are an infantry general, long schooled and experienced in infantry warfare. You must surely realize the pitiful plight of your defense forces. You know that no reinforcements can reach you. I believe, therefore, that you understand as clearly as I, that the destruction of all Japanese resistance on the island is merely a matter of days. It will entail the necessity of my destroying the vast majority of your remaining troops.

General Buckner's proposal for us to surrender was, of course, an affront to Japanese tradition. General Ushijima's only reaction was to smile broadly and say, "The enemy has made me an expert on infantry warfare."

Lying on my bed in the dark room, I thought about the history of military surrenders. In modern warfare in the West, defeated commanders usually surrendered gracefully to the victors. This was generally true of white-race societies—from Napoleonic times, the Franco-Prussian War, the American Revolution and Civil War, down to World Wars I and II. Top commanders would generally be held responsible for defeats. And where commanders were killed, units below them were generally allowed to surrender on their own. To my limited recollection, there existed no cases of Western armies fighting to the death. When an army's value as a fighting force was obviously spent, they would take the course of surrendering.

In Japan, on the other hand, it was not uncommon for a losing commander and his subordinates to commit suicide. . . .

Thus, not to be taken prisoner became a fixed principle—part of our military education. . . .

At dawn on June 22, after three hours of violent machine-gun fire, Mabuni village was silent. That meant the end of Lieutenant Matsui and his platoon. I heard nearby tanks rumbling over the savaged earth. They bombarded our headquarters cave, which was empty and still as we waited to die. Colonel Sato visited General Cho, and Lieutenant Akinaga came to chat with me. Just before noon there was a tremendous explosion at the staff headquarters entrance. Smoke and dust blew inside and soldiers came rushing back to me. It was a phosphorous bomb, and we all put on gas masks. The

entrance was still open, and I heard footsteps and arrogant laughter. The enemy was approaching the entrance, and I shouted to Lieutenant Akinaga, "Hey, it's okay here! Defend the central shaft!" He ran to the shaft.

Katsuyama brought a memorandum I had left behind and, gasping for air, reported, "The hill is completely occupied by the enemy. They exploded a satchel charge at the main shaft, and there are many casualties around General Cho's quarters."

Akinaga dashed off to the main shaft. Ten minutes passed, and I thought he had been killed. If the enemy could pass through the shaft, they would get Generals Ushijima and Cho first. The rooms of the staff officers and adjutants would be cut off, and we would have no escape.

I approached the shaft cautiously, with flashlight in hand. Smoke and dust filled the air. There was no one to talk to—they were all dead. The smell of blood was everywhere. I shone the light at the base of the shaft, revealing a pile of ten soldiers. Expecting more assaults through the shaft, I hurried to leave the area, stepping on bodies as I went. There was a groan of pain. One still lived.

General Cho's room was completely blown up. He sat silently on a bed next to General Ushijima. Soldiers stood guarding them. Alone in a dark corner sat Miss Nakamoto, pale-faced, clenching her fists to fight back tears.

What had happened was this. As soon as Lieutenant Akinaga and his men reached the hilltop, they threw grenades at the enemy and were shot down. Lieutenant Ikeda and his men then tried to reach the top, but they were all shot and fell to the bottom of the shaft. To make matters worse, several grenades accidentally went off, causing more damage. In the medical room two girls were lying on beds among the wounded soldiers. They were unrecognizably disfigured. . . .

The enemy finally occupied the hilltop. They might penetrate the shaft at any moment. The only remaining entrance, the one facing the ocean, was now within their reach. Generals Ushijima and Cho knew well that their time was up, but they had not yet given the word about *hara-kiri*. They now ordered troops to retake the hilltop by nightfall and make a suicide charge on Mabuni the next morning. The generals would then commit suicide on the hilltop. I entrusted to Colonel Katsuno the task of retaking the hilltop. I stepped over the pile of corpses one more time and went to my room. It seemed empty, but one by one my men appeared out of the darkness.

Yahara then discusses failed suicide attacks to reclaim the cliff controlled by the Americans. With their situation now hopeless, two Japanese generals plan their own ritual suicide.

At midnight on June 23 we abandoned any effort to recover the hilltop. Generals Ushijima and Cho scheduled their *hara-kiri* for the morning. Both were fast asleep. The paymaster had yet to return from General Cho's room. I stared helplessly at the stalactites—like them, devoid of all energy and emotion. Time ticked away.

At 0300 General Ushijima summoned me to his room. Dressed in full uniform, he was sitting cross-legged. General Cho was drinking his favorite King of Kings whisky, and he was very intoxicated. They were surrounded by familiar faces. I solemnly saluted them but said nothing. . . .

The two generals exchanged poems back and forth. I could not hear them clearly, but I recall their mention that Japan could not exist without Okinawa. Later, I learned their final words.

General Ushijima's last poems:

Green grass of Yukushima, withered before
    autumn,
Will return in the spring to Momikoku.

and:

We spend arrows and bullets to stain
    heaven and earth,
Defending our homeland forever.

General Cho's last poem:

The devil foe tightly grips our southwest
    land,
His aircraft fill the sky, his ships control the
    sea;
Bravely we fought for ninety days inside a
    dream;
We have used up our withered lives,
But our souls race to heaven.

Time was running out. Everyone in the cave formed a line to pay their last respects. Major Ono, a man of innocent face and indomitable spirit, returned and reported that the final message had gone to Imperial General Headquarters. It read:

Your loyal army has successfully completed
preparations for homeland defense. . . .

Officers and men who had shared the hardships of war, as well as Miss Heshikiya and the other young women, came to pay their respects. The young women were scheduled to descend with the remaining soldiers and reach the caves along the cliff before daybreak. General Cho's orderly, Nakatsuka, gave them his canteen of precious water, saying he no longer needed it. Cho's personal assistant said, "Excellency, I am sorry I must leave before offering incense at your funeral." Cho gave a wry smile.

General Ushijima quietly stood up. General Cho removed his field uniform and followed with Paymaster Sato. Led by candlelight the solemn procession headed for the exit, with heavy hearts and limbs.

When they approached the cave opening, the moon shone on the South Seas. Clouds moved swiftly. The skies were quiet. The morning mist crept slowly up the deep valley. It was as if everything on earth trembled, waiting with deep emotion.

General Ushijima sat silently in the death seat, ten paces from the cave exit, facing the sea wall. General Cho and Sato sat beside him.

The *hara-kiri* assistant, Captain Sakaguchi, stood behind them. I was a few steps away. Soldiers stood at the exit, awaiting the moment.

On the back of General Cho's white shirt, in immaculate brush strokes, was the poem:

With bravery I served my nation,
With loyalty I dedicate my life.

By first light I could see this moral code written in his own hand, in large characters. General Cho looked over his shoulder at me with a beautifully divine expression and said solemnly, "Yahara! For future generations, you will bear witness as to how I died."

The master swordsman, Sakaguchi, grasped his great sword with both hands, raised it high above the general's head, then held back in his downward swing, and said, "It is too dark to see your neck. Please wait a few moments."

With the dawn, the enemy warships at sea would begin to fire their naval guns. Soldiers at the cave entrance were getting nervous. Granted their leave, they fled and ran down the cliff.

People were still nudging me toward the cave exit when a startling shot rang out. I thought for a moment it was the start of naval gun firing, but instead it was Sato committing suicide outside the cave. When that excitement subsided, the generals were ready. Each in turn thrust a traditional *hara-kiri* dagger into his bared abdomen. As they did so, Sakaguchi skillfully and swiftly swung his razor-edged sword and beheaded them. Ushijima first, then Cho.

Like a collapsed dam, the remaining soldiers broke ranks and ran down the cliff. I sat down outside the cave with Captain Sakaguchi, who declared with solemn amazement, "I did it!" His ashen face bore a look of satisfaction. Utterly exhausted, we watched the brightening sky. What a splendid last moment!

It marked a glorious end to our three months of hard battle, our proud 32nd Army, and the lives of our generals. It was 0430, June 23, 1945.

REVIEW QUESTIONS

1. What contrast did Hiromichi Yahara draw between defeated armies in the West and the Japanese experience?
2. What was Yahara's reaction to General Cho's suicide?

CHAPTER 14

Europe: A New Era

WHEN THE WAR IN EUROPE ENDED in May 1945, many areas lay devastated, none more so than the once-picturesque German city of Dresden, in which some 30,000 people had perished in a fire bombing by Allied planes in February 1945. Europe was faced with the awesome task of reconstructing a continent in ruins. *(dpa/Corbis)*

At the end of World War II, Winston Churchill lamented: "What is Europe now? A rubble heap, a charnel house, a breeding ground for pestilence and hate." Everywhere the survivors counted their dead. War casualties were relatively light in Western Europe. Britain and the Commonwealth suffered 460,000 casualties; France, 570,000; and Italy, 450,000. War casualties were heavier in the East: 5 million people in Germany, 6 million in Poland (including 3 million Jews), 1 million in Yugoslavia, and more than 25 million in the Soviet Union. The material destruction had been unprecedentedly heavy in the battle zones of northwestern Europe, northern Italy, and Germany, growing worse farther East, where Hitler's and Stalin's armies had fought without mercy to people, animals, and the environment. Industry, transportation, and communication had come to a virtual standstill. Now members of families searched for each other; prisoners of war made their way home; Jews from concentration camps or from hiding places returned to open life; and displaced persons by the millions sought refuge. Yet Europe did recover from this blight, and with astonishing speed.

The war produced a shift in power arrangements. The United States and the Soviet Union emerged as the two most powerful states in the world. The traditional Great Powers—Britain, France, and Germany— were now dwarfed by these superpowers. The United States had the atomic bomb and immense industrial might; the Soviet Union had the largest army in the world and was extending its dominion over Eastern Europe. With Germany defeated, the principal incentive for Soviet-American cooperation had evaporated.

After World War I, divisive nationalist passions intensified. After World War II, Western Europeans progressed toward unity. The Hitler years convinced many Europeans of the dangers inherent in extreme nationalism, and fear of the Soviet Union prodded them toward greater cooperation.

Some intellectuals, shocked by the irrationality and horrors of the Hitler era, drifted into despair. To these thinkers, life was absurd, without meaning; human beings could neither comprehend nor control it. In 1945, only the naive could have faith in continuous progress or believe in the essential goodness of the individual. The future envisioned by the philosophes seemed more distant than ever. Nevertheless, this profound disillusionment was tempered by hope. Democracy had, in fact, prevailed over Nazi totalitarianism and terror. Moreover, fewer intellectuals were now attracted to antidemocratic thought. The Nazi dictatorship convinced many of them, even some who had wavered in previous decades, that freedom and human dignity were precious ideals and that liberal constitutional government, despite its imperfections, was the best means of preserving these ideals. Perhaps, then, democratic institutions and values would spread throughout the globe, and the newly established United Nations would promote world peace.

1   The Aftermath: Devastation and Demoralization

In 1945 European cities everywhere were in rubble; bridges, railway systems, waterways, and harbors destroyed; farmlands laid waste; livestock killed; coal mines wrecked. Homeless and hungry people wandered the streets and roads. Europe faced the gigantic task of rebuilding.

Theodore H. White
"GERMANY: SPRING IN THE RUINS"

Political journalist Theodore H. White (1915–1986) covered postwar reconstruction and European politics during a more than five-year residence on the Continent in the late 1940s and early 1950s. In the following account, White recounted circumstances in Germany during the initial postwar years with an eye to the transformation he witnessed by 1951–1952.

Here and there in this Germany of 1945 lay little pockets of unscarred village and hamlet, bypassed by encircling armies or ignored by marauding bombers, their brown and gray church spires rising like accusing fingers to the sky from the sturdy, field-stone house of the peasants. But the roads that ran from village to town, from town to city were torn and ruptured by the passage of war; tanks had disemboweled the roadbeds, artillery and planes had shattered the bridges. And the roads led to cities, one more appalling than the other—rubble heaps of stone and brick, rank with the smell of sewage and filth, dirty with the dust of destruction working its way into clothes, linen, skin and soul.

The forlorn people who lived in the ruins in those Winter Years could feel little beyond hunger. The clear German skin which glows so pink and ruddy in health shrunk sallow over shriveled bodies, or puffed over the unhealthy putty of children bloated by hunger edema. By April of 1947 even the conquerors' statisticians admitted that the daily German ration had fallen to 1,040 calories, or thirty-three per cent below the scientific calculation of the minimum necessary to sustain life. Allied health teams stopped Germans on street corners and weighed them bodily to confirm these figures, and found the nation

decaying. White-faced men and women collapsed at their jobs for lack of food. Dignified people sought jobs as clerks or servants in the office of the occupying armies because in the barracks of the conquerors they got one hot meal of stew a day, which kept them alive. The United States government appropriated money to give every German school child one hot meal a day in his classroom. When Germans could think of anything beyond food they thought of clothes; the leather jerkins of German workingmen and their black leather boots had frayed and cracked; the ugly woolen stockings of German women were thin and holed; children played in the streets in the cut-down Wehrmacht jackets and pants of their fathers. The search for shelter was a nightmare; for this country, forty per cent of whose homes had been smashed, was being forced to absorb and shelter eight million refugees thrust back into it. For a German the perspective of ambition was the search to find for his family two rooms with a toilet and running water, and, if this were found, he dreamed cautiously of a home where the toilet would not be in the kitchen where the food was cooked, but in a real toilet compartment of remembered privacy.

Values withered: Girls roamed the streets, sleeping with the conquering soldiers for a candy bar, a cake of soap, a tin of Quaker Oats, coming home to once-chaste beds dirty with disease. Money was meaningless, cigarettes were currency; two cartons of American cigarettes bought a set of Meissen china, three cartons bought a Leica camera, two cigarettes were a tip. Businessmen became pirates. Families dissolved.

By an enormous, instinctive act of national resolution Germans put thinking out of their minds and concentrated on simple things: how to find a job, and how to work. For only by working could one find food, find clothes, find a roof. Even work was difficult; Germany could make only a strictly limited quantity of steel, of aluminum, of sulfur, of copper. She was forbidden to

make again the vast range of intricate machinery in which lay her commercial strength; she could not build airplanes, could not fly airplanes, could not synthesize rubber or gasoline. One worked at what came to hand. In the Ruhr workmen stood in sullen silence and watched the dismantlers surveying for removal of generators, rolling mills and steel ovens. Krupp sat in his prison and British engineers carefully paced the jungle of his Essen works marking with white chalk the machine tools, the drop forges, the presses to be taken away. At the Bochumer Verein, which had made both submarine assemblies and the finest crucible steels, the newest and most efficient shops were dismantled.

Gerold Frank
"THE TRAGEDY OF THE DPS [DISPLACED PERSONS]"

The term "Displaced Persons" was coined at the end of World War II to describe the unprecedented number of people who were uprooted by almost six years of violence. The geographic and personal circumstances of these individuals, who numbered in the millions, were extraordinarily diverse: Jewish and non-Jewish concentration camp survivors; laborers from the agricultural, mining, and heavy industrial sectors forced to toil for the Nazi war effort or willing to pursue employment within the Third Reich; German nationals who fled their homes in eastern Germany, Poland, Hungary, Czechoslovakia, and Romania to escape the advancing Red Army, or who suddenly found themselves within redrawn borderlands (East Prussia, Silesia, the Sudetenland) that were no longer part of Germany; and German and non-German members of the Wehrmacht who either could not return to their homes in Soviet-occupied Eastern Europe, or sought to traverse war-torn Germany to rejoin their families.

DP camps were established by the Allies to feed and house these refugees until they could move on, but the problem was so vast that the newly founded United Nations was compelled to create a UN Relief and Rehabilitation Commission to coordinate DP assistance. The following description deals specifically with the problems confronting Jewish refugees who wished to emigrate to Palestine, then still a mandate of Britain, which restricted immigration of Jews.

Prague

One overwhelming truth emerges from a tour of investigation through displaced-persons camps in Germany. It is that these people must be taken out—at once. If we fail to act, within six months we shall run the risk of having

100,000 psychiatric cases on our hands, plus the complete demoralization of a people; and it will take not only psychiatric help but the Army to prevent the possibility not only of their killing Germans but of killing themselves. There is a limit to how long a human being can be told "no" and be denied everything he needs and on which he counts.

Constant denial, constant frustration, unending disillusion—these are driving Jews who survived concentration camps to a point beyond despair. They are on the verge of moral collapse. The only substance on which they exist is Palestine. It dominates their every waking moment. The word itself is incandescent with meaning to them. One is appalled even to contemplate what might now be taking place among them if there were no Palestine on which to fasten their hopes and with which to identify their future.

The actual liberation was a miraculous event. For the Jewish DPs it was almost like the Messianic deliverance, and with it they expected a kind of universal welcome and universal repentance by the world which had permitted them to suffer such monstrous cruelties. There was no welcome. There was no repentance. Instead, there came to them the dawning realization that they were nuisances, problems, pariahs.

So far, I've heard no talk of vengeance—only this grim determination to go to Palestine—but the path may become too difficult; the world may have learned the art of keeping them out of Palestine better than they have learned the art of getting into it. In such an event it is possible that the determination to have their own way for once, if allowed no other outlet, will explode disastrously.

No one who has visited a DP center is likely to have any illusions about it. Physically it is a transient overnight camp in which people are sitting on packed bags with no alternative but to remain day after day. Psychologically it is an institution where creative instincts are thwarted, where there is no real opportunity for work, no incentive to build, no possibility of saving for the future. . . .

And why is Palestine, as the subcommittee of the Anglo-American Committee of Inquiry

on Palestine repeatedly asked DPs in camp after camp, why is Palestine uppermost in their minds—not the United States or Britain, with their millions of free Jewish citizens? These men and women and young people replied in words not soon forgotten that Palestine has become to them a symbol with infinite meanings, of which, perhaps, the most significant is personal dignity. This is the quality of which Hitler robbed the survivors of his massacres in the eyes of the world. Palestine means security for them, not in the sense of safety but in the sense of being wanted by those among whom they live. The committee questioned a group of a dozen ragged Jewish boys and girls who infiltrated into the American zone after they returned to Poland and found none of their families alive. Who organized these youngsters into a group, the committee asked, remembering tales of well-fed Jews with pockets full of money.

"Organized?" repeated a 20-year-old girl, puzzled. "We met on the road, first three of us and then two more, and so on. Our mothers, fathers, brothers and sisters were all burned by the Germans and so we became brothers and sisters to each other." Individually they are wanted by each other, these DPs, and by no one else; collectively they are wanted by no one save the Jews of Palestine. This symbol of Palestine has in it the desire to stand up proudly, to cast off the stigma of an inferior race, to cease being objects of contempt and toleration. "When will you let us go home to Palestine and no longer hear all these terrible things said about us?" asked a 13-year-old boy at the Fahrenwald camp near Munich. "When shall I be able to be a Jew again?" In this symbol of Palestine there is above all else a desire to go to the end of the line, to cease being a wanderer, to reach *home*.

This helps to explain the poll of their attitudes on emigration taken under UNRRA auspices at the request of the committee. It resulted in more than 18,700 of 19,000 answering "Palestine"; when asked to list their second choice, 98 percent renamed Palestine. This is no rationalization of the fact that there is no chance to emigrate to the democracies.

They are convinced that their only hope is to begin life anew on their own soil. "Yes," said Israel Wilence of the Greifenberg camp, 25 miles from Augsburg, "I know that six million Jews are living happily in America. They lived happily in Germany. I don't say what happened in Germany will happen in America, but I don't want even to take the chance that it will happen." . . .

The Jewish DPs hate Germany with a pathological hate. They detest Europe and they distrust the world. The one in seven who survived starvation, torture, slave camps, gas chambers and crematoria has had agonizing time to think and draw conclusions. They wrote "Palestine" as first choice and second choice, but when they were told, as in the Fürth DP center near Nuremberg, not to make the second choice the same as the first, 500 of the 2,000 there wrote as second choice the single word "crematorium."

A German Expellee from Czechoslovakia "GERMANS WERE DRIVEN OUT OF THEIR HOMELAND LIKE DOGS"

Millions of Germans were expelled from Poland, Czechoslovakia, Yugoslavia, Romania, and Hungary, places where their ancestors had lived for centuries, by vengeful Eastern Europeans. Leaders in these countries, driven by nationalist aspirations, welcomed an opportunity to rid their nations of an ethnic minority, particularly since many of these Germans had aided the Nazi occupiers. In 1945–1946, some 12 million to 13 million Germans were driven westward either fleeing the Russians or in a massive campaign of ethnic cleansing. Expelled from their homes, often with only a few minutes' warning, they had to leave virtually all their property and possessions behind; the Nazis had done exactly the same to Jews and Poles. Herded into internment camps they were brutalized by Polish and Czech guards who relished the opportunity to torment Germans. Tens of thousands of expellees died from malnutrition, disease, exposure, and mistreatment; thousands more committed suicide. Estimates for the number of refugees who perished before reaching their destination in Germany range from 500,000 to 1.7 million. The following selection describes the suffering endured by Germans expelled from Czechoslovakia.

The Russians occupied Roemerstadt on May 4, 1945. A few days after their entry into town the Czech Svoboda Army came in and took over. All Czech soldiers were given three days' right to loot at will. They took anything they fancied. But that was just the start of the terror. An official proclamation was announced, whereby all Germans had to give up their radios and cameras. The death penalty threatened those who did not follow this order. The "N" patch (N is the first letter in the Czech word for German, *Nemec*) had to be worn by all Germans beginning in May 1945 until their expulsion.

In August 1945, the first Germans were driven out of their homeland like dogs. Individual family members were chosen at will and driven off to the railway station, where cattle cars stood ready. The cars had no roofs, and they were literally stuffed full of people. Old people as well as small children were forced into these cars, getting nothing to eat or drink. In these first days of expulsion the temperature averaged

30 degrees Centigrade [86 degrees Fahrenheit]. We were standing some 10 to 15 meters from these cattle cars but were not allowed to even once bring water or food to our relatives and friends. Even a priest, whose parents were part of the transport, was denied permission to bring something to his folks. He cried bitterly because he couldn't give his suffering parents so much as a drink of water. No one can imagine the pain and suffering that reigned over these families at such a sight, and as a consequence of these events. Probably because of protests from abroad these humiliating expulsions were stopped for a while. In any case, a second wave of expulsions began in January 1946. The regulations were that Germans could take only 50 kg of clothing and personal items, and 500 Reischsmarks with them. Whoever had more money than that had to give it up without restitution. My wife, her parents and I were expelled on March 1, 1946. First we were all assembled in a camp where our baggage was inspected, weighed and anything over 50 kg confiscated. Furthermore, things were taken from us which had been allowed by the regulations but which the Czechs took a fancy to. There were incidents where people had their whole legal 50 kg taken away from them. After this first check we were body searched. First we had to leave our rooms so that they could be searched for any hidden jewelry or other objects left behind. Even the straw mattresses were emptied. Next we were taken one by one for the body search. I even had to take off my shoes for inspection, in the soles of which I had sewn 2,000 Reischsmarks. Luckily I had been wearing them this way for a few weeks and they were worn enough to escape detection. So I got through this part with little difficulty. Had they found the money, I would have been whipped, for it had been strictly forbidden to take more than 500 Reischsmarks. On March 3, 1946, like the others before us, we were loaded onto cattle cars. The entire train was under heavy Czech military guard. As we headed off in the direction of Germany, no one knew what was to become of us.

Regarding confiscation of homes and businesses, I personally witnessed this as well. As already noted, my wife's parents owned a bakery and a store for groceries and shoes in Roemerstadt, Kirchenplatz 8. It was the last German business in the area. On the evening of October 21, 1945, around 6 P.M., a group of soldiers came in, locked us in a room, posted a guard at the door and kept us prisoner until 10 P.M. During that time two men ransacked the bakery, the other business and the apartment. Around 10 P.M. we had to go up to the second floor where we were again locked in. The next day we were taken to jail, where I was beaten. The reason for the beating was not that I had broken some law, it was because I was German. That was also the reason for our imprisonment. Moreover, as we discovered later, during the time we were in jail our home and business had been completely looted. Since they couldn't prove Party membership or any other transgressions on our part, we were released on the night of October 31 around 11 P.M. Fortunately we had a place to stay with some relatives, as we were not permitted to return to our own house. Thus, overnight, our property and possessions were gone.

REVIEW QUESTION

1. Immediately after the war, what were the main concerns of Germans? Of Jews in DP camps? Of Germans living in Czechoslovakia?

2 The Cold War

After World War II the first Western statesman to express his alarm over Soviet expansionism was Winston Churchill, the doughty and articulate wartime leader of Great Britain. While noting, on a visit to America, that the United States stood "at the pinnacle of world power," he warned of the Soviet challenge. It threatened the liberties that were a traditional part of Western democracy. Prompted by the failure of the attempt to appease Hitler and by the war experience, he urged military strength and political cooperation between Western Europe and the United States in order to stem the Communist advance.

In the United States, George Kennan, a foreign service officer with extensive experience in Eastern Europe and Moscow, soon followed Churchill's lead, advocating the thwarting of Soviet ambitions by a policy of containment. Churchill and Kennan formulated the Western outlook in what came to be called "the Cold War." At his first major Party Congress, Nikita Khrushchev, Stalin's successor in the Soviet Union, set forth the Soviet position, foreseeing the victory of Communism by peaceful means. By 1956 the ideological positions of the chief antagonists in the Cold War had been fixed.

Winston Churchill
THE "IRON CURTAIN"

In a famous speech at Fulton, Missouri, on March 5, 1946, when he was no longer in office, Churchill articulated his views on the duty of Western democracies in the face of Soviet expansion. Significant passages from that speech, in which the term *iron curtain* was first used, follow.

A shadow has fallen upon the scenes so lately lighted by the Allied victory. Nobody knows what Soviet Russia and its Communist international organization intends to do in the immediate future, or what are the limits, if any, to their expansive and proselytizing tendencies. I have a strong admiration and regard for the valiant Russian people and for my wartime comrade, Marshal Stalin. There is sympathy and good will in Britain—and I doubt not here also—toward the peoples of all the Russias and a resolve to persevere through many differences and rebuffs in establishing lasting friendships. We understand the Russian need to be secure on her western frontiers from all renewal of German aggression. We welcome her to her rightful place among the leading nations of the world. Above all we welcome constant, frequent and growing contacts between the Russian people and our own people on both sides of the Atlantic. It is my duty, however, to place before you certain facts about the present position in Europe—I am sure I do not wish to, but it is my duty, I feel, to present them to you.

From Stettin in the Baltic to Trieste in the Adriatic, an iron curtain has descended across the Continent. Behind that line lie all the capitals of the ancient states of Central and Eastern Europe. Warsaw, Berlin, Prague, Vienna, Budapest, Belgrade, Bucharest and Sofia, all these famous cities and the populations around them lie in the Soviet sphere and all are subject in one form or another, not only to Soviet influence but to a very high and increasing measure of control from Moscow. . . . The Communist parties, which were very small in all these eastern states of Europe, have been raised to pre-eminence and power far beyond their numbers and are seeking everywhere to obtain totalitarian control. Police governments are prevailing in nearly every case. . . . Turkey and Persia are both profoundly alarmed and disturbed at the claims which are made upon them and at the pressure being exerted by the Moscow government. An attempt is being made by the Russians in Berlin to build up a quasi-Communist party in their zone of occupied Germany. . . . Whatever conclusions may be drawn from these facts—and facts they are—this is certainly not the liberated Europe we fought to build up. Nor is it one which contains the essentials of permanent peace. . . . What we have to consider here today while time remains, is the permanent prevention of war and the establishment of conditions of freedom and

democracy as rapidly as possible in all countries. Our difficulties and dangers will not be removed by closing our eyes to them. They will not be removed by mere waiting to see what happens; nor will they be relieved by a policy of appeasement. What is needed is a settlement and the longer this is delayed the more difficult it will be and the greater our dangers will become. From what I have seen of our Russian friends and allies during the war, I am convinced that there is nothing they admire so much as strength, and there is nothing for which they have less respect than for military weakness. . . . If the western democracies stand together in strict adherence to the principles of the United Nations Charter, their influence for furthering these principles will be immense and no one is likely to molest them. If, however, they become divided or falter in their duty, and if these all-important years are allowed to slip away, then indeed catastrophe may overwhelm us all.

Nikita S. Khrushchev
REPORT TO THE TWENTIETH PARTY CONGRESS

After World War II, the Korean War, and the escalation of the nuclear arms race into the deployment of hydrogen bombs, the Soviets perceived themselves to be in a worldwide struggle with the Western capitalists. In the Soviet view, the socialist system was advancing, whereas the capitalist system was in decline; the Cold War represented a desperate effort to preserve capitalism. Communists especially attacked the American desire to deal with the socialist countries from a position of superior strength.

Soviet international policy gave special attention to the aspirations of "the people of the East," the Asians and Africans emerging from colonial rule. Soviets described American aid to developing countries as a new form of imperialism, whereas Soviet aid was pictured as humanitarian assistance in the struggle against colonialism.

Nikita Khrushchev summed up the Soviet perspective on world affairs for the benefit of a new generation of Soviet citizens. As first secretary of the Communist party, he delivered a report to the Twentieth Party Congress in February 1956, on the eve of his famous denunciation of the crimes of the Stalin era (see page 327). He sounded an optimistic but militant note. Alarmed by the progress of the arms race, Khrushchev gave vigorous support to an old Soviet plea for the peaceful coexistence of the two competing sociopolitical systems— a coexistence in which victory would inevitably go to Communism.

Soon after the Second World War ended, the influence of reactionary and militarist groups began to be increasingly evident in the policy of the United States of America, Britain and France. Their desire to enforce their will on other countries by economic and political pressure, threats and military provocation prevailed. This became known as the "positions of strength" policy. It reflects the aspiration of the most aggressive sections of present-day imperialism to win world supremacy, to suppress the working class and the democratic and national-liberation movements; it reflects their plans for military adventures against the socialist camp.

The international atmosphere was poisoned by war hysteria. The arms race began to assume more and more monstrous dimensions. Many big U.S. military bases designed for use against the U.S.S.R. and the People's Democracies [East European countries under Soviet control] were built in countries thousands of miles from the borders of the United States. "Cold war" was begun against the socialist camp. International distrust was artificially kindled, and nations set against one another. A bloody war was launched in Korea; the war in Indo-China dragged on for years.

The inspirers of the "cold war" began to establish military blocs, and many countries found themselves, against the will of their peoples, involved in restricted aggressive alignments—the North Atlantic bloc, Western European Union, SEATO (military bloc for South-East Asia) and the Baghdad pact.

The organizers of military blocs allege that they have united for defence, for protection against the "communist threat." But that is sheer hypocrisy. We know from history that when planning a redivision of the world, the imperialist powers have always lined up military blocs. Today the "anti-communism" slogan is again being used as a smokescreen to cover up the claims of one power for world domination. The new thing here is that the United States wants, by means of all kinds of blocs and pacts, to secure a dominant position in the capitalist world for itself, and to reduce all its partners in the blocs to the status of obedient executors of its will. . . .

The winning of political freedom by the peoples of the former colonies and semi-colonies is the first and most important prerequisite of their full independence, that is, of the achievement of economic independence. The liberated Asian countries are pursuing a policy of building up their own industry, training their own technicians, raising the living standards of the people, and regenerating and developing their age-old national culture. History-making prospects for a better future are opening up before the countries which have embarked upon the path of independent development. . . .

[T]he colonial powers . . . have recourse to new forms of colonial enslavement under the guise of so-called "aid" to underdeveloped countries, which brings colossal profits to the colonialists. Let us take the United States as an example. The United States renders such "aid" above all in the form of deliveries of American weapons to the underdeveloped countries. This enables the American monopolies to load up their industry with arms orders. . . . States receiving such "aid" in the form of weapons, inevitably fall into dependence. . . .

Naturally, "aid" to underdeveloped countries is granted on definite political terms, terms providing for their integration into aggressive military blocs, the conclusion of joint military pacts, and support for American foreign policy aimed at world domination, or "world leadership," as the American imperialists themselves call it. . . .

[In contrast,] the exceptionally warm and friendly welcome accorded to the representatives of the great Soviet people has strikingly demonstrated the deep-rooted confidence and love the broad masses in the Eastern countries have for the Soviet Union. Analyzing the sources of this confidence, the Egyptian *Al Akhbar* justly wrote: "Russia does not try to buy the conscience of the peoples, their rights and liberty. Russia has extended a hand to the peoples and said that they themselves should decide their destiny, that she recognizes their rights and aspirations and does not demand their adherence to military pacts or blocs." Millions of men and women ardently acclaim our country for its uncompromising struggle against colonialism, for its policy of equality and friendship among all nations and for its consistent peaceful foreign policy. *(Stormy, prolonged applause.)*

. . . The Leninist principle of peaceful coexistence of states with different social systems has always been and remains the general line of our country's foreign policy. . . . To this day the enemies of peace allege that the Soviet Union is out to overthrow capitalism in other countries by "exporting" revolution. It goes without saying that among us Communists there are no supporters of capitalism. But this does not mean that we have interfered or plan to interfere in the internal affairs of countries where capitalism still exists. . . . It is ridiculous to think that revolutions are made to order. We often hear representatives of bourgeois countries reasoning thus: "The Soviet leaders claim that they are for peaceful co-existence between the two systems. At the same time they declare that they are fighting for Communism, and say that Communism is bound to win in all countries. Now if the Soviet Union is fighting for Communism, how can there be any peaceful co-existence with it?" . . .

When we say that the socialist system will win in the competition between the two systems—the capitalist and the socialist—this by no means signifies that its victory will be achieved through armed interference by the socialist countries in the internal affairs of the capitalist countries. Our certainty of the victory of Communism is based on the fact that the socialist mode of production possesses decisive advantages over the capitalist mode of production. Precisely because of this, the ideas of Marxism-Leninism are more and more capturing the minds of the broad masses of the working people in the capitalist countries, just as they have captured the minds of millions of men and women in our country and the People's Democracies. *(Prolonged applause.)* We believe that all working men in the world, once they have become convinced of the advantages Communism brings, will sooner or later take the road of struggle for the construction of socialist society.

REVIEW QUESTIONS

1. Where did Winston Churchill observe evidence of Soviet expansionism? Find on a map of Europe and Asia the areas he mentioned.
2. What were Churchill's recommendations for countering Soviet expansionism?
3. What, according to Nikita Khrushchev, were the "imperialist powers" (the United States, England, and France) trying to accomplish in their pursuit of a "position of strength"?
4. How did Khrushchev describe the aims of American policy in regard to the Soviet Union?
5. What were Khrushchev's hopes for the future? What were his reasons for viewing socialism as superior to capitalism?

3 Communist Repression

When at the end of World War II the Soviet armies pursued the retreating Germans deep into Central Europe, they subjected Eastern Europe to Soviet domination. By 1948 all countries except Yugoslavia had fallen under Stalin's iron grip. Soviet domination was buttressed by the Warsaw Pact, the military alliance of all countries within the Soviet bloc formed in 1955 to counter the North Atlantic Treaty Organization (NATO). It was further strengthened by the Council for Mutual Economic Assistance (COMECON), created in 1958 in response to the emerging European Economic Community; it tried to weld the disparate economies of Eastern Europe into a viable unit for the benefit of the Soviet boss.

Yet Soviet rule did not take firm root. The peoples under Soviet domination traditionally had looked westward, benefiting from economic, religious, and cultural ties with Western Europe. They also carried over from their past a strong nationalist ambition for independence. As Western Europe recovered from World War II, the discrepancy between the poverty of the Soviet bloc and the prosperity of its Western neighbors, especially the Federal Republic of Germany, added a further source of anti-Soviet agitation.

Inevitably the craving for independence and freedom caused mounting tensions in Soviet-controlled Eastern Europe. Within each country Soviet lackeys struggled against the reformers who were asserting, however cautiously, the yearnings of their peoples. Tensions occasionally erupted in dramatic protests, as evidenced in Hungary in 1956.

Roy Medvedev
STALIN'S LAST YEARS

One of the most remarkable interpreters of the Soviet past is the philosopher and historian Roy Medvedev (b. 1925). The twin brother of biologist Zhores Medvedev, Roy has maintained a staunch belief in democratic socialism; for this reason, he has rigorously criticized those phenomena of Soviet history—Stalinism, in particular—that not only prevented its realization but also threatened to despoil it as an ideal. He spent years amassing research for his magisterial analysis of the Stalinist era, much of it from interviews with survivors. The work appeared in the West in 1972 under the title *Let History Judge.* In 1989, Medvedev released a revised and expanded edition of the book, which drew on materials that recently had become available under Mikhail Gorbachev (see page 468).

In the following selection from the 1989 edition of the work, Medvedev describes the resumption of political repression in the Soviet Union following World War II.

The victory of the Soviet people in the Great Patriotic War, though won at the price of enormous sacrifices, engendered great exaltation. People tried to heal the wounds of war as quickly as possible; they lived on the hope of a better and happier future. The land was so bloodsoaked that any thought of new deaths seemed unbearable. So strong was this sentiment that immediately after the war the Presidium of the Supreme Soviet decreed an end to the death penalty, even for the most serious crimes. The spy mania and universal suspicion that prevailed before the war tended to disappear, especially in view of the drastic change in the international situation. The Soviet Union was no longer isolated. It had become a superpower, and both its friends and its enemies abroad closely followed events inside the USSR. All this set limits on the arbitrary measures Stalin and his circle could indulge in.

Still, repression continued in the postwar period, though on a somewhat smaller scale than in the prewar years. In 1947, for example, many prominent figures in the Soviet air force and aviation industry, who had been heroes in the war, were arrested on trumped-up charges. . . . A large number of officials in the aviation industry and military aviators were also arrested on charges of producing airplanes of "poor quality," of stopping military production too soon and switching aircraft factories over to consumer production too quickly. Stalin's own son Vasily took a hand in this affair. He was a coarse, semiliterate alcoholic, who began the war as a captain and rose to lieutenant general by the end of the war, being placed in charge of the air force of the Moscow Military District, a position totally incommensurate with his abilities.

A number of other prominent military men were arrested on false charges, including major figures in the Soviet navy. . . .

Even Marshal Zhukov, who after the war remained minister of defense and deputy to the supreme commander in chief, as well as being the chief in command of the Soviet forces in Germany, fell into disfavor. . . .

Until after Stalin's death Zhukov was obliged to stay far from Moscow, at first in Odessa, later in the Urals Military District. The press stopped writing about him; people stopped talking about him. . . .

In 1949–1951 some oblast[1] party organizations were decimated. The "Leningrad Affair" was the most serious of such cases. . . . Indeed, nearly the entire staff of the Leningrad obkom[2] was arrested, and mass repression fell on officials of the local Komsomol, the Soviet executive committee, on raikom[3] leaders, factory managers, scientific personnel, and people in higher education. Thousands of innocent people were arrested, and many of them died in confinement.

Many of the officials who were cut down in 1949–1952 . . . belonged to the new generation of leaders who rose to prominence after 1936–1937 and distinguished themselves during the war. They were significantly different from the preceding generation. As a rule, they completely accepted the cult of Stalin's personality. As their careers progressed, some of them acquired the characteristic features of Stalinists: rudeness and unjustified abruptness in their treatment of subordinates, dictatorial manners, vanity. But many of these younger officials knew little about the crimes Stalin had committed. They took a creative attitude toward their work, displaying great energy and organizational talent. They were basically honorable people who tried to do their jobs as well as possible, and with increasing frequency they came into conflict with such figures in Stalin's inner circle. . . .

In the first years following the war the influence of these younger officials, who had distinguished themselves during the war, increased markedly. Voznesensky,[4] for example, was made first deputy chairman of the USSR Council of

---

[1]An oblast is a province or large administrative unit of the Communist Party.

[2]An obkom is the Party committee of an oblast.

[3]A raikom is the Party committee of a raion, or district, several of which make up an oblast.

[4]Nikolai Voznesensky (1903–1950) was a Soviet economist whose rise to administrative prominence began in the late 1930s.

Ministers. . . . Sooner or later some of them were bound to become a nuisance to Stalin, as people who might diminish his own authority. That is how death came to Voznesensky, after he had been in charge of Gosplan[5] for eleven years, since December 1937.

A major factor creating a conflict with Stalin was Voznesensky's book on the war economy of the Soviet Union, which was issued in 1947. Its detailed analysis was based on much new factual material, and despite certain mistakes, it soon became popular among economists, who began to cite it on the same level as Stalin's works. Although Stalin had read the manuscript in 1947 and had even signed the authorization for publication, the book was suddenly declared to be anti-Marxist and was withdrawn. At the beginning of 1949 Stalin removed Voznesensky from all his posts, including membership in the Central Committee. Stalin also refused to see his former aide and hear him out.

Voznesensky remained at liberty for several months following his "disgrace." Apparently there was not even a pretext for his arrest. Beria[6] tried to create one—an excuse for decimating the Gosplan leadership—by concocting a case about the loss of some secret papers in Gosplan. . . . Voznesensky spoiled the show by flatly denying the charges and exposing the provocative nature of the trial in his first statement. Fearing further exposure, Beria ordered that Voznesensky appear in court no more and that the other defendants be condemned.

This was only a postponement for Voznesensky. Yet even then, out of office, with Beria after him, he did not lose faith in Stalin. His wife relates that he repeatedly phoned Poskrebyshev, Stalin's secretary, asking him to send over a courier, with whom he sent back memoranda pleading for work

and assuring Stalin of his devotion and honesty. But he did not get an answer. He believed that there was some sort of misunderstanding. "While Stalin is getting to the bottom of his," he told his family, "I must not lose time." He continued to work on a new book, "The Political Economy of Communism," which he had begun in 1948, but it remained unfinished. In 1950 he was arrested and shot.

In the postwar period the Soviet intelligentsia was struck some particularly hard blows. Instead of serious, dispassionate analysis of both the achievements and certain errors of Soviet writers, composers, theater people, and so on, Stalin and Zhdanov[7] launched pogrom-style campaigns of denunciation, one after another, which severely damaged Soviet culture at home and its prestige abroad. The persecution began in 1946–1947 with a series of speeches by Zhdanov, resulting in the expulsion of Mikhail Zoshchenko and Anna Akhmatova from the Union of Writers. Other artists were subjected to mudslinging. . . .

Soon the arrests began. . . .

The Jewish theater was in fact destroyed by the security police, the MGB (Ministry of State Security). Many leading actors of this theater were arrested. . . . The head of the theater, Solomon Mikhoels, a prominent public figure as well as a great actor, was killed. . . . Stalin, on Kaganovich's advice, invited Mikhoels to play the role of King Lear for him in 1946. This remarkable actor was repeatedly invited to give private performances of Shakespearean roles for Stalin. Each time Stalin thanked Mikhoels and praised his acting. But in 1948, with Stalin's knowledge, if not on his initiative, Beria's agents killed Mikhoels in Minsk, then made up the story that he died in an auto accident. A few years later he was posthumously labeled a spy for Anglo-American intelligence.

Those were also the years of an ugly campaign against "cosmopolitanism" and "worship

---

[5]Gosplan is the State Planning Commission, the agency which oversees the Soviet economy and prepares Five-Year Plans for it.

[6]Lavrenty P. Beria (1899–1953) was, from 1938, the head of Stalin's secret police organization and a figure so feared that, following the dictator's death in 1953, the other members of the ruling Politburo engineered his ouster and execution.

---

[7]Andrei A. Zhdanov (1896–1948) was a junior member of the Politburo who, after the war, became Stalin's chief aide and heir apparent. He is best known for leading the ideological assault on "cosmopolitanism" in the late 1940s.

of things foreign," bringing dozens of arrests and thousands of dismissals. It was dangerous even to quote foreign sources, to say nothing of corresponding with foreign scholars. . . .

After the meetings of the Agricultural Academy and the Academy of Medical Sciences in 1948 and 1950 the medical and biological sciences were subjected to unprecedented devastation. Dozens of leading scientists were repressed and thousands were fired or demoted. . . .

Attached to prisoners' dossiers were coded initials describing their "crimes"—for example, KRTD meaning "counter revolutionary Trotskyist activity." In the postwar period new initials appeared: VAT for "praising American technology"; VAD, "praising American democracy"; and PZ, "kowtowing to the West."

In the years 1946–1949 many émigrés who had returned to the Soviet Union after the war were arrested. An intensive campaign for return to the homeland had begun in 1945–1946 among émigrés living in Western Europe and Manchuria. Several thousand people responded to these appeals, of whom most were by this time children of the émigrés of the early twenties. Yet there were some former Russian officers as well. Most of the arrests before 1950 were on the standard charges of "espionage" or "anti-Soviet activity while in residence abroad." . . .

In late 1949 the MGB cooked up a story about the existence of a "pro-American Jewish conspiracy" in the Soviet Union, which was followed by the arrests of leading officials and public figures of Jewish origin. Solomon Lozovsky (Dridzo), who had just turned seventy-four, an Old Bolshevik member of the Central Committee and deputy minister of foreign affairs, was arrested and shot. Almost all the members of the Jewish Antifascist Committee were arrested, and most were shot. . . . In the summer of 1952 a large group of Jewish poets and writers who had been arrested earlier were also shot.

Early in 1949 Mikhail Borodin was arrested and soon shot. In the twenties he had been the Soviet Communist Party's chief political adviser to the Kuomintang revolutionary nationalist movement in China and a personal friend of Sun Yat-sen. From 1941 to 1949 Borodin had worked as editor in chief of the English-language newspaper *Moscow News* as well as chief editor of the Soviet Information Bureau. . . .

The repression of former political prisoners in 1948 and 1949 deserves special attention. While the war was on, they remained in confinement, even those whose terms ended in 1942–1945. The great victory, one would think, should have relieved the tension and permitted a general amnesty. It was expected, and an amnesty was in fact declared—but not for "enemies of the people." On the contrary, in the first years after the war a wave of terror swept through the camps. A vast number of prisoners received illegal extensions of their sentences by five, eight, or ten years. Many politicals were transferred from general to special camps with an "intensified regime." On completion of their sentences some were released from the camps but condemned to "eternal settlement" in northern areas, in the Kolyma region, Siberia, and Kazakhstan. A very few received permission to return to European Russia, but not, as a rule, to the big cities. . . . Although the "lucky ones" were relatively few, almost all were rearrested in 1948–1949. They were sent back to prisons and camps, often without any concrete charges, simply for preventive custody, as it was called. Those few who by some oversight were not rearrested found themselves in a terrible position. No one would hire them or register their right to live anywhere; they often wandered through the country for months and years without roofs over their heads. Some were so desperate they committed suicide; others became beggars; there were even some who returned to "their" camps, hoping to find work as wage laborers.

On November 26, 1948, the Presidium of the USSR Supreme Soviet passed a decree that stated: "Those exiled during the Great Patriotic War to remote districts of the Soviet Union on suspicion of treason, Germans, Chechens, Ingush, Crimean Tatars, . . . are to remain in those places forever, and in the case of flight from their place of registration will be sentenced to twenty years hard labor."

In late 1951 the MGB issued an order which placed all exiles and resettled persons, regardless of how or why they had come to be in that situation, under the terms of the decree of November 26, 1948. The period of exile for all was made permanent, so that those convicted for political reasons during the Stalin years had no hope of ever returning to their families or home towns.

I have been discussing arrests and executions of completely innocent persons, but I shall also take note of a special trend in the postwar years—the emergence of small conspiratorial groups among young people in Leningrad, Moscow, and Georgia whose aim was to fight the cult of Stalin and his dictatorship and to promote the "revival of Leninism." Sometimes group members took on theoretical tasks, such as writing a true history of the party or a critique of Stalin's philosophical and political statements. But in some cases the possibility of Stalin's or Beria's assassination was considered. In Moscow, for example, there was a group of sixteen students who called themselves the "Union of Struggle for the Cause of Revolution" (SBDR—Soyuz Borby za Delo Revoliutsii). . . . As a rule, these groups had strictly Marxist programs; sometimes they put out journals and composed manifestos. . . .

Under conditions of mass terror, all-embracing surveillance, and the universal cult of Stalin these groups were usually quickly discovered and their members arrested. Although matters had never gone beyond plans and discussions and the drafting of programs with any of these groups, the sentences handed down at closed trials were very severe. Three leaders of the SBDR group, . . . who were only nineteen or twenty years old, were shot. The other members of the group were sentenced to twenty-five years imprisonment. They were freed only after the Twentieth Party Congress.

Some writers and Old Bolsheviks also spoke out clandestinely against the crimes of the Stalinist dictatorship. . . .

All such uncoordinated individual protests could not of course disturb the foundations of Stalin's despotism in the slightest.

Milovan Djilas
THE NEW CLASS: AN ANALYSIS OF THE COMMUNIST SYSTEM

Milovan Djilas's book *The New Class: An Analysis of the Communist System* (1957), from which the following excerpts are taken, provides helpful insights into the explosion of discontent in Hungary, Czechoslovakia, and Poland under Soviet control. Djilas (1911–1995), a Yugoslav author and political commentator, became a Communist after finishing his studies in 1933. Although he began as a close friend of Marshal Tito, the all-powerful leader of Yugoslavia, in 1953 he turned critic, not only of his friend, but also of Communist practice and ideology. Jailed for his heresies in 1956, he wrote his assessment of the Communist system, showing its connection to the unprecedented new class of political bureaucrats dominating state and society. Under Communism the state did not wither away, as early theorists had expected. On the contrary, it grew more powerful, thanks to that highly privileged "exploiting and governing class." Aware of the dynamics of nationalism at work underneath each Communist regime, Djilas pointed to the weaknesses of Communist rule and the growing desire for national self-assertion among the peoples of the Soviet satellite states.

Earlier revolutions, particularly the so-called bourgeois ones, attached considerable significance to the establishment of individual freedoms immediately following cessation of the revolutionary terror. Even the revolutionaries considered it important to assure the legal status of the citizenry. Independent administration of justice was an inevitable final result of all these revolutions. The Communist regime in the U.S.S.R. is still remote from independent administration of justice after forty years of tenure. The final results of earlier revolutions were often greater legal security and greater civil rights. This cannot be said of the Communist revolution. . . .

In contrast to earlier revolutions, the Communist revolution, conducted in the name of doing away with classes, has resulted in the most complete authority of any single new class. Everything else is sham and an illusion. . . .

This new class, the bureaucracy, or more accurately the political bureaucracy, has all the characteristics of earlier ones as well as some new characteristics of its own. Its origin had its special characteristics also, even though in essence it was similar to the beginnings of other classes. . . . The new class may be said to be made up of those who have special privileges and economic preference because of the administrative monopoly they hold. . . .

The mechanism of Communist power is perhaps the simplest which can be conceived, although it leads to the most refined tyranny and the most brutal exploitation. The simplicity of this mechanism originates from the fact that one party alone, the Communist Party, is the backbone of the entire political, economic, and ideological activity. The entire public life is at a standstill or moves ahead, falls behind or turns around according to what happens in the party forums. . . .

. . . Communist control of the social machine . . . restricts certain government posts to party members. These jobs, which are essential in any government but especially in a Communist one, include assignments with police, especially the secret police; and the diplomatic and officers corps, especially positions in the information and political services. In the judiciary only top positions have until now been in the hands of Communists. . . .

Only in a Communist state are a number of both specified and unspecified positions reserved for members of the party. The Communist government, although a class structure, is a party government; the Communist army is a party army; and the state is a party state. More precisely, Communists tend to treat the army and the state as their exclusive weapons.

The exclusive, if unwritten, law that only party members can become policemen, officers, diplomats, and hold similar positions, or that only they can exercise actual authority, creates a special privileged group of bureaucrats. . . .

The entire governmental structure is organized in this manner. Political positions are reserved exclusively for party members. Even in non-political governmental bodies Communists hold the strategic positions or oversee administration. Calling a meeting at the party center or publishing an article is sufficient to cause the entire state and social mechanism to begin functioning. If difficulties occur anywhere, the party and the police very quickly correct the "error." . . .

The classes and masses do not exercise authority, but the party does so in their name. In every party, including the most democratic, leaders play an important role to the extent that the party's authority becomes the authority of the leaders. The so-called "dictatorship of the proletariat," which is the beginning of and under the best circumstances becomes the authority of the party, inevitably evolves into the dictatorship of the leaders. In a totalitarian government of this type, the dictatorship of the proletariat is a theoretical justification, or ideological mask at best, for the authority of some oligarchs. . . .

Freedoms are formally recognized in Communist regimes, but one decisive condition is a prerequisite for exercising them: freedoms must be utilized only in the interest of the system of "socialism," which the Communist leaders represent, or to buttress their rule. This practice, contrary as it is to legal regulations, inevitably had to result in the use of exceptionally severe and unscrupulous methods by police and party bodies. . . .

. . . It has been impossible in practice to separate police authority from judicial authority. Those who arrest also judge and enforce punishments. The circle is closed: the executive, the legislative, the investigating, the court, and the punishing bodies are one and the same. . . .

Communist parliaments are not in a position to make decisions on anything important. Selected in advance as they are, flattered that they have been thus selected, representatives do not have the power or the courage to debate even if they wanted to do so. Besides, since their mandate does not depend on the voters, representatives do not feel that they are answerable to them. Communist parliaments are justifiably called "mausoleums" for the representatives who compose them. Their right and role consist of unanimously approving from time to time that which has already been decided for them from the wings. . . .

Though history has no record of any other system so successful in *checking* its opposition as the Communist dictatorship, none ever has *provoked* such profound and far-reaching discontent. It seems that the more the conscience is crushed and the less the opportunities for establishing an organization exist, the greater the discontent. . . .

In addition to being motivated by the historical need for rapid industrialization, the Communist bureaucracy has been compelled to establish a type of economic system designed to insure the perpetuation of its own power. Allegedly for the sake of a classless society and for the abolition of exploitation, it has created a closed economic system, with forms of property which facilitate the party's domination and its monopoly. At first, the Communists had to turn to this "collectivistic" form for objective

reasons. Now they continue to strengthen this form—without considering whether or not it is in the interest of the national economy and of further industrialization—for their own sake, for an exclusive Communist class aim. They first administered and controlled the entire economy for so-called ideal goals; later they did it for the purpose of maintaining their absolute control and domination. That is the real reason for such far-reaching and inflexible political measures in the Communist economy. . . .

A citizen in the Communist system lives oppressed by the constant pangs of his conscience, and the fear that he has transgressed. He is always fearful that he will have to demonstrate that he is not an enemy of socialism, just as in the Middle Ages a man constantly had to show his devotion to the Church. . . .

. . . Tyranny over the mind is the most complete and most brutal type of tyranny; every other tyranny begins and ends with it. . . .

History will pardon Communists for much, establishing that they were forced into many brutal acts because of circumstances and the need to defend their existence. But the stifling of every divergent thought, the exclusive monopoly over thinking for the purpose of defending their personal interests, will nail the Communists to a cross of shame in history. . . .

In essence, Communism is only one thing, but it is realized in different degrees and manners in every country. Therefore it is possible to speak of various Communist systems, i.e., of various forms of the same manifestation.

The differences which exist between Communist states—differences that Stalin attempted futilely to remove by force—are the result, above all, of diverse historical backgrounds. . . . When ascending to power, the Communists face in the various countries different cultural and technical levels and varying social relationships, and are faced with different national intellectual characters. . . . Of the former international proletariat, only words and empty dogmas remained. Behind them stood the naked national and international interests, aspirations, and plans of the various Communist oligarchies, comfortably entrenched. . . .

. . . The Communist East European countries did not become satellites of the U.S.S.R. because they benefited from it, but because they were too weak to prevent it. As soon as they become stronger, or as soon as favorable conditions are created, a yearning for independence and for protection of "their own people" from Soviet hegemony will rise among them.

The subordinate Communist governments in East Europe can, in fact must, declare their independence from the Soviet government. No one can say how far this aspiration for independence will go and what disagreements will result. The result depends on numerous unforeseen internal and external circumstances. However, there is no doubt that a national Communist bureaucracy aspires to more complete authority for itself. This is demonstrated . . . by the current unconcealed emphasis on "one's own path to socialism," which has recently come to light sharply in Poland and Hungary. The central Soviet government has found itself in difficulty because of the nationalism existing even in those governments which it installed in the Soviet republics (Ukraine, Caucasia), and still more so with regard to those governments installed in the East European countries. Playing an important role in all of this is the fact that the Soviet Union was unable, and will not be able in the future, to assimilate the economies of the East European countries.

The aspirations toward national independence must of course have greater impetus. These aspirations can be retarded and even made dormant by external pressure or by fear on the part of the Communists of "imperialism" and the "bourgeoisie," but they cannot be removed. On the contrary, their strength will grow.

Andor Heller
THE HUNGARIAN REVOLUTION, 1956

After Stalin's death in 1953, the rigid political controls in Hungary were relaxed, leading to an unstable balance between Soviet-oriented hardliners and patriotic reformers willing to grant greater freedom to the spirit of nationalism and individual enterprise stirring among the people. In 1956, the year of Khrushchev's attack on Stalin, the Hungarian yearning for escape from Soviet domination exploded. On October 23 a student demonstration in Budapest, the capital, provided the spark. Throughout the country, Communist officials were ousted and the Soviet troops forced to withdraw. A coalition government under Imre Nagy was formed to restore Hungary's independence; it even appeared that the country would withdraw from the newly formed Warsaw Pact controlled by Moscow. In Budapest especially, the popular excitement over the country's liberation from the Soviet yoke knew no bounds, as is described in the eyewitness account that follows. The author, Andor Heller, was a Hungarian news photographer. He fled to Western Europe with photographs of the invasion and published them in his book *No More Comrades* (1957).

Deep dejection followed the anger caused by the Soviet counterattack that killed thousands of people and drove 200,000 into exile. A new "peasant-worker government" under János Kádár boasted of having saved the country from "Fascist counter-revolution." Subsequently, however, Kádár transformed his country's economy. Dubbed "goulash Communism" for its mixture of state and private enterprise, it became the freest in the Soviet bloc and a model for Gorbachev's *perestroika* (restructuring) in the Soviet Union in the late 1980s.

I saw freedom rise from the ashes of Communism in Hungary: a freedom that flickered and then blazed before it was beaten down—but not extinguished—by masses of Russian tanks and troops.

I saw young students, who had known nothing but a life under Communist and Russian control, die for a freedom about which they had only heard from others or from their own hearts.

I saw workers, who had been pushed to the limit of endurance by their hopeless existence under Communism, lay down their tools and take up arms in a desperate bid to win back freedom for our country.

I saw a girl of fourteen blow up a Russian tank, and grandmothers walk up to Russian cannons.

I watched a whole nation—old and young, men and women, artists and engineers and doctors, clerks and peasants and factory workers—become heroes overnight as they rose up in history's first successful revolt against Communism.

Tuesday, October 23, 1956

No Hungarian will forget this day. . . .

. . . In spite of the cold and fog, students are on the streets early in the morning, marching and singing. No one shows up for classes at the universities. After a decade of Communist control over our country, we are going to show our feelings spontaneously, in our own way—something never allowed under Communist rules.

The students carry signs with slogans that until now we have never dared express except to members of our own family—and not in every family. The slogans read:

RUSSIANS GO HOME!
LET HUNGARY BE INDEPENDENT!
BRING RAKOSI TO JUSTICE!
WE WANT A NEW LEADERSHIP!

SOLIDARITY WITH THE POLISH PEOPLE!
WE TRUST IMRE NAGY—BRING IMRE NAGY INTO THE GOVERNMENT!

The walls of Budapest are plastered with leaflets put up by the students during the night. They list the fourteen demands adopted at the stormy meetings held at the universities:

1. Withdrawal of all Soviet troops from Hungary.
2. Complete economic and political equality with the Soviet Union, with no interference in Hungary's internal affairs.
3. Publication of Hungary's trade agreements, and a public report on Hungary's reparations payments to the U.S.S.R.
4. Information on Hungary's uranium resources, their exploitation, and the concessions given to the U.S.S.R.
5. The calling of a Hungarian Communist Party Congress to elect a new leadership.
6. Reorganization of the government, with Imre Nagy as Premier.
7. A public trial of Mihaly Farkas and Matyas Rakosi [notorious Stalinists].
8. A secret general multi-party election.
9. The reorganization of Hungary's economy on the basis of her actual resources.
10. Revision of the workers' output quotas, and recognition of the right to strike.
11. Revision of the system of compulsory agricultural quotas.
12. Equal rights for individual farmers and co-operative members.
13. Restoration of Hungary's traditional national emblem and the traditional Hungarian army uniforms.
14. Destruction of the giant statue of Stalin.

During the morning a radio announcement from the Ministry of Interior bans all public meetings and demonstrations "until further notice," and word is sent to the universities that the student demonstrations cannot be held. At that moment the students decide that the will to freedom is greater than the fear of the A.V.H.—the Russian-controlled Hungarian secret police. The meeting will be held! . . .

At 3 P.M. there are 25,000 of us at the Petofi Monument. We weep as Imre Sinkovits, a young actor, declaims the *Nemzeti Dal* ("National Song"), Sandor Petofi's [a great Hungarian poet and revolutionary hero in the anti-Austrian rebellion of 1848–1849] ode to Hungary and our 1848 "freedom revolution." With tears in our eyes, we repeat the refrain with Sinkovits: . . .

"We swear, we swear, we will no longer remain slaves."

The student voices are tense with feeling. No policeman or Communist official is in sight. The young people are keeping order on their own.

. . . [W]e have swelled to some 60,000. Someone grabs a Hungarian flag and cuts out the hated hammer and sickle that the Communists had placed at its center.

One after another of the purified Hungarian flags appear. Suddenly someone remembers to put the old Kossuth [Lajos Kossuth was the leader of the Hungarian uprising of 1848–1849] coat-of-arms on the flag, in place of the Communist emblem.

We have created a new flag of freedom!

Meantime we all sing the . . . *Appeal to the Nation*, and the *Hungarian National Hymn* that begins "God Bless the Magyar"—both of which had been banned under the Communist rule.

We cannot get enough. The actor Ferenc Bessenyei recites the *National Song* again, and follows once more with *Appeal to the Nation*. Peter Veres, the head of the Hungarian Writers' Federation, leaps to the top of a car equipped with a loudspeaker. He reads the Hungarian writers' demands for more freedom—many of them the same as those in the fourteen points of the students.

The day is ending. We begin to march toward the Parliament Building. The crowds are peaceful, marching in orderly lines. We carry the new Hungarian flag.

As we march we are joined by workers leaving their jobs. By the time we arrive in Kossuth Lajos Square there are at least 150,000 of us, in front of the Parliament Building. On the square, the traffic stops. . . .

Suddenly everyone makes torches of newspapers, and lights them. It is a marvelous spectacle—ten thousand torches burning in the Square before the Parliament Building. . . .

But finally, Imre Nagy appears on the balcony. "Comrades!" he begins, but the crowd interrupts him with a roar: "There are no more comrades! We are all Hungarians!" . . .

The crowd grows still bigger, and we head for the Stalin statue. Now the demonstration has spread so large that it is going on simultaneously in three places: at the Parliament Building; in Stalin Square, where the crowd is trying to pull down the huge Stalin statue with tractors and ropes; and at the building of Radio Budapest, where part of the crowd has gone to demand the right of patriots to be heard over the air. . . .

I go with the group that heads for Stalin Square. Some of the workers have got hold of acetylene torches. They and the students are trying to cut down the dictator's twenty-five-foot metal figure. At the edge of the crowd the first Russian tanks appear, but at the moment they are only onlookers. The crowd pulls hard at the cables that have been attached to the Stalin statue. It leans forward, but is still held by its boots—a symbol, we feel. The cables are now being pulled by tractors, and the men with the torches work feverishly. The statue, though still in one piece, begins to bend at the knees. The crowds burst into cheers. . . .

. . . [W]e watch the Stalin statue, cut off at the knees, fall to the ground with a thunderous crash. . . .

Suddenly shooting breaks out from all sides. The security police—the A.V.H.—are firing into the crowds. In minutes the streets are strewn with the dying and wounded. News of the A.V.H. attack spreads. All over Budapest the workers and students are battling the hated A.V.H.

The peaceful demonstrations of the youth and the workers have been turned by Communist guns into a revolution for national freedom.

For four days—from October 31 to November 3, 1956—Hungary was free. Although the Russian forces were still in our country, they had withdrawn from the cities and the fighting had stopped. The whole nation recognized the Imre Nagy government, which, knowing it had no other alternative, was ready to carry out the will of the people. . . .

On November 3, Radio Free Kossuth summed up: "The over-whelming weight of Hungarian public opinion sees the result of the revolution as the establishment of a neutral, independent and democratic country, and just as it was ready to sweep out Stalinist tyranny, so it will protect with the same determination and firmness its regained democratic achievement." . . .

In those four days of freedom, political liberty came quickly to life. . . .

Before October 23 there had been only five newspapers in Budapest, all under complete Communist control. On November 4 there were twenty-five. Neither news nor opinions could be suppressed any longer.

Plans for a free general election were speeded.

Religious freedom, like political freedom, came back to strong life in those four days. . . .

In the countryside, the peasants and their spokesmen were mapping the changes of the farm laws and regulations. All were agreed on the goal of a free farm economy based on the individual working farmers and peasants. Peasants would be free to join or leave the farm collectives. If the collectives were dissolved, the land, tools and stock were to be distributed to the individual peasants. Compulsory deliveries at government fixed prices were abolished.

The factory committees and workers' groups were putting forward the needs and demands of the workers, not the government. The right to strike—a criminal act under the Communists—was upheld. Wages, prices, pension rights, working conditions were eagerly discussed and debated.

The economy was slowly getting on its feet. Everyone wanted to be on the streets together. . . .

Return of the Russians

At dawn on November 4, 1956, Soviet Russia attacked Hungary with 6,000 tanks, thousands of guns and armored cars, squadrons of light bombers, 200,000 soldiers—and a tidal wave of lies.

REVIEW QUESTIONS

1. What types of people became victims of Stalin's terror after World War II?
2. How did Milovan Djilas characterize the "new class"? What were its qualities? How did it wield its power?
3. Why, according to Djilas, would the Communist governments in Eastern Europe sooner or later declare their independence from the Soviet government?
4. What would you say was the climax of the Budapest demonstration on October 23?
5. What was at stake for the workers and farmers of Hungary in the anti-Soviet uprising?
6. How did the Hungarians in those crucial October days assert their freedom? What evidence of nationalism did you observe in the anti-Soviet demonstrations?

4 The New Germany: Economic Miracle and Confronting the Past

May 1945 has long been referred to in Germany as *Stunde Null,* or "zero hour." This designation would suggest that everything prior to the end of the war had been eliminated by the defeat of the Third Reich—that the terrible destruction visited upon Germany as a result of the war launched by the Nazi government had wiped the slate clean, that Germans could only go forward, not backward. Most Germans had little inclination to reflect upon the meaning of Nazi aggression and crimes against humanity. Their priorities included clearing rubble, restoring economic life, and creating a sense of normalcy.

The consensus among the victorious Allied powers and most European leaders was that the potential for future German aggression had to be checked and that the best way to do this was to integrate Germany into broader Western European economic and security arrangements. As Cold War considerations began to determine the administration of the Allied occupation zones in Germany, however, competing visions for Germany's—and Europe's—future development manifested themselves. In the West, the reestablishment of democratic political parties, elimination of the black market, and the introduction of a market economy were central considerations. German leaders and their Anglo-American and French occupiers sought to prevent a resurgence of Nazism and to guard against Communist expansion. In the East, preparations were quickly undertaken to create a Soviet-style regime, in which the Communists sought to ground their state organization upon the principles of antifascist solidarity. Regardless of zonal administration and ideological orientation, Germans were generally more interested in rebuilding than coming to terms with the past, despite the occasional admonitions of intellectuals and critical historians.

Theodore H. White
"GERMANY IS ALIVE AND VIGOROUS AGAIN"

Upon defeat of the Nazi regime in May 1945, Germany's economy lay in ruins. Bridges, railroad lines, factories and mining operations, and urban centers had received considerable damage, in some cases much of entire cityscapes had been reduced to rubble. Damage to infrastructure was compounded by a workforce that was scattered by invasion and air raids; and millions of laborers had been killed, maimed, or taken prisoner during the course of military service, while hundreds of thousands of demobilized German servicemen found the return home delayed by transportation problems. Disruptions in foodstuff production and in distribution networks meant virtually all Germans suffered from hunger. Moreover, Soviet, British, and American officials determined in a series of meetings, which culminated in a gathering of the Big Threes' leaders at Potsdam in the summer of 1945, that a USSR devastated by four years of savage warfare would help itself to reparations of salvageable industrial infrastructure. This decision had the net effect of further depleting Germany's own industrial base. In order to stave off mass starvation, the victorious powers resolved to transfer German resources across their respective occupation zone boundaries and deliver food aid.

By 1947, mounting tensions led to increased suspicions and the separation of economic cooperation between the Soviets and the Western Allies in Germany. The United States began to increase its relief aid, particularly as British contributions became more constrained by the United Kingdom's own domestic needs. The United States extended grants, credits, and loans that culminated formally in the European Recovery Program (ERP) or "Marshall Aid". (In June 1947, Secretary of State George C. Marshall proposed massive aid to promote European recovery.) The western zones of occupation in Germany, which became the Federal Republic of Germany in 1949, were a principal beneficiary of this assistance. While ERP aid amounted to a relatively small percentage of West Germany's gross domestic product between 1948 and 1951, together with the creation of a central bank, currency reform, and integration into Western European economic networks, the importance of this assistance for foodstuffs and raw materials cannot be overemphasized. During the mid and late 1950s, the West German economy took advantage of its newly established stability and began to grow steadily as a manufacturing and consumer-based economy with a strong agricultural sector, soon becoming the most dynamic economy in Western Europe.

As of the early 1960s, the Federal Republic's "economic miracle," became an object of admiration for its neighbors. West German economic success, like that of Japan, helped to ensure social stability; this, in turn, worked against any potential embrace of Communism or a return to violent, intolerant nationalism. West Germany had undergone a transformation that no one would have dared imagine possible in the spring of 1945.

Theodore White's overview of conditions between 1945 and 1947 stand in marked contrast to what White encountered by the time Marshall Aid and initial Western European economic integration helped infuse life into the West German economy in 1952. The following selection reveals the astonishment White felt upon each of his periodic visits during his extended reportage on developments across postwar Europe.

No traveler making the seasonal circuit of Europe's political centers has failed to describe how swiftly the face of Germany has changed since the ending of the Winter Years. Once set on its upward course in 1949, Germany changed from month to month. People in the streets filled out visibly. Their clothes changed from rumpled rags to decent garments, to neat business suits, to silk stockings. Cigarettes disappeared as currency, then became available everywhere, then, finally, were sold from slot machines on every corner. Food returned, food as the Germans love it, with whipped cream beaten thick in the coffee, on cake, with fruit. The streets changed face as buildings rose, as neon signs festooned them, as their windows shone with goods. For a number of years I have visited Frankfurt twice a year, staying at the Park

Hotel opposite the railway station. On my first visit I could look out of the window on a hot day and still smell the dust of rubble rising from the ruins up and down the street, ruins all down the curving Bahnhof square, ruins on every side of the railway station. At each visit thereafter, some patch of rubble was cleared, some new construction sprouted into the sky, some long stretch of broken cobblestone yielded to smooth asphalt until, finally, on my last spring visit I woke and heard the sound of hammers under my window and looked out to see the last red walls of the last red ruin on my street crumbling under the wrecker's sledge, to be cleared for what new hotel or new office building only the next visit will reveal.

The revival offered its most dramatic contrasts in Düsseldorf, the capital both of Ruhr industry and the British Occupation of that province. Down Koenigsallee, the beautiful main street of the city, luxury shops blossomed year by year to offer the steel barons and coal merchants the delights they have always enjoyed. Today, the cigar stores of Koenigsallee and Flingerstrasse offer the greatest collection of yellow, black, tan, brown, half-white stogies in Europe, gathered from Brazil, Manila, Havana, Hamburg. The Konditorei decorate their shop-fronts in midwinter with bananas and oranges, pineapples from the tropics, cheeses from Denmark, champagne and Burgundy from France, grapes from Italy, hams from Scandinavia. Gradually, as this happened, the British Occupiers of Düsseldorf began to wonder who had won and who had lost the war. The first season it became obvious that the German ration had passed the British ration, a group of British women, wives of Occupation officials, demonstrated in the main streets outside British military headquarters to protest that the Germans they had defeated were eating fatter than British soldiers' families, who themselves were eating better than Britons back home. But no housewifely protest could stop the surge. It was the next season that Americans, visiting Cologne and stopping at one of its larger hotels, noticed that its dining room was divided in two halves—one for the British Occupation officials, living on the dull, juiceless, meat-thin rations of the Ministry of Food; the other for German civilians, eating rich, heavy, stomach-filling German food. The American visitors preferred to sit on the German or conquered side of the dining room, rather than on the side of the victorious British.

Revival throbbed on all the roads and arteries of communications. Bridges went up and spans were sutured. On my first visit to Germany, in an early Winter Year, the smooth concrete paths of the autobahns were dominated by vehicles of the Occupation. The Army's olive-drab trucks purring in convoy formation, the American jeeps wasping in and out, the glittering, shimmering sedans of the American families with white Occupation plates made the wheezing old German sedans, the bumbling old German trucks—so frequently overturned, so frequently wrecked, so frequently waiting idly by the road in breakdown—seem like strangers on their own roads. But each succeeding visit has shown the roads reconquered by Germans, even though there are now three times as many Americans and troops in Germany than on my first visit. New Kapitans, Opels, Volkswagens, Porsches, Mercedes-Benzes whiz by, obscuring from sight American sedans in the procession of the autobahn; huge German double and triple trailers with their trailing black exhaust becloud the occasional American convoys. Rhine barges, furrowing the busy waters, are new again, spick and span in gleaming brass fittings, and red, white, green coats of paint. The railways run on time, efficiently, the dining cars proud with white stiff linen and solid plentiful food.

Germany is alive and vigorous again—to the sight, to the ear, to the touch. Nor is this only a matter of appearances, for statistically the profile of German effort now traces the outline of an industrial power again equal to England, and greater than any other in Western Europe.

Economists estimate that Germany's gross national product has increased by seventy per cent since the year 1948–1949; that her industrial production is two-thirds again higher than it was in 1936, Hitler's peak peacetime year;

that her wage-earners are now numbered at an all-time high. Germany's exports have multiplied by seven times in the five years since currency reform; her Dollar Gap should vanish in 1953; her credits in the European Payments Union stand at almost half a billion dollars, higher than any other of the Marshall Plan countries.

Each set of statistics bears its own story, but none reflect the phenomenon of Germany's Renaissance better than the figures of her steel production. In 1946, the year after Germany's collapse, she poured 2,500,000 tons of steel; in 1947, 3,000,000 tons. Those were the years in which the Allies had sworn that Germany should never produce more than 5,600,000 tons again. At the end of 1947, when the Western Allies lifted Germany's limit to 11,100,000 tons, their experts assured them it would take at least five years for Germany to reach the distant level of 10,000,000 tons. By 1949, however, the Germans were pouring 9,000,000 tons of steel and had drawn abreast of the French. In the fall of 1950 the Western Allies tore up the 11,100,000 ton limit and urged Germany to go all out in producing steel for the Western defense effort. At that time Western engineers gave their solemn opinion that the old, outmoded plants of the Ruhr could not be overhauled to produce more than an outer technical maximum of 13,500,000 tons. By the end of 1951 Germany was producing 13,500,000 tons

and was racing after Britain, the leading steel producer in Western Europe. In 1953 the Germans let another notch out of their belt and poured 14,500,000 tons, in some months equaling and surpassing British production. German engineers now figure that if business holds good they can pour 18,000,000 tons in the next twelve-month period, to make them the senior steel producer of Western Europe. At that point they will be pouring more than the Ruhr ever produced before, or just slightly more than three times as much as the Allies swore, seven years ago, she would ever produce again.

All other statistics crackle with the same energy. Coal production in Germany has jumped from 60,000,000 to 100,000,000 to 125,000,000 tons. The production of radios doubled Germany's prewar production by the spring of 1951, and by the beginning of 1953 Germany was producing almost twice as many automobiles as in 1936. Starting in the rubble and disaster of defeat, the Germans began to build houses. Slowly at first, as the cramped economy put itself together again, then more swiftly German craftsmen began to house their countrymen until, by 1951, Germany was building over 400,000 dwelling units a year, or more than the total number France had built in the eight years since Liberation. Germany's home-building rate per capita is, indeed, the only major European housing effort that can match America's.

Hannah Vogt
THE BURDEN OF GUILT

In the years immediately following World War II, Germans were too preoccupied with rebuilding their devastated country to reflect on the horrific crimes committed by the Third Reich and bring the criminals to justice. Indeed, many Germans either failed to comprehend the enormity of these crimes or found the subject uncomfortable, for only a few years earlier they had faithfully served the Nazi regime and embraced its ideology. They simply wanted to sweep the extermination of European Jewry from memory. However, the public trials of war criminals starting in the 1960s and the greater attention given to the topic in books and the media, including an American television miniseries that dramatized and personalized the Jewish tragedy, stimulated open discussion and reflection within Germany.

Until the 1960s, German secondary school history courses generally ended with the beginning of the twentieth century. Few teachers discussed the Nazi regime, and appropriate books about Nazism and the Holocaust were lacking. Moreover, teachers who had previously endorsed Hitler were not eager to discuss the Holocaust with their students. Distressed by a sudden outburst of anti-Semitic incidents that afflicted Germany in 1959, notably desecrated cemeteries and swastikas smeared on the walls of synagogues, German educational authorities made a concerted effort to teach young people about the Nazi past. These same anti-Semitic outrages moved Hannah Vogt, a civil servant concerned principally with education, to write a book for students about the Nazi past. Published in 1961, *The Burden of Guilt* became a widely used text in secondary schools. In the Preface, Vogt stated the book's purpose:

> {S}elf-examination and a repudiation of false political principles are the only means we have of winning new trust among those peoples who were forced to suffer fearful things under Hitler's brutal policy of force. . . . Only if we draw the right conclusions from the mistakes of the past and apply them to our thought and action can we win new trust. . . . Anyone who makes an effort to understand recent political history will learn that in politics not every means is just {and} that law and the dignity of man are not empty phrases.

The book's conclusion, excerpted below, showed a sincere effort of German schools to come to grips with the darkest period in German history.

A nation is made up of individuals whose ideas—right or wrong—determine their actions, their decisions, and their common life, and for this reason a nation, too, can look back at its history and learn from it. As Germans, we should not find it too difficult to understand the meaning of the fourteen years of the Weimar Republic and the twelve years of the Hitler regime.

The ancient Greeks already knew and taught that no state can remain free without free citizens. If the citizens of a commonwealth are not prepared to make sacrifices for their liberty, to take matters into their own hands and participate in public affairs, they deliver themselves into the hands of a tyrant. They do not deserve anything but tyrannical rule: "A class which fails to make sacrifices for political affairs may not make demands on political life. It renounces its will to rule, and must therefore be ruled." These words of a German liberal about the educated class are valid for people everywhere.

The Greeks called a man who abstained from politics "idiotēs." The Oxford English Dictionary translates this as "private person," "ignorant," "layman," or "not professionally learned." And what are we to call those who have learned nothing from our recent history but the foolish slogan "without me" (*Ohne mich*)? Are they not like fish who expect to improve their condition by jumping from the frying pan into the fire?

We have paid dearly once before for the folly of believing that democracy, being an ideal political arrangement, must function automatically while the citizens sit in their parlors berating it, or worrying about their money. Everybody must share in the responsibility and must be prepared to make sacrifices. He must also respect the opinions of others and must curb his hates, which are too blinding to be good guides for action. In addition, we need to be patient, we must have confidence in small advances and abandon the belief in political miracles and panaceas.

Only if the citizens are thoroughly imbued with democratic attitudes can we put into practice those principles of political life which were achieved through centuries of experience, and which we disregarded to our great sorrow. The first such principle is the need for a continuous and vigilant control of power. For this, we need not only a free and courageous press but also some mechanism for shaping a vital political opinion in associations, parties, and other organizations. Equally necessary are clearly drawn lines of political responsibility, and a strong and respected political opposition. Interest groups must not be diffused too widely but must aim at maximum cohesiveness. Present developments appear to indicate that we are deeply aware of at least this necessity.

More than anything else we must base our concept of law on the idea of justice. We have had the sad experience that the principle "the law is the law" does not suffice, if the laws are being abused to cover up for crimes and to wrap injustices in a tissue of legality. Our actions must once again be guided by that idea which is the basis of just life: no man must be used as a means to an end.

This principle must also be applied to our relationships with other nations. Although, on the international scene, there is as yet no all-inclusive legal body that would have enough power to solve all conflicts peacefully, still there are legal norms in international affairs which are not at all the "sound and smoke" (Faust) Hitler had presumed them to be. In no other matter was he as divorced from reality as in his belief that it was shrewd to conclude treaties today and "to break them in cold blood tomorrow," and that he could undo 2000 years of legal evolution without having such action recoil upon him. He considered force the one and only means of politics, while, in reality, it had always been the worst. Hitler's so-called *Realpolitik* was terrifyingly unreal, and brought about a catastrophe which has undone the gains Bismarck had made through moderation. Bismarck gave Germany its unity. Hitler, goaded by his limitless drive for world power,

divided Germany and destroyed the work of generations.

Thus we are now faced with the difficult task of regaining, by peaceful means, the German unity that Hitler has gambled away. We must strive for it tirelessly, even though it may take decades. At the same time, we must establish a new relationship, based on trust, with the peoples of Europe and the nations of the world. Our word must again be believed, our commitment to freedom and humanity again be trusted. Our name has been used too much for lies and treachery. We cannot simply stretch out our hands and hope that all will be forgotten.

These are the questions which should touch the younger generation most deeply: What position could and should we have among the nations? Can we restore honor to the German name? Can we shape a new and better future? Or shall we be burdened with the crimes of the Hitler regime for generations to come?

However contradictory the problem may look at first sight, there can be no shilly-shallying, but only a clear Yes to these questions. The past cannot be erased, but the future is free. It is not predetermined. We have the power to re-examine our decisions and mend our wrong ways; we can renounce force and place our trust in peaceful and gradual progress; we can reject racial pride. Instead of impressing the world with war and aggression, we can strive for world prestige through the peaceful solution of conflicts, as the Swiss and the Scandinavians have done for centuries to their national glory. For us, the choice is open to condemn Hitler's deluded destructiveness and to embrace Albert Schweitzer's message—respect for life.

If we are really serious about this new respect for life, it must also extend to the victims of the unspeakable policy of extermination. Ever since human beings have existed, respect for life has included respect for the dead. Everywhere it is the duty of the living to preserve the memory of the dead. Should we listen to insinuations that the time has come to forget crimes and victims because nobody must incriminate himself? Is it not, rather, cowardly, mean, and miserable to deny even now the dead the honor they deserve, and to forget them as quickly as possible?

We owe it to ourselves to examine our consciences sincerely and to face the naked truth, instead of minimizing it or glossing over it. This is also the only way we can regain respect in the world. Covering up or minimizing crimes will suggest that we secretly approve of them. Who will believe that we want to respect all that is human if we treat the death of nearly six million Jews as a "small error" to be forgotten after a few years?

The test of our change of heart should be not only the dead but the living. There are 30,000 Jewish fellow-citizens living among us. Many of them have returned only recently from emigration, overwhelmed with a desire for their old homeland. It is up to all of us to make sure that they live among us in peace and without being abused, that their new trust in us, won after much effort, is not destroyed by desecrated cemeteries, gutter slogans, or hate songs. Those who will never learn must not be allowed to take refuge in the freedom of opinion. A higher value is at stake here, the honor of the dead, and respect for the living. But it is not up to the public prosecutor to imbue our lives with new and more humane principles. This is everybody's business. It concerns us all! It will determine our future.

Richard von Weizsäcker
"WE SEEK RECONCILIATION"

In recent decades there has been an open and frank discussion among Germans of the nation's crimes against the Jews during World War II. In a speech during a commemorative ceremony on May 8, 1985, the fortieth anniversary of the end of World War II in Europe, Richard von Weizsäcker (b. 1920), president of the Federal Republic of Germany from 1984 to 1994, reflected on the Holocaust and the need for remembrance.

May 8th is a day of remembrance. Remembering means recalling an occurrence honestly and undistortedly so that it becomes a part of our very beings. This places high demands on our truthfulness.

Today we mourn all the dead of the war and tyranny. In particular we commemorate the six million Jews who were murdered in German concentration camps. . . .

At the root of the tyranny was Hitler's immeasurable hatred of our Jewish compatriots. Hitler had never concealed this hatred from the public, and made the entire nation a tool of it. Only a day before his death, on April 30, 1945, he concluded his so-called "will" with the words: "Above all, I call upon the leaders of the nation and their followers to observe painstakingly the race laws and to oppose ruthlessly the poisoners of all nations: international Jewry." Hardly any country has in its history always remained free from blame for war or violence. The genocide of the Jews is, however, unparalleled in history.

The perpetration of this crime was in the hands of a few people. It was concealed from the eyes of the public, but every German was able to experience what his Jewish compatriots had to suffer, ranging from plain apathy and hidden intolerance to outright hatred. Who could remain unsuspecting after the burning of the synagogues, the plundering, the stigmatization with the Star of David, the deprivation of rights, the ceaseless violation of human dignity? Whoever opened his eyes and ears and sought information could not fail to notice that Jews were being deported. The nature and scope of the destruction may have exceeded human imagination, but in reality there was, apart from the crime itself, the attempt by too many people, including those of my generation, who were young and were not involved in planning the events and carrying them out, not to take note of what was happening. There were many ways of not burdening one's conscience, of shunning responsibility, looking away, keeping mum. When the unspeakable truth of the Holocaust then became known at the end of the war, all too many of us claimed that they had not known anything about it or even suspected anything.

There is no such thing as the guilt or innocence of an entire nation. Guilt is, like innocence, not collective, but personal. There is discovered or concealed individual guilt. There is guilt which people acknowledge or deny. Everyone who directly experienced that era should today quietly ask himself about his involvement then.

The vast majority of today's population were either children then or had not been born. They cannot profess a guilt of their own for crimes that they did not commit. No discerning person can expect them to wear a penitential robe simply because they are Germans. But their forefathers have left them a grave legacy. All of us, whether guilty or not, whether old or young, must accept the past. We are all affected by its consequences and liable for it. The young and old generations must and can help each other to understand why it is vital to keep alive the memories. It is not a case of coming to terms with the past. That is not possible. It cannot be subsequently modified or made undone. However, anyone who closes his eyes to the past is blind to the present. Whoever refuses to remember the inhumanity is prone to new risks of infection.

The Jewish nation remembers and will always remember. We seek reconciliation. Precisely for this reason we must understand that there can be no reconciliation without remembrance. The experience of millionfold death is part of the very being of every Jew in the world, not only because people cannot forget such atrocities, but also because remembrance is part of the Jewish faith.

"Seeking to forget makes exile all the longer; the secret of redemption lies in remembrance." This oft quoted Jewish adage surely expresses the idea that faith in God is faith in the work of God in history. Remembrance is experience of the work of God in history. It is the source of faith in redemption. This experience creates hope, creates faith in redemption, in reunification of the divided, in reconciliation. Whoever forgets this experience loses his faith.

If we for our part sought to forget what has occurred, instead of remembering it, this would not only be inhuman, we would also impinge upon the faith of the Jews who survived and destroy the basis of reconciliation. We must erect a memorial to thoughts and feelings in our own hearts.

REVIEW QUESTIONS

1. What evidence did Theodore H. White see indicating Germany's revival?
2. According to Hannah Vogt, what lessons should Germans learn from the Nazi era?
3. How did she suggest that Germans now confront the Holocaust?
4. What did Richard von Weizsäcker have to say about collective guilt, about the implications of forgetfulness and remembrance, and about the possibility of redemption, reconciliation, and salvation?
5. In your opinion what is the meaning of the Holocaust for Western civilization? For Jews? For Christians? For Germans?

5   The Soviet Union: Restructuring and Openness

Mikhail Sergeyevich Gorbachev, president of the USSR from 1988 to 1991, started a new era in Soviet life and government. There was need for drastic change. The Soviet system of centralized control over all aspects of life had failed alarmingly. The planned economy had fallen behind free enterprise economies; productivity had declined. The official ideology of Marxism-Leninism had been discredited, and the Soviet claim of setting a model for developing countries had collapsed. Under the slogans of *perestroika* (restructuring) and *glasnost* (openness), Gorbachev began reforming the Soviet system. He loosened the strict state controls in order to stimulate the creative energies of the people; he emphasized the need for official truthfulness and open discussion of vital issues.

Yet his domestic measures created baffling problems for him. In trying to liberate private initiative and to open discussion, he also stirred up the hidden tensions in Soviet society. Revelations of Stalin's terror and of the corruption and misrule of party officials angered public opinion. In addition, workers dreaded the prospect of unemployment in a competitive economy. Even worse, the national minorities agitated for self-determination and liberation; the unity of the multinational Soviet state was threatened. As Gorbachev himself admitted: "The Soviet Union is entering a long period of uncertainty."

Mikhail S. Gorbachev
PERESTROIKA

A man of seemingly inexhaustible energy with a sure way of building public confidence, Mikhail Gorbachev (b. 1931) talked freely to all sorts of people in his own country ever since he assumed the leadership of the Communist party. He has also taken his case to audiences in Western Europe and the United States, capturing the attention of the world as a statesman eager to reduce the threat of nuclear war and to promote awareness of the responsibilities of global interdependence. In 1987 he spelled out his political views in a book appropriately called *Perestroika*, excerpted below.

The new atmosphere is, perhaps, most vividly manifest in glasnost. We want more openness about public affairs in every sphere of life. People should know what is good, and what is bad, too, in order to multiply the good and to combat the bad. That is how things should be under socialism. . . .

Truth is the main thing. Lenin said: More light! Let the Party know everything! As never before, we need no dark corners where mold can reappear and where everything against which we have started a resolute struggle could start accumulating. That's why there must be more light.

Today, glasnost is a vivid example of a normal and favorable spiritual and moral atmosphere in society, which makes it possible for people to understand better what happened to us in the past, what is taking place now, what we are striving for and what our plans are, and, on the basis of this understanding, to participate in the restructuring effort consciously.

. . . The people should know life with all its contradictions and complexities. Working people must have complete and truthful information on achievements and impediments, on what stands in the way of progress and thwarts it. . . .

. . . {T}he concept of economic reform . . . is of an all-embracing, comprehensive character. It provides for fundamental changes in every area, including the transfer of enterprises to complete cost accounting, a radical transformation of the centralized management of the economy, fundamental changes in planning, a reform of the price formation system and of the financial and crediting mechanism, and the restructuring of foreign economic ties. It also provides for the creation of new organizational structures of management, for the all-round development of the democratic foundations of management, and for the broad introduction of the self-management principles. . . .

The essence of what we plan to do throughout the country is to replace predominantly administrative methods by predominantly economic methods. That we must have full cost accounting is quite clear to the Soviet leadership. . . .

Now, after a nationwide discussion, we have adopted programs for a radical transformation of higher and secondary schools. The main direction of efforts is training young people for future work with a view to meeting the requirements of scientific and technological progress and getting rid of everything of secondary importance which gives people little except unnecessary burdens. The humanistic education of the young, the aim of which is a proper upbringing and the acquisition of adequate cultural standards, is being improved. Colleges and secondary schools lay emphasis on stimulating creative methods of instruction and education and fostering initiative and independence in secondary and higher school collectives. The new tasks call for restructuring the material base and, most importantly,

for teachers to attain a new level in their work. Those who upgrade their skills will be encouraged materially. The programs have the necessary financial backing, and their realization is proceeding. . . .

We will firmly continue the struggle against drinking and alcoholism. This social evil has been deeply rooted in our society for centuries and has become a bad habit. Hence it is not easy to combat. But society is ripe for a radical turn around. Alcohol abuse, especially in the past decades, has increased at an alarming rate and threatens the very future of the nation. . . . The per capita consumption of alcohol has dropped by half over the past two years. However, moonshining has gone up. It is impossible to resolve this issue by administrative measures alone. The most reliable way to get rid of such an evil as alcoholism is to develop the sphere of recreation, physical fitness, sport and mass cultural activities, and to further democratize the life of society as a whole. . . .

In my talks with people in the street or at the workplace I constantly hear: "Everybody supports perestroika here." I am convinced of the sincerity and fairness of these words, yet I reply every time that the most important thing right now is to talk less about perestroika and do more for it. What is needed is greater order, greater conscientiousness, greater respect for one another and greater honesty. We should follow the dictates of conscience. . . .

Observance of law is a matter of principle for us and we have taken a broad and principled view of the issue. There can be no observance of law without democracy. At the same time, democracy cannot exist and develop without the rule of law, because law is designed to protect society from abuses of power and guarantee citizens and their organizations and work collectives their rights and freedoms. This is the reason why we have taken a firm stand on the issue. . . .

The January 1987 Plenary Meeting of the Central Committee called upon Party leaders to pay greater attention to the labor, ideological and moral steeling of young people.

A didactic tone and regimentation are intolerable in work with young people. Whatever the reasons—distrust of the maturity of young people's aspirations and actions, elementary overcautiousness, a desire to make things easy for one's children—we cannot agree with such a stand. There are two prime areas in the life and work of the young. First, they have to master the entire arsenal of the ways to democracy and autonomy and breathe their youthful energy into democratization at all levels, and to be active in social endeavors. . . . Intellectual renewal and enrichment of society are what we expect of the young. . . .

Today it is imperative for the country to more actively involve women in the management of the economy, in cultural development and public life. For this purpose women's councils have been set up throughout the country. . . . We have discovered that many of our problems—in children's and young people's behavior, in our morals, culture and in production—are partially caused by the weakening of family ties and slack attitude to family responsibilities. This is a paradoxical result of our sincere and politically justified desire to make women equal with men in everything. Now, in the course of perestroika, we have begun to overcome this shortcoming. That is why we are now holding heated debates in the press, in public organizations, at work and at home, about the question of what we should do to make it possible for women to return to their purely womanly mission. . . .

Universal security in our time rests on the recognition of the right of every nation to choose its own path of social development, on the renunciation of interference in the domestic affairs of other states, on respect for others in combination with an objective self-critical view of one's own society. A nation may choose either capitalism or socialism. This is its sovereign right. Nations cannot and should not pattern their life either after the United States or the Soviet Union. Hence, political positions should be devoid of ideological intolerance. . . .

. . . We do not claim to be able to teach others. Having heard endless instructions from others, we have come to the conclusion that this is a useless pastime. Primarily, life itself teaches people to think in a new way.

REVIEW QUESTION

1. What were the essential ideas in Mikhail Gorbachev's plea for "new political thinking"?

CHAPTER 15

The West in an Age of Globalism

THE NIQAB WORN BY THIS MUSLIM WOMAN on a street in Brussels covers the body from head to toe, leaving only a slit for the eyes. Maintaining that such dress demeans women, Europeans are increasingly urging banning it outside the home. *(JULIEN WARNAND/AFP/Getty Images)*

The most important developments in recent European history were the collapse of Communism and the end of the Cold War. With the decline of Soviet power and the discrediting of Marxism, the countries of Eastern Europe, and Russia itself, struggled to adapt to Western democratic forms and the free market. The transition to laissez-faire capitalism proved particularly difficult in Russia, which remained plagued with corruption, organized crime, and a declining standard of living.

In the closing decades of the twentieth century, ethnic conflicts grew more acute. Throughout Europe Right-wing parties protested against immigration, particularly from African, Middle Eastern, and Asian lands, complaining that the essential character of their nation was being destroyed. At times, Right-wing extremists, often neo-Nazis, employed violence against immigrants. Yugoslavia was torn apart by the worst ethnic violence since World War II.

In the twenty-first century, globalization continues relentlessly; the world is being knit ever closer together by the spread of Western ideals, popular culture (particularly American), free market capitalism, and technology. Government officials and business and professional people all over the world dress in Western clothes. Women follow Western fashions in dress and makeup. People line up to eat at McDonalds, see a Hollywood movie, or attend a rock concert. Everywhere people are eager to adopt the latest technology that originated in the West but is now also manufactured in other, particularly Asian, lands.

Advanced technology intensifies the means of communication, not only through television and radio, but also with faxes, e-mail, cellular phones, and the Internet—all means of instantaneous individual communication that have become commonplace in the past two decades.

These developments promote shared interests among individuals and businesses, some of them multinational corporations, throughout the globe, reducing the importance of national frontiers. All these factors combined are reshaping non-Western societies in a relentless adjustment that causes both deep hardships and possibilities for a better life.

The ideals of freedom and democracy, historical accomplishments of Western civilization, exert a powerful influence worldwide; they are also part of the process of Westernization. Unlike technology, they cannot easily be put into practice outside the countries of their origin. However, they inspire human ambitions everywhere. They have even become part of the rhetoric of dictatorships.

At the same time, strong cultural traditions still divide the world. The hatred of radical Muslims for the West, which they see as a threat to traditional Islam, is a striking example of the clash of cultures. These Muslim militants, organized in an international network, Al Qaeda—and now increasingly operating as individuals or in independent cells—were behind appalling attacks in Africa, Asia, and

Europe as well as the bombing of the World Trade Center and the Pentagon, the worst terrorist attack in history. Their ultimate aims are the destruction of Western civilization, which they see as immoral and an affront to God, the restoration of the Islamic empire that existed in the Middle Ages, and the imposition of strict Islamic law in all Islamic lands. Often fortified by a fundamentalist theology, these militants represent a radical attack on freedom and secularism, two hallmarks of modernity.

1   The Collapse of Communism

Throughout the 1970s and early 1980s the discrepancy between Soviet ambition and deteriorating economic conditions became apparent in the Soviet Union and satellite countries of Eastern Europe. Economic productivity declined just when increasing contact with democratic and prosperous Western countries raised consumer expectations. In addition, loyalty toward the Soviet Union in the satellite countries had been steadily eroded by nationalist resentment against Communist repression.

The reforms instituted by Mikhail Gorbachev in 1986 led to a groundswell of support for liberation in Eastern Europe. Agitation for self-determination, democracy, and the end of Communist rule spread and was not suppressed as it had been in the past. During 1989, Soviet power crumbled as one by one, the Eastern European countries declared their sovereignty and ousted their Communist governments. By the end of the year, all Communist regimes there, except in Albania, had been overthrown. (Communist rule in Albania ended in 1991.) In the Soviet Union itself the Communist empire collapsed at the end of 1991. Within three years, the once-mighty superpower had disintegrated unexpectedly and in a remarkably peaceful manner. The Cold War was over.

Vaclav Havel
THE FAILURE OF COMMUNISM

Established as a sovereign state at the end of World War I, Czechoslovakia enjoyed two decades of independence until it fell under Hitler's rule in 1938–1939; in World War II it was brutally occupied by the German army. After Czechoslovakia's liberation by Soviet soldiers, Stalin ruthlessly turned it into a Communist state in 1948.

In 1968, enlightened party members, with the support of the Czech people, sought to loosen the oppressive restraints of the Communist order and reestablish ties with Western Europe. Under the leadership of Alexander Dubček the country was intoxicated with the air of freedom. Seeking a humane version of Marxism, the reformers rehabilitated the victims of the Stalinist past and stopped censorship.

Suddenly, on August 21, 1968, Soviet troops invaded the country. Although they avoided the bloodshed that had accompanied their suppression of the Hungarian uprising in 1956, the Soviet leaders stopped Dubček's reforms; liberalization in Czechoslovakia endangered their own political system. "Socialism with a human face," as Dubček's program was called, came to an end.

Yet twenty years later, in December 1989, the Communist regime dissolved in the "Velvet Revolution." Vaclav Havel, a frequently imprisoned dissident playwright and a lively intellectual, was elected president. In his 1990 New Year's Day address, excerpted below, Havel told the Czech people how the Communist regime had abused its power.

THE TRUTH, UNVARNISHED

For 40 years you have heard on this day from the mouths of my predecessors, in a number of variations, the same thing: how our country is flourishing, how many more millions of tons of steel we have produced, how we are all happy, how we believe in our Government and what beautiful prospects are opening ahead of us. I assume you have not named me to this office so that I, too, should lie to you.

Our country is not flourishing. The great creative and spiritual potential of our nation is not being applied meaningfully. Entire branches of industry are producing things for which there is no demand while we are short of things we need.

The state, which calls itself a state of workers, is humiliating and exploiting them instead. Our outmoded economy wastes energy, which we have in short supply. The country, which could once be proud of the education of its people, is spending so little on education that today, in that respect, we rank 72d in the world. We have spoiled our land, rivers and forests, inherited from our ancestors, and we have, today, the worst environment in the whole of Europe. Adults die here earlier than in the majority of European countries. . . .

LEARNING TO BELIEVE AGAIN

The worst of it is that we live in a spoiled moral environment. We have become morally ill because we are used to saying one thing and thinking another. We have learned not to believe in anything, not to care about each other, to worry only about ourselves. The concepts of love, friendship, mercy, humility or forgiveness have lost their depths and dimension, and for many of us they represent only some sort of psychological curiosity or they appear as long-lost wanderers from faraway times, somewhat ludicrous in the era of computers and space ships. . . .

COGS NO LONGER

The previous regime, armed with a proud and intolerant ideology, reduced people into the means of production, and nature into its tools. So it attacked their very essence, and their mutual relations. . . . Out of talented and responsible people, ingeniously husbanding their land, it made cogs of some sort of great, monstrous, thudding, smelly machine, with an unclear purpose. All it can do is slowly but irresistibly, wear itself out, with all its cogs.

If I speak about a spoiled moral atmosphere I don't refer only to our masters. . . . I'm speaking about all of us. For all of us have grown used to the totalitarian system and accepted it as an immutable fact, and thereby actually helped keep it going. None of us are only its victims; we are all also responsible for it.

It would be very unwise to think of the sad heritage of the last 40 years only as something foreign; something inherited from a distant relative. On the contrary, we must accept this heritage as something we have inflicted on ourselves. If we accept it in such a way, we shall come to understand it is up to all of us to do something about it.

Let us make no mistake: even the best Government, the best Parliament and the best President cannot do much by themselves. Freedom and democracy, after all, mean joint participation and shared responsibility. If we realize this, then all the horrors that the new Czechoslovak democracy inherited cease to be so horrific. If we realize this, then hope will return to our hearts.

Everywhere in the world, people were surprised how these malleable, humiliated, cynical citizens of Czechoslovakia, who seemingly believed in nothing, found the tremendous strength within a few weeks to cast off the totalitarian system, in an entirely peaceful and dignified manner. We ourselves are surprised at it.

And we ask: Where did young people who had never known another system get their longing for truth, their love of freedom, their political imagination, their civic courage and civic responsibility? How did their parents, precisely the generation thought to have been lost, join them? How is it possible that so many people immediately understood what to do and that none of them needed any advice or instructions? . . .

RECALLING RUINED LIVES

Naturally we too had to pay for our present-day freedom. Many of our citizens died in prison in the 1950's. Many were executed. Thousands of human lives were destroyed. Hundreds of thousands of talented people were driven abroad. . . . Those who fought against totalitarianism during the war were also persecuted. . . . Nobody who paid in one way or another for our freedom could be forgotten.

Independent courts should justly evaluate the possible guilt of those responsible, so that the full truth about our recent past should be exposed.

But we should also not forget that other nations paid an even harsher price for their present freedom, and paid indirectly for ours as well. All human suffering concerns each human being. . . . Without changes in the Soviet Union, Poland, Hungary, and the German Democratic Republic, what happened here could hardly have taken place, and certainly not in such a calm and peaceful way.

Now it depends only on us whether this hope will be fulfilled, whether our civic, national and political self-respect will be revived. Only a man or nation with self-respect, in the best sense of the word, is capable of listening to the voices of others, while accepting them as equals, of forgiving enemies and of expiating sins. . . .

A HUMANE REPUBLIC

Perhaps you are asking what kind of republic I am dreaming about. I will answer you: a republic that is independent, free, democratic, a republic with economic prosperity and also social justice, a humane republic that serves man and that for that reason also has the hope that man will serve it. . . .

THE PEOPLE HOLD SWAY

My most important predecessor started his first speech by quoting from Comenius.[1] Permit me to end my own first speech by my own paraphrase. Your Government, my people, has returned to you.

---

[1]Comenius was a Czech theologian and educator of the seventeenth century. The quotation was used by Tomáš Masaryk (1850–1937), the first president of Czechoslovakia, which was created after World War I. "I, too, believe before God that, when the storms of wrath have passed, to thee shall return the rule over thine own things, O Czech people."

REVIEW QUESTION

1. What did Vaclav Havel mean when he said the Czechs had lived in a "spoiled moral environment" for the past forty years?

2   Russia: Creeping Autocracy and Burgeoning Nationalism

In August 1991, Boris Yeltsin was the world's hero, standing atop a Soviet tank in Moscow and rallying his fellow Russians to the cause of democracy in the face of an attempted coup by Kremlin hardliners. Within a few years he had become an international joke, a petty tyrant and physically spent alcoholic whose chances of surviving his term as president seemed questionable. In some respects, Yeltsin, a former devoted Communist bureaucrat, embodied the country over which he ruled. Both underwent an ideological transformation that had begun amidst widespread optimism but now threatened to spin out of control, with devastating consequences for themselves and the world at large. "Shock therapy," the economic policies that all at once established free markets and private property, enriched only those who already controlled the levers of the economy while impoverishing the large majority of the population. Meanwhile, Yeltsin found himself increasingly at odds with the parliament. Faced with deadlock, he ordered army tanks to fire on the legislature and pushed through a constitution that enhanced his own powers. By the end of the 1990s, Russia's major assets (including the media, natural resources, and banks) had been gathered up by a handful of "oligarchs" who formed a clique around the president. Corruption and violent crime became common. Ordinary Russians were often going without their paychecks or pensions. In 1998 the country defaulted on its foreign debt. In short, the dreams of a market economy and political democracy had eluded Russia, which now seemed weaker than ever, a mere shadow of the Soviet superpower whose core it had been.

That Russia would undergo a revival in less than a decade was a development that few would have dared predict toward the end of Yeltsin's term in office. Ironically, it was Yeltsin himself who laid the groundwork for the turnaround when, in 1999, he named as the last of his prime ministers a little known former KGB bureaucrat named Vladimir Putin.

C. J. Chivers
VLADIMIR PUTIN: A NEW TSAR IN THE KREMLIN?

When Vladimir Putin (b. 1952) became Russia's prime minister in August 1999, he struck many people as a fairly colorless and even grim {party bureaucrat} in the old Soviet mold. Before long, however, he proved himself a dynamic leader and intrepid political operator who began the restoration of Russian power both at home and abroad. Russia under Putin has diverged considerably from the democratic path that many in the West hoped the country had embarked on following the collapse of the Soviet Union in 1991. Indeed, if anything, he has emerged more clearly as the autocrat that Boris Yeltsin often threatened to become. At the same time, Putin is enormously popular among his countrymen, who are grateful for the economic and national revival he has overseen. In the first decade of the twenty-first century, Putin made Russia a major player in the world arena once again.

Reflecting Putin's global impact, *Time* magazine chose Vladimir Putin late in 2007 as its "Person of the Year." A few months later, in March 2008, Putin, observing the two-term limit stipulated in the Russian constitution, relinquished the reins of power to his elected successor, Dimitri Medvedev, whom he had personally chosen for the job. Medvedev then appointed Putin as his prime minister, giving rise to speculation that Putin would continue to pull the strings from behind the scenes.

Late in 2008 a profile of Putin by C. J. Chivers appeared in *Esquire*. In addition to his years covering Russia for the *New York Times*, Chivers had reported from several of the republics that at one time had made up the former Soviet Union and thus brought to his analysis both a broader and more multilayered perspective. An edited version of his article on Putin appears below.

THE MAN WHO WOULD BE CZAR

Vladimir Putin is a national savior and hero, a man, sober and exceptionally smart, who stepped from shadows to resuscitate a proud country that others had run aground, looted, and left for dead. After eight years as president, a period marked by a surging economy and an unexpectedly victorious war in Chechnya, he surrendered one of the most seductively powerful offices on earth voluntarily and according to Russia's constitution, with Moscow's influence in the world restored and with a large fraction of Russia's citizens better off than they ever had been. He has been a bridge from postcommunist chaos and hardship to national stability, freer markets, individual economic choice, and the possibility of democracy.

Or, he is a cunning, even diabolical strongman [the head] of bandit cliques. As a career officer in the KGB, an organization its members never leave, he is fundamentally anti-Western and undemocratic, and comfortable with conflict, crime, and the company of beasts. Moreover, he is nostalgic for empire and covetous of power, and he has surrendered only a title. Instead, he has manipulated Russia's loose political rules and obedient political class to install a puppet successor and transfer the levers to his new post as Russia's premier, where he continues to abuse office and direct the spoils of oil-state excess to his coterie. His talk of public stewardship and personal liberties is farce. The Kremlin has rejected democracy while pretending to embrace it, hardening into a kleptocracy with nuclear weapons and state-controlled television stations purring that all is well.

Depending on the point of view of the commentator (and sometimes the source of the commentator's paycheck), the standard assessments of Putin's nine years in public office reach these rival extremes. What makes them interesting, and makes full and accurate descriptions of Putin elusive, is that both are largely true.

Vladimir Putin is one of the central figures of our times, the man who presided at the Kremlin as the broken remains of a sprawling nation were restored to life, and who used his stature to reorder the Russian-speaking world's relations with the West and become the de facto spokesman of strongmen everywhere. No recent Western leader can claim to have changed a nation and its place in the world so fully. . . .

Is Putin's Russia a retreat to Soviet practices or a capitalist democracy sputtering through early stages of evolution? Putin's signature legacy is not Russia's new wealth and confidence, nor the subjugation of Chechnya, nor the return of an assertive foreign policy, capped by the invasion of Georgia. It is the refinement, if that word could ever be used with this phenomenon, of a more sophisticated and rational police state than the failed USSR. This is no celebration of imaginary virtues; the world of his politics remains ugly and unrepaired. It is meant to pose a question. Putin has reshaped Russian autocracy under another name. To what end?

THE STRONG MAN

From the beginning, the experts' forecasts were wrong. When an exhausted President Boris Yeltsin introduced Putin to the world in the summer of 1999, announcing that Putin was his choice as prime minister (Yeltsin's sixth in less than eighteen months), few expected him to last. It was not just that Putin, then forty-six, was charged with managing a pauper state, a government adrift in disorder, and a population soured by the unmet promises of free markets and democracy. The brewing unrest in Chechnya had drifted beyond separatism and nationalism and become an international Islamic cause. Crime and corruption were pandemic, and a circle of billionaire oligarchs controlled large fractions of the nation's resources and capital, as well as voting blocs in parliament, which was a legislature for sale. . . .

In retrospect, of course, the early assessments were wrong. . . . Putin swiftly displayed his confrontational self. He directed a renewed military campaign in Chechnya, which was foundering under the self-rule separatists had gained after fighting the Russian army to a standstill a few years before. The war had undermined Russia's standing and self-esteem, psychological injuries that Putin seemed to understand viscerally. Vladimir Putin did not just promise to restore Russian rule. He went beyond the typical language of settling unsettled scores. He vowed blood. "We will pursue the terrorists everywhere," he said. "You will forgive me, but if we catch them in the toilet, we will wet them even in the outhouse." Earlier Russian premiers had been rendered inert by the tenacity of the Chechen fighters and the reliable incompetence of Russia's army. (In 1995 Viktor Chernomyrdin had pleaded for the release of hostages with

Shamil Basayev, the terrorist, on live television. "I beg you," he had said.) Putin signaled that Russia would not beg. He came from an organization that had used fear to bring a vast nation to heel. Violence for him was a governing tool.

Putin also showed skills as a performer, peppering an understated demeanor with prison-slang coarseness. Hunting terrorists to their toilets? The Russian idiom "to wet" is inmate jargon for soaking a victim in blood. It is a knowing way of saying "to kill" and suggests killing at very close range, as with a knife. Underneath his Italian suits and aura of sobriety, Putin revealed an icy Eastwood deadpan. An ease with crudity simmered beneath what passed for Putin's style. Asked if he worried about Russia's columns inflicting civilian casualties, Putin made clear that he did not, and would not keep company with people who did. "We do not need generals who chew snot," he said.

Such was the mind behind Russia's new war. Russian troops soon leveled much of Grozny, Chechnya's capital, and launched often indiscriminate sweeps through the Chechen countryside. Victims and human-rights organizations assigned much of the blame for the troops' conduct to Putin, whose language seemed to encourage it. Putin was undeterred. He had found a persona. He was not just a stern nationalist who would restore Russian sovereignty. He was the unblinking fighter, untroubled by rules, conscience, or second thought in the pursuit of national order. Russia's losing streak had been long. Putin would be its fist. RUDEST EVER P.M. WINS OVER RUSSIA, another Western newspaper declared. His popularity climbed.

Late in 1999, Yeltsin resigned, making Putin the front-runner in the presidential race. In the spring of 2000, he was elected. His time had begun.

THE BOOM

Eight years on, Russia looks not much like it did then. The value of the Russian stock market has soared. Personal incomes have grown. A society that suffered the forced austerity of

Communism and economic collapse has entered a carnival of personal spending. Gone are empty shelves, replaced by a rollicking consumer culture that buys what it wants. French perfumes, Austrian chocolates, Japanese electronics, Scandinavian cell phones, Italian handbags, Cuban cigars, Australian wines, and single-malt Scotches—malls have opened offering all of these. Rates of car ownership have multiplied with access to personal credit, and Moscow's roads, cluttered during Yeltsin's time with Zhigulis, are jammed with BMWs and Benzes. Extravagant restaurants cater to the wealthy. Sushi, in the inland reaches of a northern forest, is a minor Russian craze. For people of even modest means, stores stock fresh fruits and vegetables year-round. Yes, *babushkas* still sell onions on the streets. And yes, rural areas are deeply depressed. But the expanding Russian wealth has grown beyond the horizon. Visit tourist destinations in Thailand, the Mediterranean, Europe, or the Red Sea and you will hear Russian. Visit a real estate office in any Western capital and you will hear tales of Russian buyers.

Such are the signs of the most tangible freedom associated with Putin's Russia—the freedom to buy whatever you can afford, except, in most cases, power.

No small part of this turnaround resulted from conditions outside Putin's control. Russia's combined oil and natural-gas reserves are the world's largest, and with timber and coal and mineral deposits, these resources positioned Russia to be a global gas pump, lumberyard, and mine long before any of us knew Putin's name. The price explosion of oil enriched Russia with head-spinning speed, creating a huge transfer of global wealth to Slavic hands. Along the way, it transformed parts of dreary Moscow into a northern Vegas and allowed the Kremlin—which not long ago could not afford the fuel in its fighter jets—to pay down foreign debts ahead of schedule. And yet the results cannot be ascribed to sheer chance. It is easy to reduce the arrival of Russian wealth to the indifferent bounty of market forces, but sound macroeconomics and fiscal restraint supported some of the boom. Stephen Kotkin, the professor

of Russian history at Princeton, said early this year that if surging oil and gas prices automatically mean that states rich with hydrocarbons will enjoy instant prosperity, ask Nigeria where its boom is.

While Russia's economy roared, Putin was benefiting from another unanticipated success. By 2005, the war in Chechnya had turned. The insurgent bands were either being thinned to pockets or, in many cases, coerced to join a pro-Kremlin government led by Ramzan Kadyrov, the rebel turned Putin loyalist who replaced the chaos of conflict with a local dictatorship. Fighting lingers nearby, in Ingushetia and sometimes Dagestan, but in scale and intensity it is a fraction of the violence of 2004. No one saw this coming. Anyone suggesting four years ago, after the school siege in Beslan, that the war would be reduced to skirmishes in Ingushetia and Dagestan, and that Grozny (think: Mogadishu) would be largely rebuilt in a thousand days, would have been dismissed as a fool. But after the school siege ended in 2004, with more than 330 victims dead and hundreds more injured, Russian counterterrorism was reinvigorated.[1] Two underground Chechen presidents were killed, and [Shamil] Basayev [a Chechen militant Islamist who waged war against Russia] died in a mysterious explosion. On both sides, the war had been a race for the bottom, with horrors trumped by horrors for several years. With Beslan, the separatists had gone too far. Chechnya's Sufi nationalists had once enjoyed a reputation as underdogs. But killing children was not an image-booster; support for them collapsed. . . .

The author then discusses the good fortune that befell Putin: Islamic freedom fighters from throughout the Middle East and Central Asia who had been pouring into Chechnya to support its war against Russia suddenly had a new enemy on which to focus—the U.S. military presence in Iraq.

---

[1] In September 2004 armed terrorists seized a school in the town of Beslan in North Ossetia, an autonomous republic in Russia's North Caucasus. Demanding an end to the Second Chechen War, they took 1,100 people hostage. Eventually Russian forces staged a massive assault on the building. The death toll among the hostages numbered 334, more than half of them children.

Putin, a student of what is wrong with the United States, had loudly opposed the invasion of Iraq. But as the United States bogged down along the Tigris and the Euphrates, the war he had stood against was making his job easier. George Bush limped toward the end of his presidency, facing public unease about his handling of the wars in Afghanistan and Iraq. Vladimir Putin's public-approval ratings exceeded 70 percent. By this year, with memories of terrorism in Moscow streets fading, the Chechen war had slipped from much of the national conversation. Putin was even able to raise the subject himself to divert uncomfortable questions about his personal life. . . .

AN AGGRESSIVE FOREIGN POLICY

There are many essential moments in Putin's consolidation of power. Most publicly, it began with the arrest of oil oligarch Mikhail Khodorkovsky, an act that propelled his long climb to what he is now. But his handling of Ukraine, at first bungled, proved to be another.

Putin's Ukraine policy had courted disaster. In the elections of 2004, he publicly backed a pro-Russian candidate, Viktor Yanukovich, who had been convicted of robbery but had the support of the sordid political machine built by Leonid Kuchma, the much-hated departing president. Putin jumped in as if the race were a domestic affair. He presided over a Soviet-style military parade in Kiev and committed Russia to an energy deal that pledged to sell natural gas to Ukraine at a deep discount through 2009. Natural gas is the lubricant of the Ukrainian economy. It heats Ukrainian cities and powers electrical plants and factories. Putin's deal—to sell gas for less than a quarter of the market rate through Yanukovich's first presidential term—was a subsidy-for-loyalty exchange, and promised Ukraine's elite ample opportunity for graft. (Reselling subsidized Russian gas at high profits is a common insiders' swindle.)

There was only one problem: Yanukovich was not elected. His rival, Viktor Yushchenko, survived dioxin poisoning and emerged from the hospital as a potent symbol against the enduring nastiness of post-Soviet rule. Kuchma's government falsified an election victory for Yanukovich, but it was not enough. Hundreds of thousands of demonstrators, and then the Ukrainian court, demanded a new vote. Putin was scrambling for credibility.

His retaliation was precise. Russia announced that the gas deal with Ukraine was off, and that Ukraine would have to pay market rates, now more than five times the previous offer. Gazprom, Russia's state gas monopoly, set a deadline for late 2005. The threat's timing was carefully chosen and the irony inescapable. Ukraine faced the prospect of gas shortages in winter. And Putin, the KGB man who had given a Soviet-style energy subsidy to a nation to buy its loyalty, was now lecturing Europe about the need for market rates.

As Yushchenko resisted through the deadline, Russia escalated again, reducing pressure in pipelines feeding Ukraine. Pressure quickly began to fall in Europe, which receives much of its gas on lines that pass through Ukraine. In his anger that Ukraine overturned a falsified election, Putin was cutting off gas to the West. European officials seethed. Could he be such a neophyte? Was he not getting any better advice? Had Putin lost his mind?

With the din rising, Yushchenko capitulated in a deal to buy gas through a mysterious company, Rosukrenergo, at a compromise price. It was an utterly nontransparent arrangement, and raised immediate suspicion that insiders were profiting. After seeming cornered only months before, Putin had won, and been successful in three ways. He had forced Ukraine to accept his terms, he had pulled Yushchenko into an agreement that sullied his government and image as a reformer, and he had shown Europe that he could stand up to it as Yeltsin never did. . . .

THE CRACKDOWN

For all of Putin's domestic success, and in spite of his good luck, Russia remains bedeviled by problems. Social services are poor, and corruption has become total. Russian public services are so wormy with dishonesty and dysfunction that patients bribe doctors for care, parents buy access to schools for their children and grades for their report cards, and the police shake down drivers with a regularity resembling taxation. The court system is a sham, vulnerable to bribery and political instruction. Racial and ethnic violence is widespread, and murders of minorities occur with morbid frequency.

Russia's army, far behind Western levels of professionalism and standards of equipment, is further weakened by high rates of draft dodging, which are elevated by traditions of conscript hazing. Its record of human-rights violations is appalling. Putin has consolidated the Kremlin's control over key economic sectors—oil, gas, pipelines, aircraft and vehicle manufacture, arms dealing, banking, and metals—and the billionaires have been brought under the Kremlin's sway. But there are more oligarchs now than in 2000, suggesting that wealth has not been redistributed in ways Putin had pledged, even as inflation and a real estate bubble have eroded middle-class spending power.

All of these are issues that might motivate a growing middle class to ask questions about its government. So how did Vladimir Putin build so much prestige and muster the strength to assert himself on the world?

The easy answer, the one you've heard, is that he rolled back civil liberties and created a neo-Soviet state, securing his own power by limiting everyone else's. Since 2000, Putin's Kremlin has replaced independent television with lapdog television, stifled political competitors, expelled foreigners and harried nongovernmental organizations that criticize the state, abolished the elections for governors and replaced them with a system in which the Kremlin appoints regional leaders. The effect has been a drought of candor and vibrancy in Russia's public conversation. These days, free speech does not extend much beyond venting online, a single bold radio station, and the work of a few small, rambunctious newspapers.

But the insistence that Russia is returning to Soviet times is a claim resting on omission and exaggeration. This is not the nightmare of Soviet rule, and not just because Russians have access to food and foreign goods. Putin's Russia is a canny autocracy, a system that exerts intensive control over political society but offers pressure-release valves in individual life. In Russia, Internet use is largely unfettered, cellphone ownership is profligate, the pursuit of money is an organizing ideology, and foreign travel is common. Under the old guard, all of these would have been regarded as threats to the state. . . .

The Kremlin's political apparatus routinely falsified elections. It compelled laborers, students, and government employees to vote for its candidates. It doctored voter lists. It used tax inspectors and police to harass opposition members. It manipulated media coverage and released invented vote results. In the daily administration of government affairs, the state perched atop a sprawling machinery of graft that spirited away money from all manner of public works. And the state's penetration of the strategic industries extended the graft throughout the economy. Although checks and balances existed in the law, in practice they had been subverted. The Kremlin controlled the legislature and courts. Law-enforcement agencies—from the tax police to the successors of the KGB—worked at its bidding. No new face could stand against Putin or his men. . . .

Put another way, Putin's autocracy is a cunning blend of ruling ideas from the old Soviet regime with many of the material pleasures of capitalist life, a form of government for strongmen who did their homework. And just as they accept that freer markets are more efficient than planned economies, and that pining for foreign goods is not treason, Putin and his circle understand that Russia's people can say what they wish in their kitchens without endangering the state. This allows for democratic pretenses with centralized rule and insider access to the profits of governing. The Kremlin today does not control everything. It does not try to. Putin's circle exerts control over the profits of the most lucrative industries, and bares its teeth at actual threats to power. Repression is no longer total. It is precise, and its weight is brought down, often publicly, on the few who stand up to the state. . . .

A KINDER, GENTLER POLICE STATE

For years after the Soviet Union's collapse, Russia's liberals and Westerners alike hoped that the freed people and new republics would form law-abiding and democratic states. Putin's rule has labored to prevent that from happening, and the old Soviet world has hardened to its new shape. Across the rolling expanse of steppe, forest, and mountain range formerly under Kremlin rule, every single government unfailingly declares itself democratic. But aside from in the Baltic states, few in the region can speak candidly on television or the radio, or watch a free and independent news broadcast of local origin, or enjoy unmolested public assembly that criticizes the government, or have a fair hearing before an impartial judge in a court where the law is the highest authority, or select leaders from a slate of candidates who have been allowed

to campaign openly and without restriction. This is the state of the Russian-speaking world nearly two decades after the wall came down. . . .

TO WHAT END?

Early this year, Putin was challenged by a reporter at a news conference over the continued vote fabrications in Chechnya. There, according to the government's figures for the parliamentary election last year, 99 percent of the voters had cast ballots, and 99 percent of the ballots were for the political party Putin leads. Such election figures have been rivaled only in Kim Jong-il's North Korea, Mao's China, Niyazov's Turkmenistan, and Saddam Hussein's Iraq. They were especially absurd for a vote in Chechnya, a land shaped by cycles of resistance to Russian rule, and that had been brought back to yoke by force. The correspondent wanted to know: Did the president of Russia find these numbers credible?

Putin declined to answer. Instead, he asked a state journalist from Chechnya to answer for him. The young Chechen quickly stood. "These are absolutely realistic figures," he said, grinning obsequiously. And Vladimir Putin watched with a mix of satisfaction and boredom, the face of unchecked power itself.

REVIEW QUESTION

1. In what direction has Putin taken Russia? How does that change affect the United States?

---

3 Globalization: Patterns and Problems

The interaction between the West and the non-Western world initiated during the Age of Exploration in the fifteenth and sixteenth centuries accelerated with the emergence of European imperialism in the late nineteenth century. Today the world is being knit ever closer together by the spread of Western ideals, free-market capitalism, and technology, particularly telecommunications (satellites and the Internet). The breakthrough in information technology, says Thomas L. Friedman, foreign affairs columnist for *The New York Times*, has enabled companies "to locate different parts of their production, research, and marketing in different countries, but still tie them together through computers and teleconferencing as though they were in one place." And it allows individuals all over the world to communicate with each other instantly and inexpensively, overcoming national borders. A distinguishing feature of globalization is the elimination of barriers to free trade and the interconnectedness of national economies. Proponents of these trends argue convincingly, as does economist Jagdish Bhagwati, that expanded international "trade enhances growth, and the growth reduces poverty." The economic growth facilitated by globalization, continues Bhagwati, also alleviates social distress, including female oppression, child labor, and illiteracy.

> Let me add that growth is also a powerful mechanism that brings to life social legislation aimed at helping the poor and peripheral groups. Thus, rights and benefits for women may be guaranteed by legislation that prohibits dowry, proscribes polygamy, mandates primary [school] enrollment for all children (including girls), and much else. But it will often amount to a hill of beans unless a growing economy gives women the economic independence to walk out and even to sue at the risk of being discarded. A battered wife who cannot find a new job is less likely to take advantage of legislation that says a husband cannot beat his wife.

Moreover, Bhagwati argues that even if the state requires primary school education, necessity will often compel impoverished parents to send their children to work rather than to school. However, as the parents' income increases because of economic growth they are likely to send their children to school.

But globalization has also created a backlash among people who regard Westernization as a threat to revered traditions. The most dramatic and dangerous reaction against Western values has occurred in Muslim lands, which have witnessed a surge of religious fundamentalism designed to counter Western influence. In their struggle against modernization and westernization, radical Islamists or jihadists have resorted to terrorism, culminating in the attack on the World Trade Center and the Pentagon on September 11, 2001.

Fareed Zakaria
"DEMOCRACY HAS ITS DARK SIDES"

In the following selection from his book *The Future of Freedom* (2003), Fareed Zakaria, editor of *Newsweek International*, discusses the implications of the spread of democracy throughout much of the globe. In many countries, he observes, the adoption of democratic procedures—parliaments and the ballot—has enabled dictators to gain and retain power.

We live in a democratic age. Over the last century the world has been shaped by one trend above all others—the rise of democracy. In 1900 not a single country had what we would today consider democracy: a government created by elections in which every adult citizen could vote. Today 119 do, comprising 62 percent of all countries in the world. What was once a peculiar practice of a handful of states around the North Atlantic has become the standard form of government for humankind. Monarchies are antique, Fascism and Communism utterly discredited. Even Islamic theocracy appeals only to a fanatical few. For the vast majority of the world, democracy is the sole surviving source of political legitimacy. Dictators such as Egypt's Hosni Mubarak and Zimbabwe's Robert Mugabe go to great effort and expense to organize national elections—which, of course, they win handily. When the enemies of democracy mouth its rhetoric and ape its rituals, you know it has won the war.

We live in a democratic age in an even broader sense. From its Greek root, "democracy" means "the rule of the people." And everywhere we are witnessing the shift of power downward. I call this "democratization," even though it goes far beyond politics, because the process is similar: hierarchies are breaking down, closed systems are opening up, and pressures from the masses are now the primary engine of social change. Democracy has gone from being a form of government to a way of life.

Consider the economic realm. What is truly distinctive and new about today's capitalism is not that it is global or information-rich or technologically driven—all that has been true at earlier points in history—but rather that it is *democratic.* Over the last half-century economic growth has enriched hundreds of millions in the industrial world, turning consumption, saving, and investing into a mass phenomenon. This has forced the social structures of societies to adapt. Economic power, which was for centuries held by small groups of businessmen, bankers, and bureaucrats has, as a result, been shifting downward. Today most companies—indeed most countries—woo not the handful that are rich but the many that are middle class. And rightly so, for the assets of the most exclusive investment group are dwarfed by those of a fund of workers' pensions.

Culture has also been democratized. What was once called "high culture" continues to flourish, of course, but as a niche product for the elderly set, no longer at the center of society's cultural life, which is now defined and dominated by popular music, blockbuster movies, and prime-time television. Those three make up the canon of the modern age, the set of cultural references with which everyone in society is familiar. The democratic revolution coursing through society has changed our very definition of culture. The key to the reputation of, say, a singer in an old order would have been *who* liked her. The key to fame today is *how many* like her. And by that yardstick Madonna will always trump Jessye Norman.* Quantity has become quality.

What has produced this dramatic shift? As with any large-scale social phenomenon, many forces have helped produce the democratic wave—a technological revolution, growing middle-class wealth, and the collapse of alternative systems and ideologies that organized society. To these grand systemic causes add another: America. The rise and dominance of America— a country whose politics and culture are deeply democratic—has made democratization seem inevitable. Whatever its causes, the democratic wave is having predictable effects in every area. It is breaking down hierarchies, empowering individuals, and transforming societies well beyond their politics. Indeed much of what is distinctive about the world we live in is a consequence of the democratic idea.

We often read during the roaring 1990s that technology and information had been democratized. This is a relatively new phenomenon. In the past, technology helped reinforce centralization and hierarchy. For example, the last great information revolution—in the 1920s involving radio, television, movies, megaphones— had a centralizing effect. It gave the person or group with access to that technology the power to reach the rest of society. That's why the first step in a twentieth-century coup or revolution was always to take control of the country's television or radio station. But today's information revolution has produced thousands of outlets for news that make central control impossible and dissent easy. The Internet has taken this process

---

*African-American opera singer.

another huge step forward, being a system where, in the columnist Thomas Friedman's words, "everyone is connected but no one is in control."

The democratization of technology and information means that most anyone can get his hands on anything. Like weapons of mass destruction. We now know that Osama bin Laden was working on a serious biological-weapon program during the 1990s. But what is most astonishing is that the scientific information and manuals found in Al Qaeda's Kabul safe houses were not secrets stolen from government laboratories. They were documents downloaded from the Internet. Today if you want to find sources for anthrax, recipes for poison, or methods to weaponize chemicals, all you need is a good search engine. These same open sources will, unfortunately, soon help someone build a dirty bomb. The components are easier to get than ever before. Mostly what you need is knowledge, and that has been widely disseminated over the last decade. Even nuclear technology is now commonly available. It is, after all, fifty-year-old know-how, part of the world of AM radios and black-and-white television. Call it the democratization of violence.

It's more than a catchy phrase. The democratization of violence is one of the fundamental—and terrifying—features of the world today. For centuries the state has had a monopoly over the legitimate use of force in human societies. This inequality of power between the state and the citizen created order and was part of the glue that held modern civilization together. But over the last few decades the state's advantage has been weakened; now small groups of people can do dreadful things. And while terrorism is the most serious blow to state authority, central governments have been under siege in other ways as well. Capital markets, private businesses, local governments, nongovernmental organizations have all been gaining strength, sapping the authority of the state. The illegal flow of people, drugs, money, and weapons rising around the world attests to its weakness. This diffusion of power will continue because

it is fueled by broad technological, social, and economic changes. In the post–September 11 world the state has returned, with renewed power and legitimacy. This too will endure. The age of terror will thus be marked by a tension between the forces that drive the democratization of authority on the one hand and the state on the other.

To discuss these problems is not to say that democracy is a bad thing. Overwhelmingly it has had wonderful consequences. Who among us would want to go back to an age with fewer choices and less individual power and autonomy? But like any broad transformation, democracy has its dark sides. Yet we rarely speak about them. To do so would be to provoke instant criticism that you are "out of sync" with the times. But this means that we never really stop to understand these times. Silenced by fears of being branded "antidemocratic" we have no way to understand what might be troubling about the ever-increasing democratization of our lives. We assume that no problem could ever be caused by democracy, so when we see social, political, and economic maladies we shift blame here and there, deflecting problems, avoiding answers, but never talking about the great transformation that is at the center of our political, economic, and social lives.

DEMOCRACY AND LIBERTY

"Suppose elections are free and fair and those elected are racists, fascists, separatists," said the American diplomat Richard Holbrooke about Yugoslavia in the 1990s. "That is the dilemma." Indeed it is, and not merely in Yugoslavia's past but in the world's present. Consider, for example, the challenge we face across the Islamic world. We recognize the need for democracy in those often-repressive countries. But what if democracy produces an Islamic theocracy or something like it? It is not an idle concern. Across the globe, democratically elected regimes, often ones that have been re-elected or reaffirmed through referenda, are routinely ignoring constitutional limits on their power and depriving their citizens of basic rights. This disturbing phenomenon—visible from Peru to the Palestinian territories, from Ghana to Venezuela—could be called "illiberal democracy."

For people in the West, democracy means "liberal democracy": a political system marked not only by free and fair elections but also by the rule of law, a separation of powers, and the protection of basic liberties of speech, assembly, religion, and property. But this bundle of freedoms—what might be termed "constitutional liberalism"—has nothing intrinsically to do with democracy and the two have not always gone together, even in the West. After all, Adolf Hitler became chancellor of Germany via free elections. Over the last half-century in the West, democracy and liberty have merged. But today the two strands of liberal democracy, interwoven in the Western political fabric, are coming apart across the globe. Democracy is flourishing; liberty is not.

In some places, such as Central Asia, elections have paved the way for dictatorships. In others, they have exacerbated group conflict and ethnic tensions. Both Yugoslavia and Indonesia, for example, were far more tolerant and secular when they were ruled by strongmen (Tito and Suharto, respectively) than they are now as democracies. And in many nondemocracies, elections would not improve matters much. Across the Arab world elections held tomorrow would probably bring to power regimes that are more intolerant, reactionary, anti-Western, and anti-Semitic than the dictatorships currently in place.

In a world that is increasingly democratic, regimes that resist the trend produce dysfunctional societies—as in the Arab world. Their people sense the deprivation of liberty more strongly than ever before because they know the alternatives; they can see them on CNN, BBC, and Al-Jazeera. But yet, newly democratic countries too often become sham democracies, which produces disenchantment, disarray, violence, and new forms of tyranny. Look at Iran and Venezuela. This is not a reason to stop holding elections, of course, but surely it should make us ask, What is at the root of this troubling development? Why do so many developing countries have so much difficulty creating stable, genuinely democratic societies? Were we to embark on the vast challenge of building democracy in Iraq, how would we make sure that we succeed?

REVIEW QUESTION

1. According to Fareed Zakaria, how has the contemporary world been shaped by democracy? What does he see as the "dark sides" of democracy?

4 Female Oppression

"The two biggest threats to women today are Islamic fundamentalism and the trafficking and normalization of prostitution," says Donna Hughes, professor of women's studies at the University of Rhode Island and an expert on the trafficking of women. As Southeast Asia opened to the West and the Soviet Union collapsed, trafficking (that is, illegal commercial trading) in women and young girls for prostitution became a major international issue. Conservative evangelical Christians in the United States had pushed the Bush administration to pressure foreign governments to curb trafficking or face sanctions. This has had some success, particularly where countries have been able to abolish the use of underage girls in brothels.

Trafficking is only one facet of the larger problem of the oppression of women. The resurgence of Islamic culture among one billion Muslims has had a marked effect on the social position of Muslim women. While women in Western-influenced Islamic countries have made progress in gaining rights and freedoms, the more conservative Islamic states have maintained traditional Islamic law that relegates women to a subordinate position in society, governing their conduct and the way they dress, and consigning them to a domestic role in a male-dominated society.

The revolution of 1979 in Iran changed a modernizing country into an Islamic republic with repressive laws governing women. The worst excesses of female oppression occurred in Afghanistan during the fundamentalist Taliban regime (1996–2001) that imposed rules for women, permitting beatings by male relatives, prohibiting females from working, barring them from schools, restricting medical treatment, and demanding that they wear the burka—a garment that covered them from head to foot. Violators could be severely beaten, imprisoned, or executed.

United Nations Secretary-General
ENDING VIOLENCE AGAINST WOMEN
"THE SYSTEMATIC DOMINATION OF WOMEN BY MEN"

In October 2006 the United Nations released the Secretary-General's in-depth study of violence against women, which concluded that "the pervasiveness of violence against women across the boundaries of nation, culture, race, class and religion points to its roots in patriarchy—the systematic domination of women by men." Excerpts from the study follow.

INTRODUCTION

65.   The recognition of violence against women as a form of discrimination and, thus, a human rights violation, provides an entry point for understanding the broad context from which such violence emerges and related risk factors. The central premise of the analysis of violence against women within the human rights framework is that the specific causes of such violence and the factors that increase the risk of its occurrence are grounded in the broader context of systemic gender-based discrimination against women and other forms of subordination. Such violence is a manifestation of the historically unequal power relations between women and men reflected in both public and private life. . . . Vulnerability to violence is understood as a condition created by the absence or denial of rights.

66.   Violence against women is not confined to a specific culture, region or country, or to particular groups of women within a society. The different manifestations of such violence and women's personal experience of it are, however, shaped by many factors, including economic status, race, ethnicity, class, age, sexual

orientation, disability, nationality, religion and culture. . . .

Patriarchy and Other Relations of Dominance and Subordination

69.　Violence against women is both universal and particular. It is universal in that there is no region of the world, no country and no culture in which women's freedom from violence has been secured. The pervasiveness of violence against women across the boundaries of nation, culture, race, class and religion points to its roots in patriarchy—the systemic domination of women by men.

72.　A number of key means through which male dominance and women's subordination are maintained are common to many settings. These include: exploitation of women's productive and reproductive work; control over women's sexuality and reproductive capacity; cultural norms and practices that entrench women's unequal status; State structures and processes that legitimize and institutionalize gender inequalities; and violence against women. Violence against women is both a means by which women's subordination is perpetuated and a consequence of their subordination.

73.　Violence against women serves as a mechanism for maintaining male authority. When a woman is subjected to violence for transgressing social norms governing female sexuality and family roles, for example, the violence is not only individual but, through its punitive and controlling functions, also reinforces prevailing gender norms. Acts of violence against women cannot be attributed solely to individual psychological factors or socioeconomic conditions such as unemployment. Explanations for violence that focus primarily on individual behaviours and personal histories, such as alcohol abuse or a history of exposure to violence, overlook the broader impact of systemic gender inequality and women's

subordination. Efforts to uncover the factors that are associated with violence against women should therefore be situated within this larger social context of power relations. . . .

76.　Impunity for violence against women compounds the effects of such violence as a mechanism of control. When the State fails to hold the perpetrators accountable, impunity not only intensifies the subordination and powerlessness of the targets of violence, but also sends a message to society that male violence against women is both acceptable and inevitable. As a result, patterns of violent behaviour are normalized. . . .

Culture and Violence Against Women

78.　While some cultural norms and practices empower women and promote women's human rights, customs, traditions and religious values are also often used to justify violence against women. Certain cultural norms have long been cited as causal factors for violence against women, including the beliefs associated with "harmful traditional practices" (such as female genital mutilation/cutting, child marriage and son preference), crimes committed in the name of "honour," discriminatory criminal punishments imposed under religiously based laws, and restrictions on women's rights in marriage. However, the cultural bases of other forms of violence against women have not been adequately examined, at least in part because of narrow conceptions of what constitutes "culture." . . .

81.　Cultural justifications for restricting women's human rights have been asserted by some States and by social groups within many countries claiming to defend cultural tradition. These defences are generally voiced by political leaders or traditional authorities, not by those whose rights are actually affected. Cultural relativist arguments have been advanced in national contexts and in international debates when laws and practices that curtail women's human rights have been challenged. The politicization of culture in the form of religious "fundamentalisms" in diverse geographic and religious contexts has become a serious challenge to efforts to secure women's human rights. . . .

84.   Various manifestations of femicide, the murder of women because they are women, illustrate the interrelationship between cultural norms and the use of violence in the subordination of women. Femicide takes place in many contexts: intimate partner violence, armed conflict, workplace harassment, dowry disputes and the protection of family "honour." For example, crimes committed in the name of "honour," usually by a brother, father, husband or other male family member, are a means of controlling women's choices, not only in the area of sexuality but also in other aspects of behaviour, such as freedom of movement. Such crimes frequently have a collective dimension, with the family as a whole believing itself to be injured by a woman's actual or perceived behaviour. They are often public in character, which is integral to their social functions, which include influencing the conduct of other women. In other cultural contexts, preoccupation with women's sexuality is manifested not only in practices for enforcing chastity but also in the way female sexuality is turned into a commodity in the media and advertising. . . .

Economic Inequalities and Violence Against Women

86.   Economic inequalities can be a causal factor for violence against women both at the level of individual acts of violence and at the level of broad-based economic trends that create or exacerbate the enabling conditions for such violence. These economic inequalities can be found at the local, national and global levels. Women's economic inequalities and discrimination against women in areas such as employment, income, access to other economic resources and lack of economic independence reduce women's capacity to act and make decisions, and increase their vulnerability to violence.

87.   Despite overall advances in women's economic status in many countries, many women continue to face discrimination in formal and informal sectors of the economy, as well as economic exploitation within the family. Women's lack of economic empowerment, also reflected in lack of access to and control over economic resources in the form of land, personal property, wages and credit, can place them at increased risk of violence. In addition, restrictions on women's control over economic resources, such as household income, can constitute a form of violence against women in the family. While economic independence does not shield women from violence, access to economic resources can enhance women's capacity to make meaningful choices, including escaping violent situations and accessing mechanisms for protection and redress. . . .

Violence Against Women Within the Family

111.   The forms of violence a woman may experience within the family across her life cycle extend from violence before birth to violence against older women. Commonly identified forms of violence against women in the family include: battering and other forms of intimate partner violence including marital rape; sexual violence; dowry-related violence; female infanticide; sexual abuse of female children in the household; female genital mutilation/cutting and other traditional practices harmful to women; early marriage; forced marriage; non-spousal violence; violence perpetrated against domestic workers; and other forms of exploitation. . . .

Intimate Partner Violence

112.   The most common form of violence experienced by women globally is intimate partner violence. The pervasiveness of different forms of violence against women within intimate relationships, commonly referred to as

domestic violence or spousal abuse, is now well established. . . .

113.   Intimate partner violence includes a range of sexually, psychologically and physically coercive acts used against adult and adolescent women by a current or former intimate partner, without her consent. Physical violence involves intentionally using physical force, strength or a weapon to harm or injure the woman. Sexual violence includes abusive sexual contact, making a woman engage in a sexual act without her consent, and attempted or completed sex acts with a woman who is ill, disabled, under pressure or under the influence of alcohol or other drugs. Psychological violence includes controlling or isolating the women, and humiliating or embarrassing her. Economic violence includes denying a woman access to and control over basic resources.

Harmful Traditional Practices

118.   Female infanticide and prenatal sex selection, early marriage, dowry-related violence, female genital mutilation/cutting, crimes against women committed in the name of "honour," and maltreatment of widows, including inciting widows to commit suicide, are forms of violence against women that are considered harmful traditional practices, and may involve both family and community. . . .

119.   The most extensive body of research concerns female genital mutilation/cutting. It is estimated that more than 130 million girls and women alive today have undergone female genital mutilation/cutting, mainly in Africa and some countries in the Middle East. The practice is also prevalent among immigrant communities in Europe, North America and Australia. Surveys revealed significant geographic variations in the prevalence rates in 19 countries: 99 per cent in Guinea, 97 per cent in Egypt, 80 per cent in Ethiopia, 17 per cent in Benin, and 5 per cent in Ghana and Niger. They also show that the practice may be slowly declining even in high prevalence countries because of increasing opposition from women's groups. Higher female educational levels, female access to and control over economic resources, ethnicity and women's own female genital mutilation/cutting status have been found to be significantly associated with their support for or opposition to female genital mutilation/cutting.*

120.   Practices of son preference, expressed in manifestations such as female infanticide, prenatal sex selection and systematic neglect of girls, have resulted in adverse female-male sex ratios and high rates of female infant mortality in South and East Asia, North Africa, and the Middle East. A study in India estimated that prenatal sex selection and infanticide have accounted for half a million missing girls per year for the past two decades. In the Republic of Korea, among pregnancies having sex-identification tests, more than 90 per cent of pregnancies with male foetuses resulted in normal births, whereas more than 30 per cent of those with female foetuses were terminated, according to the National Fertility and Family Health Survey.

121.   Early marriages involve the marriage of a child, i.e., a person below the age of 18. Minor girls have not achieved full maturity and capacity to act and lack ability to control their sexuality. When they marry and have children, their health can be adversely affected, their education impeded and economic autonomy restricted. Early marriage also increases the risk of HIV infection. Such marriages take place all over the world, but are most common in sub-Saharan Africa and South Asia, where more than 30 per cent of girls aged 15 to 19 are married. In Ethiopia, it was found that 19 per cent of girls were married by the age of 15 and in some regions such as Amhara, the proportion was as high as 50 per cent. In Nepal, 7 per cent of girls were married before the age of 10 and 40 per cent by the age of 15. A UNICEF global assessment found that in Latin America and the Caribbean, 29 per cent of women aged 15 to 24 were married before the age of 18.

---

*Removing a young girl's clitoris so she would not derive pleasure from sexual intercourse.

122.   A forced marriage is one lacking the free and valid consent of at least one of the parties. In its most extreme form, forced marriage can involve threatening behaviour, abduction, imprisonment, physical violence, rape and, in some cases, murder. There has been little research on this form of violence. A recent European study confirmed the lack of quantitative surveys in Council of Europe countries. One study of 1,322 marriages across six villages in Kyrgyzstan found that one half of ethnic Kyrgyz marriages were the result of kidnappings, and that as many as two thirds of these marriages were non-consensual. In the United Kingdom of Great Britain and Northern Ireland, a Forced Marriage Unit established by the Government intervenes in 300 cases of forced marriage a year.

123.   Violence related to demands for dowry—which is the payment of cash or goods by the bride's family to the groom's family—may lead to women being killed in dowry-related femicide. According to official crime statistics in India, approximately 6,822 women were killed in 2002 as a result of such violence. Small community studies have also indicated that dowry demands have played an important role in women being burned to death and in deaths of women labelled as suicides.

124.   Crimes against women committed in the name of "honour" may occur within the family or within the community. These crimes are receiving increased attention, but remain underreported and under-documented. The most severe manifestation is murder—so-called "honour killings." UNFPA estimated that 5,000 women are murdered by family members each year in "honour killings" around the world. A government report noted that "karo-kari" ("honour killings") claimed the lives of 4,000 men and women between 1998 and 2003 in Pakistan, and that the number of women killed was more than double the number of men.

125.   Older women, including in particular widows, are subject to harmful practices in a number of countries, which can involve both the family and the community. A study conducted in Ghana, based on data collected from news reports and interviews, found that many poor, often elderly women were accused of witchcraft. Some were murdered by male relatives and those who survived were subjected to a range of physical, sexual and economic abuses. Violence directed against widows, including sexual abuse and harassment and property-related violence at the hands of relatives, mainly in-laws, has been reported from a number of countries including India, but information remains scarce. . . .

Femicide: The Gender-Based Murder of a Woman

127.   Femicide occurs everywhere, but the scale of some cases of femicide within community contexts—for example, in Ciudad Juárez, Mexico and Guatemala—has drawn attention to this aspect of violence against women. Most official sources agree that more than 320 women have been murdered in Ciudad Juárez, one third of whom were brutally raped. In Guatemala, according to National Civil Police statistics, 1,467 women were murdered between 2001 and the beginning of December 2004. Other sources claim the figure is higher, with 2,070 women murdered, mostly aged 14 to 35. The killings have been concentrated in areas where the economies are dominated by *maquilas*, assembly plants for export products owned and operated in tax-free zones by multinational companies. Impunity for these crimes is seen as a key factor in these occurrences, and in the case of Guatemala, the legacy of the internal armed conflict that ended in 1996 is also seen as a contributing factor. . . .

Trafficking in Women

135.   Trafficking is a form of violence against women that takes place in multiple settings and usually involves many different actors including families, local brokers, international criminal networks and immigration authorities. Trafficking in human beings takes place both between and within countries. The majority of the victims of human trafficking are women and

children, and many are trafficked for purposes of sexual exploitation.

136.   A definition of trafficking is provided by the Protocol to Prevent, Suppress and Punish Trafficking in Persons, Especially Women and Children, supplementing the United Nations Convention against Transnational Organized Crime: *"Trafficking in persons* shall mean the recruitment, transportation, transfer, harbouring or receipt of persons by means of the threat or use of force or other forms of coercion, of abduction, of fraud, of deception, of the abuse of power or of a position of vulnerability or of the giving or receiving of payments or benefits to achieve the consent of a person having control over another person, for the purpose of exploitation. Exploitation shall include, at a minimum, the exploitation of prostitution of others or other forms of sexual exploitation, forced labour or services, slavery or practices similar to slavery, servitude, or the removal of organs.". . .

138.   Although various sources suggest that hundreds of thousands of people are trafficked globally every year, few come to the attention of authorities. For instance, in 2005, 506 victims were identified in Portugal, 412 in Mexico and 243 in Turkey. The number of traffickers prosecuted and convicted is also remarkably low. For instance, in 2003, 24 people were prosecuted and only 8 convicted in Lithuania, 59 were prosecuted and 11 convicted in Ukraine and, in 2004, 59 people were prosecuted and 43 convicted in the United States.

REVIEW QUESTIONS

1. List examples of violence against females discussed in the UN study.
2. What traditional practices did the study find particularly harmful?

---

5 Child Soldiers

Human rights groups estimate that some 300,000 child soldiers, some not even in their teens, serve in government or rebel armies throughout the world but particularly in Africa and South Asia. Warring groups deliberately recruit or kidnap these immature children, often poor, uneducated, orphaned, or separated from their parents because of war. At times rebel forces, commanded by thuggish warlords interested only in personal power and wealth, have destroyed whole villages and abducted the surviving children whom they train and indoctrinate for battle and threaten with death if they resist. These children can be quickly taught to fire lightweight automatic weapons, which technological advances have made simple to operate. Often sent into battle high on drugs and brainwashed into believing that the enemy is an evil force that has to be liquidated, child soldiers have become ruthless killing machines.

Ishmael Beah
A LONG WAY GONE: MEMOIRS OF A BOY SOLDIER

At age twelve, Ishmael Beah fled from rebels who were attacking his native village in Sierra Leone. Months later government forces recruited young Ishmael and turned the gentle boy into a killer. At sixteen, UNICEF removed him from the fighting and two years later he moved to the United States where he attended college. In excerpts from *A Long Way Gone*, which appear below, Ishmael Beah describes the terrifying ordeal of a child soldier.

The lieutenant asked his men to gather everyone at the square. "In the forest there are men waiting to destroy all of our lives. We have fought them as best as we can, but there are too many of them. They are all around the village." The lieutenant made a circle in the air with his hands. "They won't give up until they capture this village. They want our food and ammunition." He paused, and slowly continued: "Some of you are here because they have killed your parents or families, others because this is a safe place to be. Well, it is not that safe anymore. That is why we need strong men and boys to help us fight these guys, so that we can keep this village safe. If you do not want to fight or help, that is fine. But you will not have rations and will not stay in this village. You are free to leave, because we only want people here who can help cook, prepare ammunition, and fight. There are enough women to run the kitchen, so we need the help of able boys and men to fight these rebels. This is your time to revenge the deaths of your families and to make sure more children do not lose their families." He took a deep breath. "Tomorrow morning you must all line up here, and we will select people for various tasks that have to be carried out." He left the square, followed by his men.

We stood in silence for a while and slowly started walking to our respective sleeping places, as the curfew was approaching. Inside, Jumah, Alhaji, Kanei, Moriba, Musa, and I quietly discussed what we were going to do.

"The rebels will kill anyone from this village because they will consider us their enemy, spies, or that we have sided with the other side of the war. That is what the staff sergeant said," Alhaji said, explaining the dilemma we faced. The rest of the boys, who were lying on their mats, got up and joined us as Alhaji continued: "It is better to stay here for now." He sighed. We had no choice. Leaving the village was as good as being dead.

"Attention. This is an order from the lieutenant. Everyone must gather at the square immediately." A soldier spoke into a megaphone. Before he had finished his last word, the square was filled. Everyone had waited for this moment that would determine what we were going to do for our safety. Before the announcement, I sat with my friends near the window in the kitchen. Their faces were blank; they showed no emotion, but their eyes looked pale with sorrow. I tried to make eye contact with each of them, but they all looked away. I tried to eat my breakfast, but fear had taken away my appetite.

As we found spots in the back of the crowd, gunshots filled the air, then faded to a silence even more unbearable than the reports.

The lieutenant stood on several bricks so that he could be high enough to be seen by all. He let silence settle in our bones, then waved his hands to some soldiers who brought before us two bodies—a man and a young boy who had lived in the village. The blood that soaked their clothes was still fresh and their eyes were open. People turned their heads away, and little children and babies began to cry. The lieutenant cleared his throat and started speaking in the midst of the cries, which eventually ceased as he went on.

"I am sorry to show you these gruesome bodies, especially with your children present. But then again, all of us here have seen death or even shaken hands with it." He turned to the bodies and continued softly: "This man and this child decided to leave this morning even though I had told them it was dangerous. The man insisted that he didn't want to be a part of our war, so I gave him his wish and let him go. Look at what happened. The rebels shot them in the clearing. My men brought them back, and I decided to show you, so that you can fully understand the situation we are in." The lieutenant went on for almost an hour, describing how rebels had cut off the heads of some people's family members and made them watch, burned entire villages along with their inhabitants, forced sons to have intercourse with their mothers, hacked newly born babies in half because they cried too much, cut open pregnant women's stomachs, took the babies out, and killed them . . . The lieutenant spat on the ground and continued on, until he was sure that he had mentioned all the ways the rebels had hurt every person in the gathering.

"They have lost everything that makes them human. They do not deserve to live. That is why we must kill every single one of them. Think of it as destroying a great evil. It is the highest service you can perform for your country." The lieutenant pulled out his pistol and fired two shots into the air. People began shouting, "We must kill them all. We must make sure they never walk this earth again." All of us hated the rebels, and we were more than determined to stop them from capturing the village. Everyone's face had begun to sadden and grow tense. The aura in the village rapidly changed after the speech. The morning sun had disappeared and the day became gloomy. It seemed as if the sky were going to break and fall on the earth. I was furious and afraid, and so were my friends. Jumah looked toward the forest with his hands behind his back, Moriba was holding his head, Kanei stared at the ground, Musa wrapped his hands around himself, Alhaji covered his eyes with his left hand, and I stood akimbo to stop my legs from shaking. All women and girls were asked to report to the kitchen; men and boys to the ammunition depot, where the soldiers watched their movies and smoked marijuana. . . .

The soldiers took more than thirty boys with them. Two were seven and eleven years old. Almost all the rest were between the ages of thirteen and sixteen. Ishmael Beah then describes how the boy soldiers were fed a diet of war movies and drugs. In the following excerpt he relates an attack on a rebel camp.

Once the camp was in sight, we would surround it and wait for the lieutenant's command. The rebels roamed about; some sat against walls, dozing off, and others, boys as young as we, stood at guard posts passing around marijuana. Whenever I looked at rebels during raids, I got angrier, because they looked like the rebels who played cards in the ruins of the village where I had lost my family. So when the lieutenant gave orders, I shot as many as I could, but I didn't feel better. After every gunfight we would enter the rebel camp, killing those we had wounded. We would then search the houses and gather gallons of gasoline, enormous amounts of marijuana and cocaine, bales of clothes, *crapes,* watches, rice, dried fish, salt, *gari,* and many other things. We rounded up the civilians—men, women, boys, and young girls—hiding in the huts and houses, and made them carry our loot back to the base.

On one of these raids, we had captured a few rebels after a long gunfight and a lot of civilian casualties. We undressed the prisoners and tied them until their chests were tight as drums.

"Where did you get all this ammunition from?" the corporal asked one of the prisoners, a man with an almost dreadlocked beard. He spat at the corporal's face, and the corporal immediately shot him in the head at close range. He fell onto the ground and blood slowly leaked out of his head. We cheered in admiration of the corporal's fierceness and saluted him as he walked by. Suddenly Lansana, one of the boys, was shot in the chest and head by a rebel hiding in the bushes. We dispersed around the village in search of the shooter. When the young muscular rebel was captured, the lieutenant slit his neck with his bayonet. The rebel ran up and down the village before he fell to the ground and stopped moving. We cheered again, raising our guns in the air, shouting and whistling. . . .

"If anyone starts any funny business, shoot him." The lieutenant eyed the prisoners. We set the thatched roofs on fire and left, taking the prisoners with us. The flames on the thatched roofs waved us off as they danced with the afternoon breeze, swaying as if in agony. "We"—the lieutenant pointed to us—"are here to protect you and will do all we can to make sure nothing happens to you." He pointed to the civilians.

"Our job is a serious one and we have the most capable soldiers, who will do anything to defend this country. We are not like the rebels, those riffraffs who kill people for no reason. We kill them for the good and betterment of this country. So respect all these men"—he pointed to us again—"for offering their services." The lieutenant went on and on with his speech, which was a combination of instilling in the civilians that what we were doing was right and boosting the morale of his men, including us, the boys. I stood there holding my gun and felt special because I was part of something that took me seriously and I was not running from anyone anymore. I had my gun now, and as the corporal always said, "This gun is your source of power in these times. It will protect you and provide you all you need, if you know how to use it well."

I cannot remember what prompted the lieutenant to make this speech. A lot of things were done with no reason or explanation. Sometimes we were asked to leave for war in the middle of a movie. We would come back hours later after killing many people and continue the movie as if we had just returned from intermission. We were always either at the front lines, watching a war movie, or doing drugs. There was no time to be alone or to think. When we conversed with each other, we talked only about the war movies and how impressed we were with the way either the lieutenant, the corporal, or one of us had killed somebody. It was as if nothing else existed outside our reality.

The morning after the lieutenant's speech, we proceeded to practice killing the prisoners the way the lieutenant had done it. There were five prisoners and many eager participants. So the corporal chose a few of us. He picked Kanei, three other boys, and me for the killing exhibition. The five men were lined up in front of us on the training ground with their hands tied. We were supposed to slice their throats on the corporal's command. The person whose prisoner died quickest would win the contest. We had our bayonets out and were supposed to look in the faces of the prisoners as we took them out of this world. I had already begun staring at my prisoner. His face was swollen from the beating he had received, and his eyes looked as if they were watching something behind me. His jaws were the only tense part of his facial expression; everything else seemed calm. I didn't feel a thing for him, didn't think that much about what I was doing. I just waited for the corporal's order. The prisoner was simply another rebel who was responsible for the death of my family, as I had come to truly believe.

The corporal gave the signal with a pistol shot and I grabbed the man's head and slit his throat in one fluid motion. His Adam's apple made way for the sharp knife, and I turned the bayonet on its zigzag edge as I brought it out. His eyes rolled up and they looked me straight in the eye before they suddenly stopped in a frightful glance, as if caught by surprise. The prisoner leaned his weight on me as he gave out his last breath. I dropped him on the ground and wiped my bayonet on him. I reported to the corporal, who was holding a timer. The bodies of the other prisoners fought in the arms of the other boys, and some continued to shake on the ground for a while. I was proclaimed the winner, and Kanei came second. The boys and the other soldiers who were the audience clapped as if I had just fulfilled one of life's greatest achievements. I was given the rank of junior lieutenant and Kanei was given junior sergeant. We celebrated that day's achievement with more drugs and more war movies.

REVIEW QUESTIONS

1. What techniques did the lieutenant use to convert young boys to killers?
2. How was Ishmael's perception of the value of human life transformed?

6 Radical Islamic Terrorism

On September 11, 2001, nineteen Muslim Arabs, fifteen of them from Saudi Arabia, hijacked four planes: two of them they crashed into the World Trade Center in New York, bringing down both towers; a third plane rammed into the Pentagon in Washington, D.C., causing severe damage; the fourth plane, apparently headed for the White House, crashed in a field in Pennsylvania when passengers attacked the hijackers. In all, almost three thousand people perished. The meticulously planned operation was the work of Al Qaeda, an international terrorist network of militant Muslims, or Islamists as they call themselves.

The leader of Al Qaeda, Osama bin Laden, scion of an immensely wealthy Saudi family, operated from Afghanistan with the protection of the radical fundamentalist Taliban, who ruled the country, transforming it into a repressive regime based on a rigid interpretation of Islamic law.

When Taliban leaders refused to turn bin Laden over to the United States, President George W. Bush, supported by an international coalition, launched a military campaign whose ultimate goal was the destruction of international terrorism. Local Afghan forces opposed to the Taliban, assisted by American airpower—which proved decisive—defeated the Taliban in few weeks. The new leaders of Afghanistan no longer permitted their country to serve as a haven and training center for radical Islamic terrorists. But Taliban fighters, who found refuge in Pakistan, continue to wage guerrilla war against the American-backed government.

Seething discontent in the Muslim world, particularly among Arabs, provides Al Qaeda with recruits, including zealots willing to inflict maximum casualties on civilians, even if doing so means blowing themselves up in the process. After September 11, several Al Qaeda operations were thwarted, including attempts to explode airplanes. But terrorists, either loosely or directly affiliated with Al Qaeda, succeeded in other operations, including the bombing of a nightclub in Bali, Indonesia, that killed more than 200 people, most of them Australian tourists; a series of truck-bomb explosions in Istanbul, that wrecked two Jewish synagogues, the British consulate, and a British bank, killing more than fifty people and wounding hundreds; the blowing up of crowded commuter trains in Madrid that killed 191 people and injured more than a thousand; and the suicide bombing of the London transit system that left more than seven hundred dead and injured.

Bin Laden and his followers view their struggle against the United States as a holy war against the infidel. Their goal is the creation of an Islamic world-state governed by Islamic law, a revival of the medieval caliphate. A religious fanatic and absolutist who cannot tolerate pluralism, bin Laden wants to drive Westerners and Western values out of Islamic lands; he is also a theocrat who would use the state's power to impose a narrow, intolerant version of Islam on the Muslim world. He and his followers are zealots who are convinced that they are doing God's will. Recruits for suicide missions are equally convinced that they are waging holy war against the enemies of God and their centers of evil, for which they will be richly rewarded in Paradise. The hatred of radical Muslims for the West shows that in an age of globalism the world is still divided by strong cultural traditions.

Mary Habeck
JIHADIST IDEOLOGY

For some analysts September 11 demonstrated that after the defeat of the Nazis in World War II and the collapse of the Soviet Union, the West is now confronted with another ominous threat: Islamism or, as some prefer, Islamofascism. Islamists or jihadists, best represented by Osama bin Laden and Al Qaeda, regard terrorism, the deliberate targeting of civilian life, as a legitimate means of fulfilling their sacred mission: ending the humiliation of Muslims by the West; restoring the caliphate and Muslim hegemony over all lands where Islam once prevailed and even beyond; and imposing a strict interpretation of Islamic law throughout the Muslim world. Jihadists, a number of whom have lived in Europe, loathe Western civilization, which they view as materialistic, hedonistic, and sacrilegious; they are repelled by secular democracies, which draw a line between church and state, promote female equality, and tolerate homosexuality. In their eyes, the United States, the leading Western power, constitutes Islam's major enemy. They believed that striking at the World Trade Center and the Pentagon, symbols of American power, was fitting retaliation for American aggression against Muslims and that their act would demonstrate American weakness and the jihadists' resolve to destroy the infidels. Jihadists expected that the suicide bombers would be seen by their coreligionists as martyrs and the ensuing publicity would incite and mobilize the Muslim masses throughout the world to their cause. Al Qaeda, they thought, would be recognized as the vanguard of the global struggle against the enemies of Islam.

In the following selection, Mary Habeck, a student of international relations, analyzes the jihadist ideology that led to 9/11.

It should now be obvious why the United States had to be attacked on September 11. Inspired by their distinctive ideology, certain extremists decided that the United States had to be destroyed. There are two central innovations in the ideology that allow—even demand—the destruction of the United States and the murder of thousands of innocents: an aberrant definition of tawhid[1] and a concentration on violence as the core of their religion. Unlike the vast majority of the Islamic world, the extremists give tawhid political implications and use it to justify all their violent acts. They assert that tawhid means God alone has sovereignty and His laws alone—as laid out in the Qur'an and

hadith[2] and by certain traditional jurists—are normative. Thus the only acceptable society for the jihadis is a government that applies the tenets of Islamic law in a way that they believe is correct. Based on this definition of tawhid, the extremists argue that democracy, liberalism, human rights, personal freedom, international law, and international institutions are illegal, illegitimate, and sinful. Because it grants sovereignty to the people and allows them to make laws for their society rather than depending entirely on the God-given legal system of Islam, democracy is the focus for jihadist critiques. The United States is recognized by the jihadis as the center of liberalism and democracy, a center that is willing to spread its ideas and challenge other ways of organizing society, and thus must be destroyed along with democracy itself.

---

[1]Tawhid: The Muslim belief that there is one omnipotent God all of whose laws are binding and that God's laws are superior to all human-made injunctions.

[2]Hadith: Traditions about Muhammad's life that are an integral part of Islamic law.

The antidemocratic rhetoric of Zarqawi and bin Ladin is not, then, just a reaction to U.S. policies, but rather a reflection of their own most deeply held religio-political views of the world.

Violence also permeates jihadist thought. In their reading of history, the conflict between the United States and Islam is part of a universal struggle between good and evil, truth and falsehood, belief and infidelity, that began with the first human beings and will continue until the end of time. A literal clash of civilizations is taking place around the world and, in the end, only one system can survive: Muslims must rid the earth of democracy or else the supporters of democracy (especially the United States, but the entire "West" as well) will destroy true Islam. Jihadis do not believe that this is a theoretical or ideological struggle that can be played out peacefully; rather, the existence of a political or legal system with provisions that transgress the bounds of shari'a [Islamic law] is an act of aggression against Islam that must be dealt with through revolutionary force.

Because history is dominated by the struggle between good and evil, jihadis assert that all Muslims are called by God to participate in the fight—physically if at all possible, or at least by word or financially—acting as God's sword on earth to deal with the evildoers and their wicked way of life. Muslims who answer the call to fight must do so solely to win God's pleasure so that, in the end, it does not matter if the holy warrior accomplishes anything positive through his violence and incitement to violence: intentions alone count. If a *mujahid* is killed while slaughtering innocent civilians or soldiers on the field of battle, and he acted with pure intentions, he will be guaranteed a welcome into a paradise of unimaginable delights. At the end of time the jihadis envision a world ruled solely by their version of Islam, a world in which "the religion will be for God alone." Thus the jihadis believe that they are more than small groups of violent people who have murdered thousands of men, women, and children. Instead they are honored participants in a cosmic drama, one that will decide the fate of the world and that will ultimately end with the victory of the good, the virtuous, and the true believers.

In addition to fighting evil for God's pleasure, al-Qaida had more mundane short and long-term objectives for the 9/11 assault, objectives that have been articulated by its leaders and that they have lived out. In the short term, al-Qaida wanted to energize a war effort that they began during the early nineties, convince a larger number of Muslims to join their cause, and frighten the United States into leaving all Islamic lands. Al-Qaida's longer-term goals included converting all Muslims to their version of Islam, expanding the only legitimate Islamic state (Afghanistan) until it contained any lands that had ever been ruled by Islamic law, and, finally, taking the war beyond the borders of even this expansive state until the entire world was ruled by their extremist Islam. In pursuit of these ends, they believed that the murder of thousands of innocent civilians—including Muslims—was not only legally justified but commanded by God Himself. The jihadist war is thus, in many ways, a struggle over who will control the future of Islam: will this ancient religion become associated with the hatred and violence of the jihadis, or the more tolerant vision proposed by moderate, liberal, and traditional Muslims? . . .

How, then, should the world respond to the jihadis and their revolutionary ideology? As should be obvious from this discussion, the extremists themselves are not interested in dialogue, compromise, or participation in a political process to attain their ends. For ideological reasons, they have chosen to use violence rather than peaceful means to resolve their problems and achieve their objectives. The ultimate goals of the jihadis are likewise so radical—to force the rest of the world to live under their version of Islamic law—that there is no way to agree to them without sacrificing every other society on the planet. The United States and other countries must then find reasonable strategies that will exploit the failures of the jihadis, stop the extremists from carrying out violent attacks, minimize the appeal of their beliefs, and eventually end their war with the world.

European Union
ISLAMIST TERRORISM

Many young European Muslims, searching to give their lives a richer meaning and finding Western culture spiritually empty, are returning to their ancestral faith. Those among them who are particularly disaffected—while often seemingly assimilated and educated, even professionals—have been receptive to firebrand imams. Often imported from Arab countries and financed by the Saudi government, these imams despise Western values, demonize Jews, and preach the duty of jihad. As a result of the preaching of these radical imams and the efforts of militant recruiters who spot likely candidates, terrorist cells have been established in various European cities. The Internet has become a powerful recruiting and networking tool for Al Qaeda, one of whose goals is the Islamization of Europe. Jihadist web sites, numbering in the thousands, propagate extremism. They feature imams extolling Wahhabism, a puritanical, fundamentalist form of Islam; Islamists providing religious justification for holy war; images of dead Americans killed by "glorious" jihadists; suicide bombers giving their farewell speech; and instructions for making explosive devices. Extremist Islamic cells in Europe have engaged in numerous acts of terror.

Analysts fear that the 20 million Muslims residing in Europe, many of them alienated from European culture, poorly integrated into European society, and believing that the West has exploited Muslims and denigrated their faith, are potential recruits for extremist Islamic groups, including Al Qaeda, and that European cities could become targets of fanatical jihadists. Extremist Islamist cells in Europe have engaged in numerous acts of terror. Much of the planning for 9/11 took place in Hamburg, Germany. In 2004, Muslim terrorists of North African origin, who identified with Al Qaeda, blew up four crowded commuter trains in Madrid, Spain, killing 191 andwounding about 2,000. In July 2005, Muslim suicide bombers killed more than 50 people and injured 700 in a terrorist attack on London's transit system. In a second attack two weeks later the bombs failed to detonate and the suspected suicide bombers were arrested. The following year, British security foiled a terrorist plot to blow up several transatlantic flights departing Heathrow airport that would have killed more people than had perished on 9/11. That the planners and perpetrators of these attacks were not foreign jihadists, but British citizens raised and educated in Britain who were terrorizing their fellow citizens, was viewed by analysts as an ominous sign. German authorities reported that in 2004 some 32,000 Muslims were affiliated with radical Islamist organizations operating on German soil. Frequently these recruits have been radicalized by Arab imams trained in the Middle East, who proclaim that Islam is engaged in a holy war against the West and that martyrdom will redeem Muslim honor and assure victory.

Nor are Western-educated Muslims immune from the lure of jihad. It was a recently radicalized Dutch-born, Dutch-speaking, and Dutch-educated Muslim of Moroccan extraction who cruelly and gleefully ritually butchered Theo Van Gogh for making a film about the suppression of Women in Muslim lands. One of the terrorists sentenced to death in Pakistan for the beheading of *Wall*

Street Journal reporter Daniel Pearl was born in London and educated at exclusive British schools, including the London School of Economics. Drawn to radical Islam, several doctors and engineers have been involved in terrorist attacks in Britain. These terrorists are filled with moral outrage; they see themselves as idealists striking back at the West, which they perceive as waging a war against Islam in which their fellow Muslims are being humiliated, oppressed, and killed. European jihadists continue to recruit young Muslims to fight in Kashmir, Chechnya, Afghanistan, and Iraq.

Islam is also attracting European Christian converts whose zeal for their new religion can be harnessed for terrorist purposes. At the end of 2001, an alert flight attendant prevented Richard Reid, a recent British convert who discovered Islam while serving a prison sentence, from igniting an explosive device hidden in his shoe that would have blown up the plane in mid-air. In September 2007, German authorities charged a native German and youthful convert to Islam with heading a terrorist cell planning attacks against American targets in Germany that could have killed hundreds of people.

The following document, *EU Terrorism Situation and Trend Report 2007*, issued by the European Union, discusses recent Islamist terrorist attacks and activities in Europe.

Along with the failed terrorist attack that took place in Germany, Denmark and the UK each reported one attempted terrorist attack. No further information on prevented or disrupted Islamist terrorist attacks was made available by the Member States' law enforcement authorities.

GERMAN TROLLEY BOMB CASE

On 31 July 2006, two Improvised Explosive Devices (IEDs) packed in two suitcases were placed onboard two regional trains near Cologne in an attempted coordinated attack. The devices failed to detonate. Both so-called 'trolley bombs' were made up of a gas cylinder, an alarm clock, a functioning detonator and three PET bottles filled with petrol. Had the devices detonated, it is estimated that there would have been a significant loss of life in two trains.

Two Lebanese nationals studying in Germany were subsequently arrested on suspicion of placing the IEDs on the trains.

The suspects were reported to have been motivated by the publication of the Danish cartoons of the Prophet Muhammad in German newspapers; it was also reported that the Internet played a role in preparations. Further, there were reports that the suspects had undergone a swift radicalisation process. The suspects initially intended to carry out the attack during the FIFA World Cup but changed their plans due to the security measures in place.

UK AIRPLANE PLOT

On 10 August 2006, a series of arrests took place in the UK in connection with an alleged suicide bombing plot. The suspects planned to smuggle the component parts of IEDs onto aircrafts and assemble and detonate them on board and in flight. Liquid explosives concealed in plastic soft drink bottles were to be detonated with battery powered detonators aboard transAtlantic airliners en route from the UK to the US. If successful, the attack would have caused mass murder of potentially thousands of civilian air travellers. . . .

Eleven suspects were charged in connection with the plot. The suspects were predominantly UK citizens of Pakistani descent. They were reportedly motivated to carry out the attack by the situation in Afghanistan and Iraq, and intended to strike a target that would hit both the UK and the US at the same time. They seem to have undergone a 'rapid radicalisation': in a matter of 'some weeks and months, not years,' they were prepared to kill civilians in a suicide attack.

DANISH 'HOMEGROWN' VOLLSMOSE GROUP

On 5 September 2006, nine individuals were arrested in Vollsmose, a suburb of Odense, Denmark. Seven were remanded in custody on suspicion of preparing a terrorist attack. Allegedly, they procured material and effects for making explosives. According to one account, the explosives were produced using an unknown quantity of ammonium nitrate and Triacetone Triperoxide (TATP) supplemented by metal splinter shrapnel to increase the bombs' destructive power.

The Danish Minister of Justice stated that the group had planned one or several terrorist attacks against undisclosed targets within Denmark. The motivation of the group remains unknown. However, several commentators have pointed to Denmark's military engagement in Iraq and the global row over the cartoons depicting the Prophet Muhammad.

As in the UK case, the members of the Vollsmose group were suspected of being so-called 'homegrown' terrorists. More precisely, they were predominantly young second-generation Muslim immigrants of Middle Eastern origin with Danish citizenship. One member of the group was a Danish convert to Islam.

ARRESTED SUSPECTS

During the period between October 2005 and December 2006, a total of 340 persons were reported as having been arrested on Islamist terrorism related offences. Two hundred and sixty arrests were carried out in 2006.

Less than ten percent of the arrested individuals were suspected of preparation, planning or execution of terrorist attacks. The arrests took place in the Czech Republic, Denmark, France, Germany, Italy, Spain and Sweden.

The vast majority of the arrested individuals were suspected of being members of a terrorist organisation. Other frequent criminal activities were financing of terrorism and facilitation. . . .

The bulk of the arrests took place in France, Spain, Italy and the Netherlands and the majority of those arrested came from Algeria, Morocco and Tunisia. Arrested suspects originating from North Africa were often loosely affiliated with North African terrorist groups, such as the *Salafist Group for Preaching and Combat*. . . .

TERRORIST ACTIVITIES
Propaganda

In October 2006, an Iraqi citizen was arrested in Germany on suspicion of providing support to foreign terrorist groups. He allegedly disseminated audio and video files showing leading personalities of *al-Qaeda* and *al-Qaeda in Mesopotamia*. In addition to this, in 2006 one person was arrested in Denmark for Islamist terrorist propaganda and two in the UK for soliciting murder by publishing inciting statements and running websites inciting murder, urging to fight *jihad* and raising funds, respectively. Law enforcement agencies investigated propaganda offences in Belgium, Denmark, France and Germany. The number of police investigations into this phenomenon seems small compared to the amount of propaganda circulating on the Internet. This is partly explained by the lack of a legal basis for arrests of or investigation against persons using the Internet in this manner. Law enforcement agencies also have difficulties in identifying individuals who spread Islamist terrorist propaganda on the Internet. As an example, in autumn 2005, a suspect arrested in the UK on charges of participating in an alleged bomb plot, turned out to be a key individual that had used the Internet to spread Islamist propaganda.

Financing of Terrorism

Financing of terrorism covers two distinct aspects: financing of terrorist attacks and funding of terrorist networks.

Relatively small sums are necessary to carry out a terrorist attack; estimates for the Madrid bombings in 2004 range from EUR 8,000 to 15,000. Given the small amount of money required, the prevention of terrorist financing appears to some extent unrealistic; hence priority is given to financial investigations into the money trail left by terrorists. . . .

There is little doubt that money for funding Islamist terrorist networks or organisations is gathered in the EU through legal and/or illegal means. In this regard, the fact that almost ten percent of all suspects arrested in the EU during the reporting period were involved in financial and material support to terrorist organisations is significant. These suspects are mostly linked to terrorist organisations, such as the GSPC, the GICM, or *al-Qaeda.*

Financial and logistic support to terrorist organisations is based on funds provided legally or illegally by sympathisers of terrorist groups.

Funding is procured by establishing and managing small companies as sources of legal income, which is then used to support radical groups inside and outside the EU. Another very significant source originates from private donations, and from the misuse of *zakat** payments by Muslims. The funds are mostly collected by charitable organisations or associations and individuals. . . .

There are strong suspicions that *zakat* money collected within the EU is used to fund terrorism. A UK-based charity reportedly remitted a large amount of money declared to be relief funds for earthquake victims to suspects in Pakistan who were involved in the UK airplane plot. Funds collected legally can be transferred worldwide using the banking system without arousing suspicion. . . .

The range of illegal sources for the funding of terrorism appears to cover most criminal activities ranging from vehicle-related crimes to forgery of identity and travel documents or financial crimes, such as the use of false credit cards. . . .

Recruitment

Six Member States reported investigations into Islamist terrorist recruitment in the EU between October 2005 and December 2006.

In total, 24 individuals were arrested on suspicion of terrorist recruitment.

The individuals reported as having been arrested for recruitment were linked to the Iraqi Sunni organisation *Ansar al-Islam.* This may suggest that they were involved in recruiting volunteers in the EU for the support of the armed struggle against coalition troops in Iraq.

In most instances, the recruitment occurred in schools, spiritual meeting places like mosques, or in prisons. The modus operandi includes the use of propaganda material such as videos, tracts and movies supporting the claim that Muslims must take part in the global *jihad.*

Training

Eight persons were arrested in relation with terrorist training. The charges included plotting to establish a training camp, providing training and receiving training in terrorist techniques. . . .

In general, training in extremist ideology and terrorist techniques takes place overseas, where some of the terrorists receive military and specialist training. Nevertheless, one investigation concerned two training camps that were allegedly established in the South of England. In terrorist training camps, participants are taught a very radical interpretation of Islam and trained in handling explosives, as well as setting up and financing terrorist cells. Trainers usually belong to the militant categories of Islamists, maintaining international contacts with other members or networks.

The camps are mainly located in the Middle or Near East, or in South-East Asia. Training camps in the Sahel region, mostly controlled by *al-Qaeda in the Islamic Maghreb,* seem to acquire increasing

---

Zakat is the third pillar of Islam and refers to spending a fixed portion of one's wealth for the poor or needy.

importance and are used for the training of several terrorists originating in the Maghreb. Individuals that receive terrorist training remain in contact with both their facilitation networks and support cells. Religious or paramilitary training activities abroad might be an indicator that terrorists are in the early planning phase of an attack.

Facilitation

In 2006, a total of 52 individuals were arrested in seven Member States suspected of a wide range of offences related to facilitation of or support to terrorism. Two thirds of the suspected individuals were arrested in France and Spain.

Eighty-six percent of those arrested for facilitation were men, mainly North African or EU nationals.

In the reports contributed by the Member States, facilitation covers a wide range of support activities: provision of false identity documents, resources and fundraising for terrorist networks engaged in conflict areas. Other supporters of terrorism provide false administrative documents, consultancy services or assistance in marriages of convenience, in particular for illegal immigrants who adhere to Islamist ideologies. Several cells or networks dismantled in Spain and in Italy were found to be supporting North African groups in Europe and facilitating the dispatching of fighters to Iraq. Only a few of the cases reported concern the provision of false documentation for the use by Islamists. However, it should be noted that this offence is often considered a common law crime when no link with Islamist terrorism can be established.

SITUATION OUTSIDE THE EU

The perceived oppression of Islam or the presence of 'foreign' troops in Islamic lands is often invoked as justification for the execution of terrorist acts in several parts of the world, such as Chechnya, Kashmir, Iraq or Afghanistan. The idea that these local struggles are part of a global *jihad*, seen as a worldwide war between Islam and the non-believers, has been actively promoted by Islamist terrorist ideologues and

leaders of Islamist terrorist groups, such as *al-Qaeda*. Whereas local insurgency or resistance groups aim at overthrowing or seceding from the affected state's government, the ideology of global *jihad* identifies the Western world, including the EU Member States, as the principle enemy and target. . . .

The report then discusses attacks on Westerners and Western targets in Afghanistan, Egypt, Algeria, Bali, and Jordan.

ISLAMIST TERRORIST PROPAGANDA

For more than a decade, supporters of Islamist terror groups have published written statements, articles by ideological leaders and online magazines on the Internet, exploiting the potential for swift and anonymous communication that this medium offers.

More recently, the use of static websites for the propagation of Islamist terrorist propaganda appears to be in decline: such websites are easily closed down by hackers or law-enforcement agencies. Terrorist groups and their supporters may find online forums that support a radical view of Islam to be a more secure way of disseminating their propaganda material. These forums target a particular audience and offer details of access to files stored on so-called 'free-storage sites.' Files containing, for instance, high-quality full-length films may be obtained from such sites. Since this material is spread over numerous web servers located in different countries, blocking access to all copies of the files becomes virtually impossible.

Arguably, the most professional and most productive propaganda outlet is currently the *al-Sahab Media Production Company*. Al-Sahab mainly produces video files which can take the form of documentaries, interviews, speeches or news programmes. Another characteristic of *al-Sahab's* products is that many of them are accompanied by English subtitles. Where the speaker uses English, Arabic subtitles are added. All known speeches by members of the original *al-Qaeda* leadership released after June 2006 carry the *al-Sahab* logo.

Other Islamist terrorist groups have their own propaganda outlets. Iraqi and Afghan Islamist insurgent groups publish audio and video speeches of their leaders and videos showing attacks on Iraqi and coalition forces under their own labels, such as *al-Furqan Media Production Company* of the *Islamic State of Iraq,* formerly known as *al-Qaeda in Mesopotamia,* or the *Voice of Jihad* of the *Taliban* in Afghanistan. It is often the case that these groups attempt to emulate the stylistic features and technical professionalism of *al-Sahab*. . . .

In general, 2006 saw a rise in the frequency of statements and communiqués by Islamist groups, especially *al-Qaeda.* The quality and style of video messages and filmed attacks are more professional and the techniques used are increasingly sophisticated. English, either spoken or in subtitles, is often the language of choice. This may be an indication that propagandists are attempting to reach as wide an audience as possible. The frequency and quality of such propaganda, together with the possibilities for global access, are signs of an ongoing coordinated media offensive by Islamist terrorist groups.

KEY FINDINGS AND TRENDS

- Failed and planned attacks by Islamist terrorists as reported by Member States aimed at indiscriminate mass casualties.
- The London airplane plot and the trolley bomb case in Germany targeted civilians and transportation infrastructure in Member States.

  In both cases, the radicalisation process of the suspects is reported to have been rapid.
- The explosives of choice for Islamist terrorists are IEDs made with home-made explosives. At least two cases involved the use of TATP, a highly volatile explosive requiring a certain degree of expertise.

- The foiled plot in London demonstrates a high level of sophistication in the preparation of an attack and the ability to adapt to the latest security measures, as well as a high degree of creativity in attempting to circumvent them.
- The majority of the arrested suspects were born in Algeria, Morocco and Tunisia and had loose affiliations to North African terrorist groups, such as the GICM and the GSPC.

  However, the suspects involved in the foiled airplane plot in London and the Danish Vollsmose group were born or raised in a Member State, including converts, who had been radicalised in Europe.
- The amount of women among those arrested suspected of Islamist terrorism was less than among all terrorism suspects and a large majority were EU citizens. No female suspects were arrested for planning, preparing or executing an attack.
- Islamist terrorist networks are funded from legal and illegal sources depending on the individuals involved. The range of illegal sources for Islamist terrorism funding varied from vehicle-related crimes to forgery of identity and travel documents or financial crimes, such as the use of false credit cards.
- Volunteers are recruited in the EU to support Islamist terrorist activities in Iraq, which has been promoted as the key scene of global *jihad* by Islamist propagandists. It seems likely that, should other regional conflicts, such as those in Somalia and Afghanistan, become 'marketed' as global *jihad,* more volunteers may be recruited in the EU to support them.
- The frequency of video statements by members of the original *al-Qaeda* leadership and other Islamist terrorists has shown a marked increase. The propaganda is of greater sophistication, of high quality and more professional. English is used more often, either in direct speech or in subtitles, allowing potential access to a wider audience than previous Arabic-only publications. These facts may point to a coordinated global media offensive by Islamist terrorists.

Abdurrahman Wahid[1]
"RIGHT ISLAM VS. WRONG ISLAM: MUSLIMS AND NON-MUSLIMS MUST UNITE TO DEFEAT THE WAHHABI IDEOLOGY"

Abdurrahman Wahid (1940–2010), the former president of Indonesia, was co-founder and patron of the LibForAll Foundation, a nonprofit organization that is dedicated to reducing religious extremism and discrediting the use of terror worldwide. In the following article, which appeared in the *Wall Street Journal* on December 30, 2005, President Wahid analyzes the strength and wide appeal of a virulent Wahhabi/Salafi fundamentalism that supports Islamist terrorism. He summons both Muslims and the non-Muslims to unite in a campaign against religious extremism, "a global struggle for the soul of Islam." Such a campaign should develop strategies based on an understanding of our own strengths and weaknesses. Among our strengths, says Wahid, we should recognize that the large majority of Muslims and Muslim religious leaders have not been radicalized, that we can work with individuals and organizations that represent moderate religious views, that we can dispose of considerable resources to spread our message, that "the power of the feminine spirit" can play an important role because women have a vital stake in the outcome of this struggle, and that the "desire for freedom, justice, and a better life" is universal.

Jakarta—News organizations report that Osama bin Laden has obtained a religious edict from a misguided Saudi cleric, justifying the use of nuclear weapons against America and the infliction of mass casualties. It requires great emotional strength to confront the potential ramifications of this fact. Yet can anyone doubt that those who joyfully incinerate the occupants of office buildings, commuter trains, hotels and nightclubs would leap at the chance to magnify their damage a thousandfold?

Imagine the impact of a single nuclear bomb detonated in New York, London, Paris, Sydney or LA! What about two or three? The entire edifice of modern civilization is built on economic and technological foundations that terrorists hope to collapse with nuclear attacks like so many fishing huts in the wake of a tsunami.

Just two small, well-placed bombs devastated Bali's tourist economy in 2002 and sent much of its population back to the rice fields and out to sea, to fill their empty bellies. What would be the effect of a global economic crisis in the wake of attacks far more devastating than those of Bali or 9/11?

It is time for people of good will from every faith and nation to recognize that a terrible danger threatens humanity. We cannot afford to continue "business as usual" in the face of this existential threat. Rather, we must set aside our international and partisan bickering, and join to confront the danger that lies before us.

---

[1]Both the introduction and the selection appear in Marvin Perry and Howard Negrin, eds., *The Theory and Practice of Islamic Terrorism* (New York: Palgrave Macmillan, 2008).

An extreme and perverse ideology in the minds of fanatics is what directly threatens us (specifically, Wahhabi/Salafi ideology—a minority fundamentalist religious cult fueled by petrodollars). Yet underlying, enabling, and exacerbating this threat of religious extremism is a global crisis of misunderstanding.

All too many Muslims fail to grasp Islam, which teaches one to be lenient toward others and to understand their value systems, knowing that these are tolerated by Islam as a religion. The essence of Islam is encapsulated in the words of the Quran, "For you, your religion; for me, my religion." That is the essence of tolerance. Religious fanatics—either purposely or out of ignorance—pervert Islam into a dogma of intolerance, hatred and bloodshed. They justify their brutality with slogans such as "Islam is above everything else." They seek to intimidate and subdue anyone who does not share their extremist views, regardless of nationality or religion. While a few are quick to shed blood themselves, countless millions of others sympathize with their violent actions, or join in the complicity of silence.

This crisis of misunderstanding—of Islam by Muslims themselves—is compounded by the failure of governments, people of other faiths, and the majority of well-intentioned Muslims to resist, isolate and discredit this dangerous ideology. The crisis thus afflicts Muslims and non-Muslims alike, with tragic consequences. Failure to understand the true nature of Islam permits the continued radicalization of Muslims worldwide, while blinding the rest of humanity to a solution which hides in plain sight.

The most effective way to overcome Islamist extremism is to explain what Islam truly is to Muslims and non-Muslims alike. Without that explanation, people will tend to accept the unrefuted extremist view—further radicalizing Muslims, and turning the rest of the world against Islam itself.

Accomplishing this task will be neither quick nor easy. In recent decades, Wahhabi/Salafi ideology has made substantial inroads throughout the Muslim world. Islamic fundamentalism has become a well-financed, multifaceted global movement that operates like a juggernaut in much of the developing world, and even among immigrant Muslim communities in the West. To neutralize the virulent ideology that underlies fundamentalist terrorism and threatens the very foundations of modern civilization, we must identify its advocates, understand their goals and strategies, evaluate their strengths and weaknesses, and effectively counter their every move. What we are talking about is nothing less than a global struggle for the soul of Islam.

The Sunni (as opposed to Shiite) fundamentalists' goals generally include: claiming to restore the perfection of the early Islam practiced by Muhammad and his companions, who are known in Arabic as al-Salaf al-Salih, "the Righteous Ancestors"; establishing a utopian society based on these Salafi principles, by imposing their interpretation of Islamic law on all members of society; annihilating local variants of Islam in the name of authenticity and purity; transforming Islam from a personal faith into an authoritarian political system; establishing a pan-Islamic caliphate governed according to the strict tenets of Salafi Islam, and often conceived as stretching from Morocco to Indonesia and the Philippines; and, ultimately, bringing the entire world under the sway of their extremist ideology.

Fundamentalist strategy is often simple as well as brilliant. Extremists are quick to drape themselves in the mantle of Islam and declare their opponents kafir, or infidels, and thus smooth the way for slaughtering nonfundamentalist Muslims. Their theology rests upon a simplistic, literal and highly selective reading of the Quran and Sunnah (prophetic traditions), through which they seek to entrap the worldwide Muslim community in the confines of their narrow ideological grasp. Expansionist by nature, most fundamentalist groups constantly probe for weakness and an opportunity to strike, at any time or place, to further their authoritarian goals.

The armed ghazis (Islamic warriors) raiding from New York to Jakarta, Istanbul, Baghdad, London, and Madrid are only the tip of the iceberg, forerunners of a vast and growing population that shares their radical views and ultimate objectives. The formidable strengths of this worldwide fundamentalist movement include:

(1) An aggressive program with clear ideological and political goals; (2) immense funding from oil-rich Wahhabi sponsors; (3) the ability to distribute funds in impoverished areas to buy loyalty and power; (4) a claim to and aura of religious authenticity and Arab prestige; (5) an appeal to Islamic identity, pride, and history; (6) an ability to blend into the much larger traditionalist masses and blur the distinction between moderate Islam and their brand of religious extremism; (7) full-time commitment by its agents/leadership; (8) networks of Islamic schools that propagate extremism; (9) the absence of organized opposition in the Islamic world; (10) a global network of fundamentalist imams who guide their flocks to extremism; (11) a well-oiled "machine" established to translate, publish and distribute Wahhabi/Salafi propaganda and disseminate its ideology throughout the world; (12) scholarships for locals to study in Saudi Arabia and return with degrees and indoctrination, to serve as future leaders; (13) the ability to cross national and cultural borders in the name of religion; (14) Internet communication; and (15) the reluctance of many national governments to supervise or control this entire process.

We must employ effective strategies to counter each of these fundamentalist strengths. This can be accomplished only by bringing the combined weight of the vast majority of peace-loving Muslims, and the non-Muslim world, to bear in a coordinated global campaign whose goal is to resolve the crisis of misunderstanding that threatens to engulf our entire world.

An effective counterstrategy must be based upon a realistic assessment of our own strengths and weaknesses in the face of religious extremism and terror. Disunity, of course, has proved fatal to countless human societies faced with a similar existential threat. A lack of seriousness in confronting the imminent danger is likewise often fatal. Those who seek to promote a peaceful and tolerant understanding

of Islam must overcome the paralyzing effects of inertia, and harness a number of actual or potential strengths, which can play a key role in neutralizing fundamentalist ideology. These strengths not only are assets in the struggle with religious extremism, but in their mirror form they point to the weakness at the heart of fundamentalist ideology. They are:

(1) Human dignity, which demands freedom of conscience and rejects the forced imposition of religious views; (2) the ability to mobilize immense resources to bring to bear on this problem, once it is identified and a global commitment is made to solve it; (3) the ability to leverage resources by supporting individuals and organizations that truly embrace a peaceful and tolerant Islam; (4) nearly 1,400 years of Islamic traditions and spirituality, which are inimical to fundamentalist ideology; (5) appeals to local and national—as well as Islamic—culture/traditions/pride; (6) the power of the feminine spirit, and the fact that half of humanity consists of women, who have an inherent stake in the outcome of this struggle; (7) traditional and Sufi leadership and masses, who are not yet radicalized (strong numeric advantage: 85% to 90% of the world's 1.3 billion Muslims); (8) the ability to harness networks of Islamic schools to propagate a peaceful and tolerant Islam; (9) the natural tendency of like-minded people to work together when alerted to a common danger; (10) the ability to form a global network of like-minded individuals, organizations and opinion leaders to promote moderate and progressive ideas throughout the Muslim world; (11) the existence of a counterideology, in the form of traditional, Sufi and modern Islamic teachings, and the ability to translate such works into key languages; (12) the benefits of modernity, for all its flaws, and the widespread appeal of popular culture; (13) the ability to cross national and cultural borders in the name of religion; (14) Internet communications, to disseminate progressive views—linking and inspiring like-minded individuals and organizations throughout the world; (15) the nation-state; and (16) the universal human desire for freedom, justice, and a better life for oneself and loved ones.

Though potentially decisive, most of these advantages remain latent or diffuse, and require mobilization to be effective in confronting fundamentalist ideology. In addition, no effort to defeat religious extremism can succeed without ultimately cutting off the flow of petrodollars used to finance that extremism, from Leeds to Jakarta.

Only by recognizing the problem, putting an end to the bickering within and between nation-states, and adopting a coherent long-term plan (executed with international leadership and commitment) can we begin to apply the brakes to the rampant spread of extremist ideas and hope to resolve the world's crisis of misunderstanding before the global economy and modern civilization itself begin to crumble in the face of truly devastating attacks.

Muslims themselves can and must propagate an understanding of the "right" Islam, and thereby discredit extremist ideology. Yet to accomplish this task requires the understanding and support of like-minded individuals, organizations and governments throughout the world. Our goal must be to illuminate the hearts and minds of humanity, and offer a compelling alternate vision of Islam, one that banishes the fanatical ideology of hatred to the darkness from which it emerged.

REVIEW QUESTIONS

1. What are the fundamental components of the world-view of Islamic extremists? How do Western civilization and Zionism fit into this world-view?
2. What are the long- and short-term goals of the Islamists?
3. How do you think the world should respond to the jihadists and their revolutionary ideology?
4. What were the predominant crimes of most persons arrested for Islamic terrorism?
5. What implications do you see in the fact that many of the terrorists in the EU were "homegrown" and quickly radicalized?
6. How is the propaganda of Islamic terrorist groups becoming increasingly sophisticated and professional?
7. Why do the authorities find it difficult to contend with Islamist propaganda?
8. According to Abdurrahman Wahid, why is the Wahhabi/Salafi movement a perversion of true Islamic teaching?
9. How does Wahid propose to counter Islamic extremism?

7 Islam in Europe: Failure of Assimilation

In the 1950s and 1960s Western Europe's booming economy created a demand for cheap labor that was met by an influx of millions of Muslims from Turkey, Pakistan, and North Africa, many of them illegals. Like other immigrants, they sought to join relatives, find economic opportunities, or escape from oppressive regimes. As a result, many European countries, including France, Germany, Britain, Belgium, Holland, Sweden, and Spain, now have substantial Muslim populations.

Essentially European countries have tried two approaches to absorbing Muslim immigrants—multiculturalism and assimilation. Practiced in Britain, Holland, and Germany, multiculturalism treats Muslims as members of a separate community with a distinct religious and cultural identity; this approach assumes that the Muslims' way of life could exist side by side with the cultural norms of the host country. Assimilation, the integration model adopted in France, does not grant Muslims a special status but encourages individual Muslims to embrace the nation's culture and values, to think of themselves as proud and loyal French citizens. Both approaches are now perceived as failures, for many Muslims remain profoundly alienated from European society and at odds with its values. European liberal-democracy, which espouses religious freedom, equal rights for women, separation of church and state, and freedom of expression, conflicts with many facets of Islamic society.

In describing the failure of the multicultural approach, analysts refer to the persistence of tight-knit Muslim ghettos; the terrorist bombings in the London subway on July 7, 2005 by Muslims who were born and educated in Britain; the murder on November 2, 2004 of Dutch filmmaker Theo Van Gogh by an Islamist extremist with Dutch citizenship; the demands of some Muslim groups that they be governed by their own religious law rather than the law of the land; the perpetuation in Europe by some Muslims of cultural mores that sanction polygamy, forced marriages between young girls and much older men, wife-beating, so-called honor killings of "wayward" females, and require women to keep their bodies and faces hidden from view; the high crime rate among Muslims—in Britain Muslims are 2 percent of the population but more than 8 percent of the prison population; and the emergence in European lands of extremist cells that have participated in terrorist acts, including 9/11.

In the fall of 2005, the suburbs of Paris and scores of other French cities were convulsed by two weeks of rioting—nearly 9,000 cars set afire and schools, shops, and churches burned to the ground—by young Muslim males from the bleak housing projects inhabited principally by North African immigrants. That the great majority of rioters were not recent immigrants, but had been born in France, was particularly distressing to officials, for French government prided itself on creating a uniform French identity that superseded ethnic and religious origins. Whatever the aspirations of the government, many French citizens remain resentful of North African immigrants whom they view as an alien minority that, unlike other immigrants, has failed to integrate into French society. They point to the immigrants' preference for native cultural traditions, the high cost of welfare payments they receive, and the high crime rate among them—Muslims, about 10 percent of the nation, constitute more than 50 percent of France's prison population. Numerous commentators, however, interpreted the riots as a rebellion by a resentful underclass protesting discrimination, segregation, poverty, and a staggering unemployment rate—as much as 40 percent—for young Muslim males.

Faced with what is perceived as a rapidly growing unassimilable Muslim minority that is hostile to Western values, lives in isolated communities, often does not speak the host nation's language, and recruits and finances terrorists, Europe is experiencing a backlash against Muslim immigrants and multiculturalism. An increasing number of Europeans now say that the premise of multiculturalism—assigning equal value to and tolerating Islamic traditions that are hostile to Western values—was a mistake, for several of these traditions undermine democracy and fragment the nation. The sentiments of Jan Wolter, a Dutch judge, are shared by many native Europeans: "We demand a new social contract. We no longer accept that people don't learn our language, we require that they send their daughters to school, and we demand they stop bringing in young brides from the desert and locking them up in third floor apartments." Increasingly, governments are introducing tighter immigration laws and are deporting Muslim radicals. They are also trying to work with moderate Muslims who support integration into European society and value Europe's liberal-democratic tradition. However, successful integration, say some commentators, is a two-way street. It is necessary for European society to address the socioeconomic problems burdening Muslims, overcome racist attitudes toward immigrants, and recognize the fact that numerous Muslims do work and pay taxes, respect the laws of their adopted country, and reject extremism; most importantly, Muslims must be made to feel that their religion is not being attacked and insulted. For many years to come Europeans will be confronted with—or tormented by—the question of Islam's place in their country.

Walter Laqueur
THE LAST DAYS OF EUROPE: EPITAPH FOR AN OLD CONTINENT

In *The Last Days of Europe: Epitaph for an Old Continent* (2007), Walter Laqueur, a prominent American historian with strong ties to Europe, discusses several threats to Europe's future, one of which is the burgeoning Muslim population. Laqueur raises an important question. In the past, immigrant Jews—and recently Sikhs and Hindus—have thrived in Britain, even when confronted with prejudice. Why is the integration of Muslim immigrants in Western society so fraught with problems? Following is Laqueur's discussion of this issue.

The problem facing West European societies is more often than not the second- and third-generation young immigrants—the very people who it was expected would be well integrated, equal members of these societies but who, on the contrary, revolted against their country of adoption. The reasons usually given are poverty (two-thirds of British Muslims live in low-income house-holds), inadequate housing and overcrowding, ghettoization, unemployment, especially of the young, lack of education, racial prejudice on the part of their non-Muslim neighbors—all of which are said to lead to a lack of social mobility, crime, and general marginalization of the Muslim communities. By implication or directly, it is argued that it is the fault of the state and of society that these and other misfortunes have taken place.

However, Muslims who have had successful careers in business or the professions say almost without exception that their ethnic identity did in no way hamper them.

To what extent has ghettoization been enforced by the outside world, and to what degree was it self-imposed? That new immigrants congregate in certain parts of a city is a well-known phenomenon. It can be studied, for instance, in London, where, traditionally, Irish (Camden Town), Jews (East End and later Golders Green), Australians and Poles (near Earls Court and Olympia), blacks (Brixton), Japanese (South Hampstead), and other newcomers settled at first. They were motivated by the wish to be among people who spoke their language and have ethnic food shops, travel agencies, clubs, and other organizations. The Russian immigrants to Berlin in the 1920s congregated in Charlottenburg, while poor Jews from Eastern Europe settled in the eastern part of the city.

A similar process took place as far as the Muslim immigration was concerned, but there was a basic difference: Earlier immigration waves did not receive any help with their housing on the part of the state or the local authorities, whereas in the second half of the twentieth century such assistance was the rule rather than the exception. For this reason there was little incentive to move out from lodgings that, however inadequate or displeasing, were free or inexpensive. When Eastern European Jews first moved to Whitechapel toward the end of the nineteenth century and the beginning of the twentieth, there was no mayor of London who went out of his way to help them. They and other immigrants had to fend for themselves, facing incomparably greater difficulties—for instance, there was no health service or other social assistance—than present-day immigrants. Muslim newcomers apparently like to stick longer with their coreligionists than do other groups of immigrants, and they are encouraged by their preachers to do so. This is true even with regard to India, where there is more ghettoization than in Europe; even middle-class Muslims seem to be reluctant to leave the areas where members of their community live.

The sites around Paris where many of the French Muslim immigrants live and which exploded in November 2005 were uncomfortable and aesthetically displeasing, but they were not slums like London's East End. Yet it was precisely in these quarters that, in the words of a foreign visitor, an antisociety grew up infused with a burning hatred of the other France and deep distrust and alienation. . . . Although they enjoy a far higher standard of living or consumption than they would in the country of their parents, this is no cause for gratitude; on the contrary, it is felt as an insult or a wound, even as they take it for granted as their due. . . .

Housing has been mentioned as perhaps the main reason for the Paris riots of 2005, youth unemployment as another. Unemployment amounts to 30 to 40 percent in France and Germany and not much less in Britain and the Netherlands. As a Berlin head teacher put it, "We are creating an army of long-term unemployed." The rate of dropouts is very high among Turkish youth in Berlin and also in other European countries; it is much higher among boys than among girls. Only 3 percent of Muslim youth make it to college in Germany. Their language skills are low, which is not surprising because Turkish or Arabic is spoken at home, books are not found in many households, and the use of German (or English) is discouraged by the parents, who often do not master the language. Boys are sent to Koran schools but are not encouraged to study other subjects. Girls are often forbidden to go to school beyond the age of sixteen, let alone attend universities, because there they might be exposed to undesirable influences. When a Berlin school decided (after consultation with students and their parents) to insist on the use of the German language only at school, it came under heavy attack by the Turkish media even though most pupils and their parents favored the measure. Some well-meaning local protagonists of multiculturalism joined the protest because they believed that this was tantamount to cultural repression. But can a young generation advance socially and culturally unless they have mastered the language of the land?

Racism and xenophobia have been identified as factors responsible for the underachievement of Muslim youth. But this explanation fails to account for the scholastic success of pupils with an Indian and Far Eastern background, who score higher in most subjects than the average German or British student. Nor does it explain why Muslim girls acquit themselves much better than the boys. Could it be connected with the fact that girls are not allowed to go out in the street unaccompanied, whereas the boys spend most of their time there? Indian pupils in British schools have been doing twice as well as the Pakistanis, and those from the Far East have been outpacing almost everyone else.

There are many explanations, but the idea sometimes voiced that it is all the fault of the state or society is not plausible and will not help remedy the situation. Young people are told day in, day out, that they are victims of society and that it is not really their fault if they fail. As a result of these failures, a youth culture of violence and crime has developed that has little to do with religion. Despite attendance at Koran schools (more in Germany, with higher attendance, than in France and the United Kingdom), these young men are not well versed in their religion. They may go to the mosque on Fridays but will drink and take drugs afterward despite the religious ban. The main influence on these young people is neither the parental home nor the imams but the street gang. The parents have little authority, their way of life does not appeal to the offspring, they are not assertive enough, and they work too hard and earn too little. Old-fashioned Islam is of no great interest to many of them, either; a well-positioned imam in Britain said that "we are losing half of them." Only a few charismatic religious leaders who preach extreme action may have a certain following among young males. To understand the scenes in the schools and streets of Kreuzberg and the *banlieues,* a textbook on juvenile delinquency could be more helpful than the Koran.

School has the least authority; in France and the United Kingdom language is less of an impediment, but in Germany the pupils quite literally often do not understand what the teacher is saying and there is no effort to understand either the teacher or fellow pupils from other countries with different native languages. Many teachers do not succeed in imposing their authority, for if they dare to punish pupils for misbehavior or make any demands on them, they are accused of racism and discrimination. The streetwise pupils are adept at playing the race card.

Muslim youth culture varies to a certain extent from country to country. Common to them is the street sports gear (hooded sweatshirts, sneakers, etc.) and the machismo; their body language expresses aggression. They want respect, though it is not clear how they think such respect has been earned; perhaps it is based on the belief that

"this street (quarter) is ours." In France and the United Kingdom hip-hop culture plays a central role; the texts of their songs express strong violence, often sadism. The street gang usually has a territorial base; Turks in Berlin have their own gangs, and the same is true with regard to Arabs and Kurds who arrived later in Germany. Sometimes the street gang is based on a certain village or district in the old country where the (extended) family originated. There has been a great deal of fighting between these territorial gangs; in Britain it has been quite often blacks against Indians (or Pakistanis) or, as in Brussels, Turks against black Africans.

Street gangs linger about aimlessly and often engage in petty crime. In Britain gangs of Muslim background have largely replaced the Afro-Caribbeans as drug pushers, though the key positions are usually not in their hands. Dealing in stolen goods is another way to earn the money needed for their gear, hashish (heavier drugs are sold but seldom consumed), and other entertainment. Teachers do not dare to interfere, and the local police are reluctant to make arrests, for judges will usually release those who have been arrested, especially if they are underage. Some proceed to more serious forms of crime. This is a theme that the European Muslim communities have been very reluctant to deal with. Crime figures are difficult to obtain, but all experts agree that the percentage of young Muslims in European prisons far exceeds their proportion in the population. This also goes for cases of rape, which in many gangs have become part of the rite of passage, especially in France, and to a lesser degree in the United Kingdom, Scandinavia, and Australia. The victims are by no means always non-Muslim girls or women who "asked for it" through immodest attire and behavior but also sometimes young Muslim women; the *hijab* does not by any means always offer protection. . . .

This rise in European crime cannot, of course, be attributed only to immigration, but there is no doubt that it is one of the main reasons. The head of the London Metropolitan Police made it known that 80 percent of the crime committed on the London Underground was carried out by immigrants from Africa. The head of Berlin's police announced that one out of three young immigrants in that city had a criminal record. Such statistics mentioning ethnic or religious background are forbidden in France, but the high number of young Muslims in French prisons (70 percent of the prison population according to some estimates) is no secret.

How does one account for the great aggressiveness of these gangs, as manifested, for instance, in the French riots of November 2005 but also on many occasions before and after? Their lack of achievement undoubtedly adds to the general discontent. The issue of identity (or lack of it) is frequently mentioned in this context. Many of the young (second) generation do not feel at home in either the parents' homeland or the country in which they live. They feel that they are not accepted in Europe and may curse the host country in all languages, but they would feel even less at home in Turkey or North Africa or on the Indian subcontinent, and they have no wish to return to these homelands. . . .

Sexual repression almost certainly is another factor that is seldom, if ever, discussed within their communities or by outside observers. It could well be that such repression (as Tsvetan Todorov has explained) generates extra aggression, an observation that has also been made by young Muslim women. Young Muslim men cannot freely meet members of the opposite sex from inside their own community; homosexuality is considered an abomination, yet in fact according to many accounts it is frequently practiced—as it has been all through Muslim history. The rejection of the other society manifests itself in many ways, beginning with defacing of walls of buildings and escalating to the torching of cars, as has happened frequently in France. In extreme cases there is an urge to destroy everything at hand and to attack all comers, including the firefighters and first-aid technicians rushing to the ghettos to deal with an emergency.

REVIEW QUESTION

1. How does Walter Laqueur explain the failure of second- and third-generation Muslim immigrants to assimilate into West European societies?

---

8 Resurgence of Anti-Semitism

In the decades following the Holocaust, overt anti-Semitism appeared to have receded in Western Europe. The outbursts of the traditionally anti-Semitic far Right—nationalists, racists, Fascists, and opponents of democracy—did not greatly affect the surviving Jews and their descendants who represented a model of successful integration. In recent years, however, there has been a significant upsurge of anti-Semitic incidents in European lands, including physical assaults, the firebombing of Jewish synagogues, schools, and homes, and the desecration of Jewish cemeteries with Nazi symbols, much of it, but not all, initiated by the growing number of Muslims residing in Western Europe. Labor MP Denis MacShane, who, in 2007, chaired a committee of British parliamentarians that studied anti-Semitism in Britain concluded that "Hatred of Jews has reached new heights in Europe." Similar conclusions were reached by the United States State Department and the Parliamentary Assembly of the Council of Europe.

Reaching epidemic proportions, anti-Semitism has become a principal theme in Middle-Eastern media and motivation for attacks on Jews by Muslims living in Europe. As Cardinal Tucci, the director of Vatican Radio, stated in November 2003: "Now in the whole Muslim world, in the media, the radio, television, in schools, a whole system inciting to anti-Semitism exists. It is the worst anti-Semitism that can be imagined after Nazi anti-Semitism, if not its equal."

Contemporary Muslim anti-Semitism borrowed considerably from traditional European anti-Semitism—Christian, nationalist, and Nazi. Like the Nazis, much of the Muslim world perceives Jews as a criminal people that threatens all humanity. As in Nazi Germany, the media in the Arab/Muslim world are often filled with repulsive caricatures of Jews—dark, stooped, sinister, hook-nosed, devil-like creatures—many of them taken from Nazi works. In Arab sermons, classrooms school books, and on the Internet, Jews are often referred to as "accursed," "descendants of apes and pigs," "the scum of the human race," "the rats of the world," "bacteria," "vampires," "usurers," and "whoremongers."

The Arab media have revived the medieval blood libel that Jews are required to murder non-Jewish children to obtain their blood for making unleavened bread for Passover. Holocaust denial is widespread in the Middle East; so too is celebrating Hitler's mass murder of Jews. A columnist for *Al-Akhbar*, considered a moderate newspaper sponsored by the Egyptian government, gives "thanks to Hitler of blessed memory," for taking revenge against Jews—although Muslims "do have a complaint against him for his revenge on them was not enough." And Dr. Ahmed Abu Halabiyah, rector of advanced studies at the Islamic University of Gaza expresses similar genocidal thoughts: "The Jews must be . . . meet them, kill them. It is forbidden to have mercy in your hearts for the Jews in any place and in any land, make war on them anywhere that you find yourself. Any place that you meet them, kill them."

Propagated over the Internet and by radical imams in mosques throughout Europe, this demonization of the Jews—together with scenes of violent conflict between Israelis and Palestinians and Hezbollah frequently depicted on television—has incited Muslim youth in Europe to acts of intimidation, physical assault, and vandalism against Jews; it has also led to organized campaigns of vilification of Jews on college campuses. On a positive note, in some European lands Muslim and Jewish organizations are engaged in interfaith dialogue and some Muslim intellectuals and religious leaders have condemned anti-Semitic outbursts.

In addition to the anti-Semitic incidents initiated by Muslims residing in various European lands, analysts have pointed to the ongoing Jew-hatred of the far Right and a rather new phenomenon—a growing and insidious anti-Semitism afflicting the Left.

As in the past, European anti-Semitism remains a bulwark of the far Right who propagate Holocaust denial and Jewish conspiracy theories—Jews invented a "Holocaust hoax" to extract compensation from Germany; Jews control the world's media and finances and are conspiring to dominate the planet; Jews are the real power behind the U.S. government; Jews are a threat to the nation.

During the Nazi era and for decades before, the Left—liberals, socialists, trade unionists, and intellectuals, including many academics—had been the strongest defenders of Jews against their detractors and oppressors. But now the distinguishing feature of the "new anti-Semitism" is its adoption by the Left who employ anti-Semitic language and imagery—linking the Star of David with the swastika—to express their support of the Palestinians and to delegitimize Israel; for them, Israelis are today's Nazis and Israel is a criminal state that should disappear.

Many Europeans are concerned about the revival of anti-Semitism. They recognize that Jew-hatred and the irrational myths associated with it, which undermine rational thinking and incite barbaric violence, transcend a purely Jewish concern. They threaten the core values of Western civilization as Nazism so painfully demonstrated.

United States State Department
CONTEMPORARY GLOBAL ANTI-SEMITISM: A REPORT PROVIDED TO THE UNITED STATES CONGRESS

The following brief passages are drawn from a comprehensive study, *Contemporary Global Anti-Semitism: A Report Provided to the United States Congress*, prepared in 2008 by the United States State Department.

Over the last decade, U.S. embassies and consulates have reported an upsurge in anti-Semitism. . . .

This same trend has been reported with concern by other governments, multilateral institutions, and world leaders. . . .

In the United Kingdom, an All-Party Parliamentary Inquiry into anti-Semitism launched an investigation into anti-Semitism. The Inquiry produced a September 2006 report, which states, "It is clear that violence, desecration of property, and intimidation directed towards Jews is on the rise."

In June 2007, the Parliamentary Assembly of the Council of the Europe issued Resolution 1563, which notes, "The persistence and escalation of anti-Semitic phenomena . . . [and that] far from having been eliminated, anti-Semitism is today on the rise in Europe. It appears in a variety of forms and is becoming relatively commonplace." . . .

CONTEMPORARY FORMS OF ANTI-SEMITISM

Contemporary anti-Semitism manifests itself in overt and subtle ways, both in places where sizeable Jewish communities are located and where few Jews live. Anti-Semitic crimes range from acts of violence, including terrorist attacks against Jews, to the desecration and destruction of Jewish property such as synagogues and cemeteries. Anti-Semitic rhetoric, conspiracy theories, and other propaganda circulate widely and rapidly by satellite television, radio, and the Internet.

Traditional forms of anti-Semitism persist and can be found across the globe. Classic anti-Semitic [writings], such as *The Protocols of the Learned Elders of Zion* and *Mein Kampf*, remain common-place. Jews continue to be accused of blood libel, dual loyalty, and undue influence on government policy and the media, and the symbols and images associated with age-old forms of anti-Semitism endure. These blatant forms of anti-Semitism, often linked with Nazism and Fascism, are considered unacceptable by the mainstream in the democratic nations of Western Europe, North America, and beyond, but they are embraced and employed by the extreme fringe.

Anti-Semitism has proven to be an adaptive phenomenon. New forms of anti-Semitism have evolved. They often incorporate elements of traditional anti-Semitism. However, the distinguishing feature of the new anti-Semitism is criticism of Zionism or Israeli policy that—whether intentionally or unintentionally—has the effect of promoting prejudice against all Jews by demonizing Israel and Israelis and attributing Israel's perceived faults to its Jewish character.

This new anti-Semitism is common throughout the Middle East and in Muslim communities in Europe, but it is not confined to these populations. For example, various United Nations bodies are asked each year on multiple occasions to commission investigations of what often are sensationalized reports of alleged atrocities and other violations of human rights by Israel. Various bodies have been set up within the UN system with the sole purpose of reporting on what is assumed to be ongoing, abusive Israeli behavior. The motive for such actions may be to defuse an immediate crisis, to show others in the Middle East that there are credible means of addressing their concerns other than resorting to violence, or to pursue other legitimate ends. But the collective effect of unremitting criticism of Israel, coupled with a failure to pay attention to regimes that are demonstrably guilty of grave violations, has the effect of reinforcing the notion that the Jewish state is one of the sources, if not the greatest source, of abuse of the rights of others, and thus intentionally or not encourages anti-Semitism.

Comparing contemporary Israeli policy to that of the Nazis is increasingly commonplace. Anti-Semitism couched as criticism of Zionism or Israel often escapes condemnation since it can be more subtle than traditional forms of anti-Semitism, and promoting anti-Semitic

attitudes may not be the conscious intent of the purveyor. Israel's policies and practices must be subject to responsible criticism and scrutiny to the same degree as those of any other country. At the same time, those criticizing Israel have a responsibility to consider the effect their actions may have in prompting hatred of Jews. At times hostility toward Israel has translated into physical violence directed at Jews in general. There was, for example, a sharp upsurge in anti-Semitic incidents worldwide during the conflict between Hezbollah and Israel in the summer of 2006.[1]

Governments are increasingly recognized as having a responsibility to work against societal anti-Semitism. But instead of taking action to fight the fires of anti-Semitism, some irresponsible leaders and governments fan the flames of anti-Semitic hatred within their own societies and even beyond their borders. Iran's President Mahmoud Ahmadinejad has actively promoted Holocaust denial, Iran's Jewish population faces official discrimination, and the official media outlets regularly produce anti-Semitic propaganda. The Syrian government routinely demonizes Jews through public statements and official propaganda. In Belarus, state enterprises freely produce and distribute anti-Semitic material. And in Venezuela, President Hugo Chavez has publicly demonized Israel and utilized stereotypes about Jewish financial influence and control, while Venezuela's government-sponsored mass media have become vehicles for anti-Semitic discourse, as have government news media in Saudi Arabia and Egypt.

Elsewhere, *despite* official condemnation and efforts to combat the problem, societal anti-Semitism continues to exist. In Poland, the conservative Catholic radio station *Radio Maryja* is one of Europe's most blatantly anti-Semitic media venues. The Interregional Academy of Personnel Management, a private institution in Ukraine

---

[1]This upsurge was documented in the U.S. Department of State's 2006 annual *Country Reports on Human Rights Practices*, as well as its annual *Report on International Religious Freedom*. These reports can be found at www.state.gov/g/drl.

commonly known by the acronym MAUP, is one of the most persistent anti-Semitic institutions in Eastern Europe. In Russia and other countries where xenophobia is widespread, such as some in Central and Eastern Europe, traditional anti-Semitism remains a problem. In France, Germany, the United Kingdom, and elsewhere, anti-Semitic violence remains a significant concern. Recent increases in anti-Semitic incidents have been documented in Argentina, Australia, Canada, South Africa, and beyond.

Today, more than 60 years after the Holocaust, anti-Semitism is not just a fact of history, it is a current event. Around the globe, responsible governments, intergovernmental organizations, non-governmental groups, religious leaders, other respected figures, and ordinary men and women are working to reverse the disturbing trends documented in this report. Much more remains to be done in key areas of education, tolerance promotion, legislation, and law enforcement before anti-Semitism, in all its ugly forms, finally is consigned to the past. . . .

The European Monitoring Center on Racism and Xenophobia (EUMC) [drafted] *A Working Definition of Anti-Semitism.* The EUMC's working definition provides a useful framework for identifying and understanding the problem and is adopted for the purposes of this report. . . .

The EUMC provides explanatory text that discusses the kinds of acts that could be considered anti-Semitic. . . .

- Calling for, aiding, or justifying the killing or harming of Jews in the name of a radical ideology or an extremist view of religion.
- Making mendacious, dehumanizing, demonizing, or stereotypical allegations about Jews as such or the power of Jews as a collective—such as, especially but not exclusively, the myth about a world Jewish conspiracy or of Jews controlling the media, economy, government or other societal institutions.
- Accusing Jews as a people of being responsible for real or imagined wrongdoing committed by a single Jewish person or group, or even for acts committed by non-Jews.

- Denying the fact, scope, mechanisms (e.g., gas chambers) or intentionality of the genocide of the Jewish people at the hands of National Socialist Germany and its supporters and accomplices during World War II (the Holocaust).
- Accusing the Jews as a people, or Israel as a state, of inventing or exaggerating the Holocaust.
- Accusing Jewish citizens of being more loyal to Israel, or to the alleged priorities of Jews worldwide, than to the interests of their own nations.

Examples of the ways in which anti-Semitism manifests itself with regard to the state of Israel taking into account the overall context could include:

- Denying the Jewish people their right to self-determination. . . .
- Applying double standards by requiring of it a behavior not expected or demanded of any other democratic nation.
- Using the symbols and images associated with classic anti-Semitism (e.g., claims of Jews killing Jesus or blood libel) to characterize Israel or Israelis.
- Drawing comparisons of contemporary Israeli policy to that of the Nazis.
- Holding Jews collectively responsible for actions of the state of Israel.

The EUMC makes clear, however, that criticism of Israel similar to that leveled against any other country cannot be regarded in itself as anti-Semitic.

CONSPIRACY THEORIES

As noted in the EUMC *Working Definition of Anti-Semitism,* "anti-Semitism frequently charges Jews with conspiring to harm humanity, and it often is used to blame Jews for 'why things go wrong.'" The EUMC includes as contemporary examples of anti-Semitism, "Making mendacious, dehumanizing, or stereotypical allegations about Jews as such or the power of Jews as a collective—such as . . . the myth about a world Jewish conspiracy or of Jews controlling the media, economy, government or other societal institutions."

Anti-Semitism is at the root of numerous contemporary conspiracy theories, including the following examples of false claims.

- Four thousand Jews were falsely accused of not reporting to work at the World Trade Center on September 11, 2001, supposedly because they had been warned not to do so by those who had advance knowledge of the attack.
- The October 2002 terrorist bombing of a nightclub in Bali, Indonesia was falsely rumored to have been caused by an Israeli "mini-nuclear weapon."
- The December 2004 South and Southeast Asian tsunami, caused by an earthquake, was falsely rumored to have been caused by a joint U.S.-Israeli underground nuclear test.
- The United States and Israel are falsely accused of having created an "American Quran"—a document that does not exist.
- U.S. founding father Benjamin Franklin is falsely alleged to have said that Jews were a "great danger" to the United States and should be "excluded by the Constitution."

Anti-Semitic conspiracy theories play to widespread hatreds and suspicions. The examples above did not arise spontaneously. In many cases, they had been deliberately concocted. [Thus a Syrian diplomat stated five weeks after 9/11:]

"Syria has documented proof of the Zionist regime's involvement in the September 11 terror attacks on the United States . . . [That] 4,000 Jews employed at the World Trade Center did not show up for work before the attack clearly attests to Zionist involvement in these attacks."

The canards reviewed above appear to be 20th and 21st century variations on the classic conspiracy myth of *The Protocols of the Learned Elders of Zion*, which asserts that Jews are inherently evil, manipulate world events for their

own purposes, and dominate the world. This century-old Czarist forgery was exposed in 1921 as a fabrication, but it continues to be widely popular and influential around the world, including in bookstores throughout the Middle East, parts of Europe, and beyond.* . . .

In fact, long passages of the *Protocols* were plagiarized, word-for-word, from a book published in 1864 titled, *Dialogues in Hell between Machiavelli and Montesquieu*, a work of political satire that did not have an anti-Semitic theme but was written to discredit Emperor Napoleon III of France. Conspiracy theories about alleged predominant Jewish power can have tremendous influence. . . .

HOLOCAUST DENIAL AND TRIVIALIZATION

Efforts to deny or minimize the Nazi genocide against the Jews have become one of the most prevalent forms of anti-Semitic discourse. At its core, Holocaust denial relies upon—and furthers—the traditional anti-Semitic myth of a world Jewish conspiracy.

Holocaust deniers explicitly or implicitly reject that the Nazi government and its allies had a systematic policy of exterminating the Jews, killing between five and seven million Jews, and that genocide was carried out at extermination camps using tools of mass murder such as gas chambers. . . .

The Protocols of the Learned Elder of Zion has been a recent best seller in Turkey and Syria and once was a best seller in Lebanon. There are at least nine different Arabic translations of the *Protocols* and more editions in Arabic than in any other language. Arabic translations are prominently displayed in bookstores throughout North Africa and the Middle East, as well as Arabic-language bookstores in Western Europe. The *Protocols* also have been prominently displayed at international book fairs (e.g., by the government of Iran at the 2005 Frankfurt International Book Fair). In addition, the *Protocols* are so popular that they have inspired television broadcasts in Egypt, Syria, and other Arab states. In the past, Saudi textbooks reprinted sections and presented them as facts. Hamas and Hezbollah also teach the *Protocols* as fact. Since 2003, new editions of *The Protocols of the Learned Elders of Zion* have been printed in English, Ukrainian, Indonesian, Japanese, Spanish, Italian, Portuguese, Greek, Russian, and Serbian.

Initially, Holocaust deniers primarily were neo-Nazis interested in rehabilitating fascism and restoring the image of Nazi Germany; for such groups, Holocaust denial has an obvious appeal. The neo-Nazis then were joined by other right-wing groups, such as white supremacists, who were drawn to both Fascism and anti-Semitism. The neo-Nazis and white supremacists share a belief that Jews invented the Holocaust for financial gain (reparations) and spread this "myth" of the Holocaust via their alleged control of the media.

In addition to outright Holocaust deniers, others trivialize the Holocaust and accuse the Jewish people of exaggerating it as justification for the creation of the state of Israel.

A number of deniers have published articles or books trying to discredit well documented facts, historical research, and eye witness accounts, all the while casting themselves as martyrs standing up to public opprobrium and censorship. . . .

While Holocaust denial began in the 20th century with neo-Nazis and white supremacists in Europe and the United States, in the 21st century it also is found in the Middle East. The potent anti-Semitic assumptions upon which Holocaust denial is founded—primarily the myth of a world Jewish conspiracy—make it an attractive weapon for those seeking to demonize Jews and de-legitimize a major basis for the founding of the state of Israel. . . . [For example:]

"I agree wholeheartedly with [Iranian] President Ahmadinejad. There was no such a [sic] thing as the 'Holocaust.' The so-called 'Holocaust' is nothing but Jewish/Zionist propaganda. There is no proof whatsoever that any living Jew was ever gassed or burned in Nazi Germany or in any of the territories that Nazi Germany occupied during World War II. The Holocaust propaganda was started by the Zionist Jews in order to acquire worldwide sympathy for the creation of Israel after World War II."

—Saudi professor Dr. Abdullah Muhammad Sindi, interview with the *Iranian Mehr News Agency*, December 26, 2005.

REVIEW QUESTION

1. How does the resurgence of anti-Semitism reveal both the persistence of traditional forms of anti-Semitism and a new adaptive anti-Semitism? Give examples of both.

---

9 In Defense of European Values

Like the period between the world wars, the years leading up to the new millennium represented an appropriate time to reassess the legacy of Europe. By the late twentieth century, its status might have appeared diminished. Europe's global hegemony was dealt an irreparable blow by the World War II. Subsequent attempts by the peoples of the Third World at securing liberation sometimes elicited a shockingly brutal response from their mother countries. And even though the Common Market and later the European Union helped raise the standard of living on the Continent to unprecedented heights and rendered it an economic dynamo, some observers felt that Europe had lost its soul, opting for creature comforts over the culture that had made it great.

Nevertheless, the traditional values that have underlain and inspired European achievements in the modern age—and that represent Europe's legacy to America—continue to find their advocates. At times they have extolled European civilization in the face of critics inclined to belittle its significance. Others call for Europe to embrace its historic roots. To all such commentators, Europe in the twenty-first century remains vital and enduring.

Jacques Ellul
THE BETRAYAL OF THE WEST

Jacques Ellul (1912–1994), a French sociologist with a pronounced moralist bent, is known for his study of the impact of technology and bureaucracy on the modern world. Ellul wrote *The Betrayal of the West* (1978), excerpts from which follow, to defend Western civilization from its many detractors. His ideas remain pertinent more than thirty years after the book's appearance.

I am not criticizing or rejecting other civilization and societies; I have deep admiration for the institutions of the Bantu and other peoples (the Chinese among them) and for the inventions and poetry and architecture of the Arabs. I do not claim at all that the West is superior. In fact, I think it absurd to lay claim to superiority of any kind in these matters. What criterion would you apply? What scale of values would you use? I would add that the greatest fault of the West since the seventeenth century has been precisely its belief in its own unqualified superiority in all areas.

The thing, then that I am protesting against is the silly attitude of western intellectuals in hating their own world and then illogically exalting all other civilizations. Ask yourself this question: If the Chinese have done away with binding the feet of women, and if the Moroccans, Turks, and Algerians have began to liberate their women, whence did the impulse to these moves come from? From the West, and nowhere else! Who invented the "rights of man"? The same holds for the elimination of exploitation. Where did the move to socialism originate? In Europe, and in Europe alone. The Chinese, like the Algerians, are inspired by western thinking as they move toward socialism. Marx was not Chinese, nor was Robespierre

an Arab. How easily the intellectuals forget this! The whole of the modern world, for better or for worse, is following a western model; no one imposed it on others, they have adopted it themselves, and enthusiastically.

I shall not wax lyrical about the greatness and benefactions of the West. Above all, I shall not offer a defense of the material goods Europe brought to the colonies. We've heard that kind of defense too often: "We built roads, hospitals, schools, and dams; we dug the oil wells. . . ." And the reason I shall say nothing of this invasion by the technological society is that I think it to be the West's greatest crime, as I have said at length elsewhere. The worst thing of all is that we exported our rationalist approach to things, our "science," our conception of the state, our bureaucracy, our nationalist ideology. It is this, far more surely than anything else, that has destroyed the other cultures of the world and shunted the history of the entire world onto a single track.

But is that all we can say of the West? No, the essential, central, undeniable fact is that the West was the first civilization in history to focus attention on the individual and on freedom. Nothing can rob us of the praise due us for that. We have been guilty of denials and betrayals (of these we shall be saying something more), we have committed crimes, but we have also caused the whole of mankind to take a gigantic step forward and to leave its childhood behind.

This is a point we must be quite clear on. If the world is everywhere rising up and accusing the West, if movements of liberation are everywhere under way, what accounts for this? Its sole source is the proclamation of freedom that the West has broadcast to the world. The West, and the West alone, is responsible for the movement that has led to the desire for freedom and to the accusations now turned back upon the West.

Today men point the finger of outrage at slavery and torture. Where did that kind of indignation originate? What civilization or culture cried out that slavery was unacceptable and torture scandalous? Not Islam, or Buddhism, or Confucius, or Zen, or the religions and moral codes of Africa and India! The West alone has defended the inalienable rights of the human person, the dignity of the individual, the man who is alone with everyone against him. But the West did not practice what it preached? The extent of the West's fidelity is indeed debatable: the whole European world has certainly not lived up to its own ideal all the time, but to say that it has never lived up to it would be completely false.

In any case, that is not the point. The point is that the West originated values and goals that spread throughout the world (partly through conquest) and inspired man to demand his freedom, to take his stand in the face of society and affirm his value as an individual. I shall not be presumptuous enough to try to "define" the freedom of the individual. . . .

. . . The West gave expression to what man—every man—was seeking. The West turned the whole human project into a conscious, deliberate business. It set the goal and called it freedom, or, at later date, individual freedom. It gave direction to all the forces that were working in obscure ways, and brought to light the value that gave history its meaning. Thereby, man became man.

The West attempted to apply in a conscious, methodical way the implications of freedom. The Jews were the first to make freedom the key to history and to the whole created order. From the very beginning their God was the God who liberates; his great deeds flowed from a will to give freedom to his people and thereby to all mankind. This God himself, moreover, was understood to be sovereignty free (freedom here was often confused with arbitrariness or with omnipotence). This was something radically new, a discovery with explosive possibilities. The God who was utterly free had nothing in common with the gods of eastern and western religions; he was different precisely because of his autonomy.

The next step in the same movement saw the Greeks affirming both intellectual and political liberty. They consciously formulated the rules for a genuinely free kind of thinking, the conditions for human freedom, and the forms a free society could take. Other peoples were already living in cities, but none of them had fought so zealously for the freedom of the city in relation to other cities, and for the freedom of the citizen within the city.

The Romans took the third step by inventing civil and institutional liberty and making political freedom the key to their entire politics. Even the conquests of the Romans were truly an unhypocritical expression of their intention of freeing peoples who were subject to dictatorships and tyrannies the Romans judged degrading. It is in the light of that basic thrust that we must continue to read Roman history. Economic motives undoubtedly also played a role, but a secondary one; to make economic causes the sole norm for interpreting history is in the proper sense superficial and inadequate. You cannot write history on the basis of your suspicions! If you do, you only project your own fantasies.

I am well aware, of course, that in each concrete case there was darkness as well as light, that liberty led to wars and conquests, that it rested on a base of slavery. I am not concerned here, however, with the excellence or defects of the concrete forms freedom took; I am simply trying to say (as others have before me) that at the beginning of western history we find the awareness, the explanation, the proclamation of freedom as the meaning and goal of history.

No one has ever set his sights as intensely on freedom as did the Jews and Greeks and Romans, the peoples who represented the entire West and furthered its progress. In so doing, they gave expression to what the whole of mankind was confusedly seeking. In the process we can see a progressive approach to the ever more concrete: from the Jews to the Greeks, and from the Greeks to the Romans there is no growth in consciousness, but there is the ongoing search for more concrete answers to the question of how freedom can be brought from the realm of ideas and incarnated in institutions, behavior, thinking, and so on.

Today the whole world has become the heir of the West, and we Westerners now have a twofold heritage: we are heirs to the evil the West has done to the rest of the world, but at the same time we are heirs to our forefathers' consciousness of freedom and to the goals of freedom they set for themselves. Other peoples, too, are heirs to the evil that has been inflicted on them, but now they have also inherited the consciousness of and desire for freedom. Everything they do today and everything they seek is an expression of what the western world has taught them. . . .

. . . Everything used to be so organized that wealth and poverty were stable states, determined (for example) by the traditional, accepted hierarchy, and that this arrangement was regarded as due to destiny or an unchangeable divine will. The West did two things: it destroyed the hierarchic structures and it did away with the idea of destiny. It thus showed the poor that their state was not something inevitable. This is something Marx is often credited with having done, but only because people are ignorant [of history]. It was Christianity that did away with the idea of destiny and fate. . . .

Once Christianity has destroyed the idea of destiny or fate, the poor realized that they were poor, and they realized that their condition was

not inevitable. Then the social organisms that had made it possible to gloss over this fact were challenged and undermined from within.

Against all this background we can see why the whole idea of revolution is a western idea. Before the development of western thought, and apart from it, no revolution ever took place. Without the individual and freedom and the contradictory extremes to which freedom leads, a society cannot engender a revolution. Nowhere in the world—and I speak as one with a knowledge of history—has there ever been a revolution, not even in China, until the western message penetrated that part of the world. Present-day revolutions, whether in China or among the American Indians, are the direct, immediate, unmistakable fruit of the western genius. The entire world has been pupil to the West that it now rejects. . . .

. . . I wish only to remind the reader that the West has given the world a certain number of values, movements, and orientations that no one else has provided. No one else has done quite what the West has done. I wish also to remind the reader that the whole world is living, and living almost exclusively, by these values, ideas, and stimuli. There is nothing original about the "new" thing that is coming into existence in China or Latin America or Africa: it is all the fruit and direct consequence of what the West has given the world.

In the fifties it was fashionable to say that "the third world is now entering upon the stage of history." The point was not, of course, to deny that Africa or Japan had a history. What the cliché was saying, and rightly saying, was that these peoples were now participating in the creative freedom of history and the dialectic of the historical process. Another way of putting it is that the West had now set the whole world in motion. It had released a tidal wave that would perhaps eventually drown it. There had been great changes in the past and vast migrations of peoples; there had been planless quests for power and the building of gigantic empires that collapsed overnight. The West represented something entirely new because it set the world in movement in every area and at every level; it represented, that is, a coherent approach to reality. Everything—ideas, armies, the state, philosophy, rational methods, and social organization—conspired in the global change the West had initiated.

It is not for me to judge whether all this was a good thing or bad. I simply observe that the entire initiative came from the West, that everything began there. I simply observe that the peoples of the world had abided in relative ignorance and [religious] repose until the encounter with the West set them on their journey.

Please, then, don't deafen us with talk about the greatness of Chinese or Japanese civilization. These civilizations existed indeed, but in a larval or embryonic state; they were approximations, essays. They always related to only one sector of the human or social totality and tended to be static and immobile. Because the West was motivated by the ideal of freedom and had discovered the individual, it alone launched society in its entirety on its present course.

Again, don't misunderstand me. I am not saying that European science was superior to Chinese science, nor European armies to Japanese armies; I am not saying that the Christian religion was superior to Buddhism or Confucianism; I am not saying that the French or English Political system was superior to that of the Han dynasty. I am saying only that the West discovered what no one else had discovered; freedom and the individual, and that this discovery later set everything else in motion. Even the most solidly established religions could not help changing under the influence. . . .

It was not economic power or sudden technological advances that made the West what it is. These played a role, no doubt, but a negligible one in comparison with the great change—the discovery of freedom and the individual—that represents the goal and desire implicit in the history of all civilizations. That is why, in speaking of the West, I unhesitatingly single out freedom from the whole range of values. After all, we find justice, equality, and peace everywhere. Every civilization that has attained a certain level has claimed to be a civilization of justice or peace. But which of them has ever spoken of the individual? Which of them has been reflectively conscious of freedom as a value?

The decisive role of the West's discovery of freedom and the individual is beyond question, but the discovery has brought with it . . . tragic consequences. First, the very works of the West now pass judgment on it. For, having proclaimed freedom and the individual, the West played false in dealing with other peoples. It subjected, conquered, and exploited them, even while it went on talking about freedom. It made the other peoples conscious of their enslavement by intensifying that enslavement and calling it freedom. It destroyed the social structures of tribes and clans, turned men into isolated atoms, and shaped them into a world-wide proletariat, and all the time kept on talking of the great dignity of the individual: his autonomy, his power to decide for himself, his capacity for choice, his complex and many-sided reality. . . .

. . . Reason makes it possible for the individual to master impulse, to choose the ways in which he will exercise his freedom, to calculate the chances for success and the manner in which a particular action will impinge upon the group, to understand human relations, and to communicate. Communication is the highest expression of freedom, but it has little meaning unless there is a content which, in the last analysis, is supplied by reason. . . . Here precisely we have the magnificent discovery made by the West: that the individual's whole life can be, and even is, the subtle, infinitely delicate interplay of reason and freedom.

This interplay achieved its highest form in both the Renaissance and classical literature since the Enlightenment. No other culture made this discovery. We of the West have the most rounded and self-conscious type of man. For, the development of reason necessarily implied reason's critique of its own being and action as well as a critique of both liberty and reason, through a return of reason upon itself and a continuous reflection which gave rise to new possibilities for the use of freedom as controlled by new developments of reason. . . .

Let me return to my main argument. It was the West that established the splendid interplay of freedom, reason, self-control, and coherent behavior. It thus produced a type of human being that is unique in history: true western man. (I repeat: the type belongs neither to nature nor to the animal world; it is a deliberate construct achieved through effort.)

I am bound to say that I regard this type as superior to anything. I have seen or known elsewhere. A value judgment, a personal and subjective preference? Of course. But I am not ready on that account to turn my back on the construction and on the victory and affirmation it represents. Why? Because the issue is freedom itself, and because I see no other satisfactory model that can replace what the West has produced.

REVIEW QUESTIONS

1. What is the essential legacy of the West, according to Jacques Ellul? How may it be seen as a twofold heritage, both liberating and tragic?
2. For Ellul, what was the role of the Jews and Christianity in the shaping of the Western tradition? Of Greeks and Romans?

Credits

Chapter 1

pp. 8–9: Excerpt from Pico della Mirandola "Oration on the Dignity of Man" translated by Elizabeth L. Forbes. From *The Renaissance Philosophy of Man*, edited by Ernst Cassirer, Paul Oskar Kristeller and John H. Randall, Jr., pp. 223–225. Copyright © 1948 by the University of Chicago Press. Reprinted by permission.

pp. 14–16: Excerpts from *Luther's Works*, vol. 44, James Atkinson, ed. pp. 310–314. Copyright © 1966 by Augsburg Fortress Publishers. Reprinted with permission.

pp. 18–19: Bishop Jaques-Benigne Bossuet, *Politics Drawn from the Very Words of Holy Scripture*, trans. & ed., by Patrick Riley, pp. 57–61, 81–83 © 1990. Reprinted by permission of Cambridge University Press.

Chapter 2

pp. 29–31: Copernicus, Nicolaus, *On the Revolutions*, translated by Edward Rosen, edited by Jerry Dbrzycki. Reprinted by permission of Macmillan Ltd.

pp. 32–33: Maurice A. Finocchiaro, editor, *The Galileo Affair: A Documentary History*. Copyright © 1989 The Regents of the University of California. Reprinted by permission of the University of California Press.

pp. 34–37: From Galileo Galilei, translated by Stillman Drake, *Dialogue Concerning the Two Chief World Systems*, 1962, University of California Press. Reprinted with permission of University of California Press.

pp. 37–38: Galileo Before the Inquisition from Giorgio de Santillana, *The Crime of Galileo*, pp. 306–308, 310. Copyright © 1955 by the University of Chicago Press. Reprinted by permission.

pp. 39–40: Benjamin Farrington, ed. and trans., *The Philosophy of Francis Bacon*, pp. 114–115. Copyright © 1970 by Liverpool University Press. Reprinted with permission.

Chapter 3

pp. 52–53: From *The Philosophy of Kant* by Immanuel Kant, translated by Carl Friedrich, copyright 1949 by Random House, Inc. Used by permission of Random House, Inc.

pp. 58–61: Excerpted from *Candide and Other Writings by Voltaire*, edited by Haskell M. Block, Copyright © 1956 and renewed 1984 by Random House, Inc.

pp. 65–66: *Some Thoughts Concerning Education* by John Locke (1989): Extracts from *Essay Concerning Human Understanding* by John Locke (pp. 83, 103, 105, 111, 112, 113–114, 115–116, 134, 142). By Permission of Oxford University Press.

pp. 68–70: Denis Diderot, *The Encyclopedia Selections*, edited and translated by Stephen J. Gendzier. Copyright © 1967 by Harper. Used with permission.

pp. 71–74: From Jean Jacques Rousseau, *The Social Contract in the Social Contract and Discources*, trans. G.D.H. Cole, pp. 8–9, 13–15, 18–19, 23, and 26–28. Reprinted by permission of J.M. Dent & Sons and Everyman's Library.

pp. 74–76: *On Crimes and Punishments* by Beccaria, translated by H. Paolucci, © 1963. Reprinted by permission of Prentice-Hall, Inc., Upper Saddle River, New Jersey.

p. 78: Denis Diderot, *The Encyclopedia Selections*, edited and translated by Stephen J. Gendzier. Copyright © 1967 by Harper. Used with permission.

p. 79: From *Sketch for a Historical Picture of the Progress of the Human Mind* by Antonie-Nicolas de Condorcet, translated by June Barraclough. Copyright © Weidenfeld & Nicolson, an imprint of The Orion Publishing Group.

Chapter 4

Chapter 5

Chapter 6

Chapter 7

Chapter 8

pp. 195–198: From *German Worker: Working-Class Autobiographies from the Age of Industrialization,* by Alfred Kelly, 1987, University of California Press. Reprinted with permission of University of California Press.

pp. 204–206: From John Stuart Mill, *The Subjection of Women,* 1929, pp. 3–6, 10–12, 15, 60–61, 64, 73, 82, 161–164, 214–215.

pp. 207–209: Excerpts from a speech by Emmeline Pankhurst given October 21, 1913 from pp. 153–157 and 159–161 in *Suffrage and the Pankhursts,* edited by Jane Marcus. (New York: Routledge and Kegan Paul, 1987).

p. 210: From *Pages From the Goncourt Journal,* edited and translated by Robert Baldick, pp. 18, 27. Copyright © 1984. Reprinted by permission of Oxford University Press, England.

pp. 211–213: Almroth E. Wright, *The Unexpurgated Case Against Woman Suffrage* (London: Constable, 1913).

pp. 214–215: Houston Stewart Chamberlain, "The Importance of Race," from *Of The Nineteenth Century,* New York, Howard Fertig, 1968, 2005. Reprinted with permission of Howard Fertig, Inc., Publisher.

pp. 218–220: Hermann Ahlwardt's "The Semitic Versus the Teutonic Race" (p. 147) from *Rehearsal for Destruction: A Study of Political Anti-Semitism in Imperial Germany* by Paul W. Massing. Copyright 1949 by The American Jewish Committee. Copyright renewed 1977 by The American Jewish Committee. Reprinted by permission of Harper-Collins Publishers.

pp. 220–221: Excerpt from Henry Monument: From Michael Burns, *France and the Dreyfus Affair: A Documentary History* (New York: Bedford/ St. Martin's, 1999), p. 130.

pp. 224–226: From Theodor Herzl, *The Jewish State: An Attempt at a Modern Solution of the Jewish Question* (New York: American Zionist Emergency Council, 1946), pp. 76–77, 85–86, 91–93, 96. Reprinted by permission of the American Zionist Federation.

Chapter 9

pp. 241–244: From Colonel R. Meinertzhagen, Kenya Diary, 1902–1906. Copyright © 1957. Reprinted by permission of the Estate of Colonel R. Meinertzhagen.

pp. 244–246: From John Wellington, *South Africa and its Human Issues* (Oxford: Clarendon Press, 1967), p. 196.

p. 248: Joseph W. Esherick, *The Origins of the Boxer Uprising,* © 1987 by the Regents of the University of California. Reprinted by permission of The University of California Press.

Chapter 10

pp. 256–259: Notes from Underground, from *Notes from the Underground and the Grand Inquisitor* by Fyodor Dostoevsky, translated by Ralph E. Matlaw, copyright © 1960, 1988 by E. P. Dutton & Co. Used by permission of Dutton, a division of Penguin Group (USA) Inc.

pp. 260–264: From *The Will To Power* by Friedrich Nietzsche, edited by R.J. Hollingdale, translated by Walter Kaufmann, copyright © 1967 by Walter Kaufmann. Used by permission by Random House, Inc.

pp. 265–267: Copyright © 1959 Sigmund Freud. Reprinted by permission of Basic Books, a member of the Perseus Books Group.

pp. 272–274: Manifesto of Freedom from "The Founding and Maniefesto of Futurism" from *Marinetti: Selected Writings* by F.T. Marinetti, edited by R.W. Flint, translated by R.W. Flint and Arthur A. Coppotelli. Translation copyright © 1972 by Farrar, Straus & Giroux, Inc. Reprinted by permission of Farrar, Straus and Giroux, LLC.

Chapter 11

pp. 283–284: Roland Doregeles, "After Fifty Years," in George A. Panichas, ed. *Promise of Greatness* (New York: John Day, 1968), pp. 13–15.

pp. 284–286: From Stefan Zweig, *The World of Yesterday,* pp. 222–224, 226–227. English translation copyright © 1943, renewed © 1970 by

Chapter 13

pp. 410–412: Inge Scholl, pages 78–88 and 91 from *The White Rose*: *Munich, 1942–1943*. © 1970, 1983 by Inge Aicher-Scholl and reprinted by permission of Wesleyan University Press.

pp. 412–416: *The Ghetto Fights*: *The Warsaw Ghetto Uprising* by Marek Edelman. Copyright © 1990. Reprinted with permission from Bookmarks Publications.

pp. 416–419: *The Secret Army* by Tadeusz Bor-Komorowski. Copyright © 1984 by Battery Press. Reprinted with permission.

pp. 422–423: From *The Day of the Americans* by Nerin E. Gun, © 1966.

pp. 423–426: *Dresden 1945*: *The Devil's Tinderbox* by Alexander McKee, pp. 171–173, 175. (London: Souvenir Press, 1982).

pp. 426–428: From *Final Entries 1945*: *The Diaries of Joseph Goebbels* by Joseph Goebbels, edited by Hugh Trevor-Roper, translated by Richard Barry, copyright © 1978 by Martin Secker & Warberg Ltd and G.P. Putnam's Sons. Orig. German copyright © 1977 by Hoffman und Campe Verlag. Used by permission of G.P. Putnam's Sons, a division of Penguin Group (USA) Inc.

pp. 428–431: Alfred-Maurice De Zayas, *A Terrible Revenge,* published 2006 by Palgrave Macmillan. Reproduced with permission of Palgrave Macmillan.

pp. 434–437: *The Battle for Okinawa* by Colonel Hiromichi Yahara. Copyright © 1995 by John Wiley & Sons, Inc. Reproduced with permission of John Wiley & Sons, Inc.

Chapter 14

pp. 440–441: From *Fire in the Ashes*: *Europe in Mid-century* by Theodore H. White. (Toronto: George J. McLeod Limited, 1953), 134–136.

pp. 441–443: Excerpted from "The Tragedy of the DPS" by Gerold Frank. From *The New Republic,* April 1, 1946, vol. 114. No. 13, pp. 436–438.

pp. 443–444: Alfred-Maurice De Zayas, *A Terrible Revenge,* published 2006 by Palgrave Macmillan. Reproduced with permission of Palgrave Macmillan.

pp. 445–446: Reproduced with permission of Curtis Brown Ltd., London, on behalf of the Estate of Sir Winston Churchill. Copyright Winston S. Churchill.

pp. 446–448: From Nikita S. Khrushchev, "Report to the Twentieth Party Congress," from *Current Soviet Policies II, The Documentary Record of the Twentieth Party Congress and its Aftermath.* Reprinted by permission.

pp. 449–453: From *Let History be the Judge: The Origins and Consequences of Stalinism* by Roy Medvedev, 781–791. Copyright © 1989 by Columbia University Press. Reprinted with permission of the publisher.

pp. 453–456: Excerpts from *The New Class* by Milovan Djilas, copyright © 1957 by Harcourt, Inc. and renewed 1985 by Milovan Djilas, reprinted by permission of Houghton Mifflin Harcourt Publishing Company.

pp. 456–459: From *No More Comrades* by Andor Heller, pp. 9–10, 12, 13, 15, 18, 21, 23, 156–158, 160–163. © 1957 by Regnery Publishing, Inc.

pp. 460–463: From *Fire in the Ashes: Europe in Mid-Century* by Theodore H. White (Toronto: George J. McLeod Limited, 1953). Reprinted with permission from David F. White.

pp. 463–466: *The Burden of Guilt: A Short History of Germany 1914–1945* translated by Strauss Chp. "The Burden of German Guilt" by Vogt pp. 283–286. © 1964 by Oxford University Press, Inc. By permission of Oxford University Press, Inc.

pp. 468–470: Pp. 75, 84, 88, 99, 102, 105, 115–17, 143–44 from *Perestroika* by Mikhail Gorbachev. Copyright © 1987 by Mikhail Gorbachev. Reprinted by permission of HarperCollins Publishers.

Chapter 15

pp. 473–475: From *The New York Times* © January 2, 1990 *The New York Times*. All rights reserved. Used by permission and protected by the Copyright Laws of the United States. The printing, pp. 476–482: Copyright © 2009 by C.J. Chivers. Reprinted by permission of the Stuart Krichevsky Literary Agency, Inc. This article originally appeared in *Esquire Magazine* in March 2009.

pp. 483–486: From *The Future of Freedom: Illiberal Democracy at Home and Abroad* by Fareed Zakaria. Copyright © 2003 by Fareed Zakaria. Used by permission of W. W. Norton & Company, Inc.

pp. 487–492: Excerpted from *Ending Violence Against Women: From Words to Action; Study of the Secretary-General*, October 9, 2006, pp. 27–32, 37–43 http://www.un.org/womenwatch/daw/vaw. Reprinted with permission from the United Nations Publications Board.

pp. 493–495: Excerpts from *A Long Way Gone: Memoirs of a Boy Soldier* by Ishmael Beah. Copyright © 2007 by Ishmael Beah. Reprinted by permission of Farrar, Straus and Giroux, LLC.

pp. 497–498: Mary R. Habeck, *Knowing the Enemy: Jihadist Ideology and the War on Terror*. Copyright © 2006 by Yale University Press. Reprinted with permission.

pp. 499–504: From *EU, Terrorism Situation and Trend Report 2007*, pp. 18–26. Reprinted with permission from EUROPOL.

pp. 505–508: *Wall Street Journal,* "Right Islam vs. Wrong Islam: Muslims and Non-Muslims Must Unite to Defeat the Wahhabu Ideology" by Abdurrahman Wahid. Copyright 2005 by *Dow Jones & Company, Inc.* Reproduced with permission of *Dow Jones & Company, Inc.* via Copyright Clearance Center.

pp. 510–513: From *The Last Days of Europe* by Walter Laqueur. © 2007 by the author.

pp. 520–524: Excerpted from *The Betrayal of the West* by Jacques Ellul, trans. Matthew J. O'Connell. Copyright © 1978. Reprinted by permission of The Continuum International Publishing Group, Inc.